CONVEYANCING

AUSTRALIA
Law Book Co.
Sydney

CANADA and USA
Carswell
Toronto

HONG KONG
Sweet & Maxwell Asia

NEW ZEALAND
Brookers
Wellington

SINGAPORE and MALAYSIA
Sweet & Maxwell Asia
Singapore and Kuala Lumpur

CONVEYANCING

THIRD EDITION

By

GEORGE L. GRETTON, W.S.
Lord President Reid Professor of Law, University of Edinburgh

and

KENNETH G. C. REID, W.S.
Professor of Property Law, University of Edinburgh

Published in 2004 by
W. Green & Son Ltd
21 Alva Street
Edinburgh EH2 4PS
www.wgreen.thomson.com

Reprinted 2006

Typeset by J. P. Price, Chilcompton, Somerset
Printed in Great Britain by
Athenaeum Press Ltd., Gateshead, Tyne & Wear

No natural forests were destroyed to make this product;
Only farmed timber was used and replanted

A CIP catalogue record for this book is available from the British
Library

ISBN 0 414 01558 4

For AAG and GCR

FOREWORD

This book seeks to be of use both to the practitioner and to the student. Much of the material which will be of use to the latter will, of course, be familiar to the former. The focus of the book is residential conveyancing. Other topics, such as leases, are not covered. Being a text on conveyancing, there is little coverage of property law as such. However, we see property law and conveyancing as being two sides of the same coin, and we hope, and believe, that that outlook informs the book.

Much has changed since the publication of the last edition in 1999. The courts have been active in developing the law. The establishment of the Scottish Parliament has resulted in a flood of legislation, some of it of great significance for conveyancers. On April 1, 2003 the last counties became operational for the purposes of registration of title, with the result that most conveyancing is now Land Register conveyancing. And finally the feudal system, an integral part of Scottish land law for more than 800 years, was due to be abolished on November 28, 2004. This last change we have anticipated by a few months. While the law is generally stated as at May 10, 2004 it has been assumed that the feudal system is no more, and that the Title Conditions (Scotland) Act 2003 is fully in force. This new edition is thus entirely post-feudal in outlook.

We thank those who have contributed, directly or indirectly, to this edition, and in particular Alan R. Barr, Andrew A. Boyd and Graeme A. Reid.

CONTENTS

TABLE OF CASES

TABLE OF ACTS OF THE SCOTTISH PARLIAMENT

TABLE OF STATUTES

TABLE OF SCOTTISH STATUTORY INSTRUMENTS

TABLE OF STATUTORY INSTRUMENTS

ABBREVIATIONS

Gordon	William M. Gordon, *Scottish Land Law* (2nd ed., 1999)
Halliday	J. M. Halliday, *Conveyancing Law and Practice* (2nd ed., edited by Iain J. S. Talman, two volumes, 1996 and 1997)
Reid, *Property*	Kenneth G.C. Reid, *The Law of Property in Scotland* (1996), with contributions by George L. Gretton, A. G. M. Duncan, William M. Gordon and Alan J. Gamble (being a revised reprint of the first part of Volume 18 of *The Laws of Scotland: Stair Memorial Encyclopaedia*)
Reid and Gretton, *Conveyancing*	An annual series of update volumes, beginning in 1999, by the present authors, and differentiated by year, *e.g.* Reid and Gretton, *Conveyancing 2001.*

CML	Council of Mortgage Lenders
GRS	General Register of Sasines
MIG	Mortgage indemnity guarantee
NSEA	Non-solicitor estate agent
PEC	Property enquiry certificate
Personal Register	The Register of Inhibitions and Adjudications
Property Registers	The Land Register and the General Register of Sasines
ROTPB	Ian Davis and Alistair Rennie (eds), *Registration of Title Practice Book* (2nd ed., 2000, published by Registers of Scotland)
SDLT	Stamp duty land tax
SEA	Solicitor estate agent
SPC	Solicitors Property Centre

1868 Act	Titles to Land Consolidation (Scotland) Act 1868
1874 Act	Conveyancing (Scotland) Act 1874
1921 Act	Trusts (Scotland) Act 1921
1924 Act	Conveyancing (Scotland) Act 1924
1964 Act	Succession (Scotland) Act 1964
1970 Act	Conveyancing and Feudal Reform (Scotland) Act 1970
1973 Act	Prescription and Limitation (Scotland) Act 1973
1974 Act	Land Tenure Reform (Scotland) Act 1974
1979 Act	Land Registration (Scotland) Act 1979
1981 Act	Matrimonial Homes (Family Protection) (Scotland) Act 1981
1995 Act	Requirements of Writing (Scotland) Act 1995
2000 Act	Abolition of Feudal Tenure etc. (Scotland) Act 2000
2001 Act	Mortgage Rights (Scotland) Act 2001
2003 Act	Title Conditions (Scotland) Act 2003

CHAPTER 1

ABOUT CONVEYANCING

Who can do conveyancing?

Whereas estate agency work can be done by anyone,[1] conveyancing is 1–01
restricted to solicitors and advocates,[2] and to licensed conveyancers.[3] In
practice advocates do not do conveyancing, and the number of licensed
conveyancers is tiny.[4] More precisely, the rule is that only such persons
may do conveyancing for reward:

> "Any unqualified person (including a body corporate) who draws
> or prepares: (a) any writ relating to heritable . . . estate . . . shall be
> guilty of an offence . . . [but the foregoing] shall not apply: (a) to
> an unqualified person if he proves that he drew or prepared the
> writ or papers in question without receiving, or without expecting
> to receive, either directly or indirectly, any fee, gain or reward
> (other than by way of remuneration paid under a contract of
> employment) . . ."[5]

The final words allow an unqualified person to do conveyancing within a
law firm. Anyone can do conveyancing on an unpaid basis, whether for
themselves or for others. So do-it-yourself conveyancing is possible,
though rare. The rules do not apply to wills, powers of attorney or any
"document *in re mercatoria.*" Missives are also excluded from the Rules.[6]
The Law Society of Scotland recommends caution when an offer is

---

[1] Subject to the Estate Agents Act 1979. This Act applies only to NSEAs. It has a
"negative licensing" system whereby persons can be banned. There is strong pressure for
positive licensing. The Office of Fair Trading in its 2004 report *Estate Agency Market in
England and Wales* decided against positive licensing. But the pressure has continued, for
instance from the Consumers Association and from the National Association of Estate
Agents. Reform of the 1979 Act is probable, but whether it will include positive licensing is
uncertain. Also uncertain is whether there might be divergence between the Scottish and
English positions.

[2] Solicitors (Scotland) Act 1980, s.32. See *Council of the Law Society of Scotland v
Express Mortgages (Scotland) Ltd,* 1994 G.W.D. 14–906.

[3] Law Reform (Miscellaneous Provisions) (Scotland) Act 1990, s.17.

[4] The licensed conveyancers' professional body, the Scottish Conveyancing and Executry
Services Board, was abolished by the Public Appointments and Public Bodies etc.
(Scotland) Act 2003, and its functions were transferred to the Law Society of Scotland.

[5] Solicitors (Scotland) Act 1980, s.32.

[6] Solicitors (Scotland) Act 1980, s.32(3).

received from a unqualified person.[7] In any event it is necessary to check the identity of the agents for the other party.[8]

For whom can conveyancing be done?

1-02　　The question of capacity belongs to the law of persons. A full treatment would therefore be out of place here: a few words must suffice. First, natural persons. Those under 16 have capacity to own land, but juridical acts, such as entering into missives and signing dispositions, must be done on their behalf by their parents or guardians.[9] Where a child acquires land this may be through a legacy. Such a legacy may necessitate the involvement of the Accountant of Court.[10] Those aged 16 or above have full capacity, but juridical acts done by those aged 16 and 17 may be voidable if they are "prejudicial".[11] Someone dealing with such a person may therefore wish to insure against a subsequent challenge.

If an adult's capacity is impaired, for instance by senility, it may be that s/he can no longer validly act, in which case juridical acts, if they are to be valid, must be done by someone else of his/her behalf. This can happen in more than one way.[12] Continuing powers of attorney and welfare powers of attorney[13] must be registered with the Public Guardian,[14] and should also be registered in the Books of Council and Session. If the court has made an intervention order or a guardianship order,[15] it must be registered in the Land Register or the GRS.[16] Whether there exists power to buy or sell, or otherwise deal with heritable property, depends on the terms of the court order and whether consent has been given by the Public Guardian.

Powers of attorney must be scrutinised carefully since they are traditionally construed in a restrictive way.[17] The holder of the power is under a fiduciary duty to act in the best interests of the principal. That

---

[7] (2004) 49 J.L.S.S. January/41.

[8] The *CML Lenders' Handbook for Scotland,* para.3.2 says that "if you are not familiar with the seller's solicitors or independent qualified conveyancers, you must verify that they appear in a legal directory or they are currently on record with the Law Society of Scotland . . . as practising at the address shown on their note paper." Whilst this is explicitly required only when acting for a CML lender, it is probably an implied duty in every case. For the CML see Ch.18.

[9] Age of Legal Capacity (Scotland) Act 1991. See generally A. B. Wilkinson and Kenneth Norrie, *Law Relating to Parent and Child* (2nd ed., 1999)

[10] Children (Scotland) Act 1995, s.9, though the meaning of the section is obscure: see Gretton (1997) 42 J.L.S.S. 308.

[11] Age of Legal Capacity (Scotland) Act 1991, s.3.

[12] See generally Adrian D. Ward, *Adult Incapacity* (2003).

[13] An ordinary power of attorney is of no use for this purpose since it will lapse when the principal becomes *incapax.*

[14] Adults with Incapacity (Scotland) Act 2000, s.19. The website of the Public Guardian is *http://www.publicguardian-scotland.gov.uk/.*

[15] The guardian replaces the *curator bonis* of the common law.

[16] Adults with Incapacity (Scotland) Act 2000, ss.19, 56 and 61. Useful guidance from the Keeper can be found at *http://www.ros.gov.uk/pdfs/awi.pdf.*

[17] Halliday, para.13-03.

will normally exclude, for instance, any power to donate. There is no requirement that powers of attorney be registered in the Books of Council and Session, but it is invariable practice to do so.

The capacity of juristic persons, such as companies, depends on the terms of the legislation under which they are established. Juridical acts outwith their powers (*ultra vires*) are always unlawful and may, depending on the type of juristic person, be voidable or even void. The position of partnerships, limited liability partnerships and—the common type of juristic person in practice—companies is considered elsewhere.[18] There exist certain entities, notably trusts and trade unions, which are not juristic persons but which are subject to special rules and which function very nearly as juristic persons.[19] There exist a multitude of clubs, associations and businesses whose legal status may be obscure and which must be clarified at the outset. Sometimes there exists an entity with the appropriate capacity, but sometimes not.

Taking instructions

Solicitors are often called law agents. The term is useful because it focuses the fact that the solicitor is an agent and the client is the principal. Obvious though this is, it can too easily be overlooked in practice. Solicitors must ensure that they have been duly appointed by the principal. If someone telephones to say that her aged mother wants to sell her house, that is not enough: instructions must be obtained from the aged mother. As the Law Society of Scotland Code of Conduct 2002[20] puts it: "Solicitors must accept instructions only from clients or recognised agents authorised to give instructions on behalf of clients; for example persons authorised by power of attorney or another lawyer." The person who has telephoned is neither of these: she may or may not be a client of the firm but for this sale she is not the client. Again, if a client says that he and his wife wish to buy or sell a house, instructions must also be obtained from the wife.[21] If he says he wants to sell his house and says that "I just put it in my wife's name for tax purposes" that makes no difference. She owns the house. After all, had ownership *not* been transferred to her the very purpose of the transfer would have failed. Instructions to sell must, therefore, come from her. Families often act as a single entity, and treating the members as separate clients may

1–03

---

[18] Chs 24 and 25.

[19] For trusts see Ch.22.

[20] The Law Society of Scotland's regulations, codes and practice guidelines etc. are published in the *Parliament House Book* (W. Green, looseleaf updated regularly). Some can also be found on the Society's website: http://www.lawscot.org.uk/.

[21] See generally *Hopkinson v Williams*, 1993 S.L.T. 907; *MacDougall v Akram*, 1993 G.W.D. 33–2142; *Safdar v Devlin*, 1994 G.W.D. 17–1085; *Glasper v Rodger*, 1996 S.L.T. 44; *Merrick Homes Ltd v Duff*, 1996 S.C. 497; *Brady v Neilsons*, 1999 G.W.D. 4–209. Robert Rennie, *Solicitors' Negligence* (1997), para.6.15 suggests that each spouse can be presumed to be the agent of the other for conveyancing purposes, but we would respectfully dissent. See *Suleman v Shahsavari* [1989] 2 All E.R. 460 for an English case where one spouse authorised a sale: the other spouse was held not to be bound.

seem artificial and awkward. But it has to be done.[22] Separate instructions must be obtained from each member of the family, and any important letter should be sent under separate cover to each member.[23] If there is a family company, that is an additional party.[24] Where a company is a client, the instructions must come from someone with authority to give them on behalf of the company.

Increasingly in recent years a "terms of engagement" letter has been sent to the client at the outset. This is now compulsory. The Solicitors (Scotland) (Client Communication) (Residential Conveyancing) Practice Rules 2003 provide that "a solicitor shall at the earliest practical opportunity upon receiving instructions to undertake any residential conveyancing work on behalf of a private client, provide the following information to the client in writing . . ." The required information includes "details of . . . work to be carried out" and the fee, or the way the fee will be calculated.[25]

To give proper instructions the clients need to understand what is going on: this is the idea of informed consent. Usually there is no problem. But sometimes there is. A donation, particularly by an elderly client, needs to be handled carefully: does the client truly understand what is proposed and truly wish it? Another problem area is where the client does not speak English well and the solicitors find that the actual communications are coming from another member of the family whose grasp of the language is better. There are dangers of miscommunication or even of fraud. If the client needs to sign a deed, and there is doubt as to whether s/he understands it, it is wise to have someone who understands the language in question to swear an affidavit, deponing that s/he knows both the English and Ruritanian languages, and has explained the meaning of the deed to the client. A problem area that has recently caused great difficulty is where a deed is to be signed that may involve the grantor in liability for someone else's debts.[26]

Checking identity

1–04   If the clients are new, the solicitors must satisfy themselves as to their identity. This is a measure of self protection, for obvious reasons, but there is also a professional duty involved: other law firms are entitled to assume that when a solicitor claims to represent a person, s/he knows

---

[22] In *Broadway v Clydesdale Bank*, 2000 G.W.D. 19–763 and 2001 G.W.D. 14–552 the law firm addressed its letters to "the Broadway Family" and opened with the words "Dear All". This sort of thing can be sensible, but it also has its dangers. For an account of this case see Reid and Gretton, *Conveyancing 2000*, p.87 and Reid and Gretton, *Conveyancing 2001*, p.92. See also *Brady v Neilsons*, 1999 G.W.D. 4–209.

[23] It also must be borne in mind that family members may have interests that conflict, and in that case the same solicitor must decline to act for one or more.

[24] See for example *Thomson v Royal Bank of Scotland plc*, 2003 S.C.L.R. 964, where a man ran a company. He and his wife granted security for its debts. One and the same solicitor acted both for the lender and for the company. Whether he was also acting for either or both the spouses was unclear. It should not have been unclear.

[25] The Law Society of Scotland has issued a style letter: see (2003) 48 J.L.S.S. Nov./47. See further Janice H. Webster, *Professional Ethics and Practice for Scottish Solicitors* (4th ed., 2004), para.2.05 and Appendix XV.

[26] See para.1–11.

who that person is. Since the arrival of legislation on money laundering (see below), verification of identity has been taken more seriously. Nowadays it is normal for a new client to be asked to produce a passport, and for a photocopy of this to be put in the file.[27]

If the client is a company, or other body corporate, it is important to verify that it is duly incorporated.[28] If it is not a Scottish company this may involve obtaining a formal letter from a lawyer in the place where the company is incorporated confirming due incorporation.[29] The fact that the person who claims to speak on behalf of the company is authorised to do so should be checked. A company search will give a list of current directors. In some cases it is wise to obtain a copy of the minute of the board meeting authorising the transaction to proceed.[30] There may also be questions as to whether the company is acting within its corporate powers, especially for entities other than UK companies. Similar issues may arise in connection with trusts.

A solicitor who enters into missives on behalf of a non-existent principal is personally liable to the counterparty.[31]

The secured lender as client

If, as is often the case, solicitors are also acting for a secured lender, that lender is also a client. It is easy, psychologically, to overlook this, because the lender will be merely a one-off client who comes into the picture as an adjunct to the "real" client. But many law firms have come to grief because they have forgotten that, as a matter of law, the lender is as much a client as the "real" client.   1–05

Some consequences of the agency relationship

Solicitors are agents and so should do what the clients tell them, provided that this is legal, ethical and practicable. Decisions are for the clients to make. If a problem arises in the course of a transaction, it is for the clients to decide what to do. For instance, if on examining the title the purchasing solicitors find that there is a defect, it is for the clients to decide whether to refuse to settle,[32] not for their solicitors, though the latter's advice is obviously important. Of course, the clients do not want to be bothered by technical details. Deciding what needs to be referred to the clients and what does not can be difficult, and solicitors have often got into trouble by deciding something themselves which should have been referred. If in doubt, it is necessary to refer to the clients. The clients must always be kept informed, for instance by copying the missives to them, so that if anything worries them they can   1–06

---

[27] The *CML Lenders' Handbook for Scotland*, para.3.3 has detailed requirements where a CML lender is a client. It provides for certain alternatives to a passport.

[28] One danger, among others, is that the company was duly incorporated but has been struck off under s.652 of the Companies Act 1985. Such strikings-off are common.

[29] For a style see Ch.25.

[30] Arguably this should be done in all cases, but in practice it is done only selectively.

[31] In *City of Glasgow Council v Peart*, 1999 Hous.L.R. 117 missives were purportedly concluded on behalf of someone who was dead.

[32] The lender, if there is one, will also have a right of veto.

make their views known. Clients have an understandable expectation that their solicitors will, like a fairy godmother, bring about a happy ending, and the lower the fee being charged the stronger that expectation is likely to be. But solicitors cannot guarantee happy endings. If the clients are told what is happening, when it is happening, they will be aware of any emerging difficulties, and if problems become serious the task of explaining those problems is then less difficult. This is a matter of prudence from the standpoint of the solicitors. All legal practice has to be defensive legal practice. Every client is a potential negligence claimant. But it is not only prudence for the benefit of the solicitors. It is something that clients are reasonably entitled to. Physicians no longer administer unnamed medicines, nor do they conceal the diagnosis when the malady is serious. Nor should solicitors do the equivalent. Finally, just as solicitors are law *agents*, so also they are *law* agents. What they have is a professional knowledge of the laws of their country. They are not plumbers, surveyors, town planners, electricians, accountants, civil engineers or architects.[33] They should not give the impression that they have any expertise in such fields.

Law Society of Scotland

1-07   The Law Society of Scotland has power to promulgate rules that are legally binding on solicitors. The Society also issues guidelines, which do not have legal force but which represent good professional practice, and which may be regarded by a court as relevant in determining whether conduct was or was not reasonable. These rules and guidelines are available in the *Parliament House Book* and in the Society's *Directory of Services for Conveyancers*.[34] They vary greatly in length and in importance. But none of them can be ignored. At the time of preparing this edition, rules of particular importance to conveyancers included:

- The Solicitors (Scotland) Practice Rules 1986[35]
- The Solicitors (Scotland) Professional Indemnity Insurance Rules 1995
- The Solicitors (Scotland) Accounts, Accounts Certificate, Professional Practice and Guarantee Fund Rules 2001[36]
- The Solicitors (Scotland) (Client Communication) (Residential Conveyancing) Practice Rules 2003.

Guidelines of importance to conveyancers included:

- Guidelines on Acting for Separated Spouses 1998
- Guidelines on Avoidance of Delay in Concluding Missives 1998

---

[33] *cf. Wylie v Jeffrey Aitken*, 2002 G.W.D. 40–1360 on which see Reid and Gretton, *Conveyancing 2002*, p.70. In this case a client sued a law firm for allegedly having given wrong advice as to whether a drainage system was sufficient.

[34] Currently the 2003 edition. The Society's website, *http://www.lawscot.org.uk/*, is another source but is incomplete. Another source is Janice H. Webster, *Professional Ethics and Practice for Scottish Solicitors* (4th ed., 2004).

[35] Commonly known as the Conflict of Interest Rules.

[36] Commonly known as the Accounts Rules.

- Guidelines on Common Repairs 1999
- Guidelines on Deeds of Conditions in Housing Estates 1999
- Guidelines on Electronic Transfer of Funds 1999
- Guidelines on Exhibition of Title Deeds 1996
- Guidelines on Faxed and Email Documents 1998
- Guidelines on Fixed Price Offers 1998
- Guidelines on Letters of Obligation in Land Registration Cases 1997
- Guidelines on Postal Settlements 2001
- Guidelines on Property Schedules and Mortgage Advice Service 1998
- Guidelines on Retention of Funds 1998
- Guidelines on Settlement Cheques Sent to be Held as Undelivered 1998
- Guidelines on Closing Dates and Notes of Interest 1998
- Guidelines on Conflict of Interest 1998
- Guidelines on Conflict of Interest between Borrower and Spouse 1998
- Guidelines on Conflict of Interest in Commercial Security Transactions 1994
- Guidelines on Conflict of Interest and Ranking Agreements 1998
- Guide to the Solicitors (Scotland) Accounts, Accounts Certificate, Professional Practice and Guarantee Fund Rules 2001.

As well as regulating the profession, the Society aims to provide support, and here one must mention the Society's *Directory of Services for Conveyancers*, which has appeared in a number of editions.

Money laundering

Criminals, like other people, need to move funds, and a fashionable 1-08 tool for fighting crime is to make it harder for them to do so, and also to confiscate the profits made from their crimes. The legislation is European[37] and in the UK is implemented by the Money Laundering Regulations 2003.[38] These Regulations require those acting in the course of a "relevant business" to set up certain procedures, including procedures for verifying the identity of clients, for careful record keeping, and so forth. Conveyancing and estate agency are "relevant businesses".[39] In addition, the incomprehensible Proceeds of Crime Act

---

[37] 91/308/EEC, as amended by 2001/97/EC.
[38] SI 2003/3075. Further provision is made by the Solicitors (Scotland) Accounts, Accounts Certificate, Professional Practice and Guarantee Fund Rules 2001. At the time of preparing this edition, the Solicitors (Scotland) Accounts, Accounts Certificate, Professional Practice and Guarantee Fund (Amendment) Rules 2004 were on the verge of being passed, amending the 2001 Rules so as to take account of SI 2003/3075.
[39] Reg. 2(2)(l) refers to "participation in a . . . real property transaction", a provision drafted in that profoundly unionist spirit which has been so manifest in UK legislation ever since 1707.

2002[40] requires solicitors to tell the authorities[41] if they have reason to suspect the laundering of money from criminal sources. This will apply mainly to the solicitors acting for buyers, if they have suspicions about where the purchase price has come from. But if the sellers' solicitors have the same suspicions then they come under the same duties. Moreover the property being sold might itself represent the proceeds of crime.[42] All this is perhaps overkill, but criminals do use law firms for their wicked purposes. One practical consequence of the rules in force is that considerable care must be taken in verifying the identity of clients.

There are many tell-tale signs which will raise suspicions in the mind of the experienced conveyancer. Examples include payment in cash, payment from a third party, vague or improbable statements as to source of funds, last minute changes to the source of funds, and obscurity as to the client's permanent address.

Other fraud

1-09   As well as keeping an eye out for money laundering, the solicitor must beware of other kinds of fraud. Being a solicitor does not confer immunity from naivety.[43] The solicitor must have a suspicious mind. Clients may be misrepresenting their financial circumstances to the lenders. Or they may claim that they will be living in the property but in fact intend to let it out. That would contravene Standard Condition 6 of the 1970 Act and is likely also to be a tax fraud, in that the clients may intend to claim capital gains tax relief on the footing that the property will be their main residence. Again, there are ingenious ways for buyer and seller to collude for fraudulent purposes. For example, Adam owns a property worth £150,000. Beatrice agrees with him that she will buy it at a notional price of £200,000. Missives are concluded at that price. Beatrice persuades a bank that the property is worth £200,000 and on that basis borrows £175,000. The transaction settles at £200,000, with Beatrice paying £25,000 of her own money. The settlement is done between the two law firms.[44] Immediately thereafter Adam repays Beatrice £40,000 (keeping £10,000 for himself as his share of the scam) and Beatrice promptly vanishes into thin air. Her profit is £15,000. The bank loses £25,000, being the difference between what the property is worth and what they loaned on it.[45] There are many variants on this basic idea.

---

[40] Section 330 replacing s.39 of the Criminal Law (Consolidation) (Scotland) Act 1995.

[41] National Criminal Intelligence Service: *http://www.ncis.co.uk/*. The website has on it a valuable document called the *National Criminal Intelligence Service Guidance in Relation to Disclosures by the Legal Profession.*

[42] See *P v P* [2003] 3 W.L.R. 1350, a case which made waves. Though not a conveyancing case it is relevant to conveyancing transactions.

[43] Even worse than naivety is active participation. In *Di Ciacca v Normand*, 1995 S.L.T. 482, £18,000 of the price of land was paid in cash, and the price stated in the deed was reduced by that amount, to evade tax. A solicitor was prosecuted and convicted for his involvement.

[44] The fraud is easier if the settlement can be done direct between buyer and seller. It is always a matter for inquiry if that happens.

[45] And will consider suing the law firm.

Conflict of interest[46]

Conflict of interest primarily means the situation which arises when 1–10 two clients of the same law firm have interests opposed to each other.[47] In general, solicitors should avoid that situation, and, if it occurs, should cease to act for one of the clients. The reason is that, while they are bound to advance the interests of clients, here they cannot advance the interests of one without detriment to the interests of the other. That is common law. More importantly, it is common sense. But the scope of the common law principle is rather vague. For instance, it is obvious that the same firm should not act for both pursuer and defender, but it is not so obvious that the same firm should not act for both buyer and seller: in some cases the conflict is more pronounced than in others.[48] Because of this uncertainty, the principle has been focused and developed by rules and guidelines from the Law Society. The rules are the Solicitors (Scotland) Practice Rules 1986 (commonly called the *Conflict of Interest Rules*), and they should be read in conjunction with the *Guidelines on Conflict of Interest in Commercial Security Transactions 1994* and the *Guidelines on Conflict of Interest 1998*.[49] A firm must not act for both seller and buyer, or for both lender and borrower, or for both tenant and landlord. But there are certain exceptions. One of the most important is that a solicitor can act for both lender and borrower if the loan is a secured one whose terms have been agreed before the solicitor has been instructed by the lender. This exception covers most home loans.[50] However, there is a general proviso, to the effect that the exceptions can apply only where "no dispute arises or might reasonably be expected to arise". The potentiality which this has for annihilating the exceptions is obvious. In some of the exceptions (but not the mortgage one) the solicitor must send to the clients a "rule 5(2) letter"[51] setting forth the position and telling them that if a dispute does arise then separate legal representation will be necessary. This letter must be sent at the outset, not merely when the dispute arises.

Where co-owners sell there is not normally a problem. But they may be at loggerheads: the classic case is where a couple are splitting up in bitterness and the matrimonial home is to be sold. They may agree on

---

[46] See generally Janice H. Webster, *Professional Ethics and Practice for Scottish Solicitors* (4th ed., 2004).

[47] A secondary meaning is where the interests of the law firm become opposed to those of the client, for instance where the client accuses the firm of negligence. In this case also it is in general necessary for the law firm to advise the client to seek separate representation. But judging when that time has finally arrived can be difficult, and experience is required.

[48] Another difficult area in the common law is the question of clients waiving their rights to object to the conflict.

[49] For conflict of interest in security transactions see also (2003) 48 J.L.S.S. Oct./45 for a statement by the Professional Practice Committee. For discussion see D. J. Cusine and Robert Rennie, *Standard Securities* (2nd ed., 2002), Ch.2. See also (2003) 48 J.L.S.S. March/9.

[50] But note an important exception to the exception: a law firm cannot act for a lender if the borrower is a partner, spouse of a partner, etc. See the Solicitors (Scotland) Accounts, Accounts Certificate, Professional Practice and Guarantee Fund Rules 2001, r.22.

[51] The reference is to r.5(2) of the Solicitors (Scotland) Practice Rules 1986.

the sale but on little else.[52] For instance they may disagree on whether
the proceeds should be divided equally and they may disagree as to
whether any unsecured debts should be paid from the proceeds. Such
cases are death-traps for the law firms involved, and the advice of the
Law Society is that solicitors should not accept sale instructions until the
parties have entered into a written agreement with each other.[53] Finally,
disgruntled clients sometimes allege conflict of interest, and on that basis
claim damages. But even if conflict does exist, that does not of *itself* give
rise to any claim by a client for compensation. Often it is merely *injuria
sine damno*.

Cautionary wives

1-11   It sometimes happens that solicitors must advise someone who is
thinking of signing a deed that may involve her in liability for someone
else's debts. We say "her" because this area, though ostensibly gender-
neutral, is in substance highly gendered. The cases, which are
numerous,[54] all concern a wife incurring liability for the debts of her
husband's business.[55] This can happen in more than one way. One
variant is the nature of the husband's business. (a) He may be a sole
trader. (b) He may be a partner in a firm with unlimited liability. (c) He
may control a company (*e.g.* sole director and main shareholder) and the
debts are in fact those of the company. Another variant is the deed to be
signed by the wife. (d) It may be a straightforward cautionary obligation,
without any standard security. (e) There may be both a cautionary
obligation and a standard security securing that obligation granted over
property of which she is the sole owner or co-owner. (f) There may be
no cautionary obligation at all, but a standard security granted directly
for her husband's business debts.[56] (g) It may be a standard security for
an ordinary home loan, granted jointly by herself and her husband,
without any idea that the deed might relate to any other debts, but which
in fact is so worded that other debts may be covered by it. In all these
cases except the last there is a potential conflict of interest between the
parties,[57] and the same solicitors should not act for both.[58]

There is a danger that if, later, things go wrong and the wife suffers
loss she will say that she was not properly advised. The unanswerable
logic is that had she been properly advised she never would have signed.

---

[52] One other thing they are likely to concur in is the correct evaluation of the other's
character and reliability.

[53] Law Society of Scotland, *Guidelines on Acting for Separated Spouses* (1998).

[54] See generally S. Eden (2003) 7 *Edinburgh Law Review* 107 and (2004) 8 *Edinburgh
Law Review* 276.

[55] But in principle the issues are general ones, and might involve, for example, parent
and child, or two companies in the same group, or a businessperson and the company
through which s/he does business.

[56] In this case she has no personal liability. Suppose that the debts were £300,000 and
the property worth £100,000. She could lose the property but could not be liable for the
balance due to the bank.

[57] There may in fact be three (or even more) parties: husband, husband's company, and
wife.

[58] So advised by the Law Society of Scotland's Professional Practice Committee and the
Conveyancing Committee in (2003) 48 J.L.S.S. Oct./46.

This line of argument may in the first instance be used as a shield against the bank,[59] but if that fails it may be used as a sword against the solicitors who advised her—or failed to advise her properly. The advising solicitor must ensure that the wife fully understands the meaning and effect of the document, and should keep evidence to that effect. It is a good idea to send her a letter explaining it and asking her to acknowledge that she had read and understood the letter.[60] Naturally solicitors always have a duty to be reasonably satisfied that the client's consent is genuine and informed. But in some cases special care is advisable. Many law firms are reluctant to advise the cautionary wife, especially because of English caselaw imposing on solicitors impossibly onerous duties in such cases.[61]

In the last case,[62] where the standard security is for an ordinary home loan, and no business borrowing appears to be in contemplation, there is probably no conflict of interest as between husband and wife. But the solicitor must read the bank's standard style carefully, and if there is any possibility that the deed might cover future debts due by just one of the parties, that must be explained to the clients. It will be wise to record that advice in an outgoing letter.

Confidentiality

A client's affairs are confidential: the solicitor must not divulge them 1–12 except with the client's permission. This obligation of confidentiality does not, however, apply to information which is in any case in the public domain, for instance an entry in a public register. Solicitors are also not bound by confidentiality where they have reason to believe that the client plans to commit a crime. In such a case they may inform the appropriate authority,[63] and indeed are probably under a professional obligation to do so if the intention seems serious and the proposed crime is not of a minor nature.

Where possible past crime is involved, the Law Society has issued the following advice: "If you are asked to give a statement to the police or to the Procurator Fiscal, the Professional Practice Committee view is that you should offer to be precognosed on oath before the Sheriff. If you answer a question on the direction of the Court you would not be the subject of a complaint of breach of confidentiality."[64]

---

[59] The leading case is *Smith v Bank of Scotland*, 1997 S.C. 111. Consent improperly obtained by the husband can be pled in some cases by the wife against the bank. See further para.19–04.

[60] See previous footnote.

[61] The high-water mark was the decision of the Court of Appeal in *Royal Bank of Scotland plc v Etridge (No.2)* [1998] 4 All E.R. 705, on which see Gretton, 1999 S.L.T. (News) 53. When the case went to the House of Lords a slightly more moderate line was taken: [2002] 2 A.C. 773. The Scottish courts have declined to follow this case (see in particular *Royal Bank of Scotland plc v Wilson*, 2003 S.C. 544), but the reported cases have not so far involved actions by the cautionary wife (after her husband's business has failed) against the solicitors who advised her, and so the law remains somewhat unclear. The reluctance to advise the cautionary wife is fully understandable. See further D.J. Cusine and Robert Rennie, *Standard Securities* (2nd ed., 2002), paras 2.03 and 2.04. The latter paragraph is headed "Impossible burden for solicitors."

[62] Case (g) above.

[63] The Procurator Fiscal, the Lord Advocate, the Chief Constable, or the National Criminal Intelligence Service.

[64] Law Society of Scotland, *Guidelines on Confidentiality* (1998).

The Accounts Rules

1-13   These rules[65] have a fearsome reputation, but the basics are not especially complex. Indeed, to a large extent they are simple common sense. A law firm must segregate moneys which it holds for *clients* from its *own* funds. At any one time a law firm will hold some money on behalf of clients.[66] Usually such moneys are held only for a short time, perhaps only a few days, but at any given moment the total of such moneys may be substantial in amount. One example would be money received from the sale of property. Another would be money received from a client with which to settle a purchase, which has not yet taken place. A third example would be money ingathered in the course of executry administration. The law firm must hold a client account with a recognised bank, into which such moneys are paid, and from which they are withdrawn as and when needed. This account is in the name of the firm, but is expressly designated as the client account.[67] A fundamental principle is that the amount held in the client account must never—not for a single day—be less than the total amount held by the firm on behalf of clients.[68] If that principle is honoured, the objective of segregation has been achieved. Breaches of this principle occur too often. It is a sensible precaution for the firm to keep a float in the client account so that inadvertent errors will (it may be hoped) not cause a breach of the rules.[69] It should be noted that the principle implies that withdrawals from the client account can be made only where a disbursement is being made on behalf of a client, and out of funds which the client has on deposit with the firm. For example, suppose that a firm issues a fee note and withdraws the amount of the fee from the client account, paying it into the firm's ordinary account. That will be lawful if the client has on deposit with the firm sufficient to cover the fee.[70] But otherwise there will have been a breach of the Accounts Rules. (In effect, the firm will have been paying itself the fee out of funds held for *other* clients.) Another way in which the rules may be breached is if a disbursement is made on behalf of a client out of the client account without the client having first deposited funds to cover that disbursement. If such a disbursement is to be made without such a previous deposit it will have to be made out of the firm's own funds, and the moneys recovered from the client thereafter.

---

[65] The Solicitors (Scotland) Accounts, Accounts Certificate, Professional Practice and Guarantee Fund Rules 2001. See further Janice H. Webster, *Professional Ethics and Practice for Scottish Solicitors* (4th ed., 2004), para.2.25.

[66] This is a major practical difference between advocates and solicitors. It should be mentioned however that a few law firms do not hold such funds to any significant degree, such as firms dealing only in criminal work.

[67] A firm may hold more than one client account, and indeed in theory could hold as many client accounts as it has clients.

[68] Rule 4(1): "Every solicitor shall—(a) ensure that at all times the sum at the credit of the client account, or where there are more such accounts than one, the total of the sums at the credit of those accounts, shall be not less than the total of the clients' money held by the solicitor . . ."

[69] This goes against the principle of segregation but is permitted by rule 5.

[70] But even then it is permissible only if the fee has been rendered to the client. See rule 6.

From the external standpoint the moneys held by the firm are held in a bank account, the client account. But internally, the rules also require that the firm keep proper records and accounts. That means that each client has an account with the firm, on which all financial transactions are recorded, including moneys received from the client, from third parties for the client,[71] payments to the client, or to third parties for the client,[72] fees deducted, and so on. Of course, most firms keep these accounts in computerised form, but it is perfectly lawful to keep them in the traditional way, *i.e.* with pen, ink and paper. The total amount held for clients on all these various internal accounts should, at any moment in time, be not less than the total held on the external client account.

Interest earned on the client account is subject to two rules. If more than £500 is held for a client for more than two months, the client should normally be credited with the interest, but in other cases the firm may keep such interest for itself.

Every firm must have a "designated cash room partner" who is the compliance officer for the purposes of the rules. That partner, together with one other partner, must send to the Law Society, every six months, a certificate that the rules have been complied with. The Law Society have powers to audit the accounts to verify compliance.

The buying client's expectations

Once upon a time, solicitors were employed by clients to get a good title for them. That was, and remains, an important task. However, today clients expect more. One of the problems of modern practice is that there can be a mismatch of expectations between clients and solicitors. It can be hard to know what the clients can reasonably expect of their solicitors: reasonable expectations change over time. 1-14

Clients may well not understand the difference between open missives and concluded missives. The distinction must be explained. Furthermore clients tend to assume that if rights are created by missives then they will be enforceable. That may not be so: the counterparties may have disappeared or become insolvent, for example.

One problem area concerns the physical condition of the new house. It must be explained to the clients that sellers of heritable property (unlike sellers of moveables) do not normally warrant the condition of the property.[73] In most cases the property is not a new one,[74] and purchasers need to understand that they are buying something that is second-hand, or indeed twentieth-hand, and they must adjust their expectations accordingly. Sellers will normally warrant the title, but not the condition. If the house collapses the day after entry, the sellers have at common law no contractual liability. They warranted the title, and the purchasers' title

---

[71] For instance, the client is selling, and money is received from the buyer's solicitors.

[72] For instance, moneys paid to a lender to pay off a loan.

[73] This is, at least, the conventional view. For discussion, see Black, 1982 J.R. 31; Halliday, 1983 J.R. 1; Cusine (1983) 28 J.L.S.S. 228; Reid, in D. J. Cusine (ed.), *A Scots Conveyancing Miscellany: Essays in Honour of Professor J. M. Halliday* (1987), p.152. Exceptions can exist, *e.g.* where the seller is a builder: see *e.g. Owen v Fotheringham*, 1997 S.L.T. (Sh. Ct) 28.

[74] For new properties see Ch.27.

to the shattered bricks and splintered beams is indeed good. Clients need to understand that buying a second-hand house is like buying anything second-hand. There is always a risk. Even the best surveyor may overlook some defect, such as deeply hidden wood rot. It must be explained that the lenders' survey report may be fairly superficial, and that it is advisable for the clients to have their own survey.[75] It is necessary to explain what clauses will be put in the offer, and explain their limitations. For instance, the offer may not cover plumbing, and the rot clause is likely only to ask the sellers to warrant that there is no rot "so far as they are aware", which is obviously very different from an absolute guarantee. The clients must be asked whether they wish to have additional provisions, but it should also be explained that a seller is likely to reject any unusual terms. Often missives provide that any defects which the sellers are liable for must be notified to the sellers within, say, seven days of entry, and obviously the buying clients must be alerted to such deadlines. For instance, if the clients are concerned about the plumbing, they may be best advised to arrange for a plumber to visit the property before settlement, or before conclusion of missives. But of course this will cost money. As a checklist, the following are common physical problems: timber (wet rot, dry rot and woodworm), subsidence, roofing, electrics (wiring and appliances), gas (piping and appliances), central heating, drains, plumbing, and damp (rising, penetrating and condensing).[76]

Another problem area is that while solicitors acting in a purchase will check the planning situation for the property itself, they will not usually do so for adjacent properties. The client moves in and one month later finds that the charming field next door, over which she has views to the sea and the hills, is being converted into an all-year, open-air, 50-metre-high pop concert venue. The client's musical tastes go no later than Brahms, and she has three children under five. Why wasn't she told? Her solicitors didn't tell her because they didn't know, and they didn't know because they didn't ask the Council.[77] Why not, the client asks? Her husband has had a nervous breakdown and her house is unsellable. Here there has been a mismatch of expectations. Clarity at the outset is the aim.

A problem in modern practice is that many houses[78] have been altered at some stage without building consent from the local authority. Classic examples are ground floor extensions, removal of internal walls, and extensions at attic level. Missives almost always have a clause requiring the seller to warrant that there have been no such alterations within the past, say, ten years. But there is the usual problem that suing a seller is unsatisfactory at best and that at worst the seller may be unsueable. A

---

[75] For surveys see Ch.2.

[76] There is fashion in all things. Once upon a time, what everyone worried about was drains. When the authors did their apprenticeships, no one cared much about drains, and the fashionable worries were damp and subsidence. But damp and subsidence have gone the way of drains. The fashion for some years now has been to worry about unauthorised alterations.

[77] Modern missives often ask the seller to disclose any "neighbour notifications" received for planning applications. But the seller may fail so to disclose.

[78] No one knows how many. Estimates vary from 20 per cent to over 50 per cent.

response to this problem is for the buyer's solicitor to ask the surveyor to report on any modern alterations, and then to insist that the seller produces the requisite documentation, which will be building consent and sometimes also planning consent. These consents are then checked against the works which have actually been done, for it is not safe to suppose that if (a) works have been done and (b) building consent exists, then (c) the works conform to the consents.

Another point which needs to be explained is that in a typical conveyancing transaction the purchasers' solicitors will not visit the property. They are too busy and the fee chargeable does not cover time spent on a site visit, which in most cases would be pointless anyway. But occasionally this can cause problems. The unauthorised new garage, a problem of access rights, a boundary problem, which cause such trouble later, might all have been spotted in time if the buyers' solicitors had visited the property. But most firms will only make a site visit if the clients will pay for it. However, if at any stage it becomes clear that a site visit is advisable, then obviously it must be made. There is always the danger that if a law firm is sued for having missed something that a site visit would have revealed, a court might be unsympathetic to the plea that conveyancing fees do not justify such visits.

Another source of dispute concerns the proposed use of the property. The buyers' solicitors need to check what their clients' plans are. The real burdens may for instance forbid commercial use. If the clients wish to convert the property into a hotel, they will need to know this before they are committed to the purchase. So they must be asked. And as soon as the burdens writs have been seen, the clients must be informed of their provisions, as part of the report on title that should be given.[79] Unfortunately this does not always happen, at any stage, let alone before conclusion of missives.[80] Proposed usage has implications for planning permission and various types of licence. Such issues are, however, more likely to arise in commercial than in residential conveyancing.

However careful one is, the fact is that for many or most clients, lawyers are part of "the law" and it is the job of "the law" to ensure that their transaction proceeds reasonably smoothly, and unreasonably cheaply. For example, the typical purchasing clients regard closed missives as inviolable, so that settlement will take place when they want it even if the seller has died, been sequestrated, gone mad, run off with the barmaid/barman, or been abducted by aliens.[81] The typical client does not understand the distinction between contract and conveyance— between personal rights and real rights. Most clients do not expect there to be risks in conveyancing. The conveyancer knows that such risks exist,

---

[79] Even such an apparently minor condition as on the keeping of cats can cause major problems: see *e.g.* (1992) 37 J.L.S.S. 118.

[80] According to the Scottish Consumer Council, *Home Truths: A Report on Research into the Experiences of Recent House Buyers in Scotland* (2000), only 54 per cent of buyers questioned said that they had been given information on the burdens affecting their property; and in the case of tenements only 55 per cent said that the arrangements for common repairs had been explained. Broadly similar findings are contained in a survey carried out for the Scottish Law Commission, and reproduced at the end of the Commission's *Report on Real Burdens* (Scot. Law Com. No.181, 2000).

[81] Clients may also expect the other side to be bound by open missives, though themselves free to repudiate them.

16

and that although steps can be taken to reduce them, they cannot be eliminated. As a matter of fact the attitude of the typical client is not wholly unreasonable.[82] The conveyancer needs to be able to look at matters from the client's standpoint, so as to be able to explain the risks. Happily, there are some clients who will understand.

Getting information from the selling client

1–15   When clients decide to sell, various questions need to be asked. For example:

(1) Whether there have been any alterations in the property which would require planning or building consent.

(2) Whether the property has wet or dry rot or woodworm, whether any eradication work has been done for these recently, whether the central heating is in working order, and any other similar matters which likely to be raised in an offer to purchase.

(3) Whether any statutory repairs notice has been received.

(4) Whether the client has received any "neighbour notification" for any planning applications for nearby property.

(5) Whether the client has received any court writs. The classic example would be an inhibition, which would prevent any sale, but there are other possibilities such as a sequestration or an action by a neighbour about, for instance, a boundary dispute.

(6) What debts are secured over the property, since all secured debts will have to be paid off at sale. Typically there will be a bank or building society mortgage and the client should know roughly what is due. The lender normally sends an annual statement. The exact amount can be found out from the lender in due course. The great danger is that there is also a second security which the clients have granted. They may not reveal this unless asked.

(7) What moveables, if any, are included in the sale.

On the importance of record-keeping

1–16   As in all legal business good records should be kept. Partly this is for one's own convenience (memory is fallible) and partly in case someone else in the firm has to take over the transaction. But it also important as a defence against a later claim for negligence. When there is such a claim there is often a difference in the clients' account of events and that of the solicitor. "The solicitor is unlikely to recall after a period of several years what advice he gave to the client on a routine matter. The best that he can do is to describe his usual advice in the particular circumstances or to speculate as to what he "must" have said, which is unlikely to carry as much weight as the recollection of the plaintiff."[83]

---

[82] As to what the "system" should ideally deliver to them. What is obviously unreasonable is the desire to get a professional service at bucket-shop prices.

[83] R. M. Jackson, *Jackson & Powell on Professional Negligence* (5th ed., 2001), para.10–174.

That is common sense and it is the way the courts tend to look at the matter.[84] So the file should contain not only all incoming and outgoing correspondence, but also a note of every significant telephone conversation and meeting, and such a note should usually be backed up by an outgoing letter.[85] Significant documents should be photocopied, or digitally scanned, before being posted out.

When the transaction has been finished, fraudulent clients may request delivery of the file to them or their agents in order to destroy the evidence. When a file is given up a photocopy should be retained.[86] (Some firms maintain the file in digital form anyway.)

Negligence: delict

Negligence actions against solicitors are commoner today than they 1-17 used to be. Possibly this is because standards have declined,[87] but the major reason is probably that clients expect more. Little will be said about this unhappy subject here.[88] But it should be noted that a conveyancer is not liable merely because something goes wrong and a client loses money—though clients are likely to think otherwise.

The delictual standard of care of solicitors is generally accepted as being the same as that laid down in one of the leading cases on medical negligence, *Hunter v Hanley*.[89] There Lord President Cooper said:

> "To establish liability by a doctor where deviation from normal practice is alleged, three facts require to be established. First of all it must be proved that there is a usual and normal practice; secondly it must be proved that the defender has not adopted that practice; and thirdly . . . it must be established that the course the doctor adopted is one which no professional man of ordinary skill would have taken if he had been acting with ordinary care."

That is an undemanding standard of expertise. It is a sufficient defence to show that even some ordinarily competent solicitors would have made the same mistake.[90] But of course the solicitor cannot trust his luck too far. It must be borne in mind that what was acceptable conveyancing

---

[84] But the absence of proper records does not raise any actual presumption in favour of the clients: see *Wylie v Jeffrey Aitken*, 2002 G.W.D. 40–1360; Reid and Gretton, *Conveyancing 2002*, p.70.

[85] For a horror story see *Cheltenham & Gloucester plc v Sun Alliance & London Insurance plc (No.2)*, 2002 G.W.D. 18–605, with details in Reid and Gretton, *Conveyancing 2002*, p.68.

[86] *cf.* the *CML Lenders' Handbook for Scotland*, para.14.

[87] In the 1990s there was strong downward pressure on conveyancing fees, and it may be that there was a resulting downward pressure on standards. But the whole subject is controversial.

[88] See Robert Rennie, *Solicitors' Negligence* (1997) and Robert Rennie, *Opinions on Professional Negligence in Conveyancing* (2004). English law is highly relevant in this area. See R. M. Jackson, *Jackson & Powell on Professional Negligence* (5th ed., 2001); Hugh Evans, *Lawyers' Liabilities* (2nd ed., 2002).

[89] 1955 S.C. 200.

[90] There is a parallel doctrine in England, based on *Bolam v Friern Hospital* [1957] 2 All E.R. 118. But the *Bolam* doctrine is not an absolute one: *Bolitho v City and Hackney Health Authority* [1998] A.C. 232. Whether Scots law would follow *Bolitho* is uncertain.

practice at one period may not be so at a later period. For instance, a conveyancer acting for a seller who fails to include in the missives a clause requiring interest on the price in the event of late settlement would probably be liable in negligence to his client if the client suffered loss thereby. Such clauses, today standard good practice, were uncommon 30 years ago, and so a conveyancer could not then have been held liable. Thus changing practice itself changes the level of ordinary competence. One moral is that conveyancers must keep abreast of new developments, whether new legislation, new case law or simply new standard practices. Conveyancers must therefore, if only for their own protection, keep an eye on the law reports and legal journals.[91]

It must also be borne in mind that conveyancers often have to act under pressure. In a negligence action, counsel for the pursuer may ask the solicitors why they drafted some clause as they did. With hindsight it may seem indefensible, and in law it may indeed be indefensible. What the solicitors know, and what other conveyancers know, but what the counsel and the judge and the (former) client may not understand, is the pressure of chamber practice, when a clause must be drafted immediately, the drafting being interrupted several times by the ringing of the telephone and the consumption of aspirins, all in pursuit of a fee which, though no client ever believes it, may not do much more than cover overheads. At times like this solicitors rue the day when they filled in "law" on the UCAS form.

Negligence: contract

1-18   *Hunter v Hanley* was a delict case, and in practice actions against solicitors tend to be based on a delictual standard of care. But in the vast majority of cases the pursuer has a contract with the defending law firm,[92] and in principle there is no reason why the contractual standard of care should be the same as that in *Hunter v Hanley*. This is an area which has not been properly developed in our law, but the possibilities are clear. For instance, suppose that buyers' solicitors fail to spot a serious discrepancy between the boundaries in the title and the boundaries on the ground. Had they visited the property they would have seen the problem. Are they liable? Perhaps not under *Hunter v Hanley*. But a court might possibly accept an argument that the solicitors were in breach of an implied term of the client-agent contract. Moreover, one need not invoke implied terms to go beyond *Hunter v Hanley*. If the solicitors have not carried out express instructions, there will be prima facie liability, regardless of the practices of "ordinarily competent conveyancers". In residential conveyancing, buyers usually do not issue

---

[91] The *Journal of the Law Society of Scotland* has a regular feature called "Risk Management" (previously "Caveat"). According to the column at (1992) 37 J.L.S.S. 156, 47 per cent of claims arise in respect of conveyancing. The column is useful reading for any conveyancer, as are, unfortunately, the reports of the discipline tribunal. For a collection of these, see Ian Smith, *Procedures and Decisions of the Scottish Solicitors' Discipline Tribunal* (1995).

[92] In some unusual types of case a solicitor can be professionally liable to a non-client, in which case contractual liability will not normally be possible. For a discussion, see Sheriff Principal Risk in *Tait v Brown & McRae*, 1997 S.L.T. (Sh. Ct) 63.

much in the way of express instructions (except as to such obvious matters as price, date of entry, etc.), but commercial clients are often more insistent. Banks, when taking security, often have extremely detailed and highly demanding requirements which the solicitors are expected to agree to in writing. In such a case a defence based on the *Hunter v Hanley* standard of care is unlikely to succeed. Indeed, claims by banks for faulty security work constitute one of the most active areas of professional negligence today.

Negligence: insurance

Solicitors are insured against their own negligence: such insurance is 1–19 in fact compulsory.[93] However, the Master Policy has certain qualifications, one of which is that the solicitor must have acted honestly and in good faith. Where that condition is not met, the insurance cover is void: for a remarkable example see *Cheltenham & Gloucester v Sun Alliance and London Insurance plc.*[94]

Negligence: some examples of claims

There are, alas, many reported cases. Here is a selection: negligence 1–20 was not in fact established in all of them, and the facts given below are as averred by the pursuers and not necessarily as proved.[95]

- A house was resold within three years of having been purchased from the local authority, thus inadvertently triggering liability for repayment of discount.[96] The solicitors were sued for having failed to advise on the timing of the sale.[97]
- A client sued the law firm for having failed to ensure that the property had the appropriate planning permission, building consents and fire certificate.[98]
- A client sued the law firm for having failed to ensure that the property was properly served by servitudes of access and cabling.[99]
- Money was to be borrowed against a standard security. The lenders transferred the money to the law firm which it was using. The latter handed the money over to the borrower's solicitors, who in turn handed it over to the borrower, who

---

[93] Solicitors (Scotland) Professional Indemnity Insurance Rules 1995.

[94] 2001 S.L.T. 347 (discussed in Reid and Gretton, *Conveyancing 2000*, pp.116–7) *rev.* 2001 S.L.T. 1151 (discussed in Reid and Gretton, *Conveyancing 2001*, pp.30–32), and *Cheltenham & Gloucester plc v Sun Alliance & London Insurance plc (No.2)*, 2002 G.W.D. 18–605. (The latter summarises the proof, which is full of interest and worth reading on the Scottish Courts website: *http://www.scotcourts.gov.uk/*.) See further Reid and Gretton, *Conveyancing 2001*, p.30 and Reid and Gretton, *Conveyancing 2002*, p.68.

[95] The examples given are Scottish. In England there is a rich harvest of such cases, and the law of professional negligence is in many ways similar on the two sides of the border.

[96] For the "right to buy" legislation, see Ch.27.

[97] *Higginbotham v Paul Gebal & Co.*, 1993 G.W.D. 3–221.

[98] *Paterson v Sturrock & Armstrong*, 1993 G.W.D. 27–1706.

[99] *Watson v Gillespie Macandrew*, 1995 G.W.D. 13–750.

"dissipated" it.[1] All this was done without the standard
security having been put in place. The lenders sued both law
firms.[2]

• Land was sold. No servitude right of access in favour of the
retained land was reserved.[3] (When part of a site is sold it is
often important that servitudes and burdens or both be
created, either in favour of the disponed land, or the retained
land, or both.)

• Land was sold in a way that was not tax-efficient. The seller
sued his solicitors for not having advised him about the tax
aspects.[4]

• A title was bad. In the first place, the seller was an
undischarged bankrupt. In the second place, the property
turned out not to be belong to the seller at all, but to a
company. In the third place, that company did not in fact
exist, and never had existed.[5] (Is this the worst title in the
history of Scots law?).

Negligence: claims by lenders

1-21   In *National Home Loans Corporation v Giffen Couch & Archer*[6] Peter
Gibson L.J. remarked that increasing competition between lenders had
resulted in more speculative lending with a consequent higher level of
defaults, and "this has led mortgage lenders to seek ways to recover their
losses from others, and actions in negligence against their professional
advisers have become only too common". In that case the court held that
the solicitors were not liable merely because they had not told the
lenders that the borrowers had a rocky financial record. That may seem
like simple commonsense, but it came just after *Mortgage Express Ltd v
Bowerman & Partners*,[7] a decision that frightened every conveyancer in
the UK, and which has not been overruled, even though some later cases
have happily been able to distinguish it. In *Mortgage Express* the
defendants were instructed by a Mr Hadi to buy a house for £220,000.
They also acted for the mortgage lenders, the plaintiffs. The loan was for
£180,000. The property had been valued at £198,000. The defendants
became aware that the seller, a Mr Arrach, had just bought the property
from a Mr Khedair for only £150,000, but they did not tell the plaintiffs.
After borrowing and buying, Mr Hadi promptly defaulted. The plaintiffs
sold the property but it fetched only £96,000. The plaintiffs were
professional moneylenders, capable of forming their own assessment of
Mr Hadi's creditworthiness. They had had the property valued by
professional   valuers.   The   defendants   were   not   professional

---

[1] "Dissipation" may well describe precisely what happened.
[2] *The Mortgage Corporation v Mitchells Roberton*, 1997 S.L.T. 1305.
[3] *Moffat v Milne*, 1993 G.W.D. 8–572. But the position may sometimes be rescued by
the doctrine of access as a right inherent in ownership: see para.13–27.
[4] *Smith v Gordon & Smyth*, 2001 G.W.D. 26–1066. See Reid and Gretton, *Conveyancing 2001*, p.104.
[5] *Di Ciacca v Archibald Sharp & Sons*, 1995 S.L.T. 380.
[6] [1997] 3 All E.R. 808.
[7] [1996] 2 All E.R. 836.

moneylenders and they were not professional valuers. All the decisions were taken by the plaintiffs, and the role of the defendants was merely to put in place a registered mortgage. This they did. When it turned out that the plaintiffs had made a bad lending decision, instead of accepting the loss they took the view that they should be compensated by the defendants. The basis of the claim was that the defendants should have told them that the property might be worth less than valuation, because it had recently been sold for less than valuation. Alarmingly, the Court of Appeal held the defendants to be liable. Although *Mortgage Express* is an English case and thus of no more than persuasive authority, Scots and English law are similar in the area of professional negligence.[8]

Lenders, unlike private clients, have their own pre-printed instructions which are normally non-negotiable, detailed and onerous. The result is often that the obligations owed are stricter than those owed to a purchaser. Obviously there are dangers here, and in practice solicitors will often be wise to qualify their reports on title, especially since some of the demands may be unreasonable or of uncertain meaning.[9] The best thing to do with a noose is to keep your neck well away.

Marketing of property

Traditionally property marketing has been done mainly by law firms. 1–22 In the 1960s estate agents in the English style began to establish themselves.[10] Such estate agents are sometimes called non-solicitor estate agents (NSEAs) to distinguish them from solicitor estate agents (SEAs). Law firms responded to the challenge by improving their marketing services, especially by establishing Solicitors Property Centres (SPCs). Aberdeen is the oldest, dating from 1969.[11] The original Glasgow SPC failed, and for many years NSEAs dominated the Glasgow market. A new Glasgow SPC was founded in 1993 and has made rapid progress.

SEA properties, as well as being marketed in the ordinary way by the seller's firm (newspaper advertising, etc.), are marketed through the SPCs. This is done by having one or more SPC offices, where the public are welcome to browse, looking for suitable properties. In addition, SPCs publish magazines, and have websites, listing the properties on offer: these magazines (which also carry advertising) are issued free and have a wide circulation. The SPCs have a rule whereby only law firms

---

[8] Scottish negligence claims by lenders against solicitors include *Bristol & West Building Society v Rollo Steven & Boyd*, 1998 S.L.T. 8; *Midland Bank v Cameron Thom Peterkins & Duncan*, 1988 S.L.T. 611 (an important pre-*Mortgage Express* decision); *Royal Bank of Scotland plc v Harper Macleod*, 1999 G.W.D. 16–733; *Bristol & West Building Society v Aitken Nairn*, 1999 S.C. 678 (on which see Reid and Gretton, *Conveyancing 1999*, p.72); *Leeds & Holbeck Building Society v Alex Morison & Co.*, 2001 S.C.L.R. 41 (on which see Reid and Gretton, *Conveyancing 2000*, p.114; *Cheltenham & Gloucester Building Society v Royal & Sun Alliance Insurance*, 2001 S.L.T. 347; *Newcastle Building Society v Paterson Robertson & Graham*, 2001 S.C. 734 (on which see Reid and Gretton, *Conveyancing 2001*, p.29).

[9] And sometimes couched in terms of English law. At least one major lender requires solicitors to certify that the borrower is the "legal and beneficial owner".

[10] See John Sinclair, *Handbook of Conveyancing Practice in Scotland* (4th ed., 2002), paras 1.17–1.21.

[11] For links to the various SPCs see *http://www.sspc.co.uk/*. Some SPC websites have extensive information for the public: see *e.g. http://www.espc.co.uk/*.

can use them. The SPCs have proved very successful: potential buyers like to have a system whereby a very large proportion of the properties for sale in their area can be found out about quickly and easily.[12] Their success led to complaints by NSEAs and the Scottish Consumer Council, alleging that the SPCs were monopolistic. Action by the Office of Fair Trading under the Restrictive Trade Practices Act 1976 failed,[13] but the OFT continued its attack and in 1996 succeeded in getting the Monopolies and Mergers Commission to make a formal inquiry under the Fair Trading Act 1973. To the dismay of NSEAs and to the relief of the legal profession, the Report[14] concluded that the SPCs were not operating unfairly.

What proportion of the market was held by SEAs was unclear. The figures produced by the MMC's own research were different from those produced by an independent consultancy, Pieda plc, commissioned by the SPCs. The truth perhaps lies somewhere in the middle. The following table shows the SEA market share (by percentage) according to the two surveys. How much has changed since the mid-1990s is unknown, except that the market share of the GSPC, which was founded as recently as 1993, has increased.

	MMC	Pieda
Aberdeen	82	91
South West	79	81
Tayside	71	97
Edinburgh	67	82
Moray	67	68
Perthshire	56	88
Highland	52	49
Glasgow	22	14

The average sale commission for SEAs was 1.12 per cent, contrasted with the average NSEA figure of 1.42 per cent.[15] Both figures were higher than the average fee for conveyancing, either for sale or purchase, which were 0.81 per cent and 0.89 per cent respectively.[16] When one compares and contrasts[17] the different levels both of expertise and of risk, one has to think that something has gone wrong with conveyancing fees.

---

[12] Consumers also like the low pressure approach of SPCs.

[13] *Aberdeen SPC Ltd v Director General for Fair Trading,* 1996 S.L.T. 523.

[14] *Solicitors Estate Agency Services in Scotland* (Cm. 3699, August 1997). This is a mine of information about the housing market in the mid-1990s.

[15] *Solicitors Estate Agency Services in Scotland,* pp.250 and 286. The figures were assessed in 1996. In England estate agency fees tend to be substantially higher.

[16] *Solicitors Estate Agency Services in Scotland,* pp.256 and 268.

[17] To use the wording so loved by university examiners.

There exists a certain amount of sniping between SEAs and NSEAs as to which provide the better service to the public. The NSEAs claim to be more active in marketing while being no more expensive. The latter assertion is not supported by the statistics (see above). The first claim has not been tested empirically, but it would be hard to dispute that the SPC system means that participating law firms can usually market properties better than NSEAs.

The agency contracts which clients are asked to sign with NSEAs are sometimes draconian in their terms. Actions by NSEAs to compel payment of commission are common.[18] SEAs seldom contract on such terms and actions by them to compel commission are almost unknown.

Some figures about the housing market

Over the years there have been dramatic changes in the proportion of 1–23 residential properties under owner-occupation. The following table[19] shows the changes.

Year	Public sector rented%	Owner occupation%	Other%[20]
1921	6	14	80
1931	13	17	70
1941	22	22	56
1951	28	24	48
1961	42	27	31
1971	53	29	17
1981	55	35	10
1991	38	52	10
2001	23	64	13

[18] See *e.g. Chris Hart (Business Sales) Ltd v Cunie*, 1992 S.L.T. 544; *Chris Hart (Business Sales) Ltd v Niven*, 1992 S.C.L.R. 534; *Chris Hart (Business Sales) Ltd v Duncan*, 1994 S.C.L.R. 104; *Stuart Wyse Ogilvie Estates Ltd v Bryant*, 1995 G.W.D. 27–1429; *Chris Hart (Business Sales) Ltd v Mitchell*, 1996 S.L.T. (Sh. Ct) 132; *Robert Barry & Co. v Doyle*, 1998 S.L.T. 1238; *Christie Owen & Davis plc v King*, 1998 S.C.L.R. 786; *G & S Properties Ltd v Henderson*, 1999 G.W.D. 6–282; *G & S Properties v Francis*, 2001 S.L.T. 934.

[19] *Solicitors Estate Agency Services in Scotland*, p.165, except for the 2001 figures, which are from *http://www.scotland.gov.uk/stats/*. Figures have been rounded.

[20] Chiefly (a) private sector rented and (b) housing association. The latter has shown strong growth in recent years. Between 1991 and 2001 its share grew from 2.6 per cent to 6.3 per cent.

In 2002 the average price—taking houses and flats together—was £77,655, and the average loan was 76 per cent of purchase price. These figures include properties sold under the right-to-buy legislation,[21] but even if such properties are excluded the figures are in fact almost unchanged (£77,985 and 76 per cent).[22] Total annual house sales are about 135,000.[23]

Since the right-to-buy legislation has been in place for more than 20 years, it might be supposed that such sales would by now have dwindled to a trickle, but that is not so. Sales to sitting tenants by local authorities, by new town corporations and by Scottish Homes for the period 1991 to 2002 were as follows:[24]

Year	Right-to-buy sales	Year	Right-to-buy sales
1991	23,007	1997	16,517
1992	24,032	1998	14,105
1993	20,063	1999	13,317
1994	21,290	2000	13,981
1995	16,811	2001	13,169
1996	12,838	2002	15,824

The future[25]

1–24   Conveyancing has for decades been in a state of constant change, both as to law and as to practice.[26] Changes since the first edition of this work in 1993 have been vast. Here are just *some* of the statutes relevant to the conveyancer passed since the second edition in 1999: the Abolition of Feudal Tenure etc. (Scotland) Act 2000, the Mortgage Rights (Scotland) Act 2001, the Leasehold Casualties (Scotland) Act 2001, the Housing (Scotland) Act 2001, the Protection of Wild Mammals (Scotland) Act 2002, the Enterprise Act 2002,[27] the Title Conditions (Scotland) Act 2003, the Agricultural Holdings (Scotland) Act 2003, the Building (Scotland) Act 2003, the Finance Act 2003,[28] the Homelessness etc. (Scotland) Act 2003, and the Land Reform (Scotland) Act 2003. In 2003 the last of the 33 counties switched into the Land Register, so that the

---

[21] Whereby public sector tenants have—in most cases—a right of compulsory purchase of the properties they live in. See Ch.27.

[22] *http://www.scotland.gov.uk/stats/*.

[23] Scottish Executive, *Stewardship and Responsibility: A Policy Framework for Private Housing in Scotland* (2003), para.152.

[24] *http://www.scotland.gov.uk/stats/*.

[25] For some futurology see Mackenzie (2002) 47 J.L.S.S. Nov./21.

[26] It was not always thus. The third edition of *Conveyancing Practice* by John Burns appeared in 1926. The fourth edition, by Farquhar MacRitchie, which appeared in 1957, was remarkably little changed from the previous edition. Nowadays much more changes in a decade than it did in the 31 years from 1926 to 1957.

[27] For its provisions about receivership and company administration.

[28] For its provisions about stamp duty land tax.

old world of the GRS is now beginning to die out. Yet the problems of the Land Registration (Scotland) Act 1979 have become more and more apparent, and the Scottish Law Commission is examining that Act, with a view to recommending reform.[29]

The cyber-revolution is likely to transform conveyancing in the coming years. At the moment almost everything is based on paper. In the office paper files will tend to be replaced by digital ones, with any incoming paper being scanned into the file. The file, or parts of it, may be made available online to the clients and to lenders. Communications are likely to be increasingly by email. Already many things, including reports from the Keeper, can be obtained digitally. Digital deeds, digitally signed, are likely to be introduced as an alternative to physical deeds, physically signed. The process of registration in the Land Register is likely to move to a new system[30] in which the process is handled online by the Keeper's software, though paper transactions will remain competent.

The Housing Improvement Task Force has urged a number of changes to make conveyancing more consumer-friendly, particularly surveys commissioned by sellers and purchaser information packs.[31]

Finally, there is the possibility that the financial institutions may try to take conveyancing into their own hands using "conveyancing factories".[32] The attraction to the institutions is not so much the fee income as the influence over the clients' financial decisions. The institutions may also use the fact that they own many NSEAs to widen their attack. It is not impossible that the legal profession will lose domestic conveyancing.[33] There are even those who question whether there will be, in 20 years, anything which could be called a legal profession in the current sense.

But all this is speculative. The future cannot be known. All pasts were once futures, so that past futures can be known, but future futures cannot.

---

[29] The first discussion paper, *Land Registration: Void and Voidable Titles* (Scot. Law Com. Discussion Paper No.125) appeared in 2004.

[30] Automated registration of title to land (ARTL). See Gretton, Rennie, Paisley and Brymer (2004) 49 J.L.S.S. May/54.

[31] Its first, factual, report was *Issues in Improving Quality in Private Houses* (2002). Its second report, with recommendations, was *Stewardship and Responsibility: A Policy Framework for Private Housing in Scotland* (2003). For a summary and further references, see Reid and Gretton, *Conveyancing 2003*, pp.96–102. Two other reports deserving mention are Scottish Consumer Council, *Home Truths: A Report on Research into the Experiences of Recent House Buyers in Scotland* (2000), and Scottish Executive Central Research Unit, *House Buying and Selling in Scotland* (2002).

[32] A term used by the financial industry itself.

[33] As happened long ago in the USA.

CHAPTER 2

THE CONVEYANCING TRANSACTION

Introduction

2-01   In a typical conveyancing transaction each client is simultaneously a buyer (of the new house) and a seller[1] (of the old one), and also a borrower (in respect of the secured loan on the new house). The conveyancer thus has to handle all three aspects at the same time. It is like learning to drive a car: to change gear one must manipulate the accelerator, the clutch and the gearstick. It is tricky at first but gets easier with practice. The object of this chapter is to give an overview of the whole process of buying and selling a house, with details to follow in later chapters.

Contract and conveyance

2-02   The sale of property has two main elements: contract and conveyance. The contract usually takes the form of missives: a missive of offer to buy, generally followed by further missives adjusting terms, and finalised by a missive of acceptance. "Missive" means a letter, especially a letter intended to have legal effect. In modern usage it means an offer or an acceptance. "The missives" as a collective term means the contract as constituted by the letters. There is no reason why a contract for the sale of heritable property should not be entered into without missives. In that case there is a single document setting out the agreement, which both parties sign. This is uncommon in practice, though it is always adopted in sales by roup.[2] In such cases the seller pre-signs a document called the articles of roup,[3] and at the end of the roup the successful bidder signs too. The contract of sale itself, as created by the missive letters (or otherwise), is in practice sometimes called "the bargain". Thus "the bargain was concluded on April 12" means that the contract of sale came into existence at that date.

A contract for the sale of land is an *obligatio literis* and so must be in writing and subscribed.[4] Witnessing is not necessary but is common in

---

[1] The English term "vendor" has recently made an appearance, especially in commercial transactions, where English influence is always strong. In addition, the Inland Revenue insists that this term be used for SDLT purposes.

[2] Auction.

[3] Despite the plural form, articles of roup are a single document.

[4] Requirements of Writing (Scotland) Act 1995, s.1(2)(a)(i).

practice.[5] The missives can be direct between the parties, but normally are between their solicitors on their behalves. By the missives the sellers bind themselves to convey and the buyers bind themselves to pay. The contract is then performed by delivery of the disposition and payment of the price. This is called settlement,[6] and traditionally used to happen at a meeting between the two solicitors, but now usually happens by DX or Legal Post. In a simple case there will be just two missives, the offer and the acceptance. But in most cases there will be several missives, adjusting terms. When the last missive is sent, unconditionally accepting the terms which have been negotiated, the missives are said to be concluded.[7] Traditionally, when missives were short, missives could usually be concluded within a week of the offer. During the 1970s that period began to lengthen, and nowadays tends to last some weeks: indeed it is quite common nowadays for missives not to be concluded until shortly before settlement. The period from the original offer until settlement will vary according to circumstances (and the date of settlement will be stipulated in the missives themselves)[8] but is typically two months or so, and is seldom less than one month. After settlement, the disposition is registered by the buyer in the Land Register. It is at the moment of registration that ownership passes to the buyer,[9] though the right to take possession will usually have been given at settlement.

Co-ordinating the purchase and the sale

People need a roof over their heads. So clients do not wish to sell until they have another house to go to. But equally they do not want to buy another house until they have sold the old one because otherwise they would be faced with financing the loans on two houses, which may be ruinously expensive. On one side there is the abyss of two houses, and on the other the abyss of no house at all. The ideal is for the two transactions to be perfectly coordinated, but this is often not possible in practice. Even if the entry dates can be lined up in the missives, for one reason or another they may not line up in reality. Clients need to be asked at an early stage which they would prefer, if the choice has to be made: a period with two houses, and two loans, or a period with no loans, and no house. Most clients, but not all, regard the latter risk as preferable, if perfect coordination of the transactions proves impossible. This issue is one of the features of buying and selling houses which is distinctive from other transactions.

In Scotland the problem is handled in a way different from in England. Indeed, Scottish conveyancing is very different from English conveyancing. In England the usual practice is to have a gentleman's

2-03

---

[5] Before the 1995 Act missive letters had to be either witnessed or adopted as holograph. In practice the latter method was almost always used. The 1995 Act relaxed the law so that simple signature now suffices. That the response of solicitors to this change was to make witnessing virtually compulsory is curious.

[6] In commercial conveyancing, the English term "completion" is often used.

[7] Until then the missives are said to be "open". Open missives are not binding.

[8] But (especially in recent practice) the missives may remain open until shortly before settlement, so that the agreed settlement date is not actually binding until that time.

[9] Abolition of Feudal Tenure etc. (Scotland) Act 2000, s.4.

agreement to sell (called a sale subject to contract), which may last for a considerable period, often several months. This is mainly to enable the buyers to sell their existing property. That sale will also be subject to contract for the same reason. Hence what the English call a chain develops. This may include a dozen persons or more. Each will know only two others: the prospective buyer and prospective seller. During this period either side can walk away from the agreement. Finally something happens to switch the system on, for example at one end of the chain there appears someone who can make a cash purchase. Then the contract is made ("exchanging contracts"),[10] and the transaction is finally settled ("completed") one month later.

What happens in Scotland varies to some extent from case to case. Traditionally the tendency was to buy first and then sell, but nowadays it is usual to sell first.

If the housing market is good, and if they are rather choosey in what they want to buy, clients may decide to buy first and then sell. They look for a new house and then bid for it. If successful, they then put the old house on the market, and a purchaser is found. They will typically have to pay for the new house rather sooner than they are paid for the old house. This gap is covered by bridging, which means a short-term loan from a bank. So for a period the clients are indeed financing two houses, but the period is short.

However, it is risky to buy first because the old house may stick on the market, which would mean open-ended bridging. This is expensive if available, and may prove unavailable, for banks are reluctant to provide bridging finance when no buyer is in sight. The more sluggish the market, the greater the risk. It is usual nowadays to sell first and then buy. The clients put their old house on the market. When they find a buyer they bid for a new house. If the market is bad there will, they hope, be plenty of houses to bid for.[11] Bridging may again be necessary. In both cases careful consideration needs to be given to the entry date stated in the missives. It may be possible to achieve perfect co-ordination, but often the clients will find themselves, temporarily, either with two houses or no house. In either case the period needs to be kept as short as possible.

Can one rely on open missives?[12] Suppose—as is usual—that the clients decide to sell first. They find a buyer in July and there are open missives for settlement on September 30. On August 15 they find the new house of their dreams. Should they offer for it? To do so is to assume that the open missives for the sale of the old house will mature into a sale. That is risky. They may decide to offer, but to try to keep the missives on the new house open for some time. But that too has its risks. For instance, the seller of the new house may get fed up with the non-

---

[10] Usually the documents are posted, to be held as undelivered, and "exchange of contracts" then happens by agreement over the telephone.

[11] But one obvious drawback about selling first is that it means that the time available to find a new house is limited, and the house actually bought may prove not to be the ideal choice.

[12] There is even some risk in relying on concluded missives. A seller may turn out to be unable to grant a good title. A more common risk is that purchasers simply find themselves unable to come up with the money.

conclusion of the missives and sell to someone else. There are no magic answers. The experienced solicitor gets used to the juggling, but must explain everything to the clients and, ultimately, it is the clients who must decide what risks to take.

The secured loan

The buyer will normally need a loan, usually from a bank or building 2-04 society, and this will be secured over the property by a standard security (*i.e.* what in England is called a mortgage), which will become a real right upon its registration. The property being sold will also usually have a standard security over it and the debt secured will be paid off out of the proceeds of sale, with the lender granting a discharge which will then be registered. Thus typically a sale involves three registrations: the discharge of the seller's security, the buyer's security, and the disposition itself.

Fixed price sales and upset sales

A property may be offered at a fixed price, or by the upset system.[13] In 2-05 the first, the sellers are announcing that they will accept the first offer at that price, though they are not legally bound to do so.[14] Fixed price sales are less usual, though they become more common in property slumps, and of course builders tend to offer new houses and flats at fixed prices.[15] In the upset system, the advertisement solicits offers over a stated figure. The upset is generally lower (10 per cent or more) than the estimated value, so that if the sellers think their house is worth £200,000 they would call for offers over, say, £175,000. Interested parties are then invited to bid, and the sellers normally accept the highest offer. One problem with this system is that if, as has traditionally been the case, no offer is submitted without the offeror having first had the property surveyed, all bidders incur survey charges. Some clients spend a lot of money on surveys for unsuccessful bids, and this can cause bitter complaints about the system. It has often been suggested that sellers should obtain a survey and make this available to anyone interested. A pilot scheme in certain areas was run in 2004 to see whether such a system would be workable.[16] A very recent development in practice has been offers which are made subject to a satisfactory survey. In such cases the problem of multiple surveys may be circumvented.

If the sale is by the upset method, and more than one potential buyer is interested, it is usual to set a "closing date". This means that the interested parties are told that all offers must be received by a certain time, when they will be opened by the seller.

---

[13] A third possibility is roup (auction), though this is uncommon. A fourth possibility, also uncommon, is that the seller will find a buyer privately, without ever actually marketing the property.

[14] See the Law Society's *Guidelines on Fixed Price Sales*, published at (1998) 43 J.L.S.S. June/42.

[15] In England fixed price sales are almost invariably used, but the seller expects the buyer to negotiate downwards from that price.

[16] This is an initiative of the Housing Improvement Task Force. See Ch.1.

Initiating the sale

2-06   The estate agency side of a sale is the advising on a sale price,
advertising the property, and generally trying to find a buyer.[17] Most law
firms offer this service, and many have special estate agency departments. If the client goes to a NSEA then the first the solicitors learn of
the sale may be when the NSEA sends them an offer with instructions to
accept.

As soon as the selling solicitors are instructed, they need to obtain the
deeds, and the best advice is to check them before the property is
advertised.[18] (The traditional term is "title deeds", abbreviated to "the
deeds" or "the titles". For properties in the GRS title flows from the
recorded deeds, but for properties in the Land Register title flows from
the register itself, evidenced by the land certificate, a document which
may or may not, according to taste, be called a title deed. We use the
term "deeds" broadly, as including both the deeds in the narrow sense,
the land and charge certificate, and anything else relevant to the title,
such as affidavits.) For a property in the Land Register, that means
obtaining, above all, the land certificate. If there is a secured loan, which
is usually the case, the deeds will normally be held by the lender. A letter
needs to be sent asking to borrow the deeds. If the selling solicitors are
also acting as estate agents, there should be time enough to obtain them,
though some lenders are slow. But if the seller is using a NSEA, there
may be a problem, because the agents will not usually have done
anything about the deeds, so that one may be confronted by an offer to
purchase without having had the deeds to hand. In that case there are
various possibilities, one of which is to accept on the basis that the
purchasers may withdraw if the deeds, when available, reveal anything
unsatisfactory to the purchaser. If the sale will switch the property from
the GRS to the Land Register it is usually necessary, at the time of
marketing the property, to obtain a form 10 report (a pre-registration
report on title) and, in most cases, a form P16 (comparison of the title
boundary with the Ordnance map).

If the selling solicitors are acting as estate agents, then someone from
the firm will visit the property. In that case, an eye must be kept open for
problems. Some examples are: (1) The property has a shared private
access road. There may be problems about servitudes and maintenance.
(2) The property's physical boundaries are indeterminate or do not tally
with the boundaries in the title. (3) The house has recent alterations.
Have both planning permission and building consent been obtained? (4)
The property is tenanted. Will a purchaser be able to obtain vacant
possession?

The selling solicitors draw up a "schedule of particulars" which
describes the property in attractive, but truthful, terms, gives the upset
price (or the fixed price) and so on. These schedules are given out to
anyone interested, and (in most cases) can also be obtained through the
SPC.

---

[17] See John Sinclair, *Handbook of Conveyancing Practice in Scotland* (4th ed., 2002),
Ch.2.
[18] Though this is not always done. But if there is a title problem, the sooner it is
discovered the better, and above all before missives.

Misdescriptions

If the solicitors are marketing the property they must ensure that they 2–07
do not mislead prospective purchasers, whether in the sales particulars
or otherwise. To do so is unprofessional and might also lead to a claim
by the buyers against the sellers for misrepresentation.[19] Moreover, to
mislead prospective purchasers is an offence. Under the Property
Misdescriptions Act 1991 it is an offence to make "in the course of an
estate agency business" any statement which is "false or misleading".[20]
These words are open-ended. In *Enfield London Borough Council v
Castles Estate Agents Ltd*[21] a property was advertised as a "bungalow",
and the agents were prosecuted because the building, which was 30 years
old, did not have planning permission and therefore could not fairly be
called a bungalow. The prosecution failed, but (amazingly) only because
it was found in fact that the agents reasonably believed planning
permission to exist. However, caselaw on the Act is sparse.[22]

On receipt of the successful offer

If there is more than one offer, the selling solicitors will discuss with 2–08
the clients which to accept. They then send a copy of that offer to the
clients by first-class post, asking them to get in touch on receipt. At that
stage they go over the whole offer clause by clause, explaining the
meaning of each, and discussing points which may arise. Typical clauses
which may require discussion are those concerning the physical condition
of the property and the existence of planning and building consents for
any alterations that have taken place. Discussing the offer can be a
lengthy process. It is wise to follow this by a letter to the clients
confirming the points discussed and the instructions given. After this the
solicitor sends off the qualified acceptance, copying this to the clients. At
about this time a request should be sent for the property enquiry
certificates (PECs). These are issued by the local authority, and can also
be obtained from independent firms working from local authority
records, and cover such matters as planning, roads, statutory repairs
notices and so on.[23] Both the deeds and the certificates should be at
hand before conclusion of missives. Usually they can be obtained within
a couple of weeks.

---

[19] In *Stambovsky v Ackley*, 169 A.D. 2d. 254, 572 N.Y.S. 2d 672 (1991) the seller did not
disclose that the house was haunted. It was held by the Supreme Court of the State of New
York that this amounted to misrepresentation by non-disclosure. (For a photograph of the
house, but not, alas, of the ghost, see Jesse Dukeminier and James Krier, *Property* (4th ed.
1998), p.581.)

[20] As to whether the seller of a haunted house might commit an offence for
non-disclosure (because the buyer might object to a haunted house), or equally an offence
for disclosure (because the buyer might be disappointed if the ghost did not manifest
itself), see John Sinclair, *Handbook of Conveyancing Practice in Scotland* (4th ed., 2002),
p.43. Haunting is a sadly neglected branch of the law.

[21] [1996] 36 E.G. 145; [1996] 12 E.G.L.R. 21; 73 P. & C.R. 343.

[22] The only reported Scottish case is *George Wimpey UK Ltd v Brown*, 2003 S.L.T. 659.

[23] The cost of these varies according to the local authority in question from around £55
to around £110. For information see the *Directory of Services for Conveyancers* (Law
Society of Scotland, 2003).

What should be sent

2–09   At an early stage in the transaction the selling solicitors send to the purchasing solicitors various items. What is sent depends on whether the property is in the Sasine or Land Register. If the sale will switch the property from the GRS to the Land Register, there should be sent (a) the deeds, (b) the form 10 report, (c) if applicable, the form P16 report[24] and (d) a draft form 11. These reports can be obtained from the Keeper or from independent searchers. If the property is already in the Land Register, there should be sent (a) the land certificate,[25] (b) the form 12 report, (c) the draft form 13 report.

The purchasing solicitors may come back with queries about the title or other matters.[26] With luck the selling solicitors' answers will satisfy them. They will also send to the selling solicitors a draft disposition, which the latter approve, with any suggested changes, and send back. (The traditional practice is that a conveyancing deed is drafted by the solicitors for the grantee, and then revised by the grantor's solicitors. But there are some exceptions, notably leases, which are usually drafted by the solicitor for the grantor, and then revised by the solicitor for the grantee. All this is practice rather than law.) The purchasing solicitors will also return the draft form 11 or 13, having added the name of their client for the purpose of a personal search. After a while the selling solicitors receive the engrossment (*i.e.* a fair copy on deed paper) of the disposition from the purchasing solicitors. The selling solicitors have their clients execute it, also completing the "signing schedule" which gives details of the date and place of signing and the name and address of the witness. This schedule is for the benefit of the purchasing solicitors, who will use it after settlement to complete the testing clause. The selling solicitors now sit back doing the crossword, until the settlement date arrives.

Settlement

2–10   Settlement traditionally took place at the office of the selling solicitors. Nowadays it is usually done through DX, Legal Post or courier.[27] In a typical case the selling solicitors hand over:

(a) the executed disposition, with the signing schedule;
(b) the land certificate and charge certificate, or, in a first registration, the GRS deeds;

---

[24] This states whether the boundaries as set forth in the title correspond with the physical boundaries as shown on the Ordnance Survey map.

[25] If available. In first registrations there may be a long delay. It can easily happen that the buyer wishes to sell again before the land certificate is available.

[26] Alas, observations on title are often aggressive in tone. Having identified what is or may be a problem, there is a sort of psychological compulsion to shout about it. "A letter raising observations on title should always be courteously phrased whatever you may think of the quality of the conveyancing offered": David A. Brand, Andrew J. M. Steven and Scott Wortley, *Professor McDonald's Conveyancing Manual* (7th ed., 2004), p.726.

[27] The covering letters will state that the contents are to be held as undelivered, and then mutual delivery is agreed by telephone and confirmed by letter. See further (1998) 43 J.L.S.S. Oct./47.

    (c) the executed letter of obligation, with the draft for comparison;

    (d) the form 13 report (form 11 report for a first registration);

    (e) the executed discharge of the existing standard security;

    (f) any necessary Matrimonial Homes Act documentation;

    (g) the keys, unless this is being dealt with separately by the clients themselves; and

    (h) any other relevant documents, such as PECs, building warrants, etc.

In return, the selling solicitors receive the price. Payment is still usually by a cheque from the buyers' solicitors, but payment by bank transfer (which conveyancers commonly call telegraphic transfer) is increasingly common, especially for more expensive properties, and in commercial cases. It is of course perfectly lawful for the clients to settle between themselves, but it is rare for this to happen, and when it does the solicitors should be aware of the possibility of a fraud of some sort. Settlement between the solicitors also avoids the problem as to whether the buyers' cheque might bounce.[28]

Traditionally, a "state for settlement" was prepared—an account between the parties giving the price with any additions and subtractions, thus producing a final figure to be paid. Nowadays, however, states for settlement are often not used. Local authorities like them, as do housebuilding companies. They are certainly valuable where a number of factors have to enter into the calculation of the final sum due.

The selling solicitors then pay the old lender the amount outstanding on the existing secured loan (on all of them, if more than one), put through a fee note and send an account to the clients. Assuming, as is generally the case, that the letter of obligation will have been satisfied by the issue by the Keeper of a land certificate in satisfactory terms, the purchasing solicitors will return the letter, marked as implemented. The land certificate and the charge certificate will be sent to the lender together with any other relevant documents. At this stage it should be possible to close the file.

Council Tax

    A notification of change of ownership is sent by the selling solicitors to the local authority, which will then apportion council tax as between the buyer and seller. Local authorities have standard forms for such notices.[29]   2-11

Discharging the old standard security

    At the same time as carrying out the conveyancing for the sale itself, the selling solicitors will be arranging for the discharge of any standard security over the property. They write to the lender asking for a   2-12

---

[28] Might a law firm stop its cheque? The question cannot be discussed here. For a practical example see I. S. Smith, *Procedures and Decisions of the Scottish Solicitors Discipline Tribunal* (1995), pp.124–126. In England bank drafts are widely used.

[29] See *e.g.* the Law Society of Scotland's *Directory of Services for Conveyancers* (2003).

redemption statement, *i.e.* a letter which says exactly how much will be outstanding at settlement.[30] The draft discharge of security, once approved by the purchasing solicitors, is immediately engrossed and sent to the lender for execution and return. This should be in advance of settlement, so the deed of discharge is held as undelivered, for the loan at this stage has not been paid off.[31] At settlement the usual practice is to hand over the executed discharge to the purchasing solicitors who will then arrange for its registration. The amount outstanding will be repaid (by the selling solicitors out of funds in their hands) on the day of the settlement of the sale. If the existing secured loan is an "endowment mortgage" the selling solicitors may also have to arrange for the retrocession of the life policy, but nowadays lenders often do not require such policies to be assigned in the first place, and in that case such policies do not need to be assigned back upon repayment of the loan. Again the lender will execute this in advance, and after settlement the selling solicitors intimate the retrocession of the policy to the life assurance company. The life policy has nothing to do with the title to the house, so the purchasing solicitors are not interested in its retrocession and there will be no communication about this between the solicitors.

Insurance

2–13   After settlement the sellers' house insurance policy should be cancelled. The purchasing solicitors need to ensure that there is insurance cover from the moment when risk passes, which in current practice is normally at settlement.[32] However it is common to effect cover from the time when missives are concluded. This may mean that the house is simultaneously covered both by the sellers' insurance and by that of the buyers, but after all double insurance is better than no insurance. Whilst the purchasing solicitors need to check the point, it is usually left to the clients to effect the insurance, which in a majority of cases they will do through their lenders, who will normally insist on insurance[33] and who will typically decline to release the loan funds unless insurance cover is in operation.

Taking instructions in a purchase

2–14   Most buyers are also sellers, and vice versa, but for convenience of exposition the two sides are treated separately here. Some solicitors use a single file for both the purchase and the sale, while others use separate files: the latter practice is to be preferred. Sometimes purchasing clients contact their solicitors only when they are ready to bid for a house. If,

---

[30] See further the *CML Lenders' Handbook for Scotland*, para.17. (For the CML see Ch.18.)

[31] That is the standard practice but occasionally lenders refuse to co-operate: see *e.g.* (1999) 44 J.L.S.S. Feb./12.

[32] The default rule is that risk passes when missives are concluded (*Sloans Dairies v Glasgow Corporation*, 1977 S.C. 23) but missives usually provide that it will pass at settlement.

[33] Where there is a standard security there is an implied obligation to insure: 1970 Act, Sch.3, standard condition 5.

however, they make contact sooner, their solicitors have the chance to discuss with them the sort of property they want, current market prices for that sort of property, their finances, the sale of their present house, if any, the type of loan they need, and so on. It is not usual to charge for such advice, but as well as being useful to the clients it also helps the solicitors to keep close contact with them, which is a key element in retaining client loyalty. One thing that should be explained at the first meeting is the general outline of a purchase transaction, including the likely timetable. If there are two (or more) buyers then instructions must be taken from both and reporting must be to both. A survivorship destination must not be inserted without the informed consent of the clients. Co-owners may later become estranged and there may be disputes as to who contributed what and whether the proceeds of eventual sale should be divided equally on unequally.[34] Hence it should be explained that equal *pro indiviso* shares will mean an equal division of proceeds. If something different is desired then unequal shares may be the answer, while if one party regards himself or herself as lending part of the down payment to the other then it may be that that should be formally documented as a loan.[35] When cohabitants split up, if one of them contributed disproportionately to paying the bills connected with the house, such as the home loan, that party may demand a compensating payment from the other on the basis that no donation was intended, and so it may be wise to have a formal agreement to cover such matters in advance. But this is seldom done.

Finances of buying

Some clients have the finances of buying and selling at their finger 2–15 tips, and hardly need advice, while others are vague, and some unrealistic. It is good practice to make reasonably sure (a) that the clients will be able to come up with the purchase price at settlement date and (b) that they will be able to keep up with the monthly loan payments thereafter. The first of these is particularly important when the clients are new ones about whom the solicitor knows little. In Scotland (unlike England) it is not normal practice for sellers to demand a deposit.[36] The main reason for this is that it is assumed that the solicitors acting for buyers will have done at least a preliminary check on their clients' finances. In the typical case the finances are simple. The purchasers will have the proceeds of the sale of their old house (which are known or can be estimated) less the outstanding loan (which can be checked), less costs (which can be estimated), plus the loan which will be obtained for the new house (which can be estimated). The solicitors must stress that cleared funds be in the firm's hands by a stated date in good time for settlement. If the solicitors have real doubts about whether this will happen, they should consider declining to act. Of course, the danger that purchasers will fail to come up with the price can never be wholly eliminated. But solicitors

---

[34] See for instance *Grieve v Morrison*, 1993 S.L.T. 852.

[35] *cf.* Rennie, 2004 S.L.T. (News) 33.

[36] In residential conveyancing. In commercial conveyancing a deposit of, say, 10 per cent on conclusion of missives is common.

are under a professional responsibility to make reasonably sure that they will be able to do so before they submit any offer on their behalf.

Making the offer

2–16   The first step is to "note interest" to the selling solicitors. This is done simply by a phone call. The effect of noting interest has traditionally been considered as being that the sellers will not sell without first giving to the person who has noted interest a chance to bid.[37] Though not legally enforceable, this was considered a matter of good professional practice, and indeed it still is.[38]

The next step is to arrange for a survey. If this is a Scheme 1 survey (see below) it will usually be instructed by the buyers' solicitors, but might be instructed by the lenders. If it is Scheme 2 is will be instructed by the solicitors. The amount borrowable cannot be known until the survey report is available.[39] If, as is often the case, the survey notes that that there have been alterations, the sellers' solicitors will be asked for the appropriate public law consents. If these turn out to be unavailable— as is often the case—then there are various possible ways forward. If the problem is only with building consents and not with planning consents the most common practice is to ask the local authority to carry out a "physical inspection" which will generally—but not invariably—result in a "comfort letter".

Some offers nowadays are made with a subject-to-survey clause. In that case the survey will not be instructed unless and until the sellers have indicated that the offer is in principle acceptable. Moreover, as noted above a pilot scheme is beginning in some areas in which the sellers obtain a Scheme 2 survey and make it available to potential buyers.

The buyers' solicitors will need to discuss with their clients what figure to offer. The solicitors' own knowledge of the market will help here (and the clients may to some extent be relying on that knowledge), and it is wise to check the computer record of recent sales in the area kept at the local SPC. Another obvious factor is the valuation put on the property by the survey.

It is likely that there will be other points to be discussed such as what moveables (if any) in the property are to be included in the purchase. The purchasing solicitors should have in front of them, when preparing the offer, the schedule of particulars issued by the seller, and indeed it is common for this to be docqueted as part of the offer.

At some stage the clients will have to submit the application form for the new loan. The solicitors should check that this is done. In modern practice this is usually done after a successful offer has been made. In theory this exposes the clients to the risk that the lender might not agree to lend, but in practice the loan will have been informally agreed with the lender before submission of the offer, and the lender is unlikely to back off unless the application form discloses something unexpected.

---

[37] If there is more than one note of interest, a closing date is set: see para.2–05.
[38] See the next chapter.
[39] See Ch.18.

The survey

Although the term "survey" is generally used, surveyors themselves 2–17
distinguish "surveys" proper from mere "valuations". There are three
main types of valuation/survey that can be obtained. The first is the
"Scheme 1 Valuation Report". This is the least detailed and the
cheapest. It is aimed at valuing the property for lending purposes. The
second is the "Scheme 2 Homebuyer's Report and Valuation". This is
more detailed and more expensive. The third is the "Building Survey"
which is even more detailed, and even more expensive. A lender will
normally be satisfied with the first type, provided that the surveyor is on
that lender's "panel".

It is for the clients to decide which sort of survey to instruct. The more
detailed the survey the better the clients are protected against nasty
surprises but the more they will have to pay for the peace of mind. It
should be explained to the clients that a Scheme 1 Valuation is mainly
for the benefit of lenders, and whilst it may be sufficient for that purpose
it is less than satisfactory for buyers. In particular it contains disclaimers,
the effect of which is that if it turns out that there are problems with the
property it is unlikely that the surveyor can be held liable. However,
despite the advice, many clients will in practice opt for the simple
valuation to keep costs down. Estimates as to how many do so vary from
51 per cent[40] and 66 per cent.[41]

Where someone (typically the buyers, but in some cases it might be
another party) claims to have suffered loss as a result of a negligent
survey report, the question of the liability of the surveyor is a complex
one, which cannot be discussed here.[42]

Two recent developments about surveys have already been noted. One
is the pilot scheme of sellers' surveys, under the auspices of the Housing
Improvement Task Force, and the other is the increasing use of the
"subject-to-survey" offer.

Examining title

At an early stage in the transaction, the selling solicitors will send the 2–18
deeds and seller's drafts to the purchasing solicitors, as outlined above.
The latter then examine the title, and check, as far possible, other

---

[40] "The research commissioned for the Task Force demonstrates that 51 per cent of
buyers commission the basic mortgage valuation report and only 14 per cent the more
detailed homebuyer's survey. Most interestingly, 21 per cent of buyers did not know which
type of survey they had purchased": Housing Improvement Task Force, *Issues in Improving
Quality in Private Houses* (2002), para.142.
[41] Scottish Executive Central Research Unit, *House Buying and Selling in Scotland*
(2002).
[42] See, *e.g. Martin v Bell-Ingram*, 1986 S.L.T. 575; *Robbie v Graham & Sibbald*, 1989
S.L.T. 870; *Hunter v J. & E. Shepherd*, 1992 S.L.T 1095; *Melrose v Davidson & Robertson*,
1993 S.L.T. 611; *Leeds Permanent Building Society v Walker Fraser & Steele*, 1995 S.L.T.
(Sh. Ct) 72; *Mortgage Express Ltd v Dunsmore Reid & Smith*, 1996 G.W.D. 40–2295;
Lawson v McHugh, 1998 G.W.D. 31–1618; *Stewart v Ryden Residential Ltd*, 1999 G.W.D.
12–576; *Purdie v Dryburgh*, 2000 S.C. 497; *Douglas v Stuart Wise Ogilvie Estates Ltd*, 2001
S.L.T. 689; *Howes v Crombie*, 2001 S.C.L.R. 921; *Harrison v D. M. Hall*, 2001 G.W.D.
33–1314; *Beechwood Development Co. (Scotland) Ltd v Stuart Mitchell*, 2001 S.L.T. 1214;
Bank of Scotland v Fuller Peiser, 2001 S.L.T. 574.

matters, such as statutory notices and planning and building consents, and raise any queries with the selling solicitors. They will also send to the purchasing clients a report on title, with a plan, a note of rights and burdens, and a summary of the PECs. The purchasing solicitors then draft the disposition and send it to the selling solicitors for revision. At the same time the purchasing solicitors revise and return the seller's drafts, and return the title deeds. As settlement approaches, the purchasing solicitors must make sure that they will have sufficient funds on the day, to cover not only the price but other items such as stamp duty land tax. This may involve arranging a bridging loan for the clients until the proceeds of the sale of their old house are available. Settlement itself has already been outlined above. At settlement the purchasing solicitors should check that the terms of the letter of obligation conform to the draft, and that all the relevant deeds have been properly executed. In return they hand over the cheque.[43]

The keys

2–19   One essential thing at settlement is to obtain the keys from the selling solicitors, unless this is being arranged direct between the clients. The novice conveyancer, trying desperately to keep on top of the legal procedures, can forget that for the purchasers the main point of the whole business is to get the keys. If the purchasers are standing outside the house with a laden removal truck plus hungry family at 6 p.m. on Friday with no keys, with the seller uncontactable and their own solicitors' switchboard shut till 9 a.m. on Monday, they will have some choice remarks to make when they phone their solicitors from the hotel where they spent the weekend.

After settlement

2–20   After settlement the purchasing solicitors add the testing clause to the disposition. They then send it, with other documents, to the Land Register. What is sent typically are (i) the disposition, (ii) the discharge of the old standard security, (iii) the new standard security being granted by the buyers (iv) the SDLT certificate, and (v) other relevant deeds. If this is a first registration that will include a prescriptive progress of GRS deeds, and in other cases the existing land certificate and charge certificate. Also to be sent to the Register (vi) will be any applicable Matrimonial Homes documentation. Then there are the various Land Register forms. These will be (vii) form 2—or a form 1 if this is a first registration—in respect of the disposition. The terms of these forms will have been adjusted between the solicitors in advance. Next, (viii) form 2 (registration of a dealing, in this case the new standard security), and (ix) form 4 (inventory of writs).

---

[43] Except on the clear, and well-documented, instructions of the clients, the purchasing solicitors should not pay except in exchange for the disposition, clear reports and so on. *Mason v A. &. R. Robertson & Black*, 1993 S.L.T. 773 illustrates some of the risks of pre-payment.

The new home loan

Acting for both borrower and lender is potentially to be subject to 2–21 conflict of interest.[44] But in residential cases matters are usually routine and uncontroversial and so it is common to act for both parties. For the client there is the benefit that it is quicker and cheaper.[45] However, this will be possible only if the law firm is on the "conveyancing panel" for the lenders in question. In commercial cases the danger of conflict of interest is more serious and accordingly separate solicitors must act for the parties, except in low-value cases. Even in residential cases it can occasionally happen for some reason that a definite conflict of interest emerges, and in that case the solicitors must cease to act for one side or the other. Where the same firm acts for both the borrowers and the lenders, it must not be overlooked that the solicitors have in law two clients, the borrowers/buyers and the lender. Once the home loan has been agreed, the lender will send to the solicitors a formal letter of instruction, and this will typically include standard form documents which are to be used. The standard security is drafted and engrossed, and sent for signature to the clients (*i.e.* the borrowers) in advance of settlement. If a life policy is to be assigned in security (which until recently was common, but is much less so now), an assignation must be prepared and executed in advance of settlement. It may be that a new life policy is being taken out for this purpose, and so it may be necessary to liaise with the life assurance company to ensure that it is issued in time. Once the title has been examined a report on title, also called a certificate of title, must be sent to the lenders. Shortly before settlement the solicitors "requisition" the loan from the lenders. The funds will usually come by bank transfer (sometimes called telegraphic transfer) but the older method of a cheque is still sometimes used. If there is any significant delay in settlement the loan funds must be returned to the lenders and requisitioned a second time when the problems have been resolved.[46] After settlement the security must be registered at once, for until registration the lender is unsecured. If a life policy has been assigned to the lender, this must be intimated to the life office.

Closing the file

The purchasing solicitors then put through a fee note and send an 2–22 account to their clients. Some time later they will receive back from the Keeper the land certificate, plus a charge certificate for the standard security. These will come fairly quickly if the property was already in the new register, but if this transaction triggers a first registration, the certificates are likely to take many months and quite easily more than a year. The delays in such cases are a major problem with the new system. In the case of first registrations in particular, it is important to read the land certificate from cover to cover, checking, among other things, that the plan is accurate, that the clients are correctly named, that the sellers'

---

[44] For conflict of interest see Ch.1.

[45] In a secured loan it is almost invariable for the lenders to require the borrowers to pay their (the lenders') legal fees.

[46] *CML Lenders' Handbook for Scotland*, para.10.

security does not appear in the charges section, that the real burdens and servitudes are as expected, that there is the appropriate clause about matrimonial occupancy rights, and, vitally, that there is no exclusion of indemnity. The land certificate and charge certificate are then sent to the lender for safekeeping, and the seller's letter of obligation can be returned, marked as implemented. The Keeper will return the disposition and any other deeds submitted to him. Any of particular importance should be retained. Some solicitors simply bin the disposition. (A copy is retained by the Keeper.) Sometimes the GRS deeds are binned and sometimes sent to the clients to do with as they like.

Fees, outlays and getting paid

2-23   The solicitors need to be paid two things: fees and the outlays. The latter are moneys paid out for the benefit of clients, such as advertising charges, search fees, registration dues, SDLT and so on. Some firms require clients to pay disbursements as they are made or in advance, thus giving credit only for the fees. On being presented with the final account, clients often look only at the bottom line, and complain about how much it is all costing. The distinction between fees and outlays should therefore be explained. There was once a Law Society scale of fees for conveyancing, but this disappeared in 1984, since when charging has been unregulated. "Feeing up" a transaction is thus no longer the mechanical process it once was. The basis of charge will have been agreed with the clients at the outset. It needs to be borne in mind that the amount of work is not the only factor. For instance, the conveyancing on an expensive property may involve no more work than for a cheap one, but the fee will be higher, because the financial consequences of a mistake are greater. Part of the fee is thus, in a sense, an insurance premium.

Sometimes at the end of the transaction the solicitors will be holding funds for their clients, and so the payment of the fee is relatively painless, being simply a deduction. The clients are sent two bits of paper, namely the fee note and an account showing all the receipts and disbursements and the fee. It is important not to forget anything. There is nothing worse than having to contact clients six months after the transaction to say that one had overlooked some outlay and please could they send a cheque.

Fee levels

2-24   The old scale kept fees high, so the effect of deregulation has been that fee levels have fallen.[47] Client loyalty has been eroded and it is increasingly common for people to shop around seeking quotations. Moreover, NSEAs often do deals with law firms (typically small outfits) whereby the former feed them clients and the latter do the legal work for astonishingly low rates. This is a matter which has been troubling the

---

[47] Overall conveyancing fee levels are, in broad terms, similar as between Scotland and England. In most of Europe costs are far higher, partly because of higher stamp duty, or equivalent.

profession greatly in recent years. There have been accusations that such clients do not always receive a proper professional service, that time-bomb negligence claims are accumulating, that some firms are operating below real cost levels and so are running the risk of eventual insolvency, and so on. In this book we offer no views.

An example

The following is an example which is not untypical. But individual 2–25 cases vary enormously. For instance, several unsuccessful offers will result in a large bill for surveys. If a property is slow to sell there may be heavy advertising costs. In the example below the SDLT payable by the purchaser is £1000, but for a more expensive property the cost will rise rapidly: thus for a property costing three times as much (£300,000) the SDLT payable would be nine times as much (£9,000). If a property is disconform to building regulations there may be costs to the sellers, if only a comfort letter from the local authority at, say, £125. And so on. Obviously the clients will incur expenditure of other kinds as well.

(1) *Purchase of property at £100,000 with £75,000 secured loan*

(a)	SDLT	£1,000
(b)	Registration dues	£242[48]
(c)	Survey fee	£300
(d)	Solicitor's fee	£700
(e)	VAT thereon	£122.50

TOTAL **£2,364.50**

(2) *Sale of property for £100,000 with discharge of £75,000 secured loan*

(a)	Press advertising	£400
(b)	SPC advertising	£145
(c)	PEC	£100
(d)	Registration dues for discharge of standard security	£88[49]
(e)	form 10/12, 11/13 and P16 reports	£70
(f)	Commission on sale	£1,000
(g)	VAT thereon	£175
(h)	Solicitor's fee	£700
(i)	VAT thereon	£122.50

TOTAL **£2,800.50**

Non-standard transactions

By definition, non-standard transactions defy classification. There is 2–26 the cash buyer, who does not need a loan. There is the first-time buyer, who will not have an old house to sell at the same time. There is the

---

[48] £220 for the disposition and £22 for the standard security.
[49] Or £22 if the concession for simultaneous registration is obtained.

last-time seller, such as a widow who is selling her house and will move in with her son and family. There is the purchase by a tenant from the landlord. A variant of this is the council house purchase, where the tenant is purchasing at a discount under the right-to-buy legislation.[50] There is the sale where an owner has defaulted on a secured loan and the sale is by the lender. There is the executry sale, where the sale is by the executor of the deceased owner. There is the insolvency sale, where the owner has become insolvent and the property is being sold by the trustee in sequestration or liquidator or whatever. And there is the new house, where the client is buying from a builder. Some of these are mentioned again later, but a detailed account of non-standard transactions is outwith the scope of this book.

The course of a typical transaction

2-27   This is only a simplified version of a fairly typical transaction. Naturally, individual transactions vary widely. The middle column shows the direction of communication between the solicitors. The outside columns show communications with parties other than the solicitors, such as the clients.

	BUYER'S SOLICITORS		SELLER'S SOLICITORS	
→	Take instructions. Verify client's identity. If a business, check that the contact has authority. Agree terms of business. Send out 2003 Rules letter[51]		Take instructions. Verify client's identity. If a business, check that the contact has authority. Agree terms of business. Send out 2003 Rules letter	←
			Advertise	→
←	Check that client will have funds		Order deeds[52] from lender	→
			Check them	←
			Instruct form 10 or 12 and (if first registration) P16 report	→
			Request PEC	→
	Note interest	→		
←	Instruct survey			
		←	Set closing date	→
	If survey etc satisfactory, offer	→		
			Examine offers with client	→ ←

---

[50] Currently contained in the Housing (Scotland) Act 1987.

[51] A letter as required by the Solicitors (Scotland) (Client Communication) (Residential Conveyancing) Practice Rules 2003, necessary where a non-business client is involved in residential conveyancing.

[52] The "deeds" might be simply the land certificate. But there may be more, and if the property is still in the GRS the deeds are likely to be a substantial bundle.

	BUYER'S SOLICITORS		SELLER'S SOLICITORS	
		←	Send qualified acceptance plus deeds plus form 10 or 12 report plus (for first registration) P16 report plus PEC	
	Examine title for any matters on which "the buyers must satisfy themselves"			
→ ←	Report to client on title as soon as possible and obtain confirmation that boundaries and conditions are acceptable			
←	Ensure client has accepted loan offer			
	Further missives until bargain concluded, checking with client that terms are acceptable[53]	→ ←	Further missives until bargain concluded, checking with client that terms are acceptable	
		←	Draft and send "sellers' drafts"—(1) letter of obligation (2) discharge of standard security (3) form 11/13	
	Examine title			
←	Resolve any issues arising out of the examination of title	→ ←	Resolve any issues arising out of the examination of title	→
	Draft disposition, standard security,[54] assignation of life policy and any necessary Matrimonial Homes documentation[55]		Draft any necessary Matrimonial Homes documentation	
	Return deeds and revised sellers' drafts. Send draft disposition plus draft forms 1 (or 2) and 4	→	Prepare retrocession of life policy	
		←	Revise buyers' drafts and return	
			Engross sellers' drafts	
	Engross disposition and send	→		
	Draft and engross standard security and assignation of life policy if applicable			

[53] Missives may take some time to conclude. Conveyancing steps below must be progressed in the mean time.

[54] The standard security will normally be a printed form sent by the lender.

[55] If there is a sole buyer the standard security will need to be protected by a deed under the 1981 Act.

	BUYER'S SOLICITORS		SELLER'S SOLICITORS	
→ ←	Have clients execute the above		Send discharge (and retrocession if applicable) to lender for execution	→
			Have sellers execute disposition	→ ←
			Instruct form 11 or 13 report	→
			Receive form 11 or 13 report	←
		←	Send form 11 or 13 report	
	Prepare SDLT form			
→ ←	Have clients sign SDLT form			
←	Send report on title and requisition loan from lenders			
→ ←	Ensure that full price is available in cleared funds		Intimate to local authority forthcoming change of ownership	→
	SETTLEMENT Money	→ ←	**SETTLEMENT** Keys, letter of obligation, disposition with signing schedule, deeds, Matrimonial Homes documentation, form 13 or 11 report, discharge, signed form 2 for discharge	
←	Send SDLT form		Pay off loan	→
	Add testing clause to disposition		Intimate retrocession, if applicable	→
→	Receive SDLT certificate		Bill client for fees and outlays and pay any balance	→
←	Send to Land Register: (1) disposition (2) standard security (3) discharge of old security (4) SDLT certificate (5) deeds[56] (6) Matrimonial Homes documentation (7) forms 1 or 2 for the disposition,[57] (8) form 2 for the standard security (9) form 4			
←	Intimate assignation of life policy, if applicable			
→	Receive land certificate and charge certificate and check carefully			
←	Bill clients for fees and outlays			
←	Send deeds to lender			
	Return letter of obligation marked as implemented	→		

---

[56] Which deeds depends on the circumstances. In a first registration, they will be mainly or exclusively the relevant GRS deeds. Otherwise, only the land certificate may be needed.
[57] Depending on whether this is a first registration or not.

CHAPTER 3

MISSIVES I: MAKING THE CONTRACT

Introduction

Once upon a time conveyancing, in the narrow sense, was complex, 3–01
but missives were simple. Here is a style offer from 1881:

> "On behalf of . . . I hereby offer to purchase from you the house
> no . . . Street Edinburgh at the price of £ . . . sterling. Entry to take
> place at the term of Whitsunday next, when the price will be
> payable, you relieving me of any casualty which may be due at the
> date of entry. This offer shall be binding for . . . days from this
> date."

This offer was met by an unqualified one-sentence acceptance.[1] To
modern eyes, that offer comes from a golden age of innocence. Today
offers run for pages and are commonly met by qualified acceptances
almost as long. While conveyancing in the narrow sense has become
simpler than it was in 1881, missives have become more complex. As the
years go by they become longer, with new clauses being added. Sometimes the new clauses result from legislation. Sometimes they result from
new case law. Sometimes they result from problems which have arisen in
the practice of the law firm concerned, and sometimes from problems
highlighted in the legal press. But one way or another the clauses
accumulate, and few are ever removed. Firms keep a close eye on the
styles used by other firms, and a new clause often spreads quickly.[2]

FORMATION

Instructions

Throughout the transaction the solicitors act as agent for their clients. 3–02
Therefore the solicitors must make sure that they have authority to act.
If solicitors purport to conclude missives on behalf of clients and it turns

---

[1] From *A Complete System of Conveyancing* (commonly called *Juridical Styles*) (5th ed.,
1881), Vol.1. For a set of missives from 1948 see *Anderson v Lambie*, 1953 S.C. (H.L.) 43.
These missives are longer than the 1881 missives but still slight by modern standards, and
were concluded quickly: the offer was dated December 15, the qualified acceptance was
dated December 16 and the third missive, concluding the bargain, was dated December 17.
[2] See further Rennie, 2000 S.L.T. (News) 65, near the end of which can be found the
best missive clause in recorded history.

out that no proper agency had been constituted, there is no contract, but the solicitors are personally liable to the other would-be party to the contract for breach of an implied warranty that they had authority to act.[3] Solicitors will usually accept oral instructions, but this involves an element of risk, in that the client may subsequently deny the instructions, or admit the instructions but deny an important detail, such as the price.[4] Once appointed, the solicitors have authority to conclude the contract (in consultation with the clients) and to carry out the usual steps in a conveyancing transaction.[5]

Formal writing

3–03   The letters making up missives of sale must be in formal writing.[6] They can be signed by the parties themselves, but this is and has always been unusual in practice. Simple subscription is sufficient, and this need not even be by a partner, provided that the person signing has been authorised by the firm,[7] but in practice it is usually a partner who signs. Missives are normally done in probative form, *i.e.* witnessed, normally by someone within the firm, although it is difficult to see any good reason for this practice.[8] Since a purchaser does not normally sign either the missives or the disposition, it is possible for a person to buy heritable property without ever signing anything at all.[9] It is curious that the age-old rule requiring subscribed writing before a person can be bound to a contract for the purchase or sale of heritable property has been construed in this way. The key point is that the missives can be signed by the solicitors, and that their authority can be granted orally.[10] This may be unsatisfactory as a matter of policy, and is contrary to the system adopted by many other countries.

Missives by fax?

3–04   Sometimes fax is used as a means of transmitting an offer or a qualified acceptance. While a document arriving on a fax machine is just a photocopy of the original and so fails to comply with the rules of

---

[3] *Scott v J.B. Livingston & Nicol,* 1990 S.L.T. 305; *MacDougall v Akram,* 1993 G.W.D. 33–2142.

[4] See Ch.1.

[5] *Heron v Thomson,* 1989 G.W.D. 11–469.

[6] Requirements of Writing (Scotland) Act 1995, s.1(2)(a)(i).

[7] 1995 Act, Sch.2, para.2.

[8] The practice developed when the 1995 Act was passed. But the Act did not require missives to be probative, and before the Act missives were normally improbative.

[9] There may be a cheque to be signed, and if, as is usual, there is a loan, the loan documentation will have to be signed.

[10] Presumably the person orally authorised need not be a solicitor. Presumably, too, oral authority to sign a disposition would be possible. Neither is attempted in practice, and one might question the law which would allow such things. The law as summarised in the text was the law before the Requirements of Writing (Scotland) Act 1995, and those responsible for that Act did not intend to change the law in this respect: see the Scottish Law Commission's *Consultative Memorandum* No.66 (1985), para.8.4. But there might be an argument that the law was in fact changed by the 1995 Act. Section 2(1) says that signature must be by the grantor. Section 12(2) allows signature on behalf of the grantor by a person holding a "power of attorney". The 1995 Act does not require powers of attorney to be in writing (see s.1), but the expression "power of attorney" is generally understood to involve a written document, and it is noteworthy that s.12(2) avoids the general term "agency". The difficulty is ignored in practice.

execution of deeds, the facts (i) that there is a properly executed original in existence and (ii) that the terms of that original have been communicated to the other party, may make the sending of the original unnecessary. If that is correct, then a contract could be concluded entirely by fax, even although each party kept their own originals. It has been so held in the sheriff court.[11] It has also been so held in the Outer House, but the Inner House in the same case reserved its view on the matter.[12] We tentatively suggest that when the law requires that a contract be in writing that means a piece of paper produced to the other party,[13] and that an unsigned copy of such a document is insufficient. If that is right then missives cannot be concluded by fax.[14]

Digital missives?

Might missives be concluded by email? Not under current law. 3-05 Article 9 of the E-Commerce Directive,[15] which had to be transposed by member states by January 17, 2002, provides that "member states shall ensure that their legal system allows contracts to be concluded by electronic means." An exception is made for "contracts that create or transfer rights in real estate except for rental rights". The meaning of the exception is obscure.[16] A full analysis would be out of place here. However, it seems likely that the exception covers deeds such as dispositions and standard securities, but does not cover missives. If that is right then EC law requires that digital missives be allowed, and, presumably, at some time in the future that will happen.[17] Naturally, as and when digital missives are allowed, they will have to be digitally signed.[18]

Noting interest and closing dates[19]

The proper way of expressing interest in buying a house is to "note 3-06 interest" with the solicitors (or estate agents) representing the seller. This can be done by a phone call. Noting interest is an indication that the interested party is likely to have the property surveyed and is likely

---

[11] *McIntosh v Alam*, 1998 S.L.T. (Sh. Ct) 19.

[12] *Merrick Homes Ltd v Duff*, 1996 S.C. 497. See Rennie, 2000 S.L.P.Q. 346.

[13] Either by missive letters actually delivered or by a single piece of paper signed by or for both parties.

[14] cf. *Stamfield's Creditors v Scot* (1696) Br. Supp. IV, 344 where Sir James Stamfield signed a document and told the other party it was ready to be uplifted: immediately thereafter he was murdered. It was held that the document was ineffective.

[15] 2000/31/EC.

[16] The French text says "*les contrats qui créent ou transfèrent des droits sur des biens immobiliers à l'exception des droits de location*". The German text says "*Verträge, die Rechte an Immobilien mit Ausnahme von Mietrechten begründen oder übertragen*". As usual with EC legislation, the official English version is drafted on the basis that English law applies throughout the UK.

[17] Being a requirement of EC law it could be given effect to by statutory instrument.

[18] See the Electronic Signatures Regulations 2002 (SI 2002/318).

[19] See generally Janice H. Webster, *Professional Ethics and Practice for Scottish Solicitors* (4th ed., 2004), para.4.05.

thereafter to put in an offer.[20] Moreover, the convention is that sellers who have received notes of interest will not sell without giving those who have noted interest a chance to offer. This is a convention rather than a rule of law. To what extent solicitors are professionally bound to honour it is unclear.[21] If sellers set a closing date, that means that they (through their solicitors) tell those who have noted interest that all offers must be received by a certain date and time when they will be opened. The sellers' solicitors must go over the offers carefully, and discuss them carefully with the clients. If there is more than one offer a decision must be made as to which one to accept (usually the highest, but where there is not much between the first two offers there may be other reasons, *e.g.* better date of entry or personal reasons, for preferring the second highest). Once the sellers have made their decision, their solicitor should at once telephone the firms which submitted offers to tell them the outcome.

Gazumping and gazundering

3–07　　Seller are not bound to accept the highest offer, and indeed they can reject all offers. Unless and until missives have been concluded, which nowadays is likely to take some time, sellers are legally free to accept an offer which comes in after the closing date. They may also accept an increased offer from one of the unsuccessful bidders, or threaten to do so in order to persuade the successful bidders to up their price. This is called gazumping, and the bidder who was at first successful but later unsuccessful will be understandably incensed. There is normally no legal redress, but there is a question as to whether co-operation in gazumping is unprofessional.[22] The Law Society *Revised Guidelines on Closing Dates and Notes of Interest* (1998)[23] provide that a later offer is (from a professional standpoint) acceptable only if negotiations on the originally successful offer have "fallen through".[24] The solicitor in such cases needs to be careful not to act unprofessionally. Gazundering is the converse: it is where a buyer opts out of a purchase which is not yet binding so as to persuade the seller to sell for a lower figure, or so as to buy a different, cheaper, property. Gazumping tends to happen in rising markets and gazundering in falling ones. Gazumping and gazundering used to be

---

[20] In theory, missives could equally well be initiated by an offer to sell made by the seller. Occasionally this is seen. But in the normal case the missives begin with an offer to buy.

[21] The Law Society, *Guidelines on Closing Dates and Notes of Interest* (1998) provide that "selling solicitors are entitled to accept their client's instructions to accept an incoming offer without having a closing date and without giving other parties who may have noted interest an opportunity to offer, although every effort should be made to give them such an opportunity if at all possible". In the light of this it may be sensible, when noting interest, to obtain express confirmation that the opportunity to offer will be given. The whole issue has caused the Law Society difficulty: see (1998) 43 J.L.S.S. June/43 and Oct./47.

[22] For a case involving a late offer see *Morston Assets Ltd v City of Edinburgh Council*, 2001 S.L.T. 613.

[23] As with other Law Society guidelines these can be found in the *Parliament House Book*.

[24] para.3. Para. 4 provides that the solicitor should withdraw from acting if the reason that the first negotiations fell through was "solely" that the client could respond to another offer. Para. 5 has additional provisions whose meaning is, perhaps, not wholly clear.

regarded as English diseases, back in the days when missives were concluded promptly. Nowadays, when missives tend to remain open for a long period, the disease exists in Scotland too, though it is not so widespread as in England.[25]

How much?

In a buoyant housing market a seller will hope to collect a number of 3–08 noted interests. But once the first note of interest has come in there is immediate pressure to set a closing date: potential buyers will be looking at other houses as well, and they will not want to wait indefinitely for this one. Normally a closing date follows within a week to 10 days. It is usually at noon, and often on a Friday. The closing date is the date by which all offers must be submitted. The offerors are bidding blind. They may have a valuation figure provided by their surveyor. They will also usually know, through the local SPC, the recent selling prices of comparable properties. And they may know how many other people are bidding against them. If advising offerors, the trick is to offer enough to get the property but not so much that they pay more than absolutely necessary. But in practice there is a lot of luck involved and it is difficult to fix on the right figure. The clients may be up against another offeror who has just lost seven houses in a row, and is willing to offer an absurd figure to secure this one. If the market is weak there may be no noted interests at all. In that case offers can sometimes be enticed by making the house available at a fixed price: in principle the first person to submit an offer at that price is then the person to whom the property will be sold, although it does not always work out like that, partly because two offers may be submitted at about the same time.

Bargaining

It is seldom possible to meet the offer with a *de plano (i.e.* unqualified) 3–09 acceptance. Indeed, so rare have *de plano* acceptances become that the receipt of one may induce panic in the recipient. Why must the buyers' offer be qualified by the sellers? One reason is that the terms of the offer are likely to be unfairly loaded in favour of the buyers, so that it is necessary to redress the balance. (Indeed the temptation is to load it down the other way.) Another is that the property may not satisfy all the conditions laid down in the offer. Indeed, one reason why a typical offer is weighted down with onerous provisions is to "flush out" any problems that may exist. And indeed for this reason a *de plano* acceptance is often impracticable, since there is a good chance that the property does not come up to scratch in respect of all the provisions of the offer. In order to judge to what extent the terms of the offer can be accepted, the sellers' solicitors must consult with their clients and also have at least a nodding acquaintance with the title. (The sellers' solicitors should have the deeds and the PECs to hand before any offer is received, although for one reason or another it is not always possible to manage this.) A third reason for a qualified acceptance is that it may be necessary to

---

[25] It is a problem which exists in many other countries too.

alter, say, the date of entry, or the list of extras to be included in the price. Where possible, such qualifications should be agreed with the other side by telephone at the time when they are told that the offer is to be accepted. Not only does this cut down on work later but there is always the chance that in the immediate euphoria of success the buyers will be more accommodating than on the morning after.

The drafting of a qualified acceptance is difficult and should be done with care. As every offer is different, so is every qualified acceptance. There is no style to follow. Though there is pressure of time, it is vital to get the acceptance right: the clients will be bound and errors can be costly. It should be borne in mind that certain obligations, most notably the obligation to provide a good and marketable title, are implied by law. So in such cases it is not enough to delete the obligation as stated in the offer: the common law obligation is only excluded if the qualified acceptance expressly states that the clients will not, for instance, guarantee the absence of unduly onerous burdens.[26]

Missives nowadays may take a long time to conclude. Gone are the days of short offer met by short acceptance. To some extent the balance of work in a conveyancing transaction has swung from examination of title to conclusion of missives. After the seventh missive[27] has passed from one party to the other, examination of title may seem like light recreation. Is all this frantic negotiation really worth the effort? In many cases the answer is no. Much of the work may really be self-induced. The purchaser produces an offer, long and lethal, bristling with missiles and (more dangerous) concealed mines. The seller replies in kind: the purchaser's armoury is ruthlessly dismantled and replaced by the seller's own weaponry. And so it goes on. Qualified acceptance is met by a further qualified acceptance as each side tries to wear the other down. Sometimes it becomes unpleasant. Much may be threatened in the names of one's clients, including the ultimate threat, withdrawal. Meanwhile the clients may be blithely unaware of the war raging around them: the buyers are likely to believe from day one that they have bought the house and the sellers that they have sold it.[28] Usually neither has the slightest intention of withdrawing.[29] And of course they are right. It is rare for parties to withdraw just because their solicitors cannot negotiate precisely the contract they would like and few solicitors would dare suggest such a thing.

Of course, in some cases there are real issues between the parties, so that time spent in negotiation is time well spent. But this is more likely to occur in commercial than in residential conveyancing. In residential conveyancing there is something a little absurd about treating a transaction as a rerun of the Battle of Waterloo. (There may be psychological

---

[26] See *e.g. Baird v Drumpellier & Mount Venon Estates Ltd*, 2000 S.C. 103.

[27] By no means all missives follow the course here described. Missives are still sometimes concluded quickly, relations between the agents may be cordial, and the terms of missive letters reasonable.

[28] The solicitor will have explained that this is not so, but clients seldom seem to grasp the point.

[29] Such intentions are, however, commoner than they were a few years ago. It is more common now for clients deliberately to keep missives open so as to keep their options open.

benefits for the participants, but that is another matter.) On a practical level there is usually no point in loading the offer (or qualified acceptance) with oppressive conditions if these are merely going to be deleted by the solicitors acting for the other side. The path of wisdom is that a firm's style offer should be such that the firm would, if acting for a seller, be prepared to accept *de plano*.[30] But in practice some firms cannot resist the temptation of trying to slip something past the other side. Sometimes indeed precisely this happens. But unless one is transacting with Rip van Winkle, W.S., the final contract is likely to be much the same no matter how long is spent on negotiations. Meanwhile, as the days lengthen into weeks without the contract being concluded, the clients are being exposed to the risk that the other party may (for some quite unconnected reason) decide to withdraw. The solicitors involved will then have difficulty in justifying their tactics to their own clients.

Finally, practical problems can arise where there are several missives. An offer met by a qualification met by a final acceptance makes three missives. That is reasonable, in the sense that working out the final terms of the contract is not too difficult. But the more missives there are, the harder it is to work out which terms have been deleted, which reinstated, which modified, and so on. Trying to see whether the seller has or has not agreed to warrant the condition of the central heating becomes a brainteaser taking several minutes. Moreover, the client may be unimpressed by all this clutter. There has been judicial criticism. One judge commented that the set of papers before him was "a poor advertisement for the traditional process of developing the definition of the rights and obligations of the parties through qualification and counter-qualification."[31] One possible response to the problem is to use draft missives, whereby an offer is adjusted between the agents until it is mutually satisfactory. It can then be sent as a formal offer and met by a *de plano* acceptance. This is quite often done in commercial conveyancing, and should be adopted into residential conveyancing, at least where the number of missive letters starts to become substantial.

Delay in concluding missives

Traditionally missives were concluded within a few days. Quick 3–10 contracts were a matter of national pride: in England there was envy and admiration of what was called "the Scottish system". During the 1970s the period began to lengthen. Today it is common for missives to remain open until the eve of settlement. The reasons for this change are not wholly certain. To some extent it is due to the increasing complexity of offers. To some extent it is due to the problem of unauthorised alterations, a problem which became "fashionable" in the early 1990s. To some extent it is due to delay by lenders.[32] To some extent it is because some clients are deliberately keeping missives open so as to keep their options open. To some extent it is because some solicitors

---

[30] See Gretton (1989) 34 J.L.S.S. 19.

[31] *Evans v Argus Healthcare (Glenesk) Ltd*, 2001 S.C.L.R. 117 *per* Lord Macfadyen.

[32] All conveyancers have a rich store of horror stories about institutional lenders.

seem no longer to feel any sense of urgency about concluding missives. And there may be other reasons. Open missives are not binding, a fact which may or may not be satisfactory to the parties, or which may be satisfactory to one but not to the other. Even the party who is content for missives to be open may suddenly be of a different opinion. Clara is buying from Donald and is keeping the missives unconcluded until she has sold her old house. Donald may get fed up and resile, leaving Clara less than happy. She wanted to have it both ways, but what is sauce for the Clara-goose is also sauce for the Donald-gander. (In fact, however, cases in which one party resiles from open missives are not common.) The Law Society's *Guidelines on Avoidance of Delay in Concluding Missives (1998)* narrate, all too truly, that "it is increasingly common for missives to be in an unconcluded state until shortly before—or even at the date of entry". They go on to state that there is a "professional duty to conclude missives without undue delay". If the client instructs delay, then the professional duty is to disclose the circumstances to the other side. These *Guidelines* seem not to have made much impact.[33]

One consequence of the change in practice is that, whereas it used to be the norm for missives to be concluded before the agents for the buyers had had the opportunity to examine the title, so that the buyers' rights in respect of the title rested very much on the terms of the missives, nowadays the buyers' agents usually have plenty of time to examine title before conclusion of missives. The report on title can thus be sent to the buyers before, rather than after, conclusion of missives. In the old days, if there was something in the title which was unsatisfactory to the buyers, they would have to argue that there was a breach of the terms of the missives. By contrast, nowadays the missives will usually still be open when the difficulty comes to light, and in that case the buyers can simply choose not to conclude the missives. The new practice thus does have certain advantages to offset the drawbacks.

The future of missives?

3–11   Traditionally there was a period of, typically, several weeks when concluded missives were in force and both parties were locked into the deal.[34] Today missives are often in force only for a day or two or only for a few hours before settlement. Perhaps the question should be asked as to whether missives have any real value any longer? After all, the law does not actually require missives. Parties can, and occasionally do, go straight to settlement without any prior contract at all: the documentation consists of just the disposition, which is delivered[35] against payment of the price. Of course, missives do not only serve the function of locking the parties into the agreement, but also of dealing with matters not normally dealt with in the disposition, but such matters could be covered by collateral guarantees in a letter delivered at settlement. Such issues as

---

[33] For interesting discussion see a letter by Jenny H. Clark at (1999) 44 J.L.S.S. July/15.

[34] Of course there might be opt-out conditions, or a right to rescind for breach, and so on.

[35] Plus other documents as required, such as a discharge of any existing standard security, etc.

investigation of title, checking the planning situation, and so on, can all be done before settlement without any contractual framework. Conveyancing without missives would be possible. We are speculating, not recommending.

Law Society Standard Clauses

In an attempt to deal with some of the problems just described the 3–12 Law Society produced in September 1991 a set of standard clauses for residential conveyancing which it hoped that solicitors would use as the basis for offers to purchase. The clauses were registered in the form of a Deed of Declaration in the Books of Council and Session, so that they could be incorporated into offers by reference. The style did not prove popular[36] and in April 1992 a revised version was published and registered.[37] This also proved less than popular, and in 1995 the Law Society announced that the experiment was over.[38] In some ways this is a pity. The absence of a standard form makes the negotiation of missives burdensome, and with conveyancing fees so low the work can often not be properly charged for.[39] In some areas informal agreements between local firms as to mutually acceptable clauses have developed.[40] The underlying issues have not gone away, and at the time of writing it is understood that the Law Society's Conveyancing Committee is looking at the question once again.

Offer and acceptance

Unlike many contracts, missives fit neatly into the textbook category of 3–13 offer and acceptance. Once an offer has been made, it presumptively remains available for acceptance for a "reasonable time". The same is true of qualified acceptances, which in law are considered as new offers. In practice the initial offer will almost invariably contain an express, and short, time-limit by which acceptance must be made. In reality, though, time-limits often matter little, because most offers are met by qualified acceptances, and a qualified acceptance is regarded as an entirely new offer, which therefore need not adhere to the time-limit in the previous missive. It is only where a missive constitutes a final acceptance that it has to meet the time-limit in the immediately previous missive. In practice, however, each missive usually has a clause expressly deleting the time-limit stated in the previous missive.

Can a party withdraw an offer? The rules are as follows. (i) In general a party is free to withdraw at any time before acceptance. (ii) But if the

---

[36] Partly because the first of the three parts was declared unalterable. This was an unenforceable but irksome attempt to limit freedom of contract, particularly as many of the clauses might easily need variation in particular cases. The restriction was removed from the revised version. See a letter from P. Mann at (1991) 36 J.L.S.S. 380 for a characteristic response from the profession.

[37] The first version was registered on August 9, 1991 and the second on April 3, 1992. For discussion, see Smith (1993) 38 J.L.S.S. 60.

[38] (1995) 40 J.L.S.S. 326.

[39] In England conveyancers use nationally-standardised forms.

[40] See *e.g.* (1995) 40 J.L.S.S. 142.

offer is stated to be open for acceptance until a stated time, it cannot be unilaterally withdrawn before that time has arrived. (iii) A distinction exists between a clause saying that an offer will lapse by a certain date, if not accepted, and a clause which says that an offer is open for acceptance until a certain date. Only the latter falls under rule (ii).[41] The exact wording is therefore important. (iv) If the offer provides that it can be withdrawn, then withdrawal is competent notwithstanding rule (ii). In order to ensure that the right to withdraw exists, it is advisable to make use of this rule. For instance: "This offer, unless previously withdrawn, is open for acceptance until . . ." (v) Withdrawal is never competent if the offer has already been accepted.[42] Assuming the withdrawal to be competent, it need not be in formal writing, and indeed may be oral,[43] though of course from a practical point of view a formal written withdrawal is advisable.

On receipt of an offer two choices are in theory open: to accept or to reject. In practice a successful offer is usually met by a qualified acceptance, and a qualified acceptance is deemed to be both (a) a rejection and (b) a new offer.[44] It is easy to overlook (a). Once a qualified acceptance is sent the original offer is rejected once and for all *and cannot be revived by withdrawing the qualified acceptance.*[45] The only effect of withdrawing a qualified acceptance is that there is now no live offer available for the other party to accept. The earlier offer does not revive. Care should be taken with the use of qualified acceptances, particularly at a late stage in the negotiations where the qualification may concern a trivial point. For as soon as a qualified acceptance is sent the ball is back in the other party's court and the chance to bring about a concluded contract is lost until the ball is returned. It may not be returned.

The postal rule

3–14   Details of the "postal rule" can be found in the standard texts.[46] Its effect is that an acceptance may be deemed delivered at the time when it is posted, even though the offeror has so far received nothing back. Thus an offer to buy is posted on April 1 and the withdrawal posted on April 3. If the seller posts the acceptance on April 2, reaching the offeror on April 4, the law says that there is a binding contract. Most missive letters nowadays are sent by DX or Legal Post. Whether the postal rule applies to such forms of communication is uncertain, but probably it does.[47] The

---

[41] See William W. McBryde, *The Law of Contract in Scotland* (2nd ed., 2001), para.6–60.

[42] That is to say, genuinely accepted, as opposed to being met by a qualified acceptance.

[43] *McMillan v Caldwell*, 1991 S.L.T. 325.

[44] The term "qualified acceptance" is thus in a sense a misleading one, because in law it is not an acceptance at all. Indeed, each and every new missive is a rejection of what has gone before and is a new offer which incorporates parts of what has gone before. The exception is the final missive, which accepts the immediately previous one. This final missive is the only one which is truly an "acceptance".

[45] *Rutterford v Allied Breweries*, 1990 S.L.T. 249, and *cf. Findlater v Maan*, 1990 S.L.T. 465.

[46] See *e.g.* William W. McBryde, *The Law of Contract in Scotland* (2nd ed., 2001), paras 6–118 *et seq.*

[47] See William W. McBryde, *The Law of Contract in Scotland* (2nd ed., 2001), para.6–122 for general discussion, though DX or Legal Post are not specifically dealt with.

postal rule has many obscure aspects. It is generally regarded as a nuisance, but happily it can be excluded if the offer expressly states that the acceptance is to "reach this office" by the stated deadline.

Personal bar

Contracts for the sale of heritage must be constituted in formal 3–15 writing. But where formal writing has not been used a contract may still be set up by the operation of the doctrine of personal bar. This used to be governed by common law but is now statutory. If there is an informal contract for the sale of heritable property, and one party "has acted or refrained from acting in reliance on the contract . . . with the knowledge or acquiescence of the other party" then the other party "shall not be entitled to withdraw from the contract".[48] In general this makes personal bar rather easier to plead than it was at common law. The conduct in question must be of some significance. In one case taken at common law the purchaser had done no more than draft a disposition and prepare a few other forms and this was held not to justify a plea of personal bar.[49] The same would probably be true under the current rules.

Before this provision can apply there must be a *contract,* that is to say, an agreement which would have been legally binding had it not been for the absence (partial or total) of formal writing. This fact may mean that in one respect the new principle makes a plea of personal bar harder than it was at common law. For in the celebrated case (taken at common law) of *Errol v Walker*[50] the purchaser of a house made a formal offer, which was never accepted. Substantial actings followed on the part of the purchaser, on the basis of which the court held there to be a contract. The surprising aspect of *Errol* was that it allowed the use of *rei interventus*[51] not merely to cure the absence of form (*i.e.* of an acceptance not being in formal writing) but to cure the absence of *consensus in idem (i.e.* of there being no acceptance at all). If that is the correct interpretation of *Errol*,[52] the modern statutory law is probably different.

However, whilst the modern rules require *consensus in idem,* they do not limit the manner in which *consensus in idem* can be arrived at, or can subsequently be proved.[53]

Defects of consent

Like other contracts, missives may be affected by defects of consent 3–16 such as essential error or undue influence. This subject, which belongs to the general law of contract, will not be dealt with here, except for a few words about error. In the typical case, error is both unilateral and also

---

[48] Requirements of Writing (Scotland) Act 1995, s.1(3).

[49] *Rutterford v Allied Breweries,* 1990 S.L.T. 249.

[50] 1966 S.C. 93.

[51] Part of the common law doctrine of personal bar.

[52] There is room for argument as to how *Errol* should be interpreted. It generated a good deal of controversy. Many thought it wrong, and though it was never overruled it was frequently distinguished in later cases.

[53] Whereas the standard view of the old law was that the agreement had to be proved by "writ or oath".

uninduced. Thus it gives rise to no remedy. A standard example is where the buyers think that they are getting a larger piece of land than turns out to be the case.[54] Unilateral error may, however, be relevant where the error was known to, and taken advantage of by, the other party to the contract.[55] Where the missives misdescribe the property, or misstate some other matter, so that they fail to represent the common intention of the parties, judicial rectification may be available.[56] However, before missives, parties are still at the stage of negotiation, so that it is difficult to prove a common intention which the missives fail to give effect to. In practice, parties may be in dispute as to whether the error is unilateral (for which there is, in general, no remedy) or whether the error is in expression, misstating a prior common intention (for which rectification is competent). Unilateral error will found reduction where it has been induced by the other party to the contract; and damages are also due if the misrepresentation was either fraudulent or negligent.[57]

If there is misrepresentation in a conveyancing transaction, it is almost always by the seller. The representation may be oral, or it may be in the printed sale particulars. The effect is negatived, as far as private law is concerned,[58] by the more or less standard disclaimer that their accuracy is not guaranteed. Some contracts circumvent this disclaimer by express incorporation of the sale particulars. Typical misrepresentations by the seller are that the roof is in good condition, that the central heating system was recently overhauled, or that the next-door neighbours are aged and as quiet as mice. In *Smith v Paterson*[59] reduction was granted where the seller had, by deliberately careless words, misrepresented the extent of the front garden. But, as *Smith* itself shows, it is difficult to prove oral representations.

Promises and options

3-17   It is competent to make a gratuitous promise to transfer ownership of land. The promise must be in formal writing.[60] Naturally such promises are rare in practice. More important is the option. In an option, the owners undertake to sell[61] land on certain terms at a certain price, but the potential purchasers are not bound to buy. They may buy or not as they see fit. The option will be open for a stated period, such as a year, and if the option-holders choose not to exercise their option in that time,

---

[54] As in *Oliver v Gaughan*, 1990 G.W.D. 22–1247.

[55] This is the doctrine of "taking unfair advantage" of error. Compare *Spook Erection (Northern) Ltd v Kaye*, 1990 S.L.T. 676 with *Angus v Bryden*, 1992 S.L.T. 884. See further Thomson, 1992 S.L.T. (News) 215 and William W. McBryde, *Law of Contract in Scotland* (2nd ed., 2001), paras 15–31 *et seq.*

[56] Under s.8 of the Law Reform (Miscellaneous Provisions) (Scotland) Act 1985. See Ch.17.

[57] Law Reform (Miscellaneous Provisions) (Scotland) Act 1985, s.10. See *e.g. Palmer v Beck*, 1993 S.L.T. 485.

[58] False sales particulars may amount to an offence: Property Misdescriptions Act 1991. See Ch.2, where the law of the sale of haunted houses is also expounded.

[59] O.H., Feb. 18, 1986, unreported.

[60] 1995 Act, s.1(2)(a)(i).

[61] Options can in fact either be options to buy ("call" options) or options to sell ("put" options). So an owner might buy a put option. But this is rare for heritable property.

the option lapses.[62] Options are occasionally granted gratuitously but normally are onerous, *i.e.* the owner sells the option. If the option-holders decide to exercise the option, the price for the land will be in addition to the price paid for the option itself. If they choose not to exercise the option they then write off the price paid for it. In commercial conveyancing options are quite common,[63] but in residential conveyancing they are not.

An option, like missives, must be sufficiently definite as to parties, property and price.[64] An option must be exercised in the form and within the timescale laid down in the initial grant of the option. But unless the grant specifies otherwise, an option need not be exercised in formal writing or indeed in any writing at all, though the original option itself must have been in formal writing.[65] An option is not exercised by an offer to buy, for an offer to buy may be rejected, or accepted only conditionally, whereas an owner is immediately and completely bound by the valid exercise of an option. In other words, an option is not given effect to by later missives, unless both parties so wish. In practice, options do not usually contain the multifarious terms and conditions found in missives, but to some extent these will be implied.[66]

Finally, missives subject to a suspensive condition can in practice work very like an option in favour of the buyers, and, moreover, an option for which they do not have to pay: see below.

SUSPENSIVE CONDITIONS

Introduction

A suspensive condition,[67] at least in the normal usage of the term, is a 3–18 condition in a contract which is suspensive of performance. In other words there is a concluded contract between the parties—each is bound to the other—but neither can be made to perform unless or until the condition is purified, so that if the condition is not purified within the time-limit set for that purpose both parties are freed from its terms. While the suspensive condition remains unpurified, the contract is in suspense. Its activation depends on the purification of the condition. No obligation arises under the suspensive condition itself. Indeed, typically its purification is out of the control of both parties. If the condition is not

---

[62] There may sometimes be disputes as to whether the time-limit has been complied with: see *Fortune Engineering Ltd v Precision Components (Scotland) Ltd*, 1993 G.W.D. 1–49.

[63] They can provide commercial flexibility and can save capital gains tax. See Halliday, para.30–164.

[64] *Bogie v Forestry Commission*, 2001 G.W.D. 38–1432. For a marginal case see *Miller Homes Ltd v Frame*, 2001 S.L.T. 459.

[65] 1995 Act, s.1(2), and see *Stone v MacDonald*, 1979 S.C. 363.

[66] *Zani v Martone*, 1997 S.L.T. 1269; *McCall's Entertainments (Ayr) Ltd v South Ayrshire Council*, 1998 S.L.T. 1403 and 1421.

[67] See generally Thomson, in A.J. Gamble (ed.), *Obligations in Context: Essays in Honour of Professor D.M. Walker* (1990), and William W. McBryde, *The Law of Contract in Scotland* (2nd ed., 2001), paras 5.35–5.40.

met no damages are due. The contract simply falls away. However, in practice missives often provide that the buyers shall use their best endeavours to bring about the purification of the condition. The typical example is planning permission, with the purchasers being bound to pursue the planning application with reasonable diligence and so on.

Suspensive conditions are quite common, particularly in commercial conveyancing. Thus, a contract may be made conditional on the granting of planning permission or on the transfer of a liquor licence. However, within the past five years a new clause has become common in offers for residential property: the "subject to survey" clause. This says that the offer is subject to the buyers' obtaining a survey that is in terms satisfactory to them, as to which they themselves will be the "sole judge". This clause potentially operates as a suspensive condition. In practice, however, missives are seldom concluded with this clause still active. By the time that the parties get round to concluding missives the survey will have been obtained. If it was in unsatisfactory terms the buyers will simply have walked off, which they are entitled to so since there are no concluded missives. If its terms are satisfactory then missives will be concluded but this clause will have been superseded.

Two kinds of suspensive condition—"subject to contract"

3–19   As Professor McBryde observes, "there is a difference between a condition suspensive of a contract and a contract subject to a suspensive condition."[68] In the former case there is no contract at all. Open missives in which substantive agreement has been reached, but which still await the last missive concluding the bargain, are subject to a suspensive condition in the first sense. Either party is free to withdraw: there is said to be a *locus poenitentiae*. But if there is a contract subject to a suspensive condition then neither party is free to withdraw. It is in this second sense that we are concerned here. In England the expression "subject to contract" is sometimes used: it would appear to operate as a suspensive condition in the first sense. The expression is not in general use in Scotland.

Identifying suspensive conditions

3–20   It is not always easy to say whether a particular contractual term is an ordinary condition or a suspensive condition.[69] A well-drafted term should leave no doubt on the matter, but not all terms are well drafted. The standard way of introducing a suspensive condition is with the words "this contract is conditional on" or "this contract is subject to" (*e.g.* the obtaining of planning permission). Clauses which begin this way are usually suspensive. But less will do. In *Zebmoon Ltd v Akinbrook*

---

[68] William W. McBryde, *The Law of Contract in Scotland* (2nd ed., 2001), para.5–37. And see Stair I, iii, 8 and I, x, 3.

[69] Or a resolutive condition. In this latter case the formula is generally that if a certain condition is not met, either party may resile without liability to either side. For an example see *Ford Sellar Morris Properties plc v E. W. Hutchison Ltd*, 1990 S.L.T. 500.

Investment Developments Ltd[70] a clause which began with the words "it is an essential condition of this offer" was held to be suspensive even though these words are often found introducing non-suspensive conditions as well.

Sometimes conditions are apparently suspensive but are coupled with an express right to rescind for the purchasers if the condition is not purified. This is a natural attempt by the draftsman to protect the clients. If the condition is truly suspensive such a provision is unnecessary. (For if there is no purification the contract is automatically null.) Indeed, such a provision may be the basis for an argument that the clause is in fact an ordinary, non-suspensive, condition.[71] A possible alternative interpretation of such a clause is as a suspensive condition but with a right in the buyers to waive purification. (For if they have an express right to resile they also appear to have an implied right not to resile.)

Time-limit for purification of suspensive conditions

From the sellers' point of view it is most important that a time-limit 3–21 for purification be stipulated. Otherwise they may be left in the situation where they do not know whether the sale will proceed (and do not know when they will know) but yet cannot lawfully withdraw and remarket the property. If purification requires one of the parties to do something (such as to apply for planning permission), an alternative approach is to set out a timetable. In either case time should be made of the essence or, which comes to the same thing, a right of immediate rescission reserved in the event of non-compliance; but immediate rescission is possible even without provision in respect of "pure" suspensive conditions (*i.e.* where no obligations are imposed).[72] A right of rescission need not be exercised immediately, and can still be exercised if the condition was purified but out of time.[73]

If no date for purification is given the rules appear to be the following: (1) Where missives have a date of entry which is fixed independently of the suspensive condition,[74] the condition must be fulfilled by that date. (2) Otherwise, the condition must be fulfilled within a reasonable time.[75]

---

[70] 1988 S.L.T. 146. Compare *Khazaka v Drysdale*, 1995 S.L.T. 1108.

[71] See *Tarditi v Drummond*, 1989 S.L.T. 554 at 557–558. But no objection was raised on this account in *Zebmoon Ltd v Akinbrook Investment Developments Ltd*, 1988 S.L.T. 146.

[72] *T. Boland & Co. v Dundas's Trs*, 1975 S.L.T. (Notes) 80. If, however, a positive obligation is placed on one of the parties, an ultimatum must first be sent giving a "reasonable time" for performance: see *Miller Group Ltd v Park's of Hamilton (Holdings) Ltd*, 2003 G.W.D. 8–225.

[73] *Ford Sellar Morris Properties plc v E. W. Hutchison Ltd*, 1990 S.C. 34; *Bluestone Estates Ltd v Fitness First Clubs Ltd*, 2003 G.W.D. 27–768. A long delay will give rise to arguments of personal bar.

[74] As opposed, for example, to a clause which provided that the date of entry would be one week after the grant of a liquor licence. Such clauses tying entry to purification are common.

[75] See *T. Boland & Co. v Dundas's Trs*, 1975 S.L.T. (Notes) 80 *per* Lord Keith.

Can the purchasers waive a suspensive condition?

3–22   If a suspensive condition is not purified, the purchasers will usually wish to withdraw from the purchase and, generally speaking, the effect of non-purification is for the contract to fall. Sometimes, though, the purchasers may wish to proceed after all, and the question then arises as to whether they are entitled to waive the suspensive condition. It seems that such waiver is allowed in two circumstances only. The first is where an express right of waiver is reserved.[76] The second is where the condition was inserted solely in the purchasers' interests and it is severable from the rest of the contract. The second set of circumstances is not easily established. In only one reported case has the purchaser succeeded on this ground,[77] and that decision has been questioned in subsequent cases.[78] In these later cases the purchaser has failed either because the seller also had an express right to resile in the event of non-purification (which negatived the idea of the condition being for the sole benefit of the purchaser) or because the date of entry was tied to the date of purification (which prevented it from being severable). These were perhaps fairly straightforward cases. In *Imry Property Holdings Limited v Glasgow YMCA*[79] Lord Dunpark said that the mere fact there was nothing in the missives to show that the seller had an interest was not enough, and that the missives must give positive evidence that the suspensive condition was conceived in favour of the purchaser only. But the later cases suggest that the rule may be less strict than this. This rule restricting waiver applies to suspensive conditions only. A party is always free to waive the performance of ordinary contractual obligations incumbent on the other party to the contract. For instance, the fact that the sellers cannot produce a flawless title does not prevent the purchasers from proceeding with the contract if they wish to do so.

Suspensive conditions as quasi-options

3–23   Missives which are subject to a suspensive condition can sometimes function as quasi-options in favour of the purchasers, and furthermore this can happen without any payment for the option. Thus developers may conclude missives to purchase subject to a suspensive condition about planning. Such missives lock the sellers in (subject to the time-limit) but they leave the purchasers with a free hand. If they decide that they do not wish to proceed, they back-pedal on the planning application. In effect the developers have an option to purchase at any time within the time-limit, but, cunningly, have not paid an option price.[80] For

---

[76] Which is a wise precaution as far as the buyers are concerned.

[77] *Dewar and Finlay Ltd v Blackwood*, 1968 S.L.T. 196. The soundness of this decision may be doubted: see *Manheath Ltd v H. J. Banks & Co. Ltd*, 1996 S.C. 42.

[78] *Ellis and Sons Second Amalgamated Properties Ltd v Pringle*, 1974 S.C. 200; *Imry Property Holdings Ltd v Glasgow YMCA*, 1979 S.L.T. 261; *Zebmoon Ltd v Akinbrook Investment Developments Ltd*, 1988 S.L.T. 146; *Manheath Ltd v H. J. Banks & Co. Ltd*, 1996 S.C. 42.

[79] 1979 S.L.T. 261. This case also holds that the buyer cannot circumvent the rule simply by announcing that the condition has been purified, a point confirmed by *Manheath Ltd v H. J. Banks & Co. Ltd*, 1996 S.C. 42.

[80] Though they are likely to have invested money in professional fees.

this reason it is usual for the missives to require the purchasers to use their best endeavours to achieve the purification of the condition. However, it is in practice difficult to prove breach of such a term. In such cases sellers would sometimes be wiser to sell an option rather than to agree to suspended missives.

DRAFTING

Drafting: introduction

3–24

> "The moment a new term was invented by any body, and known, the ordinary list became enriched by it; in so much, indeed, that in many charters we find repetitions of the same thing, under different words; which proves that conveyancers were more atten- tive to the practice of each other, than to the sense of what they themselves were doing."

So said Walter Ross writing about the *tenendas* clause in a feu charter.[81] Little, it seems, has changed. Each firm maintains its own *pro forma* offer, either on the word processor or in the form of a pre-printed schedule.[82] But the offer is constantly revised and updated to take account of the practice of other firms. If firm A, being a large and well- known firm, think fit to insert a new clause in their offer, it will not be long before it appears in the offers of innumerable other firms. There are obvious advantages in this method of proceeding. But there are also disadvantages.[83] One is that offers become ever longer as new clauses are invented and then copied. Another disadvantage is that the imported clause may sit uneasily in the home style, and the problem is com- pounded where, as is often the case, clauses are imported from a number of different sources. It sometimes happens that "revising" the firm's offer means merely adding to it, without removing any existing clause or adapting old and new clauses to make them fully consistent. This can make offers difficult to understand. It can also lead to unexplained inconsistencies of language which might be treated as significant by a court when no significance was intended.

In residential conveyancing many firms use the same *pro forma* offer for quite different types of property—for Victorian flats, modern villas, urban and rural properties, houses subject to registration of title as well as for houses held on a GRS title, and so on. Hence, for any given property the offer will probably contain several redundant clauses. Put a field on the market, and one may get an offer asking the seller to warrant the condition of the central heating and to guarantee that there

---

[81] Walter Ross, *Lectures on the History and Practice of the Law of Scotland relative to Conveyancing and Legal Diligence* (commonly called *Ross's Lectures*) (1792), p.165 of the 1822 edition.

[82] A word-processed offer is better for client relations. Clients like to see an offer which has been, or seems to have been, tailored to their own case.

[83] We say nothing of possible breach of copyright. Copying styles regardless of copyright is an ancient practice in the legal profession, both in Scotland and elsewhere.

is a right to the solum. This practice is often criticised. It continues because it is convenient for the prospective buyers' solicitors. It does not impress the clients.

Drafting: some particular points

3-25   Drafting missives is a difficult and skilled business. Few sets of missives are beyond criticism. Drafting can only be learned by practice, but here are some thoughts.

(1) It may be worth defining the principal terms, *e.g.* seller, buyer and property. At all events consistency is desirable. The buyer should not be referred to as "the buyer" on one page and "our client" on the next.

(2) The introductory formula "it is understood that" should generally be avoided. Understood by whom? What if is it a misunderstanding? A sheriff has remarked:

> "The use of the introductory phrase 'It is understood' in these missives suggests to my mind that cl.7 is intended, not to create an obligation on one party, the defenders, which they have to implement, but to express the understanding of both parties as to a state of facts existing as at the time when they [the missives] were concluded. If their understanding turned out to be wrong then either party, or at least the pursuers, would be entitled to resile from the bargain."[84]

If this is correct,[85] then the phrase "it is understood" prevents the imposition of a direct obligation on the parties at whom it is directed (usually the sellers). In effect it deprives the purchasers of the two remedies of implement and damages, leaving them only with the possibility of rescission. It acts rather like a suspensive condition, at least so far as remedies are concerned, but in circumstances where that is probably not what the buyers want.

(3) The introductory formulae "it is condition that" and "it is an essential condition that" should be used with care. These formulae suggest that the clause has some special status, but it may be unclear just what that status is supposed to be. There seem to be three possibilities. The first is that the clause is a suspensive condition. The second is that it is term whose breach will constitute material breach. The third possibility is that the draftsperson simply felt that the clause was dealing with a particularly important matter. One may suspect that this is in fact the commonest meaning. In that case the introductory formula is legally meaningless.

(4) If the intention is that breach of some provision will entitle the innocent party to rescind, that should be stated expressly, and it should be stated whether the option to rescind is to emerge immediately on breach or only after a defined period. For example, it is common for missives to provide that if the buyer fails to pay within a defined period

---

[84] *Wood v Edwards*, 1988 S.L.T. (Sh. Ct) 17, *per* Sheriff R. J. D. Scott at 21.
[85] Which is perhaps arguable: see *Neilson v Barratt*, 1987 G.W.D. 13–467.

(such as 14 or 21 days) after the due date then the seller has the option to rescind.

(5) The sellers should normally delete a clause declaring all the terms of the offer to be "material" or some similar term. The idea is to allow the buyers to rescind for any breach, no matter how trivial.

(6) Where the seller is to warrant something (*e.g.* that the central heating system is in good working order or that there are no unusual or unduly onerous real burdens) the applicable date for the warranty should normally be the date of entry and not the date of conclusion of missives, though this point is less important than it was because the doctrine of supersession has been abrogated by the Contract (Scotland) Act 1997.

(7) Most positive obligations in missives (*i.e.* obligations to do something) are on the seller. Indeed, in residential conveyancing often the only obligation on the purchaser is to pay the price. But whichever party is subject to obligations it is important to stipulate the date by which the obligation in question must be performed. Normally obligations need to be performed by the date of entry. But there is a potential ambiguity here. If the transaction actually settles on the contractual date of entry, well and good. But sometimes transactions do not settle then, in which case there are two dates of entry, namely (a) the contractual date of entry and (b) the date on which entry is actually taken.[86] It is wise to anticipate this difficulty by providing in missives for two defined dates, namely the "date of entry" and the "date of settlement", the latter being the date on which entry is actually taken. For each obligation it should be made clear which of the two dates is the relevant one. Time is presumed not to be "of the essence" in a contract of sale of heritable property, by which is meant that failure to perform by the stipulated date, though it may be a breach of contract, is not in itself material breach entitling the other party to rescind. However, this is only a presumption, and so can be, and usually is, ousted by express terms in the missives.

(8) Before an offer or a qualified acceptance is sent, it should be checked for errors, bearing in mind that there is usually no remedy for a unilateral error. An offer to purchase which states the price at £175,000, being a typing error for £157,000, is likely to be binding.[87]

(9) As far as possible each clause should deal with just one item. If the item is complex it should be split into sub-clauses. It makes the offer easier to understand. Moreover, when the other side prepare the qualified acceptance, they can deal with the whole of a clause or sub-clause, and are not forced to say something like: "With reference to your fourth schedule clause, the words from 'and if' to 'penalty' are deleted and the following words are substituted." That is messy and, with drafting being done at speed, can cause errors.[88]

---

[86] For discussion see Reid (1988) 33 J.L.S.S. 431; Gretton (1989) 34 J.L.S.S. 175. See further *Spence v W. & R. Murray (Alford) Ltd,* 2002 S.C. 615, and Reid and Gretton, *Conveyancing 2002,* pp.55–57.

[87] See *Steel v Bradley (Scotland) Homes Ltd,* 1974 S.L.T. 133. However, the doctrine of "unfair advantage" may apply: see para.3–16 above.

[88] Some solicitors deliberately insert a "nasty" in a clause dealing with some other (innocuous) matter. We regard this as unethical, and in the long term disadvantageous, since it will give the firm a bad reputation in the profession.

(10) If a term is implied by general law, the deletion of an express term to the same effect does not oust the common law term: see *Baird v Drumpellier & Mount Venon Estates Ltd*[89] discussed below.

(11) To lay down some provision and then to add "or otherwise as may be mutually agreed" (for instance as to the date of entry) does not help matters since the parties are in any event free to renegotiate terms. Moreover such a clause does not make it clear whether it is intended to make possible oral variations of the contract. Clauses of this sort are better avoided.

(12) A clause saying that the property is subject to no overriding interests needs to be treated with care by the sellers, for most properties are indeed so subject.

Preparing the qualified acceptance

3-26 The offer must be gone through carefully with the clients. Are the facts as stated correct? Are the clients really willing to throw in the stair carpet and the tumble dryer? Is the date of entry suitable or should the purchasers be pushed on this? The meeting or telephone conversation with the clients must be documented by an outgoing letter to them confirming the information and instructions received.

Wherever possible the offer should be amended by outright deletion (*e.g.* "Clause 6 of your Schedule is deleted" or "The second sentence of clause 3 of your letter is deleted"). This is better than leaving the clause undeleted while adding Gothic amendments to it, resulting in a dog's breakfast. Thus in *Hood v Clarkson*[90] the offer had a clause about the planning situation. The qualification did not delete this clause or any part of it, but delivered a counter salvo, couched in different words, about local authority PECs and the right to resile. In the result it was wholly unclear whether a major road proposal which came to light was or was not covered by the clause. If the offer incorporates a schedule of conditions, it should be made clear whether the clause being qualified is a clause of the letter or a clause of the schedule.

The number of qualifications should not be excessive, lest this delay conclusion of missives unnecessarily. The sellers' solicitors should have the titles and the PECs and so should be in a position to deal intelligently with the contents of the offer. Thus, if they know from the PECs that, for example, the roads *ex adverso* the property have been taken over by the local authority, there is no point in qualifying the relevant clause in the buyers' offer.

Sometimes the selling solicitors may not have the necessary information to deal with a particular clause in an offer, or may have the information but be uncertain whether it meets the terms of the buyers' clause. The second case often arises with the "no unusual or unduly onerous burdens" clause. Typically the sellers' solicitors have the deeds in front of them, and so know what the burdens are, but may be uncertain whether they can be regarded as usual and not unduly onerous. In this situation it is acceptable, and sensible, to meet the

---

[89] 2000 S.C. 103.
[90] 1995 S.L.T. 98.

purchasers' clause with the over-used "the buyers shall satisfy themselves" provision, provided that the deeds are sent so that the purchasers' solicitors can do just that. If the deeds are not yet to hand, it is common to provide that they will be sent when available, with a time-limit of, for example, five working days after receipt for the buyers to satisfy themselves. In the absence of such a time-limit there is the danger (at least on one view of the law) that the buyers could pronounce on the morning of settlement that they were not satisfied and did not wish to proceed with the purchase.[91]

"Working days"

Disputes sometimes arise as to how such periods are to be calculated.[92] The law is probably as follows. Suppose the documents are sent by DX on Friday, April 10. They are received on Monday, April 13. This is day zero. Tuesday, April 14 is day one. Friday, April 17 is day four. Saturday, April 18 is probably not a "working day" in modern practice. So day five will be Monday, April 20. If the buyers' solicitors wish to resile, they thus have until close of business on that day to do so. "Five" days have thus become 10 days. The resiling letter must, it is thought, be actually received by the sellers' solicitors by close of business on April 20: it is probably not sufficient to put it into the Monday night post. Scottish bank holidays are presumably not "working days" though in practice law offices sometimes open on some bank holidays. Many areas also have non-statutory local holidays when local law offices are usually shut. Again, these are probably not "working days" where the holiday is in the area of the buyers' law office. Hence "five" will sometimes work out as being more than even 10 days. 3–27

INTERPRETATION

Effect of a prior deletion

If something is deleted, the fact of deletion is itself not normally relevant to the interpretation of the contract. Thus in *Baird v Drumpellier & Mount Venon Estates Ltd*[93] a provision about good title was deleted. The sellers later argued that the deletion indicated that they were not binding themselves to guarantee title. This argument was rejected. The missives, as concluded, contained nothing to oust the common law rule that the seller presumptively guarantees that the title is good. 3–28

No favour to either party

In missives both parties have usually been professionally advised and in the interpretation of the contract no favour is shown to either side.[94] 3–29

---

[91] If buyers are to "satisfy themselves" and they decide that they are not satisfied, must their decision be reasonable, or can they decide capriciously? See below.

[92] See David C. Coull, "Time", in *The Laws of Scotland: Stair Memorial Encyclopaedia*, Vol.23 (1987).

[93] 2000 S.C. 103.

[94] See *G.A. Estates Ltd v Caviapen Trs Ltd*, 1993 S.L.T. 1051 and *Park v Morrison Developments Ltd*, 1993 G.W.D. 8–571.

Reasonableness

3–30   A term is sometimes implied in missives that parties will act reasonably. So in *Gordon District Council v Wimpey Homes Holdings Limited*,[95]
where missives were subject to a suspensive condition that planning
permission would be granted "to the satisfaction of the purchaser" and
the permission ultimately granted was fenced in with conditions, Lord
Clyde rejected the purchaser's argument that what was to his "satisfaction" was a matter for him alone and not subject to challenge, and took
the view that "each party must have intended that the other would act
reasonably".[96] Presumably it would be open to the parties to contract so
as to exclude this "reasonable" criterion. It may be added that one party
to a contract (usually the seller) may be taken as bound to use "all
reasonable endeavours" to bring a particular event about.[97]

Contract (Scotland) Act 1997

3–31   At common law there was a rule that if a contract was embodied in
writing, evidence from outside that document,[98] whether written or oral,
was not admissible to prove that the terms of the contract were actually
other than those set forth in the document.[99] The Contract (Scotland)
Act 1997[1] rationalised the rule by changing it into a simple presumption:
"Where a document appears . . . to comprise all the express terms of a
contract . . . it shall be presumed . . . that the document does . . .
comprise all the express terms".[2] However, the rules about the need for
formal writing remain intact.[3]

The 1997 Act deals with evidence of terms which are inconsistent with
the terms of the written contract. It does not deal with extrinsic evidence
for the purpose of interpreting the terms of the contract. As has been
said, "the existing law on the use of extrinsic evidence in the interpretation of writings is notoriously complicated. The basic rule that extrinsic
evidence is inadmissible is subject to so many overlapping exceptions

---

[95] 1989 S.L.T. 141.

[96] *ibid.*, at 142. In the event the court in fact held that the purchaser had acted
reasonably. See also *John H. Wyllie v Ryan Industrial Fuels Ltd*, 1989 S.L.T. 302; *Rockcliffe
Estates plc v Co-operative Wholesale Society Ltd*, 1994 S.L.T. 592; *Hutton v Barrett*, 1994
G.W.D. 37–2188; *Palmer v Forsyth*, 1999 S.L.T. (Sh. Ct) 93. On this last case see Reid and
Gretton, *Conveyancing 1999*, p.40. Reading these cases together, it may be regarded as
doubtful whether there exists any settled doctrine in this area.

[97] The meaning of this phrase is discussed in *Elwood v Ravenseft Properties*, 1991 S.L.T.
44.

[98] Or set of documents, as in the case of missives.

[99] Though of course a contract could be altered, or even wholly novated, by a later
contract. Moreover, whilst extrinsic evidence was (in principle) not allowed to contradict a
written contract, it was admissible to explain points which were obscure.

[1] For background, see the Scottish Law Commission, *Report on Three Bad Rules in
Contract Law* (Scot. Law Com. No.152, 1996). The rule applied to evidence of terms
agreed at an earlier stage. The rule did not prevent contracts from being varied by
subsequent agreement.

[2] s.1(1).

[3] Contract (Scotland) Act 1997, s.1(4). There is room for argument about how the law
outlined in the text fits in with s.8 of the Law Reform (Miscellaneous Provisions)
(Scotland) Act 1985, discussed in Ch.14.

that it almost ceases to exist as a general rule. The law on this subject is confused [and] unsatisfactory."[4] We cannot here enter into this subject, but on the whole extrinsic evidence may be used to explain the meaning of a term in missives where such explanation is required. For instance, it is competent and indeed necessary to use extrinsic evidence to link the verbal description of the property to the actual property on the ground.

VARIATION AND WAIVER

Variation

The terms of missives can be varied by subsequent agreement, and 3–32 indeed this is not uncommon, but it requires the consent of both parties expressed in formal writing.[5] In the absence of actings, oral variation is ineffectual.[6]

Missives commonly contain a clause on the following lines: "Entry and vacant possession will be given on February 14, 2005 or on such other date as may be mutually agreed." Do these last words authorise an informal (unsubscribed) fixing of a fresh date of entry? Conflicting views have been expressed on this question.[7] The safe course is that if the date of entry is changed by mutual agreement, there should be two letters, both subscribed, one setting forth the new date and the other, from the other side, confirming it.

Waiver

Similar in effect to variation is waiver.[8] Apart from the special case of 3–33 suspensive conditions, it is always open to parties unilaterally to waive one or more of their rights under the contract. Waiver may be express, or be implied by actings, and in practice the latter is more common. But arguments based on implied waiver often fail. In order to succeed it is necessary to show, first, that one side to the contract has acted in such a way as to indicate clearly that they will not found on a particular contractual right, and secondly that the other side has acted in reliance on the alleged waiver.[9]

The commonest case in which implied waiver is pled is where, the sellers having failed to perform in some material respect,[10] the purchasers delay in rescinding the contract. The argument then arises that

---

[4] Scottish Law Commission, *Report on Interpretation in Private Law* (Scot. Law Com. No.160, 1997), p.1.

[5] The need for formal writing may be superseded by personal bar: 1995 Act, s.1(3), (6).

[6] *Aitken v Hyslop*, 1977 S.L.T. (Notes) 50; *Inglis v Lownie*, 1990 S.L.T. (Sh. Ct) 60. These cases predate the Requirements of Writing (Scotland) Act 1995 and the Contract (Scotland) Act 1997 but it is thought that the outcome would be the same under current law.

[7] Contrast *Imry Property Holdings Ltd v Glasgow YMCA*, 1979 S.L.T. 261 with *Jaynor Ltd v Allander Holdings Ltd*, 1990 G.W.D. 30–1717.

[8] On which see William W. McBryde, *The Law of Contract in Scotland* (2nd ed., 2001), Ch.25.

[9] *James Howden & Co. Ltd v Taylor Woodrow Property Co. Ltd*, 1998 S.C. 853. As to whether the reliance must be prejudicial, see Reid (1999) 4 *Edinburgh Law Review* 107.

[10] *e.g.* failing to produce a good and marketable title.

the buyers have implicitly waived their right to rescind. In fact mere delay by itself (unless very lengthy) is no bar to rescission. After all, the reason for delay is usually that the purchasers hope that performance will ultimately be forthcoming. Nor is taking entry to the property a bar to rescission, although rescission may then be prevented on the different ground that *restitutio in integrum* is not possible.[11] Nor does it make any difference that the contract itself contains a fixed date after which rescission is expressly permitted and the date is allowed to pass.[12] An example of waiver is *Macdonald v Newall*[13] where the buyer, having examined title and taken no objection to it (except on another unrelated point), took entry and did not then raise her objection until some further months had passed.[14]

---

[11] See *Armia v Daejan Developments Ltd*, 1979 S.C. (HL) 56.

[12] *Lousada & Co. Ltd v J.E. Lesser (Properties) Ltd*, 1990 S.L.T. 823; *Elwood v Ravenseft Properties Ltd*, 1991 S.L.T. 44; *Atlas Assurance Co. Ltd v Dollar Land Holdings plc*, 1993 S.L.T. 892.

[13] (1898) 1 F. 68.

[14] *Mowbray v Mathieson*, 1989 G.W.D. 6–267 is another example.

CHAPTER 4

MISSIVES II: CONTENT

Introductory

This chapter is divided into four parts: terms about the title, terms 4-01
about price and settlement, terms about physical condition (including
questions of risk) and, lastly, terms about public law, such as planning
and building control. The division is, however, not always perfectly
precise.

Essential terms

A contract for the sale of land requires, as a minimum, express 4-02
agreement as to the "three Ps"—the parties to the transaction, the
property being sold, and the price. Without such agreement there is no
contract.[1] At one time express agreement as to date of entry was also
thought essential, but it now seems that an appropriate date of entry will,
if necessary, be read into the contract.

Sometimes the offer to buy does not identify the seller, but just says
"your client". That is less than ideal, but is understandable in the context
of busy practice and lower-value transactions. In such cases the qualified
acceptance should identify the seller. If missives are concluded without
clear identification of the parties, the contract is valid provided that the
undisclosed principals are capable of eventual identification; but
obviously it is poor practice to conclude missives on this basis. If a law
firm concludes missives on behalf of a non-existent principal the missives
are void, and the law firm is itself liable for breach of warranty of
authority. Purported principals can be non-existent both in cases where
they are named and in cases where they are not named. Examples
include companies that have never been incorporated, companies that
were incorporated but have been dissolved, and clients who have died.[2]
A purported principal who exists but who has not authorised the
missives is also a non-existent principal for these purposes.[3]

---

[1] As in *N. J. & J. Macfarlane (Developments) Ltd v MacSween's Trs*, 1999 S.L.T. 619. The
fact that without the three Ps there is no contract does not mean that if the three Ps are
present then there is a contract: this is a common misconception.

[2] *City of Glasgow Council v Peart*, 1999 Hous. L.R. 117.

[3] These remarks are subject to the law about ostensible authority.

Property

4–03   The parties must agree on what is being sold. Therefore the missives must contain an adequate description. But only rarely is a full conveyancing description given in missives. For houses just a postal address is common. For undeveloped plots of ground or for commercial developments more is usually necessary, and, indeed, in commercial conveyancing the offer usually has a plan, which will have been made available to bidders by the seller. If the purchase is a first break-off—*i.e.* if the property has not previously been owned as a separate unit—a plan will be needed. Break-off sales are a rich source of problems. It is all too easy for communications between the clients and their solicitors, or between the neurons of the solicitors involved, to become muddled.

It is no objection to a description that it needs to be supplemented by extrinsic evidence. Thus, in the event of a dispute, it is competent to bring evidence as to which property is known, for example, as "4 High Street". But the extrinsic evidence cannot be made to do the work of the written description, and if the description itself is hopelessly vague there is no place for extrinsic evidence. *Grant v Peter G. Gauld Co.*[4] provides a cautionary tale. The missives began with the words:

> "We hereby offer to purchase from you the ground presently being quarried by our client and the surroundings thereto extending to twelve acres . . . and that on the following terms and conditions, namely: 1. The actual boundaries will be agreed between you and our client . . ."

Since clause 1 amounted to a direct admission that no agreement as to the property had been reached, it was held that there was no contract. But the court indicated that even without clause 1 the result might have been the same, on the basis that the expression "the surroundings thereto extending to twelve acres" was too vague to allow extrinsic evidence. Another description found to be too vague was:[5]

> "a part of Druim Na Pairc Buildings, comprising of two workshop units and garage unit amounting to 6140 sq. feet approx., together with adjoining land comprising of yard of approx. 1 acre and approx. 8½ acres of rough undeveloped land lying to the East of the above property."

In practice, disputes about the definition of the property are uncommon. But where a dispute does arise extrinsic evidence can be used. Roughly speaking, extrinsic evidence can be of two kinds, objective and subjective. Objective evidence answers the question: what is the property known as 4 High Street? The kinds of evidence which is relevant here are the boundaries as stated in the seller's title, physical features such as

---

[4] 1985 S.C. 251.
[5] In *N. J. & J. Macfarlane (Developments) Ltd v MacSween's Trs,* 1999 S.L.T. 619.

hedges or fences, and the position as understood by neighbours. Subjective evidence answers the question: what is the property that was agreed between the parties in the course of negotiations? In *Merrick Homes Ltd v Duff*[6] the contract was for the sale of "three separate areas of land . . . agreed between [the parties] which have been shown by [the seller] to [the purchasers]." The court considered this sufficient.[7]

Often there is only objective evidence, or if subjective evidence exists it is consistent with the objective evidence. But if the two are not the same a choice has to be made, and while each case will turn on its own facts, a major consideration seems to be whether the sellers are selling all or only part of what they own.[8] In the former case, the property will usually be construed as that described in the title (*i.e.* objective evidence). Even if the sellers in fact indicated a larger area to the purchasers (*i.e.* subjective evidence) the case will be analysed as (1) a contract for the smaller area as per the title but (2) one which is voidable at the instance of the purchasers for misrepresentation.[9] Conversely, where the sellers are selling part only of what they own there is less scope for objective evidence, and subjective evidence will often be conclusive.[10]

Since sellers are more likely to overstate than understate the extent of the property, subjective evidence usually favours the purchaser. One method commonly used to ensure that full weight is given to evidence of this kind is to incorporate it expressly into the offer to buy, typically by adding to the brief description of the property the words "all as advertised by you and as seen by the purchaser". Indeed, nowadays the sellers' schedule of particulars may well be annexed to, and adopted as part of, the offer.

Effect of error about the property

Where parties are in dispute as to the property, one of them is 4–04 presumptively in error. Thus the sellers think they sold plot A while the buyers think they bought plot B (which includes but extends beyond plot A). Since the error will have been unilateral it gives rise to no remedy against the other party, unless it has been induced, or unless, while uninduced, the other party took unfair advantage of it.[11] But occasionally it is impossible to reach a concluded view as to who is right. The evidence is consistent with plot A or with plot B—or very likely with plot C as well—and in that case there is mutual error and so no contract at all, because there is no consensus.

---

[6] 1996 S.C. 497.

[7] See also two cases involving options: *Miller Homes Ltd v* Frame, 2001 S.L.T. 459; *Bogie v Forestry Commission*, 2001 G.W.D. 38–1432.

[8] In a sense, of course, this line of approach may beg the question, for the sellers' position may precisely be that they were not selling all they owned.

[9] *Smith v Paterson*, O.H., Feb. 18, 1986, unreported. In this case reduction was granted where the seller had, by deliberately careless words, misrepresented the extent of the garden.

[10] *Houldsworth v Gordon Cumming*, 1910 S.C. (HL) 49 (especially *per* Lord Shaw); *Angus v Bryden*, 1992 S.L.T. 884; *Barratt Scotland Ltd v Keith*, 1993 S.C. 142; *Martone v Zani*, 1992 G.W.D. 32–1903.

[11] For the doctrine of unfair advantage, see para.3–16.

Fixtures and fittings

4-05   The term "fixtures" means things which were originally moveable but which have acceded to the property and thus become part of it,[12] and so are now heritable, while the term "fittings" means things which have not acceded and have retained their moveable nature.[13] If the contract is silent, a purchaser is entitled to fixtures (since they are part of the land) but not fittings. But often certain fittings, *e.g.* curtains and carpets, are in fact included in the sale. And it is not always clear whether certain other items are fixtures or fittings. The only way to avoid disputes later is to give a full list in the offer of the fittings, etc., which the purchasers expect to receive. Obviously the purchasers' solicitors must ask their clients about this. The sellers' schedule of particulars will usually form the basis of this list of extras. Because the borderline between fittings and fixtures can be arguable, it is common to list items which are probably fixtures anyway, such as built-in wardrobes and kitchen units. The sale of moveables is governed by the Sale of Goods Act 1979, and accordingly ownership passes in accordance with sections 17 and 18 of that Act and not by virtue of the disposition. It may be that the sellers do not actually own all the moveables included in the sale, but hold them subject to leasing or hire-purchase arrangements. In such cases the buyers will not normally be able to obtain a good title,[14] but will need to consider whether they wish to approach the supplier to take over the contracts. This issue is more likely to arise in commercial than in residential conveyancing, but then moveables tend to be more important in the former. In residential conveyancing the value of the moveables (if any) is usually small in relation to the value of the heritable property.[15] In commercial conveyancing the moveables may have a much higher value, and may constitute a substantial part of the total value. For instance, a hotel may be sold with the room furnishings, kitchen and dining goods, wetstock and so on, while a factory may be sold with machinery.[16] In such cases considerable attention has to be paid to questions of valuation and inventorying.[17]

Coal and other minerals[18]

4-06   Unlike legal separate tenements such as salmon fishings, the missives include the minerals unless they are expressly excluded.[19] So an offer for "4 High Street" includes the minerals unless otherwise stated. If it then turns out that the sellers have no title to the minerals (and often they were long ago reserved by the feudal superior), they are in breach of

---

[12] Such as doors.

[13] Such as carpets. The expression "heritable fittings" is sometimes encountered, but for obvious reasons is unsatisfactory.

[14] In certain cases good title can be obtained by virtue of s.25 of the 1979 Act.

[15] A fact which does not prevent clients from bickering, and occasionally even litigating.

[16] Which, however, will in some cases be fixtures.

[17] In important cases the inventory may be photographic as well as verbal.

[18] For the law of minerals, see Robert Rennie, *Minerals and the Law of Scotland* (2001), and Gordon, Ch.6.

[19] This is because they are "conventional separate tenements". See Reid, *Property*, para.209.

contract and the purchasers can rescind.[20] At one time this rule could be used by a purchaser as a handy method of escaping from a contract where it was unsatisfactory for other reasons, but nowadays it is normal for the offer to provide that the minerals are included in the sale only in so far as the sellers have right to them, so that if the sellers do own the minerals, they will pass to the purchasers, but if they do not own them, the purchasers cannot complain. This is a rare example of a clause which, although appearing in the purchasers' offer, is solely for the sellers' benefit. But the sellers' solicitors must check the point, in case the standard clause is not in fact included in the offer. If the selling solicitors overlook the point, and if the sellers in fact have no right to the minerals, this gives the purchasers the right to rescind. The purchaser of a house is seldom interested in the mineral rights.[21] But there is a danger that the minerals may be worked in the future—or, more usually nowadays, that they have been worked in the past—and while the withdrawal of support causing subsidence is a delict of strict liability, clauses of reservation of minerals sometimes vary the common law by excluding liability for subsidence. Hence it is wise for an offer to stipulate that any third party's right to the minerals must be subject to satisfactory compensation provisions and must not include any right to enter upon or change the level of the surface.[22] In the case of subsidence caused by coal mining, there is a statutory compensation scheme.[23] It is possible to obtain a coal mining report from the Coal Authority which will give such information as is contained in the Authority's records.[24]

Good and marketable title

It is provided in missives (and if it were not so provided, it would 4-07 anyway be implied) that the seller must exhibit or deliver a good and marketable title to the property sold. The meaning of this important provision is considered in Chapter 6.

Burdens

It is important for the buyers' solicitors to find out what their clients 4-08 plan to use the property for. For example, real burdens often forbid

---

[20] *Campbell v McCutcheon*, 1963 S.C. 505. On this issue as applied to tenement properties, see C. Waelde (ed.), *Professor McDonald's Conveyancing Opinions* (1998), p.238.

[21] Obviously in commercial and agricultural conveyancing the mineral rights may be of more importance.

[22] For a valuable discussion of the way minerals rights should be handled in missives, see D.J. Cusine and R. Rennie, *Missives* (2nd ed., 1999), para.4.73. As to the marketability of a title which is not protected by a right to compensation, see D.J. Cusine (ed.), *The Conveyancing Opinions of J.M. Halliday* (1992), pp.437-9.

[23] Coal Mining Subsidence Act 1991 as amended by the Coal Industry Act 1994. For the law of support to land see Robert Rennie, *Minerals and the Law of Scotland* (2001); Gordon, Ch.6; Reid, *Property*, paras 252 *et seq.*

[24] The Coal Authority, 200 Lichfield Lane, Mansfield, Nottinghamshire, NG18 4RG. Nowadays coal searches are usually done online: *http://www.coalminingreports.co.uk/*. See further (2003) 48 J.L.S.S. Sept./56.

commercial use. If the buyers' solicitors wrongly assume that their clients intend to use the property as a dwellinghouse, and accept the burdens accordingly, they may find themselves being sued for negligence. If the buyers do not have plans for change of use, the general clause that the property is subject to no "unusual or unduly onerous burdens" will normally suffice.[25] But otherwise the offer should specify the proposed use and stipulate that the title contains nothing that would prevent it.

The sellers will usually respond to this part of the offer in one of four ways. (i) First, they may simply accept it. (ii) Second, if they have the deeds[26] they may send them and ask the buyers to satisfy themselves. The qualified acceptance will delete the buyers' burdens clause, and replace it by one saying that the buyers have satisfied themselves.[27] (iii) Third, if they have the deeds they may send them to the buyers, stipulating that the latter have a certain period, such as five working days, to satisfy themselves. (iv) Fourth, the method just mentioned can also be used if the sellers do not yet have the deeds, with the five working days running from the date of ultimate receipt. This method is convenient if the parties wish to conclude missives quickly, before the deeds are available.

The third method is common. Nevertheless, it is, strictly speaking, not rational. For at this stage the missives are open anyway, and so no deadline can be imposed: deadlines of this sort have meaning only once missives are concluded. So long as the missives are still open, nobody is bound. Thus the buyers are always free, if they do not like the look of the title, simply not to conclude.

Matrimonial property

4–09   The provisions in missives about occupancy rights under the Matrimonial Homes (Family Protection) (Scotland) Act 1981 are considered separately as are Property Transfer Orders.[28]

Content of disposition

4–10   In general, a seller is only bound to grant, and a purchaser is only bound to accept, a disposition drawn up in the "usual" form.[29] Therefore, if either party wishes the disposition to contain something extra, this must be stipulated for expressly in the missives. For the relationship of the missives to the disposition, see Chapter 16, from which it will be seen that missives normally contain a clause providing that they will remain in force (except in so far as implemented) for a certain period, usually two years. This clause, which limits the time when missives can

---

[25] For the meaning of this general clause, see Ch.6.

[26] Which they usually will. But the deeds are typically held by a lender, and some lenders are slow in releasing deeds. Some of the best-known financial institutions are serial offenders. By "deeds" we mean the land certificate or the GRS deeds, as applicable.

[27] Because mere deletion would still leave in place the warranty implied by common law.

[28] Ch.10.

[29] See *Corbett v Robertson* (1872) 10 M. 329. The point seems to have been overlooked in *Morris v Ritchie*, 1991 G.W.D. 12–712.

be enforced, tends to be more for the benefit of the seller than the buyer, and so is likely to be something added in the qualified acceptance rather than found in the original offer.

TERMS ABOUT PRICE AND SETTLEMENT

Price

The contract must either state the price or give some method of 4–11 determining it. Such a method must not depend on future agreement being reached by the parties.[30]

Payment of deposit

In some countries, such as England, payment of a deposit (*e.g.* 10 per 4–12 cent of the price) is usually required. In Scottish practice such deposits are almost unknown, except in some commercial cases. The law about deposits in sale contracts is in some respects unclear. The problems tend to arise where the sale aborts because of the buyer's fault. The authorities seem to say that a deposit is presumptively not merely a partial payment but a security for performance, and that if the purchaser fails to settle the deposit is forfeited.[31] But the logic here is obscure, since the law of rights in security has a well-known principle—so strong that it defeats even stipulations to the contrary—that a security is enforceable to the extent of the obligation secured. Hence to classify a deposit as a security would lead to the conclusion that if the buyer defaults then the deposit is lost only to the extent of the loss to the seller. If a deposit is wholly forfeited that is presumably because it is to be regarded not as a security but as a pre-payment that is subject to an express or implied right to the seller to take it by way of liquidate damages. But we must repeat that the law on deposits is obscure.[32]

Date of entry

The offer should state the date of entry. It is common, though not 4–13 invariable, to state the hour as well as the date. If no hour is agreed then noon seems to be implied by law.

It was finally settled in *Gordon District Council v Wimpey Homes Holdings Limited*[33] that it is not fatal for their validity if missives fail to state an entry date. But a practical problem remains, because if there is no date of entry, the parties' obligations will never become due and missives can never be enforced. This problem has yet to be faced up to directly by the courts. But it appears that the law is more accurately

---

[30] For a case in which there was no agreed price and hence no contract see *MacLeod's Exr v Barr's Trs*, 1989 S.L.T. 392. And see *N. J. & J. Macfarlane (Developments) Ltd v MacSween's Trs*, 1999 S.L.T. 619.

[31] See *Zemhunt (Holdings) Ltd v Control Securities Ltd*, 1992 S.L.T. 151.

[32] For further discussion see William W. McBryde, *The Law of Contract in Scotland* (2nd ed., 2001) para.22–164.

[33] 1988 S.L.T. 481.

stated as being, not that a date of entry is not required, but that an express date of entry is not required. So if no express date is given the court will assume that the parties, being agreed on so much else, must be agreed that the obligations will at some stage become prestable, and an appropriate date will be read into the contract. In *Gordon* it was suggested that, where the contract depends on a suspensive condition being purified, the date of entry should be the date of purification. Otherwise, presumably, entry will be at a reasonable time after conclusion of missives, what is "reasonable" depending on the facts and circumstances of the case. It is in practice almost unknown for missives to omit a date of entry.

Delay in settlement

4–14   Missives almost invariably make provision for what is to happen if the buyers do not come up with the money when settlement is due. It is normal to provide that if the delay persists beyond a certain defined period, such as 21 days, the sellers may rescind the contract. The sellers need the protection of a clause of this sort because the common law rules about how long they have to wait before they can pull out are unsatisfactory.[34] Missives sometimes add that payment of the price on the date of entry is a "material condition" but this seems to contradict the provision just mentioned, for a "material" term is generally understood to be one the breach of which will justify immediate rescission. Clauses of this sort merely give an option to rescind. Thus if the 21 days pass and the sellers do not rescind, and a few days later the buyers finally tender the price, the sellers cannot refuse it, for they had not timeously exercised the option to rescind.[35]

But the right to pull out is not enough: the sellers also want interest to run on the price. Once again, the common law rules are unsatisfactory,[36] and so missives will have a clause which provides that if the price is paid late then interest will run on it, at a defined rate,[37] until payment is made. Such a clause, in its traditional form, deals with delayed settlement. It does not deal with the situation where the seller decides to rescind the contract so that settlement never happens at all.[38]

The common law rules about damages against a buyer where the seller rescinds are, once again, not very satisfactory, and so missives nowadays tend to have express provision about this possibility. In particular it is common for the interest clause to provide that interest will continue to run, even though the seller rescinds the contract, until the property has been sold to someone else. In our view, such clauses[39] often tilt the balance unfairly in favour of the seller and should be resisted by those acting for buyers. (Nevertheless they are usually accepted.)

---

[34] See the next chapter.
[35] *Cumming v Brown*, 1993 S.C.L.R. 707. See the next chapter.
[36] See the next chapter.
[37] Such as four percentage points above the base rate of a named bank.
[38] *Lloyds Bank plc v Bamberger*, 1993 S.C. 570. *cf. Rapide Enterprises v Midgley*, 1998 S.L.T. 504.
[39] See Rennie and Cusine (1993) 38 J.L.S.S. 450.

PHYSICAL CONDITION AND RISK

Risk: general

Risk concerns liability for accidental damage to the property in the 4–15
interval between conclusion of the contract (for pre-contractual damage
see below) and the transfer of ownership.[40] By "accidental" damage is
meant damage which is not the fault of either party to the contract. For
heritable property the common law rule[41] is that risk passes from the
sellers to the buyers when the contract of sale is concluded, except where
there is a suspensive condition, when, it seems, risk does not pass until
its purification. But this rule may be altered by agreement, and this
almost always happens in practice, so that risk does not usually pass until
the date of settlement. There are thus two possibilities, namely that the
risk remains with the sellers until settlement, and that it passes to the
purchasers on conclusion of the contract.

If risk remains with the sellers

Current practice is almost always that risk stays with the sellers. What 4–16
happens then if the house is accidentally damaged after the conclusion of
missives but before settlement? The purchasers could probably rescind if
the damage is major, though the law is not quite clear, so that it is
common for the point to be covered specifically in the missives.[42]
Alternatively they could enforce the contract by insisting that the sellers
repair the damage (the expense of which will typically be paid by the
sellers' insurance company).

If risk passes to the buyers

Occasionally, the common law position is not altered and risk passes 4–17
to the buyers as soon as the contract is concluded. This means that they
might have to buy charred remains. The fact that risk has passed does
not relieve the sellers from a duty to take reasonable care of the
property. Risk concerns accidental destruction only: if the sellers are at
fault, they must pay.[43]

Insurance

As soon as risk passes, the buyers should have insurance cover. If they 4–18
are obtaining a loan, the lenders will normally arrange cover. Otherwise,
the buyers' solicitors must do this. Temporary cover can be obtained by

---

[40] For an interesting study see Forte (1984) 19 *Irish Jurist* 1. Reform has been
recommended by the Scottish Law Commission: *Report on the Passing of Risk in Contracts
for the Sale of Heritable Property* (Scot. Law Com. No.127, 1990).

[41] *Sloans Dairies Ltd v Glasgow Corporation*, 1977 S.C. 223.

[42] Care must be taken with the drafting: see *Hall v McWilliam*, 1993 G.W.D. 23–1457.

[43] This rule was applied in *Meehan v Silver*, 1972 S.L.T. (Sh. Ct.) 70 even though
settlement had been delayed and the damage happened after the contractual date of entry.
But a different view was expressed, without reference to *Meehan*, in *Chapman's Trs v Anglo
Scottish Group Services Ltd*, 1980 S.L.T. (Sh. Ct.) 27 at 28.

phoning an insurance broker, and thereafter the clients will have to complete a proposal form.

Moveables

4-19   A typical house purchase will include some moveables, such as carpets, and here the legal presumption as to risk is different, risk not passing until the passing of ownership: Sale of Goods Act 1979, s.20. There may be difficulty in establishing when ownership of the moveables passes.[44] But s.20 of the 1979 Act can be contracted out of, and missive clauses which provide that risk passes at settlement are often so worded as to cover moveables.

Pre-contractual damage

4-20   Damage prior to conclusion of the contract is not governed by risk. But such damage occurs more often than might be thought. Thus, suppose that after viewing a house the clients make an offer for it. The offer is accepted in principle but it takes three weeks for missives to be concluded, during which time the house is damaged by fire. What then is the position? The answer seems to be that, unless the contract provides otherwise, the buyers have no remedy and must accept the house in its damaged state. Until the contract is concluded, the sellers have no duty of care to the buyers; and the buyers' error as to the physical state of the house is unilateral and uninduced. Missives sometimes have a clause stipulating that the property must be in substantially the same state at settlement as at conclusion of missives,[45] but this will be of no help, since the damage was already in place at conclusion of missives. One way of dealing with the danger is to use such a clause but making the date of the original offer the reference date for the condition of the property.

Warranties of quality

4-21   The sellers warrant the title but they do not usually warrant the physical state of the property. The default rule here is *caveat emptor*: it is for the buyers to have the property surveyed. The parties are, of course, free to insert into the missives warranties as to physical quality. This was seldom done until the late 1970s, but since then such contractual warranties have become standard. The items typically covered are the central heating, dry and wet rot, and woodworm. Sometimes there are other items such as gas and wiring and damp.[46] The sellers are sometimes asked to give an absolute guarantee (which they should

---

[44] On one view, if the missives make no special provision as to passing of the ownership of the moveables, ownership will pass at missives: Sale of Goods Act 1979, s.18, r.1. As against this, it could be argued that ownership passes at settlement since this is presumably the intention of the parties: s.17(1).

[45] *Hall v McWilliam*, 1993 G.W.D. 23-1457.

[46] Damp may be rising damp (from the ground), or penetrating damp (rain or snow meltwater coming through the roof, walls, etc.) or condensing damp (water vapour bedewing surfaces).

generally resist[47]) and sometimes a guarantee that these items are satisfactory as far as they are aware. This latter formula (often with a "consistent with age" proviso) is generally regarded as reasonable. Often there will be a further provision, typically inserted in the qualified acceptance, that the buyers must notify any defects within, say, seven days after entry, failing which they will be deemed to have waived their rights.[48] A common problem with these clauses is that the sellers may have lived happily with their central heating for years, regarding it as being in reasonably good working order, while the purchasers see all sorts of defects. Hence disputes.

There is no perfect way of drafting such clauses. What is vital is that both clients be aware of the position. Thus, if the missives are silent as to the plumbing, the purchasers must know this, so that if they find the plumbing to be defective, they cannot complain. In general, a buyer of a second-hand house is in the same position as the buyer of anything else second-hand, such as a car. There is always the risk of defects. To the extent that purchasers wish to take no risks, they must have surveys done. If they are worried about, say, the plumbing, they may need to have a plumber visit the property before missives are concluded.

Access

Before settlement the buyers have no right to visit the property, or 4–22 have anyone visit the property on their behalf to inspect it, except by the permission of the sellers. This fact can be unsatisfactory and hence it is common for the missives to make provision for such access.

Rot

An offer will typically require the sellers to warrant that as far as they 4–23 know there is no timber rot, and that if rot eradication has been carried out there is a valid guarantee which will be transferred to the buyers. The latter part of such a clause seems rather pointless since such guarantees are in practice never assigned, either because they are non-assignable or because they enure to the benefit of future owners without need of assignation. Moreover, such a clause is odd in as much as a seller who never obtained a guarantee is in a better position, in this respect, than one who did. It also seems unreasonable for the sellers to warrant the guarantee to be completely valid, and in addition it is unclear what their liability would be if the guarantee were defective.

---

[47] They should also think twice before giving any undertaking that the gas and electricity systems comply with applicable regulations. Such an undertaking may sound innocuous, but the regulations change constantly, so that a system which is in perfect working order, and which complies fully with the regulations applicable at the time of installation, may not comply with whatever the current regulations may happen to be.

[48] See *Williams v Mutter*, 2002 S.C.L.R. 1127 for difficulties in phrasing and interpreting a clause of this sort.

PUBLIC LAW AND PUBLIC SERVICES[49]

Property enquiry certificates (PECs)

4–24   The solicitors buying a house for clients are concerned with a number of matters which come under the control of local authorities. The main ones are planning law, building control law, the provision of certain services, and statutory notices requiring the building to be repaired or, worse, demolished.

Does the local authority provide all the normal services, *e.g.* roads and sewerage, or are they a private responsibility, in which case the maintenance costs will have to be met by the purchasers? The solicitors must find out the position and advise the clients accordingly. The normal practice is to specify in the offer that these services are available so that, if they are not, it is for the sellers to say so. In towns and cities all services are usually provided by the local authority.

On payment of a fee local authorities will issue standard-form certificates, called property enquiry certificates (PECs), giving certain information in relation to the property.[50] PECs are also issued by independent firms, working from local authority records. Without these certificates the sellers' solicitors would not be able to respond properly to the clauses in the offer dealing with such matters, and indeed offers usually require the sellers to produce evidence on such matters, which effectively means production of the PECs.[51] It is important, in requesting PECs, to identify the property adequately. A postal address is generally sufficient, but sometimes more precision is needed, especially in rural areas or for urban development sites. In some cases a plan should be sent.

The buyers' solicitors must check the certificates carefully.[52] PECs are seldom wrong, but if they are, and if loss results, the issuer may be liable in damages.[53] Usually the certificates are clear, *i.e.* they disclose nothing adverse to the property. This, however, is a matter for two cheers rather than three, for their scope is limited. They will not normally show whether there have been any breaches of planning or building law. Nor does it follow from the absence of statutory notices in the certificates that the house is actually in a good state of repair. The technical services

---

[49] The subject is a large one and the following treatment is selective and brief, especially since much public law about land and buildings is aimed at commercial property whereas this book is mainly about residential property. Whether any particular point about public law or services needs to be dealt with in the missives depends on the circumstances of the case.

[50] Contact details, costs etc. can conveniently be obtained from the Law Society of Scotland's *Directory of Services for Conveyancers* (2003). PECs vary somewhat between different local authorities—as does the price, which is usually about £100 but may be more or less.

[51] Sometimes an offer merely requests exhibition of the PECs. If when the PECs are exhibited their content proves unsatisfactory, the sellers can argue that the contract provision has nevertheless been satisfied. PECs are merely evidential. It is the underlying facts that are important.

[52] For a cautionary tale see (1992) 37 J.L.S.S. 408.

[53] *Runciman v Borders Regional Council*, 1988 S.L.T. 135; *National Children's Home and Orphanage Trs v Stirrat Park Hogg (SPH)*, 2001 S.L.T. 469; *Maypark Properties Ltd v Stirrat (SPH)*, 2001 S.L.T. (Sh. Ct) 171; *Anderson v Perth & Kinross Council*, 2000 S.C.L.R. 987.

departments of local councils do not maintain a large and vigilant band of inspectors who ceaselessly patrol the streets looking for cracks in stonework. Moreover, PECs may not disclose older statutory notices, even if the notice has not been obtempered. These, then, are the limitations, but PECs are nonetheless an important part of the conveyancing system.

One practical problem is that by the time of settlement the certificate may be some months old and the purchaser may naturally be unhappy with this. Offers sometimes insist that the certificate be dated not more than a certain period (*e.g.* 28 days) prior to conclusion of missives. This is a wise precaution but sellers may not like having to pay for an updated certificate.

Roads[54]

The buyers will be concerned about the road outside their new house 4–25 in two respects. They wish to be sure that they have a right of access, and they will not wish to have to maintain the road at their own expense. If the road is a publicly maintained road it will also be a public right of way. But the converse does not always hold good, in that some public rights of way are private as far as upkeep is concerned. Private rights of way, *i.e.* servitude roads, are of course privately maintained. The PECs will show whether the road is publicly maintained, which it usually is. If it is not publicly maintained, the purchasers are likely to be liable for upkeep, and moreover it will be necessary to inquire whether there is a right of access, either public or private (by servitude).

Roads can be divided into those in which there is a right of way in favour of the public, and those where no such right exists. Use of the latter is based on ownership, or co-ownership, of the road itself, or on the existence of a servitude over it. Roads are sometimes called "public" or "private" according to this classification. However the public/private distinction is also applied in a different way, according to whether the roadway is or is not maintained at public expense. Private roads (in the sense of no public right of way) are naturally maintained at private expense. But public roads (*i.e.* public right of way) are sometimes maintained at public expense and sometimes at private expense, and the expressions "public road" and "private road" are often used in this latter sense. It is this latter usage which is employed in the Roads (Scotland) Act 1984 ("the 1984 Act"), which is the main Act.[55] It is the "roads authority" which is responsible for the upkeep of roads which are public in the latter sense. For most roads the roads authority is the local council. Scottish Ministers are the roads authority for "trunk" roads.

Where a road is constructed by a roads authority, the land on which the road is built will first have been acquired by the authority either by agreement or by compulsory purchase. Such roads are public from their birth. But many roads are built by private builders in the course of developing a housing estate. These begin life as private roads, but the

---

[54] See Ann Faulds and June Hyslop, *Scottish Roads Law* (2000).
[55] s.151(1) defines "road". See *Viewpoint Housing Association Ltd v Lothian Regional Council*, 1991 G.W.D. 39–2408.

idea is that, by the time the development is completed, the roads authority will have taken them over. By s.16 of the 1984 Act, a roads authority must "take over" a road[56] provided it has been constructed to a sufficient standard. It used to be a worry, in buying a new house, that the builder might become insolvent[57] before completing the development, so that the bill for making up the road would have to be picked up by the houseowners. To meet this risk builders commonly obtained a commercial guarantee (called a road bond) to cover the costs of completing the roads. Nowadays the problem has been more or less solved by s.17 of the 1984 Act and regulations made thereunder[58] which provide that no building work can begin until the developer grants a road bond in favour of the local authority.[59] There are potential liabilities if the road outside (*ex adverso*) the newly purchased house has not been taken over by the council. For if the road is public in the sense of being subject to a public right of way, which it usually will be, the council can require the purchaser, as a "frontager", to maintain both the road and the pavement.[60] And even if there is no public right of way the road will require a certain amount of upkeep if it is to remain passable.

Who owns the solum beneath the road? There are three main possibilities. (1) It may belong to the roads authority. This will usually be the case with major roads. (2) It may belong to the frontagers, in sections. When houses are built—or plots sold for building—the boundaries between individual properties are often the centre line of the road. And this ownership is not affected by the road subsequently being taken over by the local authority for maintenance. (3) It may belong to the original developers or their successors, simply because on conveying the houses they never parted with ownership of the solum. Often it can be difficult to find out who owns the solum. Ownership is seldom of much practical significance except when a road is "stopped up" by the roads authority so that the former road becomes available for other purposes. By section 115 of the 1984 Act, ownership of a stopped up road vests in the frontagers "subject to the prior claim of any person by reason of title".[61]

---

[56] "Take over" means to assume responsibility for upkeep. A road which has been taken over is thus a public road in the second sense. The statute is not clearly drafted, but the idea is that if a road is taken over, it thereby becomes public in both senses.

[57] Insolvency has always been especially common in the construction industry.

[58] Security for Private Road Works (Scotland) Regulations 1985 (SI 1985/2080) as amended by the Security for Private Road Works (Scotland) Amendment Regulations 1998 (SI 1998/3220).

[59] But some developers flout the law and fail to obtain a road bond. Unfortunately, it is precisely this type of developer that is most likely to become insolvent, at which point the absence of a road bond becomes a disaster. So an offer for a house being built should still stipulate that a road bond exists and must be exhibited.

[60] Roads (Scotland) Act 1984, s.13.

[61] Presumably this is to cover the case where ownership is vested in another party such as the original developers or their successors—case 3 in the text. But the provision is odd, because if the frontagers own it already, it is superfluous, while if they do not, it is inoperative. (Because if they do not own it already, somebody else must do so, and that person's title is declared to prevail.)

Sewerage

The purchaser will normally expect public sewerage[62] provision and 4-26
indeed public water, electricity and gas. In towns this may usually be
taken for granted (except for gas), but in the countryside there may be
no public supply and each public utility has its own rules about
entitlement. Where public provision is made, the rule is usually that the
local authority (or other utility) will bring the resource in question up to
the property but the cost of making and maintaining connections
remains with the owner.

Sewerage is governed by the Sewerage (Scotland) Act 1968, as
amended. By section 1 the sewerage authority[63] must construct adequate
sewers. If impatient developers construct the sewers themselves, they
cannot recover the cost under the law of recompense.[64] The obligation to
construct adequate sewers is qualified by the proviso that nothing need
be done "which is not practicable at a reasonable cost".[65] So in many
rural areas there is no public system, and the outflow drains into a septic
tank.[66] If the tank is located in a neighbouring property, which it
sometimes is, a servitude of drainage is necessary.[67] The permission of
the Scottish Environmental Protection Agency (S.E.P.A.) may be
required.[68] Any discharge of "trade effluent or sewage effluent" into any
"controlled waters"[69] requires the consent of the S.E.P.A.[70] Any "new
discharge of trade effluent" from "trade premises" into the sewerage
system requires the consent of Scottish Water.[71]

Water

Public water supplies are provided by Scottish Water.[72] The law 4-27
relating to supply is governed by the Water (Scotland) Act 1980, as
amended, section 6 of which imposes a general duty (but subject to a
reasonable cost proviso) to supply "wholesome" water for domestic
purposes. As with sewerage, in some rural areas there will be no public
supply, with the owner taking water from a well. If the private water
supply comes from an adjacent property, it should be established by the

---

[62] Sewerage is the system. Sewage is what passes through the system.

[63] Which is, tastefully, the same as the Water Authority. As a result of the Water
Industry (Scotland) Act 2002 this is now Scottish Water for the whole of Scotland.

[64] *Varney (Scotland) Ltd v Burgh of Lanark*, 1974 S.C. 245.

[65] s.1(3).

[66] On septic tanks see Macrae (2001) 46 J.L.S.S. March/48.

[67] The relevant servitude is that sometimes called "sinks" or "outfall" which is the
servitude right to discharge foul water into a neighbouring property. See *e.g. Cochrane v
Ewart* (1861) 4 Macq. 117. See generally D.J.Cusine and R.R.M Paisley, *Servitudes and
Rights of Way* (1998), paras 3.80 *et seq.*

[68] S.E.P.A. is governed by s.20 of the Environment Act 1995. Its website is
http://www.sepa.org.uk/.

[69] This term is broadly defined to include the sea, lochs, rivers and burns.

[70] Control of Pollution Act 1974. Sections 30A, 30F and 30I of this much-amended
statute have to be read together.

[71] Sewerage (Scotland) Act 1968, s.26.

[72] Water Industry (Scotland) Act 2002. Unlike England, water supply is not privatised.
Scottish Water replaced the three water and sewerage authorities set up by the Local
Government etc. (Scotland) Act 1994.

appropriate servitudes.[73] Private water supplies must also be wholesome.[74]

Statutory notices: general

4-28 Local authorities have wide-ranging statutory powers to require the repair or demolition of buildings.[75] There are a number of different statutory provisions, but most work in much the same way. First the council is alerted to a defective building either by its own inspectors or, very often in the case of tenement property, by a telephone call from a proprietor who cannot persuade the other owners to carry out repairs. The council serves on the proprietor or proprietors of the building a formal statutory notice which requires specified works to be carried out within a specified (and usually short) time. The notice must specify adequately the work to be carried out.[76] In the case of tenements some councils serve a notice on all the proprietors in the building even for repairs which concern only one or more individual flats.[77]

There is a right of appeal against the notice, usually to the sheriff, but the right must be exercised within the statutory time-limit which, typically, is 21 days.[78] Once a notice is served the proprietors must carry out the work. If they fail to do so the council may and often does instruct contractors to do the necessary work,[79] recovering the cost from the proprietors. The amount then due to the council can be secured by a charging order (a statutory heritable security) on the building. It is always more expensive in the end if the council has to carry out the work but, particularly in a tenement, the proprietors may be unable to reach agreement on carrying out the work themselves.

If the property is subject to a statutory notice, the purchasers' solicitors must find out more details. If the notice has been complied with, well and good. If the notice is about to be complied with, that is also acceptable provided that there is clear agreement that the sellers are

---

[73] Aquaehaustus (the right to water from a source in another property) and aqua-eductus, also called watergang (the right to pipe water across or underneath another's land).

[74] The current statutory instrument on water quality is the Water Supply (Water Quality) (Scotland) Regulations 2001 (SSI 2001/207).

[75] Chiefly under the Building (Scotland) Act 1959, the Housing (Scotland) Act 1987, and the Civic Government (Scotland) Act 1982. The Building (Scotland) Act 2003, when in force, will repeal and replace the Building (Scotland) Act 1959 and parts of the Civic Government (Scotland) Act 1982.

[76] In practice, the specification is sometimes vague. It is, however, unusual for the notice to be challenged. For an example of a successful challenge see *Gardner v City of Edinburgh District Council*, 1992 S.L.T. 1149.

[77] They are entitled to do this: *University of Edinburgh v City of Edinburgh District Council*, 1987 S.L.T. (Sh. Ct.) 103; *City of Edinburgh District Council v Gardner*, 1990 S.L.T. 600. See, further, Reid (1990) 35 J.L.S.S. 368.

[78] On rights of appeal, see *Norcross v Kirkcaldy District Council*, 1993 G.W.D. 3–146; *Lindsay v City of Glasgow District Council*, 1998 Hous. L.R. 4; *Boutineau v City of Glasgow District Council*, 1998 Hous. L.R. 121.

[79] *Crawford v City of Edinburgh District Council*, 1994 S.L.T. 23. In practice, however, councils often delay taking this step for long periods.

to pay the costs.[80] The main problem which arises is where the notice has not been complied with and the council has, or is about to, carry out the work itself. Thereafter the council is entitled to recover the cost from the new owner,[81] and there seems to be no satisfactory right of relief under the general law[82] Therefore, if the agreement is that the sellers are to be liable, this should be stated expressly in the missives.

Offers vary considerably as to how they handle the possibility of statutory notices. A common approach is for the sellers to be asked to warrant that there are no such notices at the time of missives, and that any notices issued between missives and entry shall be the sellers' responsibility. If there is an existing notice the selling solicitors will so state in the qualified acceptance, and this may then lead to an agreement that the seller will be responsible for the costs. Further provision is sometimes made that in the latter event there shall be a retention from the purchase price of enough money to cover the costs, this sum to be put on deposit receipt in the joint names of the solicitors.[83] A simpler solution is to agree to reduce the purchase price by the amount of the estimated costs, which will then be the responsibility of the purchaser.[84] The main statutory notices concern dangerous buildings, buildings not of a tolerable standard, and buildings in disrepair.[85]

Statutory notices: dangerous buildings

If a building is actually dangerous, whether to its occupants or to the public at large, the council can serve a notice under section 13 of the Building (Scotland) Act 1959, or, when it is in force, under section 30 of the Building (Scotland) Act 2003 requiring the owner either to demolish the building or to secure and repair it. 4–29

Statutory notices: buildings not of tolerable standard

"Tolerable standard" is concerned less with structural stability than with the provision of basic facilities.[86] Where a house falls below the tolerable standard the council has a choice of courses of action.[87] (1) It 4–30

---

[80] Missives commonly contain a two-year supersession clause. In some types of case this can be too short a period, and where money is retained pending repairs a longer period than two years is generally advisable. For an example of what can go wrong, see *Hamilton v Rodwell*, 1998 S.C.L.R. 418 and *Hamilton v Rodwell* (No.2), 1999 G.W.D. 35–1706.

[81] *Purves v City of Edinburgh District Council*, 1987 S.L.T. 366; *Pegg v City of Glasgow District Council*, 1988 S.L.T. (Sh. Ct.) 49. But there are limits: see *Smith v Renfrew District Council*, 1997 S.C.L.R. 354.

[82] See the discussion of the obligation of relief clause in para.11–20.

[83] This is because the sellers might later turn out not to be good for the money. The retention is often augmented by *e.g.* 25 per cent to cover cost overruns. When the work is finished and paid for the proceeds of the deposit receipt are then paid to the sellers. If, however, the work is not done the purchasers will wish to obtain the contents of the deposit receipt and this can cause technical difficulties. See *Hamilton v Rodwell*, 1998 S.C.L.R. 418.

[84] Logically, the purchase price offered should already have taken account of the state of the building. A building in poor repair will attract lower bids than a building in good repair. In practice, however, purchasers usually take into account only imminent repair bills in making their bids.

[85] For background, see C. Himsworth, *Housing Law in Scotland* (4th ed., 1994).

[86] Housing (Scotland) Act 1987, s.86 as amended by the Housing (Scotland) Act 2001.

[87] s.85(1).

may serve an improvement order requiring the owner to bring the house up to tolerable standard within 180 days.[88] (2) It may serve a demolition order.[89] (3) Where a demolition order would be appropriate but for the fact that the house forms part of a larger building in which the other houses are satisfactory it may serve a closing order which prevents the house being used for human habitation.[90] Closing and demolition orders can be revoked or suspended, at the council's discretion, where either the house is brought up to the tolerable standard or where the owner plausibly undertakes to do so. Where a number of houses in the same area are sub-standard the council can declare a housing action area, which gives it additional powers, including the power of compulsory purchase, and which removes the need for individual statutory notices.[91]

Statutory notices: buildings in disrepair (defective buildings)

4–31   This is the commonest in modern practice, especially in tenement property. There are two statutory provisions, section 87 of the Civic Government (Scotland) Act 1982 and section 108 of the Housing (Scotland) Act 1987. Some councils tend to use the 1982 Act and others the 1987 Act, while sometimes local statutes are used.[92] Section 87 of the Civic Government (Scotland) Act 1982 will in due course be replaced by section 28 of the Building (Scotland) Act 2003.

Planning permission

4–32   Planning law is a large subject in its own right[93] and the treatment here is necessarily brief. Planning permission is required for any significant building work and for certain changes of use. The purchaser's agents will have four main concerns. The first is whether planning permission has been obtained for the present buildings, and for their present use. PECs will very probably not disclose the answers to these questions, except in the unusual situation of an enforcement notice having been served. For the purposes of planning law, there are various defined types of use, called Use Classes, and a change of use *within* a Use Class does not require planning permission.[94] For instance an office used by an accountancy firm could be taken over by a law firm without need for planning permission.

The second concern is whether any conditions are attached to the grant of planning permission, and if so, whether they have been observed. In commercial developments there may also be section 75 agreements.[95]

---

[88] s.88.

[89] s.115.

[90] s.114.

[91] ss.89–92.

[92] Such as the City of Edinburgh District Council Confirmation Order Act 1991, Part VI.

[93] Jeremy Rowan-Robinson, Eric Young, Michael Purdue and Elaine Farquharson-Black, *Scottish Planning Law and Procedure* (2001); Neil Collar, *Planning* (2nd ed., 1999); Angus McAllister and Raymond McMaster, *Scottish Planning Law* (2nd ed., 1999). See also the journal *Scottish Planning Law and Practice*.

[94] Currently regulated by the Town and Country Planning (Use Classes) (Scotland) Order 1997 (SI 1997/3061) (as amended), commonly called the Use Classes Order.

[95] Town and Country Planning (Scotland) Act 1997, s.75.

The third concern is whether the building is listed, or in a conservation area.[96] The PECs usually reveal this. One of the many consequences of being in a conservation area is that demolition requires permission.[97] Outwith such areas an owner is generally free to demolish without permission, except where the property is listed,[98] or is an ancient monument.[99]

The fourth concern is whether the property is affected, directly or indirectly, by planning applications for neighbouring property. For instance the next door neighbours may have applied for, or even obtained, planning permission to build 10 flats in their garden, overlooking the house being purchased. The PECs will not normally disclose this. If the purchasers wish this checked, it will have to be done as an extra request to the council. Apart from that, the missives will normally require the sellers to warrant that they have received no notification of any planning application for neighbouring property.[1]

The local authority's right to object to breaches of planning law prescribes after either four or 10 years, depending on the nature of the breach.[2]

Finally, it is important to grasp that the fact that something has planning permission does not mean that it is therefore lawful from the standpoint of public law. Other consents may be required. The most obvious one, which will be relevant in the case of most new buildings, is building consent (see below). Many particular activities also require particular consents. For instance, use of land as a caravan site requires special permission.[3]

Building control: the Building (Scotland) Act 1959

Building control[4] is concerned with the practicalities of building and   4-33
not with aesthetics or community amenity. The governing legislation is the Building (Scotland) Act 1959, as amended, together with regulations made thereunder, notably the Building Standards (Scotland) Regulations 1990.[5]

Building control: the Building (Scotland) Act 2003

The 1959 Act is prospectively repealed and replaced by the Building   4-34
(Scotland) Act 2003, and in due course there will be new Building (Scotland) Regulations made under the 2003 Act. The new Act will

---

[96] Currently regulated by the Planning (Listed Buildings and Conservation Areas) (Scotland) Act 1997. They are very common. Within the boundaries of the City of Edinburgh alone there are 36 such areas.

[97] Planning (Listed Buildings and Conservation Areas) (Scotland) Act 1997, s.66. This Act does not contain all the law on conservation areas: trees in such areas are covered by the Town and Country Planning (Scotland) Act 1997, s.172.

[98] Currently regulated by the Planning (Listed Buildings and Conservation Areas) (Scotland) Act 1997.

[99] Currently regulated by the Ancient Monuments and Archaeological Areas Act 1979.

[1] The Town and Country Planning (General Development Procedure) (Scotland) Order 1992 (SI 1992/224), art.9.

[2] Town and Country Planning (Scotland) Act 1997, s.124.

[3] Caravan Sites and Control of Development Act 1960.

[4] Not much is written on this important subject.

[5] SI 1990/2179, as amended, for instance by the Building (Scotland) Amendment Regulations 1997 (SI 1997/2157). See George Bett, Frith Hoehnke and James Robison, *The Scottish Building Regulations Explained and Illustrated* (3rd ed., 2003).

probably not come fully into force until 2005 or 2006. The new legislation makes a number of important changes but also leaves much of the existing system intact. There is to be a new supervisory agency, the Scottish Building Standards Agency (SBSA). There is also to be a new Building Standards Register (BSR) in which information about status, from the standpoint of building law, will be registered. The existing non-statutory system of building standards assessments will be put on a statutory footing. Building warrants and completion certificates, currently issued by the local authority, will in future be issued by "verifiers", although at least to begin with they are likely to be local authorities. The new Act will also introduce a greater degree of flexibility in building standards.

When is a building warrant required?

4-35   Section 8(1) of the 2003 Act provides that:

"A warrant granted under section 9 (a 'building warrant') is required for—

(a) any work for—

(i) the construction or demolition of, or
(ii) the provision of services, fittings or equipment in or in connection with,

a building of a description to which building regulations apply,
(b) any conversion of a building."

Failure to comply is an offence. Section 6 of the 1959 Act is in substantially similar terms.

The Building Standards (Scotland) Regulations 1990 run to hundreds of pages and are incomprehensible except to experts. They apply not just to the initial construction of buildings but to a whole host of fairly minor operations, for example, altering windows.[6] Whilst in practice warrants are obtained for major works, *e.g.* the construction of a new house or major alterations to an existing house, they are often not obtained for minor alterations. One reason for this was and is ignorance: most people do not realise that a warrant is needed. Tradesmen do not always know either, and if they do they may not tell their customer. A second reason is that, even where people are aware in general terms about building warrants they may be uncertain as to precisely what does and what does not require a warrant. And no wonder. The rules are technical and obscure. Thirdly, councils in practice seldom enforce the law in relation to minor alterations. Fourthly, no special simplified procedure exists for where the work is minor, so that the applicant who wishes to move a sink a metre must submit the same forms and detailed drawings as the applicant who wishes to build an entire house.[7] In practice, it is difficult

---

[6] Even where no warrant is needed, alterations must still conform to regulations.
[7] See the Building (Procedure) (Scotland) Regulations 1981 (SI 1981/1499).

to get a warrant without professional help in preparing the application, preferably from an architect. This is expensive, so that for minor works the expense of the application may exceed the cost of the work itself. No one knows what proportion of the housing stock has alterations that are unauthorised, in the sense that no warrant was issued, or, if it was issued, was not followed up by a completion certificate. But the proportion is certainly substantial: probably more than 25 per cent. One reason that no one knows is that minor alterations are often invisible.

Completion certificates

The building warrant must be obtained before work is started, and it 4–36 will not be granted unless the proposed work appears to conform to the building standards regulations. On completion, the work is inspected and if it appears to conform to the original warrant and to the building regulations a completion certificate is granted. The certificate should not be regarded as a guarantee that all is well. There will be much that the inspector has been unable to see and this is so even where, as with the construction of a new house, several visits are made during the course of building. If the inspection has been negligent, a purchaser relying on the completion certificate cannot normally hold the authority liable in damages.[8] Under the Building (Scotland) Act 1959 the completion certificate is issued by the local authority. Under the Building (Scotland) Act 2003 it will become a different kind of document. It will be signed by the applicant and submitted to the verifier, who will either accept it or reject it: rejection will correspond in substance to non-issue under the 1959 Act.

Consequences of failure to obtain a warrant or certificate

There are two possible consequences of failing to comply with the 4–37 above rules. First, it is an offence to carry out the work in the first place without a warrant,[9] and it is also an offence to occupy or use the building without a completion certificate.[10] Secondly, the local authority can serve an enforcement notice.[11] In practice, the local authority may never take any enforcement action, but this does not mean that there will be no problem, partly because the unauthorised work may be unsound and eventually have to be repaired, altered or even demolished even without any official action, and partly because when the owners come to sell they may find that prospective purchasers object to the lack of building consent.

Alterations, authorised and unauthorised: practice

Once upon a time, solicitors acting for purchasers checked building 4–38 consents for major works, but seldom bothered about minor works. Practice began to change about 1990. The main reason was a change in

---

[8] *Taylor v City of Glasgow District Council*, 1997 S.C. 183. But *cf. Perth & Kinross Council*, 1998 Hous. L.R. 78.

[9] Building (Scotland) Act 1959, s.6; Building (Scotland) Act 2003, s.8. However, prosecutions seem to be almost unknown in practice.

[10] 1959 Act, s.9(5); 2003 Act, s.21.

[11] 1959 Act, s.10; 2003 Act, s.27.

the attitude of surveyors. As a result of negligence claims, surveyors became more cautious. Nowadays they will comment on evidence they detect of recent works which might have required building consent. Of course, they can only mention what they notice, and minor alterations are often invisible. Surveyors do not have time-machines by means of which the present state of the building can be compared with earlier states. It is possible, and common, to ask the local authority for a building standards assessment, to determine whether the building is or is not in breach of building regulations.

Usually the existence of unauthorised alterations will come to light before missives are concluded, in which case the matter can be dealt with in the missives themselves.[12] Precisely what the missives will say varies from case to case. Usually the offer will have a clause saying something like: "All necessary consents including planning permissions building warrants and completion certificates have been obtained and satisfactory evidence to this effect will be exhibited at or before settlement." The sellers may, in the qualified acceptance, simply delete the whole clause, or limit it to the past ten years, or add a qualification about specified alterations. As with other missive provisions, some arm-wrestling may ensue. The outcome depends on the circumstances. During this process both solicitors have some knowledge of the premises and what altera-tions there seem to have been, and what documentation is available.

Assuming that the problem has come to light before settlement, and assuming that the missives are in standard form, what can be done by the sellers? There are three possible solutions which sellers can adopt to deal with the absence of building warrants and/or completion certificates:

(1) Obtain retrospective consents from the council. The whole process is likely to take months rather than weeks and will cost money. The costs will not be too high unless the council insists on remedial work being done before consents are issued. One of the difficulties is that the work may have complied with earlier versions of the building standards regulations but not with the current version.

(2) Obtain a "letter of comfort" from the council, *i.e.* a letter stating that enforcement proceedings will not be taken.[13] This is the cheapest solution, although in some cases it may still be necessary to employ an architect to make representations to the council. Purchasers are not, however, bound to accept such a letter, but can insist that the full terms of the missives be honoured.[14] But the missives may provide that the buyers must be satisfied with such a letter. If the sellers know that there are unauthorised alterations, it often makes sense to obtain a comfort letter in advance and then to make it clear in the missives that this is all that the purchasers can require. Different local authorities have different policies as to letters of comfort.[15]

---

[12] See *e.g.* a letter at (1999) 44 J.L.S.S. Feb./12.

[13] For an example see J. H. Sinclair, *Handbook of Conveyancing Practice in Scotland* (4th ed., 2002), p.285.

[14] See *Hawke v Mathers*, 1995 S.C.L.R. 1004.

[15] Details can be found in the Law Society of Scotland's *Directory of Services for Conveyancers* (2003).

(3) Apply for a relaxation of the building regulations in relation to the alterations in question.[16] This is not likely to be an attractive solution unless expensive remedial work would otherwise be required to comply with the regulations.

How far back need one go?

The solicitors for the purchasers will need to see both building warrant 4–39 and completion certificate for all works which require them. But for how long? For works in the last 10 years? Or 20 years? Or 50 years? Or 100 years? This question is not easily answered for, unlike planning permission, the legislation does not impose a cut-off period for enforcement by the local authority. Some help may be had from long negative prescription: it is arguable that the obligation to obtain a building warrant or completion certificate prescribes after 20 years. Some local authorities have a policy of not enforcing the requirements after a certain number of years. But it must be borne in mind that, whether or not warrant and certificate were obtained, section 11 of the 1959 Act gives the council the power to require buildings at any time to conform to current building regulations where this is necessary for "health, safety and convenience".[17]

There are practical difficulties about going back too far. Although councils maintain registers of building warrants and completion certificates, the longer ago the greater the possibility that the records cannot be located.

Since there is no clear legal cut-off period, there is no logically defensible place to stop, so that in the purchase of a flat in Edinburgh's New Town one might in theory need to see the original Dean of Guild consents for its construction in 1788, plus consents for all subsequent alterations.[18] But this would be absurd. Missives in practice vary considerably on this point. Some have no cut-off period. Some cover the period back to 1964, when the Building (Scotland) Act 1959 came into force. Others have a 20-year cut-off, and others a 10-year period.[19] Others again cover the period in which the building has been in the ownership of the present seller. The agent for the seller should certainly resist an unlimited period. In any event, not many local authorities have proper records for building warrants and completion certificates before 1975.[20] As the law stands there is no correct solution. There is also the obvious practical difficulty of showing that an alteration (for which no documentation exists) was indeed done outwith the defined period.

---

[16] Building (Scotland) Act 1959, s.4 as amended by the Building (Scotland) Act 1970; Building Standards (Relaxation by Local Authorities) (Scotland) Regulations 1997 (SI 1997/1872). See also, prospectively, s.3 of the Building (Scotland) Act 2003.

[17] See also, prospectively, s.25 of the Building (Scotland) Act 2003.

[18] For although the current law is regulated by the Building (Scotland) Act 1959, as amended, and prospectively by the Building (Scotland) Act 2003, the need for building consent has existed for hundreds of years. Before 1975 consents were given (in burghs) by the Dean of Guild Court. Such consent originally bore the curious name of the "jedge and warrant of the Dean of Guild".

[19] This was the period in the Law Society's Standard Clauses.

[20] When the Local Government (Scotland) Act 1973 came into force. The Act caused a major disruption to local authority records.

Alcohol licensing

4–40   The law relating to the sale of alcohol is too complex and extensive to be dealt with here. See the undernoted texts.[21]

Trees

4–41   There is a great deal of legislation about trees. Residential conveyancers probably need to know (and tell their clients) only that cutting down a tree in a conservation area normally requires permission, and that even outside such areas a tree preservation order can be made having the same effect.[22]

Fire prevention and employee safety

4–42   Buildings in public or commercial use, such as factories, hotels and shops, generally require a fire certificate.[23] Such buildings must also meet a minimum standard for the health and safety of employees, for instance in such matters as heating, toilet facilities and so on.[24] The cost of adapting a building so as to meet such requirements can be high.

Contaminated land

4–43   Environmental law is a large subject in its own right.[25] Numerous statutes regulate it, and more than one public agency may be involved, especially the Scottish Environment Protection Agency (SEPA). The most important legislative provisions are in Part IIA ("Contaminated Land") of the Environmental Protection Act 1990.[26] If a client plans any activity with a possibly negative environmental impact, it may turn out to be lawful, or unlawful, or lawful with the requisite permissions, and the client must be advised accordingly. Missives may need to stipulate that any necessary consents already exist.

The main worry in most cases, however, is not so much what the buyer can do but whether the land is already contaminated. Contamination

---

[21] Sir Crispin Agnew and Heather Baillie, *Allan and Chapman's The Licensing (Scotland) Act 1976* (5th ed., 2002); J. N. St C. Jameson, *A Practical Guide to Scottish Licensing Law* (3rd ed., 1998).

[22] Town and Country Planning (Scotland) Act 1997, ss.159 *et seq.*

[23] Fire Precautions Act 1971, plus statutory instruments. The certificate is issued by the Fire Authority for the area in question. For useful information see the Law Society of Scotland's *Directory of Services for Conveyancers* (2003).

[24] Mines and Quarries Acts 1954 and 1969; Factories Act 1961; Offices, Shops and Railway Premises Act 1963; Health and Safety at Work etc. Act 1974, plus numerous statutory instruments.

[25] The literature is vast. See *e.g.* Colin T. Reid, *Green's Guide to Environmental Law in Scotland* (2nd ed., 1997); Andrew Waite and Tim Jewell, *Environmental Law in Property Transactions* (2nd ed., 2001); Vincent Brown, *Environmental Pollution Law and Commercial Transactions* (2003). For recent practical advice see Lewin (2003) 48 J.L.S.S. April/30; Ross (2003) 71 *Scottish Law Gazette* 141; Ross (2003) 48 J.L.S.S. May/65; Atkins (2003) 64 Prop. L.B. 3; Brymer (2004) 68 Prop. L.B. 1.

[26] As inserted into that Act by the Environment Act 1995. There are various relevant statutory instruments, including the Contaminated Land (Scotland) Regulations 2000 (SSI 2000/178). Other relevant legislation includes the Pollution Prevention and Control Act 1999.

may be obvious but may also be hard to detect. Contamination is an issue that must be considered in every transaction.[27] The missives should require that the PECs disclose the environmental position and should give the buyers the option of having an environmental audit carried out. There should be a right to rescind if the environmental position turns out to be unsatisfactory. What the buyer should be looking for can be found in the *CML Handbook for Scotland.*[28] It should be borne in mind that even if the PECs are clear that does not necessarily mean that the land is uncontaminated.

The buyers would usually like a warranty from the seller that the land is uncontaminated, for the buyers do not want to find themselves lumbered with possible cleanup costs. However, in practice sellers are usually unwilling to grant any such warranty. In some cases (especially commercial purchases) the buyers may wish to know something of the environmental history of the site and its immediate surroundings beyond what is disclosed in the PECs. Such reports are commercially available. They can be either "desktop" searches, in which the provider gathers data from old local maps, old planning permissions and so on, or there can be a more expensive "environmental audit" in which environmental experts make a site visit and may take and test samples, make trial bores, and so on.

Access rights in favour of the public

It may be that the property is subject to a public right of way. The existence of such a right will in most cases be fairly obvious. As a result of the Land Reform (Scotland) Act 2003 the general public has access rights to the whole of Scotland, subject to a variety of exceptions. For instance, the access right does not include access to buildings, nor does it extend to "sufficient adjacent land" to allow occupiers a reasonable amount of privacy.[29] Thus gardens are exempted as well as houses. **4-44**

Liability to compulsory purchase

All land is potentially liable to be compulsorily purchased for public purposes.[30] This is a risk that a buyer has to take, like the risk of taxation. In addition, in certain cases local community organisations may have a right of compulsory purchase under the Land Reform (Scotland) Act 2003. This Act creates two sorts of purchase right. One is the "community right to buy" and which is only a pre-emption right, that is to say a right that can be exercised only if the owner puts the property up **4-45**

---

[27] Not only purchase, but also lending on heritable security and taking a lease.

[28] paras 5.2.5, 5.2.6. and 5.2.6.1. However, these provisions seem not to have been properly adapted for Scotland and may in future be amended. See Brymer (2004) 68 Prop. L.B. 1.

[29] Land Reform (Scotland) Act 2003, s.6(1). See Steven and Barr, in Reid and Gretton, *Conveyancing 2003*, pp.131 *et seq.*

[30] See Jeremy Rowan-Robinson, *Compulsory Purchase and Compensation* (2nd ed., 2003). For a useful summary of the law see David A. Brand, Andrew J .M. Steven and Scott Wortley, *Professor McDonald's Conveyancing Manual* (7th ed., 2004) paras 29.19–29.23.

for sale. The other is the "crofting community right to buy". This is geographically much more restricted, but is a stronger right, since it can be exercised at any time, and not merely if the owner happens to put the property up for sale. These rights tend to apply to larger rural estates rather than to residential or commercial property.

CHAPTER 5

MISSIVES III: BREACH OF CONTRACT

Introduction

This chapter deals with breach of contract, on the basis that settlement 5–01
has not yet taken place, or never takes place. What happens if settlement
does take place and thereafter, a remedy is sought for breach of contract,
is considered later.[1]

In residential conveyancing, payment of the price is often the only
obligation on the buyers, the remaining obligations being the sellers'.
But, so far as breach is concerned, the same general principles apply
regardless of where the obligation lies.

This chapter has four parts. The first two parts consider the two
methods of responding to breach of contract, namely (i) pulling out and
(ii) keeping going but claiming damages for any loss. The third part
considers the particular problems which arise where the breach leads to
a delay in settlement. The last part deals with settlement by special
agreement, varying the terms of the missives.

Breach, or alleged breach, may lead to litigation. Litigation is something that both the loser and the winner will in all probability end up
regretting. As well as the stress and worry, and as well as the time
consumed, even the winner is likely to end up out of pocket. The best
advice is to avoid litigation if at all possible. Clients usually underestimate the human and financial costs of litigation and overestimate their
chances of success, and are often more legalistic than lawyers.[2] But
sometimes the combativeness comes from the solicitors themselves, who
should know better, but who rush into head-on conflict on behalf of their
unfortunate clients.

PULLING OUT

Rescission

Sometimes clients change their minds about the sale, even after 5–02
missives are concluded, and wish to pull out, in which case their
solicitors may find themselves casting around for excuses for rescission.
But usually clients will not wish to withdraw from a contract unless there

---

[1] Ch.16.
[2] An insightful observation of Professor Paisley's.

is a serious breach by the other party, such as the persistent failure of a purchaser to come up with the money or failure of a seller to produce an acceptable title. Most clients will thus not wish to exercise a right to rescind the moment it emerges, but will hope that the deal can be put back together. Purchasers may be willing to disregard altogether some defect (*e.g.* in title). But if secured lenders are involved in the purchase, the decision to disregard defects must be cleared with the lenders as well as with the purchasers.

Pulling out can happen in more than one way. The basic classification is repudiation (by the party in breach) and rescission (by the innocent one).[3] In practice, conveyancers often use the term "resile" rather than "rescind". However, some contract lawyers argue that one "resiles" when one withdraws from an agreement which is not yet legally binding (*e.g.* open missives), and that the term "rescind" should be used where one party withdraws from a binding contract because of breach by the other party. This terminological approach has some judicial support.[4] There are other possibilities as well, such as withdrawing on the basis of an express contractual right to do so in certain circumstances, or, again, withdrawing on the ground that the contract was voidable. For all such possibilities conveyancers tend, rightly or wrongly, to use the word "resile".

Repudiation

5-03   One party may repudiate the contract, *i.e.* declare that s/he does not intend to perform.[5] Unless the repudiation is justified—in which it is to be classified as rescission rather than as repudiation—repudiation gives the other party an option: either to accept the repudiation, which will end the contract and normally give rise to a claim for damages, or to reject the repudiation and insist on performance.[6] The innocent party should intimate to the counterparty which option s/he is choosing. If s/he fails to do so, problems can arise as to whether s/he has implicitly accepted or rejected the repudiation.[7] In most cases s/he will wish accept the repudiation, and claim for the loss (if any) suffered as a result. Trying to compel an unwilling counterparty to go through with a conveyancing contract seldom makes sense.

---

[3] See generally William W. McBryde, *The Law of Contract in Scotland* (2nd ed., 2001), Ch.20.

[4] *Zemhunt (Holdings) Ltd v Control Securities Ltd*, 1992 S.L.T. 151; *Lloyds Bank plc v Bamberger*, 1993 S.C. 570. For discussion of terminology see William W. McBryde, *The Law of Contract in Scotland* (2nd ed., 2001), paras 20–02—20–06.

[5] *Grant v Ullah*, 1987 S.L.T. 639 is a typical example: the buyer failed to settle at the due date, and a week later wrote to say that he was unable to pay the price and was pulling out of the deal.

[6] *White & Carter (Councils) Ltd v McGregor*, 1962 S.C. (HL) 1. The abolition of this rule has been recommended: Scottish Law Commission, *Report on Remedies for Breach of Contract* (Scot. Law. Com. No.174).

[7] See below.

Rescission: positive obligations

Unless the defaulting party repudiates the contract, the mere fact that 5-04
s/he has failed to perform a positive obligation timeously does not of
itself normally amount to material breach, entitling the innocent party to
rescind. For, subject to the exceptions mentioned below—exceptions
which in fact usually apply in modern practice—time is not "of the
essence" in a contract of sale, meaning that the defaulting party must be
given a reasonable time to perform the obligation which s/he has
undertaken (and hitherto failed) to perform.[8] Only after the expiry of a
"reasonable time" does the breach become material, permitting rescission. The fact that "time is not of the essence" does not mean that delay
is not breach. It is breach, and thus will presumptively give rise to a
claim for damages. The issue being considered here is whether it is a
breach that will justify the other party in rescinding.

The ultimatum procedure

The standard method of dealing with default, if the innocent party 5-05
wishes to rescind, is to employ the ultimatum procedure laid down in
Rodger (Builders) Limited v Fawdry.[9] The chronology of this procedure is
as follows:

(a) The date for performance of the obligation passes without
performance being tendered.
(b) The defaulting party is then allowed a "reasonable time" to
perform.
(c) After expiry of the "reasonable time" the aggrieved party
serves an ultimatum, demanding performance within a further "reasonable time".
(d) If performance is still not tendered the aggrieved party may
rescind.[10]

Whether stages (b) and (c) are independently necessary is very doubtful,
but in practice it is safer to assume that they are.[11] How long is
"reasonable" will depend on the facts and circumstances of the individual case. In one case[12] the following timescale was approved by the court
for failure to pay the price: the contractual date of entry, at which the
price was due, was December 15; the ultimatum was sent on January 13;

---

[8] See generally McBryde (1996) 1 *Edinburgh Law Review* 43 at 58–60, and for further
discussion see William W. McBryde, *The Law of Contract in Scotland* (2nd ed., 2001),
paras 20–128—20–131. The rule is in some ways a curious one. If the innocent party can be
compensated by damages the rule is, on the whole, not unfair. But it seems to be applied
in other situations: see *e.g. Khazaka v Drysdale*, 1995 S.L.T. 1108. Perhaps the correctness
of that decision could be doubted.
[9] 1950 S.C. 483.
[10] For damages claims, see below.
[11] *cf. George Packman & Sons v Dunbar's Trs*, 1977 S.L.T. 140 *per* Lord Stott.
[12] *Lloyds Bank Ltd v Bauld*, 1976 S.L.T. (Notes) 53.

the expiry date of the ultimatum was January 31. However, a longer period may be necessary for other types of failure, or where, as in *Rodger (Builders) Ltd v Fawdry*,[13] eventual performance is likely. So where a seller has applied for, say, confirmation as executor or for a local authority completion certificate, "reasonable time" probably means the time that it usually takes to obtain a document of the kind in question.[14] There may, of course, be difficult cases and it is always open to a party to seek a declarator[15] that he has validly rescinded the contract.

It is the practice in a notice of rescission to state the reason for it. It has been held that rescission can be effectual even if the wrong reason is given, provided of course that a good ground for rescission does actually exist.[16] If that is so, then presumably it also follows that it is not necessary to give the reason in the first place. The decision may be correct, but we feel that the subject is a difficult one, on which the last word has not been said.

When immediate rescission is possible: (i) where the law implies such a right

5–06   The presumptive rule that time is not "of the essence" does not apply to suspensive conditions. If a condition is suspensive, then non-purification by the agreed date means that the contract falls at once,[17] but we are here dealing with positive obligations.

Rescission is also permitted as soon as the contractual settlement date arrives if the sellers turn out to have no title whatsoever to all or part of the property. If the sellers cannot produce a title by the date of entry they are not entitled to further time in which to acquire one.[18] It has been held in the Outer House that immediate rescission may be available in a third situation, namely where the sale is primarily of a business. In the case in question the business was conducted from premises which were held on lease, and the breach was a failure to obtain the landlord's consent to the assignation by the date of entry.[19]

When immediate rescission is possible: (ii) express agreement

5–07   In practice, not being able to rescind immediately where the other side has broken a positive obligation can be unsatisfactory. There may be good reason to believe that the other party will never perform. But unless the other party absolutely refuses performance (thus repudiating the contract) s/he must be given the benefit of the doubt, possibly for a number of months. Meanwhile, the innocent client is in a difficult situation. Sellers will be itching to re-sell. Meanwhile, they may be

---

[13] 1950 S.C. 483.
[14] *McLennan v Warner & Co.*, 1996 S.L.T. 1349.
[15] As in *Lloyds Bank Ltd v Bauld*, above.
[16] *Owen v Fotheringham*, 1997 S.L.T. (Sh. Ct) 28.
[17] *T. Boland & Co. Ltd v Dundas's Trs*, 1975 S.L.T. (Notes) 80.
[18] *Campbell v McCutcheon*, 1963 S.C. 505.
[19] *Ahmed v Akhtar*, 1997 S.L.T. 218.

involved in bridging finance on another house. Buyers have the difficult decision as to whether to take entry. On the one hand they may have nowhere else to live; but on the other hand if they do take entry and if the seller ultimately cannot perform they will have to move out again. The way out of these difficulties is to have an express provision in the missives about rescission for breach. This is almost always done nowadays in respect of payment of the price, but it is less common in respect of the seller's obligations, notably the obligation to produce a good and marketable title. So far as payment of the price is concerned, the clause providing for the right to rescind will normally make its appearance in the seller's qualified acceptance.

It can be done in either of two ways. One is for the missives to state that timeous payment of the price is "of the essence", thereby implying that breach will constitute material breach, so that the seller will be able to rescind immediately.[20] An alternative is to provide that if the price is not paid by a defined date, the seller may rescind. If the defined date is the contractual date of settlement, the two possibilities come to the same thing. But missives usually provide that the seller's right to rescind emerges not immediately on default but after a defined period, such as 14 or 21 days. Clauses of this sort provide a fair balance between the interests of the two parties.

Such time-is-of-the-essence or right-to-resile clauses commonly state that rescission is available only where the fault is exclusively on one side. This is a rule which would almost certainly be implied even though not expressed.[21]

Care must be taken in the wording. Sometimes one sees both forms in the same clause, *i.e.* a clause saying both (a) that timeous payment of the price is a "of the essence" and (b) that if the default persists for (*e.g.*)14 days the seller may rescind. This is self-contradictory. In one case[22] sellers found themselves having to persuade the court that the phrase, "the sellers have the option immediately thereafter [*i.e.* on non-payment] to resile" meant, not that the option must be exercised immediately but merely that it arose immediately but could be exercised at any time.

Rescission before date of entry?

Could purchasers rescind *before* the contractual date of settlement? 5–08 The answer is that this is not normally possible, but there are two, or perhaps three, exceptions. The first is where the missives confer such a right. The second is where the sellers repudiate the contract. The third, and doubtful, case is where the sellers have no title to all or part of the property. As mentioned earlier, this fact will justify rescission at the

---

[20] Sometimes the formula is that that timeous payment is an "essential condition" or "material condition". This is an ambiguous expression, for it can indicate that the condition is a suspensive one, but as applied to timeous payment the meaning is presumably that breach will constitute material breach.

[21] See *Davidson v Tilburg Ltd*, 1991 G.W.D. 18–1109.

[22] *Toynar Ltd v R. & A. Properties (Fife) Ltd*, 1989 G.W.D. 2–82. The sellers were successful.

settlement date, but in *Campbell v McCutcheon*[23] it was held that the purchaser's rescission before the settlement date was valid. This is, however, contrary to the general principle of contract law that a party need not be in a position to perform at the time of the contract, but only at the time when performance is due. Sellers might have no title when missives are concluded but still be confident that they can obtain such a title in time for settlement. *Campbell* may create an exception, but it is arguable that the approval of pre-settlement rescission was *obiter*. If not *obiter*, it is submitted that the decision was simply wrong on this issue.

Restrictions on the right to rescind

5-09   Several restrictions on the right to rescind should be noted. (1) Where, as occasionally happens, entry has been taken before settlement, it is probably the law that the buyer can rescind only if *restitutio in integrum* remains possible. *Restitutio* would be barred if the purchaser made alterations to the property to any significant extent. (2) If the other party performs, albeit late, but before rescission, then the right to rescind is probably lost.[24] (3) If a buyer delays in rescinding the contract, there may be an argument that the right to do so has been impliedly waived.[25] Closely related to this is the case where the party with the right to rescind allows that other party to change his position in reliance on the contract. Here the right to rescind may be defeated by personal bar. Such things happen surprisingly often. One party sends out a letter of rescission as a sort of bargaining move, and thereafter continues to process the transaction. Everything here depends on the exact facts, but the rescission may be held by the court to have been implicitly waived.

Rescission: warranties

5-10   Apart from positive obligations, missives may also include warranties. Examples are provisions that there are no outstanding statutory notices, that all necessary consents have been obtained for alterations, and that there are no unusual or unduly onerous burdens. If properly drawn, they will state the date at which the particular thing is guaranteed (generally the date of conclusion of missives or date of entry). It seems that breach of a warranty, provided it is material, gives entitlement to immediate rescission.[26] The warranty is either satisfied or it is not, and if it is not the

---

[23] 1963 S.C. 505.

[24] *Cumming v Brown*, 1993 S.C.L.R. 707; *Grovebury Management Ltd v McLaren*, 1997 S.L.T. 1083. But compare *Ford Sellar Morris Properties plc v E. W. Hutchison Ltd*, 1990 S.C. 34, and McBryde (1996) 1 *Edinburgh Law Review* 43 at 60–62. The rule may be different for suspensive conditions: see *Bluestone Estates Ltd v Fitness First Clubs Ltd*, 2003 G.W.D. 27–768.

[25] Though this argument in practice usually fails. See *e.g. James Howden & Co. Ltd v Taylor Woodrow Property Co. Ltd*, 1998 S.C. 853, and see further Ch.3.

[26] It seems that the point has never been expressly decided. See, however, *Morris v Ritchie*, 1992 G.W.D. 33–1950. In any case the purchasers can achieve virtual rescission simply by refusing to settle. Under the mutuality principle, they cannot be required to settle while the counterparty (here the sellers) persists in breach (unless the breach is trivial). If the sellers cannot purge their breach, they can never require the purchasers to settle.

seller is in immediate and conclusive breach. There seems no place here for the ultimatum procedure because, unlike a positive obligation, there is nothing for the seller still to do. If this is correct, then, at least in this respect, a warranty is superior to a positive obligation. In practice, though, warranties often concern relatively minor matters and often the purchaser will not wish to rescind.

Rescission: the risk of getting it wrong

Rescission can be a wise decision, but it carries a risk: unjustified 5-11 rescission is itself a breach of contract. Suppose that Jack is selling to Jill. Missives have been concluded and settlement day has been and gone, but Jill has not settled because of problems raising the money. Jack is fed up and rescinds. If he rescinds prematurely, he is in breach. If, as is usually the case, the missives provide for a deadline—for instance that if Jill fails to pay within three weeks of the due date then Jack may rescind—it is important not to send the letter of rescission too soon. Moreover, if Jack unlawfully rescinds and resells the property to Jenny, Jill may even be able to reduce the resale, whether she can or not depending on the state of Jenny's knowledge.[27]

Damages

Rescission is often accompanied by a claim for damages. This subject 5-12 is simply part of general contract law. Before looking at that law as applied to the sale of heritable property, two general remarks are worth making. The first is that the ascertainment of damages is not an exact science. The second is that the innocent party must mitigate, or minimise, his loss. However, the duty[28] to minimise does not begin until the contract comes to an end, *e.g.* by formal rescission, which may be some time after the contractual date of entry.[29] Under what heads can damages be recovered? There is surprisingly little case law on this important subject, and what follows is only an educated guess.

Damages: (i) sellers in default

Purchasers who rescind following the sellers' failure to produce a good 5-13 title, or other material default, will have to begin all over again finding a house. The expenses incurred on the abortive purchase will have been wasted. The only reported case dealing with damages in this situation is *Fielding v Newell*.[30] Unfortunately, the report is not very full and gives only the heads of damage which were disputed. These were: (a) legal fees for the unsuccessful contract; (b) survey fee; (c) travel and

---

[27] This is the "off-side goals rule", as to which see *Rodger (Builders) Ltd v Fawdry*, 1950 S.C. 483; Reid, *Property*, paras 695 *et seq*; Wortley 2002 J.R. 291.

[28] Strictly speaking, there is no "duty". Rather, the rule is that if the injured party does not mitigate, the damages are calculated as if he had done so. See William W. McBryde, *The Law of Contract in Scotland* (2nd ed., 2001) para.22-31.

[29] *Johnstone's Firs v Harris*, 1977 S.C. 365.

[30] 1987 S.L.T. 530.

accommodation costs to inspect the property; (d) cost of telephone calls to solicitor and surveyor. The reason for the dispute was that all these expenses were incurred prior to the contract being concluded. No final view was reached by the court, which instead allowed proof before answer.

Damages: (ii) buyers in default

5-14   If the buyers fail to pay, the sellers will normally re-market the house.[31] Often they will have bought another house in reliance on the sale and so will be faced with interest payments on two loans. Fortunately there is more authority here.[32] The subject may be divided into six parts.

(a) In the first place, the sellers are entitled to the difference (if negative) between the price in the first, abortive, sale and the price in the second, successful sale.[33] If the difference is not negative but positive, *i.e.* the price in the second sale is higher than the price in the first, abortive, sale, then there is a profit to the seller. Any such profit is set off against other heads of loss. The consequence may be that no damages are due.[34] This is indeed quite often the result in practice.

(b) In the second place, the sellers are entitled to the legal, advertising and other expenses of the abortive sale; but not the expenses of the second sale: since the sellers were always going to sell, it is only fair that they meet one set of expenses themselves.[35]

(c) In the third place, if the house is no longer being used (the sellers having moved into their new house), the sellers are entitled to the cost of running the house from the abortive date of entry until entry is taken on the second sale. This includes insurance and routine maintenance. In one case the cost of employing a caretaker was not allowed as being too remote.[36]

(d) In the fourth place, under the general law there is no entitlement to interest on the unpaid price unless entry is taken by the buyers, which is unusual. Interest may be recovered if special provision is made in the missives, but it must be made clear that interest is due in the event of non-payment and not only in the case of late payment.[37] Buyers should, however, normally resist such clauses, which are draconian, at least if

---

[31] However, they might decide not to sell after all. That does not preclude them from claiming damages. In that case the value of the property is assessed not according to the price achieved at resale, for there is no resale, but at a fair value at the date when the contract was rescinded. This is so even if at a later date the sellers change their minds again and do resell: see William W. McBryde, *The Law of Contract in Scotland* (2nd ed., 2001), para.22-45.

[32] *Grant v Ullah*, 1987 S.L.T. 639; *Voeten v Campbell Brook & Myles*, 1987 G.W.D. 26-1009; *Hopkinson v Williams*, 1993 S.L.T. 907; *Field v Dickinson*, 1995 S.C.L.R. 1146.

[33] *King v Moore*, 1993 S.L.T. 1117. This is on the assumption that the seller has taken proper steps to obtain a good price. If not, that means that the seller has failed to mitigate, and the first buyer can use this fact as a defence.

[34] See William W. McBryde, *The Law of Contract in Scotland* (2nd ed., 2001), para.22-46.

[35] *Johnstone's Exrs v Harris*, 1977 S.C. 365.

[36] *Chapman's Trs v Anglo Scottish Group Services Ltd*, 1980 S.L.T. (Sh. Ct.) 27.

[37] *Lloyds Bank plc v Bamberger*, 1993 S.C. 570, but *cf. Grant v Ullah*, 1987 S.L.T. 639.

they stipulate for interest not only between the contractual settlement date and the date of the sellers' rescission, but until the date when the sellers finally sell the property to another purchaser.[38]

(e) The fifth issue is whether the sellers can recover the costs caused by having to service two loans. The fact that payment was not tendered on the date of entry may place the sellers in financial difficulties, and this is especially so where, as often occurs, they have bought a new house in reliance on the sale of the old one. In this situation the sellers will be financing two loans: on the one hand they typically will still be paying the loan on the old house, and on the other hand (the sale price not having materialized) they will be paying bridging finance on the full purchase price of the new house. This can be ruinously expensive. And it is no fault of the sellers. Can the sellers recover the cost of servicing one of these loans from the purchasers?[39] In *Tiffney v Bachurzewski*[40] a claim in respect of a bridging loan failed because the possibility of the seller having to bridge was said not to be within the reasonable contemplation of the parties at the date of the contract and so not allowable under the second rule in *Hadley v Baxendale*.[41] Not many conveyancers or indeed housebuyers would accept that the possibility of bridging is as remote as this and it may be that the decision will not stand the test of time.[42] The best way round *Tiffney* is to ensure that the buyers know at the time the contract is made that the sellers have a mortgage or are otherwise relying on borrowed money. The possibility of interest payments will then be within their "reasonable contemplation".[43] If, as occasionally happens, the purchasers have paid a deposit, the sellers may be able to keep it.[44]

(f) Sixth, a claim for general inconvenience, but not for solatium, is also possible.[45]

KEEPING GOING

Introduction

Usually the parties will try to keep the contract going. Where they succeed there are two possible outcomes. One is that the defaulting side ultimately performs in full. The other is that they do not. In the second case damages are due for non-performance. In the first case damages may be due for late performance. 5–15

---

[38] See the previous chapter.

[39] They cannot recover both, and it is not wholly clear which is appropriate.

[40] 1985 S.L.T. 165. The sale eventually proceeded to settlement, but the principles are the same. See also *Hopkinson v Williams*, 1993 S.L.T. 907.

[41] (1854) 9 Ex. 341.

[42] However, *Tiffney* was followed in *Rapide Enterprises v Midgley*, 1998 S.L.T. 504. Oddly, the position seems to be different where it is the seller who is in default and the buyer who incurs interest charges. See *Caledonian Property Group Ltd v Queensferry Property Group Ltd*, 1992 S.L.T. 738.

[43] See *Grant v Ullah*, 1987 S.L.T. 639, and the *Stair Memorial Encyclopaedia*, Vol.12, paras 1009 *et seq.*

[44] See *Zemhunt (Holdings) Ltd v Control Securities plc*, 1992 S.L.T. 151.

[45] *Mills v Findlay*, 1994 S.C.L.R. 397.

Late (but complete) performance

5-16   Performance may be satisfactory but late, as where the purchasers pay the price two weeks after the date of entry, or the sellers need an extra month to obtain confirmation of executors or a building warrant. Occasionally, the defaulting party may require the stimulus of an action of specific implement. Where the problem is that the sellers refuse to sign the disposition, the court can order its execution by the Deputy Principal Clerk of Session.[46] But four points should be borne in mind in relation to actions for implement. First, implement is not available for warranties, for there the sellers are under no positive obligation. Secondly, implement will be refused if performance is impossible (*e.g.* defaulting sellers with no title cannot be ordered to acquire one). Thirdly, by virtue of the mutuality principle, implement will not be granted if the pursuers are also in breach of contract. Finally, implement against the purchasers runs into the problem that their chief obligation is to pay money, and decree of specific implement is incompetent to compel the payment of money.[47] Overall, an action of implement is usually unwise. If the counterparty simply will not settle, it is almost always better to rescind and then claim any damages which may be due.

Late performance may produce consequential loss for the innocent party, and in that case damages are usually due.[48] The possible heads of damage are the same as those which arise on rescission. The question of interest on the price is discussed below in the context of delay in settlement.

Incomplete performance

5-17   If there is incomplete performance in domestic conveyancing it is normally by the sellers. The typical situation is that the central heating system does not work properly or that there is some minor blemish in the title. In this situation the purchasers will usually wish to proceed with the sale but may also claim damages. The issue can arise in either of two ways. The problem may arise before settlement, in which case the buyers may wish to go ahead, but against a reduction of the price. Or it may emerge after settlement, in which case the buyers want to get part of the price back again, by way of damages. Such a claim is known as an *actio quanti minoris.* It was allowed in Roman law, but strangely our common law did not allow it except in certain types of case.[49] At common law, disgruntled purchasers had to choose between accepting the thing sold at

---

[46] *Mackay v Campbell*, 1966 S.C. 237; *Boag, Ptr*, 1967 S.L.T. 275; *Hoey v Butler*, 1975 S.C. 87. For the sheriff court see the Sheriff Courts (Scotland) Act 1907, s.5A as inserted by the Law Reform (Miscellaneous Provisions) (Scotland) Act 1985, s.17.

[47] An action for payment could be raised instead. But the crave or conclusion would have to be conditioned on the pursuer himself tendering performance.

[48] Notwithstanding the statement to the contrary by Lord Hunter in *Tiffney v Bachurzewski*, 1985 S.L.T. 165.

[49] For detailed discussion of this complex subject, and for more extensive citation of authority, see Stewart (1966) 11 J.L.S.S. 124; Reid (1988) 33 J.L.S.S. 285; Evans-Jones (1991) J.R. 190; Evans-Jones (1992) 37 J.L.S.S. 274. In *Fortune v Fraser*, 1995 S.C. 186 the Second Division declined to extend the scope of the *actio.* The decision was much criticised.

the agreed price, or rejecting it and claiming damages. They could not have it both ways, *i.e.* both to accept and to claim damages, unless, of course, the contract gave them that option. Traditionally missives did not confer this option, but latterly they did.[50] However section 3 of the Contract (Scotland) Act 1997 brought the law back into line with Roman law, and allows the *actio* in every case.[51] Special provision in the missives is therefore now unnecessary.

The method of calculating *quantum* is not free from doubt. The usual approach in measuring the loss recoverable by way of damages in sale is to take the difference in value between the promised and the actual performance. But there is nothing in principle to prevent the adoption of a "cost of cure" approach if that provides a more accurate measure of the loss.[52]

DELAY IN SETTLEMENT

Introduction

"Delay in settlement" has two meanings, one wider and the other   5–18
narrower. In the narrow sense it means the case where settlement does happen, but late. But this can be known only by hindsight, and when settlement fails to take place at the agreed date, the parties may not know whether the settlement is merely delayed or whether it will never take place at all. The term is thus sometimes used in a wider sense to cover any situation where settlement is not made on the due date, whatever may happen thereafter. Here, however, we use the term in the narrower sense.

The mutuality principle

If one party cannot or will not perform by the stipulated date, the   5–19
other side have the option of delaying settlement. The reason for this is the mutuality principle[53] in the law of contract, which is that if one side are in breach, then so long as they remain in breach, they cannot insist that the other side should perform. For example in *Bowie v Semple's Exers*[54] the buyer was held entitled not to pay where the seller, an executor, had still not obtained confirmation.

The limits of the mutuality principle are unclear. What are the counter-stipulations for payment of the price? Missives usually provide that "in exchange for the purchase price . . . the seller will deliver" certain specified items. Clearly purchasers could delay settlement if any

---

[50] The issue seems to have come to the general attention of conveyancers only as a result of the case of *Finlayson v McRobb*, 1987 S.L.T. (Sh. Ct.) 150.

[51] For the background see the Scottish Law Commission's *Report on Three Bad Rules in Contract Law* (Scot. Law Com. No.152, 1996).

[52] *Tainsh v McLaughlin*, 1990 S.L.T. (Sh. Ct) 102; *Hardwick v Gebbie*, 1991 S.L.T. 258; *Stair Memorial Encyclopaedia*, Vol.15, para.911. For the difficulties of this approach see *Ruxley Electronics and Construction Ltd v Forsyth* [1996] 1 A.C. 344.

[53] Or, in the language of the *jus commune*, the *exceptio non adimpleti contractus*.

[54] 1978 S.L.T. (Sh. Ct.) 9. Compare *Moor v Atwal*, 1995 S.C.L.R. 1119.

of these were missing. But presumably these are not all the counter-stipulations, for there are a number of other obligations on the sellers (such as the obligation to produce building consents) which are not included in the list. Indeed, the phrase quoted is arguably a dangerous one, in that it might be construed as meaning that if these items are produced then the buyers must pay up, even if there are other breaches by the seller.

As to the limits in the other direction, the sellers are bound to provide a good and marketable title. The question arises as to whether absolutely everything must be in place before the purchasers can be required to pay. The answer appears to be affirmative, so that the selling solicitors must take great care to obtain in good time all the deeds that are required by purchasers.

It is sometimes said that the principle becomes operative only if the breach is a material one. That appears to be incorrect.[55] A material breach is one that justifies rescission by the innocent party. The mutuality principle does not involve rescission, but merely suspension of performance until the other side is prepared to perform. Thus, suppose that the buyers fail to pay on the contractual date of entry. Unless otherwise provided by the missives, the sellers cannot rescind.[56] But nevertheless the mutuality principle applies, and they can suspend performance (*i.e.* refuse to hand over the disposition) until the buyers are prepared to perform (*i.e.* to pay). The mutuality principle applies to all breaches, except (probably) those that are trivial. If a breach is not material but in fact cannot be remedied, the mutuality principle is effectively equivalent to rescission, for the innocent party can suspend performance for ever.

Interest on the price: the common law

5–20   One almost inevitable consequence of delay in settlement is that, regardless of which party caused the delay, the price is withheld by the purchasers. Eventually, of course (unless the transaction collapses), settlement will occur and the price will then be paid. But a problem may then arise as to interest on the price during the period between the contractual date of entry and the ultimate date of settlement. The common law position is clear. It depends on whether or not entry is taken by the purchasers. If entry is taken interest is due. If entry is not taken, interest is not due. This is because the "fruits" of the price (*i.e.* interest) are treated as the equivalent of the "fruits" of the land (*i.e.* possession). If one party has one, the other party must, in equity, have the other.[57] It should be observed that entitlement to interest is not regarded as damages and is not tied to any loss that may or may not have been sustained. In practice, the rule is less fair than it sounds, especially where the delay is caused by the purchasers. Unless the purchasers take entry (and often they will not) there is no entitlement to interest. (Interest is not due merely *ex mora*.) It is true that the sellers

---

[55] *cf.* McBryde (1996) 1 *Edinburgh Law Review* 43 at 65.
[56] For the moment. But eventually they can.
[57] See Erskine III, iii, 79.

have the benefit of possession, but usually they have bought another house and it is a benefit they could do without. In practice, the house often lies empty.

Can the sellers do anything to improve their position? Halliday[58] suggests that interest will run if the sellers vacate the premises and make a formal offer of entry to the purchaser, but this does not find support in the case law.[59] Another possibility is to raise an action for payment, in which case interest will run from the date of citation.[60] As well as claiming interest the innocent party may also have a claim in damages.[61]

Where interest does run, no one seems to know what the appropriate rate is.[62] The only rule which is reasonably certain is that if the purchaser takes entry on the basis of putting the purchase price on deposit receipt (this only happens where it is the seller who is in default), the interest due is the interest actually obtained.[63]

Interest on the price: contractual provision

Because the common law can be unfair to the innocent sellers, it is 5–21 now almost universal to have a clause in missives providing that if the purchasers fail to pay at the due date, the price payable shall be augmented by interest on it at a defined rate, typically stated as being 4 per cent above the current base rate of one of the major Scottish banks. It is normal to add the words "notwithstanding consignation" in order to prevent the argument that interest should be payable at the rate actually earned.[64] It is also usual to state that interest will be due even though the purchasers do not take entry, so as clearly to exclude the common law rule. The clause often provides that the sellers are entitled to interest only where they are able to settle and the purchasers are not, though in fact this qualification is implied by law.[65]

SETTLEMENT BY SPECIAL ARRANGEMENT

Introduction

Although the party not in breach cannot be forced to settle (because 5–22 of the mutuality principle), they may often wish to do so. In that case there may be settlement by special agreement. The form that the agreement takes depends on which party is in default.

---

[58] para.38–62.

[59] See, in particular, *Thomson v Vernon*, 1983 S.L.T. (Sh. Ct.) 17.

[60] See *Tiffney v Bachurzewski*, 1985 S.L.T. 165 at 168 and 1988 G.W.D. 37–1530. However, compare *Thomson v Vernon*, 1983 S.L.T. (Sh. Ct.) 17.

[61] *Brown v Gamsu*, 1992 G.W.D. 40–2429.

[62] For discussion see Cusine and Love, in D. J. Cusine (ed.), *A Scots Conveyancing Miscellany: Essays* in *Honour of Professor J. M. Halliday* (1987).

[63] *Prestwick Cinema Co. Ltd v Gardiner*, 1951 S.C. 98.

[64] As has been said, this is the common law rule following consignation: see *Prestwick Cinema Co. Ltd v Gardiner*, above. The point of course is that the seller wishes an interest rate higher than that obtainable at current deposit receipt rates.

[65] *Davidson v Tilburg Ltd*, 1991 G.W.D. 18–119. Once again, this is the mutuality principle.

If the purchasers are in default (*i.e.* the price is not paid), it is unlikely that settlement will proceed. This is because, so long as they are protected by an interest clause, the sellers have nothing to gain by permitting entry and indeed have something to lose, because the purchasers may never come up with the money and, once in the house, may be difficult to dislodge. The purchasers, by contrast, may be keen to take entry: after all, interest is running on the price and they have nothing to show for it. And they may have nowhere else to live. What this means in practice is obtaining bridging finance (so that the price can be paid in full) until permanent finance is available. Typically, the purchasers are waiting for a loan to come through, or for the sale of their existing house.

If the sellers are in default this is usually because they have failed to come up with a sufficient title or other documentation by the contractual date of settlement. Almost invariably, the sellers will be keen to settle, because, being themselves in default, they cannot claim interest on the price, and will lose heavily if settlement is delayed. The purchasers may be less keen. Their attitude will depend partly on the seriousness of the default and partly on whether they have sold their own house. Purchasers who have sold will have nowhere to live and so will be keen to settle; purchasers who have not sold may welcome an excuse to delay settlement.

Possible arrangements

5-23   Purchasers are not, of course, bound to settle where the sellers are in default; but if they agree to settle, the agreement usually takes one of the following forms (sometimes in combination).

In the first place, if the default is minor, settlement might take place on the basis of a letter of obligation granted by the sellers' solicitors and undertaking to deliver the missing document.[66] Payment is then made in full, except that there is sometimes a small retention (*e.g.* £1,000) if the thing missing involves the expenditure of money. Note, however, that the sellers' solicitors are likely to be unwilling to grant a letter of obligation in such terms. Indeed, most firms will refuse to do so unless they are quite certain that the document is one that can be obtained. Why should the firm put its neck on the block?[67] This is a matter for negotiation, and a buyer may sometimes be willing to do without a letter of obligation. (After all, the sellers are in any case already bound to perform in terms of the missives.)

In the second place, if the default is more serious, the purchasers may not be willing to hand over the money. Indeed, it may be impossible for them to do so, at least without bridging, because the lenders may not be willing to release the loan cheque until the default is put right. The purchasers' solicitors, who are also acting for the lender, must not let

---

[66] This will be a "non-classic" letter of obligation and therefore the undertaking will not be covered by the master policy.

[67] There may, however, be strong pressure from the client, and this pressure may be hard to resist if the firm feels in some way responsible for the problem. Giving in to the pressure leads to instant relief and to non-instant problems and costs.

their sympathy for the purchasers interfere with their professional duty to the lenders. As a general rule, purchasers should never hand over the price if a valid disposition cannot be produced in exchange. The main, but not only, danger here is of the risk of supervening insolvency.[68] And even for less serious defaults the purchasers may not be willing to pay the sellers. But it may be possible for settlement to take place without the sellers actually being paid. What happens is that the purchase price is placed ("consigned") on deposit receipt with a bank in the joint names of the solicitors for the sellers and the purchasers.

A third method of settlement sometimes found is where the purchasers take entry on the basis of a deposit, which is either paid over to the sellers or put on joint deposit receipt. This will be attractive to purchasers where the loan has been withheld, so that they could not pay the full amount without bridging. Obviously, it is less attractive to the sellers. Whether the sellers are also due interest on the unpaid balance is a matter for negotiation. If nothing is said, interest is due because the purchasers have possession.

A note on D/R settlements

The precise legal effects of consignations on deposit receipt are 5–24 surprisingly obscure. One possibility is that a trust is created, with the two law firms being joint trustees.[69] But this view does not have support in the case law, and it might perhaps be better to regard the arrangement as a four-handed contract. In one case, where settlement proved impossible, the buyer was held entitled to the money on the basis of the doctrine of *causa data causa non secuta*.[70] An alternative basis for the decision would have been implied contractual terms. In addition to the theoretical problems as to the nature of the arrangement, there are two other problems. One is that the two law firms will have different loyalties, and will find it almost impossible to agree as to what is to happen to the money if their clients cannot so agree. Indeed, there are difficulties as to whether a firm will agree to the uplift of the deposit receipt without the instructions of its clients.[71] The other is that "D/R settlements", as they are sometimes called, are often made at the last minute, often on the telephone, in a desperate attempt to get a quick solution, so that written evidence of what was agreed is slight or even absent.[72]

The money cannot be released from D/R without the consent of both firms, and in practice this often puts the purchasers in a strong position,

---

[68] See the classic case of *Gibson v Hunter Home Designs Ltd*, 1976 S.C. 23.

[69] This view was adopted in the first edition of this book, but we now incline to think it incorrect. It would, however, be possible for an express trust to be created, with the money constituting the trust fund. Invoking trust law is not necessary in order for the arrangement to survive the insolvency of one of the parties: *cf. Craiglaw Developments Ltd v Wilson*, 1998 S.L.T. 1046.

[70] *Singh v Cross Entertainments*, 1990 S.L.T. 77.

[71] Logically, if the terms of the settlement are clear, the firm should release the D/R when certain conditions are satisfied, whether or not its client so agrees. But in practice no firm wishes to act without instructions, and, moreover, the terms of the settlement are often unclear.

[72] The pressure on the solicitors will be even greater if the problem exists because of their own earlier delay or negligence.

for they have what they want, namely possession, and there is no reason why they should agree to release the money until the sellers have met their obligations in full. However, if time goes by and the problem in respect of which consignation was made fails to be resolved, the buyers may wish to take the consigned sum as compensation. But it can be unclear as to whether they are so entitled. Even if they are so entitled, getting both firms to agree can be highly problematic. Moreover, in practice the missives may have lapsed by this time as a result of a supersession clause.[73] Finally, if litigation is necessary, the existence of up to five parties[74] can cause great difficulty. All this is not to say that D/R settlements should never be used. They can be extremely convenient. But they should be used sparingly, with an awareness of the potential problems, and with the fullest documentation of the agreed basis.

---

[73] *Hamilton v Rodwell*, 1998 S.C.L.R. 418, *Hamilton v Rodwell (No.2)* 1999 G.W.D. 35–1706. These two connected decisions seem to mean that, under these circumstances, *neither* party is entitled to the money. If that is so, that is good news for banks. But it cannot be so.

[74] The sellers, their solicitors, the buyers, their solicitors, and the bank itself.

CHAPTER 6

GOOD AND MARKETABLE TITLE

MEANING OF GOOD TITLE

Introduction

In a contract for the sale of land the sellers normally give an absolute 6-01 guarantee of title.[1] This is implied by law,[2] but in practice an express clause is included in the missives.[3] Naturally the parties are free to modify the obligation to give a good title, and sometimes they do so. The importance of the idea of "good and marketable title" has declined somewhat over the past 25 years or so. The older practice was, in the typical case, to conclude missives within a few days. Thus at the time of conclusion of missives the buyers' agents had not usually had the opportunity to investigate the title. The provision in the missives—and a provision implied by law—that the title had to be good and marketable was thus of great importance. If the title fell short of the required standard, the buyers would found on their contractual rights. But nowadays it is usual for the agents for the buyers to have had the opportunity to examine the title before missives are concluded. If a problem comes to light the buyers do not need to found on their right to a good and marketable title. (Indeed, they have no such right, since as yet there is no contract.) Instead, they can protect their interests simply by declining to conclude missives. Nevertheless, the concept of good and marketable title is still of considerable importance, especially in respect of problems which, for one reason or another, come to light after missives have been concluded.

The idea of a good title involves two essential elements. First, the buyers are to be made the owners.[4] Second, after acquiring ownership, they will not be subject to any third-party rights,[5] with the exception of title conditions of an ordinary nature, and with the possible exception of title leases.

---

[1] This obligation can be characterised as warrandice, and it covers much the same ground as the obligation of warrandice normally contained in a disposition. See Reid, *Property*, paras 702–14.

[2] cf. *Baird v Drumpellier & Mount Vernon Estates Ltd*, 2000 S.C. 103.

[3] For the standard clause inserted in missives, see ROTPB, para.8.9 (first registration) and para.8.37 (transfer of registered land).

[4] In the normal case. If what is being sold is a lease, then obviously the buyers are to become the new lessees of the property, not the owners of it.

[5] As far as private law is concerned. The buyers may be subject to various rights under public law.

Ownership

6–02   The sellers must offer a title to the whole of the property described in the missives. But while on general principles of landownership that necessarily includes a title to the minerals, this is usually negatived by a clause to the effect that the minerals are included only in so far as the sellers have right thereto.

Third-party rights

6–03   The third party rights may be subordinate real rights. In practice the most likely such right is a heritable security. But there exist other third party rights which may prevent the title from being a good one. One example would be occupancy rights under the 1981 Act. Another would be where the buyer's title is voidable at the instance of a third party. In such cases the Keeper would register the title with an exclusion of indemnity in relation to the right of challenge. Hence the obligation to give a good title is roughly speaking an obligation to give a title that the Keeper will neither (a) reject nor (b) accept with exclusion of indemnity. But the identity of good title with (a) and (b) is not a complete one, as two examples will show. In the first place, suppose that Jack sells land to Jill. The property is subject to an undischarged standard security. The Keeper will register Jill as owner with no exclusion of indemnity, though the security will still appear in Section C. But unless Jill was happy about taking a title subject to a security, Jack has not complied with his obligation to give a good title. In the second place, suppose that the Keeper registers Jill as owner but excludes indemnity in relation to part of the property because he thinks that Jack's title was of uncertain validity. In fact the Keeper has misread the relevant deeds and Jack's title was a perfect one. Here Jack has complied with his common law obligation to give a good title. He may, however, still be in breach of his obligations under the missives,[6] because missives usually state that the buyer will be registered as owner without exclusion of indemnity.[7]

Title conditions

6–04   Title conditions[8] such as servitudes and real burdens are a partial exception to the common law rule that a good title is a title that is not subject to third party rights.

Most properties are subject to title conditions of one kind or another. Thus, there may be real burdens regulating use and apportioning maintenance costs, or there may be servitudes. Purchasers (or at least their solicitors) know about these things. They are expected. In themselves they give no ground for complaint: a title subject to title conditions is in most cases still a good title.[9] This is common sense, for otherwise, as Lord Young observed:

---

[6] For the standard clause inserted in missives, see above.

[7] Though since the Register can be rectified so as to remove the exclusion of indemnity, it may be that the quantum of Jack's liability is zero.

[8] For title conditions generally, see Ch.13.

[9] *Urquhart v Halden* (1835) 13 S. 844; *Whyte v Lee* (1879) 6 R. 699; *Smith v Soeder* (1895) 23 R. 60; *McConnell v Chassels* (1903) 10 S.L.T. 790.

"[I]t would generally be impossible to make an effective sale of a house in town without a very minute and ponderous written contract specifying all restrictions and conditions, however usual, that applied to it. If a man simply buys a house he must be taken to buy it as the seller has it, on a good title, of course, but subject to such restrictions as may exist if of an ordinary character, and such as the buyer may reasonably be supposed to have contemplated as at least not improbable."[10]

As Lord Young indicates, however, not absolutely all title conditions are acceptable. Some may amount to a breach of the sellers' obligations to provide a good title. This is a difficult and uncertain area, both in theory and in practice. It is necessary to distinguish (1) the obligation implied by law; (2) the standard express obligation; and (3) special express obligations.

The implied obligation about title conditions

The obligation implied by law sets three criteria which must be met 6–05 before a condition of title can be objected to by the purchasers. These are: (i) that the condition must be unknown to the purchasers at the date of conclusion of missives; (ii) that it must be unusual or unduly onerous[11]; and (iii) that it must materially diminish the value of the property. In practice the second criterion is the most difficult to apply. A condition is unusual in the sense of criterion (ii) if it is unusual in relation to the type and location of the property in question. But how unusual does it have to be? The question is important because a wide interpretation would open up an all-too-convenient escape route from missives.

Unfortunately, the case law is insufficiently developed to provide a clear answer. The leading case is *Armia v Daejan Developments Ltd*,[12] in which a property in Kirkcaldy High Street bought for redevelopment was found to be subject to a wide servitude right of access affecting the frontage with the street. Although, as will be explained later, the case was actually decided on the basis of a special clause in the missives, the House of Lords indicated that even without such a clause the servitude would have constituted a breach of the seller's obligation to furnish a good title. But it is difficult to generalise from this. Would it have made any difference if the servitude had not prejudiced the redevelopment? Is the position for rural properties different? A servitude of way in itself is presumably not "unusual".[13] The test is whether it is "unusual" for a property of a particular type.

As for criterion (iii), burdens do commonly diminish the market value of a property. For example, lower flats in a tenement are usually burdened with a share in the upkeep of the roof, and this obviously

---

[10] *Whyte v Lee* (1879) 6 R. 699 at 701.

[11] "Unusual" and "unduly onerous" probably mean the same in this context. In *Umar v Murtaza*, 1983 S.L.T. (Sh. Ct.) 79 this criterion was overlooked.

[12] 1978 S.C. 152, reversed 1979 S.C. (HL) 56.

[13] *Morris v Ritchie*, 1991 G.W.D. 12–712; 1992 G.W.D. 33–1950.

means that their market value is less than it would be otherwise. But purchasers can object to a burden only if *all* three criteria are met. A burden of the type mentioned is not unusual, and so the purchasers must accept it, unless the missives provide otherwise. Likewise, a burden on a house forbidding commercial use is common and so cannot be objected to. More problematic is the situation where a burden is common in the particular locality but not elsewhere. Thus, in some urban areas burdens forbidding the sale of alcohol are common. Such a burden is usual for that area, but arguably unusual in the broader context. The law here seems unclear.

The standard express obligation about title conditions

6-06   It is normal practice for the obligation about unusual conditions to be made express in the offer. In GRS transactions the clause typically reads something like this: "There are no unusual, unduly onerous or restrictive conditions of title affecting the subjects." This differs from the implied obligation in making no mention of the state of the buyers' knowledge.[14] But while this opens up the argument that buyers could rescind even though they knew of the condition of title before entering missives, it is thought that the argument would not succeed. In Land Register transactions the recommended clause is: "There are no outstanding charges, no unduly onerous burdens, and no unusual or unduly onerous overriding interests which adversely affect the subjects of offer."[15]

In practice, it is common for the entire clause about burdens to be deleted by the sellers' solicitors in exchange for an opportunity to inspect the deeds. Provided that the selling solicitors have the titles to hand, this is usually the best practice. It avoids all dispute as to what is or is not unusual or unduly onerous. The purchasers are able to see what they are getting before becoming contractually committed to proceed. In particular, they can verify that the use they propose to make of the property is not excluded by the terms of the titles. In return the sellers have the reassurance of knowing that the purchasers will not start making difficulties on the eve of settlement on some merely technical point about the state of the burdens.

Special express obligations

6-07   The standard obligation, whether in its express or its implied form, may not always give the buyers sufficient protection. Consider the following example. Suppose that the purpose behind a particular purchase is to rent the property to students. And suppose further, which is not improbable, that the titles contain a real burden limiting the use of the subjects to occupation by "one family only". The purchasers have a problem. The standard obligation will probably not help them. The restriction is a fairly common one, and so is probably not "unusual". Consequently, the title is probably good and marketable. Unless the discovery is made before the conclusion of missives, the purchaser must

---

[14] *i.e.* criterion (i) above.
[15] ROTPB, para.7.37.

proceed. The lesson to be drawn here is, of course, simple. Where buyers intend to use the property other than simply to live in (or, in commercial properties, to work in), or where their purpose is otherwise esoteric, they should include a special clause in the missives to the effect that the proposed use is not excluded by the terms of the title.

This is what was done in the leading case of *Armia v Daejan Developments Ltd*,[16] though ironically litigation nevertheless ensued. The buyer, intending to redevelop the land, included the following clause in his offer: "There is nothing in the titles of the said subjects which will prevent demolition and redevelopment." It was held by the First Division that this clause replaced the obligation implied by law against unusual burdens, and that since the burden in question (the servitude) could not be said actually to *prevent* demolition and redevelopment, the purchaser must proceed with the purchase. This was a harsh and, with respect, implausible construction. Fortunately, it did not survive the appeal to the House of Lords, where it was decided that the special clause must be read as adding to and not as replacing the implied obligation. Further, the seller was found to be in breach of the special clause, giving the buyer the right to rescind. The interpretation adopted by the First Division was criticised as placing the buyer at a disadvantage in consequence of a clause which had clearly been intended to strengthen his position.[17]

Leases

It is not clear whether the existence of a lease, at least where the duration and rent are reasonable, prevents a title from being a good one.[18] In practice, therefore, both the missives and the disposition will normally stipulate for "actual occupation" or "vacant possession". In the disposition this is coupled with the clause of entry, which will typically read: "With entry and actual occupation (or 'vacant possession') as at the . . . day of . . . two thousand and . . ." If the buyers are acquiring leased property, typically as an investment, the missives and disposition will omit any reference to vacant possession, or actual occupation, and indeed will normally refer to the existing lease.

6–08

Pertinents

In some cases the full use of a property may require rights over neighbouring property, and in particular servitudes. Whether, in such cases, the absence of such rights would mean that the title was not a good and marketable one is uncertain, but probably they would not be regarded as prejudicing the title.[19] Hence where they are required they ought to be stipulated for in the missives.

6–9

---

[16] 1978 S.C. 152, reversed 1979 S.C. (HL) 56.

[17] The view that special clauses generally augment rather than replace the implied obligation has since been given effect to in *Umar v Murtaza*, 1983 S.L.T. (Sh. Ct.) 79.

[18] *Lothian and Borders Farmers Ltd v McCutchion*, 1952 S.L.T. 450 (which was decided on the warrandice clause in a disposition).

[19] It is to be noted that the law will often allow at least some form of access rights: *Bowers v Kennedy*, 2000 S.C. 555, discussed in para.13–27.

EVIDENCE OF GOOD TITLE

Sellers must produce evidence

6-10   It is not sufficient for the sellers to have a good title. They must also be in a position to demonstrate that fact to the buyers. If they cannot do so, then, even if their title is in fact good, they have failed in their obligation and the buyers need not proceed with the purchase.

What needs to be produced (Land Register properties)?

6-11   If the property is in the Land Register, the sellers can be expected to appear as proprietors in the land certificate. Assuming that there is no exclusion of indemnity, all that is required is that the certificate be updated through form 12 and 13 reports. If for some reason the sellers do not appear as proprietors it is necessary to produce writs (*e.g.* confirmation as executor) showing why the sellers have the right to deal with the property. Where, however, the Keeper's powers of rectification[20] are unrestricted—which will normally occur only if indemnity has been excluded—it will be necessary to go behind the land certificate in much the same way as if the title had not been registered.

Even without exclusion of indemnity the purchasers may in theory be vulnerable to judicial rectification of the deed on which the sellers' title is based,[21] and, depending on the outcome of any litigation currently before the court, may be vulnerable in certain other circumstances also.[22]

What needs to be produced (GRS properties)?

6-12   For properties that are still in the GRS—meaning that the current sale will trigger the switch into the Land Register—the rule is, in the words of Hume,[23] that the sellers must "furnish him [the buyer] with a sufficient progress of titles to the subject such a progress (for aught that can be seen) as shall maintain his right against all pretenders." The sellers' obligation ends with *prima facie* validity (Hume's "for aught that can be seen"). They need not prove that each individual writ actually is good and unchallengeable. That would be impossible. It is enough to produce writs that appear to be valid and it is then for the purchasers, if they can,

---

[20] Land Registration (Scotland) Act 1979, s.9.
[21] Law Reform (Miscellaneous Provisions) (Scotland) Act 1985, s.8. See Ch.17.
[22] *Short's Trs v Chung (No.2)*, 1998 S.C. 105, affirmed 1999 S.C. 471, in which the proprietor in possession was ordered to convey the property to the person challenging the title.
[23] *Lectures*, ii, 38.

to show that a particular writ is bad. This rule was settled by the leading case of *Sibbald's Heirs v Harris.*[24] There the purchaser refused to accept a prescriptive progress containing a decree of general service on the basis that such a decree was vulnerable to future reduction, for example by the emergence of a closer heir. But this objection was rejected by the court. A decree of special service was *prima facie* valid. It was no more vulnerable to reduction than any other writ. Unless, therefore, the buyer had concrete grounds for fearing reduction, and he had not, the title was one which he was bound to accept.

What writs must the sellers actually produce? They must produce a good prescriptive progress (including any midcouples), together with a GRS search. The length of the search will be as agreed in the missives. The obligation implied by law is that it must go back at least to the foundation writ. If, as is usually the case, the foundation writ is less than 40 years old, there is a view that the implied obligation entitles the purchaser to a search going back 40 years, this being on the basis of traditional conveyancing practice, but the point is unclear. The sellers must also produce all writs referred to for burdens and descriptions. But they need not produce writs affecting other properties, and the buyers who want evidence that, for example, roof burdens are fairly allocated in a tenement must probably stipulate for this, as in practice they invariably do. The deeds must actually be produced: it is not sufficient to invite the buyers to inspect them themselves on the register.[25] It is arguable, although undecided, that all deeds within the prescriptive progress must be probative.

Personal and company searches

With both registered and unregistered land it is necessary to produce 6–13 a search in the personal register and, where the sellers are a company, in the Companies Register also. In view of the strict rule about clear searches (see below) the sellers should take care that the list of persons to be searched against is not longer than is absolutely necessary. Searches are considered elsewhere.[26]

Occupancy rights

Though there is no authority, the general view is that if a property is 6–14 or may be affected by occupancy rights under the 1981 Act, then it is necessary, for the title to be good and marketable, for the sellers to produce the affidavits or consents or renunciations contemplated by that Act.

---

[24] 1947 S.C. 601. There is some tension between this decision and *Duke of Devonshire v Fletcher* (1874) 1 R. 1056 and *Bruce v Stewart* (1900) 2 F. 948. However, it is difficult to state a confident view on this question.

[25] *Sutherland v Garrity*, 1941 S.C. 196.

[26] See Ch.9.

Is the history of possession relevant?

6–15   For property in the Land Register, the history of possession is seldom of relevance, since title flows from the Register itself, not from prescriptive possession. However, if the title contains a restriction of indemnity, possession may become more important.

If the property is still in the GRS, then title rests on positive prescription. Positive prescription in turn presupposes possession for the requisite period, currently 10 years. Do the sellers have to offer to prove this? In practice, the answer is no, the purchasers taking the fact of possession on faith. This is generally safe enough. But take this case: Donald records in the GRS an *a non domino* disposition in 1994, and in 2005 offers to sell the land to Elaine. Donald can give a good title if, but only if, he has had 10 years of possession.

Disputes as to sufficiency of title

6–16   Inevitably, buyers and sellers do not always agree as to the sufficiency of the title offered, though such disagreements are more common for GRS titles than for Land Register ones. The reason is evident: if the Land Register shows the sellers to be registered as owners, without exclusion of indemnity, someone taking title from them will almost invariably acquire ownership without fear of challenge. However, even with properties in the Land Register there is still some scope for dispute. For instance, the sellers might not be registered, but be selling under a power of sale, for instance as judicial factors, or executors, or heritable creditors and so on. Or there may be a question as to whether the title the sellers have meets what the missives require. If the title is still in the GRS there is evidently even more scope for disagreement.

In the event of disagreement, there are various possibilities short of litigation. Thus, the parties may accept the opinion of a third party. This is quite common, and while occasionally done as a formal arbitration is more usually done informally. Or the sellers may be prepared to give, and the buyers to accept, a title insurance policy. Or again one of the parties may yield. But if both parties remain entrenched in their respective positions, litigation may be unavoidable. It may take a number of forms: for example, an action by the sellers to enforce the contract, or an action by the purchasers for declarator of entitlement to rescind, or a special case brought by both parties. But whatever form it takes the sellers are at a disadvantage. In order to succeed they must satisfy the court that the title tendered is good beyond "rational doubt";[27] and that high standard is not attained unless the only step asked of the court is to apply clearly settled law to the facts of the instant case.[28] If the law itself is in doubt the court will not normally resolve that doubt in an action between purchasers and sellers because the "proper contradictors" (*i.e.* the parties entitled to found on the alleged defect) are absent. Hence, the title will not be forced on reluctant buyers unless it is clearly a good

---

[27] *Brown v Cheyne* (1833) 12 S. 176 *per* Lord Meadowbank. See also *Dunlop v Crawford* (1849) 11 D. 1062.
[28] See *Lamb's Trs v Reid* (1883) 11 R. 76.

one. As Lord Deas put it in *Duke of Devonshire v Fletcher:*[29] "No purchaser is obliged to take the risk of law suits. If, as the sellers say, the adjudications[30] are nullities, they are such nullities as I should be sorry to have anything to do with."

It is always open to the sellers to avoid the difficulty of no "proper contradictors" by an action of declarator against the appropriate parties to have the alleged defect found ineffective. Precisely this had been done in the *Duke of Devonshire* case. But it was held that because the action of declarator had been undefended, there was the theoretical danger, however slight, that it might one day be reduced. Hence this case is authority that a title based on a decree in absence is unmarketable,[31] until the possibility of such a reduction has been removed by prescription, or, of course, by registration without exclusion of indemnity. There are a number of reasons for doubting the correctness of this view, and in practice decrees in absence are generally regarded as sufficient.

As has already been said, disputes about whether a title is good and marketable are rarer in Land Register cases, and the facts of *Duke of Devonshire* illustrate why. If those facts happened today, and if the sellers could have persuaded the Keeper that the adjudications were null, the Keeper would have deleted them from the title sheet, and the purchasers could have relied on that deletion. But the effect is often simply to shift the forum of the dispute, so that instead of being a dispute between the buyers and the sellers it becomes a dispute between the owner and the Keeper.

Title insurance

In practice, disputes are often settled by the sellers obtaining, at their 6–17 expense, a policy of title insurance, though purchasers cannot be compelled to accept this (unless the missives so provide). If the sellers are a major corporation of undoubted financial standing a policy is arguably pointless. The sellers are usually bound in absolute warrandice in any event, and the danger that the major corporation would not be able to pay up on a warrandice claim is as small, or perhaps smaller, than the danger that the title insurance company would be unable to pay up on a title policy.

Where a policy is obtained, a one-off premium is paid. The premium is calculated according to the value of the property, the risk involved, and so forth. The cover should last until the problem will have been removed by prescription. The amount of the cover should not be the present value of the property but its expected maximum value during the cover period. Thus, if a house is bought for £300,000, and seven years later the owners are evicted due to a defect in the title, their loss will probably be more than that sum, because the house will probably be

---

[29] (1874) 1 R. 1056.
[30] Which were the defects in title that the purchaser was objecting to.
[31] *Bruce v Stewart* (1900) 2 F. 948 is to the same effect.

worth more at that stage. There is obviously no way of predicting the future value. But a commonly used method is to calculate the future value on the assumption that the movement of property prices in recent years will continue into the future. If a percentage figure is used that must be projected into the future on a compound basis.

Title insurance policies are less likely to be needed for property in the Land Register. The need may arise, however, where there is an exclusion of indemnity. Suppose that Shona buys 50 hectares from Tom. The Keeper issues a land certificate, but in respect of half a hectare indemnity is excluded. Title insurance may be advisable for the half hectare until the exclusion of indemnity is deleted, after 10 years' possession. Whether it is Tom or Shona who pays the premium depends on the circumstances. If the missives are unqualified, Tom will be in breach of his obligations, and the quantum of loss to Shona is the cost of a policy, so Tom will have to reimburse her for this. If the problem comes to light before missives, then it is a matter for negotiation. In general, if the price is a full price, Tom should pay, but if the price reflects the title problem, Tom should not pay, since effectively he is already paying through the lower price.

CLEAR SEARCH

General

6-18   "Search" is the traditional term though, strictly, it is not used for the Land Register, where the official term is "report". On a first registration the seller will produce form 10/11 reports, and on a subsequent sale form 12/13 reports. In form 10/11 reports, the search is in the Personal Register and the GRS, plus a search of the Land Register to check that the property has not in fact already been registered there. In form 12/13 reports, the search is in the Personal Register and the Land Register. Where a company has been involved it will also be necessary to produce a search in the Companies Register. In the old GRS system there was an interim report followed by a final search. In the Land Register the form 10/11 or form 12/13 corresponds to the interim report and the land certificate itself has the function of the final search (and of course a broader function as well).

Missives used typically to provide for "clear searches". The usual provision now is that the form 10/11 or form 12/13 reports will "show no entries adverse to the seller's interest" and that the land certificate will "disclose no entry deed or diligence prejudicial to the purchaser's interest other than such as are created by or against the purchaser."[32] As far as the second provision (about the land certificate) is concerned the change is one of wording rather than of substance. But the modern provision that the interim report (*i.e.* the form 10/11 or form 12/13 reports) will be clear may be an innovation.

---

[32] See ROTPB, paras 8.9 and 8.37.

The obligation to demonstrate a good title includes an obligation to produce a search: that the search so produced be clear is, however, a separate and distinct obligation. It is probably implied by law, but in any event it is always expressly stipulated for, both in missives and also in the letter of obligation subsequently granted by the selling solicitors. The obligation is, of course, closely related to the wider obligation to demonstrate a good title. Usually an unclear search indicates a bad title and the former obligation becomes subsumed in the latter. But it can occasionally happen that a title is good when the search is not clear. For example, a search may disclose a standard security for a fixed sum of £40,000, which has, in fact been repaid, though no formal discharge has been registered. Since there is no debt the security is implicitly discharged. So the title is good. But nonetheless the search is not clear as it discloses an apparently undischarged security. It is only in odd cases of this kind that the separate obligation to provide a clear search is of importance. In other words, a title may be good, but the search not clear, if the title looks bad from what appears in the public registers, but is in truth good because of off-register facts.

When is a search clear?

The question of whether a search is clear arises less often as a result of 6–19 registration of title. The reason is that if the Keeper thinks that something does not affect a title he has the ability simply to omit it from the land certificate.[33] Nevertheless the basic issues remain the same.

According to Burns's *Conveyancing Practice*[34] "[if] deeds or diligences appear on record[35] the search is not clear till they are disposed of, though it is doubtful whether they really affect the purchaser's title, or even, it may be, though the contrary is true in law." The final few words of Burns's definition rest on certain remarks in *Dryburgh v Gordon*.[36] In *Dryburgh* the search disclosed two inhibitions predating the sale. Such inhibitions would in the normal course of events strike at the sale, but the seller's agents, whose letter of obligation was the subject of the action, argued that their client's title (a reversionary right under an *ex facie* absolute disposition) was in its nature incapable of being affected by these inhibitions. It was held that the search was not clear. Whatever the merits of the case against the inhibitions, on which the court expressed no decided view, there was an apparent encumbrance on the face of the search which the buyer was entitled to have discharged.

It is suggested that this case is less far-reaching than Burns seems to have feared. The point about the inhibitions in *Dryburgh* is that no one could say for certain whether or not they affected the sale, in the absence

---

[33] For instance, suppose a seller is inhibited after missives but before settlement. In such a case the Keeper will, if satisfied of the facts, issue an unqualified land certificate: ROTPB, para.6.19. In the equivalent situation in old GRS conveyancing the search was not clear.

[34] (4th ed.), p.303.

[35] That is, in a public register.

[36] (1896) 24 R. 1.

of litigation involving the inhibitors themselves. The issue was not, or at any rate was not perceived to be, one of settled law.[37] In short, the title was not good and marketable, and the remarks of the court must be read against this background. The rule, therefore, is not, as Burns appears to contemplate, that any apparent encumbrance prevents a search from being clear. The facts are subject to the law. And where the encumbrance is one which, as a matter of settled law, could not possibly affect the sale, the search is clear.[38] A search is only not clear, therefore, where either the title is actually affected by the encumbrance or where, as in *Dryburgh,* the law, or the application of the law, is in doubt.

This view appears to be confirmed by *Newcastle Building Society v White,*[39] seemingly the only reported case on the point since *Dryburgh.* There, security subjects were sold by a heritable creditor on the default of the debtor. The interim report on the search disclosed an inhibition against the debtor which postdated the granting of the standard security in favour of the creditor. A dispute arose as to whether the search was clear. It was held that it was. In terms of section 26(1) of the 1970 Act the recording of a disposition in such circumstances disburdened the security subjects of all diligences ranking *pari passu* with or postponed to the security. "Accordingly merely by applying the law any future purchaser can establish *ex facie* of the records and without reference to extrinsic material that the inhibition no longer has any relevance to the property."[40]

In evaluating the form 10/11 reports, the form 12/13 reports and the land certificate (or the interim and final searches in an old GRS transaction) it is therefore necessary to apply the relevant law to the relevant facts. But while the only limitation as to the law is that it should be certain, there is an important limitation as to the facts to which that law may be applied. Were this not so, the obligation to deliver a clear search would collapse into the more general obligation to demonstrate a good title. The limitation, in the words already quoted of the Sheriff Principal in *Newcastle Building Society v White,* is that the facts must be "*ex facie* of the records". Off-register information is irrelevant—not irrelevant in a broader sense, but irrelevant for present purposes. This rule, which is now well established, seems first to have been laid down in *Cargill v Craigie.*[41] The search in that case disclosed three inhibitions against the seller. These had in fact been discharged, but the discharges had not been registered. Thus, the title was good, but the buyer was held entitled by the House of Lords (reversing the Court of Session) to have the record cleared.[42]

The rule against extrinsic material must be set in the broader context of the need for such evidence of title as will satisfy buyers without at the

---

[37] In fact, the inhibitions probably did strike at the sale: Gretton, *The Law of Inhibition and Adjudication* (2nd ed., 1996), p.190.

[38] *Cameron v Williamson* (1895) 22 R. 293.

[39] 1987 S.L.T. (Sh. Ct.) 81.

[40] At p.85. In fact, at common law also the inhibition could not strike at the sale.

[41] (1822) 1 Shaw App. 134.

[42] In such cases, where the title is good, but appears from the searches not to be good, the title is sometimes said to be "good" but not "marketable". But this distinction between good and marketable is not universally adopted. The point is purely semantic.

same time placing an unfair burden on sellers. For the most part the rule seems to draw the line in the right place. Thus, it is not unreasonable that buyers faced with an apparent standard security or, as in *Cargill v Craigie,* with an apparent inhibition, should be entitled to more than informal evidence that the debt to which they relate has been repaid. If the debt really has been repaid the sellers can readily enough obtain and register a discharge. It seems just that they should be made to do so.

CHAPTER 7

EXAMINATION OF TITLE

INTRODUCTORY

Introduction

7–01   This chapter deals with examination of title, both for property in the Land Register and for property still in the GRS.[1] The latter is more complex, and so more space is devoted to it. A complete account of examination of title is impossible, since examination of title potentially involves the whole of property law and conveyancing. In this chapter it is assumed that title is being examined by solicitors for a buyer, but the same principles will in general apply in relation to a heritable creditor.

Procedure

7–02   A report on title must be sent to the clients. This will include a copy of the plan, a statement of any relevant pertinents (such as servitudes in favour of the property), title conditions to which the property is subject, information in the PECs and anything else of relevance. The clients should be asked for any comments, and in particular should be asked to confirm that the plan correctly shows what they think they are buying. But it needs to be borne in mind that the clients will perhaps only have visited the property a couple of times, for a total of perhaps an hour, and they may be fuzzy about the boundaries. The plan will in most cases use colour, and in that case the clients must receive a coloured plan. If the office photocopier is monochrome that means hand-colouring.

Once examination of title is complete the deeds are returned to the sellers' solicitors, with the disposition drafted by the purchasers' solicitors, and with any observations arising out of the examination. A photocopy of the land certificate, or of the key deeds if the title is still in the GRS, should be retained on file.

Tenement titles

7–03   Tenement titles pose special difficulties, and these difficulties can exist not only for GRS titles but also for titles in the Land Register. The title may be unclear as to which parts of the building are included, and as to

---

[1] On examination of title see further Halliday, Ch.36; J.H. Sinclair, *Handbook of Conveyancing Practice in Scotland* (4th ed., 2002), Chs 7 and 8; David A. Brand, Andrew J.M. Steven and Scott Wortley, *Professor McDonald's Conveyancing Manual* (7th ed., 2004), Ch.32.

the rights to the attached ground. It occasionally happens that title is taken to the first floor south when the clients think they are buying the first floor north.[2] Compass directions sometimes turn out to be approximate only, and there is sometimes confusion as to the floors. Take, for instance, a tenement with a half-sunk basement. Is that the "first" floor? Or perhaps the floor above is the first floor? Or perhaps the latter is the "ground" floor so that the third[3] storey is the "first"?

Feudalism

Feudal law was gradually sliced away by legislation stretching over many centuries. What remained was abolished by the Abolition of Feudal Tenure etc. (Scotland) Act 2000 (with effect from November 28, 2004).[4] No account of the subject will be given here. But although feudalism is abolished, conveyancers will need to know something of it for many years to come, since references to feudal writs (notably feu dispositions, feu charters, feu contracts, charters of novodamus and blench dispositions) litter existing titles.[5] 7-04

What is being looked for?

In examining a title the purchasers' solicitors seek the answers to the following (not exhaustive) list of questions: (a) Do the sellers have power to convey the property? (b) What are the title conditions and are they acceptable? (c) Are there any securities?[6] (d) Are the searches clear? (e) Are there any occupancy rights under the 1981 Act? (f) Have the necessary planning and building consents been obtained? This chapter deals with the first three questions.[7] 7-05

LAND REGISTER TITLES[8]

The land certificate

Whereas GRS titles depend on a mass of recorded deeds, to be read in the light of the complex statutory and common law rules, and with positive prescription playing a large role, where the title is in the Land 7-06

---

[2] In such cases the sellers will also typically have been under the same error, and possess the "wrong" flat which the buyers then blithely move into. It will be found that the descriptions were muddled up when the individual flats were first sold off.

[3] This word begs the question, of course.

[4] Implementing Scottish Law Commission, *Report on Abolition of the Feudal System* (Scot. Law Com. No.168, 1999). For a detailed account of the legislation, see K. G. C. Reid, *The Abolition of Feudal Tenure in Scotland* (2003).

[5] There are many sources on feudal tenure. See *e.g.* Reid, *Property*, paras 41–113; Gordon, Ch.2; K. G. C. Reid, *The Abolition of Feudal Tenure in Scotland* (2003), Ch.1. See also Ch.23 of the 2nd edition of the present book.

[6] Until recently it was also important to check whether the feuduty had been redeemed, but all remaining feuduty has now disappeared as a result of the 2000 Act, s.7. Any compensatory payment due under the Act but still unpaid is a personal debt of the person who was owner on November 28, 2004 (the day on which the feudal system was abolished), and does not transmit to purchasers: see s.8.

[7] For the others, see Chs 9, 10 and 4 respectively.

[8] For the Land Register more generally, see paras 8–08 *et seq.*

Register, there is a land certificate and little else. The role of prescription is slight.[9] Reading the certificate takes a matter of minutes. At a glance it is possible to see the boundaries of the property, the name of the current owner, and the securities and real burdens which affect the property. Further, there is little in the way of evaluation to be done. Most of the information in the land certificate is correct as a matter of law—even in the rare cases where it should not have been entered in the first place.[10] The rule is that title flows from the Register and not from the deed which gave rise to the entry. So if the land certificate shows the sellers as owners of the property, then they are indeed the owners, and the purchasers' solicitors need look no further. Naturally, the land certificate will be examined in conjunction with the form 12 and 13 reports which bring it up to date. Although land certificates enable the title to be reviewed quickly and with confidence, they are not necessarily perfect. Indeed, errors or obscurities of one sort or another are unfortunately quite common. Many are trivial, but not all. For example whilst the Land Register is map-based, there is also a verbal description, and in some titles the verbal description is obscure.

Do the sellers have power to convey the property?

7-07   *Nemo plus juris ad alium transferre potest quam ipse haberet.*[11] Buyers will receive a good title only if the sellers (or consenters, if any) own the property, and are not limited in their power of disposition by some factor such as sequestration, inhibition or mental incapacity. Alternatively, buyers will receive a good title if the sellers, though not themselves the owners, have power of sale. So the first task is to check the sellers' title, including, of course, the boundaries. In a land certificate the boundaries are usually defined with a fairly high degree of precision. The main exception is tenemental property. Here the land certificate will show the footprint of the building and will show the ground attached, but it may not indicate with precision what parts of the building are included in the title, and there may be imprecision as to what rights exist in the ground attached. But whether the land certificate is precise or not, it should be borne in mind that the task is not only to determine what the sellers own, but also to determine whether that corresponds with what the buyers think they are buying. In this connection it must be borne in mind that the missives will seldom be plan-based so that there may be a question of interpreting them. A copy of the land certificate must be sent to the clients as soon as possible with a request for comments. Since the land certificate uses colour, the photocopy sent to the clients should be coloured too.

---

[9] The 1979 Act's approach to prescription seems excessively narrow: see David Johnston, *Prescription and Limitation* (1999), para.15.63 and Scottish Law Commission, *Discussion Paper on Land Registration: Void and Voidable Titles* (Scot. Law Com. D.P. No.125, 2004), para.3.4.

[10] 1979 Act, s.3(1). This of course assumes that the land certificate is an accurate copy of the title sheet.

[11] Or, in a briefer version, *nemo dat quod non habet*: no one can transfer greater rights to another than he has himself.

In the normal case one is checking that the sellers are the owners. In the Land Register that is straightforward. On occasion the sellers may not be the registered owners but may nevertheless have a valid power of sale. For example, the seller might be a judicial factor, or an executor, or a heritable creditor enforcing a security, or a trustee in sequestration. In all such cases it will be necessary to check that the seller does indeed have power to convey.

What are the title conditions and are they acceptable?

Title conditions (real burdens and servitudes) are considered in a 7–08 separate chapter[12] and only a few remarks will be made here, beginning with real burdens. Almost all property is subject to real burdens of one kind or another. Old burdens writs, although often long and sometimes irrelevant, have usually been transcribed faithfully into the D (burdens) section of the title sheet. The purchasers' solicitors must wade through them in case something important to the clients is lurking there.

The clients are going to have to live with such burdens as have continuing force.[13] So they need to be told what they are. If possible this should be done before conclusion of missives, so that if the burdens are unacceptable the remedy is simply not to conclude missives. If that is not possible the clients must at all events be told what the burdens are before settlement. If missives are concluded without the land certificate having been exhibited, the missives will typically stipulate that the burdens shall not be "unusual or unduly onerous", an expression the meaning of which is discussed in the previous chapter. Most burdens are neither. If the buyers want to develop the property it is therefore particularly risky to conclude missives without having seen the land certificate. One possible approach in that case is for the buyers to insert in the missives a provision that, for instance, "there is nothing in the title of the property which will prevent demolition and redevelopment".[14]

Whilst a real burden, to be valid, must enter the Register, there is no corresponding rule that all burdens on the Register are valid. A burden which has been properly registered might still fail because of the nature of its terms, or because it is too vague, or because there is no one with title and interest to enforce. In fact a significant number of burdens which appear on land certificates—how many is hard to say—are invalid and unenforceable.[15] Here the solicitors' skill continues to be necessary. A real burden which can be shown to be invalid can be removed by an application for rectification,[16] while valid burdens must be evaluated, in the usual way, against the sellers' obligation to produce a good title.[17]

---

[12] Ch.13.

[13] Typically these control either maintenance or use. Many burdens, particularly in older deeds, impose one-off obligations (*e.g.* to build a house) and can be disregarded.

[14] These words are from the missives in *Armia Ltd v Daejan Developments Ltd*, 1979 S.C. (HL) 56.

[15] See para.13–17. It is for this reason that no indemnity is payable for loss arising from inability to enforce a real burden, unless (which seems unknown) the Keeper expressly assumes responsibility for its enforceability. See 1979 Act, s.12(3)(g).

[16] *Brookfield Developments Ltd v Keeper of the Registers of Scotland*, 1989 S.L.T. (Lands Tr.) 105.

[17] Usually the sellers warrant in the missives that there are no unusual or unduly onerous burdens. See para.6–06.

For servitudes burdening the property, much the same considerations apply as for continuing real burdens. But there are certain differences. Servitudes, unlike real burdens, can be constituted by prescription and also by implication. If created by grant before the 2003 Act, they need not be registered (though in practice they usually are). Hence, it may be that the purchasers' solicitors cannot discover their existence. Servitudes created in writing after the 2003 Act must be registered against both the dominant and servient properties.[18]

Two other points may conveniently be mentioned here, even though they do not involve real burdens or servitudes. The first is that the land certificate should contain a statement, in the proprietorship section, that there are no subsisting occupancy rights in terms of the 1981 Act.[19] If this statement is absent, it will be necessary to make inquiries about possible occupancy rights.[20] The second is that the land certificate should show any entry in the personal register which is adverse to the title. Thus if the sellers have been inhibited, the inhibition will be mentioned.[21]

Are there any securities?

7-09   Heritable securities, as subordinate real rights, are unaffected by a change of ownership of the encumbered land. So if a security affects the property in the hands of the sellers it will continue to affect the property in the hands of the buyers, unless it has been discharged. It is an implied term of the contract of sale that the title will not be encumbered by any security. This term can be changed by agreement, but that is rare in practice. It is thus the duty of the buyers' solicitors to ensure that all securities have been or will be discharged.

If the seller is a company (or a limited liability partnership) there may be a floating charge, but since a floating charge is not, until crystallisation ("attachment"), a real right it will not run with the property and no discharge is necessary, though it is normal to require a certificate of non-crystallisation from the chargeholder.[22] This is the case where title is being examined on behalf of a buyer. But if it is being examined on behalf of a lender the position is different, for in that case the floating charge will be unaffected. Floating charges will not be discovered from the land certificate, or form 12/13 reports, but from a search of the Companies Register.

Other documentation

7-10   The information on the land certificate is correct only at its date, which, typically, is the date on which the sellers acquired.[23] In order to find out what, if anything, has happened since it is necessary to see a

---

[18] Title Conditions (Scotland) Act 2003, s.75, but subject to the qualifications in s.75(3).
[19] Land Registration (Scotland) Rules 1980, r.5(j).
[20] See Ch.10.
[21] 1979 Act, s.6(1)(c). For some of the difficulties with this provision, see G. L. Gretton, *The Law of Inhibition and Adjudication* (2nd ed., 1996), pp.39–43; Scottish Law Commission, *Discussion Paper on Diligence against Land* (Scot. Law Com. D.P. No.107, 1998), paras 3.97–3.111.
[22] See Ch.25.
[23] However, a procedure exists for updating the land certificate at any time. See Land Registration (Scotland) Rules 1980, r.24 and form 8.

form 12 report, updating the land certificate. The report also includes a search in the personal register against anyone listed in the initial form 12 application, typically the sellers and the purchasers. If necessary, the form 12 report can itself be updated by a form 13 report.[24]

Not everything will appear on the land certificate. The property may be affected by overriding interests, which is to say rights affecting the property even though not appearing on the Register. Some overriding interests will in fact appear if the Keeper knows about them, servitudes being one example, but others, such as short leases, cannot appear on the land certificate. And the purchasers will still require to pay attention to matters such as planning permission and building consents, in the usual way.[25]

Looking behind the land certificate

A difficult question is whether it is ever necessary to go behind the 7–11 land certificate and examine the deed or deeds which led to the sellers being entered as owners.[26] The orthodox view is that this is unnecessary, unless indemnity has been excluded. Exclusion of indemnity not only indicates that the Keeper is unhappy with the title, but also makes rectification relatively easy in the event of a future challenge. This is the only case in Land Register titles where positive prescription is allowed to run.[27] In effect, the title can be treated almost like a GRS one. Since in such cases the Register can readily be rectified it is necessary to examine the underlying deeds; and since prescription runs, the examination should encompass the normal prescriptive period.[28]

Whilst this orthodox view is generally correct, case law shows that certain exceptions may exist.[29] In *Kaur v Singh*[30] the defender became registered owner on the basis of a disposition purportedly granted by the pursuer and her husband. The pursuer, alleging that her signature had been forged, sought reduction of the disposition and rectification of the Register. As matters initially stood it was plain that the pursuer could not succeed. For even if the disposition were reduced, the Register could not be rectified to the prejudice of the defender, who was a proprietor in possession and who had not been fraudulent or careless. (Since the alleged defect in the disposition was latent, there had of course been no exclusion of indemnity.) The pursuer responded by forcing the door, changing the locks and resuming possession. The defender, stripped of his possession, could no longer resist rectification. So he responded in kind and resumed possession in turn. These events suggest shortcomings

---

[24] See generally on forms 12 and 13 reports, ROTPB, Ch.3.

[25] See Ch.4.

[26] The principle that one should not have to go behind the Register is sometimes referred to as the "curtain principle".

[27] 1973 Act, s.1(1).

[28] For examination of title by reference to positive prescription, see paras 7–18 *et seq.*

[29] For a discussion, see Steven, 1999 S.L.T. (News) 163. The Scottish Law Commission has since made a number of proposals aimed at restoring the curtain principle: see *Discussion Paper on Land Registration: Void and Voidable Titles* (Scot. Law Com. D.P. No.125, 2004; available on *www.scotlawcom.gov.uk*), especially Part 4.

[30] 1999 S.C. 180.

in the legislation.[31] Protection depends on possession, but possession is easily lost. Purchasers who lose possession face the prospect of rectification on the basis of any defects contained in the underlying deeds.

Another case illustrating the limits of the orthodox view is *Short's Trustee v Chung (No.2)*.[32] This was the last in a protracted series of litigations arising out of a gratuitous alienation by Mr Short in 1986. Short's trustee in sequestration reduced the offending disposition[33] but could not rectify the Register because Mrs Chung was a proprietor in possession.[34] So instead he sought a fresh court order ordaining Mrs Chung to grant a disposition in his favour. Such a disposition could enter the Land Register by registration, thus circumventing the rules that make rectification so difficult. The trustee was successful.

A *non domino* conveyances

7-12   A *non domino* conveyances,[35] important under the GRS system, continue to play a role in registration of title.[36] Suppose that there is a conveyance from Adam to Beth, and Beth applies for registration, but the Keeper considers that Adam had no right to grant the deed. The Keeper then has two choices. The first is to reject the application.[37] The second is to accept it, but with exclusion of indemnity.[38] If the second course is adopted, Beth is now the owner, but the effect of exclusion of indemnity is that if Caroline (the rightful owner)[39] turns up within 10 years and objects, Beth's name can be deleted,[40] and she will have no claim for compensation.

In certain cases it is the Keeper's practice to enter both names on the title sheet, *i.e.* both Beth's and Caroline's.[41] If the latter applies for

---

[31] A cynic might add, unkindly, that it seems to revive the priority system of the Stone Age, though perhaps that is unfair to our ancestors. For another case where matters degenerated into an unseemly struggle for possession, this time benefiting local divers rather than locksmiths, see *Safeway Stores plc v Tesco Stores Ltd*, 2004 S.C. 29. For discussion, see Reid and Gretton, *Conveyancing 2003*, pp.91–6.

[32] 1998 S.C. 105 affirmed 1999 S.C. 471. For an overall account of this saga see Reid and Gretton, *Conveyancing 1999*, pp.69–71.

[33] *Short's Tr v Chung*, 1991 S.L.T. 472 affirmed 1991 S.L.T. 751.

[34] We should be relieved that he did not try to deprive her of possession. An earlier attempt to register the extract decree of reduction had failed: see *Short's Tr v Keeper of the Registers of Scotland*, 1996 S.C. (HL) 14.

[35] *i.e.* a conveyance by a person who does not own the property in question.

[36] ROTPB, para.6.4. For *a non domino* conveyances in the GRS system, see para.7–25.

[37] As he is entitled to do under s.4(1) of the 1979 Act.

[38] In certain exceptional cases, the Keeper may choose not to exclude indemnity.

[39] She will not be the actual owner, who at this stage is Beth. Rather, she is the person entitled to ownership.

[40] In other words, the Register can be rectified under s.9(3)(a)(iv) of the 1979 Act.

[41] For example, in *B. G. Hamilton v Ready Mixed Concrete (Scotland) Ltd*, 1999 S.L.T. 524 one party was registered as owner in 1985 and then another party was registered in 1990 in pursuance of an *a non domino* disposition. The latter received a land certificate with the following exclusion on it: "Indemnity is excluded in terms of s.12(2) of the Land Registration (Scotland) Act 1979 in respect (1) that a Disposition to the Proprietors in Entry 1, of *inter alia* the subjects in this Title was registered on Jan. 19, 1985 and ranks prior to the Disposition to the Proprietors in Entry 2, registered 26 Nov. 1990 on which their entitlement was founded and also (2) that no evidence of Title prior to said Disposition to the Proprietors in Entry 2 has been produced to the Keeper".

rectification, Beth's name is deleted. Otherwise, after 10 years' prescriptive possession Beth can apply for Caroline's name to be deleted. It is, however, open to serious question whether this double entry, whereby two persons can be simultaneously on the register as owners (other than co-owners or joint owners), is a competent procedure.[42] There is nothing in the legislation which warrants an entry of this sort. Indeed, to the contrary, it is suggested that the legislation actually excludes any such possibility. Section 3 of the 1979 Act roundly declares that registration vests the interest (here, ownership) in the person registered; and it is simply not possible for two different persons both to be owners at one and the same time.[43] The word "rank" which the Keeper uses[44] betrays the truth. For ranking is possible only between compatible rights. For instance, two standard securities have a mutual ranking, precisely because one property can be subject to two standard securities. But two ownerships cannot rank with each other. If one ownership is superior to the other, the other is not merely postponed: it is null. The same problem arises when there is a boundary problem and the Keeper decides to register both parties as owners of the disputed area.[45]

GRS TITLES[46]

Introduction

The General Register of Sasines (GRS) dates from 1617 and is in the   7–13
process of being replaced by a new property register, the Land Register. The transition, however, is a gradual one so that for many years to come both registers will remain in operation. A title which is in the Land Register consists, usually, of a single document, the land certificate. Examination of Land Register titles is thus usually a relatively straightforward task. A GRS title, by contrast, comprises a bundle of deeds, often numerous and usually uninviting. Reading and evaluating such a title is difficult.

If the property is still in the GRS, a sale will trigger a change of registers.[47] The current transaction, in other words, will be a "first registration" in the Land Register. Thus the examination of title in a transaction where the property is in the GRS and will stay in the GRS seldom happens. Examples are gratuitous transfers, either by way of donation or by way of succession. Since one does not look a gift horse in the mouth, in such cases examination of title may be cursory or non-existent. However, there is still one major type of case where property may stay in the GRS (for the time being) and where examination of title is important. That is where a standard security is being granted.

From the point of view of examination of title there is little difference between (a) the case where the property is in the GRS and will remain

---

[42] See Reid, 1991 J.R. 79.
[43] Other than as co-owners.
[44] See above.
[45] For an example see *Safeway Stores plc v Tesco Stores Ltd*, 2004 S.C. 29. See Reid and Gretton, *Conveyancing 2003*, pp.95–96.
[46] For the GRS more generally, see paras 8–23 *et seq.*
[47] 1979 Act s.2(1)(a)(ii).

there (for the time being) and (b) the case of first registration in the
Land Register. In both cases what is being examined is a GRS title. But
on a first registration there is the stimulus of knowing that the title will
be immediately re-examined by the Keeper, and that if the Keeper is not
satisfied he is entitled either to refuse registration, or to allow registration only on the basis of exclusion of indemnity.[48]

Which deeds?

7-14   A GRS title comprises an unappetising bundle of deeds, many of
which are likely to be irrelevant. Conveyancers traditionally never throw
anything away. The size of the bundle depends on the length of time the
property has existed as a separate entity. A late eighteenth-century villa
will have a large number of titles. A recently-built house will have few,
and it may be necessary to borrow the prior titles (which will deal with
the whole development from which the house has been split off) from
the builders' solicitors. It is rash to assume that the buyers' solicitors will
be given all the titles that they need. What they need, and what therefore
they are entitled to receive,[49] are the following. (a) A prescriptive
progress of titles, *i.e.* the foundation writ for the purposes of positive
prescription, plus all subsequent conveyances. (b) All security deeds and
discharges of security deeds of the recent past—in practice 40 years is
usually regarded as sufficient and people sometimes make do with less.
(c) All deeds which impose real burdens and servitudes. (d) The
principal deed, or deeds, describing the property, if not already included
under (a) or (c) above. (Usually they are included.) (e) Searches in the
GRS, the Register of Inhibitions and Adjudications, and, where applicable, the Companies Register. In the case of a first registration, these
are supplemented by a form 10 report. Searches are considered further
in Chapter 9. (f) Miscellaneous other documents, most notably documentation under the 1981 Act. In first registrations there is usually a
form P16 report, indicating whether the boundaries in the title coincide
with those on the ordnance survey.[50]

If any of the above items are missing the buyers' solicitors should ask
for them. For deeds within the prescriptive progress the sellers should
produce either the originals or extracts (the validity of which is guaranteed by the 1970 Act, s. 45). Quick copies (*i.e.* ordinary photocopies) are
acceptable for burdens writs. To what extent sellers are bound at
common law to deliver the deeds (principals or extracts) and to what
extent they are bound merely to exhibit them, is not wholly clear. In the
absence of special agreement, the matter is now regulated by statute,
obliging the sellers to deliver all deeds and searches relating exclusively
to the land conveyed.[51]

---

[48] 1979 Act, ss.4(1) and 12(2). Both are rare, especially the former.
[49] As part of the obligation for good and marketable title, for which see Ch.6
[50] ROTPB, Ch.4.
[51] 1979 Act, s.16(1)(a)(i). The word "all" here is odd. Why should some trivial deed, 50
or 150 years old, perhaps long since lost, have to be delivered?

How exacting?

The buyers' solicitors must examine the title carefully. This is one of 7–15 the main things they are being paid for. It is obviously better to discover a title defect before, rather than after, settlement. The buyers can refuse to settle (or conclude missives), as opposed to trying later to pursue the sellers for damages. In practice, most GRS titles contain something or other which is not quite perfect. How exacting should the buyers' solicitors be? Three types of defect may be distinguished. There is the obviously trivial, for instance an alteration of an inessential word in one of the deeds which has not been declared in the testing clause. Such defects can be ignored. Next there is the obviously fatal defect. For instance, one of the deeds has not been signed, or the seller turns out just to have been sequestrated. In that case the title must be rejected. Third, there is the intermediate defect. Many defects are sufficient to put the sellers in breach of their obligation to produce a good title, without being particularly serious. They are technical defects only. Something has not been done completely correctly. The title may be satisfactory, but it is impossible to be absolutely sure. In other words, there is "rational doubt".[52] Usually there is no real danger of the defect coming home to roost. Even if there is some third party out there who might, in theory, be able to found on the apparent defect, this will almost certainly never happen in practice. The buyers' solicitors know that. So do the sellers' solicitors. Nonetheless, the buyers' solicitors may well object to the title and insist on remedial measures. Traditionally the main reason for this was that they were worried that when their clients came to resell the property, the solicitors acting for the then buyers would be less accommodating, with the result that the sale would fall through. Nowadays the worry is more likely to be that the Keeper may take a strict line and exclude indemnity from the title (which would itself make the title unmarketable). And in either case since there has been no judicial eviction there will then be no remedy against the original sellers under the warrandice clause in the disposition. So the buyers' solicitors will be reluctant to take any risk. Risk-averseness is understandable but it does not make for speedy (or harmonious) conveyancing.

Examination of title is a skilled task. Possible defects can arise in many different, and unexpected, ways and it is impossible to examine title properly without a good working knowledge of the whole of conveyancing law. It is important not only to spot defects but to classify them properly. Minor errors should not be confused with more serious ones. The most irritating person to do business with is the smart Alec who reads conveyancing books (such as this one) on the bus on the way to work and who sees it as his duty to give free conveyancing lessons to the solicitor acting for the other party. If a defect is trivial, it should be ignored. There is no need to point it out to the other side. That merely wastes time, a point all the more worth remembering today when conveyancing fees have become so unremunerative. The conveyancer must know when to speak up and when to shut up.

---

[52] The phrase of Lord Meadowbank in *Brown v Cheyne* (1833) 12 S. 176. See para.6–16.

Notes on title

7-16   In examining a GRS title, the buyers' solicitors traditionally made an elaborate summary of the various deeds. This summary was called notes on title.[53] Such notes had two main purposes. In the first place, before photocopiers came into use, the notes would provide a substitute for the deeds themselves, which might well leave the law office quickly, for instance to go to secured lenders. The law firm could thus answer questions about the title without having to call up the deeds. In the second place the making of the notes was a useful discipline, whereby the conveyancer forced him/herself to check everything systematically. Any points arising that needed to be pursued—for instance deeds not seen—would be marked prominently, for instance in red ink. In recent years notes on title have tended to become less elaborate, and if the title is in the Land Register the buying solicitor is unlikely to write anything that a traditional solicitor would recognise as notes on title.

Do the sellers have power to convey the property?

7-17   The basic issues here are the same as for a property in the Land Register but the way of establishing the seller's right is very different. Suppose that the client, Ian, is buying a house from Harriet. Ian will receive a good title only if (i) Harriet is the owner (or has power to convey as, for instance, executor or judicial factor or heritable creditor etc.) and (ii) the disposition by Harriet to Ian is valid (*i.e.* properly executed and so on). Point (ii) is easily checked. But what of point (i), namely, whether Harriet was owner, or at least had power to convey? The answer is: as for Ian, so for Harriet. Harriet owned the property if, and only if, (i) the person from whom she acquired (George) owned the property, or at least had power to convey, and (ii) the disposition from George to Harriet was valid. So one must consider George's title, and then Frank's title (George's author)[54] and then Emma's title (Frank's author), and so on. The problem is that title is derivative. Harriet has a good title only if George had a good title, whose title in turn depends on Frank and on Emma. Where does it all stop? Is it necessary to go right back to the original Crown grant by Alexander III or by God to Adam and Eve? The answer is no, because of the doctrine of positive prescription.

Positive prescription[55]

7-18   The basis of positive prescription is section 1 of the Prescription and Limitation (Scotland) Act 1973.[56] Its importance in conveyancing law and practice for GRS titles cannot be overstated: its role in the Land

---

[53] For an example see J.H. Sinclair, *Handbook of Conveyancing Practice in Scotland,* (3rd ed., 1995) p.262. It is a sign of the times that the current edition (4th ed, 2002) omits this section.

[54] By "author in title" conveyancers mean the person from whom the property was acquired.

[55] On prescription generally see David Johnston, *Prescription and Limitation* (1999) and D. M. Walker, *The Law of Prescription and Limitation of Actions in Scotland* (6th ed., 2002).

[56] As amended by the Abolition of Feudal Tenure etc. (Scotland) Act 2000, s.76(1) and Sch.12, para.33(2).

Register is different and much less important. Positive prescription is the acquisition of real rights in land by possession or use for a certain period of time.[57] The chief real rights in land are (a) ownership (b) heritable security (c) lease (d) proper liferent (e) servitude, and (g) real burden. However, real burdens cannot be acquired by prescription,[58] while special provision is made for servitudes in section 3. Also excluded are short leases, *i.e.* leases of 20 years or less, as section 1 covers only real rights that can be registered, and short leases cannot be registered.[59] This chapter is concerned only with ownership, but the same rules apply to other real rights in land, and indeed must be applied in, for instance, the purchase of a leasehold title, the latter being common in commercial conveyancing. In practice, prescription is almost never encountered with reference to the remaining real rights in land, *i.e.* security and proper liferent.

There are two main requirements if prescription is to operate. First, there must be an appropriate deed which has been recorded in the GRS (called the foundation writ or the prescriptive writ). Secondly, the land must be possessed for 10 years.

Identifying the foundation writ

Examination of title begins with a bundle of deeds, sometimes a large 7–19 one, tied up with red tape.[60] Which is the foundation writ? The rule for prescription is that the 10 years of possession must follow and be founded on (hence "foundation" writ) the recording of the deed. So the foundation writ is the first property writ recorded more than 10 years before the current transaction. By "property writ" is meant a deed which conveys the property: usually this will be a disposition or feu disposition, but it may also be[61] a notice of title or a judicial decree having the effect of a conveyance. Thus, if it is now 2005, and Sarah is selling to Thomas, and Sarah bought the property in 2001 from Rona, and Rona bought the property in 1997 from Paul, and Paul bought the property in 1989 from Norah, the foundation writ is the disposition of 1989.[62] (If there is a qualifying writ which is not quite 10 years old this can be treated as the foundation writ provided that the 10-year period will have expired by the time the clients' disposition is recorded.)

Once the foundation writ has been identified, it must be read to ensure that it complies with section 1. For this purpose only the deed

---

[57] David Johnston, *Prescription and Limitation* (1999), para.14.04 says that positive prescription does not result in acquisition, but we would respectfully disagree.

[58] 1973 Act, s.1(3).

[59] However, it must not be supposed that only long leases can be real rights. Short leases generally are real rights too, by virtue of the Leases Act 1449.

[60] It is one of the mysteries of existence that red tape is pink. And one of the skills to be learned by the novice, apart from trying to find out how the dictaphone works, and where the loo is, is how to tie the writs up again so that they won't promptly spill out all over the floor. (The secret is to tie the tape as tight as possible, leaving one deed out, and then slide that one in.)

[61] See 1973 Act, s.5(1).

[62] The foundation writ can sometimes be very old. One of the authors once acted in the purchase of property from a corporation which had bought it in 1646 and was now selling for the first time. The 1646 deed in favour of the corporation was thus the foundation writ.

itself should be considered[63] and extrinsic evidence is disregarded. This is less straightforward than it sounds. By the deed itself is meant (a) the actual words of the deed including schedules, plans and other annexations[64] and (b) any other words which are formally imported by reference, typically descriptions and real burdens. Other deeds which are referred to but are not formally imported are not part of the foundation writ and fall to be disregarded for this purpose. This includes any midcouples (also called links in title) mentioned in the foundation writ for the purposes of deduction of title.[65]

"Sufficient in respect of its terms"

7–20   In the words of section 1(1), the foundation writ must be sufficient in respect of its terms to constitute a real right in the land or to land of a description habile to include the particular land.[66] To test this, the description given in the dispositive clause must be examined. All that is required is that the words of description are capable of including the land in question, even if this is not the only, or even the most natural, interpretation of the words.[67] For instance, it is common to find that the description is little more than a glorified postal address. In that case, the property actually possessed for the prescriptive period will be owned. By contrast, a bounding description excludes land lying beyond the stated boundary. This is the maxim of "no prescription beyond a bounding title". Thus, if the description states a boundary line, and the successive owners have in fact possessed beyond that line, there will be no ownership of the extra land, no matter how long the possession has endured.[68]

Not *ex facie* invalid or forged

7–21   The foundation writ must not be invalid *ex facie* or forged.[69] If a deed is forged it is not a good foundation writ. But this case aside, defects which are not apparent from a visual inspection of the deed do not matter. The concern is only with *ex facie* validity and, as explained earlier, extrinsic evidence is irrelevant. Thus, so long as the deed looks correct, it does not matter (for the purpose of qualifying as a foundation writ) if it is actually fundamentally defective, *e.g.* if it was granted by a non-owner, or if an inspection of the midcouples listed in the deduction of title clause would reveal that they are inept or even non-existent. Nor

---

[63] s.1(1)(a): "Sufficient in respect of its terms".

[64] The schedules, plans and annexations must, however, be incorporated into the deed in conformity with s.8 of the 1995 Act (discussed in para.14–08).

[65] See Halliday, para.36–07.

[66] s.1(1)(a).

[67] *Auld v Hay* (1880) 7 R. 663; *Suttie v Baird*, 1992 S.L.T. 133. For a qualification of the doctrine see *Michael v Carruthers*, 1998 S.L.T. 1179.

[68] The rule is the same even where it is argued that the land is possessed as a part and pertinent: see *Cooper's Trs v Stark's Trs* (1898) 25 R. 1160.

[69] s.1(2).

does it matter that such defects are actually known about. The law is concerned only with the appearance of the foundation writ. Good faith is irrelevant in positive prescription. The test is whether, if there were no extrinsic defects, the deed would be sufficient to confer the right in question. If the answer is yes, the deed is good as a foundation writ. In marginal cases the test may be difficult to apply, but it appears from the wording of section 1(2) of the 1973 Act that doubts should be resolved in favour of validity. Only a deed bearing clear evidence of its own invalidity fails to make the grade.[70]

The requirement of possession

Possession must follow the recording of the foundation writ. The period is 10 years.[71] The possession must be continuous, by which is meant, not that the possessors must be there all that time, but that they must not have yielded possession to anyone else (*e.g.* a squatter) who does not recognise their title. Possession may be civil, for example through a tenant. Section 1(1) of the 1973 Act says that possession may be "by any person and his successors". So the fact that the property has changed hands does not matter, so long as the new proprietor or proprietors also took possession. Section 1(1) provides that the possession must be exercised "openly" (*i.e.* not just when the neighbour is out shopping), "peaceably" and "without any judicial interruption". Possession must be founded on the foundation writ, by which is meant that the possession must be "adverse" (*i.e.* attributable to the foundation writ) and not of consent (*i.e.* attributable merely to the consent of the true owner).

Both a foundation writ and 10 years' possession are required for prescription. But while foundation writs are anxiously examined and argued about by solicitors, possession is usually taken for granted and no evidence is required. Whether this is entirely wise seems open to question. But, of course, verifying past possession is difficult. What in practice usually happens is that the purchasers' agent checks the search for the past 40 years. If there is a competing title, this will be shown up by the search, and in that case it may be necessary to investigate the history of the possession. There is no magic about the figure of 40 years. It is a practical point. Thus, suppose the foundation writ is 12 years old, and in fact was invalid at the time, someone else owning the property. A 40-year search will, in practice, reveal this fact, in which case it would be necessary to verify that the sellers, or their predecessors, have had 10 years of possession. Conversely, if a 40-year search throws up no competing title, almost certainly there is no competing title.[72]

7–22

---

[70] See further John Burns, *Conveyancing Practice* (4th ed., by F. MacRitchie, 1957), p.201.

[71] In certain questions with the Crown, the period is 20 years: s.1(5). Generally, on the calculation of time, see s.14.

[72] For the potential risks in taking possession for granted, see *Hamilton v McIntosh Donald Ltd*, 1994 S.C. 304. For discussion see Rennie, 1994 S.L.T. (News) 261.

Effect of prescription

7-23   According to section 1(1) of the 1973 Act, the effect of prescription is that "the validity of the title . . . shall be exempt from challenge". This means that even if the foundation writ was voidable or, worse, void, this no longer matters, and the title based on that deed can no longer be challenged. Of course, in practice, most foundation writs are perfectly good anyway; but the value of prescription is that it is not necessary to prove that this is so. It no longer matters whether it was good or not. Take the example given above. It is now 2005, and Sarah is selling to Thomas, and Sarah bought the property in 2001 from Rona, and Rona bought the property in 1997 from Paul, and Paul bought the property in 1989 from Nora. The foundation writ is the disposition of 1989. The title is now good, provided that there has been possession, even if Nora had no title, so that the 1989 deed was void. Prescription cuts off any right to reduce the title. But it will not cut off other rights. For instance, the ordinary running of positive prescription will not cut out real burdens or servitudes or heritable securities.[73] (If it did, then anyone with a mortgage more than 10 years old would be happy.)

A quirk: prescriptive reacquisition

7-24   There is a curious quirk which arises from the law of prescription. Suppose that in 1995 Alan disponed 50 hectares to Beth, who recorded her disposition in the GRS. Beth took possession, but due to a misunderstanding about boundaries only took possession of 49 hectares, Alan remaining in possession of the extra hectare. In 2005 Alan would have reacquired, by prescription, title to that hectare. For Alan would have had 10 years of possession and this would be attributable to the deed by which he had (sometime before 1995) acquired the property. Correspondingly, in 2005 Beth's ownership of that hectare would cease.[74]

A note on the disposition *a non domino*

7-25   It sometimes happens that someone notices that a piece of ground is unoccupied and apparently abandoned. Using prescription, it is possible to acquire ownership. What happens is that the person gets a friend[75] to grant to him a gratuitous disposition of the land, and the disposition is recorded. This is called a disposition a *non domino, i.e.* "by a non-owner". The disponee takes possession, and 10 years later will become the owner. This may seem like theft, but good faith is not a requirement of positive prescription.[76] Moreover, the true owner has 10 years to reclaim the property, and the policy of the law is that an owner who

---

[73] Such rights may be extinguishable by negative prescription, but not merely by possession for 10 years.

[74] See Hume, *Lectures*, iv, 549; *Wallace v University of St Andrews* (1904) 6 F. 1093; *Love-Lee v Cameron of Lochiel*, 1991 S.C.L.R. 61.

[75] Who should, of course, exclude warrandice. It is sometimes said that it is sufficient to grant a disposition in favour of oneself but this is somewhat doubtful, for such a writ does not bear to be a transfer. See further David A. Brand, Andrew J .M. Steven and Scott Wortley, *Professor McDonald's Conveyancing Manual* (7th ed., 2004) para.12.7.

[76] And as far as the criminal law is concerned, heritable property cannot be stolen.

abandons property cannot expect indefinite protection. When purchasing from someone who purports to have acquired ownership in this manner, it is obviously wise to verify that there has been 10 years of possession, unless the acquisition took place long ago, such as more than 40 years ago.

A disposition *a non domino* must not reveal that the disponer is not the owner, or it will lose its potential status as a foundation writ.[77] Here candour does not pay. So a deed which admitted, in the narrative clause, that "we have occupied the subjects hereinafter disponed continuously since 1955, openly, peaceably and without any judicial interruption, but without a title" was held to fail as a foundation writ.[78] However, the cautious words "only so far as I have right thereto" do not amount to a denial of title and do not prevent the running of prescription.

Traditionally the Keeper would accept dispositions *a non domino* for the GRS without querying them. However, his practice changed in 1996, and he will now accept them only in certain types of case, though what those types of case are is not wholly clear.[79]

As well as unoccupied property, the *a non domino* disposition will sometimes be encountered where a person has long been in possession of land but without a good title. One example would be a company which possesses land under a 999-year lease granted in the eighteenth century. No rent has been paid for many decades and indeed the lessee does not even know who the landlord is. The lessee registers an *a non domino* disposition in its favour. After 10 years it will have a good title. One problem, in cases of this sort, is that it could be argued that the possession for 10 years is referable to the lease rather than to the disposition, in which case the title would not be good. The position probably depends on whether rent is being paid.[80] If it is, the possession is referable to the lease. If not, possession is capable of being founded on the disposition.[81]

Writs subsequent to the foundation writ

Assuming a good foundation writ followed by 10 years' possession, the 7–26 title 10 years ago today can be treated as having been good. But what has happened since? The owner may have been inhibited, or sequestrated, or have died, or have disponed the property to someone else. The task of the buyers' solicitor is to connect the current sellers with the good title of 10 years ago. If the property has not changed hands during that period, the sellers will have been the grantees of the foundation writ, and there is nothing further to be checked in this respect. But in many cases the property will have changed hands. If so, the dispositions or other writs

---

[77] This is because it would be invalid *ex facie*.

[78] *Watson v Shields*, 1994 S.C.L.R. 819 affirmed 1996 S.C.L.R. 81.

[79] See (1997) 42 J.L.S.S. 72. There may be room for doubt as to whether the Keeper has the right to reject which he asserts, as far as the GRS is concerned. He does of course have that right in respect of the Land Register.

[80] *Houstoun v Barr*, 1911 S.C. 134; *B. G. Hamilton v Ready Mix Concrete (Scotland) Ltd*, 1999 S.L.T. 524.

[81] *Grant v Grant* (1677) Mor. 10876; David Johnston, *Prescription and Limitation* (1999), para.16.27.

connecting the current sellers to the good title of 10 years before must be examined. Such writs must be absolutely, and not merely *ex facie,* valid, for prescription has not yet operated on them. So extrinsic defects matter as much as intrinsic defects, although in practice it may not always be possible to find out about such extrinsic defects. Each title is different and an exhaustive list of things to look out for cannot be given, but some of the more important points are given below.

Each consecutive deed must follow on from its predecessor. This means either that the granter of deed 4 was the grantee of deed 3, or that, the grantee of deed 3 having died or been sequestrated, etc., without having conveyed the property, the property has passed to the granter of deed 4 in some other way, *e.g.* as a result of a grant of confirmation of executors or act and warrant in favour of a trustee in sequestration. In such cases the confirmation, etc., is called a midcouple or link in title and, of course, must be checked.

Another example is the special destination. For instance, a house is conveyed to Alan and Beth and the survivor of them. Alan dies, and the next deed is a disposition by Beth alone. These issues are considered elsewhere in this book.[82]

Each deed must be checked for errors, such as the designations of the parties, the description of the property, and the mode of execution.[83] In principle, the warrants of registration should be checked, as should the stamp duty, though in practice it is most unlikely that the Keeper would have accepted a deed with errors of these kinds. The conveyancer should consider whether there is anything in a deed which raises reasonable suspicions and suggests that further evidence is needed. It must be remembered that the deeds after the foundation writ must be absolutely (and not merely *ex facie*) valid. A party who signs as "Postman Pat" is probably under age and unable to convey property. Further inquiries must be made of the sellers' solicitors.

There is also the possibility that a deed, while not void, might be voidable. Examples of potentially voidable deeds include: (i) deeds by persons aged 16 or 17 which are "prejudicial";[84] (ii) gratuitous alienations and unfair preferences granted by persons when insolvent; (iii) deeds by a party who has been inhibited; (iv) disposals by a spouse within five years prior to a claim by the other spouse for aliment or financial provision.[85]

Voidable titles and good faith

7-27   Where a deed within the prescriptive progress is voidable (not void), there are two possibilities. The first possibility is that the purchasers do not know about the problem and have no reasonable means of knowing

---

[82] Chs 22, 23 and 26.
[83] This can require historical knowledge of the law. For instance, the current rules on execution of deeds only go back to August 1, 1995, when the 1995 Act came into force. See further Ch.14.
[84] Age of Legal Capacity (Scotland) Act 1991, s.3.
[85] Family Law (Scotland) Act 1985, s.18.

about it, for example because it appears neither from the deed itself nor from the search. In such a case they are protected, because voidability does not affect a subsequent purchaser in good faith.[86] Unless the deed is reduced, and the extract decree recorded[87] before the purchasers record their own disposition, there is no danger from a subsequent reduction. The right to reduce is a personal right which does not transmit against successors in good faith.

The other possibility is that the purchasers do know, or ought to know, that the deed is voidable. In that case, the right to reduce will normally transmit against them, with the result that the sellers are not offering a good and marketable title and must take steps to buy off the party with the right to reduce.

Gratuitous alienations[88]

A "gratuitous alienation" means any act (or, in some cases, omission) 7-28 whereby the value of the debtor's patrimony is diminished. The main example is a donation—*i.e.* a gratuitous transfer. Gratuitous alienations are normally valid, and are common between family members. But persons who are insolvent are forbidden to give away property, and if they do so, the donation is voidable at the instance of the creditors. However, since the donation is voidable only and not void, a third party acquiring for value and in good faith has nothing to fear.[89] Thus suppose Mark gratuitously transfers title to his house to his wife, Nicole. He is insolvent, and a year later is sequestrated. In the meantime, Nicole has sold the property to Oliver. If Oliver was in good faith, his title cannot be reduced by Mark's trustee in sequestration, who in that case can do no more than sue Nicole for the value of the property. The trouble is that if the fact that Nicole's acquisition was gratuitous appears from the face of the title, which in a GRS case it usually does, Oliver is probably barred from pleading good faith.[90] So Oliver is at risk, at least in theory. In practice, of course, most gifts are not made by insolvent donors. The law is probably that unless there is some particular ground for suspecting voidability, or unless there is some special clause in the missives, a purchaser cannot object to a title which includes a gratuitous transfer.[91] The creditors' right to reduce depends on the donor being sequestrated or granting a protected trust deed within five years.[92] Hence, provided that the personal search is clear, there is no reason to worry about a donation which is more than five years old.

---

[86] Stair, IV, xl, 21; Erskine, III, v, 10; Hume, *Lectures*, iii, 236–238. See, further, Reid, *Property*, para.692.

[87] Conveyancing (Scotland) Act 1924, s.46(1).

[88] Bankruptcy (Scotland) Act 1985, s.34. And see William W. McBryde, *Bankruptcy* (2nd ed., 1995).

[89] Bankruptcy (Scotland) Act 1985, s.34(4), *proviso*.

[90] *Hay v Jamieson* (1672) Mor. 1009; Erskine, IV, i, 36; Bell, *Comm.*, ii, 183.

[91] *cf. Sibbald's Heirs v Harris*, 1947 S.C. 601, discussed in para.6–12.

[92] Bankruptcy (Scotland) Act 1985, s.34(3). The period is only two years if the alienation is not to an "associate" (defined in s.74 to include close relative, business partner, employer, and employee).

Identification of property

7-29   It is pointless establishing that the sellers have a good title, unless it is a good title to the property which the purchasers have contracted to buy. But in practice this is easier said than done, not least because missives are themselves often dangerously vague in describing the property. In a GRS title all deeds within the prescriptive period will usually contain the same description, which will normally consist of (a) a general description and (b) a particular description imported by reference from the break-off writ.[93] The general description may not take matters very far. But unless there is a good plan, the particular description may also be of limited help. Old particular descriptions are often vague. They may refer to boundary features which no longer exist. In *Anderson v Lambie*[94] Lord Reid remarked that "the lands were described as 'parts of the twenty-six shilling and eightpenny land of old extent[95] of Blairmackhill' and otherwise were only identified as having been possessed by persons long since forgotten or bounded by other lands apparently now unidentifiable".

Although a plan-based title is in general preferable, for obvious reasons, planless ones are often fine, while plans often turn out to be inadequate. Some employ the dreaded "floating rectangle",[96] *i.e.* a plan showing a plot of ground apparently in the middle of nowhere and which is not anchored to any recognisable and permanent landmark such as a public road. Even if the plan shows a road, this may not be sufficient. Thus, the plan may show the property next to "the public road from Drumbeg to Balnacraig" with no indication of where on that road (which is 5 kilometres long) the property actually lies. Some plans lack a north sign,[97] and some lack measurements. It is common to see plans which can only be understood on the basis of colouring: for instance, the property is defined as the area coloured red. But if the principal deed is lost, the plan may prove uninterpretable, since in the GRS everything is in monochrome. Even if the deed is not lost, a deed whose terms do not appear in its recorded version is unsatisfactory. If there is no plan, or if the plan is inadequate, then a new plan will be required, assuming that the transaction is a first registration.

In some cases the plan or other description looks first-class but in truth does not correspond to the property as actually possessed. Assuming that the transaction is a first registration this problem will normally be brought to light by a P16 report.

---

[93] In other words, the successive deeds will not normally contain the full description, but refer to an earlier deed by A to B. (Clients are often puzzled why the deed in their favour should refer to other people.) For descriptions, generally, see Ch.12.

[94] 1954 S.C. (HL) 43.

[95] *Anderson v Lambie* was half a century ago but even now there are some GRS titles that are defined by reference to the "old extent". The old extent was an official land survey made in the 13th century. It was the subject of a classic work of Scottish legal historiography: *Memorial on Old Extent* (1816) by Thomas Thomson, published as Vol.10 of the Stair Society series (1946).

[96] Occasionally also called the "floating shape" because of course it may not be an actual rectangle.

[97] Some helpfully include a north sign which in fact points south.

What are the title conditions and are they acceptable?

The issues here are substantially the same as for properties in the 7–30
Land Register, already discussed.[98] The main difference is that whereas
in a land certificate all the real burdens are set out in type, in the land
certificate, in a GRS title the burdens may be scattered among numerous
different deeds. Older ones will be handwritten and perhaps barely
legible.

Are there any securities?

The issues here are substantially the same as for properties in the 7–31
Land Register.[99] One difference is that if the property is in the Land
Register, discharged heritable securities will simply be invisible. They
will be omitted from the land certificate. But in a GRS title the
conveyancer must examine the discharges to check that they are valid.[1]
In the case of discharges more than five years old the rule is that a defect
not discoverable from the face of the deed will not affect purchasers
unless they know about it.[2] So only *ex facie* validity matters. This rule
does not apply to discharges within the last five years, but at common
law a *bona fide* purchaser is only affected by defects sufficiently serious
to make the deed void (as opposed to voidable), and such defects are
usually discoverable from an examination of the deed itself.

---

[98] para.7–08.
[99] para.7–09.
[1] See Halliday, para.36–60.
[2] Conveyancing and Feudal Reform (Scotland) Act 1970, s.41.

CHAPTER 8

REGISTRATION

INTRODUCTION

General

8-01   The Land Register and the General Register of Sasines (GRS) are often referred to as the property registers. Registration in the property registers is described as registration for "publication",[1] as opposed to registration for "preservation" (or for "execution") in the Books of Council and Session.[2] Like other registers, the property registers are open to the public. Both are divided into 33 registration areas, corresponding to the traditional counties, except that Glasgow is a separate registration area. Despite being so divided, both the Land Register and the GRS are registers for the whole of Scotland, and are based in Edinburgh.[3] Unlike many countries, property registration in Scotland is done on a national rather than a local basis.[4]

The Land Registration (Scotland) Act 1979, which is the basis of the Land Register, is unsatisfactory in a number of respects, and the Scottish Law Commission is reviewing it. Future legislation is thus a possibility.[5]

---

[1] The reason being that real rights must be made public: this is the publicity principle.

[2] This is the register of the Court of Session. But it is administered by the Keeper rather than by the Court. Typically this register is used for the safekeeping ("preservation") of deeds which cannot be registered in the property registers (*e.g.* deeds of trust or powers of attorney). But since any probative deed can be registered, it is competent to register deeds such as dispositions, standard securities and so on. As well as preservation, registration is useful as proving conclusively that the deed existed not later than the date of registration. The register is public, and anyone can obtain an extract. The register has other functions too. In particular, a probative document of debt, with a consent clause, can be registered for "execution", allowing the creditor to do summary diligence. The Sheriff Courts have similar registers, called the Sheriff Court Books.

[3] These registers are based at Meadowbank House, 153 London Road, Edinburgh EH8 7AU. The website is *http://www.ros.gov.uk/*. This is full of valuable information and advice. Administratively the body in charge is the "Registers of Scotland Executive Agency" but in law, and in conveyancing parlance, everything is done by "the Keeper" (*i.e.* the registrar), more properly "the Keeper of the Registers of Scotland".

[4] There used to be a system of local Registers of Sasines, with both county registers (called the "particular" registers) and burgh registers. People had the option to use the local register or to use the GRS. These local registers were gradually phased out, under the Land Registers (Scotland) Act 1868 and the Burgh Registers (Scotland) Act 1926. The last to close was the Dingwall Burgh Register of Sasines, on June 30, 1963.

[5] The first of two discussion papers has already been published: see *Discussion Paper on Land Registration: Void and Voidable Titles* (Scot. Law Com. D.P. No.125, 2004; available on *http://www.scotlawcom.gov.uk/*).

Introduction of the new register

The GRS, which was established in 1617,[6] is being phased out, with 8–02
properties being gradually transferred to the Land Register. There are
roughly two million title units in Scotland, and at the time of this edition
about one half were in the Land Register and about one half were still in
the GRS. However, if one looks at it not from the standpoint of the
numbers of title units but from the standpoint of area, the picture is very
different. The reason is that market turnover is higher for smaller urban
units than for larger rural ones. The movement of individual units is one-
way, from the old register to the new.

The new register was brought into operation county by county. The
first county to become "operational" was Renfrewshire, on April 6, 1981.
The original plan was to have all 33 counties operational by 1992, but in
fact the process took until 2003 to complete. The 33 counties are listed
below, with the date when they became operational in the new register.

Aberdeen,[7]	1 April 1996	Kirkcudbright[8]	1 April 1997
Angus[9]	1 April 1999	Lanark	3 January 1984
Argyll	1 April 2000	Midlothian[10]	1 April 2001
Ayr	1 April 1997	Moray	1 April 2003
Banff	1 April 2003	Nairn	1 April 2002
Berwick	1 October 1999	Orkney & Shetland[11]	1 April 2003
Bute	1 April 2000	Peebles	1 October 1999
Caithness	1 April 2003	Perth	1 April 1999
Clackmannan	1 October 1992	Renfrew	6 April 1981
Dumfries	1 April 1997	Ross & Cromarty[12]	1 April 2003
Dunbarton	4 October 1982	Roxburgh	1 October 1999
East Lothian[13]	1 October 1999	Selkirk	1 October 1999
Fife	1 April 1995	Stirling	1 April 1993
Glasgow[14]	30 September 1985	Sutherland	1 April 2003
Inverness	1 April 2002	West Lothian[15]	1 October 1993
Kincardine	1 April 1996	Wigtown	1 April 1997
Kinross	1 April 1999		

---

[6] Registration Act 1617.

[7] The practice of conveyancers is to refer to the "County of Aberdeen" rather than
"Aberdeenshire", and likewise for the other counties.

[8] Stewartry of Kirkcudbright.

[9] At one time called the County of Forfar.

[10] At one time called the County of Edinburgh.

[11] Orkney and Shetland form a single area.

[12] Ross and Cromarty form a single area.

[13] At one time called the County of Haddington.

[14] Barony and Regality of Glasgow.

[15] At one time called the County of Linlithgow.

Transfers into the new register

8-03   When each county became operational, that did not mean that all the properties in that county promptly switched into the new register. Individual properties remain in the GRS until they are individually transferred to the new register, which may not happen for years or decades. The basic idea[16] is that when a property is sold, it switches to the new register, but until that happens it stays in the GRS. That not only means that properties remain in the GRS while they continue in the hands of the owner at the time the county became operational, but they will even stay in the GRS if the property is transferred for reasons other than sale, such as a disposition by an executor to a beneficiary, or a disposition in implement of a donation.[17] So not only are many properties still in the GRS, but registrations of deeds in the GRS are still taking place. Since sometimes the same property stays in the hands of the same family for generations, with transfers from one family member to another happening on the basis of donation or inheritance rather than sale, there will still be deeds being recorded in the GRS for many decades to come—subject, of course, to possible future changes in the law. Likewise, and subject to the same qualification, first registrations[18] will still be happening for many decades into the future.

To speak of an individual property changing from the old register to the new one is actually an oversimplification, for it is possible for a given property to be, for a time, in both registers, in the sense that some rights in it are in the one register while others are in the other. This can happen when there exists a long lease, for a long lease can be in the GRS while the right of ownership is in the Land Register, and also conversely.[19]

Primary and secondary rights

8-04   For the purposes of land registration a distinction can be made between primary and secondary real rights in land. The Act itself does not express matters thus,[20] but the distinction is implicit. The primary real rights are ownership[21] and long lease, which is to say a lease for more than 20 years. All other real rights in land are secondary. The sale of a primary real right triggers a compulsory switch to the new register.[22]

---

[16] What follows is slightly simplified. For all details, see the 1979 Act. For instance, a disposition "in consideration of marriage", though not a sale, triggers the switch. Why this was thought worthy of special statutory provision is but one of the many mysteries of the 1979 Act.

[17] But, of course, once a property has been switched into the Land Register, non-sale dispositions will enter the Land Register, not the GRS.

[18] That is to say, the switch of a given property from the old register to the new.

[19] Before the abolition of feudalism it could also happen in respect of different feudal rights. Thus it was common for the superiority to be in the GRS while the *dominium utile* was in the new register.

[20] And indeed shows its origins in, still feudal, times by the use of "interest in land" instead of the more precise "real right in land" found in modern statutes.

[21] Before the abolition of feudalism, there was *dominium utile* (which is now simple ownership) and also various levels of superiority, all of which were primary real rights for the purposes of land registration.

[22] 1979 Act, s.2(1)(a)(ii). However, the assignation of a lease triggers a switch even without payment of consideration: see s.2(1)(a)(v).

This means that the first time a property is sold after the county became operational there is a first registration in the Land Register. The same is true for the first transfer of an existing long lease. Similarly, if a primary real right is still in the GRS but another primary real right is carved out of it, the new primary real right goes into the new register while the balance of the existing primary real right remains, for the time being, in the old register.[23] This happens when a long lease is granted.[24] The ownership retained by the landlord remains, for the time being, in the old register, while the newly created long lease enters the new register. It is also possible for a lease to be in the old register while the property is in the new one. This would happen if the lease was granted before the county became operational, and thereafter the property was sold, while the lease remained in the hands of the original lessee.

The rule for secondary real rights is different. The rule is that a newly created secondary real right is entered in the same register as the primary real right to which it relates.[25] For example, if a standard security is granted over land which is still in the old register, the security is also entered in the old register. But a standard security over land which is in the new register will itself enter the new register.

The switch operates in one direction only. Once a title is registered in the Land Register, all subsequent rights are registered there also.[26] To the GRS there is no return.

How soon should the grantee register?

There is no time-limit for registration in either the Land Register or 8–05 the GRS. The grantee can rush or dawdle to Register House. The disposition (or other deed) remains valid indefinitely.[27] However, the grantee, if a natural person, must still be alive at the time of registration.[28] If the grantee has died, the disposition does not cease to be valid, and the executor can complete title using the disposition and the confirmation as the midcouples.[29] If the grantee is a company, or other juristic person, it must still exist at the time of registration. But although there is no time limit for registration, in practice it should be done as soon as possible. One reason is to protect the grantee against the possible insolvency of the granter.[30] The standard letter of obligation stipulates for registration within 21 days.[31] Unless the application is later rejected or withdrawn, the date of receipt is the date of registration. Two deeds arriving on the same day rank equally.[32]

---

[23] 1979 Act, s.2(1)(a)(i).

[24] Before the abolition of feudalism, it could also happen if the land were feued.

[25] 1979 Act, s.2(3).

[26] 1979 Act, s.2(3), (4).

[27] By law. Occasionally (and this was especially the case in feu dispositions) one sees an express time-limit of, say, six months.

[28] 1868 Act, s.142.

[29] In a GRS case where the grantee has died without recording there will normally have to be a notice of title in favour of the executor. See further Ch.22.

[30] *Burnett's Tr v Grainger*, 2004 S.L.T. 513.

[31] For letters of obligation, see Ch.9.

[32] 1868 Act, s.142 as amended by the 1979 Act; 1979 Act, ss.4(3) and 7. Before the 1979 Act, deeds ranked not only by date but by hour of registration.

Registration dues

8–06   The idea is that the registers should be self-financing. Registration costs money, and has become more expensive since the introduction of registration of title. The fees for registration in the two property registers are the same; but since running the Land Register is more expensive, fees paid for the GRS subsidise the Land Register. The current registration fees are to be found in the Fees in the Registers of Scotland Order 1995.[33] The fee is payable when the application is made.[34]

For dispositions the fee is based on the price paid, or, where there is no price, on the value of the property. For dispositions the fee is £22 for a value up to £10,000, and thereafter £11 per £5,000 or part thereof. So the fee for registering a disposition for a price of £40,000 is £88. The scale goes up to a value of £200,000, on which the fee is thus £440. For a value over £200,000 but under £300,000 the fee is £500, and it then goes up £50 for every £100,000 of value, so that the registration fee for a disposition of a £350,000 property would be £550. A new scale operates for values over £800,000. For standard securities, the fee is also based on the value, but not of the property, but of the secured loan.[35] It is basically one-half that for a disposition, though the equivalence is not quite exact. Up to £20,000 the fee is £22, and thereafter £11 per £10,000 or part thereof. After £200,000 a new scale operates. However, an important qualification is that a standard security registered at the same time as a disposition is charged a flat fee of £22. Hence, the practice is to register both deeds together wherever possible. Thus, a disposition of a £152,000 house plus a standard security for £74,000 would cost either £429 (£341 + £88) or £363 (£341 + £22).

For registrations in the Land Register part of the fee is a premium for title insurance. It is thus curious that the same fee is payable even if such insurance is refused (by exclusion of indemnity). It is equally curious that the fee is the same in the GRS, where no title insurance is obtained.

The Land Register and the GRS compared

8–07   The Land Register and the GRS work in different ways. The GRS is a register of deeds. It consists of countless deeds stretching back to the establishment of the register in 1617. These are divided by county, but apart from that there is no arrangement, except chronological. The deeds affecting a given plot are thus scattered in an unconnected way over vast numbers of record volumes. They are traceable by the indexes and by the search sheets. The GRS is not a register of title, as such. Nowhere in the register is there anything which gathers together the real rights in a plot of land and states authoritatively who holds them. Moreover, although, subject to minor qualifications, registration in the

---

[33] SI 1995/1945.

[34] Land Registers (Scotland) Act 1995. See a note by the Keeper at (1995) 40 J.L.S.S. 482.

[35] "The fee to be charged shall be calculated on the amount of the heritable security" says the statutory instrument. However, there is a problem: few standard securities are for fixed loans. For instance, a standard security might be granted to secure an overdraft. At the time of the security the overdraft is zero. A month later it is £1,000,000.

GRS is a *necessary* condition of obtaining a real right, it is not a *sufficient* condition, for a deed in the GRS may be void. Suppose that Rachel dispones her farm to Tara. A small strip of land which is included in the disposition, and which is possessed as part of the farm, actually belongs to a neighbour. Despite the recording of the disposition, Tara does not acquire ownership of that strip. *Nemo plus juris ad alium transferre potest quam ipse haberet.* The disposition would be ineffectual to that extent and the neighbour would still be the owner. Thus, the fact that there exists in the GRS a deed ostensibly passing ownership to X does not necessarily mean that X thereby became the owner. Hence, the task of ascertaining from the GRS what are the real rights in a plot of land or a house, and in whom such rights are vested, is not a straightforward one. It is a task for a trained conveyancer.

The Land Register employs a different system, which is used in a number of other countries, called registration of title. In registration of title the register maps the boundaries of each plot, or title unit, and says who has what real rights in it. The Register, as well as being divided into counties, is divided into the various title units, so that each unit has its own title sheet, identified by letters (indicating the county) and numbers, such as REN123456. To change the real rights the same deeds are used as in the GRS system—dispositions, standard securities, and so forth—but such deeds, instead of being recorded,[36] are used by the Keeper as the basis for altering the title sheet. Registration (*i.e.* alteration of the title sheet) is necessary, in the sense that, subject to minor qualifications, there can be no real right without registration. But the system goes further than this. In registration of title, there is, again subject to minor qualifications, no such thing as a void registration.[37] Registration is, thus, not only necessary to obtain a real right, but it is also sufficient. Whereas in the GRS the role of the Keeper is limited and passive, in registration of title the Keeper's role is extensive and active.

In the GRS system, title—good, bad or indifferent—flows from the recorded deed. In the Land Register, by contrast, title does not flow from the deed, but from the Register. The deed is not registered. Its function is, so to speak, to persuade the Keeper to make an entry in the Register. This principle has many consequences. For instance, whereas in the GRS system a void *deed* will mean a void *title*, in the Land Register if the Keeper makes an entry on the basis of a void deed, the entry is not void and so the title is not void. Again, if a deed that is not void but is voidable is reduced, the consequences in the GRS system are dramatic, for the effect of the reduction is that the deed becomes void, and as a result the title becomes void. But in the Land Register the reduction of a voidable deed has, in itself, no real effect. Title does not flow from the deed, so its reduction does not alter the title. It will merely make the title inaccurate, and hence subject to the possibility of rectification.

From what has just been said it will be seen that the Land Register cannot normally be wrong. Nonetheless, "inaccuracy" can still happen.[38]

---

[36] Though the Keeper does retain a copy of all such deeds.

[37] One possible exception would be where a registration was made in the name of a non-existent person.

[38] See para. 8–13, below.

But here again the users of the system are protected, for a person who suffers as a result of an inaccuracy is normally entitled either to demand "rectification" of the Register, or, in the alternative, "indemnity" *i.e.* compensation from the Keeper. If rectification is granted, then the person who loses the property normally gets compensation. So whether rectification is allowed or refused the Keeper will usually end up paying compensation. As between the two competitors for title, one gets the mud (*i.e.,* the property), and the other the money.[39] That is a great advantage of the system over the GRS, where it is possible (if unusual) to end up with neither the mud nor the money. However, one advantage of the GRS is that once one does have the mud one is absolutely secure. By contrast, a Land Register title is always slightly precarious. The fact that title flows from the Register makes it certain that one gets the mud in the first place—but also means that one can lose it, if the Register proves fickle in its affections. "Easy come" leads inexorably to "easy go."[40]

With the GRS the question "who is the owner?" can be difficult to answer. With the Land Register it is almost always easy to answer. But it must not be supposed that in consequence the Land Register is always plain sailing. Once the easy question of ownership has been answered, there sometimes remain difficult questions, notably: (i) is the Register inaccurate? (ii) if so is it rectifiable? and (iii) is indemnity payable, and if so to whom? Similar remarks can be made about subordinate real rights such as standard securities.

THE LAND REGISTER

Primary and secondary real rights

8–08   As mentioned above,[41] the 1979 Act divides real rights into two classes, primary and secondary. There are two kinds of primary real rights, namely ownership and long lease, *i.e.* a lease of over 20 years.[42] Other interests are secondary. Examples are standard securities, real burdens, and servitudes. Primary real rights have their own title sheet. Secondary real rights do not, and are registered on the title sheet of the primary real right to which they relate.[43]

The title sheet

8–09   The title sheet is part of the Register: the Register is composed of title sheets. Nowadays the Register is kept in digital form. The title sheet is divided into four parts.[44] (a) The property section defines the property.

---

[39] This turn of phrase comes from T. W. Mapp, *Torrens' Elusive Title* (1978), para.4.24. "Torrens" systems of land registration are common round the world. The 1979 Act system has important affinities with the Torrens family.

[40] This phrase too is that of the perceptive Mapp: see *Torrens' Elusive Title*, paras 3.13 and 4.26.

[41] para.8–04.

[42] Before the entry into force of the 2000 Act there were three kinds of primary real right, namely *dominium utile*, *dominium directum* and long lease.

[43] 1979 Act, s.5(1).

[44] Land Registration (Scotland) Rules (SI 1980/1413), Pt II.

There is a verbal description, typically little more than the postal address, coupled with a detailed plan, based on the Ordnance Survey map.[45] (b) The proprietorship section names the person who owns the property. (c) The charges section lists any heritable securities which affect the property. (d) The burdens section lists the real burdens and, sometimes, servitudes. Only those real rights (burdens, securities, etc.) listed in the title sheet affect a proprietor, except for overriding interests.[46] The title sheet thus gives an almost complete picture of the state of the title. Any educated person can understand it.

Certificates of title (i): the land certificate

There are two kinds of "certificate of title", namely the land certificate 8-10 and the charge certificate. The land certificate is a certified paper copy of the title sheet. This is what the owner will receive.[47] A land certificate is thus an extract from the register. But whereas with other registers any number of extracts can be obtained by anybody, on payment of the appropriate fee, only one land certificate is normally issued for each title sheet. If it is lost, however, the Keeper may issue a substitute.[48] The point is significant because the land certificate must be produced for any registration,[49] though certain exceptions exist.[50] But additional copies of the title sheet, called, somewhat mysteriously, "office copies", can also be obtained.[51]

Certificates of title (ii): the charge certificate

A standard security is not a primary real right and so does not attract 8-11 its own title sheet (or land certificate). Instead it is registered in the charges section of the title sheet to which it relates. However, the Keeper issues to the creditor a document called a charge certificate which contains the security deed itself, with certification that it has been entered on the title sheet.[52] As with a land certificate, the role of this type of certificate is purely evidential. The security exists as a real right by virtue of its entry in the title sheet.

Overriding interests

The principle of registration of title is that all real rights affecting a 8-12 property are entered in the title sheet, and that, consequently, any right not so entered has no real effect. But this ideal is not fully realisable in

---

[45] For descriptions see Ch.12.

[46] 1979 Act, s.3(1)(a). For overriding interests, see below.

[47] 1979 Act, s.5(2); Land Registration (Scotland) Rules 1980, r. 14 and form 6. A long lease has its own title sheet and there will be a separate land certificate. Thus for a single property subject to a long lease there will be two title sheets and two land certificates.

[48] See Rennie (2001) 46 J.L.S.S. Feb./34.

[49] Land Registration (Scotland) Rules 1980, r.9(3), r.17(2).

[50] Land Registration (Scotland) Rules 1980, r.18.

[51] 1979 Act, s.6(5). An office copy is also a form 15 report since it is requested on a form 15.

[52] 1979 Act, s.5(3); Land Registration (Scotland) Rules 1980, r.15 and form 7.

practice.[53] Hence, there exists a category of rights called overriding interests[54] whose validity is unaffected if they are omitted from the title sheet. Servitudes are one example, the reason for this being that a servitude can be created by unregistered deed, or by implication, or by prescription, so that the Keeper can never be certain that he knows of all servitudes. Other important examples are short leases, floating charges, and occupancy rights under the 1981 Act. Even here the ideal is for overriding interests to be noted in the title sheet, and (with some exceptions) the Keeper may note them if he knows of their existence.[55]

Inaccuracy

8–13   The 1979 Act makes certain provisions for the situation where the Register is "inaccurate". At first sight it might seem impossible that the Register could ever be inaccurate. It is not as if real rights existed independently of the Register, so that the Register could somehow fail to reflect their existence or nature.[56] To say that the Register is wrong is thus rather like saying that a passage in Hamlet is a misquotation from Shakespeare. Suppose that Oliver owns land, and Charles forges Oliver's signature on a disposition in favour of Barry. Barry applies for registration, and is successful. Barry is now owner. He is owner because the Register says so, and the Register cannot be wrong.[57] That being the case, what is "inaccuracy" and how is inaccuracy possible?

While no definition is given in the 1979 Act, it seems to be that an entry on the Register is inaccurate if it was not justified, or is no longer justified, by the deed which induced it. An entry can be inaccurate in two ways. Either it can be inaccurate from the beginning, as in the example just given; or it can start life as an accurate entry but become inaccurate as a result of events. For instance, suppose that Oliver is owner, and then Charles, by fraud, induces Oliver to dispone to him. Charles is registered as owner. The disposition is voidable by reason of the fraud. Oliver reduces it. At this stage (but only at this stage) the Register becomes inaccurate.

An entry does not cease to be effective just because it is, or has become, inaccurate. Inaccuracy may not matter at all. Whether or not it matters depends on whether rectification[58] is possible. Sometimes it is, and sometimes it is not.

Inaccuracies can arise for a variety of reasons, not least the fault of the applicant. One source is error at Register House, especially on first registration. The Law Society of Scotland's Conveyancing Committee has noted the following as being complained about by solicitors:

---

[53] Any more than it is realisable under the GRS system, which has an almost identical class of overriding interests (not so-called).

[54] Defined in the 1979 Act, s.28. Not all overriding interests are real rights.

[55] 1979 Act, s.6(4)(b). In certain situations the Keeper is actually obliged to note them if he knows of them: s.6(4)(a). The exceptions are short leases and occupancy rights.

[56] Overriding interests, however, do exist independently of the Register, and are not made any more real merely by being noted there.

[57] It is otherwise for the GRS, where the disposition, though recorded, would still be void, and since title flows from recorded deeds, the title would be void.

[58] Rectification within the meaning of the 1979 Act is not to be confused with judicial rectification in the sense of s.8 of the Law Reform (Miscellaneous Provisions) (Scotland) Act 1985, on which see Ch.17.

(i) An incorrect postcode or address. (ii) The title number is not consistent throughout the document. (iii) The plan does not show the boundaries correctly. (iv) The proprietorship section does not contain the correct details and designations. (v) There is an unexpected exclusion of indemnity. (vi) All prior charges[59] have not been discharged or ranking agreements have been incorrectly shown. (vii) Burdens are not corrected stated or irrelevant burdens have not been excluded. (viii) There are grammatical or spelling errors.[60]

Rectification

In principle an inaccuracy on the Land Register can be rectified by the 8-14 Keeper, whether on request,[61] on his own initiative, or on being ordered by the court.[62] Rectification, if allowed, does not have retrospective effect.[63] The past cannot be altered. Title flows from the Register, whether the Register is accurate or inaccurate. Rectification cannot normally proceed if it would prejudice a proprietor in possession.[64] Sometimes rectification is to the benefit of such a proprietor, for example the removal of real burdens or other encumbrances.[65] More usually it is not.

If rectification is competent, it is unclear whether it could still be refused on a discretionary basis, with indemnity being paid instead. It depends on what "may" means in section 9(1). In one case it has been interpreted as conferring not only a power but also a discretion.[66]

If an application for rectification is successful, any party prejudiced will normally be entitled to compensation. If an application for rectification is unsuccessful, even though the Register is shown to be inaccurate, the applicant will normally be entitled to compensation. Rectification of an inaccuracy is barred only where it would prejudice a proprietor in possession.

Proprietor in possession: general

Perhaps surprisingly in view of its importance, the term "proprietor in 8-15 possession" is not defined in the legislation. For example it is not stated whether the "possession" can be civil (indirect) as well as natural (direct) possession. The meaning of the expression was considered in *Kaur v Singh*.[67] There the First Division, having decided that a heritable creditor

---

[59] Heritable securities.

[60] (2003) 48 J.L.S.S. Nov./61.

[61] An application for rectification is made on form 9.

[62] 1979 Act, s.9(1). The court includes the Lands Tribunal.

[63] *Stevenson-Hamilton's Exrs v McStay*, 1999 S.L.T. 1175; *Keeper of the Registers of Scotland v M.R.S. Hamilton Ltd*, 2000 S.C. 271.

[64] 1979 Act, s.9(3).

[65] An example is *Brookfield Developments Ltd v Keeper of the Registers of Scotland*, 1989 S.L.T. (Lands Tr.) 105.

[66] *Kaur v Singh*, 1998 S.C. 233 *per* Lord Hamilton. With respect we have reservations about this interpretation.

[67] 1999 S.C. 180. For commentary, with some facts not in the reports, see 1997 S.C.L.R. 1075 and 1998 S.C.L.R. 862. This litigation is of considerable significance for registration of title. For the sequel see *Kaur v Singh (No.2)*, 2000 S.L.T. 1323, dealing with the quantum of the Keeper's liability.

was not a proprietor in possession, inclined to limit "proprietor" to the holder of a primary real right. "Possession", however, was thought to include civil possession, so that owners who let their houses would still be proprietors in possession. There is authority that one cannot be a proprietor in possession in relation to a servitude.[68]

The criterion is perhaps a crude one.[69] If a disposition erroneously conveys part of a neighbouring property, the neighbour is expropriated,[70] and if the disponee has taken possession of the extra area the neighbour cannot normally get title back, but is limited to claiming compensation. Compensation may be sufficient, but often is not. Cases of this sort have happened and have led to much criticism of the 1979 Act. The rule about possession also encourages self-help as between parties, with results that may be unacceptable or absurd.[71]

When being a proprietor in possession is no defence

8–16   Even a proprietor in possession is not always secure against rectification. The legislation provides five situations where rectification remains possible.[72] The *first* is where the purpose of rectification is to note or correct an overriding interest. The *second* is where all parties having an interest agree in writing.

The *third* is where the inaccuracy has been caused by the "fraud or carelessness" of the proprietor. Carelessness requires reasonable foresight of the inaccuracy and therefore a degree of knowledge on the part of the proprietor.[73] Further, in order to "cause" an inaccuracy, the carelessness must be present at or before the time of registration. The evidence is often the application form for registration.[74] If the statements on the form turn out to have been incorrect the Keeper has the possibility of arguing that the proprietor was careless (or even fraudulent) and so not protected against rectification.[75] Needless to say, the Keeper retains the application forms for future scrutiny. One might say, with only a small degree of exaggeration, that a registered title is only as good as its underlying application form.[76] In this connection, it should be noted that the application forms, as well as containing a battery of particular questions, have a catch-all question[77] asking whether there are "any facts and circumstances material to the right or title of the

---

[68] *Griffiths v Keeper of the Registers of Scotland*, Lands Tribunal, December 20, 2002, unreported. See Reid and Gretton, *Conveyancing 2003*, pp.88–91.

[69] Scottish Law Commission, *Discussion Paper on Land Registration: Void and Voidable Titles* (Scot. Law Com. D.P. No.125, 2004), paras 4.1–4.28.

[70] Because title flows from the Register.

[71] See para.7–11.

[72] 1979 Act, s.9(3).

[73] *Dougbar Properties Ltd v Keeper of the Registers of Scotland*, 1999 S.C. 513.

[74] Forms 1–3.

[75] *e.g. Stevenson-Hamilton's Executors v McStay (No.2)*, 2001 S.L.T. 694. Fraud/carelessness has a double effect: it opens the door to the possibility of rectification, even against a proprietor in possession, and it cancels or restricts the Keeper's indemnity. For the latter see ss.12(3)(n) and 13(4).

[76] There is an obvious analogy here with insurance law. The proposal form becomes the basis of the contract of insurance, and a misstatement in it may vitiate the contract.

[77] Question 14 in form 1 and question 8(c) in form 2.

applicant which have not already been disclosed in this application or its accompanying documents". Causation is required as well as fraud or carelessness. So if the Keeper knows of a defect but proceeds to register nonetheless, it seems that the resulting inaccuracy is caused by the Keeper and not by the proprietor in possession. In practice, purchasers are most at risk in first registrations, where a new title sheet is made up partly in reliance on the statements in the forms. In subsequent transactions, purchasers are entitled to rely on the Register, and are not careless merely because they happen to know that the Register is in fact inaccurate.[78]

The *fourth* case is where the point is one about which indemnity has been excluded. For example, Sandra applies for the first registration of a plot of land. The Keeper checks her (GRS) title and finds that, although good for the most part, there is doubt about its validity in respect of a small area. He registers Sandra as owner of the whole, but in respect of the small area he excludes indemnity. A neighbour, Nigel, now points out that he was[79] the owner of this area and asks for rectification in his favour. Since indemnity had been excluded, rectification is possible. It will be observed that exclusion of indemnity has a double consequence, both as to indemnity and as to rectifiability. Conversely, if indemnity is not excluded the proprietor has a double protection: normally the title will not be subject to rectification, and, if for some reason it is nevertheless rectified, he or she should be protected by indemnity.

The *fifth* case is where rectification is consequential on the judicial rectification of the underlying deed. This topic is explored further in Chapter 17.[80]

Reduction

Reduction of a disposition[81] has, of itself, no effect on a registered title, because title flows from the Register and not directly from the deed. The deed is important, but only indirectly, as being the justification for what the Register says. So how can the reduction of the deed be given effect to? Normally there are just two ways in which the Register can be changed: by registration and by rectification.[82] In GRS titles the extract decree of reduction is registered. But protracted litigation has established that this cannot be done in the Land Register. If a decree of reduction is to enter the Land Register, this can only be by rectification and not by registration as such.[83] But even rectification may not be

8-17

---

[78] *Dougbar Properties Ltd v Keeper of the Registers of Scotland*, 1999 S.C. 513.

[79] "Was" not "is" because the registration in favour of Sandra, albeit wrong, made her the owner.

[80] para.17–11.

[81] Reduction is aimed at the deed, not at the title. The title is affected only in so far as the deed is affected.

[82] One of a number of conceptual difficulties with the 1979 Act is a failure to distinguish adequately between the two.

[83] *Short's Tr v Keeper of the Registers of Scotland*, 1996 S.C. (HL) 14. See Reid (1996) 1 S.L.P.Q. 265. This litigation, the costs of which doubtless exceeded the value of the property many times over, well illustrates the shortcomings of the legislation.

possible to give effect to a decree of reduction.[84] If rectification turns out to be barred (typically because there is a proprietor in possession, who has not been guilty of "fraud or carelessness", and there is no exclusion of indemnity) then the reduction cannot be given effect to at all, in which case the deed is void but the title based on the deed is unaffected. However, in such a situation pursuers can in some cases achieve their objective by another route, namely an action against the owner compelling the grant of a disposition.[85] The disposition could then be registered as of right.[86]

Rectification: further restrictions

8-18   The legislation says that the Keeper must rectify when so ordered by the court, but may also rectify by his own administrative act. This can lead to problems. It can be argued that a person adversely affected by the rectification is deprived of property without due process of law, in a manner inconsistent with the European Convention on Human Rights.[87] As a public official, the Keeper is bound to respect the Convention. If the argument is correct, it may suggest that the Keeper should not rectify unless those involved have consented or the court has so ordered.[88]

Even without the human rights dimension, the Keeper has no power to rectify (except with the consent of those involved) where the alleged inaccuracy derives from a deed which, though voidable,[89] stands unreduced. The reason is simple: until such reduction has happened, the Register is accurate.[90] A voidable deed remains valid unless or until it is reduced, and in practice voidable deeds are often never reduced at all, for a variety of reasons.

Indemnity

8-19   The Keeper is obliged to indemnify, *i.e.* to pay compensation to, certain persons who suffer loss.[91] He may be liable not only for loss caused by his fault, but also for loss arising without any fault on his part.

---

[84] Procedurally the simplest course is often to have conclusions for (a) reduction of the deed and (b) rectification of the Register. See *e.g. Stevenson-Hamilton's Exrs v McStay (No.2)*, 2001 S.L.T. 694. The Scottish Law Commission has suggested that rectification should always be allowed in respect of the reduction of voidable deeds: see *Discussion Paper on Land Registration: Void and Voidable Titles* (Scot. Law Com. D.P. No.125, 2004), Part 6.

[85] *Short's Tr v Chung*, 1998 S.C. 105 affirmed 1999 S.C. 471. This was the third and last stage of an astonishing saga. For the first two stages see *Short's Tr v Chung*, 1991 S.L.T. 472 and *Short's Tr v Keeper of the Registers of Scotland*, 1996 S.C. (HL) 14. For discussion see Reid and Gretton, *Conveyancing 1999*, pp.68–71.

[86] The protection of the proprietor in possession is confined to rectification and has no application to registration.

[87] Specifically article 6 read with article 1 of the First Protocol.

[88] For fuller discussion see Gretton, in Alan Boyle, Chris Himsworth, Andrea Loux and Hector MacQueen (eds), *Human Rights and Scots Law* (2002).

[89] If the deed is void then the issues are not quite the same, but whether a deed is voidable or void itself may need judicial determination.

[90] See further Reid and Gretton, *Conveyancing 2000*, p.110. *Higgins v North Lanarkshire Council*, 2001 S.L.T. (Land Court) 2 is a valuable case in many respects but may be criticised on the various grounds mentioned above.

[91] See McDonald (2001) 55 Prop. L.B. 3 and (2002) 56 Prop. L.B. 1.

Compensation payments are funded by the fees charged for registration. It is a title insurance scheme.[92] Indemnity is normally payable when loss is caused by an inaccuracy in the Register, and is payable to the person who suffers that loss. Who suffers that loss depends on whether the inaccuracy, on being discovered, is rectified or not. There are thus two possibilities. The first is that the Register is rectified, in which case the person who suffers loss is the person against whom the rectification is made.[93] The second is that the Register is not rectified, in which case the person who suffers loss is the person who suffers by the fact that the inaccuracy stands uncorrected.[94] For example, suppose that there are two neighbouring plots of land, owned by Alan and Beatrice respectively, and by some error the Register has the boundary wrong, giving Alan a strip of what should be Beatrice's land. The Register is inaccurate. If it is rectified, Alan loses ownership of the strip, and so he is presumptively entitled to be compensated by the Keeper. If the Register is not rectified, Beatrice fails to recover what should be hers, and she is therefore presumptively entitled to be compensated by the Keeper. In short, if the Register is inaccurate, then indemnity is presumptively payable whether it is rectified or not, but to different persons in each case: indemnity for rectification, and indemnity for non-rectification.[95]

But there are important exceptions. Exclusions of indemnity may be either express or implied. The Keeper can expressly exclude indemnity either for the whole title, or in respect of particular aspects only,[96] although this is uncommon. Any exclusion of indemnity will be stated on the land certificate and so will be obvious to purchasers. In addition, there are implied exclusions of indemnity. Section 12(3) of the 1979 Act contains a long and miscellaneous list of exclusions which apply to all titles. These include: reductions under the Bankruptcy (Scotland) Act 1985 and certain other statutes;[97] minor inaccuracies in boundaries;[98] inability to enforce real burdens; matters concerning overriding interests; and fraud or carelessness on the part of the claimant.[99] The precise meaning of many of these exclusions is unclear. The last is of particular

---

[92] 1979 Act, s.24.

[93] 1979 Act, s.12(1)(a).

[94] 1979 Act, s.12(1)(b). Section 12(1) also imposes liability on the Keeper in two other cases, namely if he loses a document and if he issues a land certificate with an error. On the latter provision, see *Keeper of the Registers of Scotland v M.R.S. Hamilton Ltd*, 2000 S.C. 271.

[95] Because of the way the 1979 Act is framed, it is sometimes said that "whoever wins, the Keeper loses." This is not entirely true, but there is much truth in it.

[96] 1979 Act, s.12(2). Just as the Act gives little guidance as to when the Keeper should accept or reject an application, so it gives little guidance as to when, on accepting an application, he should grant or withhold indemnity.

[97] For a strained and unsatisfactory interpretation of this provision, see *Short's Tr v Keeper of the Registers of Scotland*, 1996 S.C. (HL) 14.

[98] Section 12(3)(d) provides that "there shall be no entitlement to indemnity in respect of loss where . . . . the loss arises as a result of any inaccuracy in the delineation of boundaries shown in a title sheet, being an inaccuracy which could not have been rectified by reference to the Ordnance Map . . . " The ROTPB, para.4.26 says this is "to cover the limitations in scaling." That interpretation may be right, but we confess to finding s.12(3)(d) hard to understand.

[99] For the fraud and carelessness exclusion, see *e.g. Dougbar Properties Ltd v Keeper of the Registers of Scotland*, 1999 S.C. 513, and *Stevenson-Hamilton's Executors v McStay (No.2)*, 2001 S.L.T. 694.

importance, because it means that any inaccuracy or omission in the form 1 or form 3 has the potential to count as carelessness, with consequences that may be serious: this is very like the rule in insurance law that the proposal form is the "basis of the contract" and that the proposer must disclose everything material.

Application forms

8-20   An application for registration in the Land Register must be made on the appropriate form. There are three.[1] Form 1 (pink) is used for a first registration, *i.e.* for the disposition or other deed which triggers the switch from the GRS to the Land Register. Form 2 (blue) is the standard form for other cases. However, where part only of registered land is being transferred, form 3 (yellow) should be used. The forms contain a number of questions not all of which can be answered by the grantee's solicitor, and the normal practice is for the form to be completed in draft and then revised by the solicitor for the granter. Usually a separate form is required for each deed, and all deeds submitted at the same time are listed in a single inventory, known as form 4 (white).[2] Thus, buyers of land already registered in the Land Register who are also taking out a loan must complete two forms 2, one for the disposition and another for the standard security. A form 4 is also completed listing the land certificate,[3] the disposition and the standard security. However, a discharge of an existing security submitted at the same time as a disposition does not require its own form 2 provided it is listed on the form 4.[4] Application forms must be signed by the grantees or (as usually in practice) by their solicitors.

The questions must be taken seriously: the resulting land certificate is only as good as the application form. Because of its importance a copy should be retained (as should a copy of the form 4). The Keeper retains a copy, and if any problems subsequently arise he will check it carefully.

The registration process

8-21   We begin with a historical analogy. Before 1858 conveyances could not be recorded in the GRS. Subject to certain exceptions, notarial instruments of sasine were recorded. The actual conveyances were mere midcouples or links in title, the deeds that underlay and justified the notarial instrument. After 1858 conveyances could be directly recorded.[5] The Land Register reverts, in this respect, to the pre-1858 position. The form 1 or 2 is like a notarial instrument of sasine. The role of the actual

---

[1] Land Registration (Scotland) Rules 1980, r.9(1). For practical guidance, see ROTPB, Ch.5. Appendix A of David A. Brand, Andrew J .M. Steven and Scott Wortley, *Professor McDonald's Conveyancing Manual* (7th ed., 2004) contains useful examples of completed application forms.

[2] Form 4 is submitted in duplicate, with one copy being returned as a receipt.

[3] For registered land, applications must normally be accompanied by the land certificate and, where appropriate, by the charge certificate also. See Land Registration (Scotland) Rules 1980, r.9(3).

[4] ROTPB, para.5.30. In a first registration it is not necessary to record the discharge separately in the GRS.

[5] Except for general conveyances.

deed of conveyance is reduced to that of a midcouple or link in title that underlies and justifies the entry in the Land Register, in that it connects the current applicant with the existing registered proprietor.

The Keeper can refuse an application if it is not accompanied by the appropriate deeds and other documentation.[6] So, for example, an a *non domino* disposition can be refused on the ground that there are no supporting deeds to vouch for the granter's ownership. Further, the legislation requires the Keeper to refuse an application in cases where (a) the land is not sufficiently described (b) it relates to a right abolished by the Abolition of Feudal Tenure etc. (Scotland) Act 2000[7] (c) the land is a souvenir plot (d) the application is frivolous or vexatious (e) (except in first registrations) the deed does not refer to the title number, and (f) the registration fee is not tendered.[8] Unless an application is refused or withdrawn, the date of registration is the date on which the application is received.[9] The date of registration is the relevant date for the creation of any real right which flows from registration.[10] Ranking is by day and not by time within a particular day, so that two applications received at different times on the same day carry the same date of registration and, in a competition between them, rank equally.[11]

It sometimes happens that the documentation submitted with an application is insufficient for the Keeper to make an informed decision. In that case he can formally request that the applicant submit the missing documentation within a stated period of not less than 60 days.[12] The sanction for non-compliance is that the application will either be rejected, or accepted with an exclusion of indemnity. Although the rule allows the Keeper to set a period longer than 60 days, he does not usually do so.

In the Land Register what is registered is the grantee's title and not the deed evidencing that title, though a copy of that deed will in fact be kept, together with the application form. In first registrations the Keeper must convert the GRS title into a Land Register title by making up a new title sheet.[13] Otherwise, his task is to make the necessary alteration to an existing title sheet.[14] So if William is acquiring registered land from Margaret, and at the same time granting a standard security, the Keeper will substitute "William" for "Margaret" in the proprietorship section, and add the standard security to the charges section. If registered land is to be divided, a new title sheet is opened up for the property being split off, and corresponding adjustments are made to the parent title sheet.

---

[6] 1979 Act, s.4(1).

[7] A provision designed to prevent applications in respect of superiorities, or of the superiority element of a mixed estate (*i.e.* a title which comprises a mixture of superiority and *dominium utile*).

[8] 1979 Act, s.4(2).

[9] 1979 Act, s.4(3).

[10] 1979 Act, s.3(4).

[11] 1979 Act, s.7(2), (4). Ranking in this sense is only really appropriate for standard securities. If two applications for ownership are accepted, only one can confer ownership. Here s.3(1) appears to turn the normal rules on their head by preferring the later application: see Reid, *Property*, para.685.

[12] Land Registration (Scotland) Rules 1980, r.12.

[13] 1979 Act, s.5(1)(a)(i).

[14] 1979 Act, s.5(1)(a)(ii), (b).

Registration of a primary real right is followed by the issue to the new registered proprietor of the land certificate, which is an authenticated copy of the title sheet.[15] No one else is entitled to a land certificate and at any given time only one such certificate exists for any given real right in land.[16] There is no equivalent certificate for secondary real rights except in the case of heritable securities, where a charge certificate is issued.[17] The land certificate should be carefully checked by the grantee's solicitors, particularly in a first registration. The land certificate replaces the old GRS deeds which, in theory at least, cease to be relevant, except where indemnity has been excluded.

The Keeper also returns the deed which induced the registration, and this should be kept with the land certificate. While in practice copies of all deeds submitted are retained by the Register, only those referred to in the land certificate are available for inspection under the 1979 Act,[18] although a wider right of access is conferred by the Freedom of Information (Scotland) Act 2002.[19]

First registration

8–22   In a first registration the Keeper must carry out a full examination of the GRS title, with the result that the process is more complicated. If problems are anticipated the Keeper should be contacted in advance: at the Registers of Scotland there is a Department of Pre-Registration Enquiries.[20]

The following must be sent to the Keeper:

    (i) the disposition;
    (ii) the new standard security (if there is one);
    (iii) the discharge of the old standard security (if there was one);
    (iv) the deeds comprising the GRS title;
    (v) any other relevant documents such as matrimonial affidavits and death certificates;
    (vi) form 1, in respect of the disposition;
    (vii) form 2, in respect of the standard security;
    (viii) form 4, in duplicate, listing the writs being submitted and any other deeds referred to but not submitted.

The disposition will trigger first registration, and thereafter the standard security will be in respect of an interest which has already (by a single

---

[15] 1979 Act, s.5(2). For the form, see Land Registration (Scotland) Rules 1980, r.14 and Sch.A, form 6. By s.5(4) a land certificate is "accepted for all purposes as sufficient evidence of the contents of the title sheet of which the land certificate is a copy".

[16] But a substitute copy, marked "substitute", may be issued where the original has been lost or destroyed. See Land Registration (Scotland) Rules 1980, r.19. Anyone may apply (on form 15) for a simple copy ("office copy") of the title sheet or part thereof: s.6(5).

[17] 1979 Act, s.5(3), (4). For the form, see Land Registration (Scotland) Rules 1980, r.15 and Sch.A, form 7.

[18] 1979 Act, s.6(5).

[19] Subject to exceptions, any Scottish public authority (such as the Keeper: Sch.1, para.11) must make available any information which it holds: see s.1(1). The Act is expected to come fully into force on January 1, 2005.

[20] The URL is *http://www.ros.gov.uk/solicitor/prereg*.

moment) become a registered interest. However, the title number cannot be inserted because at this stage it has not been allocated. If the standard security is submitted later, the title number, which by this stage will be known, can simply be written in at the top of the first page: a new deed is not required.

Form 1, read with the notes thereto[21] and the guidance in the ROTPB, is fairly self-explanatory. The section headed "schedule of heritable securities, etc." is for existing, undischarged securities, including those to be discharged as part of the application, but not including the new security being granted by the purchasers. The section headed "schedule of burdens" should simply list the burdens writs by reference to the form 4. The "FAS" number is the Keeper's account number for the law firm submitting the application. Where a question is inapplicable, instead of answering yes or no, one simply writes "N/A". For instance, where the disposition is from one individual to another, "N/A" will be the response to questions 6, 7 and 8, which are concerned only with bodies corporate.

Under head (iv) above (GRS title) only the relevant deeds need to accompany the application, *i.e.* chiefly the foundation writ, the deeds since then, the burdens deeds, and the deeds referred to for descriptions. A specimen list is given at para.5.5 of the ROTPB. Thus, many of the deeds handed over at settlement need not, and should not, be forwarded to the Keeper.

THE GENERAL REGISTER OF SASINES

Structure and contents

The General Register of Sasines ("GRS") was established by the Registration Act 1617[22] and is now regulated chiefly by the Land Registers (Scotland) Act 1868.[23] At first dispositions, and other conveyancing deeds, were not recorded directly. What was recorded was the instrument of sasine, which was a notarial deed that followed on from the conveyancing deed itself, and which would reflect its substantive provisions. But since the Titles to Land (Scotland) Act 1858 conveyancing deeds can themselves be recorded. About half of all title units are still in the GRS. Moreover, deeds are still being recorded[24] there, in cases where the property in question is still in the GRS and the deed is not one that triggers the change to the new Register, such as a standard security, or a disposition by way of donation.

Unlike the Land Register, the GRS is a register of deeds not of rights, though of course rights flow from the deeds. Physically the Register is

8-23

---

[21] The notes are not on the forms themselves, but are in a schedule to the Land Registration (Scotland) Rules 1980.

[22] Still in force. For the history, see L. Ockrent, *Land Rights: An Enquiry into the History of Registration for Publication in Scotland* (1942).

[23] See also the Register of Sasines (Scotland) Act 1987 which authorises the keeping of the Register otherwise than in paper form. See, further, a note from the Keeper at (1989) 34 J.L.S.S. 235.

[24] Although one can speak of "registration" in the GRS, the word traditionally favoured by conveyancers is "recording".

nothing but a massive collection—one might liken it to a warehouse, not in physical terms but in functional terms—of copy deeds, stretching back hundreds of years.[25] Originally the copies were made by hand, by clerks with quills and ink. Early in the 20th century photocopying was introduced, and nowadays the copying is on microfilm.[26] The full-sized pre-microfilm copies are bound up into large and heavy record volumes. There is no arrangement by property. The only division is by county. Thus for, say, East Lothian one deed might be a disposition of a house in North Berwick, the next a standard security over a shop in Haddington, and the third a servitude over a farm near Tranent. The next deed affecting the farm might be thousands or tens of thousands of pages later. And in all this mass of paper and microfilm, there is nothing which actually states, in an authoritative manner, who has right to what. Of course, if there is a recorded disposition by Jack to Jill then Jill is probably the owner, but it is possible for deeds in the GRS to be voidable or actually void.[27] Deeds of every kind, it is true, can be voidable or void, and not just deeds in the GRS, but in the GRS title rests on the recorded deed, so voidability or nullity of the deed will result in voidability or nullity in the real right itself.[28] By contrast, real rights in the Land Register are rather more insulated (but not wholly insulated) from the deeds on which they are based.

Indexes and search sheets

8-24   The GRS is indexed both by person and by property.[29] Most important of all are the search sheets.[30] For any given property a separate sheet is maintained for all the primary real rights therein, that is to say for ownership, and any recorded leases and sub-leases.[31] Whenever a deed is recorded, a brief summary is prepared and entered into the appropriate search sheet. The summary also states the place in the register itself where the deed can be found. The search sheet system is powerful and efficient. It enables the state of the title to virtually any plot of land still in the GRS to be investigated quickly and easily. An example will give the idea. Mary owns Whiteacre. There is a search sheet for the ownership, and the disposition in favour of Mary (from Louis) is mentioned there, as are previous dispositions of the property (Kate to Louis, Ian to Kate and so on) as far back as the property has been a

---

[25] Herein lies one of the many differences between the GRS and the Land Register. The GRS offers a complete history of the title of a property going back centuries. The Land Register is non-historical, and one knows nothing of the past history of the property. There is nothing but a memory-less moving present. This aspect of the Land Register has a number of unsatisfactory consequences.

[26] Register of Sasines (Scotland) Act 1987.

[27] This presents obvious difficulties for examination of title, discussed in Ch.7.

[28] This statement is a little oversimplified. In particular, prescription may cure defects.

[29] For examples of the persons index and property index see G. L. Gretton, *Guide to Searches* (1991), pp.6 and 8.

[30] For an example of a search sheet, see G. L. Gretton, *Guide to Searches*, p.12. Search sheets have no statutory basis, though without them modern conveyancing would be impossible. They were introduced in 1871. Hence it can be difficult to trace pre-1871 deeds in the Register unless one knows the date of registration.

[31] This is the same as in the Land Register, with title sheets.

separate unit—or back to the start of the search sheet system in the 1870s. Also listed will be other relevant deeds such as standard securities. Suppose that, before the county became operational for the Land Register, Mary granted a 25-year lease to Nigel. This would be noted on the title sheet, but at the same time a new title sheet for the leasehold would be created.

Warrants of registration

Until recently, all deeds presented for registration had to contain a warrant of registration.[32] Broadly speaking, the warrant replaced the instrument of sasine, which was mandatory until 1858.[33] The warrant was a request by the grantees (or in practice their solicitors) to record the deed. There was a statutory form.[34] The warrant could appear anywhere on the deed but in practice was usually placed at the foot of the last page. Warrants of registration ceased to be required on November 28, 2004 for the GRS.[35] They were never required for the Land Register. 8–25

The registration process

The deed is accompanied by an application form. The same form is used for any deed.[36] The deed must be accompanied by the appropriate SDLT certificate.[37] The extent of the Keeper's power to reject deeds for the GRS is uncertain. Probably it is not very extensive, although there are remarks in *Macdonald v Keeper of the Registers*[38] which might suggest otherwise. Recently the Keeper has begun to reject a *non domino* dispositions, except in certain circumstances,[39] but his right to do so has not been judicially tested. Three clear reasons exist for refusal to register: (a) no SDLT certificate; (b) insufficient identification of the property (the situation in *Macdonald*); (c) deed not properly executed. Much more common than unilateral rejection is an invitation by the Register to withdraw a deed. It then becomes necessary to weigh up the seriousness, or otherwise, of the error in question. It may be so minor that withdrawal is unnecessary; and occasionally the "error" turns out to be no such thing. 8–26

Once a deed has been accepted for recording it goes through various registration processes.[40] The Presentment Book,[41] which is used as a receipt book for all writs, and which gives the date of presentment, the name of the writ, and the parties, has been computerised since April 1, 1992. The Keeper takes a copy of the deed, nowadays by microfilm. The

---

[32] 1868 Act, ss.15 and 141.

[33] Titles to Land (Scotland) Act 1858.

[34] Conveyancing (Scotland) Act 1924, s.10(1), (3) and Sch.F.

[35] Abolition of Feudal Tenure etc. (Scotland) Act 2000, s.5.

[36] At the time of writing the non-statutory CPB2 form, in use since 1992, was about to be replaced by a new form prescribed under the 2000 Act, s.5.

[37] For SDLT certificates, see paras 15–13 and 15–14.

[38] 1914 S.C. 854.

[39] See (1997) 42 J.L.S.S. 72.

[40] See the *Stair Memorial Encyclopaedia*, Vol.6, paras 452 *et seq*.

[41] For an example of the Presentment Book in its traditional (pre-computerisation) form, see G. L. Gretton, *Guide to Searches*, p.2.

original deed is then returned to the grantee. A certificate of registration is stamped on the original of the deed and gives details of (a) the date of recording and (b) the fiche and frame number (or previously book and folio number[42]) of the copy preserved in the Register.

Since all recorded deeds are preserved, in copy, anyone can obtain copies of such copies.[43] Copies come in two varieties. First there is the so-called quick copy, which is a simple photocopy. Then there is an extract,[44] which is also a photocopy, but which comes complete with a backing and a certificate that it is a true copy. By section 45 of the 1970 Act an extract copy is as good as the original deed.[45]

---

[42] The folio is the page.

[43] Here there is a strong contrast with the Land Register. That register is not a register of deeds, and even though the Keeper actually keeps copies of important deeds, he will not normally release them to the public.

[44] An extract of a document is not a short version of it but a full official authenticated copy.

[45] Quick copies and extracts can be obtained direct from the Keeper, or can be obtained through firms of searchers.

CHAPTER 9

SEARCHES, REPORTS AND LETTERS OF OBLIGATION

INTRODUCTORY

Introduction

To search the registers is simply to look to see what they say. The   9–01
registers that are most important for the conveyancers, and the ones
covered in this chapter, are the Land Register, the General Register of
Sasines ("GRS") and the Register of Inhibitions and Adjudications. The
word "search" is sometimes used to mean the act of searching. But it is
also used to mean the report on what was discovered. The tendency
nowadays is to use the word "report" if that is what is meant.

If the sellers' title is in the Land Register there will be a land
certificate. But that certificate will not be up-to-date. The sellers may
assert that nothing has appeared in the Land Register since the
certificate was issued, but the buyers would be unwise to rely on such
assurances. The same is true for property still in the GRS. The sellers
will hold the deeds, including the disposition in their favour, and they
may say that the deeds produced are all the relevant deeds. But there is
no way to verify that without checking the GRS itself. The risk is less
with the Land Register than with the GRS, for in the case of the Land
Register a change on the register will normally be accompanied by an
updating of the land certificate. But even with the Land Register there is
some element of risk.

In this chapter it is assumed that separate solicitors act for the
granters and the grantees. However, where there is a secured loan the
same solicitors will usually act for both parties.[1] Moreover, in
remortgages it is quite common for the borrower to be unrepresented. In
that case everything is done by the lenders' solicitors, who are acting
exclusively for the lenders.

Who searches?

The registers are public and so anyone can search them. In practice,   9–02
searches are usually done either by the Keeper[2] or by firms of professional searchers. The Land Registration (Scotland) Rules 1980 seem to

---

[1] Assuming that the loan is an ordinary home loan.

[2] The Keeper offers searches in Land Register, the GRS and the Register of Inhibitions
and Adjudications except in the unusual case where the property is in the GRS and is, for
the time being, staying there. Searches in the Companies Register cannot be obtained from
the Keeper. Searches can be instructed and transmitted digitally through the Keeper's
eFORMS ONLINE system on *http://www.ros.gov.uk/*.

have assumed that searching would be a monopoly of the Keeper. It gave a "list of forms to be used in connection with registration"[3] and these forms were all addressed to the Keeper. But there was nothing in the 1979 Act to support that view of matters. When the dust had settled, independent searchers[4] were providing searches as well as the Keeper. Independent searchers are normally instructed on forms substantially the same as those prescribed by the Rules for use by the Keeper. But they are free in principle to offer any kind of search, whereas the Keeper can offer only searches of the kinds prescribed by the 1980 Rules. Anyone can instruct a search, but in sales the search is in practice instructed by the sellers' solicitors, and the reports are then forwarded by them to the buyers' solicitors. Production of search reports being the sellers' responsibility, the cost falls on them, unless otherwise agreed.

Liability for mistakes

9–03   A searcher is liable for loss caused by an inaccurate search. This liability is statutory in the case of the Keeper, and would seem to extend not only to the person who instructed the search but also to third parties who have relied on it.[5] Independent searchers are liable in contract to those who have instructed them. Whether they are liable to third parties who rely on the search seems not to have been tested in reported caselaw. But on the general principles of the law of delict it would seem that such liability does exist. It is certainly the general understanding that searchers are liable to third parties.

When searches are and are not made

9–04   Searches are made before money changes hands, whether the payment of a price or the release of a loan to be secured on heritable property. The final search will, however, not come in until after settlement. Searches are mainly for the benefit of buyers and lenders. The sellers, or the borrowers, may claim to have a good title, but that needs to be checked against the registers themselves. As well as sales and secured loans, there may be other circumstances in which a search may be made. A person acquiring a subordinate real right will usually wish to check the granter's title. When someone dies the executor may wish to check the title even if no sale is being contemplated. And a person may simply be curious to know who has what rights in a certain building or plot of land.

An obligation is probably implied by law that sellers shall exhibit or deliver clear searches.[6] The rule seems to be that delivery is required for such searches as relate exclusively to the property conveyed.[7] Missives usually have a clause which repeats the implied rule. Occasionally, a contract will say that the sellers need neither exhibit nor deliver a search. That will not of itself free them from an obligation to grant a valid title.

---

[3] Opening words of Sch.A.
[4] Such as Millar & Bryce: *http://www.millar-bryce.com/*.
[5] Land Registration (Scotland) Act 1979, s.12(1)(d).
[6] See para.6–18.
[7] 1979 Act, s.16(1).

It merely shifts the onus on to the purchasers to make the necessary searches themselves. But the granter of a non-onerous deed in general does not need to show good title (you don't look a gift horse in the mouth) and hence need not exhibit searches. Examples are donations and conveyances by an executor in implement of a legacy.

Some other registers

The registers that are most important to the conveyancer are the Land 9–05 Register, the GRS, and the Register of Inhibitions and Adjudications.[8] But there exist many other registers, which may be of relevance. We shall mention a few of them. (i) One is the Companies Register.[9] (ii) Another is the Register of Community Interests in Land, which was set up by the Land Reform (Scotland) Act 2003 and which also has a role for the Agricultural Holdings (Scotland) Act 2003. If the property is registered in this register then the owner is not free to sell it.[10] (iii) A third is the Building Standards Register, established by the Building (Scotland) Act 2003, which will, when the provisions are in force, contain information on the building law status of individual properties. (iv) Another is the Planning Register which records the planning applications for particular properties.[11] (v) The Books of Council and Session are a register too well-known to require explanation:[12] in practice many deeds relevant to conveyancing practice are registered there.

Registers Direct: on-line access

The Land Register can be accessed online. One must first register as a 9–06 user, but there is no subscription charge: payment is by use. The system is called Registers Direct. It also covers parts of the GRS. The use of the system by the legal profession seems to be rather limited, and it has not replaced searches and reports from the Keeper and from independent searchers.

PROPERTY IN THE LAND REGISTER[13]

Form 12/13 Reports

Where the property is in the Land Register the usual method of 9–07 search is a form 12 report, either from the Keeper or from independent searchers. This discloses any changes in the title sheet since the date that the land certificate was issued. In most cases there will have been no changes. If there is a significant gap between the date of the form 12 report and settlement, it can be updated by a form 13 report. In all cases

---

[8] The first two were the subject of Ch.8.
[9] See Ch.25.
[10] For a missive clause dealing with this register see Reid and Gretton, *Conveyancing 2003*, p.140.
[11] Town and Country Planning (Scotland) Act 1997, s.36.
[12] But see Ch.8, n.2.
[13] See generally paras. 8–08 *et seq.* and the ROTPB, Ch.3.

the title number must be given to enable the search to be effected. The form 12 should be sent to the Keeper in duplicate. The form 12 report he sends back is normally headed "12A", but for special cases the response may be a 12B, 12C, 12D or 12E.[14]

A form 12/13 report is double search. It searches not only the Land Register but also the Register of Inhibitions and Adjudications. The form needs to give the names and addresses of the relevant parties. More detailed consideration of the Register of Inhibitions and Adjudications will be found later in this chapter.[15]

Form 12/13 is drafted by the sellers' solicitors. They will insert the names and designations of the sellers to the part of the form requesting a search in the Register of Inhibitions and Adjudications. The draft is sent, accompanied by the land certificate, to the buyers' solicitors for revisal. The latter will add the names and designations of the buyers in the part of the form dealing with the Register of Inhibitions and Adjudications. If separate solicitors are acting for the buyers' lenders they too should have the opportunity to revise the draft. The form 12 report will be obtained, and exhibited to the buyers or lenders, before settlement. After settlement the Keeper will in due course issue a new land certificate and, in the case of a standard security, a charge certificate. These also are reports. In the GRS system searches are divided between interim and final, and in the Land Register the form 12/13 report corresponds to the interim report and the land certificate and charge certificate correspond to the final search.

Other methods of searching the Land Register

9-08   There are two other methods of searching the Land Register. One is to have the land certificate updated.[16] Evidently this can be done only by the Keeper and not by independent searchers. This method is in practice not used in sales and loans, partly because it is relatively slow and partly because it may be inconvenient for the land certificate to be at Register House precisely when it is most needed by the parties. The other is a form 15 report, also called an office copy. This is the same as a land certificate except that it does not have the same evidential status. It can be obtained either from the Keeper or from independent searchers. Once again this method is seldom adopted.

FIRST REGISTRATION

Introduction

9-09   If the property is still in the GRS the present transaction will normally switch it into the Land Register, *i.e.* a first registration. All relevant deeds should be among the deeds sent for examination. The buyers would however be unwise to take this on trust, for there might be one or

---

[14] ROTPB, para.3.7.
[15] paras 9–15 *et seq.*
[16] This is requested on a form 8.

more deeds recorded in the GRS which are not among the deeds which the sellers produce. This might be as a result of fraud by the sellers, or mere inadvertence. Here are some examples.

(i) The estate is a large one and over the years the sellers have sold off various small parcels of land. Indeed, this is the norm for large estates. In that case, copies of the break-off deeds should have been put up with the titles. But it can happen that one or more such deeds have been overlooked, so from the deeds in the possession of the sellers it looks as if they own rather more than they actually do.

(ii) It might be that the sellers have granted a standard security without telling their solicitors. This is uncommon, but far from unknown. The sellers may not be fraudulent in not telling their solicitors. They may not realise what they have done. Such securities are commonly called "double-glazing standard securities" because they are often presented to a householder for signing for credit deals, such as for double-glazing.

(iii) There might be an adjudication against the sellers. In that case, the sellers should know of it, but a copy will not be with the title deeds, and the sellers may conveniently forget to tell their solicitors.

So it is necessary for the GRS to be searched.[17] The Land Registration (Scotland) Rules 1980 prescribe forms to be used by the Keeper. These are forms 10 and 11. Generally only the form 10 is used but if there is a significant gap between the date of the form 10 report and settlement, it can be updated by a form 11 report. Parties are free to instruct independent searchers. Although a form 10/11 report is primarily a search of the GRS and the Register of Inhibitions and Adjudications, the Land Register will also be checked, to ensure that the property, or part of it, has not already been registered in the Land Register. In practice the key to searching the GRS is the system of "search sheets". Each unit of property has its own sheet—rather like the title sheet in the Land Register—and this gives a brief summary, chronologically, of the deeds affecting that property. Details of the deeds can then be found in the register itself.

Form 10 was intended to be used when the property is first marketed, and form 11 was intended as an update to be used shortly before settlement. But in modern practice only the form 10 is generally used, this happening shortly before settlement, and a form 11 continuation is used only if there is a delay. The two forms instruct both a GRS search and also a personal search.

The form 10 must identify the property sufficiently. It cannot identify the property by title number since no title number yet exists. It may be that the existing GRS description is sufficient. If not, a new plan will have to be prepared, and submitted with the form 10. A copy of this plan

---

[17] And also the Register of Inhibitions and Adjudications and, if appropriate, the Companies Register. See below and, for the Companies Register, Ch.25.

can then be used for the disposition. In most cases the seller will, at the same time as submitting the form 10, also submit a P16.[18] Whilst some difficult questions exist as to what the proper length of the GRS search should be, going back in time, such questions are less important if the property is entering the Land Register since the effect of registration will normally be to protect the acquirer. Although there will almost always be an existing search report among the deeds (see below) the Keeper will not refer to it, but will search afresh.

THE GRS SYSTEM

Introduction

9-10   If the property is still in the GRS the present transaction will normally switch it into the Land Register, *i.e.* a first registration. The exceptions are (a) where the property is being transferred but not by reason of sale, such as by reason of donation or succession, and (b) where the transaction is not a transfer but the grant of a subordinate real right such as a standard security. Where one of these exceptions applies the old form of search will be required.

The memorandum

9-11   The purpose of a GRS search is simply to identify all deeds registered there, affecting a defined property, within any defined period.[19] Almost always there will be an existing search report among the deeds, prepared at the time of the last transaction. In that case, the practice is to send this off to the searchers with a request that they continue it to the present. This is called a continuation of search. The letter of request to the searchers is called a memorandum for continuation of search (or a memorandum for search if there is no existing search report), and follows a standard format. It is drafted by the granters' solicitors and sent to the grantees' solicitors for approval, revision and return. The granters' solicitors then extend it (*i.e.* make a principal version) and send it off to the searchers, and it will be returned to them when complete. The granters pay the searchers' fee. Occasionally, there is no existing search and in that case it will be necessary to instruct a new search.

Period

9-12   How far back a search should go depends on various factors, but the general rule is that it should go back 40 years or to the date of the foundation writ, whichever is the longer. Some consider it sufficient to go back only to the foundation writ, since any prior writ will be irrelevant by reason of positive prescription. There are, however, several reasons

---

[18] See Chs 7 and 12.

[19] For an example of a GRS search, combined, as usual, with a search of the Personal Register, see David A. Brand, Andrew J. M. Steven and Scott Wortley, *Professor McDonald's Conveyancing Manual* (7th ed., 2004), Appendix A.

why the standard advice is to go back 40 years. One is that there might be undischarged securities. As a rule of thumb, any security older than 40 years has probably been extinguished by payment or by the long negative prescription. A second is that positive prescription works only if there has been possession. In practice, one does not normally check the fact of possession. A 40-year search is a sort of substitute, for if there were a competing title, such a search would almost certainly show it up, and in that event further inquiry could be made. If there is an existing search, it should be checked back either to the foundation writ or for 40 years whichever is the longer, for the same reasons.

Interim reports

A GRS search report comes in two forms: interim and final. The final 9–13 report will be sent by the searchers some time after settlement. Processing deeds in the GRS takes some time, so that a search carried out on a given day will not give a conclusive view of the deeds that are on the register on that day. The searchers will be asked for an interim report, shortly before settlement. This corresponds to the form 10/11, or the form 11/12. The final search report corresponds, in a sense, to the land certificate.

Start and close dates for the GRS search

The memorandum for the searchers gives both the start date and the 9–14 closing date for the search. The start date will be a specific date, normally the day after the close of the existing search. The closing date will not be a specific date, but will list the deed being recorded. If there is more than one, the relevant deed will be the last one. For instance in a remortgage, two deeds will be recorded, namely the new standard security and the discharge of the old standard security. The memorandum will tell the searchers to close the search as soon as both of these have been recorded. When the searchers find both these deeds on the register they will then close off the search.

The Personal Search

The Personal Register

The personal search is a search in the Register of Inhibitions and 9–15 Adjudications. (That is its official name, but in practice it tends to be called the Personal Register or the Diligence Register, or the ROI.) Whereas the Land Register is a register of properties and the GRS is a register of deeds, the Personal Register is, roughly speaking, a register of names. The main things it includes are inhibitions and sequestrations. Despite the name, adjudications normally go into the Land Register or the GRS and not the Personal Register. A person who is inhibited or sequestrated is, of course, barred from selling.

Types of entry

There are various kinds of entry which may be found in the Personal 9–16 Register. The following is a non-exhaustive list:

(a) Inhibition, usually in the form of letters of inhibition or summons and inhibition.

(b) Notice of inhibition.[20]

(c) Discharge, or restriction, by inhibitor.[21]

(d) Certified copy interlocutor, or decree, of recall.

(e) Decree of dismissal or absolvitor where inhibition was used on dependence.[22]

(f) Notice of litigiosity, which may take the form either of a summons of adjudication or a summons of reduction.[23] These have an effect similar to inhibition.

(g) Decree of adjudication. However, such decrees are not normally registered here at all, but in the Land Register or GRS as appropriate.

(h) Notice concerning sequestration.[24]

(i) Trust deed for behoof of creditors.[25]

(j) Company administration order and interlocutor refusing or discharging such order.[26]

(k) Application for rectification.[27]

(l) English bankruptcy order.[28]

Inhibitions[29]

9-17   Inhibition forbids the inhibited person from selling or otherwise alienating heritable property. It also strikes at a subsequent grant of heritable security, and probably a subsequent floating charge in so far as the charge affects heritage. Breaches of inhibition are not void, but are voidable at the instance of the inhibitor. This is done by an action of reduction *ex capite inhibitionis,* though in certain types of case it is possible for the inhibitor to enforce without any action of reduction. An inhibition endures for five years, after which it prescribes.[30] An inhibition can be used not only in execution of a decree but also on the dependence.[31] In the latter case it will become void if the pursuer fails in the action. The sheriff court has no jurisdiction in inhibition, and so if pursuers wish to inhibit in such an action they must obtain letters of

---

[20] Titles to Land Consolidation (Scotland) Act 1868, s.155.

[21] A restriction leaves the inhibition partially in force.

[22] This will have the effect of discharging the inhibition.

[23] 1868 Act, s.159 as amended by the Law Reform (Miscellaneous Provisions) (Scotland) Act 1985, Sch.2, para.4.

[24] Bankruptcy (Scotland) Act 1985, s.14. See also ss.15(5) and 17(8).

[25] Bankruptcy (Scotland) Act 1985, Sch.5, para.2. This provides that the trustee "may" register. The provision is thus non-mandatory.

[26] Insolvency (Scotland) Rules 1986, r.2.3 as amended by the Insolvency (Scotland) Amendment Rules 2003.

[27] Under s.8 of the Law Reform (Miscellaneous Provisions) (Scotland) Act 1985. See Ch.17.

[28] These are registered if the English trustee so wishes but not otherwise. Their effect is uncertain.

[29] See G. L. Gretton, *Law of Inhibition and Adjudication* (2nd ed., 1996).

[30] Conveyancing (Scotland) Act 1924, s.44.

[31] There has been a recent change in the procedure for inhibition on the dependence: see Act of Sederunt (Rules of the Court of Session Amendment No.6) (Diligence on the Dependence) 2003 (SSI 2003/537).

inhibition from the Court of Session. Letters of inhibition can also be used in Court of Session actions, but usually a warrant to inhibit is included in the signeted summons, in which case what will appear on the search will be the words "summons and inhibition".

Inhibition may be discharged voluntarily by the inhibitor, the discharge being registered in the Personal Register. Or it may be discharged by interlocutor of the Court of Session, this being called a recall. Recalls likewise are registered in the Personal Register. Partial discharge and partial recall are possible, whereby the inhibition is discharged from certain property or a certain transaction, while retaining its effect as against other property and transactions. Such a partial recall is sometimes called a restriction.

Inhibition simply identifies the person inhibited, without specifying any particular property, as all heritable property in Scotland (whether in the Land Register or the GRS) is automatically affected. It is purely a negative diligence, and confers on the inhibitor no real right. A creditor who wishes to obtain a real right by diligence must use adjudication. Adjudication need not be preceded by inhibition, though in practice it usually is. A decree of adjudication, upon being registered in the Land or Sasine Register, gives the adjudger a real right, being a type of judicial heritable security.[32]

Inhibition takes effect on the day when it is registered. However, the inhibitor may first register a notice of inhibition.[33] If so, the inhibition takes effect from the date of the registration of the notice, provided that the inhibition itself is registered within 21 days of the notice. If the inhibition itself is registered outwith that period, the notice is void, and the inhibition takes effect from its own date of registration. The reason for the notice procedure is speed and surprise: in practice, it is usually possible to register a notice several days earlier than the inhibition itself.

Sequestration and trust deeds

After inhibitions, the most important entries on the Personal Register   9–18 are sequestrations.[34] Trust deeds for behoof of creditors may also appear.[35] Naturally, a purchaser wishes to be sure that the seller has not been sequestrated, and has not granted a trust deed. In the case of sequestration, what enters the register is normally the "warrant to cite". This does not mean that the person has in fact been sequestrated, but only that there is a petition for sequestration. However, the warrant to cite, upon being recorded, bars the debtor from alienating heritable property. Moreover, if the warrant to cite is not followed by registration of an interlocutor dismissing the petition, it is normally a fair inference that sequestration has taken place. Occasionally a sheriff clerk will fail to register some warrants to cite in the Personal Register. The effect of

---

[32] The Scottish Law Commission has suggested that adjudication be replaced with a new diligence known as land attachment. See *Report on Diligence* (Scot. Law Com. No.183, 2001). At the time of writing legislation was expected.

[33] See s.155 of the 1868 Act.

[34] Bankruptcy (Scotland) Act 1985, s.14.

[35] Bankruptcy (Scotland) Act 1985, Sch.5(2). These may be registered in the Personal Register, but they do not have to be.

such omission on a *bona fide* third party is unclear. An alternative source of information on bankruptcies is the Register of Insolvencies.[36] On the matters that it deals with (which do not include inhibitions) the information in this register is more detailed than what can be found in the Personal Register.

Occasionally, it happens that a seller is sequestrated about the time of the sale, so that the warrant to cite does not appear on the interim report. In that case there follows what is traditionally called the "race to the register".[37] The trustee in sequestration can complete title in the Land Register or GRS, and if s/he does so before the buyers have registered their disposition, the trustee will have won the race. S/he will be the owner, in trust for the creditors, and the buyers will have nothing, except a claim in the sequestration. The reason is that at the time when the buyers register their disposition, the granter is no longer owner, so that the deed is, by this time, an *a non domino* deed. Conversely, if the buyers complete title first, they win the race. In practice, it is difficult for the trustee to act quickly, so that the race is more of a stroll for the buyers.[38]

Instructing the personal search

9-19   It is normal to instruct the search in the Personal Register as part of the form 12. But if the transaction will switch the property for the first time into the Land Register it is normal to instruct the personal search as part of the form 10.[39] In these two cases the form 10/11 report, or the form 12/13 report, will expressly state whether there is any relevant entry in the Personal Register, but the land certificate will be silent, unless there is a relevant entry, in which case it will be stated on the certificate.[40] Thus if the certificate says nothing, that means that the Personal Register was, or appeared to be, clear. If the property is, for the time being, staying in the GRS a personal search will be instructed together with the search in the GRS, and the same pattern of interim and final report exists. The Personal Register has the advantage that it is always up to date, so that a search done today will show entries made yesterday. Consequently, the need for the letter of obligation is less. Still, the latter covers the Personal Register also.

When the sellers' solicitors draft the form 10/11 or form 12/13, or the memorandum for search, they will put the sellers' names on it. When the buyers' solicitors revise it they will normally add the buyers' name. The main reason for this is that the buyers will normally be granting a security and the lenders will want to know if the buyers are inhibited or sequestrated.

---

[36] Bankruptcy (Scotland) Act 1985, s.1.

[37] *Burnett's Tr v Grainger*, 2004 S.L.T. 513.

[38] Scottish Law Commission, *Discussion Paper on Sharp v Thomson* (Scot. Law Com. D.P. No.114, 2001), para.4.8.

[39] The pattern thus follows the old GRS practice, whereby an instruction for search would usually be for both the GRS and the Personal Register, and the resulting report would include both in a single document.

[40] 1979 Act, s.6(1)(c).

Identifying the person to be searched against

The object of the personal search is to ensure that there are no entries 9–20 against the person being searched against. The search is by name and address. A danger here is that entries, such as inhibitions, may not have quite the same name as the name stated in the search memorandum: see *Atlas Appointments v Tinsley*.[41] It is important that if the name of the person being searched against has any variants, these should also be searched against. Foreign names present a problem, partly because it may be unclear which part of the name is to be regarded as the surname and partly because there may be problems in transcribing from a non-Latin script. An inhibition against Mao Tse Tung would be indexed against Tung, or, if the name is spelt in the Pinyin transcription, in which the name is written as Mao Zedong, against Zedong. But in Chinese usage the surname is Mao, and the search instruction might have been against Mao. Hence, with such names, the search should be against all possible forms. Saddam Hussein's surname was Saddam, not Hussein. Although such problems are especially prevalent with non-European names, European ones can also be problematic. For instance, an inhibition against Otto von Bismarck would be indexed under V rather than B.

Another problem concerns addresses. If the name is uncommon, the searchers will report entries against it even if the address in the search instruction does not match the address in the inhibition or other entry. But if the name is common (Macdonald, Smith, Campbell, Jones, etc.) they are less likely to do this. A typical danger would be that an inhibition is made against James Campbell at his business address, but the search is instructed against James Campbell at his home address. Or the inhibition might state a previous address. The name is so common that the searchers may not report it. Their guarantee extends (or is said to extend) only to exact matches. So it is important that all addresses are stated in the memorandum, and solicitors are under a professional duty to find out from their clients all potentially relevant addresses.

Against whom, and how far back?

Against whom should personal searches be made, and for how far 9–21 back? We begin with the case where the property is in the GRS. The predominant view is that there should be a personal search against every grantor of every conveyance since (but not including) the foundation writ, the period of search running back for five years from the date when that conveyance was registered. In the case of the present seller, that simply means searching back for five years from the present date. Prior parties will normally have already been searched against in the previous transaction, but of course this must be checked. Thus, suppose that it is now 2004 and Adam is buying from Boris. Boris bought from Carla in 2000, Carla bought from Dorothy in 1995, and Dorothy bought from Euan in 1988. The foundation writ is the 1988 disposition. Hence Boris must be searched against for the period 1999 to 2004, Carla for 1995 to

---

[41] 1997 S.C. 200.

2000, and Dorothy for 1990 to 1995. Euan need not be searched against. As already mentioned, in practice the existing search will normally show searches against these parties (except the current seller) for precisely these periods. Notwithstanding what has just been said, the form 10 requests a search only for five years back from 2004. If the property is in the Land Register matters are simpler: only the registered owner, and the buyer, normally need to be searched against.

Sales by special parties

9–22   Where the current sellers are heritable creditors exercising a power of sale, a personal search is necessary against the sellers It is also standard practice in such a case to search against the debtor, though in general no entry in the Personal Register against the debtor after the date of the creation of the heritable security can affect the creditors' power of sale.[42] Where the sale is by an executor the practice is to search against both the deceased and against the executor *qua* executor. It is not necessary to search against the executor as an individual since any inhibition or sequestration against her/him as an individual could not affect his/her powers as executor. Much the same considerations apply to sales by trustees. If the disposition contains the consent of a beneficiary, the practice is to search personally against that beneficiary as well. Indeed, in all cases where a disposition involves a consenter, the consenter should in general be searched against.[43]

If the sale is by a trustee in sequestration, a personal search is probably unnecessary. For instance, any inhibition against the bankrupt has no effect on the trustee's power of sale,[44] and it is difficult to see how a trustee in sequestration himself could competently be inhibited in his/her capacity as trustee. In practice, however, there is usually a personal search against the bankrupt, and this may be wise so as to check that the sequestration notice was properly registered. Where the sale is by a trustee acting under a trust deed for behoof of creditors, the practice is to search against both the debtor and the trustee, though the latter is probably unnecessary if the trust is "protected".[45]

If the sale is by a liquidator, receiver or administrator the position is less clear.[46] A personal search against the actual liquidator, receiver or administrator is probably unnecessary, though it is sometimes done. A personal search against the company is normally carried out, but the

---

[42] cf. *Newcastle Building Society v White*, 1987 S.L.T. (Sh. Ct.) 81.

[43] An exception is where the consent is by a spouse so as to waive occupancy rights under the Matrimonial Homes (Family Protection) (Scotland) Act 1981. Another possible exception is where A sells to B on missives and B sells to C, and the disposition is granted by A to C with B's consent. If *Leeds Permanent Building Society v Aitken Malone & Mackay*, 1987 S.L.T. 338 is correct, an inhibition against B will not affect C's title. However, the practice in such cases is to search against B as well as against A. The point is complex and cannot be discussed further here.

[44] Bankruptcy (Scotland) Act 1985, s.31(2).

[45] Bankruptcy (Scotland) Act 1985, Sch.5, as amended by the Bankruptcy (Scotland) Act 1993.

[46] The law is governed mainly by the Insolvency Act 1986, which, however, gives no guidance on this matter. See, further, G. L. Gretton, *Law of Inhibition and Adjudication* (2nd ed., 1996), Ch.11.

seller will often seek to stipulate in the missives that the purchaser cannot object to the title on the ground of any inhibition. This is probably safe for the purchaser, subject to two qualifications. The first is that it seems not to be safe where the sale is by an administrator, since an inhibition against a company probably, though not certainly, prevents sale by its administrator. The other is that where a company is in receivership, an inhibition against the company registered, not merely prior to the onset of the receivership, but prior to the original creation of the floating charge, will probably prevent sale.[47] Because the law on such matters is not clear, it is especially important to have clear provision in the missives, whatever that provision may be.

There are also problems about how a partnership should be searched against. Practice varies, but a standard practice is to search against the firm name and against the names of the persons who hold the property for behoof of the firm.

Personal search against the purchaser

An inhibition does not prevent the inhibitee from acquiring heritable 9–23 property. But the practice is for the purchasers to be personally searched against, as well as the sellers, especially at least if they are at the same time granting a heritable security to finance the purchase.[48] More serious is the possibility that a purchaser might be an undischarged bankrupt, a fact which would be disclosed by the personal search.

Inhibition against the sellers after missives

Sometimes sellers are inhibited after conclusion of missives but before 9–24 the purchasers' title is recorded. In that case the inhibition is ineffective because the sellers were under an obligation to sell before the inhibition was registered.[49] Nevertheless, in this situation the search is not clear because *ex facie* of the registers the inhibition predates the sale, as the missives are not recorded.[50] In this case, the general view is that the purchasers can refuse to settle. In practice, various possibilities are open. The purchasers may choose to settle. Or they may agree to settle only if the sellers obtain a title insurance policy. Or they may insist that the sellers obtain a discharge or recall of the inhibition, or a consent to the sale by the inhibitor. The Keeper will register the buyers without exclusion of indemnity if he is satisfied as to the dates.[51]

---

[47] See *Iona Hotels Ltd v Craig*, 1990 S.C. 330, an arrestment case, but the principle seems the same.

[48] However, in such a case a lender is in fact usually protected against any such inhibition. See G. L. Gretton, *Law of Inhibition and Adjudication* (2nd ed., 1996), pp.203–06. Nevertheless, the solicitor has a professional duty to disclose an inhibition even if it does not strike at the security: Janice H. Webster, *Professional Ethics and Practice for Scottish Solicitors* (4th ed., 2004), para.4.06(h).

[49] Inhibition does not strike at future voluntary acts, *i.e.* acts which the inhibited person was already under an obligation to perform when he was inhibited.

[50] See para.6–19.

[51] ROTPB, para.6.19.

LETTERS OF OBLIGATION

Letters of obligation

9-25   Letters of obligation are needed partly because the information
available from the registers may not be wholly up-to-date, partly because
there will usually be a short delay between the receipt of the report and
settlement, and partly because the buyers may not be able to complete
their title instantly, so that there may be a period of a few days between
the date of settlement and the date of completion of title.[52] Thus there is
a risk, albeit a very small one, that the land certificate will disclose
something that was not discoverable from the form 12 or 10 report.

A letter of obligation is a formal undertaking by the sellers' solicitors
that that the land certificate will contain no exclusion of indemnity and
show no entries prejudicial to the purchasers, and also that the answers
in the form 1 or 2 remain correct as far as the sellers are concerned.[53] It
is limited to entries existing at settlement or made within 21 days[54]
thereafter. If the property is still in the GRS and is, for the time being,
remaining there, the letter of obligation undertakes that the final search
will be clear. The letter of obligation takes the form of a signed letter,
addressed to the purchasers' solicitors. The letter may be enforced either
by the purchasers' solicitor or by the purchasers.[55] For the question of
the joint and several liability of the sellers and their solicitors see the
undernoted case.[56]

The undertaking is normally given by the sellers' solicitors, so that
they are liable on it.[57] This is the whole point. The sellers are liable
anyway, in terms of the missives: the buyers want something better than
that. In effect, the sellers' solicitors are acting as guarantors for their
clients.[58] There is no legal obligation to grant a letter of obligation,
unless the missives so provide, which would be most unusual.[59] However,
it is ordinary practice for such a letter to be granted,[60] although practice
is sometimes different where the seller is a company.[61] The solicitor's

---

[52] A reason for this last delay is the need to obtain an SDLT certificate: see paras 15–13
and 15–14.

[53] For styles see ROTPB, paras 8.14 and 8.43. These styles have no official status, but
are in general use.

[54] This is the standard modern period. Until 2002 it was 14 days. What determines the
period is the attitude of the professional insurers. See Most (2002) 47 J.L.S.S. Oct./12.

[55] See *Emslie v James Thomson & Sons*, unreported but summarised at (1991) 36 J.L.S.S.
349 and *Warners v Beveridge & Kellas*, 1994 S.L.T. (Sh. Ct) 29

[56] *McGillivray v Davidson*, 1993 S.L.T. 693.

[57] However, if (as occasionally happens) it is expressly granted "on behalf of our clients"
then the firm itself is not bound. For an example see *Digby Brown & Co. v Lyall*, 1995
S.L.T. 932. For an unsuccessful attempt to escape liability see *Cheval Property Finance plc v
Hill*, 2003 G.W.D. 36–999.

[58] If the solicitors are compelled to incur loss under their letter of obligation they may be
able to recover from their clients: *Marshall Wilson Dean & Turnbull v Feymac Properties
Ltd*, 1996 G.W.D. 22–1247.

[59] The Law Society's standard offer had such a clause. Such a clause probably does not
bind the sellers' solicitors directly, but rather binds the sellers to ensure that their solicitors
grant the obligation.

[60] See (1991) 36 J.L.S.S. 171.

[61] For the position with companies, see Ch.25.

duty to honour a letter of obligation is a professional as well as a legal one.[62]

The profession's insurers compensate solicitors for payments under letters of obligation provided that the solicitors took proper steps to minimise risk. This means instructing a search, and asking the clients to disclose any secured loans (such as "double-glazing" standard securities). Full cover is given only to "classic" letters of obligations, *i.e.* those granted in ordinary form. A letter of obligation is non-classic to the extent that it undertakes to deliver such items as planning or building consents.[63] The sellers' solicitors should beware of undertaking to deliver any document unless they can be sure that it will be obtainable. For instance, a letter of obligation should not promise delivery of a retrospective building consent unless the sellers' solicitors can be certain that the local authority will issue this. The point may seem obvious, but law firms do sometimes fall into this trap, thereby exposing themselves to a damages action if and when they fail to deliver the necessary document. Extras of this sort go beyond the "classic" letter of obligation and will be subjected to a double excess by the profession's insurers.

---

[62] Janice H. Webster, *Professional Ethics and Practice for Scottish Solicitors* (4th ed., 2004), para.4.03.

[63] Rennie (1993) 38 J.L.S.S. 431; Sim (2001) 46 J.L.S.S. April/40; note from the Conveyancing Committee of the Law Society (2003) 48 J.L.S.S. April/26.

CHAPTER 10

MATRIMONIAL HOMES AND HOMES IN CO-OWNERSHIP

Introduction

10–1   At common law, if the matrimonial home was owned by just one spouse, the other spouse had no rights in it, and, if the marriage broke down, the owning spouse could insist that the non-owning spouse leave. The position was not as bad as it sounds, partly because the ejected spouse could, if necessary, claim aliment to cover housing costs (and, in the event of divorce, other rights), and partly because in practice most matrimonial homes are (unless rented) owned in common by both spouses, and when two persons own in common, the common law is that neither can require the other to leave. However, the law was felt to be unsatisfactory, and the Matrimonial Homes (Family Protection) (Scotland) Act 1981 changed it, giving a set of statutory rights called "occupancy rights" to the non-owning spouse.[1] The Act is important to conveyancers because of the need to ensure, on behalf of a grantee, that there are no outstanding occupancy rights.

As well as covering the case where the house is owned by one spouse only, the Act also has certain provisions that apply where it is co-owned. This chapter will, in addition, consider the position where residential property is co-owned by persons who are not spouses, such as cohabitants and siblings. In such cases the Act does not apply.[2]

At the time of preparing this edition the Civil Partnerships Bill was before the Westminster Parliament. It contains provisions conferring on partners substantially the same rights as are conferred on spouses by the 1981 Act.

The nature of occupancy rights

10–2   Occupancy rights are conferred by the 1981 Act where title[3] is held by only one spouse, and are conferred on the other spouse. The Act calls the spouse who holds the title the "entitled spouse", and the other the "non-entitled spouse". The non-entitled spouse is thus the spouse who is entitled to occupancy rights. The chief element of occupancy rights is the

---

[1] See generally E. M. Clive, *The Law of Husband and Wife in Scotland* (4th ed., 1997), Ch.15.

[2] In general. It has limited provisions about cohabitants.

[3] Occupancy rights also apply to leases.

right to occupy the matrimonial home even if the entitled spouse withdraws consent to such occupation.[4] In other words, if Mr and Mrs Smith live together, and title is held by Mrs Smith, she cannot throw Mr Smith out, except with the consent of the court. Indeed, he can, with the consent of the court, throw her out, for another aspect of occupancy rights is that the non-entitled spouse can obtain a court order excluding the entitled spouse from the home, this being called an "exclusion order".[5]

The matrimonial home

The Act applies to "matrimonial homes". Although the title of the Act 10-3 uses the word "family", it is not necessary that there be any children for the Act to apply.[6] "Matrimonial home" is defined as:

"Any house, caravan, houseboat or other structure which has been provided or has been made available by one or both of the spouses as, or has become, a family residence and includes any garden or other ground or building attached to, and usually occupied with, or otherwise required for the amenity or convenience of, the house, caravan, houseboat or other structure but does not include a residence provided or made available by one spouse for that spouse to reside in, whether with any child of the family or not, separately from the other spouse."[7]

Three consequences of this definition are worth noting. In the first place, suppose that Mr and Mrs White live in a flat together. Mrs White then moves out, and buys a house for herself, and lives there without her husband. The new house is not a matrimonial home.[8] Mr White has no rights to it. He could not insist on moving in against her wishes. But the flat where her husband is living remains a matrimonial home.[9] She could insist on moving in to that flat, against his wishes. Not only could she insist on moving in, but she could in appropriate cases compel him to move out, by means of an exclusion order. In general, once a property is a matrimonial home, it retains that status until something happens which

---

[4] Matrimonial Homes (Family Protection) Scotland) Act 1981, s.1(1).

[5] There seems to be a logical problem here. Section 4(1) defines an exclusion order as an order "suspending the occupancy rights of the other spouse". But since it is only Mr Smith who has "occupancy rights", how can he have Mrs Smith's "occupancy rights" suspended? Mrs Smith has no "occupancy rights". Her right to occupy exists, not because she has statutory "occupancy rights", but simply because she is the owner of the property. See Gretton, 1981 S.L.T. (News) 297. The amendments to the Act do not seem to have affected this point.

[6] The titles of statutes are often like advertising copy. Who could fail to approve of a statute for "family protection"?

[7] 1981 Act, s.22. Simplicity of drafting is not a feature of this Act. For discussion of this definition see D. I. Nichols and M. C. Meston, *The Matrimonial Homes (Family Protection) (Scotland) Act 1981* (2nd ed., 1986), and E. M. Clive, *op. cit.* (4th ed., 1997), paras 15.005 to 15.010.

[8] Hence, she could sell it, truly swearing an affidavit (see below) that it was not a matrimonial home.

[9] Thus, in effect he could not sell it without his wife's consent.

takes it outwith the definition, or until something happens to bring the occupancy rights to an end—typically the dissolution of the marriage by divorce or death.

In the second place, only something which can be lived in can be a matrimonial home. Thus, the Act can be ignored in, for instance, the sale of a factory. Or again, if Mary grants a standard security to Norah and Norah assigns this to Olga, Olga need not worry that Norah might be married, because a standard security cannot be a matrimonial home.[10]

In the third place, only natural persons—human beings—can be married. Suppose that Alan sells a house to Brian Ltd and Brian Ltd later sells it to Charles. The house cannot be a matrimonial home in relation to Brian Ltd, though Charles will still need to be sure that it is not a matrimonial home in relation to Alan.

Why the Act affects conveyancing

10-4   Much of the 1981 Act is of only limited interest to conveyancers, and occupancy rights would be of only limited interest to them as well, were it not for the fact that such rights are not merely rights by one spouse against the other. In certain cases they can affect third parties, such as a purchaser or heritable creditor. This is because section 6(1) of the Act provides that, subject to certain qualifications, a "dealing" by the entitled spouse does not affect the occupancy rights of the other spouse. "Dealing" includes sale, so that if Mrs Smith sells the house (even after Mr Smith has moved out), his occupancy rights can survive and be enforceable against the buyer. In other words, occupancy rights are not ordinary personal rights, but can behave rather like real rights. It is because occupancy rights are quasi-real that they are important in conveyancing. They are, however, not true real rights. They do not affect certain types of third party. Thus, as will be seen later, they affect some purchasers but not others, some creditors but not others, and so on. Occupancy rights are probably to be classified as personal rights that in some situations can bind third parties.

If a "dealing" by Mrs Smith is subject to the occupancy rights of Mr Smith, that does not mean that the dealing is void or even voidable at Mr Smith's instance. Thus, suppose that Mrs Smith dispones to Mr Jones, and there is no matrimonial homes documentation. Mr Smith's occupancy rights survive. He can stay in the house, and Mr Jones cannot move in. But nevertheless Mr Jones is the owner, and has all the rights incidental to ownership, except the right to possess.[11] That right is temporarily suspended, until, for one reason or another (*e.g.* the termination of the Smiths' marriage) the occupancy rights come to an end.

Two other types of right, similar to occupancy rights, deserve brief mention. The 1981 Act gives, in certain situations, equivalent rights to cohabitants.[12] But these are of little conveyancing importance because

---

[10] But Olga may be affected by possible occupancy rights in the house in favour of Mary's spouse.

[11] Of course, the right to possess is of great importance. But it is not everything.

[12] 1981 Act, s.18.

they cannot normally affect third parties. Again, rights somewhat similar to occupancy rights are created by the Bankruptcy (Scotland) Act 1985 in favour of the family of a bankrupt.[13]

Response to the Act—reform

The Act proved a conveyancing disaster, and even after two rounds of 10–5 reform[14] much remains that is unsatisfactory from the conveyancing standpoint. In 1990 the Scottish Law Commission conceded that the conveyancing aspects of the Act "have proved to be inconvenient and unpopular",[15] and suggested possible further reforms.[16] However, conveyancers have gradually learned to cohabit with the Act.

Restriction and ending of occupancy rights

Occupancy rights are the rights of a spouse as such, and so end when 10–6 the spouse ceases to be a spouse, which is either by the death of one party or by divorce. In addition, a spouse can renounce occupancy rights,[17] though this is uncommon in practice. It is also possible for occupancy rights to be extinguished by prescription.[18] Where occupancy rights exist, and have not been set aside by death, divorce or renunciation, a third party who buys the house, or acquires any rights in it, will normally need the consent of the non-entitled spouse. In the absence of such consent the non-entitled spouse could occupy the house to the exclusion of the purchaser. That does not mean that the purchaser would not be owner, but the ownership would be subject to the occupancy rights.

If that were all, the Act would not have been such a headache for conveyancers. Purchasers would simply have checked whether the property was subject to occupancy rights, and, if so, would have asked for the consent of the spouse holding those rights. However, what of the case where there appear to be no such rights, typically the case where the seller is said to be unmarried? The reality might be different. The seller, who says she is unmarried, might not be telling the truth. Perhaps it would have been reasonable for the Act to have made no special provision for such a case: in this imperfect world there is always a risk that people will not tell the truth, and special legislative provisions to deal with that danger are not normally thought necessary. If special provision was thought necessary, the natural rule would have been that a purchaser in good faith would be protected. But in fact the legislation is more demanding. It gives protection to purchasers, provided that they are both in good faith and hold an affidavit from the seller. Possibly the most sensible response of conveyancers would have been to ignore

---

[13] s.40.
[14] Law Reform (Miscellaneous Provisions) (Scotland) Act 1985 and the Law Reform (Miscellaneous Provisions) (Scotland) Act 1990.
[15] *Discussion Paper on Family Law: Pre-consolidation reforms* (Scot. Law Com. D.P. No.85, 1990), p.1.
[16] Scottish Law Commission, *Report on Family Law* (Scot. Law Com. No.135, 1992).
[17] 1981 Act, s.1(5), (6).
[18] See para.10–14, below.

this strange and complex procedure designed to guard against remote possibilities, especially since purchasers regularly run greater risks (albeit still remote) all the time. However, since the Act laid down this rigmarole, conveyancers felt obliged to go along with it, and, this being universal practice, a solicitor who fails to demand an affidavit in such cases is likely to be guilty of negligence.

The three kinds of deed

10-7   The conveyancing side of the Act revolves around three deeds, namely (i) the renunciation (ii) the consent and (iii) the affidavit. These are sometimes confused (at least by legal typists). For instance, one sometimes sees the word "affidavit" on the backing of a deed which, when opened, turns out to be a consent or a renunciation.

In the renunciation a spouse wholly gives up occupancy rights. It can, however, only refer to "a particular property", so that a deed renouncing such rights in any *future* matrimonial home would presumably be invalid.[19]

In the consent, also called the "consent to dealing", a spouse consents to a particular transaction, but does not otherwise give up occupancy rights. Thus, if the husband is sole owner, and grants a standard security, and the wife consents, her occupancy rights remain intact as against the husband himself and as against all third parties except the heritable creditor and any parties deriving right from the heritable creditor.

Lastly, there is the affidavit. Whereas the renunciation and consent waive occupancy rights, either wholly or in part, the affidavit has a different purpose. It is not a waiver of occupancy rights, but a statement that no such rights exist. This is typically where the owner is unmarried, but a married owner can sometimes grant an affidavit too, where the property is for some other reason not a matrimonial home. It is thus evidential rather than restrictive or extinctive. Another important difference is that, whereas a renunciation or consent is granted by the owner's spouse, an affidavit is granted by the owner.

Styles: (i) Renunciations

10-8   The renunciation has no prescribed form,[20] except that the renouncer must swear or affirm before a notary[21] that it is made "freely and without coercion of any kind".[22] In practice, the renunciation will have three signatures, namely those of the renouncer, the notary, and a witness. The Act does not require a witness, but renunciations will normally be registered in the Books of Council and Session, for that that a witnessed deed is necessary.[23]

---

[19] 1981 Act, s.1(5).
[20] See Halliday, para.36–32 for a style.
[21] Thus, it seems that a justice of the peace could not do this. But an independent conveyancing practitioner can: Public Appointments and Public Bodies (Scotland) Act 2003, s.14.
[22] 1981 Act, s.1(6).
[23] 1995 Act, s.6.

If made outwith Scotland a renunciation may be sworn or affirmed before "any person duly authorised by the law of the country (other than Scotland) in which the swearing or affirmation takes place to administer oaths or receive affirmations in that other country".[24] In England, commissioners for oaths are more common than notaries, and all English solicitors are now, *ipso facto*, commissioners for oaths.[25] For renunciations done abroad there is the problem that there is no easy way of checking whether the person administering the oath is duly authorised. (Where can you lay your hands on the current list of notaries in Burkino Faso?[26]) Sections 6 and 8 of the Act help by providing that a *bona fide* purchaser or heritable creditor will be protected if the renunciation "bears to have been properly made". It should probably bear the seal of the foreign notary.[27]

Styles: (ii) Consents

For the consent, there is a prescribed style.[28] It can either be in a   10–9
separate deed or be incorporated in the deed to which it consents. Both are common and indeed often both are used in the same transaction, that is to say, there is a consent given at the beginning of the transaction followed by a second consent incorporated in the final deed. The prescribed style needs attestation, but does not need a notary.

Styles: (iii) Affidavits

There is no prescribed style for affidavits.[29] Though the Act requires a   10–10
notary for a renunciation, it makes no corresponding provision for affidavits, nor, again in contrast to the provisions for renunciations, is there any provision for execution outwith Scotland. The law is not wholly clear.[30] The Keeper's practice is to accept affidavits made outwith Scotland if sworn or affirmed before a person who is there authorised by law to receive sworn statements. Thus he will accept an affidavit sworn in England before a commissioner for oaths. He requires evidence that the person receiving the affidavit was authorised by law.[31] Within Scotland not only notaries but also independent conveyancing practitioners can

---

[24] 1981 Act, s.1(6). This was added by s.13(4) of the Law Reform (Miscellaneous Provisions) (Scotland) Act 1985.

[25] Solicitors Act 1974, s.81. There may, however, be a problem here. The Commissioners for Oaths Act 1889, s.1 says that a commissioner may administer an oath "for the purposes of any court or matter in England". See Styles (1991) 36 J.L.S.S. 444.

[26] Actually an international system exists. The old one was the so-called legalisation process. The Hague Convention of October 5, 1961 replaced this by the apostille procedure. Most but not all states are parties to the Convention (including the UK but not, it may be of help to know, Burkino Faso.)

[27] See Ferguson (1992) 37 J.L.S.S. 10; Swinney (1992) 37 J.L.S.S. 141.

[28] SI 1982/971. See, further, Halliday, para.36–31.

[29] For a style see Halliday, para.36–33. Generally on notarial deeds see para.14–27.

[30] See D. I. Nichols and M. C. Meston, *The Matrimonial Homes (Family Protection) (Scotland) Act 1981* (2nd ed., 1986), p.52, and the contributions by Styles, Ferguson and Swinney (above).

[31] ROTPB, para.6.44. This paragraph applies to affidavits but not to renunciations, as to which the ROTPB says little. But affidavits are much commoner than renunciations.

act.[32] There is no requirement for witnessing, but this is usually done. Affidavits are sometimes registered in the Books of Council and Session, in which case witnessing is essential.[33]

The 1985 reforms[34] made no difference to renunciations (except as to execution abroad) or to consents, but they did make changes to affidavits.[35] The 1981 Act lays down a style not directly but indirectly. In its original form it provided for "an affidavit sworn or affirmed by the entitled spouse declaring that there is no non-entitled spouse". This was bizarre, for "an entitled spouse" implies a non-entitled spouse, so that any affidavit in these terms could only be false.[36] The replacement wording in s. 6 is "an affidavit sworn or affirmed by the seller declaring that the subjects of sale are not a matrimonial home in relation to which a spouse of the seller has occupancy rights".[37]

Unlike a renunciation or consent, an affidavit can cover only two types of "dealing", namely sales and securities.[38] In particular, gifts, trusts, leases and servitudes are apparently not covered.[39] Thus, if a married woman gives property to her daughter, the donor's husband can consent.[40] But if the woman is a widow, no matrimonial documentation is possible in terms of the statute. Nor is such documentation possible for the grant of a lease by a bachelor, or where a divorcee grants a trust deed for behoof of creditors. In all these cases the grantee must take the chance that there might be a spouse with occupancy rights in the woodwork. However, because of these gaps in the legislation, the practice has developed of taking non-statutory affidavits in such cases, and the Keeper generally will accept them[41]

What is a dealing?

10–11   As has been seen, occupancy rights concern the conveyancer because they can survive "dealings".[42] What, then, is a "dealing"? It is not a term of art in Scots law, and the 1981 Act nowhere explains it. Section 6 tells us only that the term "includes the grant of a heritable security and the creation of a trust but does not include a conveyance under section 80 of the Lands Clauses Consolidation (Scotland) Act 1845". That is all. It does not mention sale. It is only by inference that it is clear that a sale is a "dealing", because s. 6(3)(e) has a provision for the case where "the dealing comprises a sale". So, apart from heritable security, trust, and

---

[32] Public Appointments and Public Bodies (Scotland) Act 2003, s.14.
[33] Requirements of Writing (Scotland) Act 1995, s.6.
[34] Law Reform (Miscellaneous Provisions) (Scotland) Act 1985, s.13.
[35] For the background to these reforms, see an unsigned article at (1982) 27 J.L.S.S. 455.
[36] See the definitions in s.1 of the 1981 Act.
[37] Corresponding new wording was introduced to s.8, for heritable securities.
[38] 1981 Act, ss.6(3)(e) and 8(2A).
[39] D. I. Nichols and M. C. Meston, *op. cit.*, p.53 say that excambion is covered, but this seems questionable.
[40] Note, however, that the protection to *bona fide* third parties against the possibility of latent invalidity is also confined to sales and securities. See the 1981 Act, ss.6(3)(e) and 8(2A). Thus, a forged consent produced in association with a gift would be ineffective.
[41] For donation see ROTPB, para.6.45
[42] s.6.

sale, it is a matter of speculation as to what is or is not a "dealing". The cautious view is that a "dealing" might be any juridical act which might adversely affect occupancy rights. Thus, gifts, leases and servitudes are probably "dealings". With no case law, the prudent conveyancer must assume that they are.

Agreeing to the shortening of a calling-up notice for a standard security is, perhaps, not a "dealing" since there is specific provision for it in section 20,[43] the effect of which, however, is virtually to make it a "dealing". A sale by a heritable creditor is not a "dealing" because it is not an act of a spouse. But the original grant of the security is a "dealing", which may taint a subsequent sale by the creditor. Thus, if Ms Gray owns a house and grants a standard security to the bank, without any matrimonial homes documentation, that is a dealing, and a subsequent sale by the bank, though not itself a dealing, will be subject to any occupancy rights which a Mr Gray (if he exists) may have in the house. Hence a purchaser from a heritable creditor will check the matrimonial documentation produced when the security was granted. Subject to section 2 of the 1981 Act, an adjudication is not a "dealing" since again it is not the act of a spouse. For bankruptcy, see below.

A borderline case is a further advance made by a heritable creditor. Usually there is no difficulty, as normally the spouse will already have consented to the security. But suppose that Mr Green, a bachelor, grants a standard security to the bank, and later marries. So far so good, because even though Mrs Green has not consented, the security was a pre-marriage transaction and so cannot be subject to the new spouse's occupancy rights. (Mrs Green has occupancy rights, indeed, but Mr Green's prior acts are not subject to them.) But what if Mr Green then borrows more money from the bank? This does, in a sense, put Mrs Green's occupancy rights at risk, for a larger loan must increase the danger of default. So is the further advance a "dealing"? No one knows. The prudent course is therefore to obtain matrimonial documentation for a further advance. The current practice of the Keeper is to turn a blind eye.[44]

Timing

Sections 6(3)(e) and 8(2A) in their pre-1991 form[45] said that pur- 10–12
chasers and heritable creditors are protected against latent occupancy rights if both (a) they are in good faith and (b) "at or before" the time of the transaction there is produced a renunciation or consent or affidavit. This meant that retrospective affidavits were worthless, and this caused a good deal of bother in practice. The Law Reform (Miscellaneous Provisions) (Scotland) Act 1990 changed this by removing the "at or before" clause.[46] Retrospective deeds are thus now competent.

---

[43] Amending s.19(10) of the 1970 Act.

[44] ROTPB, para.6.46.

[45] *i.e.* prior to the coming into force of the Law Reform (Miscellaneous Provisions) (Scotland) Act 1990.

[46] Law Reform (Miscellaneous Provisions) (Scotland) Act 1990, Sch.8, para.31.

Co-ownership

10–13   Where title is in the name of both spouses there are no occupancy rights. Of course, if property is co-owned, both co-owners have the right to occupy it, as a matter of common law, but that is not the same as the "occupancy rights" created by the Act.[47] Any deed granted by just one co-owner can have no effect on the rights of the other spouse, again as a matter of common law. However, the Act does have certain provisions about co-ownership by spouses.

One is section 9. Suppose that Mr and Mrs Beige are co-owners, and become estranged, and Mr Beige leaves the house and conveys his one-half share to his brother. At common law, that could not prejudice Mrs Beige's right to possession, but the brother would also have the right to share the possession with her.[48] Section 9 goes further and says that the brother has no right to occupy, except with Mrs Beige's consent. Furthermore, section 19 gives the court a discretion to refuse, or postpone, decree in an action of division and sale raised by one spouse against the other. This provision is obviously of key significance, in a world where most matrimonial homes are co-owned.[49]

Consider, next, the case where title is held in common by two persons who are not married, at least to each other, and likewise the case where title is held by three persons, two of whom are spouses. In such cases the Act has virtually no conveyancing implications, because of section 6(2), which defines "entitled spouse" for the purposes of the section thus:

" 'entitled spouse' does not include a spouse who, apart from the provisions of this Act,—

(a) is permitted by a third party to occupy a matrimonial home; or

(b) is entitled to occupy a matrimonial home along with an individual who is not the other spouse, whether or not that individual has waived his or her right of occupation in favour of the spouse so entitled."

This convoluted provision means that where there is common ownership involving a party other than the spouses, there can be no "entitled spouse" for the purposes of section 6, and hence a spouse in such a case has no protection against a "dealing". In other words, in the case of common property, occupancy rights do not affect successors, and are purely personal. Thus, if two sisters own a house in common and sell it, there is no need for affidavits (if they are spinsters) and no need for renunciations or consents (if they are married). However, the provision quoted is to be found only in section 6 (protection to purchasers) and not in section 8 (protection to lenders). The practical result of the omission has been that where, in such a situation, the parties wish, not to

---

[47] See the definition scheme in s.1.

[48] A potentially unworkable situation, but any co-owner can always terminate such a situation by insisting on a sale of the whole property.

[49] For cases on s.19 see *e.g. Rae v Rae*, 1991 S.L.T. 454 and *Milne v Milne*, 1994 S.L.T. (Sh. Ct) 57.

sell the property, but to grant a *heritable security,* matrimonial documentation is often demanded. This practice is understandable but, it is thought, not necessary. Broadly speaking, section 6 does three things: (1) It lays down the general principle that occupancy rights are unaffected by "dealings". (2) It states exceptions to this rule, including the common ownership exception. (3) It has specific provisions for sales. The first two of these are of general application, and are not confined to sales. Section 8 deals with heritable securities, but its provisions correspond only to what is here called part (3) of section 6. Parts (1) and (2) of section 6 apply equally to heritable securities, and indeed to all "dealings".[50] Hence the conclusion, that in the common ownership situation, a heritable creditor does not need to be protected by matrimonial documentation.[51] However, if a lender insists on documentation, then documentation must be obtained.

Lastly, cohabitants. If they are co-owners, the case is the same as before. Matrimonial documentation is not required. If one party only is the owner, section 18 may apply to confer occupancy rights on the non-entitled cohabitant, but this is purely a personal right. It cannot survive a "dealing" and so it is not normally of interest to conveyancers.

Prescription

The importance of prescription to the conveyancer is where there has 10–14 been a "dealing" which has not been supported by the proper matrimonial documentation. The provision about prescription[52] applies only where both (i) the entitled spouse has ceased to be entitled to occupy the house and (ii) starting from that date, five years[53] have passed during which the non-entitled spouse has not occupied the house. The first of these can, in most cases, be easily established as being the date of sale. But the second is not so easily established. Thus, suppose it is 2004 and Fergus is selling to Gina. Gina notices that when Fergus bought in 1999 from Edgar no matrimonial documentation was obtained. It is clear that as far as Edgar is concerned requirement (i) was met in 1999. But one also needs to know that since 1999 the house has not been occupied by anyone who might have been a spouse of Edgar. There is no easy way to prove this. The practice has developed of getting Fergus to swear a (non-statutory) affidavit that during that period no one has occupied the house who might have been a spouse of Edgar. This seems a reasonable procedure, though it is doubtful whether Gina could be required to accept it, unless there was a stipulation to that effect in the missives. The Keeper is prepared to accept such an affidavit.[54]

---

[50] Here, as elsewhere in the Act, it is difficult to admire the drafting.

[51] See also ROTPB, para.6.35.

[52] 1981 Act, s.6(3)(e), as amended by s.13 of the Law Reform (Miscellaneous Provisions) (Scotland) Act 1985. The only reported case is *Stevenson v Roy,* 2003 S.C. 544.

[53] Scottish Law Commission, *Report on Family Law* (Scot. Law Com. No.135, 1992), para.11.11 recommended that the period be reduced to two years.

[54] (1994) 8 Prop. L.B., p.5. ROTPB, para.6.30 says that "The Keeper is normally prepared to take a pragmatic view where Question 9 in . . . form 1 is answered in the affirmative." This seems to pin the risk on the purchaser.

Dispensation

10-15   The Act[55] empowers the court to dispense with the consent of a
spouse to a dealing. The three main grounds are (a) that the spouse
cannot be traced (b) that the spouse is incapax and (c) that the spouse
has unreasonably withheld consent. There are problems as to the exact
meaning of the last of these, but we will not deal with dispensation to
any great extent since it is mainly a matter for court practitioners rather
than conveyancers.[56] Mention must, however, be made of *Fyfe v Fyfe*.[57]
Here the husband wanted to sell the house but his estranged wife
refused to consent. He applied for a dispensing order. The court refused,
on the ground that dispensation is competent only in relation to a
specific transaction, and marketing a property is not a specific transaction. Just how specific one has to be is not clear from the case. Possibly
the stage of concluded missives must be reached, or perhaps it is only
necessary that a formal offer has been received. But whatever the exact
rule may be, the effect is that dispensation is likely to be a pointless
exercise. The missives would have to be conditional upon the obtaining
of the dispensing order, and few buyers would be prepared to wait while
an action, whose outcome must be uncertain, drags its way through the
courts.[58]

Guardians, attorneys, executors, trustees

10-16   Before the Adults with Incapacity (Scotland) Act 2000 there was some
doubt as to whether a sale by a *curator bonis* of an incapax was or was
not a "dealing" for the purposes of the 1981 Act. The Keeper's view was
that it was not.[59] The same issue arises, since the 2000 Act, for sales by
intervenors and by guardians. The Keeper adheres to his previous
position.[60] Whilst this may be right the issue is arguable. At a policy level
it is not clear why a wife should cease to be protected when her husband
loses his reason. The cautious approach is to assume that a "dealing" by
a guardian may be covered by the Act. So if the incapax is married, the
spouse should consent. If the incapax is unmarried, there is a problem,
for it seems pretty clear that a guardian could not swear an affidavit
under the Act.[61] But this is just one of several cases where no
matrimonial documentation is possible. As in the other cases, non-
statutory affidavits are in practice used, coupled with evidence of the fact
of the incapacity.[62] If the incapacity affects the spouse whose consent is
needed, again there is a problem because although a dispensation is
competent, there is the *Fyfe v Fyfe* problem (above).

---

[55] s.7.

[56] For procedural problems see *Longmuir v Longmuir*, 1985 S.L.T. (Sh. Ct.) 33.

[57] 1987 S.L.T. (Sh. Ct.) 38.

[58] Reform has been recommended: see Scottish Law Commission, *Report on Family Law*
(Scot. Law Com. No.135, 1992), paras 11.13 and 11.14.

[59] ROTPB, para.6.41.

[60] See Reid and Gretton, *Conveyancing 2002*, p.106.

[61] At present. The Scottish Law Commission has recommended that the position be
changed: see *Report on Family Law* (Scot. Law Com. No.135, 1992), para.11.22.

[62] This approach is acceptable to the Keeper: see (1997) 42 J.L.S.S. 266.

The general view, with which we would concur, is that it is not competent to include in a power of attorney a power to swear an affidavit, but that it is competent to include a power to sign a consent or a renunciation.[63]

The 1981 Act did not make it clear how a transaction by an executor or other trustee is to be treated. Clearly, no one could have occupancy rights against a trustee *qua* trustee. But might a beneficiary's spouse have occupancy rights? Under section 1, occupancy rights arise not merely where the entitled spouse is owner but where he is entitled to occupy, with the consequence that a right less than ownership can be a ground for occupancy rights. Thus, if a beneficiary is entitled to occupy, his spouse might have occupancy rights. But that of itself does not prove that a purchaser, say, from the executor or other trustee needs to obtain matrimonial documentation. For section 6 says that occupancy rights will survive a "dealing" only where the "dealing" is done by the "entitled spouse". It could be argued that a sale or other transaction by an executor or other trustee is done only by the trustee and not by the beneficiary, so that no documentation would be required, since no occupancy rights could survive the transaction. A strong example would be where a trust deed directs the property to be sold. Such a sale could hardly be a "dealing" by the beneficiary. Another strong example would be if the sale is necessary to raise funds to pay off debts. Arguably, a transaction is never a "dealing" by the beneficiary except where his consent to it is necessary. But because of the uncertainties, the safe course, and the one generally adopted, is to obtain matrimonial documentation in relation to the beneficiary, *i.e.* either an affidavit from the beneficiary himself or a renunciation or consent from his spouse. Thus, suppose that Kate owns a house. She dies. Her widower, Lucas, is her sole legatee and executor. He sells *qua* executor. An affidavit from him *qua* beneficiary should be obtained. (He might have remarried.)

Often the beneficial right will be vested in more than one person. In that case section 6(2)(b) will apply and there will be no need for matrimonial documentation. But if there is any room for doubt, documentation should be obtained.[64]

Noting in the Land Register[65]

The 1979 Act (as amended) provides that occupancy rights are   10–17 overriding interests. But rule 5(j) of the Land Registration (Scotland) Rules 1980 (as amended) requires the Keeper to add a note that there are no subsisting occupancy rights of spouses of former owners if he is satisfied that this is the case. (If not satisfied, he will qualify the note.) Naturally, the occupancy rights of the *existing* owner's possible spouse are not covered. The Keeper's note is not conclusive as to occupancy rights. As overriding interests they either exist, or do not exist, independently of what he says. The advantage of the Keeper's statement is simply that if it turns out to be incorrect he will be liable to pay

---

[63] ROTPB, para.6.42.

[64] For the Keeper's practice on dispositions by executors see ROTPB, para.6.40.

[65] See generally ROTPB, para.6.28.

compensation. At first sight it would appear that such compensation is not in fact available, because section 12(3)(h) of the 1979 Act excludes liability where "the loss arises in respect of an error or omission in the noting of an overriding interest". But the view generally taken, and taken by the Keeper himself, is that the Keeper would be liable because a statement under rule 5(j) is, strictly speaking, not a "noting of an overriding interest".

Examination of title

10-18   Once created, occupancy rights do not prescribe except by non-exercise for a continuous period of five years.[66] This creates a risk of elderly rights lingering on. Thus even although Mr Brown sold his house in 1995, it is possible, if unlikely, that Mrs Brown might continue to have occupancy rights which would affect a buyer today. This has implications for examination of title. In the typical case the Keeper will insert a statement, under rule 5(j), that there are no subsisting occupancy rights. If so, that disposes of the historical position, and purchasers need concern themselves only with the possible spouse of the current seller. But in first registrations and in GRS transactions the historical position needs to be checked. This means checking (in principle all the way back to the commencement of the Act on September 1, 1982) that for each disposal the appropriate documentation was obtained.[67] If documentation is missing, it can often be obtained now; or it may be possible to rely on negative prescription, provided a (non-statutory) affidavit can be produced to the effect that a non-entitled spouse has not been in occupation for a period of five years.

Missives

10-19   Some offers make no provision at all about matrimonial documentation. This is presumably on the view that such documentation will have to be produced anyway because of the general obligation to produce a good and marketable title. Doubtless this is correct, but the usual practice is to have a clause in the offer dealing with the matter. The clause should provide that the land certificate will contain an unqualified statement in terms of rule 5(j).

There are two common errors in such clauses. The first is to use the prefatory words: "Where the subjects are a matrimonial home within the meaning of . . .". The trouble with this is that matrimonial documentation is normally required whether or not the property is a matrimonial home. Thus, if the seller is a spinster, the property cannot be a matrimonial home, but the purchaser still wants to get an affidavit. The other error is that such clauses, though requiring documentation from the seller, sometimes fail to require that the property be free of rights under the 1981 Act in respect of prior transactions.

---

[66] 1981 Act, s.6(3)(f). See para.10–14.

[67] In some cases subsequent events may mean that the absence of documentation no longer matters.

Death

Death dissolves marriage. Hence it ends all rights under the 1981 Act.   10–20

Bankruptcy

If one spouse becomes bankrupt, the matrimonial home has limited   10–21
protection under s. 40 of the Bankruptcy (Scotland) Act 1985.[68] Beyond
that the trustee in sequestration is probably free to do what the bankrupt
himself could not have done, namely to ignore the non-bankrupt
spouse's rights under the 1981 Act. The point is, however, not wholly
free from doubt.[69]

If the house is co-owned, the trustee in sequestration has the right to
insist on a sale, and can, if need be, compel this by an action of division
and sale. In most cases he will first approach the non-bankrupt spouse
(Mrs Smith) and offer to sell to her Mr Smith's *pro indiviso* share at a
fair market value. Thus, if the house is worth £150,000 and there is a
secured loan of £60,000, Mrs Smith could buy her husband's half share
for £45,000, provided that she agreed to assume sole responsibility for
the secured loan. In practice, of course, she may not have the financial
resources to do this.

Separation and divorce[70]

When a marriage breaks down there is often a separation agreement,   10–22
and, if so, it will deal with the house. The agreement should normally
contain a renunciation of all occupancy rights, and a discharge of any
succession rights in the house, including any right under any special
destination. If the house is co-owned by Mr and Mrs Ochre with a
survivorship destination and Mr Ochre is to dispone his half share to
Mrs Ochre, such a disposition should be in the form of a deed by both
Mr and Mrs Ochre to Mrs Ochre, so as to ensure that the destination is
wholly deleted from the title.[71] The agreement should, of course, deal
with any secured loan. If Mrs Ochre is to become sole owner then
normally she will be assuming sole responsibility for the secured loan,
but it should be recalled that as far as the bank is concerned this is just
an agreement between the Ochres, and the original loan documentation
still stands, whereby Mr and Mrs Ochre will be jointly and severally
liable to the bank for the whole loan. Hence Mr Ochre has the risk that
Mrs Ochre might default and the bank might then claim from him. The
best arrangement is to have a deed of variation signed by the bank
releasing Mr Ochre from his obligation. Moreover, many banks have
standard form documentation forbidding any disposition without their
consent, so that the transfer of the half share to Mrs Ochre ought to be

---

[68] For collusive sequestrations, see s.41 of the 1985 Act.

[69] On this and other matters, see William W. McBryde, *Bankruptcy* (2nd ed., 1995),
Ch.9.

[70] For practicalities, see Bett (2000) 48 Prop. L.B., p.1; Bett (2004) 68 Prop. L.B., p.5.
See also E. M. Clive, *The Law of Husband and Wife in Scotland* (4th ed., 1997),
para.19.035.

[71] See para.23–15.

cleared with the bank. In the interval between the separation agreement and the actual conveyance Mrs Ochre's right to her husband's half share is, of course, personal, not real, and so she is exposed to an element of risk.

Divorce, like death, dissolves marriage and so brings to an end all rights under the 1981 Act.

Section 8 of the Family Law (Scotland) Act 1985 (as amended) empowers the court in divorce actions to make an order for the transfer of property (property transfer order—PTO) from one spouse to the other.[72] "Property" includes heritable property, and the order may relate to *pro indiviso* shares. A PTO is not itself a transfer: like missives, it imposes an obligation to convey. The spouse who is to acquire the property does not become owner until there has been a registered disposition in the ordinary way. The rights of heritable creditors are protected.[73]

The risk for a purchaser of a matrimonial home is that the court might have made such an order, which the owner is, by selling to someone else, defying. Does this matter to the buyer? The answer is that it depends. Since a PTO is not in itself a conveyance, both the purchaser and the transferee spouse are entitled to demand a disposition. Whoever registers first will become owner. But if it is the buyer who wins, but did so in the knowledge of the prior existence of the PTO, then an "offside goal" has been scored, meaning that the title is voidable at the instance of the disappointed spouse.[74] There is little to worry about here in practice. Sales in defiance of a PTO are as rare as fraudulent double sales. No special provision is required in missives—it is covered by the good and marketable title obligation—though in practice it is quite common to put in a special clause.

An estranged couple will often agree to the sale of the home. If so, well and good. But experience shows that the parties may fall out over numerous issues, and especially the question of how the proceeds are to be divided. Hence the path of wisdom is that the sale should be conducted by a firm of solicitors which acts for neither party in any other respect.[75]

Division and sale

10–23   If a co-owned property is not a matrimonial home, then either party can insist that the property be sold, and if necessary force matters by an action of division and sale.[76] This is a matter of right: outwith the context of the 1981 Act the court has no discretion to refuse.[77] The court will order either (a) division of the property (which is rare in practice) or (b) sale of the whole property followed by division of the price.

---

[72] The Act also empowers the court to make "incidental orders" in relation to matrimonial property, but it is difficult to see how these could affect a purchaser.

[73] For details see *MacNaught v MacNaught*, 1997 S.L.T. (Sh. Ct) 60.

[74] For the "offside goals rule" see Reid, *Property*, paras 695 *et seq.* See further Cusine (1990) 35 J.L.S.S. 52.

[75] See further the Law Society of Scotland's *Guidelines on Acting for Separated Spouses.*

[76] Reid, *Property*, paras 32 and 33.

[77] *Burrows v Burrows*, 1996 S.L.T. 1313. If the parties are married, s.19 of the 1981 Act gives the court a discretion.

Out of the proceeds the fees and outlays in the sale must be paid, as must debts secured on the property.[78] The net proceeds of sale fall to be divided between the parties according to the size of their share of ownership, which in most cases will be equal.[79] Claims which one party may have against the other can, however, be taken into account in the division.[80] The disposition needs to be executed by both parties, but if one refuses the court can pronounce an interlocutor authorising the clerk of court to execute it.[81]

Sometimes one party does not wish the property to be sold on the open market, but wishes to buy the other's share at a fair price. If the other party agrees, then there is no problem, but what if the other party refuses? Can such an arrangement be forced through by court action? The authorities are conflicting.[82]

---

[78] It is assumed that such debts are secured over the whole property. Very rarely debts will be secured only over one share, and in that case they fall to be deducted from that share.

[79] If the title is in more than one person, without specifying the size of the shares, then the shares are equal.

[80] *Ralston v Jackson*, 1994 S.L.T. 771; *Gray v Kerner*, 1996 S.C.L.R. 331; *McMahon's Tr v McMahon*, 1997 S.L.T. 1090. cf. *Johnston v Robson*, 1995 S.L.T. (Sh. Ct) 26, though that case is odd because it is not clear what the basis of the counterclaim was. The mere fact that the defender had made the original deposit on the house was, in itself, irrelevant (though it could have become relevant had it been averred that it had been a loan, for instance).

[81] For procedure see I. D. Macphail, *Sheriff Court Practice* (2nd ed., by C. G. B. Nicholson and A. L. Stewart), Vol.I (1998), para.23-37 *et seq.*

[82] *Scrimgeour v Scrimgeour*, 1988 S.L.T. 590; *Berry v Berry*, 1989 S.L.T. 292; *Gray v Kerner*, 1996 S.C.L.R. 331; *Ploetner v Ploetner*, 1997 S.C.L.R. 998. And see also *Wilson v Harvey*, 2004 S.C.L.R. 313.

CHAPTER 11

DISPOSITIONS

INTRODUCTION

Deeds of constitution, deeds of transfer, and deeds of extinction

11-01   Conveyancers traditionally distinguish three classes of deed: (i) deeds of constitution (also called deeds of creation), (ii) deeds of transfer, and (iii) deeds of extinction. A deed of constitution creates a new real right. Examples are leases and standard securities.[1] In such cases the granter retains a real right, but the grantee also acquires a real right of some type, newly created. A deed of transfer, or transmission, simply transfers from one person to another an existing real right. Dispositions and assignations are the sole examples for heritable property. So if Mary leases land to Nick, that is a deed of constitution, but if Nick then assigns the lease to Olga, that is a deed of transfer. A deed of extinction brings a real right to an end: it is not transferred but ceases to exist. Examples are renunciations of leases and discharges of standard securities. This chapter deals with one type of deed of transfer, the disposition. The disposition is the most important deed encountered in conveyancing.

Dispositions

11-02   A disposition is the deed used to transfer ownership[2] of land. So if Jack sells a house to Jill, the sale is effected by a disposition[3] by him in favour of her and registered in the Land Register. This is a standard disposition. What is happening is that Jack is selling what he owns. By contrast, there can also be a break-off (also called break-away or split-off) disposition, in which Jack conveys only a part of what he owns. Break-off dispositions have all the terms of a standard disposition but also some additional terms.

Unlike many other deeds, there is no statutory form of disposition, although certain individual clauses have prescribed statutory forms. In theory, therefore, any form can be used provided it is clear. In practice,

---

[1] And, before the abolition of feudal tenure, feu dispositions. Feu charters and feu contracts were in substance the same as feu dispositions.

[2] When they still existed, superiorities were also transferred by disposition.

[3] Very occasionally a property is held on ultra-long lease, in which case the sale of the lease will be implemented by an assignation rather than by a disposition. For ultra-long leases, and for plans for their conversion into ownership, see Scottish Law Commission, *Discussion Paper on Conversion of Long Leases* (Scot. Law Com. D.P. No.112, 2001).

there is a standard method of drafting a disposition which, with minor local and personal differences, is in universal use. This is not a pretty deed. It is written in the first person,[4] and, although long, is usually all one sentence, the different parts of the deed being marked off by a battery of colons, semi-colons and commas. Some of it is redundant, mere empty words of style. The language is to some extent archaic.[5] The client may not understand it, and may, not unreasonably, wish it to be explained. The deed is unilateral in form—only the granter signs[6]—but bilateral in effect: the grantee is considered bound by its terms on accepting delivery at settlement.[7] There are two forms of disposition in current use, namely dispositions of property in the Land Register and dispositions of GRS land (*i.e.* land not yet registered in the Land Register). They are similar but not identical.

Structure of the disposition

A disposition is divided into several clauses.[8] What, precisely, is meant 11–03 by a "clause" is perhaps not wholly determinate, but the issue is largely semantic. There can be some variation in practice, but in a typical modern disposition these are as follows:

(a) The narrative clause, also called the inductive clause, stating the parties and the cause of transfer.
(b) The dispositive clause, identifying the property and conveying it.
(c) The burdens clause, mentioning existing burdens and stating new ones, if any.[9]
(d) The entry clause, stating the date when the disponee is to take possession.
(e) The warrandice clause, whereby the granter warrants the title.
(f) Miscellaneous clauses.
(g) The testing clause, with details of how and when the deed was signed.

There is sometimes a clause declaring that the granter holds in trust for the grantee, pending registration.[10] In some cases involving property still in the GRS there has to be a clause of deduction of title after the entry clause. Until 1979 there were three other clauses, namely the writs

---

[4] If the granter is a company or other juristic person then the deed will run in the first person plural.

[5] Conveyancing deeds often have a long history. The disposition has been evolving for more than 800 years.

[6] There is nothing to stop the grantee signing, but it is not done in practice, certain special cases apart. It might, however, be argued that the law ought to require the grantee to sign. It is curious that it is possible to acquire heritable property without ever signing anything.

[7] See, *e.g.*, *Hunter v Boog* (1834) 13 S. 205.

[8] See *e.g.* John Sinclair, *Handbook of Conveyancing Practice in Scotland* (4th ed., 2002), para.9.2.

[9] If the property is in the Land Register it is normal to omit reference to existing burdens.

[10] See para.11–27.

clause, the rents clause and the relief clause, which came before the warrandice clause, but these are now implied[11] and are thus invariably omitted.

Two examples will be given. The first is of property that is in the Land Register. The second is of property that is still in the GRS: such a disposition will normally trigger a first registration in the Land Register but the form is the same even in the case where it will be recorded in the GRS.

Disposition of property in the Land Register

11–04   *[Narrative]* I, Kevin Kennedy, born on sixth May nineteen hundred and sixty four,[12] residing formerly at fifty-two Cornwall Street, Aberdeen and now at fifty-five Emily Drive, Kirkcudbright, regis-tered[13] proprietor of the subjects hereinafter disponed, in consid-eration of the price of two hundred thousand pounds (£200,000) paid to me by Donald Henry McQuoist, born on eleventh August nineteen hundred and sixty nine, and Sara Jane Cumming or McQuoist, born on twelfth April nineteen hundred and seventy seven, residing together at thirty Fairholm Drive, Paisley, of which I hereby acknowledge receipt, *[Dispositive]* do hereby dispone to the said Donald Henry McQuoist and Sara Jane Cumming or McQuoist equally between them All and Whole that area or plot of ground with the dwelling-house erected thereon and garden ground effeiring thereto known as fifty-five Emily Drive, Kirkcudbright, being the subjects registered under Title Number KRK12345: *[Entry]* With entry and actual occupation as at the fourth day of October two thousand and five; *[Warrandice]* and I grant warrandice; *[Trust]*[14] and I hereby declare that, until title is registered in the Land Register in pursuance of these presents, I hold the said subjects as trustee for behoof of the said Donald Henry McQuoist and Sara Jane Cumming or McQuoist : *[Testing]* In witness whereof these presents are subscribed by me at Kirkcudbright on the first day of October in the year two thousand and five in the presence of Arlene Duguid, trainee solicitor, fourteen Waterperry Street, Kirkcudbright.

Disposition of property in the GRS

11–05

[Narrative] I, James Jameson, born on third January nineteen hundred and fifty nine,[15] residing formerly at forty-two Sauchiehall Square, Glasgow and now at five Frances Street, Stornoway, heritable[16] proprietor of the subjects hereinafter disponed, in consideration of the price of two hundred thousand pounds

---

[11] Land Registration (Scotland) Act 1979, s.16.
[12] It is good but not (yet) standard practice to give dates of birth: see para.11–06.
[13] Or "heritable": see para.11–07.
[14] Whether a trust clause ought to be inserted is arguable: see para.11–27.
[15] It is good but not (yet) standard practice to give dates of birth: see para.11–06.
[16] Or "registered": see para.11–07.

(£200,000) paid to me by Alan Dewar Johnston, born on tenth May nineteen hundred and sixty three, and Clare Janet Macleod or Johnston, born on tenth June nineteen hundred and sixty seven, residing together at thirty-two Fairlie Drive, Dundee, of which I hereby acknowledge receipt, *[Dispositive]* do hereby dispone to the said Alan Dewar Johnston and Clare Janet Macleod or Johnston equally between them All and Whole that area or plot of ground with the dwelling-house erected thereon and garden ground effeiring thereto known as five Frances Street, Stornoway,[17] in the County of Ross and Cromarty, being the subjects described in Disposition by Fergus Chalmers Campbell in favour of Donald Macleod dated first, and recorded in the Division of the General Register of Sasines applicable to the County of Ross and Cromarty on eleventh, both days of May in the year nineteen hundred and thirty-five: together with (one) the fittings and fixtures (two) the parts and pertinents and (three) my whole right title and interest present and future *[Burdens]* But always with and under in so far as valid subsisting and applicable the burdens conditions and others specified and contained in the said Disposition by Fergus Chalmers Campbell in favour of Donald Macleod dated and recorded as aforesaid: *[Entry]* With entry and actual occupation as at the fourth day of October two thousand and five; *[Add deduction of title if granter's title not completed by registration] [Warrandice]* and I grant warrandice; *[Trust]*[18] and I hereby declare that, until title is registered in the Land Register in pursuance of these presents, I hold the said subjects as trustee for behoof of the said Alan Dewar Johnston and Clare Janet Macleod or Johnston: *[Testing]* In witness whereof these presents are subscribed by me at Stornoway on the first day of October in the year two thousand and five in the presence of Elspeth Marie Macdonald, trainee solicitor, fourteen Pinwherry Gardens, Stornoway.

NARRATIVE CLAUSE

Designation

The parties to a deed—granter, grantee and consenter (if any)—must 11–06 be designed (*i.e.* described and identified). But other people mentioned in a deed normally need not be designed.[19] Thus, when a deed refers to prior deeds for real burdens, there is no need to design the parties to those prior deeds. Where designation is required, the approved technique is to design a party on the first occasion in which he appears in the deed and thereafter to refer to him as "the said Alan Dewar Johnston".

The test of a successful designation is that the party in question can be identified. The normal practice is to provide the full name and address.

---

[17] In practice, for no good reason, the postcode is usually omitted. It is sometimes said that this is because postcodes can change. But so can street numbers and street names.

[18] Whether a trust clause ought to be inserted is arguable. See para.11-27.

[19] An exception is a clause of deduction of title. See Conveyancing (Scotland) Act 1924, Schs A and B.

Some solicitors add occupations, although strictly this is only necessary where two people of the same name live at the same address (*e.g.* father and son). In most legal systems a designation will state the date of birth, and often the place of birth and nationality as well. Scotland is unusually lax in its standard of designations in conveyancing deeds. Dates of birth ought to be included, not as a matter of legal necessity, but as a matter of good practice. In the usual case the granters of the present disposition will be the grantees of the immediately previous disposition of the same property (or, in the case of Land Register titles, the person listed in the title sheet). But their address will typically have changed. In the older disposition they will be designed as living at their former address. It is good practice to link up the two deeds by giving both addresses as in the style above. This demonstrates that the James Jameson who was designed as living in Sauchiehall Square is the same James Jameson who now lives at Frances Street.

If a married woman adopts her husband's name, her maiden name should nevertheless be given as well. Thus if Clare Janet Macleod marries and chooses to become Clare Janet Johnston, she should be designed as "Clare Janet Macleod or Johnston". Where a party acts in a representative or fiduciary capacity, such as a trustee or as a liquidator, this fact should be added to the designation, together with details of the appointment. Thus, for an executor the designation will refer to the confirmation, mentioning its date and the court which issued it. For a trustee in sequestration the reference will be to the act and warrant, its date, and the court issuing it. In the case of a trustee under a deed of trust, the deed of trust must be identified, typically by reference to the Books of Council and Session where it will (at least if good practice has been followed) have been registered.

Juristic persons such as companies are designed by reference to their official address (in the case of a company this is known as the registered office) and to the statute under which they are incorporated. In the case of a company it is nowadays invariable practice to include the company's registration number. The reason is that it is easy for a company to change its name, and indeed a company can have a name which was formerly held by another company. Only the registration number is an unchangeable birthmark by which the identity can be unambiguously determined.

Heritable proprietor and unregistered holder

11–07   The traditional practice was to follow the name and designation of the granter with either the words "heritable proprietor" or the words "uninfeft proprietor". "Heritable proprietor" meant that the granter was, or at least claimed to be, the owner of the property, implying a title completed by registration. A granter who was "uninfeft proprietor" held the property under an unregistered conveyance. To be infeft literally meant to have taken feudal entry with the superior.

Although hallowed by long usage, "uninfeft proprietor" suffered from the obvious objection that a person who was uninfeft could not be the "proprietor" of the land; and today, following feudal abolition, it is no longer possible to be either "infeft" or "uninfeft". A replacement term is needed. The Title Conditions (Scotland) Act 2003 proposes "unre-gistered holder".[20] "Unregistered proprietor" would be closer to the previous terminology but suffers from the objection already mentioned. "Unregistered granter" is accurate but does not fit readily into the narrative clause of the typical deed.[21] Our own preference, following the 2003 Act, is for "unregistered holder".

The Keeper's view has been that "heritable proprietor" and "uninfeft proprietor" should not in any event be used for dispositions of proper-ties in the Land Register.[22] But while it is true that these terms are unnecessary in such dispositions, they are unnecessary even in disposi-tions recorded in the GRS. Notwithstanding the Keeper's view they continue to be widely used. When it comes to tradition, the force is strong. For those who choose to continue to use these terms, we tentatively suggest the terms (a) "heritable proprietor" and (b) "unre-gistered holder".

Cause of granting, and consideration

Although the cause of granting is in practice always stated, in the 11–08 narrative clause, it is not a requirement of law. In most cases a disposition is in implement of a contract of sale, so the price is narrated. Where the disposition is by way of gift, the traditional style is to narrate that the deed is granted for the "love, favour and affection" borne to the grantee.[23] A disposition by an executor or trustee will usually narrate the will or deed of trust, explaining that the grantee is a beneficiary. Occasionally one sees the formula "for certain good and onerous causes and considerations". This is a legalistic way of saying that the reason for the deed is not being disclosed.

There can be many reasons, apart from sale,[24] why a disposition is granted. While silence is possible, it is normal to explain, and sometimes this becomes something of a story. Indeed, one could begin by narrating the creation of the heaven and the earth, getting on, at about page four, to the bit about Almighty God feuing Scotland to Adam and Eve and the survivor of them.[25] It is a matter of judgment how much to include. If in

---

[20] Title Conditions (Scotland) Act 2003, s.128(1), Sch.14, para.7(3)(a), substituting "unregistered holder" for "uninfeft proprietor" in s.3(6) of the Land Registration (Scotland) Act 1979.

[21] Especially in the grant of a subordinate real right, where one can hardly be the "unregistered granter of the subjects aftermentioned".

[22] ROTPB, para.8.47.

[23] These words acquire a certain irony where the disposition arises from marital breakdown.

[24] Sale is a reason ("cause") for a conveyance, but is not a conveyance itself. This is perhaps obvious enough for heritable property, but the same is true for other property as well.

[25] In fact, we have it on good authority that God did not convey Scotland to Adam and Eve. "In the 28th verse [of the first chapter of Genesis], God saith to Adam and Eve, 'increase and multiply, and replenish the earth, and subdue or subject the same, and have dominion over the fishes of the sea, the fowls of the heaven, and all living things which move upon the earth.' This gift, therefore, could not be to Adam and Eve, who could neither replenish the earth nor subjugate nor subdue it; but it was to mankind which then was in their persons only; and it did not import a present right of property, but only a right or power to appropriate by possession, or *jus ad rem*, not *jus in re*." Stair, II, i, 1.

doubt, include it, because the effect is to preserve evidence as to the background circumstances. Sometimes there have been conveyancing problems in the past which the present deed is intended to correct, and if so it is helpful to outline the background.

While in practice the sellers will not release the disposition until payment is made, the buyers ought nonetheless to have a formal receipt. This is achieved by including words such as "of which we acknowledge receipt". A receipt in this form raises a strong presumption that payment has been made.[26]

One reason why care needs to be taken to state the cause accurately is that inaccuracy may cause problems later. Where two people buy a house it is easy to assume that both are contributing to the price and to so state in the narrative clause.[27] But that is not always true. The potential difficulties caused by inaccuracy are all the greater because the courts have sometimes declined to allow extrinsic evidence to contradict the narrative clause.[28] However, an inaccurate narrative clause can be in principle rectified under section 8 of the Law Reform (Miscellaneous Provisions) (Scotland) Act 1985.[29]

Consenters

11–09   Where a third party has, or may have, some right in relation to the property which might prove damaging to the position of the grantee, it is wise to ensure that s/he signs the deed as a consenter. Most dispositions do not have consenters, but if there is one the relevant details are given in the narrative clause.

Sometimes the intended effect of the consent is stated in the deed itself. A common example is where a heritable creditor consents, with the effect of discharging the security. Or again the effect may be defined by statute. An example is a consent given by the spouse of the disponer in terms of the Matrimonial Homes Act.[30] These are the simple cases. In other cases there are two, mutually exclusive, effects of signing as consenter. In the first place, if it turns out that the consenter, and not the granter, was the true owner, the fact that the consenter signed is sufficient to transfer ownership to the grantee.[31] In the second place, if the consenter is not owner but has some other real right in the land,[32] or,

---

[26] Erskine, II, iii, 22.

[27] As in the example above.

[28] *Gordon-Rogers v Thomson's Exrs*, 1988 S.L.T. 618; *McCafferty v McCafferty*, 2000 S.C.L.R. 256. By contrast, such evidence was held admissible in *Nottay's Tr v Nottay*, 2001 S.L.T. 769. *Gordon-Rogers* involved a survivorship destination. Such a destination is normally non-evacuable if both parties paid the price, and the consequences of that fact can be profound. Other examples where it was later asserted that the narrative clause was inaccurate include *Aitken's Tr v. Aitken*, 1999 G.W.D. 39–1898 and *Bank of Scotland v Reid*, 2000 G.W.D. 22–858.

[29] The subject of Ch.17.

[30] Matrimonial Homes (Family Protection) (Scotland) Act 1981, s.6(3)(a)(i). See paras 10–7 and 10–9.

[31] Stair II, xi, 7; *Mounsey v Maxwell* (1808) Hume 237. Erskine (II, iii, 21), however, argues that there is no transfer of ownership, although the consenter is under a personal obligation to grant a new disposition. The view of Stair is correct.

[32] *e.g.* a lease or a heritable security.

alternatively, if he has only a personal right in relation to the land, he cannot[33] thereafter exercise the right to the prejudice of the grantee or the grantee's successors. A common example is where Alan sells on missives to Beth and Beth resells to Chris and the disposition is from Alan to Chris with Beth's consent. Another example is where a trustee dispones with the consent of a beneficiary. Unless otherwise stated in the deed, the consenter corroborates only the conveyance of the land contained in the dispositive clause. The consent does not touch the other clauses, *e.g.* the warrandice clause.

DISPOSITIVE CLAUSE

Dispositive words

The dispositive clause is introduced by the words "do hereby dispone". 11-10 "Dispone" means "transfer",[34] so "hereby dispone to the said Alan Dewar Johnston and Clare Janet Macleod or Johnston" has the effect (upon registration) of transferring ownership of the property to the Johnstons. At common law "dispone" was a magic word, without which ownership could not pass. Synonymous terms were unavailing. By statute this rule has been abrogated,[35] and all that is now needed is some term that makes the intention plain. But in practice the word "dispone" continues to be used.

Common property or joint property

The only case where heritage can (and indeed must) be held in joint 11-11 property is where it is held by trustees. All other cases of *pro indiviso* ownership are cases of common property.[36] It should be observed, however, that ownership in common is often referred to, loosely, as ownership "in joint names". That, for example, is the terminology that clients generally use. It is not usual to specify in the disposition whether the multiple ownership being conferred is common or joint. The law is clear. But since common property, unlike joint property, can involve shares of different sizes, it is good practice to specify the size of individual shares ("to the said Alan Dewar Johnston and Clare Janet Macleod or Johnston equally between them"). If the shares are intended to be equal, which is generally the case, this is not strictly necessary, for if the size of the shares is not stated, the law will presume that equal shares are intended.

Description

The question of how the property is to be identified—the law and 11-12 practice of descriptions—is the subject of the next chapter.

---

[33] Unless the contrary intention can be gathered.
[34] Or, more strictly, "transfer the ownership of heritable property".
[35] Conveyancing (Scotland) Act 1874, s.27.
[36] Reid, *Property*, para.34.

Burdens

11–13   The creation of new real burdens and servitudes is discussed in Chapter 13. Here we consider the conveyancing practice where there are existing burdens, which is usually the case.

In dispositions of property in the Land Register no reference to existing burdens is necessary.[37] The grantee takes the property as set out in the title sheet, and the title sheet lists the burdens.[38] What follows is therefore applicable to dispositions of property which is still in the GRS, which is to say mainly first registrations. Traditionally deeds imposing burdens contained a provision requiring all future deeds to refer to the burdens. Whether such provisions were enforceable is an open question, but at all events section 68 of the Title Conditions (Scotland) Act 2003 now declares all such provisions unenforceable.

Nonetheless existing burdens should be referred to in the disposition. This is partly to avoid claims in warrandice: in granting warrandice the granter guarantees the terms of the dispositive clause, and if the dispositive clause makes no reference to burdens, the granter is taken as guaranteeing that there are none.[39] Another reason is purely practical: when faced with a bundle of title deeds it is difficult to know which writs contain real burdens. The list in the disposition saves time and energy.

In practice existing burdens are almost never repeated in full. The usual formula is: "But always with and under the burdens, conditions and others, so far as valid, subsisting and applicable, specified in . . . " [then list the deeds in which the burdens appear].[40] The significance of "so far as valid, subsisting and applicable" is that real burdens can become spent, and the grantee does not wish to be committed to the proposition that all the burdens in the title remain live and enforceable. In practice, the list is simply copied from the immediately preceding disposition. But if a burden is obviously spent it can safely be omitted.

Typically there are two or three deeds listed. All deeds older than 1858 will be instruments of sasine, because until that year dispositions and feu dispositions could not be registered directly and their contents were summarised in the instrument.

Reservations

11–14   The dispositive clause also includes details of anything which is being reserved to the granter. In most cases nothing is reserved. But in a break-off disposition part of the land is reserved. Where that happens it may be that the mineral rights under the ground being disponed are also reserved, though that will be possible only if the disponer has them in the first place, which may not be the case. In a break-off deed the disponer is likely also to reserve real burdens and servitudes over the

---

[37] Land Registration (Scotland) Act 1979, s.15(2).

[38] *ibid.*, s.3(1)(a).

[39] However, if the grantee knows of, or is deemed to know of, the burden, there will be no remedy in warrandice.

[40] This formula has its origins in a statutory style which has now been repealed. See Conveyancing (Scotland) Act 1874, s.32 and Sch.H, repealed by the Title Conditions (Scotland) Act 2003, s.128 and Sch.15. There is now no prescribed form of wording.

disponed property. Whether these should strictly be called "reservations" is arguable, for it might be said that only something that already exists can be reserved, and before the break-off happens no real burdens or servitudes can exist between the two parts of the as-yet undivided property. But at all events in practice conveyancers often speak of "reserving" real burdens and servitudes. In a complex deed it can sometimes be unclear whether some item is being disponed or reserved, and the practice is to say something like "together with (by way of grant not exception) . . ." or vice versa.

THE IMPLIED ASSIGNATIONS

Introduction

The narrative and dispositive clauses are the two most important 11–15 clauses in a disposition. But there are also a number of ancillary clauses. Two of these (neither usually of much importance) are the clause of assignation of writs and the clause of assignation of rents. Until the passing of the 1979 Act these clauses were set out in full.[41] But by section 16 of the Act these two clauses[42] are implied and accordingly in practice are now omitted.[43] These clauses are "assignations" since what they transfer is incorporeal, intimation being effected by registration.[44]

Assignation of writs

The assignation of writs has two effects. The first is to transfer certain 11–16 personal rights. Conveyances contain a number of contractual obligations by the granter to the grantee, the two most important being the obligation of warrandice and the obligation of relief.[45] These obligations can sometimes be enforced by successors of the original grantee. Suppose, for example, that Amy dispones to Beth, Beth dispones to Chris, and Chris dispones to David. In the dispositions Amy, Beth and Chris will have entered into certain obligations. But since these are personal, not real, they can, on general principles, be enforced only by Beth, Chris and David respectively. Unless, of course, they are assigned. By section 16(1) of the 1979 Act the implied assignation of writs imports "an assignation to the grantee of the title deeds and searches and all deeds not duly recorded". What this appears to mean is that some, but not all, of the obligations in dispositions are assigned. In past times this was important (*e.g.* for unexecuted precepts of sasine, procuratories of resignation, and other antiquarian exotica). Today what it all appears to mean is that (a) obligations of warrandice are assigned[46] and that (b)

---

[41] In the form prescribed by s.8 and Sch.B of the Titles to Land Consolidation (Scotland) Act 1868.

[42] Together with the clause of relief, for which see below.

[43] This section applies to dispositions both of GRS property and registered property.

[44] *Paul v Boyd's Trs* (1835) 13 S. 818; *Edmond v Magistrates of Aberdeen* (1855) 18 D. 47, (1858) 3 Macq. 116.

[45] See below.

[46] Stair, II.iii.46.

obligations of relief are not. Why both should not be treated in the same way is a mystery.[47]

The practical effect is this. In the above example, when Amy dispones to Beth, Amy grants warrandice.[48] So Beth has a right against Amy. When Beth dispones to Chris, Beth in turn grants warrandice to Chris. So Chris has a right of warrandice against Beth. But he also has a right of warrandice against Amy, for Amy's former right has passed to Chris by the assignation of writs. Likewise, when Chris dispones to David, David comes to hold three rights of warrandice, against Amy, Beth and Chris.

The second aspect of the assignation of writs concerns the delivery of the title deeds. The law here depends on whether the property is in the Land Register or not. If it is not, then section 16(1) of the 1979 Act places the granter under certain obligations as to the title deeds, including the obligation to deliver all titles relating exclusively to the land conveyed.[49] Since the title deeds are normally delivered at settlement,[50] along with the disposition, the section 16 obligation is usually fulfilled at precisely the same moment as it is incurred. If the property is in the Land Register, the obligation normally relates only to the land certificate and the charge certificate (if any). The exception is where indemnity is excluded.[51] It is common practice, upon first registration, to destroy the existing deeds, or to hand them to the purchasing clients. In the latter case they will usually cease to be available. This may occasionally cause difficulties, particularly if the title comes to be challenged by reference to an underlying deed.

Quite separately, there is a statutory right to consult title deeds for anyone who has, or is entitled to acquire, a real right in the land in question.[52] Until 1979 dispositions usually included, as an appendix, an inventory of writs listing the principal title deeds. This practice, never required by law, has now disappeared.

Assignation of rents[53]

11–17   The clause of assignation of rents, though included, expressly or by implication, in all deeds, is relevant only if the property disponed is tenanted. Its object is twofold. In the first place, it enables the disponee to draw the rents as soon as the disposition has been delivered and its terms intimated to the tenant. This point was important long ago when a disponee might be slow in completing title. Nowadays, when disponees almost invariably complete title at once, this aspect no longer matters. The other purpose of the clause is to arrange, as between disponer and disponee, the point in time after which the rents payable will go to the

---

[47] Similar difficulties apply to s.8 of the 1868 Act.

[48] In the normal case, at least. See also para.16–13.

[49] Presumably one must read into the provision an implied term that the obligation relates only to deeds which the granter has or can obtain.

[50] The only common exception is in a break-off disposition, where the granter will usually retain them.

[51] 1979 Act, s.3(5).

[52] Abolition of Feudal Tenure etc. (Scotland) Act 2000, s.66.

[53] See Halliday, para.37–13.

disponee. For instance, if the disposition is granted in August, and the rent is payable twice a year, at Whitsunday and Martinmas, is the disponer to keep the Whitsunday rent, and the disponee to take the Martinmas rent? Or should the rent for Whitsunday to Martinmas be split? And so on.

Before the 1979 Act, the disposition could either have a detailed clause, or could simply say "I assign the rents", the meaning of which expression was defined by statute.[54] Under section 16 of the 1979 Act the assignation of rents is implied.[55] However, the implied statutory meaning is extremely hard to understand,[56] involving as it does problems about forehand rents, backhand rents, arable farms, pastoral farms, conventional terms and legal terms.[57] Conveyancers who are unwilling to take a month or two off to investigate the law should avoid the statutory provisions by making express, detailed and clear provision as to how the rental income is to be apportioned as between disponer and disponee.

THE CONTRACTUAL OBLIGATIONS

Contractual effect of the disposition

As well as being an executory deed, conveying the land (and the writs 11–18 and rents), a disposition is also a contract imposing obligations, usually on the granter. As personal rights, these obligations do not transmit for the benefit of future owners unless assigned. Whereas ownership passes to the disponee only on registration, the contractual obligations generally take effect immediately, on delivery of the disposition.[58] The contractual obligations are: (i) entry; (ii) warrandice;[59] and (iii) obligation of relief.[60]

Entry

Entry is the date at which the granter is bound to yield possession to 11–19 the grantee. In a sale this will already have been contracted for in the missives. The date of entry must be distinguished from (i) the date of the disposition and (ii) the date when the disposition is delivered.

---

[54] Titles to Land Consolidation (Scotland) Act 1868, s.8.

[55] 1979 Act, s.16. The meaning of this implied clause is very similar to the meaning defined in s.8 of the 1868 Act.

[56] See J. Rankine, *Law of Leases* (3rd ed., 1916) and G.C.H. Paton and J.G.S. Cameron, *The Law of Landlord and Tenant in Scotland* (1967).

[57] Not to mention quantum mechanics, special relativity theory, and the meaning of love. (Which, however, are, by comparison, easy topics.) An example will illustrate the sort of problems that can be encountered. A pastoral farm is let with the rent one term backhand. The landlord sells with entry at August 1. The rent "conventionally" payable at Martinmas is "legally" payable at the previous Whitsunday. Therefore, by the statutory provisions it goes to the disponer, even though actually paid when the disponee is already the owner.

[58] Of course, the missives will already contain contractual obligations, but we are dealing with those which derive from the disposition.

[59] See Ch.16.

[60] Sometimes a supersession clause is also found, repeating (unnecessarily) the clause found in missives. See Ch.16.

The date of the disposition is the date of execution (signature) or, if there is more than one signature, of last execution. This date will be found from the testing clause. It has little legal significance. Usually it is before the date of entry. If it is after the date of entry (*e.g.* because something has gone wrong with the transaction and settlement is delayed) it is usual to add to the entry clause the words "notwithstanding the date hereof", which indicates that the unusual sequence is not just a typing error. It sometimes happens (*e.g.* with gifts or with sales to sitting tenants) that entry is to be on the same day as the deed is executed, and in that case the entry clause reads "with entry at the date hereof".

The date of delivery is, in a sale, the date of settlement, the date at which the transaction actually settles, that is, when the disposition is handed over in exchange for the price. In a normal sale the date of entry and date of settlement are the same day. But if things go wrong (*e.g.* the purchasers cannot pay) the date of entry may pass without the transaction being settled. Before delivery, the disposition has no effect. After delivery, but before registration, its effect is limited, since at this stage ownership has yet to pass. But the deed still has various effects. Its contractual clauses have full effect, and the disponees, though not owners, have the status and privileges of unregistered holders.

Entry is the date at which the granter must yield possession.[61] But possession may either be natural (*i.e.* physically by the owner) or civil (through another person, such as a tenant) and the entry clause in its statutory form is satisfied by either. This means that purchasers who arrive with their removal van only to find that the property is tenanted have no redress under the statutory clause. Nor, probably, do they have redress under the warrandice clause.[62] The solution is to contract specifically for vacant possession, thus: "With entry and actual occupation[63] on twenty second November Two Thousand and Five".[64]

The meaning of vacant possession or actual occupation has occasionally caused problems. In *Stuart v Lort-Phillips*[65] cattle belonging to a neighbour were found grazing on about one-third of the subjects of sale. The neighbour claimed he had an agricultural tenancy. Both facts were held to be a breach of the obligation to give vacant possession. This was so even although the claim to the tenancy might (and in fact did) turn out to be spurious.[66] If an express entry clause is omitted, it is implied that entry is at the next term of Whitsunday or Martinmas.[67] But in practice the clause is never omitted, except by accident.

---

[61] Until feudal abolition, "entry" also had another sense, that of entry with the superior. Until 1874 this meant obtaining a further deed, a "charter by progress". There were various forms of charter by progress. For a buyer there was a choice of two, the charter of confirmation and the charter of resignation. The former was commoner in practice. The Conveyancing (Scotland) Act 1874 Act, s.4 (applied to the Land Register by s.29 of the 1979 Act) provided that the disponee was deemed to take entry with the superior upon registration. Entry in the feudal sense has died with feudalism itself.

[62] *Lothian & Border Farmers Ltd v McCutchion*, 1952 S.L.T. 450, though the soundness of this decision is uncertain.

[63] Or "vacant possession".

[64] The wording here can be traced back at least as far as Sch.B to the Titles to Land Consolidation (Scotland) Act 1868.

[65] 1977 S.C. 244.

[66] See also *Scottish Flavour Ltd v Watson*, 1982 S.L.T. 78 where it was held that the presence of rubbish was too trivial.

[67] 1874 Act, s.28.

Obligation of relief

An owner of land has certain obligations *qua* owner, some of the main 11–20
ones being (a) real burdens (b) non-domestic rates (c) council tax and
(d) statutory notices, *e.g.* notices served by the local authority under
section 28 of the Building (Scotland) Act 2003[68] requiring the repair of
buildings and empowering the authority to carry out the work itself and
recover the cost from the owner. Difficult questions can arise as to when
these obligations pass to the grantees, and to what extent the grantees
have relief against the granters.

For council tax[69] and rates, the grantees become liable on taking entry.
For real burdens[70] and, probably,[71] for statutory notices also, the
grantees become liable on acceptance of delivery of the disposition.
Usually entry and acceptance of the disposition occur on the same day,
i.e. on settlement. However, the fact that the grantees become liable
does not mean that the granters cease to be liable, provided that the
obligation has already been incurred. In such a case both the incoming
and the outgoing owners are liable, and the latter, if they pay, have,
unless otherwise agreed, a right of relief against the former. That is so
for real burdens.[72] It is also true for council tax and rates, as to which the
right of relief is based on the obligation of relief clause. This clause,
formerly express, is now implied by the 1979 Act, to the effect of
imposing on granters an obligation to relieve grantees of a variety of
burdens exigible prior to the date of entry.[73] Whether this clause includes
statutory notices is uncertain.[74] But in any event the missives should, and
normally do, make provision for liability as between seller and purchaser.

TESTING CLAUSE

Testing clause

Probative deeds finish with a testing clause giving details of execution. 11–21
Although the testing clause appears above the signatures, it is not
possible to complete it until the deed has been signed. When a deed is
being prepared for signature the traditional practice was to finish with
the words "In witness whereof." Granters were then asked to leave a
substantial gap between the end of the deed and their signatures so that
the testing clause could be added. However, it is commonly done in
other ways. One is for the testing clause to be completed before
signature except for blanks which are later filled in by hand.[75] Execution
of deeds is considered in Chapter 14.

---

[68] Not in force at the time of writing, but due to replace s.87(1) of the Civic Government
(Scotland) Act 1982, which is to similar effect.

[69] Local Government Finance Act 1992, s.75.

[70] Title Conditions (Scotland) Act 2003, s.9 read with s.123.

[71] *Pegg v City of Glasgow District Council*, 1988 S.L.T. (Sh. Ct.) 49.

[72] 2003 Act, s.10. And see para.13–13.

[73] 1979 Act, s.16(3).

[74] *McIntosh v Mitchell Thomson* (1900) 8 S.L.T. 48 suggests that it may.

[75] para.14–07.

EXCAMBIONS AND SECTION 19 AGREEMENTS

Excambions

11-22   An excambion is where A dispones land to B and B dispones other land to A. In other words it is a swap. The deed of excambion[76] is usually called a "contract" of excambion, a somewhat misleading term since in fact it is a two-way disposition and will normally have been preceded by a contract, typically in the form of missives. Of course, it is possible to have two separate dispositions instead of a deed of excambion. Excambions may be used in all sorts of cases, but the typical one is where two adjacent landowners agree to swap certain areas, perhaps so as to straighten out a zigzag boundary.[77]

Section 19 agreements

11-23   A deed granted under section 19 of the 1979 Act[78] is available where the title boundaries of neighbouring properties are mutually inconsistent, and the parties agree on a solution. A deed is registered with an agreed plan, and the matter is thus settled.

REVISIONS AND ALTERATIONS

Revisions

11-24   By convention dispositions are drafted by the solicitors for the grantees. This is because the disposition will be basis of the grantees' title and the grantees have the stronger interest in ensuring that it is correct. However, in large developments, such as housing estates, the granters' solicitor will usually produce a *pro forma* style of disposition to be used in all cases. Once a deed has been drafted it is sent to the solicitors acting for the other party to be revised, that is to say checked for errors, both legal and clerical. The revising solicitor marks "revised" on the draft, and adds the firm name and the date. The deed is then returned to the other solicitors who prepare an engrossment, which is a fair copy on deed paper. This process is usually sufficient to eliminate both drafting and clerical errors.[79] Nonetheless it may sometimes happen that an engrossed disposition requires to be altered.

Alterations[80]

11-25   First, alterations before execution. Before execution there is no restriction on alterations. The alteration was on the deed when executed, and so is part of the deed. Minor alterations can be made by interlineation, marginal addition or erasure (known collectively as vitiations) or

---

[76] For a style see Halliday, para.37–73.

[77] In such a case a deed under s.19 of the 1979 Act is not appropriate, since that section applies only where there is a discrepancy as between the existing title boundaries. In the typical case of excambion, there is no such discrepancy.

[78] For a style see Halliday, para.33–91.

[79] Word processors have helped to eliminate clerical errors.

[80] See also para.14–09.

more simply, in the age of word processors, by reprinting the offending page. For probativity the testing clause must declare that the alteration was already part of the deed by the time of subscription.[81]

Secondly, alterations after execution. Such alterations need to be re-executed by the signatories,[82] so that in practice one may as well prepare a new (and correct) deed. Apart from that, after execution a deed cannot lawfully be altered. Alteration amounts to the crime of forgery.[83] But in practice deeds are sometimes altered by one of the solicitors involved, the alteration being cheerfully and dishonestly declared in the testing clause as having been made before subscription.[84] The most brazen case of alteration is the substitution of one page for another, which is possible now that the granter does not have to sign each page.[85] Such dishonesty cannot be condoned.

INTERPRETATION

Interpretation

Each clause in a disposition has its own recognised function, and in all 11–26 questions involving that function the clause is treated as the principal provision. If therefore there is a repugnancy between the principal clause and the rest of the deed the principal clause prevails. But if the principal clause itself is ambiguous, that ambiguity may be resolved by reference to the rest of the deed.[86]

Extrinsic evidence can be used to interpret and explain the wording of the deed, but not to modify it.[87] There are two main examples of the explanatory role of extrinsic evidence. The first is to link up words used in the deed to physical objects or people. For example to say that a property is "bounded on the south by the road known as Buchanan Street, Glasgow" might require extrinsic evidence as to the location of Buchanan Street. The second is to resolve ambiguity. If something is ambiguous, extrinsic evidence is admissible.

---

[81] Requirements of Writing (Scotland) Act 1995, s.5(4), (5). If the testing clause fails to do this, the court naturally has power to declare the altered deed to have been the deed which was executed: s.5(6).

[82] 1995 Act, s.5(1) and Sch.1.

[83] Hume, *Commentaries*, i, 159.

[84] The alteration is then probative (presumptively valid) but latently invalid. Sometimes (perhaps as a result of the voice of conscience) the testing clause asserts that the alteration has been made, but does not say that it was made before execution. That achieves nothing.

[85] The change was made in 1970. The current law is in ss.2 and 3 of the 1995 Act. The wisdom of the modern law may be questioned.

[86] *e.g. Orr v Mitchell* (1893) 20 R. (HL) 27.

[87] Except by judicial rectification, for which see Ch.17. The Contract (Scotland) Act 1997, s.1 (which allows the admission of additional terms in certain circumstances) applies only to contracts and promises. For an analysis of the present law, and recommendations for its reform, see Scottish Law Commission, *Report on Interpretation in Private Law* (Scot. Law Com. No.160, 1997).

EFFECT OF DELIVERY OF THE DISPOSITION

Effect of delivery of the disposition

11-27   Before delivery of the disposition, the right of the buyers is simply a
personal right under the missives. The sellers have a right to be paid, and
the buyers have a right to receive a valid disposition, and to obtain
possession of the property. At settlement the parties perform their
respective obligations, namely payment by the buyers, and delivery of the
deed and transfer of possession by the sellers. But the buyers at this
stage still do not have ownership. Ownership is a real right (indeed, the
chief kind of real right), and a real right can be obtained only by
registration in the Land Register or GRS.[88] Until the buyers register, the
sellers remain owner. The interval between the delivery of the disposition and its registration is short—seldom more than a few days. In this
period the buyer (call her Betty) is in theory at risk simply because the
seller (call her Alice) is still the owner. Thus, Alice could fraudulently
convey the property to someone else, say Ciaran. In that case there
would be what is called a race to the register between Ciaran and Betty,
and whoever registered first would win.[89] Much the same would apply if
Alice were to be sequestrated. If Alice delivers a disposition to Betty,
and Alice is then sequestrated, there is a race to the register between
Betty and Alice's trustee in sequestration. Whoever wins that race takes
the property, although in practice trustees in sequestration are generally
so slow off the mark as to pose no danger to a buyer who registers with
reasonable dispatch.[90] If, however, no disposition has been delivered
then Betty is doomed to lose the race. There is a special rule where the
seller is a company and goes into receivership after having delivered a
disposition. In that case the buyer, when she registers, takes the property
free from the receiver's rights. This exception derives from the controversial 1997 case of *Sharp v Thomson*.[91] At one time there was
speculation that *Sharp v Thomson* had a broad *ratio* to the effect that
some sort of "beneficial interest", neither a personal right nor a real
right, passed to the buyer upon delivery of the disposition, but that view
has not prevailed.[92]

---

[88] This was always the rule and is confirmed by s.4 of the Abolition of Feudal Tenure
etc. (Scotland) Act 2000.

[89] Though Ciaran, if in bad faith, would be subject to the "off-side goals rule". See
further, Reid, *Property*, paras 695 *et seq.*

[90] For a celebrated case where the buyer was even slower than the trustee, see *Burnett's
Tr v Grainger*, 2004 S.L.T. 513. The same is equally true in the case of a creditor of Alice
attaching the property.

[91] 1997 S.C. (HL) 66.

[92] *Burnett's Tr v Grainger*, 2004 S.L.T. 513. For the *Sharp v Thomson* saga, see Scottish
Law Commission, *Discussion Paper on Sharp v Thomson* (Scot. Law Com. D.P. No.114,
2001; available on *http://www.scotlawcom.gov.uk*), which contains an extensive bibliography
on a case which has probably generated more writing than any other in Scottish legal
history except *Donoghue v Stevenson* 1932 S.C. (HL) 31. The decision in *Burnett's Tr v
Grainger* has confirmed that, although the decision of the Inner House in *Sharp v
Thomson*, 1995 S.C. 455 was reversed by the House of Lords, the Inner House's exposition
of Scots property law was correct and was not superseded by the decision of the House of
Lords.

At first instance, in 1994, *Sharp v Thomson* was decided in favour of the receiver.[93] The result was that solicitors became more conscious than before of the potential danger to buyers, and accordingly it became fairly common for the disposition to contain a clause declaring that the property would be held by the sellers in trust for the buyers until the latter registered. These trust clauses remain common. The point is that the rights of a beneficiary in a trust normally are protected against the insolvency of the trustee. Because of the House of Lords' ultimate decision in *Sharp v Thomson* such clauses are not needed to protect against receivership. Whether buyers have much to fear as to the sequestration or liquidation of the sellers, or diligence against them, is doubtful, unless they are quite extraordinarily slow in registering. Hence the usefulness of a trust clause is open to question. It might also be doubted whether the trust so created is valid. If valid it gives a certain protection against unlikely possibilities, but also imposes certain duties on the sellers[94] and also creates new risks for the buyers.[95] The whole issue is complex and unclear.[96]

---

[93] 1994 S.L.T. 1068.

[94] The duties of trusteeship are potentially onerous.

[95] If there is no trust clause the buyers have some protection against a fraudulent double sale by virtue of the offside goals rule. But if there is a trust clause this protection seems to be lost on account of s.2 of the Trusts (Scotland) Act 1961.

[96] For further discussion see Steven and Wortley, 1996 S.L.T. (News) 365; Chalmers, 2002 S.L.T. (News) 231.

CHAPTER 12

DESCRIPTIONS

Introduction

12-01   The subject of descriptions[1] is divided in this chapter into six unequal parts:

(i) Descriptions in the Land Register.
(ii) Descriptions in deeds where the property is in the Land Register.
(iii) Descriptions in deeds triggering first registration.
(iv) Descriptions in GRS deeds, *i.e.* deeds recorded, or to be recorded, in the GRS.
(v) Descriptions in missives.
(vi) Final observations.

DESCRIPTIONS IN THE LAND REGISTER

General

12-02   In the Land Register each property unit is identified by a plan. The plan is part of the title sheet itself, and hence is also contained in the land certificate, for the land certificate is an extract of the title sheet. The plan in the title sheet is known as the title plan, and the plan in the land certificate is known as the certificate plan, but they are the same plan. In this respect the system in Scotland differs from that of many other countries, where there exists a single registration plan of the whole country, or province, called a cadastral plan,[2] divided into numbered title units, and the property register describes the property only by reference to the relevant cadastral number. Our system is more convenient for the user. A downside is that overlaps between two properties can happen in a way that would hardly be possible in the cadastral system. Whilst we have no cadastral map as such, there is something very like it in the Index Map.[3] This is a map of all title units that are in the Land Register. As properties gradually switch from the GRS to the Land Register, the Index Map covers more and more of the surface of Scotland. In the early days of registration of title, the map system was a paper one. Nowadays

---

[1] As to which Ch.4 of the ROTPB is essential reading.
[2] In French, *le cadastre*, in German *das Kataster*, etc.
[3] Land Registration (Scotland) Rules 1980, r.23.

it is digital, though since land certificates are in paper form the certificate plan is a paper version of the digital original. Both the title plans and the Index Map are based on what the legislation calls the Ordnance Map.[4] The legislation speaks of "the" Ordnance Map, as if it were something fixed. In fact the Ordnance Survey's maps are in a state of constant revision. New versions are sent to the Keeper on a monthly basis. The Keeper not only uses the latest map for new registrations, but will also take "remedial action" where necessary for existing title sheets.[5] However, despite the constant updating, the map for a given area may, at a given time, be significantly out of date. Indeed, whilst the surveying standards of the Ordnance Survey are high, all human endeavours are fallible, so that a map may contain surveying inaccuracies, quite independently of the question of whether it is up-to-date. The problem of inaccurate or out-of-date Ordnance Survey maps is significant and perennial.

The plan in the title sheet will have a north sign, and will state the scale, but it will not usually show area measurements[6] or boundary measurements, and these have to be discovered by using the scale. If the Keeper does show these measurements he will in practice exclude indemnity as to their accuracy. The scales used by the Keeper are 1:10000, 1:2500 and 1:1250. The Keeper decides which scale to use. For urban properties he will normally use 1:1250. He can use more than one plan, with different scales. Whatever the scale, plans are limited in their accuracy. Even on the 1:1250 scale, the tiny distance of one millimetre on the plan represents 1.25 metres on the ground. The problem is worse with the other scales. The result is that descriptions in the Land Register cannot be more than approximate, and so there is scope for neighbours to war with each other.

Precision is further limited by the fact that normally "indemnity is . . . excluded is respect of information as to the line of the boundary."[7] This exclusion applies where (as is typically the case) a boundary coincides with a physical feature on the ground, such as a wall or fence. The plan will show that feature, with the title boundary on it, but the Keeper is not guaranteeing that the title boundary actually corresponds precisely to the physical line. The Keeper will sometimes, by the use of arrows,[8] attempt to state whether the boundary is the middle, or nearside, or farside, of a physical feature, but once again he excludes indemnity in respect of these arrows. There is also a verbal description, but in most cases this is little more than a postal address. However, the verbal description can be fuller when this is appropriate, as in tenemental property. Often the mineral rights are excepted from the title. This fact will be indicated verbally. Pertinents will also be indicated verbally. The Land Registration Act[9] requires the Keeper to enter into the title sheet

---

[4] See in particular the Land Registration (Scotland) Act 1979, ss.4(2)(a) and 6(1)(a), and the Land Registration (Scotland) Rules 1980, r.23.

[5] ROTPB, para.4.26. The law hereabouts is boggy.

[6] Unless 2 hectares or more: see 1979 Act, ss.6(1)(a) and 12(3)(e).

[7] See 2(d) of the "General Information" printed inside every land certificate. This derives from form 6 of the Land Registration (Scotland) Rules 1980.

[8] The use of the arrow system is explained in the printed information in each land certificate.

[9] Land Registration (Scotland) Act 1979, s.6(1)(e).

particulars of "any enforceable real right pertaining to the interest". Thus, if the property is the benefited (dominant) property in a servitude or real burden, this should be mentioned, if known, to the Keeper. Usually, and especially with real burdens, it is not known to the Keeper.[10] However, the position is now changing, for real burdens and servitudes granted after November 28, 2004 have to be registered in the titles of both the benefited and the burdened properties.[11]

Tenements

12-03   With tenement properties the plan shows the "footprint" of the tenement, and also the "steading", which is the footprint plus the attached land, but it does not have a "sectional" view, and so the only way the individual unit can be identified within the tenement is by the verbal description.[12] For instance, it will say something like "the eastmost house on the third or top floor" typically adding "within the land edged red on the title plan." The "land edged red" will be the steading. A casual look at the plan might suggest that the owner owns everything within the red line, but of course that is not so. As for the back green, the rights will usually be stated verbally. If a particular part of the back green is exclusively owned, that may be indicated either verbally or by a plan.[13] In tenemental property the verbal description is, indeed, of central importance. In practice the verbal description tends to be copied more or less verbatim from the GRS title. The GRS description may well have been somewhat vague, and even sloppy, and that vagueness and sloppiness thus tend to migrate from the GRS to the Land Register. There may be no alternative in practice, but such titles hardly display the Land Register to best advantage.

Migration to Land Register of sloppy GRS descriptions

12-04   The problem of vague, obscure or sloppy verbal descriptions migrating verbatim from the GRS to the Land Register can sometimes also arise with non-tenemental properties, especially with pertinents. The GRS title may have purported to confer on plot X rights over neighbouring plot Y, and yet the purported rights may in fact not be valid as servitudes or real burdens or indeed anything else, for descriptions are done by fallible human beings whose knowledge of the law of Scotland is not always perfect. Yet such descriptions often migrate to the new title sheet verbatim without being seriously queried by the Keeper's staff. Vague and sloppy conveyancing is not confined to GRS deeds. Modern deeds, and perhaps especially deeds of conditions, are often unsatisfactory, and the unsatisfactory wording will tend to end up unchanged in the title sheet.

---

[10] See Ch.13.

[11] Title Conditions (Scotland) Act 2003, ss.4 and 75. See paras 13–12 and 13–26.

[12] Occasionally GRS titles have sectional plans, so in this respect transfer into the Land Register may cause a loss of information.

[13] For the Keeper's current practice in this respect see (2003) 71 *Scottish Law Gazette* 123–4. In cases of doubt he may require affidavits about exclusive possession, or consents from the other owners in the tenement.

Deeds of conditions

Deeds of conditions[14] are meant to be used for burdens. But in 12–05 practice they are sometimes used not only for burdens but also for rights, such as co-ownership of amenity areas. In such cases the title sheet will usually follow suit, so that the Property Section will say something like "together with the rights set forth in item 4 in Section D". Though common, the practice is arguably wrong. Some solicitors return such land certificates to the Keeper, insisting that the rights be inserted in Section A.

Physical features as boundaries

Where the boundary is a physical feature such as a wall, the title sheet 12–06 and land certificate may state whether the line of the boundary is (a) the middle line (*medium filum*) or (b) one face or (c) the other face. The statement can be verbal or by the use of arrows.[15] The plan will have a north sign, and will state the scale, but it will not usually show area measurements[16] or boundary measurements, and these have to be discovered by using the scale. If the Keeper does show these measurements he will in practice exclude indemnity as to their accuracy.

Water boundaries, whether the sea, lochs, rivers or burns are not uncommon and present special problems, especially as they may shift over time.[17]

Approved estate layout plans

Where an owner plans to build new houses and sell them off 12–07 individually, the owner can agree with the Keeper what is called an "approved estate layout plan", showing the whole proposed development with proposed boundaries. This procedure is not compulsory, but it is normal practice. It has many benefits, including avoiding muddles as to boundaries, and avoiding the need for each form 12 for each unit to have a precise description, since a plot number will suffice. The scheme is available only if the whole development site is in the Land Register, but so useful is the scheme that if the site, or a part of it, is in the GRS the Keeper will normally be happy to accept a voluntary first registration for the whole site.

---

[14] For which see para.13–11.

[15] The arrow points to the face that is the boundary. If the arrow lies across the boundary feature, that means that the boundary is the middle line.

[16] Unless 2 hectares or more: see 1979 Act, ss.6(1)(a) and 12(3)(e).

[17] For the common law position see *Stirling v Bartlett*, 1994 S.L.T. 763. For the Keeper's practice see ROTPB, paras 6.99–6.101, read in the light of the Keeper's statement at (2002) 47 J.L.S.S. May/11.

Descriptions in Deeds Where The Property is in The Land Register

Dealings with whole

12-08   If a title is in the Land Register, and the deed is dealing with the whole of the registered title—which of course is usually the case—then the description in the deed is simply a reference to the title number,[18] plus a brief verbal description. There is an approved statutory style: "the subjects[19] registered under Title Number . . .".[20] Thus in practice the wording would be something like "ALL and WHOLE Number Four Beech Drive Perth being the subjects registered under Title Number PER 12345." A disposition of the whole of an existing title unit is sometimes called a standard disposition, both for the purposes of the Land Register and for the GRS.

The postal address is an example of a "general description".[21] General descriptions are of little importance for deeds dealing with property in the Land Register, except for tenemental property. They are much more important for GRS deeds, and accordingly will be discussed below. The words "ALL and WHOLE . . ." (formerly "All and Haill", and before that "*Totas et Integras*") are of great antiquity and considerable theoretical obscurity. According to Craig:

> "The words 'all and whole' are exegetical and mean that the subject is conveyed as a complete unit with all its parts. In ordinary language the word 'all' is used with reference to things differing in kind, and the word 'whole' with reference to things of the same kind. Anyhow, the effect of these words is to show that the entire or universal subject is carried by the disposition. For the person who sells an estate or transfers it for some onerous cause is bound in law to hand it over complete and perfect, clear of all burdens, servitudes, and encumbrances whatsoever."[22]

But in modern practice the words have become rather like a mere punctuation mark. They are usually written in capitals, and help show at a glance where the description is starting.

---

[18] This is required by the 1979 Act s.4(2)(d). Actually this provision is not always workable and is sometimes disregarded (*e.g.* an application by an uninfeft proprietor based on a midcouple which contains a general description).

[19] "The subjects" is a traditional conveyancing term meaning the property in question. It can be criticised on the ground that in legal theory the term "subjects" refers to the subjects of rights, which is to say persons, in contrast to "objects" which themselves may be divided into rights and things. Land is thus an object rather than a subject.

[20] Land Registration (Scotland) Rules 1980, r.25 and Sch.B.

[21] The general description is not to be confused with the general disposition. A general description (or general conveyance), like a special description, is used in a special disposition, *i.e.* a disposition of one or more identified properties. A general disposition is a disposition of all the disponer's heritable property, without description. An example of a general disposition is a trust deed for behoof of creditors, in which the granter conveys all his or her property to the trustee. See Ch.21.

[22] *Jus Feudale*, II, iii, 23 (translation by J. A. Clyde, 1934).

Break-off deeds

If a disposition or other deed[23] is a break-off deed (also called a 12–09 break-away deed or a split-off deed), that is to say, if it is one that deals with only part of an existing title unit, then it must contain a "particular description", which is to say a description with precise identification of the boundaries. Except in the case of a unit in a tenement such a description must be plan-based.[24] If there is in place an approved estate layout plan (see above) the deed plan should normally be copied from that and should bear a docquet so stating.[25] The plan should be at one of the scales used by the Keeper, except that he will accept deeds containing 1:500 plans, and these are widely used for residential property. In some cases the deed will need a second plan, a "location" plan at a different scale, so as to anchor the first plan to surrounding features that can be identified on the Ordnance Map. Either the body of the deed or the plan itself should make clear whether the boundaries follow the middle, nearside or farside of the boundary features. Any measurements should be metric and should normally be to an accuracy of two decimal places, *i.e.* to an accuracy of one centimetre. The traditional detailed verbal description which used to be the norm in break-off deeds in the GRS[26] is unnecessary.

In a break-off conveyance, after the description there follows a clause identifying, by reference, the larger property of which the present property was hitherto a part. The official clause is: "being part of the subjects registered under Title Number . . ."[27] In practice "part" is often expanded to "part and portion", because that is the expression traditionally used in GRS deeds. Indeed, the name of this clause, both for GRS and Land Register deeds, is the "part-and-portion" clause.

Break-off dispositions are more difficult to handle than standard dispositions. Often servitudes and real burdens need to be granted (over the retained land), or reserved (over the disponed land), or both. Factual information will be needed on a variety of matters such as services and access routes. Whilst such matters ought to have been expressly provided for already in the missives, sometimes they have not been, or only in general terms, and the disposition needs to make specific provision. Care needs to be taken as to precisely what is being conveyed: it sometimes happens that after settlement one party or the other claims that the area conveyed was not what the missives provided.

Common parts

In many types of development there will be areas which will be co- 12–10 owned by the various proprietors. The break-off dispositions will need to identify these areas in a suitable manner. A practical problem is that the development may alter after the first break-off disposition has been

---

[23] Break-off writs are usually dispositions. But it is competent to have a standard security or a lease of only part of a registered title.

[24] By contrast, in GRS deeds a particular description can be purely verbal. See below.

[25] ROTPB, para.8.47 at p.338.

[26] See below.

[27] Land Registration (Scotland) Rules 1980, r.25 and Sch.B.

granted. Indeed, developers often wish to reserve the right to vary their plans in response to varying commercial demands. Thus, in a residential development instead of 20 houses the developer may wish to increase the number to 25. If that is done after the first break-off, and the first break-off granted a 1/20 share of the common parts, there is a problem. This problem is usually fudged by conveying "a right in common with the other proprietors in the said development to . . ." without specifying the proportion. It is a fudge because at the time of the first conveyance a definite share must be conveyed, and, once conveyed, cannot be changed except by corrective conveyancing. A problem of the same sort, but more serious, is that the developer may wish to change the physical extent of the areas which are to be common parts. Once the first break-off has been granted, containing a share of those parts, any alteration becomes impossible without corrective conveyancing. This problem also is sometimes fudged by granting in the first disposition a right in common to the common areas which are not defined in the plan but only in a vague verbal formula, the pith of which is that the common parts will be all parts of the development which will not be specifically conveyed to individual purchasers. But it is incompetent to convey an area which is indeterminate and potentially fluctuating and whose extent can be discovered only by future circumstances.[28] Under present law there exists no neat solution to this kind of problem.

DESCRIPTIONS IN DEEDS TRIGGERING FIRST REGISTRATION

General

12-11   The existing GRS description may well be sufficient for the purposes of a first registration, bearing in mind that the Keeper must be able to plot the boundaries with reasonable precision by reference to the Ordnance Map at the appropriate scale. What is required is either: (a) that the existing title is plan-based, the plan being an adequate one, or (b) that the existing title has a "full bounding title with measurements".[29] If neither requirement is met,[30] a plan will have to be drawn up, signed by both disponer and disponee, and submitted to the Keeper.[31]

The simplest way to do this is for the disposition that is inducing first registration to contain a new, plan-based, description, conforming to the criteria applicable to the Land Register (above). The alternative is to submit to the Keeper a separate plan, signed by both disponer and disponee.[32] If it is going to be necessary to have a plan prepared, it is

---

[28] See also s.4(2)(a) of the 1979 Act.

[29] Land Registration (Scotland) Rules 1980, Sch.A, form 1, part B, question 1. The form is prescribed by statutory instrument, and thus has legal force, but it is nevertheless curious that what is legally required can be discovered only from an application form. One would expect the requirements would be laid down directly, and that the terms of the application form would merely reflect those norms.

[30] As for the nature of descriptions in GRS deeds, and some of the problems that can exist with such descriptions, see below.

[31] Land Registration (Scotland) Rules 1980, Sch.A, form 1, part B, question 1.

[32] *ibid.*

simpler to have it as part of the disposition itself. If the disposition is a break-off disposition, it will need a new plan in any case. The deed will also need a part-and-portion clause. This will refer back to the descriptive deed, which is to say the earlier deed in the GRS that describes the property from which the new title unit is being broken off. This earlier descriptive deed will in the typical case itself have been a break-off disposition (or, very commonly, a feu disposition, feu charter or feu contract).

Tenements

There is one exception to the rule that in a first registration the title 12–12 must be plan-based: this is where the property is a tenement flat.[33] However, even here a plan may be needed, for instance to identify a part of the adjacent ground that is exclusively allocated to the particular flat.[34]

P16 Report

The applicant's solicitors need to check whether the title boundaries 12–13 correspond to what is actually possessed.[35] The usual way to do this is to ask the Keeper for a P16 Report, or to ask independent searchers for a P16 equivalent. Here there is a comparison of the title boundaries with the physical boundaries as shown in the Ordnance Map.[36] Alternatively the applicant's solicitors can do this themselves. The usefulness of a P16 Report is that a discrepancy between the title boundaries and the physical boundaries is a warning sign that there may exist a potential boundary dispute. The fact that the applicant's alleged title boundaries exceed the physical boundaries does not necessarily mean that the Keeper will decline to register the applicant for the excess, or that he will register the applicant for the excess only with exclusion of indemnity, for it might be that the title is definitely good.[37] But, as has been said, a discrepancy is a warning sign.

DESCRIPTIONS IN GRS DEEDS

Introduction

Since 2003 the Land Register has been "operational" in all counties in 12–14 Scotland, cases when a deed will be recorded in the GRS are increasingly rare. It happens when the existing title is still in the GRS, and the deed being granted is not one that triggers the switch to the new register. Examples are standard securities and gratuitous dispositions,

---

[33] Land Registration (Scotland) Rules 1980, Sch.A, form 1, part B, question 2.

[34] ROTPB, para.4.14.

[35] Land Registration (Scotland) Rules 1980, Sch.A, form 1, part B, question 2.

[36] ROTPB, paras 4.8–4.12.

[37] What has just been said is, we believe, the law. The Keeper's practice may not be the same. Thus para.4.16 (at p.94) of the ROTPB says that "if the extent of the property as defined in the deeds is found to be larger than the occupational extent . . . verification that the applicant is willing to accept the smaller extent *must* be given." (Emphasis added.)

such as dispositions by executors to legatees, and dispositions for "love favour and affection". Such cases will continue to arise for many years, and perhaps decades, into to future. Moreover, since so many titles are still GRS titles, an understanding of GRS descriptions will long remain important for the conveyancer.

The distinction between descriptions in the Land Register itself and descriptions in deeds has no counterpart for the GRS. The reason is that the GRS is in essence a warehouse of deeds, and nothing more than deeds, apart from a superb system of indexes and so on. Whereas in the Land Register map-based precision is vital, in the GRS deeds do not have to be map-based. Indeed, before 1924 deed plans could not enter the GRS at all. In principle, all that is required of a description is that it enables the property to be identified. Extrinsic evidence is permitted,[38] a rule which allows considerable vagueness in the description. Thus, in *Murray's Trustee v Wood*[39] the description was: "All and Whole that piece of ground fronting Baker Street of Aberdeen, in the burgh and county of Aberdeen". Since it could be established by extrinsic evidence that the granter owned only one property in Baker Street, this was held to be a sufficient description. The Keeper can reject deeds if the description is insufficient, but since for GRS deeds much latitude is allowed such rejections are rare. The only reported case is *Macdonald v Keeper of the Registers.*[40] There the Keeper was held entitled to reject a deed with the description "the house in No.140 McDonald Road, Edinburgh, the title to which is in my name" on the basis that, since No.140 was a tenement building, he could not tell which flat was being conveyed. There would seem to be some tension between this decision and *Murray's Trustee v Wood*. It is generally accepted that *Macdonald v Keeper of the Registers* was correctly decided, so there seem to be two thresholds of imprecision: the lowest level, below which a description becomes meaningless and without effect, a threshold that the description in *Murray's Trustee v Wood* did not fall below, and a higher threshold, where the description, though it might be sufficient if accepted for recording, is still so vague that the Keeper is entitled (but not obliged) to reject.

Old units of measurement

12–15   Many descriptions of property in the GRS are based on the imperial units of measurement, and, surprising though it may seem, some are still based on the old Scots units.[41]

The imperial linear measures are:

> 1 mile = 8 furlongs
> 1 furlong = 10 chains
> 1 chain = 22 yards

---

[38] Which is just as well, for otherwise the traditional type of estate title would be invalid.

[39] (1887) 14 R. 856. See also *Cattanach's Tr v Jamieson*, (1884) 11 R. 972 where the court looked for help in other parts of the deed.

[40] 1914 S.C. 854.

[41] Article XVII of the Treaty of Union abolished the Scots units, but this was widely ignored in practice.

1 yard = 3 feet
1 foot = 12 inches.

One yard = 0.9144 metres, 1 foot = 0.3048 metres and 1 inch = 25.4 millimetres. A shorthand is widely used for feet and inches: thus 16'7" means 16 feet and 7 inches.

As to imperial superficial measure,[42] 1 acre = 4840 square yards, *i.e.* a furlong by a chain (0.4047 hectares). The acre is divided into 4 roods, and each square rood into 40 square poles. A square pole is thus 30.25 square yards.[43] A square yard = about 0.836 square metres.

The old Scottish units generally had the same names as the imperial measures, but were different in size. The fall = about 5.65 metres, and the chain = 4 falls. Forty square falls (also called simply a fall) = a square rood (also called simply a rood), and 4 square roods = 1 acre. The Scots acre = about 1.26 imperial acres = about 0.51 hectares.

General descriptions

Land may be described in a GRS deed without reference to bound- 12–16 aries. This is known as a general description. Such a description may not enable the property to be identified from the Ordnance Map on its own: local information may be necessary.

The following are examples of general descriptions.

"ALL and WHOLE that detached dwelling-house number twelve Appletree Lane, Cupar, Fife."

"ALL and WHOLE that flatted dwelling-house[44] entering by the common passage and stair number fifteen Montrose Crescent, Dumfries, being the southmost dwelling-house on the second floor above the street or ground floor."

"ALL and WHOLE the lands of Cottown of Fetterletter, Ardlogie, Little Gight, Blackpool, Little Milbrex, North Faddonhill, Bruckleseat, Letherty, Myre of Bedlam, Moss of Blackhillock, West Auchmaliddy, Dens, Middlemuir, Belnagoak, Gowanwell, Middlethird, Backhill of Ardo, Merdrum, Cairnorrie, North Arnybogs, Auchencrieve, Auchnagatt, Skilmafilly, Mains of Inkhorn, Quilquox, Mains of Schivas, Greenness, Lethen, Mill of Crichie Den, Hornscroft, Flobbets, Milton of Fochel, and Redmoss in the County of Aberdeen".[45]

---

[42] "Superficial measure" refers to area, as opposed to "linear measure" which refers to length.

[43] The square pole is also called simply "the pole". Since the pole is also a linear measure of 5.5 yards, the word "pole" is ambiguous, but context generally makes it clear whether the linear or superficial measure is meant. "Perch" means the same as pole.

[44] "Flatted dwelling-house" is the standard expression. Not "flat" since "flat" traditionally means "floor".

[45] The two previous examples are imaginary, but this is a GRS title in Aberdeenshire, with much verbiage omitted for the sake of brevity. Sir John Rankine (*Land Ownership* (4th ed., 1909, p.101), wrote disapprovingly of descriptions by "a string of uncouthly-spelt names". This was the standard form of description for estates in the old days, and is sometimes still encountered, with no plans to help. To those interested in place names or local history, these deeds are poems, and the uncouthness is a delight.

General descriptions continue to be used, both in deeds used for the registered properties and for properties still in the GRS. But in the former they are of little significance, since the core of the description is the title number. As for the GRS, one usually sees a particular description in addition to the general one.

Particular descriptions

12-17   A particular description (also called a bounding description) identifies the property by its boundaries, normally with measurements. When property is[46] first conveyed as a separate unit (a split-off or break-off) it is usual[47] to have a particular description. This is also occasionally done even where the disposition is not a split-off, but where the existing description is inadequate. There is, however, one type of case where a property being conveyed for the first time as a separate unit does not need a bounding description. Suppose that a part of a field is split off. That deed needs a particular description. But when the remainder comes to be conveyed later on, the description of the original subjects can be repeated, "under exception of" the subjects already split off, defined by a reference to the earlier break-off deed.

A particular description can be done (a) purely verbally, or (b) purely by a plan, or (c) by both.[48] Traditionally it was done purely verbally. Sometimes a plan was attached, but there was originally no means of copying plans into the GRS, and so such plans had limited importance, and what mattered was the verbal description. Eventually, in 1924, it became competent to lodge in the GRS a duplicate copy of the deed plan,[49] and when the Keeper adopted the practice of photocopying deeds not long after, plans began to be recorded without the need for a duplicate. As a result purely verbal bounding descriptions, which are on the whole less informative than a good plan, should have been abandoned, but in practice they tended to be used in addition to the plan. It was only in the 1990s that particular descriptions without verbal bounding descriptions began to become common. A particular description using both a verbal description and a plan is given below.

Not all plans in GRS deeds were good. Indeed, the same is true today, for deeds for the Land Register, but today poor plans will usually get nowhere, because the Keeper will reject them and ask for a better one. But in the GRS the role of the Keeper was an essentially passive one, and many poor plans entered the register. Some had no north sign.[50]

---

[46] The present tense is used, but break-off conveyances would today be recorded in the GRS only in very special cases, such as where a testator, holding a GRS title, leaves part of a farm to one child and another to another.

[47] But far from invariable. Descriptions of residential property were often mere postal addresses, plus words of style that meant little.

[48] It must be emphasised that this concerns the GRS. For the Land Register deeds a verbal particular description in a break-off deed is not sufficient, except for tenement units. There must be a plan.

[49] Conveyancing (Scotland) Act 1924, s.48.

[50] For an example of the potential consequences see William Jardine Dobie, *Plain Tales from the Courts* (1957), pp.12–14.

Others, more creatively, had a north sign pointing south, or, even east or west. Some had neither scale nor linear measurements. Some were "floating rectangles",[51] which showed only that Fergus McFeu owned 1.23 hectares of a certain shape somewhere, the only definite information being that it was in Argyll. A common fault was to identify boundaries or areas by colours so that the plan became meaningless in a monochrome copy. The reason that this was a fault was that the GRS is a monochrome register.[52]

Verbal particular description

In a verbal particular description the conveyancer mentally stands in the middle of the plot, and turns round clockwise, describing the boundaries and their lengths as seen from the central point. It is usual to start from the northern boundary. 12–18

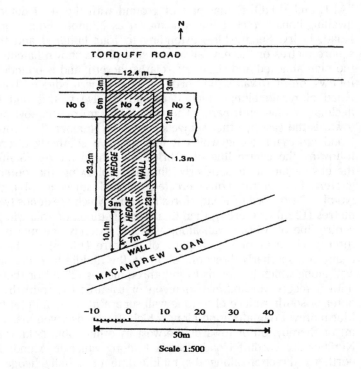

Measurements are followed by the words "or thereby" since absolute accuracy is not normally attainable. It is usual to give the measurement in both figures and words. Decimals are often worded thus: "along which boundary it extends seven metres and eighty-five decimal or one-hundredth parts of a metre (7.85 m) or thereby". Or "seven metres and eight decimal or one tenth parts of a metre (7.8 m) or thereby". This is

---

[51] To use the common term. The shape might of course be anything at all.
[52] Except where the procedure under s.38 of the Conveyancing (Scotland) Act 1924 was used, but such cases were rare.

cumbersome and confusing, but is standard practice. It is usual, though not invariable practice, to have a statement of area: *e.g.,* "extending to one hectare and two hundred and twenty-five decimal or one thousandth parts of a hectare (1.225 ha) or thereby".

Where the title boundary follows a physical one, such as a road or a wall, the description ideally states whether the title boundary is the nearside or farside or middle line (*medium filum*). If the deed is silent on the point, the expression "bounded by" is generally construed as meaning the nearside, so that, for example, "bounded by a stone wall" excludes the wall from the property.[53] But there are exceptions, and the expression "bounded by a road" means, where the road is public, that the boundary is the *medium filum*.[54]

The following is a typical example of the traditional sort of verbal bounding description:

"ALL and WHOLE that plot of ground with the semi detached dwelling-house erected thereon known as Number Four Torduff Road, Dalry, Selkirkshire, extending to four hundred and thirty square metres or thereby, all as the said plot is shown hatched on the plan annexed and signed as relative hereto, and is bounded as follows: on or towards the north by the southern edge of Torduff Road aforesaid along which it extends twelve metres and four decimal or one-tenth parts of a metre (12.4 m) or thereby; on or towards the east by other subjects known as Number Two Torduff Road aforesaid, along which it extends in a southerly direction following the centre line of a brick wall three metres (3 m) or thereby, again in a southerly direction following the outer or western face of the house erected on said adjacent subjects at Number Two Torduff Road aforesaid along which it extends twelve metres (12 m) or thereby, then in a westerly direction following the centre line of a brick wall along which it extends one metre and three decimal or one-tenth parts of a metre (1.3 m) or thereby, again in a southerly direction following the middle line of a stone wall along which it extends twenty-three metres (23 m) or thereby, until it meets Macandrew Loan; on or towards the south by the outer or southern face of a stone wall separating the said plot from Macandrew Loan aforesaid along which it extends seven metres (7 m) or thereby; on or towards the west by other subjects known as Number Six Torduff Road aforesaid, along which it extends in a northerly direction along the middle line of a holly hedge ten metres and one decimal or one-tenth part of a metre (10.1 m) or thereby, then in a westerly direction following the middle line of said hedge along which it extends three metres (3 m) or thereby, then in a northerly direction following the middle line of said hedge along which it extends twenty-three metres and two decimal

---

[53] See Halliday, para.33–11; *Butt v Galloway Motor Co. Ltd,* 1996 S.C. 261.
[54] *Magistrates of Ayr v Dobbie* (1898) 25 R. 1184; *Baillie v Mackay,* 1994 G.W.D. 25–1516 (reported in part, 1996 S.L.T. 507). Compare *Harris v Wishart,* 1996 S.L.T. 12. See also Gordon, paras 4–35 and 4–36.

or one-tenth parts of a metre (23.2 m) or thereby, then in a northerly direction following the middle line of a mutual gable wall between the house erected on the plot hereby disponed and the house erected on the said adjacent subjects at Number Six Torduff Road aforesaid along which it extends six metres (6 m) or thereby, then in a northerly direction following the middle line of a wooden fence along which it extends three metres (3 m) or thereby until it reaches Torduff Road aforesaid."

The deed would then normally continue with a part-and-portion clause.

Demonstrative plans and taxative plans

If a deed has both a detailed verbal description and a plan these are to be read together. But occasionally there are irreconcilable discrepancies between them. In that case, which prevails? That depends on whether the plan is—to use the strange but time-honoured terminology—"taxative" or "demonstrative". If the deed declares the plan to be "taxative", that means that in the event of such irreconcilable inconsistency, the plan is to be deemed correct, while if the plan is stated to be "demonstrative" that means that the verbal description is to prevail.[55] The difference between a demonstrative plan and a taxative one only arises where the difference is an irreconcilable one. If it is reconcilable then there is no difference: in every case the effort has to be made to read the verbal description and the plan as two views of a single truth. 12–19

Good practice was traditionally to state that a plan was demonstrative where it was only a sketch, but if the plan was a good-quality one it was better to declare it taxative. Most conveyancers, however, routinely declared a plan to be "demonstrative not taxative" as words of style. Occasionally, a deed is silent as to the point. In that case the resolution of the discrepancy can be difficult.[56] If a property is described solely by plan, without a detailed verbal description, a discrepancy cannot arise and no purpose is served by declaring the plan either taxative or demonstrative. Obvious though that fact is, such declarations were common. The taxative/demonstrative distinction remains important for interpreting existing descriptions in GRS deeds, but modern deeds do not normally have detailed verbal bounding descriptions.

Descriptions by reference, and part-and-portion clauses

Only break-off conveyances are likely to contain a particular description. Subsequent deeds normally just refer to some earlier deed in the GRS, the descriptive deed, where that description can be found. This saves unnecessary repetition. There is a special statutory procedure set 12–20

---

[55] For an example see *Royal and Sun Alliance Insurance v Wyman-Gordon Ltd*, 2001 S.L.T. 1305.
[56] For the reported decisions on such cases, see Halliday, para.33–13 and Gordon, para.4–08.

out in the 1874 Act[57] and the 1924 Act.[58] The earlier descriptive deed will almost always have itself been a break-off disposition, or a feu disposition, feu charter or feu contract, that is to say, a deed conveying the property as a unit for the first time. However, occasionally one finds that on account of inadequacies in the description in the existing descriptive writ, a later standard disposition—that is, a disposition that is not a break-off disposition—contains a new particular description.

In a break-off disposition there is a part-and-portion clause identifying the larger property from which the property being conveyed is being broken off. The principle is precisely the same as for dispositions for the Land Register. The larger property will normally be identified by means of a description by reference.

Standard securities

12-21   In a standard security the secured property must, of course, be identified. It would be natural to suppose that the applicable rules would be the same as for dispositions, and indeed that is now the case.[59] But for GRS properties (including first registrations) the position was, until recently, not the case.[60] The 2000 Act has now rationalised the law, and the special rules for descriptions in standard securities have been done away with.[61] The change is retrospective.[62] If there is a split-off disposition, and a standard security is being simultaneously granted by the disponee, the plan must be prepared in duplicate, one copy being attached to the standard security.[63]

Parts and pertinents: an excursus

12-22   The description is concerned with the land conveyed. But the grantee receives more than the bare land. The generic term for the extras which also pass to the grantee is "parts and pertinents". In so far as there is any sustainable distinction between "parts" and "pertinents" it is that "parts" are those rights which are exercisable over the land itself, while "pertinents" are those rights exercised in association with the land but beyond its boundaries.[64] Since the parts and pertinents pass automatically, there is no need for them to be mentioned. Despite this, it is usual to add "together with the parts and pertinents" in GRS deeds. This is not done in deeds relating to property in the Land Register, but

---

[57] s.61.

[58] s.8 and Sch.D. Since at common law it is competent to incorporate into a deed all or part of any other deed, provided that the deed so incorporated is adequately identified, it is not clear why the special statutory provisions were thought necessary.

[59] 1979 Act, s.15(1), which excludes 1970 Act, Sch.2, note 1.

[60] For details see the 2nd edition of this book (1999), para.12–23.

[61] Abolition of Feudal Tenure etc. (Scotland) Act 2000, Sch.12, para.30(23).

[62] 2000 Act, s.77(3).

[63] ROTPB, paras 6.70 and 8.47.

[64] Reid, *Property*, paras 199–206.

that is not because such properties do not have parts and pertinents. The words are omitted because they are implied by statute.[65]

Land is owned *a coelo usque ad centrum* (from the sky to the centre, *i.e.* of the earth). What is built on or lies underneath the land is a "part" of the land. So houses and trees and minerals are parts. But this is subject to the exception of legal separate tenements,[66] *i.e.* property reserved from the land by legal implication. Of these, two (gold and silver, and oil and gas) are the property of the Crown. A third, coal, was at one stage nationalised but has since been denationalised.[67] The remaining legal separate tenements are the right to fish for salmon and the right to gather mussels and oysters.[68] Minerals are conventional separate tenements. As such, they are not reserved by legal implication but are capable of being reserved and hence owned separately from the land. In practice, minerals were usually reserved by the superior when land was feued. Such rights are unaffected by the abolition of feudal tenure since the reserved minerals were held by the superior not as *dominium directum* but as *dominium utile*. If minerals are held by someone other than the owner of the land, then they do not pass as a part of the land. If the mineral rights have not been separated then they pass as part of the land, unless expressly reserved.

Pertinents form a ragbag. Whereas "parts" are parts by necessary implication, this is only true of pertinents in two cases. One is title conditions, such as real burdens and servitudes: if Blackmains has a servitude right over Whitemains, then that right is inseparable from Blackmains, and passes *ipso facto* in any conveyance thereof. The other is a speciality of the law of the tenement: in a flatted building each individual flat has, as a pertinent, a right of common property in respect of the common passage and stair. These two cases apart, a pertinent is usually another, and smaller, piece of land which is subordinate in some way to the principal land. A garage or cellar are examples. In practice, land A only becomes a pertinent of land B by express grant or by positive prescription.[69]

In an ordinary disposition the granters dispone all that they own. Nothing is retained. Accordingly, new pertinents cannot be created, for there is no retained land in respect of which a valid grant can be made. So an ordinary disposition is simply a disposition with the existing parts and pertinents. Since parts and pertinents, by definition, pass with the land, no clause is actually necessary. "A grant of the lands of A . . . is as extensive as a grant of A with parts and pertinents."[70] Nonetheless, as already mentioned, it has been the traditional practice to include a clause as a matter of style. At one time the clause was long. Craig offers the following:

---

[65] 1979 Act, s.3(1)(a). But they could equally well be omitted in GRS deeds too.

[66] *Tenementa separata*. See Reid, *Property*, paras 207–213.

[67] Coal Industry Act 1994. Nowadays coal is obtained by quarrying ("open-cast") and so the operator needs to obtain surface rights. See generally Robert Rennie, *Minerals and the Law in Scotland* (2001).

[68] Another separate tenement, teind, is abolished by s.56 of the 2000 Act.

[69] See *Cooper's Trs v Stark's Trs* (1898) 25 R. 1160.

[70] *Gordon v Grant* (1850) 13 D. 1 at 7. For the Land Register the rule is statutory: 1979 Act, s.3(1)(a).

"along with the houses, buildings, woods, plains, muirs, marshes,
ways, paths, rivers, streams, lakes, meadows, pastures, and pas-
turages, mills, multures and the sequels thereof, fowlings, buntings,
fishings, peat-mosses, turbaries, rabbits, rabbit-warrens, doves and
dove-cots, gardens, orchards, smithies, malt-kilns and brewhouses,
brooms, woods, forests, and coppice, timber, quarries of stone and
lime, courts and their suits, herezalds, bloodwites, and merchets of
women, together also with grazings, free ish and entry, and all
other liberties, conveniencies, profits, easements, and pertinents
whatsoever, named as well as unnamed, under the ground as well
as above the same, pertaining, or which may in any manner
whatsoever lawfully pertain in the future, to the fore said lands,
including the castle, mills, parts, pendicles, and pertinents thereof,
freely, fully, quietly, wholly, honourably, happily and in peace,
without any impediment, revocation, contradiction, or obstacle
whatsoever."[71]

Modern practice is, alas, more restrained. A typical GRS clause is:
"Together with (One) the fittings and fixtures (Two) the parts, privileges
and pertinents, and (Three) my whole right, title and interest, present
and future, in and to the subjects hereby disponed". In dispositions of
property in the Land Register even this tends to be omitted.

The reference to "fittings" is odd. In *Jamieson v Welsh*[72] Lord Kinnear
justly commented that "a sound conveyancer in framing a disposition . . .
will not think it necessary to insert a futile conveyance of the moveables
which would carry nothing".

In GRS deeds, the reference to "whole right, title and interest" is to
cover accretion. If the granter does not own the property at the time of
the grant but comes to own it later, ownership will accresce automatically to the grantee. But in fact the same effect is achieved by the
clause of absolute warrandice.[73]

Legal separate tenements (such as salmon fishings) will not be
included unless listed in the title sheet or, in GRS titles, expressly
mentioned in the deed, this usually being done in the pertinents clause.[74]

The parts and pertinents clause is likely to be different, and more
extensive, in a break-off conveyance. Here, it is often necessary to confer
on the grantee rights over land being retained by the granter, and these
rights appear either directly in the pertinents clause, or sometimes in a
separate deed of conditions which is then incorporated by reference into
the pertinents clause. Typically the rights are servitudes (such as a right
of way or a right to lead pipes and cables)[75] and rights of common
property.

---

[71] *Jus Feudale*, III, iii, 30 (Clyde's translation).
[72] (1900) 3 F. 176 at 182.
[73] Stair, III, iii, 2; Bankton, III, ii,16 and 18; Erskine, II, vii, 3. For accretion see Reid,
Property, para.677.
[74] *McKendrick v Wilson*, 1970 S.L.T. (Sh. Ct.) 39.
[75] See further Ch.13 for real burdens and servitudes.

MISSIVES

Missives

For missives the only requirement is that the property be described in such a way that it can be identified. In practice the description is often simply a postal address, usually with the addition of some such words as "as shown to our clients", and sometimes with the sales particulars included as part of the missives. If the description is too vague the missives will be void. Descriptions in missives are discussed further in Chapter 4.[76]

12-23

FINAL OBSERVATIONS

Dispositions: a summary of practice for both GRS and Land Register transactions

A deed relating to property in the Land Register only needs to state the title number,[77] while for GRS dispositions (other than first registrations) a general description is sufficient.[78] But conveyancers prefer to describe property twice. So most dispositions contain both a general and also a particular description. Except with break-off deeds, the particular description will be by reference to the title number, or, if the property is not yet in the Land Register, to the break-off disposition. A break-off deed will contain a particular description, which will normally be plan-based, and a part-and-portion clause, identifying the larger property from which the present property is being broken off. The part-and-portion clause must refer to the title number, or, if the property is not yet in the Land Register, to the earlier break-off conveyance. A parts and pertinents clause may be added to taste. Current practice may be summarised in the following table:

12-24

---

[76] para.4–03.
[77] 1979 Act, s.15(1).
[78] The sufficiency of such descriptions was discussed at para.12–16.

Table

Deed	Description
Standard disposition (registered land)	(i) general description + (ii) particular description by title number[79]
Standard disposition (first registrations and GRS transactions)	(i) general description + (ii) particular description by reference back to the GRS descriptive deed[80]
Break-off disposition (registered land)	(i) general description + (ii) particular description + (iii) part-and-portion clause by title number[81]
Break-off disposition (first registrations and GRS transactions)	(i) general description + (ii) particular description + (iii) part-and-portion clause by reference back to the GRS descriptive deed[82]

Different meanings of "boundary"

12–25   "Boundary" has four possible meanings in the context of land registration, and these different meanings are so easy to confuse that they are in fact confused by the legislation itself. The four meanings of "boundary" are (i) the title boundary, *i.e.* the limit of what is owned, (ii) the occupational boundary, *i.e.* the limit of what is actually occupied, (iii) a physical feature such as a wall or hedge of the sort that is typically, but not necessarily, a boundary feature and (iv) the physical boundary feature as shown on the Ordnance Map.

Not all four will exist in all cases: sometimes only the first two exist, there being no physical boundary feature at all. But all four may exist, and usually do exist. All four may coincide, but any two may differ and in theory all four could differ. Thus a title boundary might stop a metre short of a wall, but occupation might extend five metres to the other side

---

[79] For instance: "ALL and WHOLE the subjects known as Two Main Street, Renfrew and registered under Title Number . . .".

[80] For instance: "ALL and WHOLE the subjects known as Two Main Street, Inverness in the County of Inverness being the subjects described in the Disposition by . . . in favour of . . . dated . . . and recorded in the Division of the General Register of Sasines for the County of Inverness on . . . together with (1) the parts and pertinents (2) the fixtures and fittings and (3) my whole right, title and interest, present and future".

[81] For instance: "ALL and WHOLE the semi-detached house number 53 William Road, Dunkeld, being the subjects delineated in red on the plan annexed and signed as relative hereto, being part and portion of ALL and WHOLE the subjects registered in the Land Register under title number PER 88888."

[82] An example would be the description of the property at 4 Torduff Road, given in para.12–18, followed by something like: "which said subjects hereby disponed are part and portion of ALL and WHOLE the subjects described in the Disposition by . . . in favour of . . . dated . . . and recorded in the Division of the General Register of Sasines applicable to the County of Selkirk on . . .".

of the wall, while the Ordnance Map might show the wall but in the wrong position, either because of inaccurate cartography or because the wall has been rebuilt on a different line since the area was last surveyed.

As an example of how easy it is to be confused, consider form 1, part B, question 2.[83] This has an odd logical structure. The first bit asks whether a P16 report confirms that the title boundaries coincide with the boundaries as shown on the Ordnance Map. The answer may be positive. If it is negative it will be either because such a report has been issued but it does not so confirm, or it has not been issued. If the answer to the first bit is negative, the applicant is asked to state whether the title boundaries coincide with the "occupational extent". Thus if the title boundaries coincide with the boundaries as shown on the Ordnance Map, and yet do not coincide with the occupational boundaries, this fact will not be brought to light by form 1.

Problems with tenements

Tenements have already been mentioned, but problems are so 12–26 common that something more needs to be said. In descriptions of tenement flats, whether in deeds or missives, there is plenty of scope for muddle. Some people call the lowest storey the ground storey while others call it the first storey. In some tenements the lowest storey is a basement below street level. In that case the storey two floors up from the basement level might be called the first, or the second, or the third storey. In GRS titles where the units have been sold off over many years inconsistent numbering systems are sometimes encountered. Even if the titles are consistent a flat may be marketed with a different storey number and this is likely to be followed in the missives. Sometimes, too, there is a muddle about compass directions. If there are two units on the second floor and the only distinction between them is that one is east and the other west, a muddle may cause serious problems. In a 2004 case a bank called up a standard security over a flat in Firpark Terrace, Dennistoun. It took possession of the wrong flat. On discovering the mistake it took possession of a second flat in the tenement. It advertised this second flat for sale and sold it. It was only when the owner of the second flat turned up (it had been vacant for some weeks) that it was discovered that this too was not the right flat, which was in fact yet another flat in the same tenement.[84] Because of inadequate descriptions tenements also frequently give rise to other problems, such as title to cellars and to the backgreen. Obscurities in tenemental titles often are transferred from the GRS to the Land Register.

---

[83] Land Registration (Scotland) Rules 1980.
[84] *The Times* (Scottish edition), March 16, 2004, p.9 and March 17, 2004, p.7.

CHAPTER 13

TITLE CONDITIONS

INTRODUCTION

Real burdens and servitudes compared

13-01   Real burdens, servitudes, and conditions in long leases are the main examples of title conditions,[1] but, leases being beyond the scope of the present work, this chapter concerns only real burdens and servitudes. They have much in common. With one minor exception,[2] each is a right held by the owner of one parcel of land (known as the "benefited property" or "dominant tenement") in respect of another, and neighbouring, parcel of land (known as the "burdened property" or "servient tenement"). In each case the right "runs with the land", that is to say, is enforceable by the owner for the time being of the benefited property against the owner for the time being of the burdened property.[3] And each is used by conveyancers in much the same types of situation, most typically when land is being divided and split off, or for developments such as housing estates. Thus in practice real burdens and servitudes often jostle together in the same deed, usually break-off dispositions or deeds of conditions.

But there are important differences. Like so much of property law, the law of servitudes derives ultimately from the law of Rome. Real burdens, by contrast, are home-grown, dating only from the late eighteenth century. Something like one half of all real burdens originated in feudal writs and so were enforceable, at first, by feudal superiors.[4] Many of these were lost following the abolition of the feudal system although, for the time being at least, they remain as a ghostly presence on the Land Register.[5] But many also survived by being attached of new to a benefited property. The rules for such attachment were complex but transitional and are referred to in this chapter only where necessary to

---

[1] Title Conditions (Scotland) Act 2003, s.122(1).

[2] Personal real burdens, discussed in para.13–19.

[3] This over-simplifies. As will be seen (para.13–13) title conditions are sometimes enforceable by, and against, occupiers even if they do not own.

[4] But, quite often, by neighbours ("co-feuars") as well. The enforcement rights of neighbours are unaffected by feudal abolition.

[5] Abolition of Feudal Tenure etc. (Scotland) Act 2000, ss.17(1) and 46.

understand the present law.[6] As well as removing the enforcement rights of superiors, feudal abolition was also the occasion for a more general reorganisation of the law. The Title Conditions (Scotland) Act 2003, which came into force on the first post-feudal day,[7] re-states the law of real burdens in statutory form but with important changes.[8] One of those is to re-draw the boundary between real burdens and servitudes. Today only positive servitudes are recognised, that is to say, rights to make limited use of another's land, for example for access or the laying of a pipe. The former class of negative servitudes is now subsumed within real burdens.[9] Real burdens are of two types. An "affirmative burden" is an obligation to do something, such as to maintain a wall or pay for the cost of common services. A "negative burden" is an obligation *not* to do something, such as not to erect a building or not to use the burdened property for commercial purposes.[10] In creating title conditions, it is necessary to be clear what kind of condition or conditions is intended. As will be seen, the rules of creation are by no means the same.

When are title conditions needed?

There are two main occasions when title conditions are likely to be   13–02
needed. One is when land is divided. The other is when land is developed, typically by a volume builder for housing. If these two situations are kept in mind, both the law and the practice are easier to understand.

The subdivision case

Suppose that Donald owns a house surrounded by a hectare of land.   13–03
He sells half the land to Edmund, who wishes to build a house there. Donald might require the use of a septic tank lying in the area sold. This can be achieved by the servitude of "sinks".[11] Again, Donald may wish to

---

[6] 2000 Act, Part 4; 2003 Act, Part 4. For a full account, see K. G. C. Reid, *The Abolition of Feudal Tenure in Scotland* (2003).

[7] Martinmas 2004, the "appointed day" under the Act. The term and quarter days were formerly of great importance. The term days are Whitsunday and Martinmas, and the quarter days are Candlemas and Lammas. True, *i.e.* ecclesiastical, Whitsunday is variable. The other true dates are February 2 (Candlemas), August 1 (Lammas) and November 11 (Martinmas). But for legal purposes the term and quarter days are now fixed as the 28th days of February, May, August and November: Term and Quarter Days (Scotland) Act 1990. So feudal abolition was on November 28, 2004.

[8] This was based on the Scottish Law Commission's *Report on Real Burdens* (Scot. Law Com. No.181, 2000; available on *http://www.scotlawcom.gov.uk*), which remains an indispensable guide to the legislation.

[9] 2003 Act, ss.79 and 80. Former negative servitudes were automatically converted into (negative) real burdens.

[10] 2003 Act, s.2. By s.2(3), however, a right to enter or otherwise make use of property, which must normally be a servitude, can be created as a real burden if it is for a purpose ancillary to a positive or negative burden, *e.g.*, a right to enter in order to carry out repairs which the burdened owner has failed to make.

[11] The curiously named servitude right to discharge "foul water"—to use the polite term—into another person's land.

continue to use a path through the land being sold, which will require a servitude of way. Donald may wish to impose an affirmative burden, for instance an obligation to share equally in the maintenance of a common boundary wall. He may also wish to impose negative burdens, to protect the amenity of his retained property. So for instance he may impose an obligation not to build more than one house, and not to use the sold property for commercial purposes. In all of these cases the burdened property is the land sold to Edmund and the benefited property the land retained by Donald. Of course, if Donald wishes to impose such servitudes and burdens, he should so specify in the missives.[12] The general principle of law is that if missives do not provide for the imposition of title conditions, a purchaser can refuse to accept such imposition.[13] Equally, Edmund may wish to have burdens and servitudes imposed on the land retained by Donald, and for similar reasons.

The development case

13-04   A standard example of a development is a block of flats. When a block of flats is first built, it will be in unitary ownership—that of the developer. It may remain in unitary ownership, with the owner renting out the flats rather than selling them. But if the flats are sold off individually, either immediately after construction or at some later stage, it is normal to insert real burdens, regulating both maintenance and use. Another standard case is where a volume builder develops a housing estate. Affirmative burdens will be imposed for such things as mainten- ance of mutual boundary walls, and there will also be negative burdens, restricting use. One might ask why, for, once the houses are sold, the builder no longer has any commercial interest. The reason is that burdens are believed, rightly or wrongly, to increase the attractiveness of the estate to potential purchasers. Of course, as far as a purchaser's own house is concerned, he or she would prefer it to be burden-free. But a purchaser wants burdens on the *other* houses, to keep up the amenity of the area. The price for burdens on the other houses is to accept burdens on one's own.

Once all the flats or houses have been sold the burdens can no longer be enforced by the developer, and the normal arrangement is for the burdens to be mutually enforceable within the development. Thus each flat, or house, is at the same time both a burdened property and also a benefited property. It is a burdened property because, like every other flat or house, it is subject to the burdens. But it is a benefited property because the owner can enforce the burdens against any other property. In effect, the burdens form a set of local laws for the administration of

---

[12] There has been some litigation about the degree of precision needed in an obligation to create a servitude. See *Callander v Midlothian District Council*, 1996 S.C.L.R. 955; *Brennan v Robertson's Exrs*, 1997 S.C. 36; *Inverness Seafield Development Co. Ltd v D C S Mackintosh*, 2001 S.L.T. 118.

[13] *Corbett v Robertson* (1872) 10 M. 329. *cf. Morris v Ritchie*, 1991 G.W.D. 12–712, 1992 G.W.D. 33–1950.

the development. Burdens which are mutually enforceable in this way are referred to in the 2003 Act as "community burdens"[14] and are subject to a number of special rules, especially in relation to variation and discharge.[15] This reciprocal enforceability of community burdens may be contrasted with the typical product of subdivision, which is for burdens to affect one property (Edmund's in the example given above) but not the other (Donald's).[16] Edmund's property is a burdened property but not a benefited property. Donald's property is a benefited property but not a burdened property.

Real burdens and planning law

The question is sometimes asked, why negative burdens continue to be 13–05 used when modern planning law protects amenity. For example, if a neighbour in Edinburgh's Heriot Row wishes to turn the house into a nuclear reprocessing factory, there is no need to worry, because planning consent will be refused.

There are three answers to this question. The first is that negative burdens can cover points which could not be covered by planning law. The second answer is that the planning authorities often fail to enforce planning law, especially in respect of minor infringements. The third reason is that the planning authority can always grant planning consent, leaving the outraged neighbour fuming but powerless.[17] These two latter points arise from the fact that planning law is part of public law. It is enforced or waived by a public authority. Neighbours have a right to voice their objections, but the planning authority makes up its own mind. The value of real burdens is that they are part of private law, and can be enforced by the owner of the benefited property. This is true even if planning consent has been given. Thus, suppose that planning consent is given to convert a dwelling-house into a public house, but there is a real burden forbidding any "trade, business or profession", and the benefited property is the house next door. The owner of that house can interdict use as a pub, notwithstanding the grant of planning consent.[18]

Importance of use in practice

With new developments, title conditions are imposed almost as matter 13–06 of course. But with subdivisions too it should be instinctive for the conveyancer to consider the possible need for servitudes and real burdens. This applies to both parties to the deal, for it is not only the seller but also often the buyer who may need the benefit of such

---

[14] 2003 Act, s.25(1).

[15] 2003 Act, Part 2. For variation and discharge of community burdens, see para.13–22. The other rules confer a right on the owners of a majority of units to appoint a manager, and to carry out repairs such repairs as are sanctioned by real burdens. These are default rules and subject to different provision by community burden.

[16] In contrast with "community burdens" these are sometimes described as "neighbour burdens" although the term does not appear in the 2003 Act.

[17] K. Gray and S. F. Gray, (1999) 3 *Edinburgh Law Review* 229.

[18] The fact that planning permission has been granted may, however, help the burdened owner in an application to the Lands Tribunal for variation. For the Tribunal's powers, see para.13–24.

conditions. The clients may not have thought about this question clearly, and so an active approach is necessary. A site visit is desirable. This will, for example, reveal if there is a path to the public road from the retained subjects over the subjects to be sold. Or it will reveal problems about pipes and cables. Or it will indicate the existence of a boundary wall which will need to be kept up.[19] In addition to affirmative burdens, the clients must be asked about negative burdens which may be needed for amenity.

Occasionally, split-offs happen where the lawyers involved have failed to do these things. Such failure can cause problems to the clients in future years and may even give rise to a negligence action against the solicitors involved.[20] Sometimes, however, the position can be saved by arguing that a servitude exists by implication, or, after 20 years,[21] by prescription. However, unlike servitudes real burdens cannot arise either by implication or by prescription.

Permissible content

13-07   As already mentioned, a real burden must usually comprise an obligation to do something or an obligation not to do something, while a servitude confers a right of limited use. Since it runs with the land, a title condition must affect the land itself and not merely the person who happens to be its owner for the moment. And both properties must be affected: a title condition burdens one parcel of land for the benefit of another parcel of land. It must, in other words, be "praedial" at both ends. Thus an obligation to repay a loan of £1000 could not be a real burden. Nor could a right to take exercise be a servitude. In practice the praedial rule is sometimes difficult to apply, particularly in relation to the benefited property. For if a condition confers obvious benefit on a person it may be a matter of debate as to whether it confers benefit on a property as well. In one case, for example, it was doubted whether a prohibition on playing tennis on a Sunday conferred more than personal benefit on the original disponer, whose religious views, it was assumed, had led to the imposition of the burden.[22] But it is possible to argue than even here a praedial benefit arises,[23] for tennis can be a noisy game and hence disruptive to those living in an, otherwise quiet, residential area. To ban it on Sundays is to preserve tranquility on a day when most people are at home.

Other restrictions apply. A title condition must not be contrary to public policy.[24] It must not impose a periodical payment in respect of the use of land.[25] It must not be "repugnant with ownership", that is, it must

---

[19] If there is no boundary wall there may be a need to impose a burden requiring one to be built and maintained.

[20] *e.g. Moffat v Milne,* 1993 G.W.D. 8-572.

[21] The period for the prescriptive constitution of a servitude is 20, not 10, years: 1973 Act, s.3.

[22] *Marsden v Craighelen Lawn Tennis and Squash Club,* 1999 G.W.D. 37-1820.

[23] As the Scottish Law Commission has done: see *Report on Real Burdens* (Scot. Law Com. No.181, 2000) para.2.13.

[24] 2003 Act, s.3(6).

[25] 1974 Act, s.2.

not impose an obligation so severe as to remove the normal rights of an owner.[26] Thus a real burden cannot forbid the performance of ordinary juridical acts such as a disposition or the grant of a lease.[27] Burdens prohibiting division of the title are not uncommon but are invalid. (By contrast prohibitions of functional division, such as the subdivision of a house into two units, can be valid.) Under the 2003 Act redemption rights are no longer valid as real burdens, but pre-emption rights remain competent.[28] A real burden must not create a monopoly, for instance in relation to management of a development,[29] although the 2003 Act allows developers to reserve a power to manage, or to appoint a manager, for as long as they continue to own property in the development, but restricted to a maximum period which is normally five years.[30]

Unlike in other countries, servitudes in Scotland have traditionally been limited to a fixed list of a dozen or so "known" types, although the precise content of the list has been a matter of dispute.[31] It is only recently, for example, that parking has been recognised as a possible servitude.[32] The 2003 Act abolished the fixed list in the case of servitudes created by writing and registration,[33] but it remains in place for servitudes created by prescription or other means. For the first of these a more adventurous use of servitudes may now be anticipated.

Existing title conditions: burdened property

If the burdened property is in the Land Register, all the real burdens 13–08 will be set forth in full in the burdens section of the title sheet (and land certificate). This includes burdens which were created, prior to first registration, by a deed recorded in the GRS. Understandably, the Keeper's practice here is to copy the original wording, even though this may be archaic or unclear or verbose.[34] Servitudes can be created without registration and so are overriding interests for the purposes of registration of title. They may or may not appear on the title sheet; and even if some are mentioned, there may be others which are not mentioned.

---

[26] 2003 Act, ss.3(6), 76(2).

[27] *Moir's Trs v McEwan* (1880) 7 R. 1141 at 1145. As Lord Young said, "you cannot make a man proprietor and yet prohibit him from exercising the rights of proprietorship". See also *Calder v Police Commissioners of North Berwick* (1899) 1 F. 491 at 493. However, restrictions on use can go very far. A prohibition of any building has been recognised since Roman times as a valid servitude (now, under the 2003 Act, a real burden) and in *Lees v North East Fife District Council*, 1987 S.L.T. 769 a real burden forbidding all use except that of a swimming pool was upheld.

[28] 2003 Act, s.3(5). For pre-emptions, see para.13–31.

[29] 2003 Act, s.3(7).

[30] This is done by a special type of real burden known as a "manager burden". See the 2003 Act, s.63. The period is three years in the case of sheltered housing and thirty years in the case of council houses being sold under the right-to-buy legislation.

[31] D. J. Cusine and R. R. M. Paisley, *Servitudes and Rights of Way* (1998), Ch.3.

[32] And then perhaps only if ancillary to a right of way: see *Moncrieff v Jamieson*, 2004 S.C.L.R. 135, discussed in Reid and Gretton, *Conveyancing 2003*, pp.68–70; *Nationwide Building Society v Walter D. Allan Ltd*, August 4, 2004, OH.

[33] 2003 Act, s.76.

[34] 1979 Act, s.6(2). This can have a curious psychological impact. A burden which formerly existed in some 19th-century deed, written by hand, on paper dirtied and frayed by a century and a half of use, and legible only with great effort, tends to seem unimportant. The same burden, neatly word-processed and appearing on a fresh land certificate, looks very different and rather threatening.

There is no equivalent display of title conditions for GRS property, and the practice is to list the burdens writs in each new conveyance of the burdened property[35] (including a conveyance inducing first registration). In practice, the listing is done after the description. The relevant clause begins with such words as: "But always with and under, in so far as valid subsisting and applicable, the following real burdens conditions servitudes and others namely . . .". The list then refers to the various deeds which created the burdens or servitudes.[36] It is a mere reference, not a full repetition. Those deeds, or photocopies of them, will commonly be among the titles themselves, or a copy can be obtained from the registers. Dispositions of property in the Land Register are taken to incorporate the whole terms of the title sheet and so do not list the burdens and servitudes.[37] Traditionally, deeds which created real burdens imposed an obligation to make reference to the burdens in all future conveyances, but under the 2003 Act this is of no legal effect.[38]

Existing title conditions: benefited property

13–09   Title conditions are pertinents of the benefited property, and thus pass with that property by implication.[39] So they need not be mentioned in a disposition of the benefited property, although in the case of a GRS title it is helpful if this is done.[40] In a title in the Land Register real burdens may be listed in the property section of the title sheet of the benefited property,[41] if brought to the Keeper's attention, but any list is likely to be incomplete. The position is transformed for the future by the requirement that new real burdens be registered against the benefited property as well as the burdened.[42] Servitudes are only likely to appear on the title sheet if created by registration, typically in a disposition of the benefited property. The Keeper's practice is not now to list servitudes created by implication or prescription unless supported by a court declarator.[43] Even if title conditions are listed, however, their validity is not absolutely assured, for a title condition which is fundamentally bad can be removed from the property section by rectification, leaving the registered proprietor with, at best, a claim for indemnity from the Keeper.[44]

---

[35] Including notices of title (1924 Act, Sch.B) but not standard securities (1924 Act, s.9(1) as applied by s.32 of the 1970 Act).

[36] See further para.11–13.

[37] 1979 Act, s.15(2).

[38] 2003 Act, s.68.

[39] 1979 Act, s.3(1)(a). For pertinents see Ch.12.

[40] "Together with the servitudes and other rights created in . . .".

[41] Land Registration (Scotland) Rules 1980, r.4(c).

[42] 2003 Act, s.4(5).

[43] ROTPB, paras 6.54–6.58.

[44] Rectification is possible because one cannot be a "proprietor in possession" in respect of subordinate real rights such as servitudes and real burdens. That, at least, was the view taken in *Griffiths v Keeper of the Registers of Scotland*, Lands Tribunal, December 20, 2002, unreported; but compare *Mutch v Mavisbank Properties Ltd*, 2002 S.L.T. (Sh. Ct) 91. In at least some cases, payment of indemnity will be prevented by the obscurely-worded s.12(3)(g) of the 1979 Act. See further Reid and Gretton, *Conveyancing 2003*, pp.88–91.

REAL BURDENS[45]

Preparing the deed

In principle only an owner can burden land,[46] real burdens must be 13–10 created in a deed granted by the owner of the property that is to be burdened.[47] However, the holder of an uncompleted title can also burden land.[48] Any probative deed will do, but in practice real burdens are created mainly in dispositions (in the case of subdivisions) and deeds of conditions (in the case of developments).

The deed must nominate and identify both the benefited property and the burdened property (*e.g.* "the benefited property is . . .").[49] For the purposes of registration, a proper conveyancing description is needed, typically by reference to a plan or title number. In the case of a disposition, one of the properties (usually the burdened) will be the property that is being conveyed. The burdens themselves must be set out in full, preferably in numbered paragraphs. In the case of dispositions this is best done in a separate schedule:[50] particularly to be avoided is the traditional practice of cramming burdens into the dispositive clause as part of the notionally single sentence which constitutes a disposition. It is a statutory requirement that the words "real burden" (or some permitted equivalent) be used (*e.g.* "but always with and under the real burdens contained in the schedule annexed and signed as relative hereto").[51] A possible style is given at the end of this chapter.

The drafting of real burdens is difficult and requires close attention, particularly in view of the strict rules of interpretation (discussed below). Since burdens are potentially perpetual, the wording must be intelligible not only to the parties to the deed but to successors 100 years hence. As a general rule the terms of the burden must be found within the "four corners of the deed".[52] In the leading case of *Aberdeen Varieties Limited v James F. Donald (Aberdeen Cinemas) Limited*[53] a real burden was held invalid because it referred to an Act of Parliament and so could

---

[45] A detailed study of the new law is still lacking, and the fullest treatment remains the Scottish Law Commission's *Report on Real Burdens* (Scot. Law Com. No.181, 2000; available on *http://www.scotlawcom.gov.uk/*). A number of summary accounts can be found, for example: K. G. C. Reid, *The Abolition of Feudal Tenure in Scotland* (1993), Ch.7; Reid and Gretton, *Conveyancing 2003*, pp.106–31; D. A. Brand, A. J. M. Steven and S. Wortley, *Professor McDonald's Conveyancing Manual* (7th ed., 2004), Chs 15, 17, and 18. Since much of the common law is re-enacted by the 2003 Act, the older texts also remain of value.

[46] However, in some cases the holder of a long lease can create conditions that bind subsequent holders. See Reid and Gretton, *Conveyancing 2003*, p.60–63.

[47] 2003 Act, s.4(2)(b).

[48] 2003 Act, ss.60(1), 123(1). If the title is in the GRS a clause of deduction of title is required.

[49] 2003 Act, s.4(2)(c).

[50] As indeed recommended 40 years ago by the Halliday Report: see *Conveyancing Legislation and Practice* (1966, Cmnd. 3118), para.77.

[51] 2003 Act, s.4(2)(a). As an alternative it is permissible to use the name of a type of burden (such as community burden or conservation burden) as long as it is a name provided by the Act: see s.4(3).

[52] 2003 Act, s.4(2)(a). *cf.* Lord Guthrie in *Anderson v Dickie*, 1914 S.C. 706 at 717: "The extent of it must be ascertained by a singular successor without travelling beyond the four corners of his titles."

[53] 1939 S.C. 788; 1940 S.C. (HL) 52.

not be understood on its own. This is not an isolated example. Purported burdens can be found which refer to statutes such as the Town and Country Planning (Scotland) Acts,[54] while in older deeds the terms of prior articles of roup are sometimes declared to be real burdens, without, however, setting these terms out in the deed itself. Such provisions may be valid contractually between the original parties but are not valid as real burdens. There is one exception. In tenements or other developments it is common for maintenance costs to be apportioned according to some external measure such as feuduty or rateable value. This is allowed by the 2003 Act provided that, as in the examples given, the necessary information is contained in an enactment, a public register, or a record or roll to which the public readily has access.[55]

Deeds of conditions

13–11　　As the name suggests, deeds of conditions are simply deeds which set out the conditions which are to affect land.[56] Servitudes are quite often included as well as real burdens. In practice, deeds of conditions are used where a disposition would not be appropriate. That might because no disposition is in prospect, as in the case where established neighbours agree that certain matters between them should be regulated by real burdens (or servitudes). But more usually it is because, in a development, each property is to be made subject to the same burdens, and rather than repeat the burdens in every disposition it is easier to set them out in advance in a single deed which applies to the whole development.[57] Thus most deeds of conditions are granted and registered before any individual unit has been sold.

In practice deeds of conditions usually create community burdens, that is, burdens which are mutually enforceable as among the individual units in the community or development. A number of drafting specialities then arise. First, so long as the conditions are declared "community burdens", there is no need to provide separately that they are "real burdens".[58] Secondly, a mere declaration that the conditions are community burdens creates mutual enforceabilility without further provision.[59] Thirdly, provided the "community" is nominated and identified in the deed, there is no need for separate nomination and identification

---

[54] *i.e.* a burden providing that the owner can make no development or change of use which would require planning consent. The effect (if valid) would be that for any such development or change of use the owner would need both planning consent and the consent of the creditor in the burden.

[55] 2003 Act, s.5(1)(b), (2). The provision is retrospective.

[56] Until 1874 real burdens could only be created in conveyances. Section 32 of the 1874 Act introduced the deed of conditions as a statutory facility for setting out burdens in advance of a conveyance of the land. With the repeal of s.32 by the 2003 Act, Sch.15, deeds of conditions have ceased to have a specific statutory basis, but their continued use is anticipated.

[57] An alternative way of providing for a development is to use the development management scheme, introduced by Part 6 of the 2003 Act. See para.27–11. The conditions are then part of the scheme and not real burdens, although many of the same rules apply.

[58] 2003 Act, s.4(2)(a), (3).

[59] 2003 Act, s.27.

of the benefited and burdened properties.[60] This is because, with community burdens, the same properties are both benefited and burdened. Indeed the "community" is usually the whole development. Fourthly, the 2003 Act implies certain default rules for communities in respect of the appointment of a manager and the carrying out of repairs.[61] These rules can be modified or excluded by contrary provision in the deed of conditions. Otherwise they apply in full. Finally, while community burdens may ordinarily be varied or discharged by agreement of the owners of a majority of units, it is competent to raise or lower this threshold in the deed of conditions.[62] Usually the alteration will be in a downwards direction, for example to 40 per cent or 30 per cent of units, in recognition of the difficulty of obtaining large numbers of signatures. Different percentages can be provided for different classes of burden. At the same time it is competent, if desired, to exclude section 35 of the 2003 Act, which gives the alternative of variation and discharge by signature of all neighbours within four metres.[63]

Deeds of conditions often specify what parts of the development are to be owned in common, *e.g.* parking areas. However, a deed of conditions cannot actually convey the common parts. This must be done, separately, by the dispositions. Hence, it is necessary for each break-off conveyance to say not only that the property is subject to the burdens in the deed of conditions, but also that it includes the appropriate share in the common areas specified in the deed of conditions. In other words, the deed of conditions needs to be referred to twice, once for the burdens and once (in the parts and pertinents clause) for the common parts.

Registration

Unlike other types of real right, title conditions affect not one 13–12 property but two. Nonetheless the former law required registration against only one of these properties, the burdened. While, therefore, an owner knew from the Register about the burdens to which the property was subject, he or she might have little or no idea as to whether that same property carried enforcement rights in respect of other burdens against other properties. The position was changed by the 2003 Act. The deed creating a real burden must now be registered against both the benefited and the burdened property.[64] If one of the properties is in the Land Register and the other in the GRS, registration in both registers is needed. In the case of a deed of conditions creating community burdens, however, there is only a single property (the community) and hence only single registration. The burdens are entered in the property section of the title sheet of the benefited property and in the burdens section of the title sheet of the burdened property, although they are set out in full only in the latter. Once burdens have been transcribed on to the Register

---

[60] 2003 Act, s.4(2)(c), (4).
[61] 2003 Act, ss.28–31.
[62] 2003 Act, s.33(1)(a).
[63] 2003 Act, s.35(1)(b).
[64] 2003 Act, s.4(1), (5).

it has been doubted whether it is competent to refer back to the original deed in order to assist interpretation.[65]

Normally real burdens are created on registration,[66] although they do not take effect in a practical sense unless the benefited property is in separate ownership.[67] In developments this does not occur until the first property is disponed. But while developers are keen that the burdens should affect any properties which are sold, they may be less keen that they should affect such property as remains in their hands. For that would be to commit them to a building plan from which they may later need to depart. The solution, permitted by the 2003 Act, is to postpone the date of creation; but if burdens are not to be created on registration, the deed must either specify a later fixed date or must tie creation to the registration of some other deed.[68] With deeds of conditions a common practice is to defer creation, for any individual plot, until registration of a break-off disposition into which the deed of conditions has been duly incorporated.[69] If there is then no break-off conveyance, or if the conveyance does not incorporate the deed of conditions, the burdens never become live in respect of the plot in question.

Enforcement

13-13   A real burden is enforceable by anyone with both title and interest.[70] Title is tied to the benefited property. Its owner has title to enforce, but so too do tenants, proper liferenters, and non-entitled spouses with occupancy rights under the 1981 Act.[71] Some of the difficulties of identifying the benefited property are explored in the next section. Normally a person has interest to enforce only if failure to comply with the burden will, in the particular circumstances, result in material detriment to the value or enjoyment of that person's right in the benefited property.[72] Since a reduction in *value* may be difficult to demonstrate, the enforcer's task will often be to demonstrate material detriment to *enjoyment*. In fact the test is quite exacting, with the result that many people with title to enforce, especially in large housing estates, will lack the necessary interest in respect of the particular breach in question. It will be difficult, for example, to demonstrate interest in relation to a breach taking place several streets away.

---

[65] A rule which does not seem entirely satisfactory. See *Marshall v Duffy*, 2002 G.W.D. 10–318, discussed in Reid and Gretton, *Conveyancing 2002*, pp.86–7.

[66] 2003 Act, s.4(1). By s.61 they cease to be binding as a matter of contract.

[67] But the burdens are in existence nonetheless. The rule for servitudes is different: see 2003 Act, s.75(2).

[68] 2003 Act, s.4(1).

[69] In fact this was the law between 1874, when deeds of conditions were first allowed, and 1979 when, by s.17 of the 1979 Act, such deeds took effect immediately on registration. But the effect of s.17 could be excluded and this was commonly done.

[70] 2003 Act, s.8(1).

[71] 2003 Act, s.8(2). But, by s.8(4), only owners can enforce pre-emptions, redemptions and other options.

[72] 2003 Act, s.8(3). But a person also has interest to enforce obligations to defray some cost (*e.g.* the cost of maintenance) if he or she has some proper basis for seeking payment (such as that he or she incurred the cost).

Negative burdens can be enforced against any person having the use of the burdened property, including an owner, tenant, or even a squatter.[73] Otherwise real burdens could be made difficult to enforce merely by the granting of a lease. By contrast, affirmative burdens (such as obligations of maintenance) are considered too onerous for a merely temporary occupier and may only be enforced against the owner of the burdened property.[74] Sometimes leases are drawn so as to allow the owner to recover in turn from the tenant. If the property is co-owned, each owner has joint and several liability.[75] Similarly, if property is transferred at a time when an affirmative obligation remains outstanding,[76] recovery may be made from either the new owner or from the old. A new owner who is made to pay can recover in turn from the old, unless the missives provide otherwise.[77]

For negative burdens the most common, and most useful, remedy is interdict. But it is necessary to act quickly, for once a breach is completed, no remedy may be available. For by then it is too late for interdict; courts are reluctant to order the demolition of completed structures;[78] damages are available only where loss can be shown, which may be unusual; and irritancy has been abolished.[79] Moreover, even if a remedy can be found, the enforcer is likely to be met with the plea of acquiescence.[80]

Finding the benefited property: in general

The two main occasions on which the benefited property or properties 13–14 must be found are enforcement (for title to enforce is tied to the benefited property)[81] and discharge (for a real burden is discharged by the owner of the benefited property);[82] and in practice, discharge being a great deal more common than enforcement, the search for the benefited property is normally led by the owner of the burdened property, who is seeking to be relieved of the burden. Often the search is an arduous one. In the case of burdens created under the 2003 Act there is no difficulty, because the burdens must be registered against both properties.[83] But for burdens created before November 28, 2004 the position is a great deal more complex, for three reasons. First, there was no requirement under the former law to identify the benefited property at all, although this was sometimes done in practice. Where it was not, benefited properties would be implied in various circumstances. The relevant rules were largely abolished by the 2003 Act and replaced by the new rules,

---

[73] 2003 Act, s.9(2).

[74] 2003 Act, s.9(1).

[75] 2003 Act, s.11(5).

[76] As to when an obligation is outstanding, see 2003 Act, s.10(4).

[77] 2003 Act, s.10. At the time of writing it was possible that this provision would be amended to restrict the liability of the new owner in certain cases.

[78] Reid, *Property*, para.423.

[79] Irritancy was the remedy of bringing the grant to an end, without payment of compensation. It was abolished by the 2000 Act, s.53 and the 2003 Act, s.67.

[80] para.13–25.

[81] para.13–13.

[82] para.13–22.

[83] para.13–10.

discussed in the next paragraph.[84] Difficult as these rules are, they are simpler than those that they replaced.[85] Secondly, perhaps as many as one half of all real burdens were created in, or in association with, grants in feu. Hence they were enforceable by the feudal superior. In some cases superiors' rights were extinguished, with the feudal system, on November 28, 2004. In others they were reallocated to other properties in accordance with rules set out in the 2000 and 2003 Acts. Thirdly, there is frequently more than one benefited property. The search cannot be abandoned, therefore, when the first such property is uncovered, for there may be others, and only an exhaustive investigation will reveal the true position.

Finding the benefited property: seven rules

13–15   How then are the benefited property or properties to be found? For burdens created before November 28, 2004[86] it is possible to reduce a complex body of law to seven main rules. As more than one rule may apply, it is necessary to consider each rule, if only briefly, in relation to each burden. It should not be supposed, however, that different rules will necessarily lead to different results, for the rules overlap both in scope and effect. The rules are as follows:

(i) *Any express nomination of a benefited property is to be given effect.*[87] Thus if a deed of conditions provides that the burdens are to be enforceable by the owners of every unit in a development, each unit is a benefited property (and the burdens are community burdens). Or if a break-off disposition nominates land kept back by the granter as the benefited property, that nomination stands.

(ii) *Where burdens are imposed on related properties under a common scheme, each property is a benefited property.*[88] This rule, and the next, are concerned with common schemes. A "common scheme" is where the burdens on a group of properties are the same or similar, and were imposed by the same person (or by that person and a successor). With a deed of conditions there is almost always a common scheme, for usually the whole point of such a deed is that the same burdens should be imposed on a number of different properties. Rule (ii) further requires that the properties be "related", and a non-exhaustive list of criteria is set out in the legislation.[89] For properties to be "related" there must

---

[84] 2003 Act, s.49. The replacement rules are set out in ss.52—57.

[85] Insofar as they are complex this is usually because they are based on the previous rules, thus ensuring that no enforcement rights are lost as a result of the change.

[86] Usually the deed must be registered before that day, being the appointed day for the abolition of the feudal system. But in the case of rule (ii), it is sufficient if the deed imposing burdens on *one* of the units is registered before the appointed day: see 2003 Act, s.53(1).

[87] The legislation, in other words, leaves express nomination untouched.

[88] 2003 Act, s.53. See further K. G. C. Reid, *The Abolition of Feudal Tenure in Scotland* (2003), paras 5.7–5.12. The rule does not apply to rights of pre-emption, redemption or reversion, or to maintenance obligations (*e.g.* in respect of roads or sewers) which have been taken over by a public authority. See ss.53(3) and 122(2).

[89] 2003 Act, s.53(2).

normally be physical connection or proximity, or shared facilities or obligations. A deed of conditions is usually sufficient indication that the properties are related.[90] Most cases involving rule (ii) are obvious. In practice this is the development case (as opposed to the subdivision case),[91] so that the standard examples are housing estates and tenements. The effect of the rule is to create community burdens, for each property, already a burdened property, is elevated into a benefited property as well. A special variant of rule (ii) applies in respect of sheltered housing.[92]

(iii) *Where burdens are imposed on unrelated properties under a common scheme, each (or any) property is a benefited property if the deed creating the burdens for that property (a) gives notice that a common scheme exists and (b) contains nothing to exclude mutual enforceability.*[93] This is a statutory restatement of the former law, and the previous case law will continue to be of some help.[94] A typical example of "unrelated"[95] properties is a scattering of individual plots sold by a rural estate over a number of years and made subject to the standard estate conditions. In many such cases, however, the other requirements of rule (iii) will not be met. Thus it is unusual for individual conveyances to refer, even obliquely, to a common scheme;[96] and even where this is done there may be contra-indicators which exclude mutual enforceability, such as the reservation of a right to vary or waive the burdens.[97] Unlike rule (ii), therefore, rule (iii) is not often encountered in practice.

(iv) *In a facility burden the benefited properties are (a) the facility itself and (b) any properties which benefit (and are intended to benefit) from the facility.*[98] A "facility burden" is one which regulates the maintenance, management, reinstatement or use of facilities such as the common parts of a tenement, a common area for recreation, a private road, private sewerage, or a boundary wall.[99] In a tenement, for example, the effect of rule (iv) is that maintenance burdens are enforceable by everyone, for each flat will be a benefited property. In the case of a garden wall, a maintenance obligation would be enforceable by the owners of the land

---

[90] 2003 Act, s.53(2)(c).

[91] See paras 13–02—13–04.

[92] 2003 Act, s.54. The effect is to confer the status of benefited property even on a unit which is unburdened, provided it is used in "some special way" (*e.g.* as accommodation for a resident warden). Many sheltered housing developments contain such a unit.

[93] 2003 Act, s.52. See further K. G. C. Reid, *The Abolition of Feudal of Tenure in Scotland* (2003), paras 5.13–5.17. As with rule (ii), the rule does not apply to rights of pre-emption, redemption or reversion, or to maintenance obligations (*e.g.* in respect of roads or sewers) which have been taken over by a public authority. See ss.52(3) and 122(2).

[94] For which see Reid, *Property*, paras 399–401.

[95] Section 52 does not provide as such that the properties be "unrelated"; but if they are "related" the much wider s.53 applies (*i.e.* rule (ii)), and there is no need to consider s.52.

[96] There is sufficient notice if the burdens were imposed in a single conveyance followed by subdivision. But the fact that a single conveyance was used will often indicate that the properties are "related" and hence subject to rule (ii).

[97] 2003 Act, s.52(2).

[98] 2003 Act, s.56(1)(a). See further, K. G. C. Reid, *The Abolition of Feudal Tenure in Scotland* (2003), paras 6.1–6.5. As with rules (ii) and (iii), the rule does not apply to maintenance obligations assumed by public authorities: see s.122(2).

[99] 2003 Act, s.122(1), (3).

on either side. As the first example shows, rule (iv) will often overlap with rule (ii), with the same results, for many facility burdens are imposed on related properties under a common scheme.[1]

(v) *In a service burden the benefited properties are any property to which the services are provided.*[2] A "service burden" is a burden on one property to supply services to another, for example water or electricity.[3] Such burdens are rare, and rule (v) correspondingly unimportant.

(vi) *In a (formerly) feudal burden the benefited property is any property nominated in a notice registered under s.18 of the 2000 Act.* For the final two rules it is necessary to divide burdens into "feudal" and "non-feudal". The distinction turns on provenance. The former were created in a grant in feu (such as a feu disposition) or in a deed of conditions granted in association with a grant in feu. The latter were created in a disposition or in a deed of conditions associated with a disposition. Under the old law, feudal burdens were always enforceable by the feudal superior, and were sometimes also enforceable by neighbours ("co-feuars") as a result of express provision in the deed or by legal implication. The Acts of 2000 and 2003 extinguished the rights of superiors, while at the same time amending and re-stating the rights of neighbours in the manner summarised as rules (i)–(v) above. But superiors could sometimes avoid the extinction by "reallotting" the enforcement right to other land in their ownership. This was done by registering a notice under section 18 of the 2000 Act prior to November 28, 2004.[4] The result was for the nominated land to become a benefited property in the burden (and hence for the burden to survive feudal abolition). Normally, land could be nominated only if it contained a building used as place of human habitation or resort and lying within 100 metres of the feu (*i.e.* the burdened property).[5]

(vii) *In a (formerly) non-feudal burden the benefited property is, transitionally, such property in the neighbourhood as was still retained by the granter at the time of creation.* This is the subdivision case. Thus suppose, as in the example given earlier,[6] that Donald disponed half of his land to Edmund while retaining the other half. Real burdens were imposed on Edmund's land. Under rule (vii) the benefited property would be the land retained by Donald. This is not a new rule but an old

---

[1] Rule (iv) was enacted before there were any plans to have rule (ii): see 2000 Act, s.23 (now repealed). Its importance has been much reduced by rule (ii).

[2] 2003 Act, s.56(1)(b).

[3] 2003 Act, s.122(1).

[4] For a detailed account, see K. G. C. Reid, *The Abolition of Feudal Tenure in Scotland* (2003), Ch.3. In a few cases there was the alternative of converting the feudal burden into a personal real burden such as a conservation burden: see para.13–19.

[5] If the 100-metres rule could not be satisfied, the superior could attempt to reallot by agreement under s.19 of the 2000 Act, or apply to the Lands Tribunal under s.20 for the 100-metres requirement to be waived. Either case leads to an entry on the property register.

[6] para.13–03.

one.[7] It is preserved by the 2003 Act but only for ten years.[8] An owner such as Donald who wishes his property to remain a benefited property must execute and register a notice in the prescribed form before November 28, 2014.[9] Otherwise the status of benefited property under rule (vii) will be lost (although it may continue by virtue of one of the other rules).

Although intricate and, as yet, unfamiliar, these rules may turn out to 13-16 be easier to use than first impressions suggest. Rules (i) and (iii) presuppose a statement in the deed, which will in turn appear in the property register. Rule (vi) involves the registration of a separate notice. Rules (iv) and (v) depend on a straightforward classification by type of burden. Rule (ii) involves a consideration of the properties to determine whether or not they are "related". The most difficult rule is the last, requiring as it does an investigation into the landholdings of the granter at the time when the deed was first registered.[10] Fortunately, rule (vii) is temporary and its replacement, from 28 November 2014, requires the registration of a notice. From that day too the Keeper must note on the Land Register the applicability of any of rules (ii)—(v) and, where possible, identify the benefited property.[11] After an awkward period of transition, therefore, it should become much easier to find the benefited property. Already it is easier than under the law which is being replaced.[12]

Unenforceable burdens

The mere fact that a burden is on the Land or Sasine Register does 13-17 not guarantee its validity or enforceability.[13] A surprising number of "burdens" on the registers are unenforceable, for various reasons. First, as with any other real right, there may have been an error of constitution—for example, absence of title or capacity or a defect of execution. Admittedly, registration in the Land Register cures errors of this kind,[14] but many burdens originated in the GRS and are not cured merely by being listed in the Land Register following first registration.[15] Second, the burden may fail as to content. Third, it may be expressed in language which is insufficiently certain. Fourth, there may be no

---

[7] It derives from *J. A. Mactaggart & Co. v Harrower* (1906) 8 F. 1101. See Reid, *Property*, para.403. This is the only rule of the old law in relation to implied rights to survive. There have been few reported cases and the rule is undeveloped. A modern, and controversial, case is *Marsden v Craighelen Lawn Tennis and Squash Club*, 1999 G.W.D. 37–1820, discussed in Reid and Gretton, *Conveyancing 1999*, pp.59–61.

[8] 2003 Act, s.49(2).

[9] 2003 Act, s.50.

[10] A practical difficulty is that the Land Register does not disclose previous owners.

[11] 2003 Act, s.58. Before that date he is entitled, but not bound, to make such an entry.

[12] For a discussion of the difficulties with that law, see Scottish Law Commission, *Report on Real Burdens* (Scot. Law Com. No.181, 2000), paras 11.21–11.25.

[13] The converse proposition, however, is true: a burden which is *not* on the Register is invalid and unenforceable. In the case of the Land Register this rule is statutory: see 1979 Act, s.3(1)(a).

[14] 1979 Act, s.3(1).

[15] Since they are not "registered" in the Land Register, s.3(1) does not apply.

benefited property, for the application of the seven rules just described may yield a negative result. Fifth, a feudal burden may have been extinguished by feudal abolition, especially if the burden was neither imposed under a common scheme nor the subject of a notice registered by the superior.[16] Ultimately the plan is that burdens extinguished in this way be removed from the Land Register, at the prompting of the owner of the burdened property, but the relevant provision is not yet in operation.[17] Finally, the burden may have been extinguished in some other way but not involving registration, for example by negative prescription or acquiescence. If a burden appearing in the title sheet turns out to be invalid, no compensation is payable by the Keeper.[18]

For the conveyancer, the possibility that a burden is unenforceable should always be borne in mind. Sometimes this can be a welcome, and cost-free, solution to an apparently intractable problem. In practice, the approach to be taken depends very much on the situation one is in. Purchasers are bound to be cautious. It is not enough that a burden is probably invalid, or, though valid, probably does not strike at the use proposed. Purchasers want certainty, or something near it. By contrast, suppose that owners are using their property in a certain way, and the use is objected to. Here the law agent for the owners will be only too glad to seize upon any argument that will tend to show that the burden is invalid or is to be construed in a narrow sense. And the same, of course, applies if litigation takes place. A probable argument once accepted by a court becomes a certainty.

Division of benefited and burdened properties

13–18   Particularly in the case of older burdens, the original benefited or burdened property will often have been divided, so that one plot of land has become two or four or more, with a corresponding number of separate owners. Division of the *burdened* property in this way has no effect on the burdens as such, and each plot remains burdened as the undivided property was before.[19] For the *benefited* property, however, division results in the proliferation of enforcement rights. In place of the single owner of an undivided property there are now as many owners, and enforcers, as there are plots. Admittedly, not all owners may have interest to enforce, for some plots may be too remote. Nonetheless the overall result is unwelcome to owners of burdened properties. Some control is now exercised by the 2003 Act.[20] Unless the disposition provides otherwise, any part of a benefited property which is split off will immediately cease to be a benefited property. Sometimes there may be good reasons for overriding this default rule and allowing the disponee the benefit of the burdens. But in the long term there will be a welcome tendency for benefited properties to shrink. The provision is not

---

[16] In the cases mentioned the burdens would survive under one of rule (ii), (iii) or (vi).
[17] 2000 Act, s.46.
[18] 1979 Act, s.12(3)(g).
[19] 2003 Act, s.13. In the case of an affirmative burden, each owner is liable jointly and severally, while the owners are generally liable among themselves in proportion to the area of each plot: see 2003 Act, s.11.
[20] 2003 Act, s.12.

retrospective, however, and so has no effect on divisions occurring before November 28, 2004.

Personal real burdens

Some countries allow title conditions without a benefited property.[21] 13–19 In Scotland this is not possible for servitudes, but a limited class of "personal real burdens" was introduced by the 2003 Act. The dissonance in the name is deliberate. The burden is "real" in the sense that all real rights are real, that is to say, as a right in a thing (the burdened property). But it is "personal" in the sense that it held by a person without reference to a benefited property. A personal real burden is thus, in this respect, closer to a standard security or lease than to a servitude. "Personal" real burdens may be contrasted with ordinary or "praedial" real burdens—that is, a real burden *with* a benefited property.[22]

Eight types of personal real burden are listed in the 2003 Act.[23] No others are permitted. Most of the eight are unusual and some are practically unknown. In the narrow sphere in which they operate they can be seen as a replacement for feudal burdens, allowing a person (generally a public body) to dispose of all of its land and yet still impose real burdens. Indeed any feudal burden which had the characteristics of a personal real burden could be converted into such a burden by registration of a notice prior to November 28, 2004.[24] Thus most of the first personal real burdens came about by conversion rather than by creation of new; and two such burdens (personal pre-emption burdens and personal redemption burdens) can only be created in this way.

Personal real burdens are restricted both by content and by holder. Only two need be mentioned. A "conservation burden" protects the built or natural environment for the benefit of the public,[25] and may be held only by Scottish Ministers, by local authorities, and by certain other designated conservation bodies (mainly private trusts).[26] Thus if a conservation body restores property and sells it, conservation burdens can be included in the disposition to ensure that the historic features of the building are duly preserved. Quite different in character is the "economic development burden". As the name suggests, this has as its purpose the promotion of economic development—a rather vague

---

[21] For example, South Africa and the United States of America.

[22] There is a corresponding distinction between personal and praedial servitudes, which is well-known throughout the civil law world. See Stair II.7.pr, and Erskine II.9.5. "Praedial" is from the Latin word *praedium* meaning land or an estate. The only personal servitude (in this sense) recognised in Scots law is proper liferent.

[23] 2003 Act, s.1(3). The list comprises: conservation burdens, rural housing burdens, maritime burdens, economic development burdens, health care burdens, manager burdens, personal pre-emption burdens, and personal redemption burdens.

[24] 2000 Act, ss.18A, 18B, 18C, 27, and 27A. Maritime burdens (burdens over the foreshore or sea bed held by the Crown) did not require a notice: see s.60. For a full account, see K. G. C. Reid, *The Abolition of Feudal Tenure in Scotland* (2003), Ch.4.

[25] 2003 Act, s.38.

[26] For the list of conservation bodies, see the Title Conditions (Scotland) Act 2003 (Conservation Bodies) Order 2003 (SSI 2003/453). Amendments to the list are likely in the future.

notion which will no doubt be tested in the courts.[27] Such burdens can be held only by Scottish Ministers and by local authorities, and they are the rough equivalent of the statutory agreements which were already available for Scottish Enterprise and Highlands and Islands Enterprise.[28]

For the most part, personal real burdens are governed by the same rules as praedial real burdens. In the absence of a benefited property, however, personal real burdens are transferred by assignation followed by registration.[29] But only a qualified holder can take, and some burdens (such as economic development burdens) are not assignable at all. Only the holder of a personal real burden has title to enforce, and interest is presumed.[30]

Interpretation[31]

13-20   In construing real burdens there is a presumption for freedom. Thus if the validity of a condition is uncertain, it will generally be construed as invalid,[32] while if its scope is doubtful, it will generally be construed according to its narrowest possible meaning,[33] and the courts are reluctant to extend the scope of a burden by implication. Hence, the vital importance of accuracy when drafting new burdens. Unfortunately, a burden which looks clear, and perhaps even elegant, to its author may appear in a different light to a court which has the benefit of hindsight and of knowledge of events that no one may have foreseen.[34]

The case law is voluminous and, for the draftsman, disheartening. For example, an obligation to build cannot be extended to imply an obligation to maintain.[35] In one case an obligation to build a house "which may include a garage" was held not to imply a prohibition on building a second garage.[36] An obligation to supply water was held not to

---

[27] 2003 Act, s.45.

[28] Enterprise and New Towns (Scotland) Act 1990, s.32 (as amended by the 2003 Act, s.113).

[29] 2003 Act, s.39.

[30] 2003 Act, s.47.

[31] On interpretation, see Reid, *Property*, paras 415–422; Gordon, paras 22–41—22–50; Halliday, paras 34–31–34–34.

[32] But in practice it can be difficult to predict what a court would say. Thus, in *Lothian Regional Council v Rennie*, 1991 S.L.T. 465 two judges held a burden to be ineffectual as being hopelessly imprecise in its scope, while the third judge thought that its meaning was perfectly clear. Similarly, the Lord Ordinary and the First Division took opposed views in *Grampian Joint Police Board v Pearson*, 2000 S.L.T. 90, 2001 S.C. 734.

[33] For illustrative examples, in addition to the cases cited below, see *Graham v Shiels* (1901) 8 S.L.T. 368, *Shand v Brand* (1907) 14 S.L.T. 704, *The Walker Trustees v Haldane* (1902) 4 F. 594, and *Heritage Fisheries Ltd v Duke of Buccleuch*, 2000 S.L.T. 800. But the court will not adopt a narrow reading unless it is a reasonable one: *Cochran v Paterson* (1882) 9 R. 634 at 638; *Frame v Cameron* (1864) 3 M. 290 at 294.

[34] e.g. *Heritage Fisheries Ltd v Duke of Buccleuch*, 2000 S.L.T. 800 at 802 D-E ("language which is at once obscure and infelicitous and which seems calculated to maximise the scope for misunderstandings and disputes.")

[35] *Peter Walker & Son (Edinburgh) Ltd v Church of Scotland General Trustees*, 1967 S.L.T. 297. Contrast *Clark v Glasgow Assurance Co.* (1854) 1 Macq. 668. Though a House of Lords case, it is out of line with current judicial attitudes.

[36] *Carswell v Goldie*, 1967 S.L.T. 339. And see *Ross v Cuthbertson* (1854) 16 D. 732 and *Buchanan v Marr* (1883) 10 R. 936.

imply an obligation that it be of drinkable quality.[37] The terms "conventional dwelling-house"[38] and "buildings of an unseemly description"[39] have both been held to be too vague as a basis for real burdens, although it has been also held (it is submitted incorrectly) that "not of a class inferior to the houses some time ago built by" is valid as the basis of a real burden.[40] In a remarkable series of cases an obligation that a dwelling-house must be "self-contained" has been held to refer to structure not use. Thus, such a burden does not prevent division into flats, provided that the structure remains *capable* of use as a single dwelling-house.[41] An obligation to erect buildings of a certain type does not imply a prohibition of additional buildings of a different type.[42] An obligation to erect houses[43] (or anything else) is invalid as a real burden if no time-limit is expressed.[44] Where a burden forbids a certain use, it is presumed not to forbid such use as is merely "ancillary". For example, a prohibition of commercial use would not prevent a house being used commercially, provided that its main use continued to be that of a dwelling-house.[45] Because of this, it may be desirable when drafting a burden to add a clause expressly forbidding ancillary use, and this is sometimes done.

The traditionally hostile approach to real burdens was due in part to the difficulty of procuring their discharge prior to the introduction of the Lands Tribunal jurisdiction in 1970. With the further reforms in the 2003 Act, discussed below, there is now no reason for a court to attempt discharge by means of interpretation, and indeed the 2003 Act expressly provides that "real burdens shall be construed in the same manner as other provisions of deeds which relate to land and are intended for registration".[46] As a result, it should no longer be true in the future, as it has sometimes been in the past, that real burdens are interpreted more strictly than servitudes; and some at least of the cases in the previous paragraph may no longer be good law. But even before the changes brought about by the 2003 Act the courts sometimes read deeds with a

---

[37] *Anstruther's Trs v Burgh of Pittenweem*, 1943 S.L.T. 160.

[38] *Lawson v Hay*, 1989 G.W.D. 24–1049.

[39] *Murray's Trs v Trustees for St Margaret's Convent* (1906) 8 F. 1109, 1907 S.C. (HL) 8.

[40] *Morrison v McLay* (1874) 1 R. 1117. See also *Middleton v Leslie's Trs* (1894) 21 R. 781.

[41] The distinction seems odd but is well supported by authority, *e.g. Moir's Trs v McEwan* (1880) 7 R. 1141; *Buchanan v Marr* (1883) 10 R. 936; *Miller v Carmichael* (1888) 15 R. 991; *Porter v Campbell's Trs*, 1923 S.C. (HL) 94.

[42] *Cowan v Magistrates of Edinburgh* (1887) 14 R. 682; *Fleming v Ure* (1896) 4 S.L.T. 26. For whether the burden implies a prohibition of altering the buildings see *Cochran v Paterson* (1882) 9 R. 634, *Thom v Chalmers* (1886) 13 R. 1026, and *Johnston v MacRitchie* (1893) 20 R. 539.

[43] Burdens of this nature were once very common. The superior wanted to keep up the value of the land as a security for his feuduty. Clauses requiring insurance and rebuilding in the event of destruction were common for the same reason. Such clauses (except in so far as they might protect amenity) are now pointless.

[44] *Gammell's Trs v The Land Commission*, 1970 S.L.T. 254, distinguishing *Anderson v Valentine*, 1957 S.L.T. 57.

[45] *Colquhoun's C.B. v Glen's Tr*, 1920 S.C. 737; *Low v Scottish Amicable Building Society*, 1940 S.L.T. 295.

[46] 2003 Act, s.14. For a discussion, see Scottish Law Commission, *Report on Real Burdens* (Scot. Law Com. No.181, 2000) paras 4.61–4.67. Much earlier, the Halliday Report para.81 had advocated a similar change.

sympathetic eye. Where, for example, there was an obligation to maintain a boundary fence it was held that it could fairly be implied that the fence should be stockproof.[47] And a rather vague power for factors to act "in their sole discretion" was held enforceable, on the basis that they could not go beyond the specific obligations imposed on the owners by other clauses in the deed of conditions.[48]

It is common to find burdens which forbid "nuisances". There is only one reported case[49] where such a clause has been challenged as too vague. In that case the burden forbade: "any soap work candle work tan work slaughter house cattle mart skin work dye work oil work lime work distillery brewery or other manufacture or chemical process of any kind, nor to deposit nauseous materials thereon nor to lay any nuisance or obstructions on the roads or streets adjoining said ground nor to do any other act which may injure the amenity of the said place of the neighbourhood for private residences". The challenge failed. Clauses with this sort of wording are often to be found in older deeds.[50] The modern tendency is simply to forbid any "trade business or profession", and there can be little doubt that this expression is acceptably precise. Reference to "nuisance" as such is rare in modern burdens. One interpretative problem is that "nuisance" is a delict against neighbours in any case.[51]

Extinction: in general

13-21   Quite often owners want to do something which is prohibited by a real burden. There is then a choice. One option is to seek the agreement of those with rights to enforce, formalised in a minute of waiver. Another option is to apply to the Lands Tribunal for variation or discharge. If the burden is more than 100 years old, it can often be brought to an end under the "sunset rule" merely by service and registration of a notice of termination. And finally the owner can ignore the burden and do the forbidden thing anyway. Until the 2000 Act this last course was risky because the superior might have a right to irritate the feu and so reclaim the property without compensation. Today the worst that can happen is a court order to stop, or to undo, the breach. Even that is rare. In practice, burdens are not often enforced, and where they are enforced the available remedies may turn out to be unsatisfactory.[52] Indeed often the real concern is not enforcement but rather the possible reluctance of a future purchaser to accept a title where there has been a blatant breach of one of the burdens. Minutes of waiver, in particular, are often sought long after the breach has occurred, under stimulus of an anxious or demanding purchaser.

---

[47] *Church of Scotland General Trustees v Phin*, 1987 S.C.L.R. 240.

[48] *Crampshee v North Lanarkshire Council*, 2004 G.W.D. 7-149.

[49] *Mannofield Residents Property Co. Ltd v Thomson*, 1983 S.L.T. (Sh. Ct.) 71. See also *Meriton Ltd v Winning*, 1993 S.C.L.R. 913, 1995 S.L.T. 76.

[50] "The usual grotesque enumeration of noxious and offensive businesses and trades"—Lord Shaw in *Porter v Campbell's Trs*, 1923 S.C. (HL) 94.

[51] On nuisance as a delict, see N. R. Whitty, "Nuisance", in *Stair Memorial Encyclopaedia* Reissue (2001).

[52] para.13-13.

Not only does breach of a burden avoid the cost and inconvenience of a discharge, or the pain of compliance: it may also bring the burden to an end altogether, through the doctrines of acquiescence and negative prescription. This is not, of course, to advocate breach. Where possible, obligations should be complied with. But breach is common in practice, not least because the burdened owner is often quite unaware of, or indifferent to, the conditions in his or her title.

Minute of waiver

A standard method of removing or restricting real burdens is by a 13–22 written minute of waiver.[53] There is no prescribed form. In practice waivers usually discharge the burden only to the extent of allowing the activity proposed by the burdened owner, so that in all other respects the burden remains in force. Although burdens can be enforced by occupiers as well as by owners, only the owner of the benefited property grants the deed. A registered title is not required provided that, in the case of GRS property, the deed includes a clause of deduction of title.[54] The burden is not varied or discharged until the deed is registered, against the burdened property. Superiors did not usually grant minutes of waiver without payment, but in the post-feudal world waivers will often be gratuitous.

It is important to identify all of the benefited properties. There is no point in obtaining a minute of waiver from the owner of one property only to find that the owner of another seeks and obtains an interdict. This obvious point was sometimes overlooked in the past, especially in respect of feudal burdens, and the register is full of minutes of waiver granted by superiors alone without regard to the, admittedly difficult, question of whether neighbours (co-feuars) had enforcement rights as well.[55] Even today the identification of benefited properties may not be a straightforward task;[56] and if the numbers go far into double figures there may be little prospect of persuading everyone to sign, at least within a reasonable period of time.

Some help is provided by the 2003 Act in respect of community burdens, *i.e.* the burdens that typically regulate "communities" such as tenements and housing estates. For community burdens not every benefited owner need sign. Instead a minute of waiver is valid if granted and executed (i) by the owners of a majority of the "units" (houses or flats) in the community (or by the owners of such units as may be specified in the constitutive deed) or (ii) by the manager of the community, if duly authorised, whether in the constitutive deed or by the owners.[57] But any owner who did not sign must be sent a copy of the deed and a notice in prescribed form, and allowed a period of eight weeks to apply to the Lands Tribunal for preservation of the burden.[58]

---

[53] 2003 Act, ss.15 and 48.
[54] 2003 Act, s.60.
[55] D. J. Cusine and J. Egan, *Feuing Conditions in Scotland* (1995).
[56] paras 13–14 and 13–15.
[57] 2003 Act, s.33.
[58] 2003 Act, s.34.

Assuming that no such application is made, the Tribunal endorses the deed accordingly and it can then be registered.[59]

An alternative method is slightly less cumbersome. This allows for the variation or discharge of a community burden (other than a facility burden) by a deed executed by the owners of the burdened property and of all benefited properties which lie within four metres (but disregarding roads of less than 20 metres in width).[60] The advantage, as compared to the previous method, is the relatively small number of signatories. The disadvantage is the possibility of defeat by a single unco-operative neighbour. As before, intimation must be given to the other owners, but it is sufficient to fix a notice to the burdened property and to one or more lamp posts, and nothing need be sent.[61]

Sunset rule

13–23   A minute of waiver needs the consent of the benefited owner or owners. But for burdens which are more than 100 years old the burdened owner can act alone. In terms of a procedure first introduced by the 2003 Act,[62] the owner[63] draws up a notice of termination in statutory form. A copy is sent to the owners of all benefited properties within four metres (disregarding roads), and also fixed on the burdened property and on a lamp post or lamp posts. If, after eight weeks, no application has been made to the Lands Tribunal by a benefited owner, the notice is endorsed with a certificate by the Tribunal and registered against the burdened property. Registration marks the moment of extinction. The procedure is not restricted to community burdens but is available for all real burdens other than conservation burdens, facility burdens and one or two other minor cases. Furthermore, it can be used for any number of qualifying burdens, thus allowing a title to be "cleansed" of elderly burdens in a single act. It may be that such cleansing will become a matter almost of routine.

Lands Tribunal

13–24   Since 1971 the Lands Tribunal[64] has had an equitable power to waive or vary title conditions, and the Tribunal's powers are now refined and re-enacted by Part 9 of the 2003 Act. Most applications to the Tribunal are in respect of real burdens, and because the jurisdiction is essentially

---

[59] 2003 Act, s.37(2) (as applied by s.34(4)). By s.37(4) the deed must also be endorsed with a docket, sworn before a notary public and signed by the grantee, that intimation was properly carried out

[60] 2003 Act, s.35. This method is also unavailable in respect of service burdens and of burdens in sheltered housing developments.

[61] 2003 Act, s.36. But sending is available as an alternative.

[62] 2003 Act, ss.20–24.

[63] Or any other person (such as a tenant) against whom the burden is enforceable: see 2003 Act, s.20(1).

[64] The Lands Tribunal is not to be confused with the Land Court. The Lands Tribunal, as well as having the jurisdiction mentioned in the text, also has an important role in hearing and determining disputes about the "right to buy" legislation, and also disputes in relation to the Land Registration (Scotland) Act 1979.

discretionary, within the limits of certain statutory criteria,[65] the outcome is often difficult to predict. Further, the criteria in the 2003 Act are different in some respects from those in the previous legislation, making past case law an even less certain guide than before.[66] It is common for applications to be unopposed, in which case they are granted without further inquiry.[67] Even in opposed cases, however, applications are quite often successful, with expenses generally following success.[68] In the past the Tribunal has tended to be under-used, but with the proliferation of enforcement rights brought about by the 2003 Act[69]—and the consequent difficulty or impossibility of obtaining minutes of waiver—it is likely to seem increasingly attractive.

Extinction by breach: negative prescription and acquiescence

After five years of breach a real burden is extinguished by negative 13–25 prescription.[70] But the burden may have been brought to an end much earlier owing to acquiescence. Specific provision for acquiescence is made in the 2003 Act.[71] The breach must involve material expenditure the benefit of which would be substantially lost if the burden were now to be enforced. Unauthorised building is the typical case. The burden is extinguished if either the owner of the benefited property or properties consented to the work, however informally, or if all those with enforcement rights (which might include tenants and other occupiers) consented or at least failed to object within the period ending 12 weeks after the work was substantially completed. The work must be sufficiently obvious that the enforcers knew of it or ought to have known. In effect, enforcers must object at once or lose their rights.

It is easy to see why these provisions are important. Suppose, for instance, that a deed of 1899 conveyed plots of ground for the erection of tenements. The deed will have imposed various real burdens. Some, such as restrictions on use, are likely still to be enforceable. But suppose that one of the burdens concerned the building line. It may, for instance, have provided that there should be no building nearer than four feet from the inner line of the pavement. This is unlikely to matter today, for if the builder in fact built up to three feet from the pavement, negative prescription will long ago have barred any objection. Much the same is true even of more recent works—extensions, garages, porches, greenhouses and the like. If more than five years have passed, the matter is taken care of by prescription; if less than five years, acquiescence may

---

[65] Set out in the 2003 Act, s.100.

[66] See, for that case law, Sir Crispin Agnew of Lochnaw, *Variation and Discharge of Land Obligations* (1999), and also the much briefer accounts in Halliday, Ch.34 (Part C) and Gordon, Ch.25.

[67] 2003 Act, s.97. But this does not extent to facility burdens, service burdens, burdens in sheltered housing developments, and servitudes.

[68] 2003 Act, s.103.

[69] Particularly due to s.53: see para.13.15.

[70] 2003 Act, s.18—on the assumption that prescription has not been interrupted. Under the previous law the period was 20 years. For transitional provisions, see s.18(5), (7).

[71] 2003 Act, s.16. Specific but not exhaustive: the common law doctrine of acquiescence remains applicable insofar as not replaced by the new provision.

usually be assumed to have operated. In relation to the latter it is true that a potential purchaser cannot be sure that the unauthorised works were not objected to at the time, but there is a statutory presumption that no objections were made and hence that acquiescence operated.[72] For practical purposes this will usually be enough, even without a formal minute of waiver.

Prescription and acquiescence extinguish burdens only to the extent of the breach. So if a greenhouse is built, contrary to a general prohibition on building, the greenhouse is allowed, but in all other respects the burden remains in force and could be used to prevent further building operations.

SERVITUDES[73]

Creation by deed

13–26   A conveyancer who is instructed to create a servitude will naturally do so by deed. And if, as typically, this affects land which is being sold, the servitude will be included in the disposition (in subdivision cases) or in the deed of conditions (in development cases).[74] In a disposition a servitude can either be reserved (in favour of any land being kept back by the granter) or granted (in favour of the land being disponed), and both are common. From time to time a servitude is also created between established neighbours, without a sale, in which case the deed used is a (freestanding) deed of servitude. In all cases the deed must be granted by the owner of the burdened property and, except where a disposition is used, the granter's title must have been completed by registration.[75] To allow registration the deed must be probative.

No particular words are necessary, although "servitude" avoids any suggestion that the right is merely contractual and should always be used.[76] For servitudes of a familiar and well-established type, not much more than the name is needed, but the new servitudes permitted by the 2003 Act[77] will require to be more closely defined. In drafting it should be borne in mind that land is presumed free of burdens and that servitudes, like real burdens, are interpreted strictly.[78] The basic grant of servitude is sometimes supplemented by conditions as to its exercise, and such conditions are in any event implied by law.[79] As well as giving the

---

[72] 2003 Act, s.16(2).

[73] The standard work is D. J. Cusine and R. R. M. Paisley, *Servitudes and Rights of Way* (1998). Useful shorter accounts can be found in works such as Gordon, Ch.24 and Reid, *Property*, paras 439–93 (A. G. M. Duncan).

[74] For the distinction between subdivision and development, see paras 13–02—13–04.

[75] D. J. Cusine and R. R. M. Paisley, *Servitudes and Rights of Way*, para.4.08.

[76] See *e.g. Robertson v Hossack*, 1995 S.L.T. 291; *Moss Bros Group v Scottish Mutual Assurance plc*, 2001 S.C. 779.

[77] As to which see para.13–07.

[78] For real burdens, see para.13–20. The courts are, however, realistic as to the amount of detail that can reasonably be expected: see *Axis West Developments Ltd v Chartwell Land Investments Ltd*, 1999 S.L.T. 1416.

[79] For the conditions that are implied, see D. J. Cusine and R. R. M. Paisley, *Servitudes and Rights of Way*, Ch.12.

terms of the servitude the deed must also nominate and describe both the benefited and the burdened properties. Under the old law, there was no requirement that the deed be registered, although registration was normal in practice, but the 2003 Act requires registration against both properties.[80]

Probably the commonest servitude is that of way,[81] and as there are two main types (pedestrian and vehicular) it is important to specify which is intended. To avoid any doubt as to whether vehicular access includes pedestrian access, the phrase "pedestrian and vehicular" should be used. If the nature of the servitude has not been specified, a court will, it seems, construe the servitude on the basis of actual usage.

Creation by implication or prescription

Unlike real burdens, servitudes can also be created by implication 13–27 from the terms of a conveyance, and by positive prescription. The first of these is usually the mark of conveyancing negligence, for if a servitude is needed, it should be created expressly. It will not be discussed further here.[82] In *Bowers v Kennedy*[83] it was held that, for landlocked property, there is always a right of access over land of which it was formerly part, and that this is attributable, not to servitude, but to an inherent quality of ownership itself. As such it is imprescriptible and so is not lost even by long periods of non-use. The court, however, declined to be drawn on the more important question as to whether such a right arises even where there was no previous connection with the surrounding land.

Servitudes by prescription are, again, only marginally a conveyancing matter and so will not be discussed here. The relevant prescriptive period is 20 years.[84]

Division of the benefited property

A familiar problem is whether, on the division of the benefited 13–28 property into separate plots, a servitude enures to the benefit of all the various plots which now make up the original property. A farmer who happily granted a servitude of way for a neighbouring farmer may be less happy if he finds that, instead of the occasional tractor, countless cars drive up and down day and night because the neighbouring farm is now a housing estate. In at least some cases, such use would disturb the principle that the burden of a servitude is not to be increased; but because of uncertainties in the law, the ideal is to make clear provision

---

[80] 2003 Act, s.75-except for pipeline servitudes, in recognition of the fact that the sheer number of burdened properties may make registration impractical.

[81] Also called "passage", "access", "free ish and entry", etc.

[82] For discussion and authorities see D. J. Cusine and R. R. M. Paisley, *op. cit.*, Chs 7, 8 and 9; Gordon, *op. cit.*, paras 24–34-24–41; and Reid, Property, paras 452–457. Some important cases are *Cochrane v Ewart* (1861) 23 D. (HL) 3; *Gow's Trs v Mealls* (1875) 2 R. 729; *Murray v Medley*, 1973 S.L.T. (Sh. Ct.) 75; *King v Brodt*, 1993 G.W.D. 13–886.

[83] 2000 S.C. 555. For commentary, see Reid and Gretton, *Conveyancing 2000*, pp.52–4; R. R. M. Paisley (2002) 6 Edin. L.R. 101.

[84] 1973 Act, s.3.

on the point in the original deed, either allowing such future use or alternatively forbidding it.[85]

Extinction

13–29   A servitude is brought to an end by a formal discharge executed by the owners of the benefited property or properties. If the servitude was entered on the Register against the burdened property, the discharge must likewise be registered against that property,[86] but otherwise registration is not required. In practice formal discharges are uncommon, and if a servitude is extinguished it is usually because it has not been exercised for the twenty years of negative prescription.[87] Extinction may also come about by acquiescence in a building project—such as a wall across a path—which is inconsistent with the future exercise of the servitude.[88] A servitude is extinguished by confusion if the benefited and burdened properties come into the ownership of the same person, but with the possibility of revival (although the law is not certain) if the properties later come to be separated.[89] Finally, and as with real burdens, a servitude may be varied or discharged by application to the Lands Tribunal.[90]

PRE-EMPTIONS, REDEMPTIONS AND REVERSIONS

Pre-emptions

13–30   Sometimes, when land is split off and sold, the seller reserves a right of first refusal on a subsequent re-sale. This gives the option of buying back before the land is sold to someone else. Rights of pre-emption are common only in rural areas, and are found particularly where land is sold from a large estate. Sometimes a pre-emption is contractual in nature but more usually it is included within a conveyance with the idea (not always successfully realised)[91] that it should be a real burden. The price is typically that which a future potential purchaser is willing to pay, although sometimes it is a fixed sum which, with inflation, will rapidly represent a bargain for the pre-emption holder.[92] From an owner's point

---

[85] Relevant cases include *Keith v Texaco Ltd*, 1977 S.L.T. (Lands Tr.) 16, *Alvis v Harrison*, 1991 S.L.T. 64, and *Alba Homes Ltd v Duell*, 1993 S.L.T. (Sh. Ct) 49. For an excellent and persuasive study of the whole question see D. J. Cusine and R. R. M. Paisley, *Servitudes and Rights of Way*, Ch.14.

[86] 2003 Act, s.78.

[87] 1973 Act, s.8.

[88] See, *e.g.*, *Millar v Christie*, 1961 S.C. 1.

[89] D. J. Cusine and R. R. M. Paisley, *Servitudes and Rights of Way*, paras 17.22–17.31. A real burden is not extinguished by confusion: see the 2003 Act, s.19.

[90] See para.13–24.

[91] *e.g.* because there is no benefited property, as in *Macdonald-Haig v Gerlings*, Inverness Sheriff Court, December 3, 2001, unreported; discussed in Reid and Gretton, *Conveyancing 2002*, pp.63–5. Disappointments of this kind are apt to lead to actions for professional negligence against one's law agents: see *MacDonald-Haig v MacNeill & Critchley*, 2004 S.L.T. (Sh. Ct) 75.

[92] In *Macdonald-Haig v Gerlings* (above) a low price was held not to breach article 1 of the First Protocol to the European Convention on Human Rights.

of view, a pre-emption is irksome and can delay sales and put off potential purchasers. There is also the danger that it is overlooked, at least in the initial stages of a sale.

For reasons which are largely historical, the law distinguishes between (i) real burden pre-emptions created in a grant in feu, or in a non-feudal deed executed after September 1, 1974, and (ii) real burden pre-emptions created in a non-feudal deed executed before 1 September 1974.[93] Pre-emptions of the second type are normal real burdens which run with the land and affect all future sales, thus allowing the holder to choose when to buy. Pre-emptions of the first type are, in principle, available only on the first sale. By virtue of a provision which dates from 1938 but was re-enacted in a revised form by the 2003 Act,[94] the property is offered back only on the first occasion on which it is sold. The pre-emption holder then has 21 days to accept the offer or to reject it, but in either case the pre-emption comes to an end:[95] if the holder chooses not to buy, there is no second chance. However, a proper written offer is needed, and on terms which are both reasonable and in conformity with the clause of pre-emption. Thus it is not sufficient, under the Act, merely to write to the holder asking whether the pre-emption will be exercised (although this is commonly done in practice); and even if the answer to such a letter were to be "no", the pre-emption would live on and could be exercised on the occasion of the next sale.

In practice the requirement of a formal offer is often highly inconvenient. Since the price is generally that which a purchaser is willing to pay, no offer can be made until the property is marketed and offers from third parties received. There is then a delay while the formal offer is made to the pre-emption holder. Naturally, potential purchasers are resentful and may lose interest. For pre-emptions of the first type, however, a solution is provided by the 2003 Act.[96] Holders who do not want to exercise the pre-emption can make their position clear in advance by executing a pre-sale undertaking in statutory form. This lasts for a specified period and can be subject to conditions, such as that the price at which the property is sold be above a certain figure. If the property is sold during this period, a disposition duly registered, and any conditions in the undertaking complied with, the pre-emption is extinguished automatically.[97] Unsurprisingly, however, not all pre-emption holders are willing to commit themselves in advance in the manner required by the legislation.

It should not be assumed that a pre-emption is still "live" merely because it appears on the Register. All pre-emptions in grants in feu

---

[93] 2003 Act, s.82.

[94] 2003 Act, s.84. The former provision was s.9 of the Conveyancing (Scotland) Act 1938.

[95] Except in the case of rural housing burdens, where the pre-emption is considered to be complied with for the current sale but is not extinguished for the future: see 2003 Act, s.84(1). A rural housing burden is a right of pre-emption constituted in favour of a designated rural housing body: see 2003 Act, s.43.

[96] 2003 Act, s.83.

[97] As before, however, rural housing burdens are extinguished only in respect of the current sale: see the 2003 Act, s.83(1).

were extinguished on November 28, 2004 unless preserved by registration of a notice under sections 18 or 18A of the 2000 Act;[98] and many other pre-emptions were extinguished on the first occasion on which the property was offered back on the basis of the rule already described. If, however, the position is in doubt, as it may be, it is wise to assume that the pre-emption remains good, and to offer the property back to the holder. A disposition granted in breach of a pre-emption is vulnerable to reduction for a period of five years.[99]

Redemptions

13-31   More onerous still are rights of redemption. These are rights of repurchase at the option of the holder, sometimes exercisable at will and sometimes tied to the occurrence of a particular event. Importantly, it does not matter that the owner does not want to sell. Since November 28, 2004 it has no longer been competent to create redemptions as real burdens,[1] and those created on or after September 1, 1974 were restricted to 20 years.[2] Further, all redemptions created in grants in feu expired on November 28, 2004 unless preserved by registration of a notice under sections 18 or 18A of the 2000 Act. Nonetheless some elderly redemptions remain on the Register and may still be enforceable.

Reversions: School Sites Act 1841

13-32   A redemption is an example of a reversion.[3] The only other example of importance is reversions under the School Sites Act 1841. Here some background is necessary. The 1841 Act allowed owners to convey land (including entailed land) for the building of schools and schoolhouses. Originally these grants were to private trustees, but in due course title passed, first to education boards and ultimately to local authorities. Many of these schools and schoolhouses have now closed and the site sold by local authorities. And typically such sales disregard the third proviso to section 2 of the 1841 Act, which is to the effect that, on the land ceasing to be used for the statutory purposes, it "shall thereupon immediately revert to and become a portion of the said estate". For a long time, indeed, this proviso was forgotten about, but in recent years there has been a spate of claims by those entitled, or allegedly entitled,

---

[98] Section 18 provides for preservation as a praedial real burden, and s.18A as a personal pre-emption burden. See K. G. C. Reid, *The Abolition of Feudal Tenure in Scotland* (2003), paras 4.21–4.23.

[99] *Matheson v Tinney*, 1989 S.L.T. 535; *Roebuck v Edmunds*, 1992 S.L.T. 1055. Although usually a proprietor in possession, the acquirer would have at least constructive knowledge of the pre-emption and so would probably be unprotected against rectification of the Register: see the 1979 Act, s.9(3)(a)(iii). After five years the pre-emption is extinguished and (except in the case of rural housing burdens) cannot be exercised in respect of future sales: see the 2003 Act, s.18(2), (6).

[1] 2003 Act, s.3(5)(a).

[2] 1974 Act, s.12.

[3] For classification and analysis of reversions, pre-emptions and other options to acquire land, see Scottish Law Commission, *Report on Real Burdens* (Scot. Law Com. No.181, 2000), paras 10.1ff.

to the reversion. In a case where the site has been sold, this presents a threat to the title of the acquirer.

The 2003 Act contains a provision designed to secure the acquirer's title and, more generally, to regulate the making of claims under the statutory reversion.[4] The details are complex but in essence the reverter, on the site ceasing to be used as a school, must choose between a conveyance of the site or a sum of money representing its value (although the local authority can insist on payment of money). Where the trigger event for the reversion occurred after April 4, 2003 (the date the provision came into force), the reverter is denied the benefit of improvements made to the land and, in the case of a reconveyance, must pay a sum representing their value. The provision leaves open the question of entitlement to the reversion, and here the law has yet to make a definitive choice as to whether the reversion is personal to the original granter (and so passes to the granter's heirs) or whether it is praedial (and so attaches to the estate from which the land was originally taken).[5] A practical difficulty with the second view is that the original estate may have been broken up. In England and Wales, where the 1841 Act also applied, the reversion is treated as personal.[6]

STYLE DISPOSITION WITH REAL BURDENS AND SERVITUDES

Suppose that Jack owns a house and a substantial amount of land. 13–33 Jack is selling part of the land to Jill. He will want her property to be subject to certain burdens and servitudes, and likewise she will want the same, vice versa. There will thus be (a) servitudes in favour of Jack (b) real burdens in favour of Jack (c) servitudes in favour of Jill and (d) real burdens in favour of Jill. The disposition could be drafted in many different ways, but something on the following lines would make sense. First, there would be the two clauses following within the body of the deed:

TOGETHER WITH the right to (one) the real burdens set out in part II of the schedule annexed and signed as relative hereto and (two) the servitudes set out in part III of the said schedule . . .

. . .BUT ALWAYS WITH AND UNDER (one) the real burdens set out in part IV of the said schedule, and (two) the servitudes set out in part V of the said schedule . . .

---

[4] 2003 Act, s.86

[5] Scottish Law Commission, *Report on Real Burdens*, para.10.47.

[6] *Fraser v Canterbury Diocesan Board of Finance* [2000] Ch. 669; *Bath and Wells Diocesan Board of Finance v Jenkinson* [2002] 3 W.L.R. 202.

Then the schedule would be on the following lines:

SCHEDULE

Part I: Interpretation

In this Schedule—

'the retained property' means ALL and WHOLE [*the property being retained by Jack*];
'the disponed property' means ALL and WHOLE the subjects disponed by the foregoing Disposition by Jack . . . in favour of Jill . . . ;
'the disponer' means Jack . . . and his successors as owners of the retained property; and
'the disponee' means Jill . . . and her successors as owners of the disponed property.

Part II: Real burdens affecting the retained property

The following real burdens are imposed on the retained property in favour of the disponed property [*there follow the real burdens in numbered paragraphs*]

Part III: Servitudes affecting the retained property

The following servitudes are imposed on the retained property in favour of the disponed property [*there follow the servitudes in numbered paragraphs*]

Part IV: Real burdens affecting the disponed property

The following real burdens are imposed on the disponed property in favour of the retained property [*there follow the real burdens in numbered paragraphs*]

Part V: Servitudes affecting the disponed property

The following servitudes are imposed on the disponed property in favour of the retained property [*there follow the servitudes in numbered paragraphs*]

The Schedule would be doqueted:

This is the Schedule referred to in the foregoing Disposition by Jack . . . in favour of Jill . . . dated [*date of execution*].

CHAPTER 14

EXECUTION OF DEEDS

Execution on or after August 1, 1995

The law of execution of deeds was recast by the Requirements of 14-01
Writing (Scotland) Act 1995, which applies to all documents executed on
or after August 1, 1995. To a substantial extent, however, the 1995 Act
follows the previous law, and many cases decided under that law
continue to be of relevance.

A summary account of the old law will be found at the end of this
chapter. But for the most part we consider only the law introduced by
the 1995 Act.[1]

Subscribed writings and probative writings

By section 2 of the 1995 Act a deed is valid if it is subscribed by the 14-02
granter. Nothing further is needed. But for conveyancers this will rarely
be enough. If a deed is to be registered in the GRS or the Books of
Council and Session or the sheriff court books it requires to be
"probative".[2] In practice the same rule is also applied to deeds presented
to the Land Register. A probative deed is one which, from its
appearance, is presumed to be validly executed. Under the 1995 Act
there are two routes to probativity. One is to supplement the signature
of the granter with a witness—or some equivalent of a witness.[3] The
other is to apply to the court for a judicial docquet, endorsed on the
deed, to the effect that the deed was subscribed by the granter.[4] In
practice docquets are used almost exclusively for wills,[5] and they will not
be considered further here.[6]

---

[1] For accounts of the 1995 Act see Kenneth G. C. Reid, *The Requirements of Writing
(Scotland) Act 1995* (1995); Robert Rennie and D. J. Cusine, *The Requirements of Writing*
(1995); Currie on Confirmation of Executors (8th ed., by Eilidh M. Scobbie, 1995), Ch.4.
In addition much useful material may be found in the Scottish Law Commission's report
on *Requirements of Writing* (Scot. Law Com. No.112, 1988).

[2] Requirements of Writing (Scotland) Act 1995, s.6(1), (2). Some exceptions are set out
in subs.(3). The word "probative" had a range of meanings under the old law and is
avoided in the 1995 Act, but it is too convenient to abandon.

[3] s.3.

[4] s.4.

[5] A will cannot be used as the basis of an application for confirmation of executors
unless it is probative. See Succession (Scotland) Act 1964, s.21A.

[6] For the procedure, see Act of Sederunt (Requirements of Writing) 1996 (SI
1996/1534).

The relationship between validity and probativity is not always understood. A formally valid deed is one which has been properly executed. This means that it has been subscribed by the granter. A probative deed is one which is presumed to have been subscribed by the granter and hence is presumed to be formally valid.[7] This presumption is of value. After a gap in time the authenticity of deeds can be difficult to prove. But if a deed is probative, no proof need be brought. Rather it is for a person disputing authenticity to prove that the execution was not properly conducted. In practice this means that probative deeds can be relied on. That is one reason why conveyancers use them. Of course even probative writs may sometimes fail. It is possible for a deed to be both probative and invalid. Probativity confers only a presumption of validity, and the presumption can be rebutted. If George forges the granter's signature and then adds his own as a witness, the deed is probative under section 3 of the 1995 Act. But it is also invalid, because the granter did not in fact sign. In practice, however, probative deeds are rarely challenged, and even more rarely with success.

Making probative deeds

14-03　　Two things are required to make a deed probative. First, the granter must have subscribed, or, rather, must seem to have subscribed. And secondly the subscription must be attested by a witness, or, rather, seem to have been so witnessed. Special rules, considered later, apply where the granter is a company or other juristic person.

The granter subscribes

14-04　　The sovereign superscribes, that is to say, signs at the top of deeds.[8] According to Stair this is because "Princes have not the time to peruse the whole body [of the deed], wherein there is much of formality".[9] Everyone else, being members of the more leisured classes, must "subscribe", defined in the 1995 Act as meaning to sign at the end of the last page, but excluding any annexation such as a plan or schedule.[10] With multiple granters there may not be enough room for all of the signatures, in which case it is permissible to sign on an additional page or pages provided at least one granter signs at the end of the deed proper.[11] A person who grants in more than one capacity—for example as both an executor and an individual—need sign only once.[12] In addition to subscription, a will or other testamentary writing requires to be signed at least once on every sheet,[13] and the practice is for the testator to sign at the foot of each page.

Normally a party must sign by forename or initial plus surname.[14] An abbreviated or familiar form of the forename is also acceptable. The

---

[7] See para.14–12.
[8] A rule preserved by s.13(1)(a) of the 1995 Act.
[9] Stair IV, xlii, 3.
[10] s.7(1). For plans and schedules, see below.
[11] s.7(3).
[12] s.7(4).
[13] s.3(2).
[14] s.7(2)(b).

surname must come last. Thus Margaret Agnes Brown (nee Black) could sign as "Margaret Brown" or "Peggy Brown" or "Agnes Brown" or "Maggie Brown" or "Nancy Brown" or "M Brown" or "A Brown" or "M A Brown". Alternatively she could use the surname of "Black". But she could not sign as "Brown M A" (more an educational statement than a signature) or as "N Brown"[15] or "Brown" or "Margaret".[16] As an alternative, the 1995 Act also allows signature by the full name by which the granter is identified in the deed,[17] but this is uncommon in practice. There is no requirement that the signature be the granter's usual signature. Some people have a number of "usual" signatures as well as some which are distinctly unusual. The signature must, however, be legible, for probativity requires that the deed "bears" to have been subscribed by the granter.[18] It is prudent to warn clients of this in advance. A deed bearing an illegible signature will usually be formally valid, as having been subscribed by the granter,[19] but it will not be probative.

Once subscribed, a deed is already formally valid. Adding a witness adds nothing to validity.[20] But without a witness the deed is not probative.

The witness attests

Only one witness is needed. Even a deed with multiple granters can 14–05 make do with a single witness provided that all the granters sign at the same time. In that case the witness need sign only once.[21] But if the granters sign at different times a separate witness[22] is needed for each occasion.

Like the granter, the witness must be of normal legal capacity. This means that the witness must be 16 or over, and mentally capable of acting.[23] A witness can be a grantee of the deed (for example a beneficiary under a will) although this is usually inadvisable as running the risk of challenge on other grounds, such as undue influence. A witness cannot be one of the granters.[24]

The witness attests to two distinct things. The first is the identity of the granter. The witness is required to "know" the granter.[25] But the standard is not exacting, and it is sufficient if the witness has credible information at the time of the witnessing. Prior acquaintance is not

---

[15] "N" is not "an initial of a forename", as required by s.7(2)(b), but an initial of a familiar form of a forename.

[16] However, "Margaret" would be sufficient on non-probative documents (*e.g.* informal wills), provided it could be shown that that was the usual method of signature or was intended as the signature. See s.7(2)(c).

[17] s.7(2)(a).

[18] s.3(1)(a).

[19] s.2. And see *e.g. Stirling Stuart v Stirling Crawfurd's Trs* (1885) 12 R. 610.

[20] Compare here the old law where (except in the case of holograph deeds) a deed was not formally valid until it had been witnessed.

[21] s.7(5). And see also s.3(6).

[22] Who could, in theory, be the same person.

[23] s.3(4)(c)(ii) and (iii).

[24] s.3(4)(b).

[25] s.3(4)(c)(i).

required.[26] It is good practice to ask for some form of identification, such as a passport or driving licence.

Secondly, the witness attests to the fact of subscription. Usually this means watching as the granter signs, but the 1995 Act allows a granter who has already signed to acknowledge the signature to the witness.[27] Acknowledgment is normally by words, but in theory might also be non-verbal.[28] There is no need for the witness to read the deed. The attestation relates to execution and not to content.

The witness must then sign.[29] Although the 1995 Act does not say so, the practice is to sign at the end, and by convention the granter signs on the right-hand side of the page and the witness on the left. The rules about methods of signing are the same as for granters.[30] The signature must occur immediately after the event which is witnessed, as "one continuous process".[31] This is to avoid possible substitution of documents: a witness who signs at once can have no doubts that the correct deed is being signed. Even a short time gap might be treated as fatal.[32] In cases where the signature is acknowledged by the granter, the relevant event is acknowledgment and not the initial signature. Thus a witness can sign 20 years after the granter, so long as the signature follows on immediately from the granter's acknowledgment.

Finally, the witness must be designed, by name and address.[33] Usually the full name is given, although this is more than the 1995 Act requires. The name must be given even in a case where it is clear from the signature itself. A business address is sufficient, and is common in practice. At one time occupations were given,[34] but this is not required by the 1995 Act and the practice is dying out. The designation can be added at any time before the deed is founded on in legal proceedings or registered for preservation in the Books of Council and Session or in sheriff court books.[35] Usually it appears in the testing clause, which is added within a few days of execution.

Sanctions for breach of the witnessing rules

14-06   Since probativity is concerned only with the appearance of a document, it may be asked what sanction exists for breaches of these various requirements, for instance that the witness should know the grantor.

---

[26] s.3(5). There is continuity here with the old law, for which see *Walker v Adamson* (1716) Mor. 16896 and *Brock v Brock*, 1908 S.C. 964.

[27] s.3(7).

[28] *Cumming v Skeoch's Trs* (1879) 6 R. 963; *MacDougall v MacDougall's Exrs*, 1994 S.L.T. 1178; *Lindsay v Milne*, 1995 S.L.T. 487; *McLure v McLure's Exr*, 1997 S.L.T. 127.

[29] s.3(1)(b). Compare s.3(1)(a) which requires that the deed is "subscribed" by the granter.

[30] s.7(5).

[31] s.3(4)(e); and see s.3(6) for cases of multiple granters.

[32] Since the result of invalid attestation was invalid execution, the old law was more forgiving than the new law seems likely to be. See e.g. *Thomson v Clarkson's Trs* (1892) 20 R. 59 (gap of 45 minutes allowed).

[33] s.3(1)(b).

[34] Not always accurately. In *Braithwaite v Bank of Scotland*, 1999 S.L.T. 25 a witness gave his occupation, as a joke, as "consultant gynaecologist".

[35] s.3(3)(a).

After all, even if the witness did not know the granter, the deed is still both probative and—as a witness is not needed for formal validity— valid. If, however, there is a court action and it emerges that there has been a material breach (*e.g.* that the witness did not know the granter) then the deed loses the benefit of the presumption that it was subscribed by the granter.[36] In other words it becomes improbative, thus easing the task of a challenger.[37] Two other possible sanctions must be mentioned. One is that the solicitor who condones a breach may be guilty of professional misconduct, and the other is that the witness may be guilty of a criminal offence.

Testing clause

As its name suggests, a testing clause narrates the details of the 14–07 attestation. Strictly, a testing clause is not required, except where there are alterations in the deed which need to be declared.[38] In practice, one is almost always used, and it contains the designation of the witness, and the date and place of execution.

Since the testing clause contains details of execution, it cannot be finalised until after the deed has been signed. The traditional practice was to finish the deed with the first words of the testing clause ("IN WITNESS WHEREOF"), and then to ensure that the granter and witness left a suitable gap above their signatures for the testing clause to be added later.[39] But quite apart from the awkwardness of asking clients to sign a deed containing a gap, this method was open to the risk of new material being added, without the client's knowledge, after execution had taken place. Its diminishing popularity today, however, is due less to fear of fraud than to the virtual disappearance of the typewriters used for the testing clause. Today it is common for deeds to be printed with an outline testing clause, but with blanks for the date and place of execution and the name and address of the witness, which can be completed (in ink) after execution.

In the case of a disposition, the deed is prepared by the buyers' solicitors but executed by the sellers. Once the final version (the "engrossment") is ready, it is sent to the sellers' solicitor, along with a signing schedule.[40] After it is signed, it is retained by the sellers' solicitor until settlement, when it is handed over to the buyers' solicitor. It is only then that the testing clause is completed, by the buyers' solicitor. The deed is then ready and can be sent to the Register once the appropriate SDLT certificate has been obtained.

---

[36] s.3(4).

[37] See para.14–13.

[38] For alterations see para.14–09.

[39] One might ask why the testing clause is not simply added after the signatures. Originally, the reason was to meet the requirement of the Subscription of Deeds Act 1681 that the designations of witnesses be "in the body of the deed". But while this requirement disappeared as long ago as 1874, the practice remains.

[40] A form on which the date and place of signing and the designation of the witness are to be filled in. Its only purpose is to enable the testing clause to be completed, after which it can be torn up.

Schedules and plans

14–08   Usually schedules and plans are signed by the granter, but this is a
formal requirement only for annexations which contain a visual or verbal
description of land.[41] Under the Act, plans and other visual representations must be signed on each page (if there is more than one), while a
schedule containing a verbal description need be signed only on the last
page. The requirement is for signature and not subscription. The witness
need not sign and in practice does not usually do so. Indeed an
annexation can be signed at a different time from the deed proper,
provided only that it is signed prior to litigation or registration (including
registration in the Land Register or the GRS).[42] But that would be
unusual.

Two further steps are required if the annexation is to be treated as
part of the deed.[43] First, the annexation must be referred to in the deed
itself (*e.g.* "which subjects are hatched and delineated in red on the plan
annexed and subscribed as relative hereto").And secondly, the annexation must contain some kind of identifying tag, to link up with the
reference in the deed. In the Keeper's view, this should normally include
a reference to the parties to the deed and (preferably) to the date: for
example "This is the plan referred to in the foregoing Disposition by
Elizabeth Anne Mackie in favour of James Murray dated August 11,
2004."[44]

There is no requirement that an annexation be physically attached to
the deed, whether by stapling or otherwise, but this may often be good
practice if the two are not to become separated.

Alterations

14–09   Occasionally a deed is altered after it has been typed. Usually this
involves either (1) the deletion of words, whether by erasure or by
scoring out, or (2) the addition of words, whether by writing over words
previously erased or by interlineation or by marginal addition (*i.e.*
additional words written in the margin of the deed).[45] Until the 1980s
alterations were quite common. Now, with word processors in almost
universal use, they are rare, although not unknown.

There is no objection to alterations provided that they were made
before the granter signs. They are then part of the deed as signed by the
granter. No special steps need be taken.[46] By contrast, an alteration
made after execution is not part of the deed and has no legal effect
unless it is separately executed.[47] An obvious difficulty is dating alterations. A person reading a deed a year or two after execution can see the
alteration but has no ready means of discovering when it was made. In

---

[41] s.8(1), (2).

[42] s.8(5).

[43] s.8(1), (2).

[44] See (1995) 40 J.L.S.S. 405.

[45] s.12(1) (definition of "alteration").

[46] Under the old law it was sometimes the practice to sign marginal additions, typically
with the forename of the granter on one side and the surname on the other. But this is not
required under the 1995 Act.

[47] s.5(1).

probative deeds the problem is solved by means of a presumption. If the deed or (in practice) the testing clause contains a declaration that the alteration was made before subscription, the declaration is presumed to be true and the alteration is treated as part of the deed.[48] The presumption can of course be rebutted, but in practice contrary evidence may be hard to come by.[49]

Avoiding mistakes

Things can go wrong in the execution of deeds. For instance, the 14–10 granter might sign in the wrong place or in the wrong way, or the witness might not know the granter or might sign before the granter rather than after. The best way of avoiding mistakes is for the solicitor to supervise the whole process.[50] Where this cannot be done, the client must be sent clear instructions written in a simple and non-technical style. In practice this is often done by a pre-printed schedule of signing particulars, which the client is asked to complete with details of the place and date of signing and the name and address of the witness.

Identifying a deed as probative

Often solicitors have to look at deeds which they had no part in 14–11 executing. An obvious example is in examination of title on the purchase of land. In such cases the solicitor will be concerned to check that the deed is probative. Fortunately, that is easily determined. Probativity is about what appears to have happened rather than about what actually happened. A deed is probative if it appears to have been validly subscribed and witnessed. More precisely, section 3(1) of the 1995 Act provides that a deed is probative ("presumed to have been subscribed by that granter") if four conditions are satisfied. These are (1) that the deed bears to have been subscribed by the granter; (2) that it bears to have been signed by a witness; (3) that it bears to state the name and address of the witness; and (4) negatively, that nothing in the deed indicates that it was not so subscribed and witnessed.

One presumption plus four

If a deed is probative, it is presumed to have been subscribed by the 14–12 granter, and hence (under section 2 of the 1995 Act) to be formally valid.[51] That is the main presumption created by probativity, and its main value. But, depending on the circumstances, subsidiary presumptions may also operate.[52] (1) If the deed gives the date of subscription, the deed is presumed to have been subscribed on that date. (2) If the deed gives the place of subscription, the deed is presumed to have been subscribed at that place.[53] In practice testing clauses invariably give both

---

[48] s.5(4), (5).
[49] By s.5(3) all relevant evidence may be used for this purpose, whether written or oral.
[50] *Lindsay v Milne*, 1995 S.L.T. 487 at 488H *per* Lord Prosser.
[51] s.3(1).
[52] They are, however, contingent on the main presumption—except in the case of testamentary documents—or which see s.3(10).
[53] s.3(8).

the date and place of execution, although the place is usually no more specific than the name of the town or city. (3) If the deed includes an annexation with a visual or verbal description of land (for example, a plan), and the annexation bears to have been signed by the granter, the annexation is presumed to have been so signed.[54] (4) Finally, as already mentioned, any statement in the deed or testing clause that an alteration was made before subscription is presumed to be true, and the alteration is presumed to form part of the deed.[55]

The presumptions are concerned solely with the formalities of execution. There is no presumption that the granter had title, or was mentally capable of making the grant, or, more generally, that the deed is legally effective. A deed may fail for reasons which have nothing to do with execution.

Disputing authenticity

14-13   A person wishing to challenge the authenticity of a probative deed has a choice of approach. One possibility is to attack the deed directly by seeking to prove that the granter did not subscribe. If this can be done the deed is shown to be invalid. The other possibility is to attack the deed indirectly by proving merely that the attestation by the witness was not properly conducted.[56] In that case the deed is not shown to be invalid, but equally it is no longer presumed to be valid.[57] In other words, the deed ceases to be probative, so that a person seeking to found on it must then bring positive proof of its authenticity. After an interval of time that may be an impossible task. Since a deed is not probative in the first place unless it appears to be properly attested, it follows that an attack on the attestation process must depend on factors which are not patent from the deed itself. Section 3(4) of the 1995 Act gives an exhaustive list of such factors. They include: forgery of the witness's signature; non-age and mental incapacity; not knowing the granter; and failure to see the granter sign or acknowledge the signature, and failure to sign immediately thereafter.

Powers of attorney

14-14   A person can authorise someone to sign a deed on his behalf. This is just an application of the law of agency. Common examples are where a person is going to be out of the country for some time, or where a person has become physically or mentally frail.[58]

The usual way of authorising another person to sign is by executing a deed known as a power of attorney,[59] although companies and other

---

[54] s.8(3), read in conjunction with s.3(1).

[55] s.5(4), (5).

[56] The fact that the onus of proof lies with the challenger shows, in effect, the existence of a further presumption that the deed was properly attested.

[57] s.3(4).

[58] Not too mentally frail, for an *incapax* cannot do any juridical act, and thus cannot grant a mandate or agency.

[59] This is the English term, which has now come into general use in Scotland. The traditional term is "factory and commission". For styles see Halliday, *op. cit.*, paras 13–12—3–21.

juristic persons often proceed with less formality, and there is nothing in the 1995 Act which requires writing for the constitution of agency.[60] Where a power of attorney is used, it is normally registered for safekeeping in the Books of Council and Session. A power of attorney executed before April 2, 2001 is unaffected by the subsequent mental incapacity of the principal,[61] but powers granted since that date lapse on incapacity unless they were constituted as continuing powers of attorney under Part 2 of the Adults with Incapacity (Scotland) Act 2000.[62] In order to qualify as a continuing power of attorney within the Act the deed must (i) state that the power is intended to be a continuing power (ii) incorporate a certificate in prescribed form[63] by a solicitor, practising advocate or registered medical practitioner to the effect that the principal understands the nature and extent of the power, and (iii) be registered with the Public Guardian.[64]

Powers of attorney are restrictively construed, at least by conveyancers.[65] The agent has power to do only such things as the deed clearly envisages, and where a deed is signed under a power of attorney, the power of attorney must be examined to establish that the agent was acting lawfully. Where a conveyancing deed is executed under a power of attorney, this power should have been expressly conferred. A person holding a power of attorney cannot normally donate the property, since to do so would be contrary to the duty to act in the interests of the principal.

The *Encyclopaedia of Scottish Legal Styles*[66] gives two different methods of drawing up a deed which is to be signed by an attorney. One is to have the deed run in the name of the attorney. ("I, AB, attorney of CD, conform to Power of Attorney in my favour, etc."). In that case the testing clause runs "IN WITNESS WHEREOF these presents are subscribed by me as attorney foresaid". The other method is not to mention the attorney in the deed (which runs in the name of the principal) but to say in the testing clause "IN WITNESS WHEREOF these presents are subscribed by me the said CD *per* my attorney AB (design) acting under Power of Attorney, etc". In both cases the deed is subscribed by the attorney, in the attorney's own name.[67]

Granter mentally incapable

A continuing power of attorney survives supervening mental inca- 14–15 pacity, as just seen, and the disposition or other deed can be granted by the attorney on behalf of the *incapax*. In the absence of a continuing

---

[60] See in particular s.1(1).

[61] Adults with Incapacity (Scotland) Act 2000, Sch.4, para.4. Previously, only powers of attorney granted on or after January 1, 1991 had this privilege: see Law Reform (Miscellaneous Provisions) (Scotland) Act 1990, s.71 (repealed by the 2000 Act, Sch.6).

[62] Adults with Incapacity (Scotland) Act 2000, s.18. For further details, see Adrian Ward, *Adult Incapacity* (2003), Ch.6.

[63] For which see The Adults with Incapacity (Certificates in Relation to Powers of Attorney) (Scotland) Regulations 2001 (SSI 2001 No.80).

[64] Adults with Incapacity (Scotland) Act 2000, ss.15 and 19.

[65] Halliday, *op. cit.*, para.13–03.

[66] Vol.4, p.166.

[67] s.12(2). There is thus no need, as sometimes happened under the old law, for the attorney to sign in both names ("CD *per* his attorney AB").

power it is necessary to apply to the sheriff court for an intervention order or guardianship order under Part 6 of the Adults with Incapacity (Scotland) Act 2000.[68] This replaces the former procedure of seeking the appointment of a *curator bonis*.[69] The application is required to give a conveyancing description of the property (including the title number if the property is registered in the Land Register), and the sheriff's interlocutor must itself be registered in the Land Register or the GRS.[70] Once appointed, an authorised person (intervenor) or guardian is in the position of an agent, and the disposition or other deed is drawn up and executed in the manner already described in relation to attorneys. Property used as the principal's house cannot be sold without the further consent of the Public Guardian.[71]

Granter blind or unable to write

14–16   A granter who is blind could choose to sign the deed himself or herself, or grant a power of attorney giving authority to sign to someone else.[72] A granter who is not blind but merely unable to write could in theory give oral authority to an attorney,[73] although this invites problems of proof.[74] In practice both categories of granter are likely to use the special procedure set out in section 9 of the 1995 Act. This allows the giving of oral authority to sign, but only to a restricted class of persons— solicitors with practising certificates, advocates, justices of the peace, sheriff clerks, licensed conveyancers (for dispositions and standard securities) and licensed executry practitioners (for testamentary documents).[75] The idea is that those mentioned can be trusted to follow the instructions of the person in question and not to take advantage of the opportunity for fraud. Under the old law, execution by this method was known as notarial execution,[76] but notaries are no longer listed by name in the legislation,[77] except in relation to execution taking place outside Scotland. In practice, the signatories under the section 9 procedure are almost always solicitors.

---

[68] See Adrian Ward, *Adult Incapacity* (2003), Ch.10, and for the conveyancing aspects Reid and Gretton, *Conveyancing 2002*, pp.100–111 (A. J. M. Steven and Alan Barr).

[69] Which is no longer competent: see Adults with Incapacity (Scotland) Act 2000, s.80.

[70] Adults with Incapacity (Scotland) Act 2000, ss.56 (intervention order) and 61 (guardianship order).

[71] Adults with Incapacity (Scotland) Act 2000, s.53(6) (authorised person) and Sch.2, para.6(1) (guardian).

[72] s.9(7).

[73] The 1995 Act neither asserts nor denies that oral authority is competent. But the general rule under the Act is that writing is required only in the cases set out in s.1(2). Powers of attorney are not listed.

[74] Alternatively such a person could sign by mark, which is sufficient for improbative deeds. See s.7(2)(c).

[75] 1995 Act, s.9(6); Public Appointments and Public Bodies etc. (Scotland) Act 2003, s.14(3). Outside Scotland the facility is extended to notaries public and any other person with official authority to execute documents on behalf of persons who are blind or unable to write.

[76] And indeed often still is.

[77] This is because the category is widened from notaries to all solicitors with practising certificates.

Although the section 9 procedure can be used for deeds of all kinds, the typical case is the execution of a will on behalf of an old and frail testator.[78] A deed executed under section 9 can be either probative or improbative, but here we are concerned only with the former.[79] The procedure, which must be strictly adhered to, is as follows:

(i) The granter, solicitor and witness[80] assemble.

(ii) The granter declares that he or she is blind or unable to write.[81] There is no requirement that this statement be true, and no duty on the solicitor to investigate its truth.

(iii) The solicitor reads the document to the granter.[82] If there is a plan or equivalent, the solicitor must describe it—in some cases a challenging task.[83] Both steps can be dispensed with by the granter, even in cases of blindness.

(iv) The granter authorises the solicitor to subscribe.[84] This may be in words, or merely implied from the circumstances.[85]

(v) The solicitor subscribes.[86] In the case of a will a signature is also required on every sheet.[87]

(vi) The witness signs.[88] In signing, the witness attests to steps (3) to (5).[89] The actual subscription must have been observed and there is no question of mere acknowledgment of signature.

(vii) The testing clause is added. It (or the deed proper) must contain a statement that the deed was read (or as the case may be, not read), and that the granter gave the solicitor authority to sign.[90]

Under the pre-1995 law, stages (i) to (vi) required to be carried out as one continuous process,[91] and while this rule is not repeated by the 1995 Act (except in relation to the witness signing immediately after the solicitor),[92] a cautious view would be that the continuity requirement of the former law continues to apply. The final stage (the testing clause) can presumably be completed at any time.

---

[78] Of course the person must be *capax*. Wills are often made by the dying, who may no longer be physically capable of writing.

[79] For improbative deeds (*i.e.* deeds formally valid under s.2), see s.9(1), (2).

[80] s.3(4)(dd). All references to s.3 in the context of this procedure are references to that section as amended by Sch.3.

[81] s.9(1).

[82] s.9(1).

[83] s.9(5).

[84] s.9(1).

[85] s.12(1) (definition of "authorised").

[86] s.9(1).

[87] s.3(2).

[88] s.3(1).

[89] s.3(4)(d), (dd).

[90] s.3(1).

[91] *e.g. Hynd's Tr v Hynd's Trs*, 1955 S.C. (HL) 1.

[92] s.3(4)(e).

A deed which bears to be executed in the manner just described is probative, *i.e.* is presumed to have been validly executed[93] on behalf of the granter.[94]

A solicitor who executes a deed under s. 9 must not take benefit from the deed, and the rule is extended to close relatives (spouse or children). This means that in the case of a will, for example, the solicitor must not be included among the beneficiaries. Any purported conferral of benefit, direct or indirect, is invalid, but the deed is otherwise unaffected.[95]

Companies

14–17   In recent years the law of execution of deeds by companies has changed with bewildering frequency. The following table shows the changes, and the dates from which they took effect.

Execution of Deeds by Companies

Date	*Method of Execution*	*Statutory basis*
October 1, 1874 to June 30, 1948	(i) Subscription of two directors and company secretary + common seal (ii) Subscription in accordance with articles of association[96]	1874 Act, s.56[97]
ditto	(iii) Subscription of one signatory authorised by company + two witnesses	Subscription of Deeds Act 1681
July 1, 1948 to July 30, 1990	(i) Subscription of two directors + common seal (ii) Subscription of one director and company secretary + common seal (iii) Subscription in accordance with articles of association[98]	Companies Act 1947, s.82(1)[99]; Companies Act 1948, s.32(4); Companies Act, 1985, s.36(3)
ditto	(iv) Subscription of one signatory authorised by company + two witnesses	Subscription of Deeds Act 1681

[93] s.3(1).

[94] s.3(4)(dd). The effect of this provision seems to be to create a presumption that the solicitor signed with the authority of the granter. It is, however, troublesome that the presumption mentioned at the end of subs.(4) goes further than the presumption mentioned at the end of subs.(1).

[95] s.9(4). Under the previous law the conferral of benefit invalidated the entire deed.

[96] Some doubt surrounds the validity of this method: see an article published at (1987) 32 J.L.S.S. 148.

[97] This provision came into force on October 1, 1874. It was the first attempt to make special provision for company execution. Later it was restated in successive legislation on companies: see Companies (Consolidation) Act 1908, s.76(3), and Companies Act 1929, s.29(4).

[98] Some doubt surrounds the validity of this method: see an article published at (1987) 32 J.L.S.S 148.

[99] This provision came into force on July 1, 1948: see S.R. & O. 1948 No.439.

July 31, 1990 to November 30, 1990	(i) Subscription of two directors (ii) Subscription of one director and company secretary (iii) Subscription by two signatories authorised by company	Companies Act 1985, s.36B(3)[1]
ditto	(iv) Subscription of one director + one witness (v) Subscription of company secretary + one witness (vi) Subscription of one signatory authorised by the company + one witness (vii) Subscription of one director + common seal (viii) Subscription of company secretary + common seal (ix) Subscription of one signatory authorised by company + common seal	Law Reform (Miscellaneous Provisions) (Scotland) Act 1990, s.72(3)
December 1, 1990 to July 31, 1995	(i) Subscription of two directors (ii) Subscription of one director and company secretary (iii) Subscription of two signatories authorised by company	Companies Act 1985, s.36B(3)[2]
ditto	(iv) Subscription of one signatory authorised by company + two witnesses	Subscription of Deeds Act 1681
August 1, 1995 onwards	(i) Subscription of two directors (ii) Subscription of one director and company secretary (iii) Subscription of two signatories authorised by company (iv) Subscription of one director + one witness (v) Subscription of company secretary + one witness (vi) Subscription of one signatory authorised by company + one witness	Requirements of Writing (Scotland) Act 1995, s.3[3]

[1] As inserted by the Law Reform (Miscellaneous Provisions) (Scotland) Act 1990, s.72(1).

[2] As inserted by the Law Reform (Miscellaneous Provisions) (Scotland) Act 1990, s.72(1).

[3] In relation to companies, s.3 has to be read subject to the amendments in Sch.2, para.3(5) of the 1995 Act.

14-18   It is not necessary to explore here the reasons for these changes. The complex position in 1990 was caused by doubts over the effectiveness of new rules introduced on July 31 of that year.[4] As a result, the rules were replaced before the end of the year, and for a transitional period of four months (July 31 to November 30) two sets of rules were declared, retrospectively, to have been simultaneously in operation. This meant that deeds by companies during that period could be executed in no fewer than nine different ways. The rules were changed again by the 1995 Act, but there is some continuity with the rules previously in force.

The current rules apply to all companies incorporated under the Companies Acts, whether in Scotland or in England and Wales, in any case where the applicable law is the law of Scotland.[5] This covers all deeds which create real rights over Scottish land, even where the granter is an English company. The rules are straightforward. The company has a choice. Like a natural person, it can decide to use a witness. In that case the deed must be subscribed by a person representing the company—a director, the secretary, or an authorised person—and attested by a witness.[6] The usual rules of attestation, described earlier, apply. Alternatively the deed can be subscribed by two representatives of the company, without a witness. This means subscription by (a) two directors or (b) a director and the company secretary or (c) two authorised persons.[7] Mixed doubles are not permitted, so that a deed subscribed by a director and an authorised person would not be probative.[8] There is no requirement that the second representative sign on the same day as the first. Whichever method is used, there is no longer any role for the company seal.

A deed executed in the manner described above is probative, *i.e.* it is presumed to be subscribed by the company. That at least is what the Act says.[9] But the presumption is promptly negatived by a further rule that the person signing is not presumed to be authorised to sign.[10] The net result of these two somewhat inconsistent provisions is probably that the deed is presumed to be signed by the person who bears to sign it, but no more than that; so that a person relying on the deed should check out the signatory's credentials. If the signatory purports to be a director or the secretary, the position is easily verified by a search of the company file. If the signatory purports to be an authorised person, it will be

---

[4] For the background, see articles published at 1990 S.L.T. (News) 241 and 369. In brief, the Companies Act 1989, s.130, introduced s.36B into the Companies Act 1985, effective on July 31, 1990. But the new section was found to be flawed. Accordingly, s.72(1) of the Law Reform (Miscellaneous Provisions) (Scotland) Act 1990, which came into force on December 1, 1990, substituted a new version of s.36B with its operation made retrospective to July 31, 1990.

[5] s.12(1) (definition of "company").

[6] s.3(1).

[7] s.3(1A) as substituted by Sch.2, para.3(5).

[8] Unless either (i) one could be regarded as a witness to the signature of the other or (ii) a director can be regarded as an authorised person. But while not probative, such a deed would be formally valid under s.2 and Sch.3, para.3(1).

[9] s.3(1A) as substituted by Sch.2, para.3(5). For validity see para.25.04.

[10] s.3(1C) as substituted by Sch.2, para.3(5).

necessary to see evidence of authority, for example a power of attorney or board minute.[11]

Less is required for improbative deeds, *i.e.* for deeds which are merely formally valid under section2 of the 1995 Act. A deed granted by a company is formally valid if it is subscribed by a director or the secretary or an authorised person.[12]

Limited liability partnerships

The rules for limited liability partnerships follow those for com- 14–19 panies.[13] Thus an LLP executes deeds through the signature of a member; and the deed is probative as well as merely valid if the signature is witnessed or the deed is signed (without a witness) by two members. But there is no presumption that a person bearing to sign as a member of an LLP was such a member, and the position requires to be verified.

Receivers, administrators and liquidators

Receivers, administrators, and liquidators are authorised by statute to 14–20 execute deeds on behalf of the company.[14] It follows that a deed by a company in receivership, administration or liquidation is formally valid if subscribed by, respectively, the receiver, administrator or liquidator,[15] and is probative if the subscription is attested by a witness.[16]

Partnerships

Partnerships execute deeds through the signature of a partner or some 14–21 other person authorised for this purpose.[17] So, for example, a law firm might authorise a legal assistant to sign missives of sale. Signatories can use either their own name or the name of the firm.[18] As usual under the 1995 Act, bare subscription is enough for formal validity, but probativity requires attestation by a witness.[19] By contrast with the position for companies and LLPs, in a probative deed the authority of the signatory is presumed.[20]

---

[11] Sometimes there may be nothing in writing. The 1995 Act, s.12(1) defines "authorised" as to mean expressly or impliedly authorised. The definition also makes clear that the authority can be given generally, or only in relation to a particular deed.

[12] Sch.3, para.3(1). For the tension between this provision and the rules of company law as to the power of directors, see para.25.3.

[13] 1995 Act, Sch.2, para.3A (inserted by the Limited Liability Partnerships (Scotland) Regulations 2001 (SSI 2001/128), Sch.4, reg.5, para.6).

[14] Insolvency Act 1986, Sch.1, para.9 (administrators), Sch.2, para.9 (receivers), Sch.4, para.7 (liquidators). These provisions are expressly saved by Sch.2, para.3(2) of the 1995 Act.

[15] 1995 Act, s.2.

[16] s.3(1).

[17] Sch.2, para.2(1).

[18] Sch.2, para.2(2).

[19] ss.2 and 3.

[20] The presumption conferred by s.3(1) is that the deed is presumed to be subscribed by "that granter" (*i.e.* the partnership).

Local authorities

14–22   Local authorities execute deeds through the signature of an employee authorised for this purpose (a so-called "proper officer").[21] The deed is probative if either the subscription is witnessed, or the deed is sealed with the common seal of the authority.[22] The authority of the signatory is presumed.[23] A deed which is subscribed without a witness or seal is formally valid but not probative.[24]

Other bodies corporate

14–23   Among the many other juristic persons, not yet mentioned, are building societies, industrial and provident societies, and universities. A small number of these have their own rules of execution contained in the applicable statute or statutory instrument. But in all other cases[25] execution is governed by paragraph 5 of Schedule 2 to the 1995 Act. This provides for subscription by a person representing the body corporate— either a member of the governing body (*i.e.* a director or equivalent), or the secretary, or an authorised person.[26] As usual, bare subscription achieves formal validity but not probativity.[27] For probativity there must also be attestation by a witness, or sealing with the common seal.[28] If sealing is used, it must be carried out on the same day as the signatory signed, and by a person with authority to do so.[29] Authority to sign is not presumed and should be investigated wherever possible.[30]

Foreign companies

14–24   Paragraph 5 of Schedule 2 to the 1995 Act also applies to foreign companies. It should be noted that Scots international private law provides that deeds relating to immoveable property in Scotland must be executed as required by Scots law rather than the law of the place of incorporation or the law of the place of execution.[31] It seems to be the case that execution in terms of the 1995 Act is not only necessary but is also sufficient, so that the deed will be validly executed even if the foreign law would impose a stricter standard.

With foreign companies there are practical difficulties in verifying that those who sign for the company are indeed authorised to do so. A

---

[21] Sch.2, para.4(1). For the definition of "proper officer", see s.12(1).

[22] S.3(1) (as amended, for local authorities, by Sch.2, para.4(5)).

[23] Sch.2, para.4(2). Unusually, the presumption applies even to improbative deeds.

[24] s.2.

[25] Sch.2, para.5(1), (2).

[26] Sch.2, para.5(2).

[27] s.2.

[28] s.3(1) (as amended, for bodies corporate, by Sch.2, para.5(5)).

[29] s.3(4)(h) as substituted by Sch.2, para.5(6).

[30] s.3(1B) as substituted by Sch.2, para.5(5).

[31] Erskine III, ii, 40. For a full discussion see A. E. Anton and P. R. Beaumont, *Private International Law* (2nd ed., 1990), Ch.24.

solution commonly adopted is to obtain a letter from a law firm in that country confirming that the deed has been properly executed.[32]

Excessive informality

It is possible for law to be too simple. If it is too easy to execute deeds, 14–25 there is a danger that people will undertake obligations either unintentionally or with insufficient reflection. The 1995 Act requires no more than a signature at the end of the document. In some cases this may seem too low a threshold. The risk of unintentional obligations greatly exercised solicitors at the time when the 1995 Act was passed. Like other people, solicitors sign their letters; and this gave rise to the fear that letters which were intended to do no more than state a negotiating position would be treated as having formal, contractual effect. Some solicitors reacted by adding at the end of all letters an express statement that no contractual effect was intended (which must often have puzzled their clients). In fact the fear is largely misplaced. The rule is not that all subscribed documents are contractual in effect. Rather it is that contracts in relation to land must be subscribed.[33] Most letters could not conceivably be read as imposing contractual obligations. A docquet of denial is necessary only in the small number of cases where there is genuine danger of misinterpretation.

A more serious criticism is the opportunity for fraud. In many countries, deeds of a certain class require to be executed in front of a notary, who is regarded as a state official. In Scotland deeds have always been executed privately. For a person determined on fraud, the rules in the 1995 Act do not form much of an obstacle. The possibilities here are numerous. The granter's signature could be forged.[34] Or the granter could be persuaded to sign by misrepresentation,[35] or by force and fear,[36] or by the application of undue influence.[37] Another approach would be to allow the granter to sign normally, but then to alter what has been signed. Since the granter only signs at the end (except in the case of probative wills), it would be possible to substitute some of the earlier pages. If the document is too short to have earlier pages, it would still be possible to add text into the space reserved for the testing clause, or to make alterations elsewhere in the deed which are then declared in the testing clause (falsely) to have been added before subscription. There are, of course, some protections. The requirement that a witness must "know" the granter is at least a modest hindrance to forgery (except, of course, where the witness is also the forger). And after execution, deeds are usually handled by solicitors, who are in general trustworthy and can

---

[32] Such a letter is likely to be needed for other purposes, including to confirm that the company was duly incorporated, that it has not been dissolved, that it is not in some form of bankruptcy process, and generally that it has full right and power to grant the deed in question. For a style, see para.25–13.

[33] s.1(2)(a)(i).

[34] *Kaur v Singh*, 1999 S.C. 180.

[35] As often argued in the so-called "cautionary wife" cases such as *Smith v Bank of Scotland*, 1997 S.C. (HL) 111.

[36] *Russo v Hardey*, 2000 G.W.D. 27–1049.

[37] *MacGilvary v Gilmartin*, 1986 S.L.T. 89.

be relied on not to tamper. But the opportunities for fraud remain, and there is evidence that its incidence is increasing.

There are, of course, arguments the other way. A system which depends on execution in front of notaries is likely to be slow and expensive. The Scottish system is fast and cheap. These are important advantages, particularly in the commercial world.[38] Whether these advantages outweigh the drawbacks is a matter on which opinions may differ.

Execution before August 1, 1995

14-26   The 1995 Act applies to deeds executed on or after August, 1, 1995. But in the course of conveyancing it is often necessary to read and evaluate deeds executed before that date. The relevant rules may be summarised briefly.[39]

The normal method of executing a deed was by subscription of the granter and of two witnesses.[40] Such a deed was both formally valid and also probative. At one time the granter was also required to sign each separate sheet,[41] but this rule was abandoned with effect from November 29, 1970, except in the case of wills.[42] The rules for witnessing were broadly the same as they are under the 1995 Act.

In general, a deed was not valid without witnesses. Hence an error in attestation was fatal to the deed.[43] But if the deed was in the handwriting of the granter (*i.e.* "holograph"), or if the signature was preceded by the words "adopted as holograph" in the granter's hand, the deed was formally valid although not probative. The "adopted as holograph" formula was used by solicitors for missives of sale and letters of obligation and its withdrawal is still resented by some. Holograph documents tended to be home-made wills. Conveyancing deeds, then as now, were always attested.

Affidavits and other notarial documents[44]

14-27   An affidavit (also called a deposition) is a declaration made in writing and subscribed by the deponent, and the truth of which is sworn (or affirmed) by the deponent to a notary (or other person authorised by law

---

[38] This is hardly a new thought. In his important work on *Testing of Deeds*, written in 1795, Robert Bell wrote that (pp.3–4) "although we may be forced to acknowledge, that a greater degree of security exists in some of these regulations [on notarial execution in other countries] than our own law admits of, we shall find that they are incumbered with unwieldy forms, and that the publication on which principally their security depended, must have unfitted them for many of the transactions of business; while . . . our own law joins to a sufficient degree of security, a facility and ease in the execution of our deeds, admirably fitted for the purposes of a rich and commercial people".

[39] For a fuller account, see Ch.15 of the first edition of this book.

[40] Subscription of Deeds Act 1681.

[41] Deeds Act 1696.

[42] 1970 Act, s.44. Even in the case of wills, a failure to sign on each sheet could be cured by a petition under s.39 of the 1874 Act, as an informality of execution.

[43] For example, in *Williamson v Williamson*, 1997 S.C. 94 a will was denied effect because one of the witnesses had absent-mindedly signed using the surname of the testator instead of his own surname. Under the 1995 Act the will would have been perfectly valid, as having been subscribed by the testator.

[44] For more detail see (1997) 42 J.L.S.S. 50.

to "receive" affidavits), the notary also signing. In receiving the affidavit the notary is acting as a public official. The law assumes that he will act conscientiously.

Affidavits are not covered by the 1995 Act, but are subject to common law. Witnessing is not necessary, though it is not uncommon, especially for affidavits under the 1981 Act. As far as Scots law is concerned, the notary need not use his or her seal, but if the affidavit is needed in a foreign matter the seal should always be used. If the affidavit consists of more than one sheet, it is probably necessary only that the last sheet be signed, but it is prudent for both notary and deponent to sign every sheet, especially if the affidavit is needed in a foreign matter. Again, if the affidavit is for foreign use the designation of the deponent should be fuller than is customary in Scots law: for instance, the date of birth should be stated.

The notary is professionally bound to be satisfied as to the identity of the deponent, and this duty must be taken seriously, because this lies at the very heart of the notarial system. It is good practice, especially if the affidavit is for foreign use, to append a docquet stating in what manner the notary was satisfied on this matter.[45] The notary is also under a professional duty to be satisfied that the deponent understands the document, which may give rise to problems if there are linguistic difficulties. It is indispensable that the notary should administer an oath or affirmation, for failure to do so renders the affidavit void.[46] There is no fixed form, but "I [swear by Almighty God] [solemnly and sincerely affirm] that to the best of my knowledge and belief the contents of this affidavit are true" is an appropriate style. The usual practice is for the deponent to stand and raise his right hand.[47]

A typical affidavit would begin: "At Dundee on the tenth day of November in the year two thousand and four compeared[48] Mungo Park of 41 St Mary's Road Milnathort in the County of Kinross who being solemnly sworn and examined[49] hereby depones . . ." and would end "all which is truth as the deponent shall answer to God".

Scots law does not make much use of notaries, apart from affidavits, though Scottish notaries will find themselves asked to notarise all sorts of things for foreign use. However, one Scottish document which does need notarisation and which must be mentioned here is the deed of renunciation of occupancy rights under the 1981 Act.[50]

---

[45] *e.g.* "I satisfied myself as to the identity of the deponent by examination of her Spanish passport number 987654321."

[46] *Blair v North British and Mercantile Insurance Co.* (1889) 16 R. 325.

[47] Some notaries ask the deponent to hold a Bible in the left.

[48] *i.e.* appeared.

[49] Meaning that the notary has checked that the deponent understands the meaning of the affidavit.

[50] See Ch.10.

CHAPTER 15

STAMP DUTY LAND TAX

Introduction

15-01   Most conveyancing transactions are subject to stamp duty land tax (SDLT), which replaced stamp duty on December 1, 2003.[1] Stamp duty, long-established if little admired, was a tax on deeds. If there was no deed, no tax was due. Further, stamp duty could not be sued for directly, and its collection depended largely on the rule that a deed not properly stamped would not be accepted for registration in the Land Register or GRS. This meant that if registration was not needed a deed might not be stamped, and even in the case of registrable deeds, such as dispositions, purchasers occasionally preferred the risks of non-registration to the cost of stamp duty. This benign regime is now at an end.[2] SDLT is a tax on transactions and not on deeds. And while, as before, registration requires evidence of payment, the tax is due whether registration takes place or not. Indeed, even if no disposition is ever delivered, SDLT is due on missives alone once possession is taken or the price substantially paid.[3]

Which transactions?

15-02   In principle SDLT is payable on any *land transaction*, that is to say, on the *acquisition* of a *chargeable interest*.[4] "Acquisition" extends to initial creation, transfer, variation and extinction, and the person so acquiring, in this extended sense, is referred to in the legislation as the "purchaser".[5] So a tenant is a purchaser, or the grantee of a minute of waiver of a real burden. A "chargeable interest" is either (i) a right or power in or over land or, more mysteriously, (ii) the benefit of an obligation, restriction or condition affecting (i).[6] The typical chargeable interest is a real right in land, such as ownership, lease, real burden or servitude. The limitation to land will be noted: no SDLT is payable in relation to the sale of goods or the assignation of a life policy.

Even for land there are exceptions. Rights in security, such as standard securities and floating charges, are exempt.[7] So are donations.[8] Thus if

---

[1] See generally Finance Act 2003, Part 4, as amended.
[2] For stamp duty, see Ch.15 of the second edition of this book.
[3] Finance Act 2003, s.44. If a disposition is eventually delivered, it is then a separate land transaction, but the SDLT already paid is set off against any SDLT now due: see s.44(8).
[4] Finance Act 2003, s.43(1).
[5] Finance Act 2003, s.43(3), (4).
[6] Finance Act 2003, s.48(1).
[7] Finance Act 2003, s.48(2)(a).
[8] Finance Act 2003, Sch.3, para.1.

Mrs Smith makes a present of a house to her husband, no SDLT is payable. The same is true if the conveyance is by Mrs Smith's executor, in implement of Mrs Smith's will. For the same reason SDLT is not due on deeds of assumption of trustees or on gratuitous declarations of trust. Further, even if the transaction is not an outright donation, nothing is due unless the consideration reaches the applicable threshold, currently £60,000 in the case of residential property.[9] As a result, some standard transactions are likely to escape payment, including grants of servitude, deeds of conditions, minutes of waiver, and variations of leases. Other exemptions are more esoteric. They include purchases by charities, and certain transactions in connection with divorce.[10] Even if no tax is due, however, it may still be necessary to make a return to the Inland Revenue.[11]

In practice, SDLT is payable mainly in two cases. One is the purchase of land, or of a lease over land. The other is the grant of new lease. Thus, although, strictly, SDLT is not deeds-based, payment is typically prompted by dispositions, by leases, and by assignations of leases. In addition, SDLT is payable in respect of involuntary transactions including acquisitions by statute, by common law, and by court order,[12] but only in the unusual case of consideration being paid.

Like stamp duty before it, SDLT is payable by the purchaser.[13] Purchasers may be unaware of this, or be aware of it but underestimate the amount which will be due. It is important that they are told at the start that the funds to be made available at settlement must include provision for SDLT. Even after such advice some clients resentfully regard SDLT as something charged by "the lawyers" and as such practically indistinguishable from fees.

Rates

Except in the case of the grant of leases, discussed later,[14] SDLT is based on the price paid by the purchaser ("chargeable consideration"), rounded down to the nearest £1.[15] For payments in kind, the relevant figure is the market value of the consideration.[16] As with all taxes, the rates change from time to time, and in recent years there were sharp increases in the rate of stamp duty, now reflected in SDLT. Reduced rates, however, apply to land in disadvantaged areas.[17] At the time of writing the normal rates are: 15–03

---

[9] Strictly this is not an exemption but a case where the relevant rate is, currently, 0 per cent.

[10] Respectively Finance Act 2003, s.68, Sch.8 and Sch.3, para.3.

[11] para.15.12.

[12] Finance Act 2003, s.43(2).

[13] Finance Act 2003, s.85. While this was true as a matter of practice under stamp duty, it is formally so under SDLT.

[14] para.15.09. Special rules are necessary only because the consideration involves rent. The assignation of a lease, however, follows the normal rules.

[15] Finance Act 2003, s.55, Sch.4, para.1.

[16] Finance Act 2003, Sch.4, para.7. For other cases, see Sch.4 generally.

[17] See para.15.11.

Category	Rate
Not more than £60,000 (residential property) or £150,000 (other property)	0%
From £60,001 (residential property) or £150,001 (other property) to £250,000	1%
From £250,001 to £500,000	3%
More than £500,000	4%

It will be seen that, at the lowest rate, residential property is treated less favourably than other property. "Residential property" means a house and its garden, including houses in the process of construction.[18] Where any of the land is not residential, the whole transaction is classified as non-residential and benefits from the lower initial rate.[19] The same is true of a transaction comprising the sale of six or more separate houses.[20]

It would be natural to suppose that the first £60,000 (or £150,000) of the price will be charged at zero, the next slice at 1 per cent, and so on, rather in the way that the income tax band rates are applied, so that if a house were sold at £80,000 the duty would be (0 per cent × £60,000) + (1 per cent × £20,000) = £200. That would be reasonable. It is not the law.[21] If a house is sold for £50,000 the duty is zero. If a house is sold for £80,000, the duty is £800. If a house is sold for £245,000, the duty is £2,450. If a house is sold for £255,000 the duty is £7,650. Thus, a 4 per cent increase in price (from £245,000 to £255,000) results in a 212 per cent increase in the tax payable. Hence, when a property is near one of the band boundaries, the exact price can assume considerable significance.[22]

Value added tax

15-04   In cases where value added tax (VAT) is payable on the price, the price is grossed up for SDLT purposes to include the VAT.[23] There is thus a tax on a tax. VAT may be payable in two main types of case. One is the sale of new,[24] non-domestic property. The other is the sale (or lease) of older non-domestic property, but only if the seller (or lessor) has waived exemption from VAT. Where exemption is waived only after

---

[18] Finance Act 2003, s.116(1). Some special rules, *e.g.* for student halls of residence, are given in s.116(2), (3).

[19] Finance Act 2003, s.55(2).

[20] Finance Act 2003, s.116(7).

[21] Except for the SDLT due on rent under leases, for which see para.15.10.

[22] All taxes result in distortions of the economic activities which they feed on, and SDLT is certainly no exception. Keeping SDLT to a minimum can be a major issue in commercial transactions. A sale of land for £5 million is impossible unless £200,000 can be found to pay the Inland Revenue.

[23] Finance Act 2003, Sch.4, para.2.

[24] Meaning not more than three years old.

settlement,[25] SDLT is not payable on the resulting VAT.[26] Although VAT is an important question in conveyancing, it is essentially a matter for commercial conveyancing, and so will not be further dealt with here.

Linked transactions

Parties might seek to avoid SDLT by packaging a large transaction 15–05 into a series of small ones, the price for each part being less than one of the threshold figures. This obvious evasion is prevented by the idea of linked transactions. Where transactions are linked, they are treated as a single transaction, and SDLT is paid on the total price.[27] Transactions are "linked" in the required sense "if they form part of a single scheme, arrangement or series of transactions between the same vendor and purchaser or, in either case, persons connected with them".[28] So if Alan sells Barbara a house for £200,000, SDLT cannot be avoided by having (for instance) four separate dispositions of one quarter *pro indiviso* shares, each with a price of £50,000. And given the wide definition of connected persons,[29] the same is probably true if some of the sales involve spouses, siblings or in-laws rather than Alan and Barbara themselves.

Sale of house with contents

Where a house or other building is sold together with moveable items 15–06 such as carpets, the moveables are not part of the price for SDLT purposes.[30] Therefore, only that part of the price applicable to the heritage should be given as the price in the disposition. Missives often provide how the total price in a sale should be apportioned as between heritage and moveables, and the legislation requires that such apportionment be "on a just and reasonable basis".[31] Nonetheless the temptation may be to overstate the value of the moveables, so that SDLT is reduced or even (if the figure can be brought below £60,000) eliminated. This temptation should be resisted. A contract which falsely apportions price as between heritage and moveables might be unenforceable as contrary to public policy.[32] At any rate it is probably professional misconduct on the part of the solicitor.[33] And the fraudulent evasion of SDLT is an offence punishable by up to seven years' imprisonment.[34] Whilst, however, a false apportionment is unacceptable, "no man in this country is under the smallest obligation, moral or other, so to arrange his legal relations to his business or to his property as to enable the Inland

[25] *i.e.* the "effective date of the transaction", discussed in para.15.13.
[26] Finance Act 2003, Sch.4, para.2.
[27] Finance Act 2003, s.55(4).
[28] Finance Act 2003, s.108(1).
[29] Section 108(1) incorporates the definition in the Income and Corporation Taxes Act 1988, s.839.
[30] See para.15.02.
[31] Finance Act 2003, Sch.4, para.4(1).
[32] *Saunders v Edwards* [1987] 2 All E.R. 651, esp. at p.665 *per* Nicholls L.J.
[33] *ibid.*
[34] Finance Act 2003, s.95.

Revenue to put the largest possible shovel into his stores".[35] Drawing the line between a false, and a merely generous, estimate of the value of the moveables can be difficult, both morally and legally.

Sale of a business

15–07   In commercial cases, different types of property may be sold in the course of the same transaction, for example, land, goodwill, receivables, stock in trade, and so on. SDLT is payable only in respect of land.[36]

Options

15–08   The grant of an option to buy land is itself a land transaction separate from its ultimate exercise.[37] So if A Ltd has an option to purchase land from B Ltd for £1 million, and if the option itself carried a price of £200,000, the result is two separate land transactions: the grant of the option, and the eventual disposition by B Ltd to A Ltd. The fact that the option is taxable prevents avoidance of SDLT by ascribing to the option a price which is really part of the price for the land.

Excambions

15–09   Where Alan and Beth agree to excamb (*i.e.* exchange) land this can be effected either by two separate dispositions, or by a single deed (known as a contract of excambion) in which Alan conveys to Beth and Beth conveys to Alan. Whichever method is chosen, SDLT is payable on the value of each property.[38] For instance, if Alan dispones to Beth a property worth £270,000, and Beth dispones to Alan a property worth £240,000 plus £30,000 in cash, SDLT will be payable on the first transaction at 3 per cent and on the second transaction at 1 per cent. This unfavourable outcome is modified where a person buys a new house from a house-building company and pays partly by the exchange of his existing house. No SDLT is then payable on the conveyance of the existing house.[39]

Leases

15–10   Leases are taxed both on the rent and on any premium paid for the grant of the lease. The position of the premium is straightforward. SDLT is paid at the rates already described[40] except that, where the annual rent exceeds £600, the 0 per cent band is replaced by 1 per cent.[41]

Rent is, by its nature, more difficult to tax. Stamp duty was payable on the annual rent but on a scale which rose with the duration of the lease.

---

[35] The immortal words of Lord President Clyde in *Ayrshire Pullman Motor Services v Commissioners of Inland Revenue* (1929) 14 T.C. 754.

[36] para.15.02.

[37] Finance Act 2003, s.46. The same rule applies to pre-emptions reserved by the seller, although in practice there will either be no consideration or one too small to attract SDLT.

[38] Finance Act 2003, s.47, Sch.4, para.5(3).

[39] Finance Act 2002, s.58. There are some qualifications.

[40] para.15.03.

[41] Finance Act 2003, Sch.5, para.9.

SDLT applies a uniform scale, but to the total rent payable during the lease, discounted at 3.5 per cent a year in respect of future payments.[42] This is known as the *net present value* of rent. Rent reviews are disregarded if five or more years from the start of the lease.[43] There is a threshold, for the net present value, of £60,000 for residential property and £150,000 for land which is not wholly residential.[44] If the net present value is below the threshold no SDLT is payable. If it is above the threshold, SDLT is payable at 1 per cent but only to the extent that the threshold is exceeded.[45] So for example if the net present value of the rent for a shop is £250,000, the SDLT due is £1000 (1 per cent of £100,000).

In practice, a lease often takes the form of missives of let, which may or may not ultimately be followed by a formal lease. If possession is taken and rent paid on the basis of missives, SDLT is payable as if it were a formal lease. A subsequent grant of a lease might be a notifiable transaction[46] but no further tax would be due.[47]

Disadvantaged areas

As latterly under stamp duty, transactions in so-called disadvantaged 15-11 areas are given quite substantial relief from tax. Disadvantaged areas in Scotland are identified by postcode, and in cases of doubt it is important to check whether a property qualifies.[48] In disadvantaged areas no SDLT at all is payable in respect of non-residential properties, while for residential properties the threshold for tax is raised from £60,000 to £150,000 although higher bands are unaffected.[49] Where property is partly residential and partly non-residential, the consideration falls to be apportioned as between the two categories and SDLT is payable only on as much consideration as is attributable to residential property.[50]

Notifiable transactions

A key distinction is between those transactions which must be notified 15-12 to the Inland Revenue and those which need not. It would be natural, but mistaken, to suppose that this is the same as the distinction between

---

[42] Finance Act 2003, Sch.5, paras 2, 3, and 8. Para.6 contains rules for calculating the terms of a lease.

[43] Finance Act 2003, Sch.17A, paras 7(3) and 14.

[44] For the meaning of residential property in this context, see para 15.03.

[45] Finance Act 2003, Sch.5, para.2, as amended by the Stamp Duty Land Tax (Amendment of Schedule 5 to the Finance Act 2003) Regulations 2003 (SI 2003/2914), Sch, para.1. This use of the threshold is in contrast to that which applies in sales: see para.15-03.

[46] For notifiable transactions, see para.15.12.

[47] Finance Act 2003, s.44.

[48] The legislation has adopted the list of disadvantaged areas already made for the purposes of stamp duty by The Stamp Duty (Disadvantaged Areas) Regulations 2001 (SI 2001/3747). See Finance Act 2003, Sch.6, para.2. The complete list is given in Reid and Gretton, *Conveyancing* (2001), pp.41-3. Postcodes can also be checked against http://www.inlandrevenue.gov.ukso/pcode_search.htm.

[49] Finance Act 2003, Sch.6, paras 4 and 5. For leases the threshold is raised also in respect of the net present value of rent. For the meaning of "residential property" see s.116.

[50] Finance Act 2003, Sch.6, para.6.

transactions which attract tax and transactions which do not. Admittedly no SDLT is due in respect of transactions where notification is not required, but by no means all transactions which are notifiable will involve the payment of tax. This is a trap for the unwary. It should not be assumed that because no tax is due, no return need be made to the Revenue.

The transactions which are notifiable are:[51]

    (i) the transfer of ownership or of a lease for consideration;[52]
    (ii) the grant of a lease for seven years or more;
    (iii) and any other transaction if SDLT is due, or would be due but for a relief.

Thus all dispositions must be notified other than those in implement of a gift. The position is the same for assignations of leases. A new lease must always be notified if for seven years or more. Otherwise notification is necessary only where SDLT is due or would be due but for a relief (such as disadvantaged areas relief, mentioned above). In practice the consideration for most other transactions will fall below even the lowest threshold for tax (currently £60,000) and so will not be notifiable. Common examples will include deeds of trust, minutes of waiver, deeds of conditions, deeds of servitude, and deeds of assumption and conveyance of trustees. And of course no notification is required in respect of deeds, such as standard securities, which are wholly exempt from SDLT.[53]

Administrative arrangements depend on classification. If a transaction is notifiable, a land transaction return must be sent to the Revenue. If it is not notifiable, but it leads to registration, a self-certificate is needed. Both routes must now be considered in greater detail.

Land transaction returns

15–13   A transaction which is notifiable is duly notified by sending to the Inland Revenue a land transaction return accompanied by payment of any tax that is due.[54] This must be done within 30 days of the "effective date of the transaction", normally the date on which the transaction is settled.[55] The obligation rests on the purchaser, lessee, or other grantee of the deed.[56] If two people are buying together—a husband and wife, for example—each is liable jointly and severally.[57] There are penalties for late notification and interest is due in the event of late payment.[58]

The basic land transaction return (SDLT 1) runs to six pages.[59] While the long-term aim is for electronic submission, at present the return

---

[51] Finance Act 2003, s.77.
[52] Except where the consideration for residential property does not exceed £1000: see Finance Act 2004.
[53] para.15.02.
[54] Finance Act 2003, ss.76(1), (3), 86(1).
[55] Finance Act 2003, ss.119 and 121 (meaning of "completion").
[56] "Purchaser" is given an extended meaning by Finance Act 2003, s.43(4).
[57] Finance Act 2003, s.103.
[58] Finance Act 2003, ss.87 and Sch.10, paras 3–5.
[59] For that, and other, forms, see the Stamp Duty Land Tax (Administration) Regulations (SI 2003 No.2837), reg.9 and Sch.2.

must be completed in black ink and sent or delivered to the Inland Revenue, SDLT, Netherton, Merseyside L30 4RN. Other forms are used for more complex transactions. For example, SDLT 3 must be used where the property has no postal address, and SDLT 4 for grants of lease or where the purchaser is a company. The return includes a declaration, signed by the purchaser, that it is correct and complete to the best of his or her knowledge.[60] If there is more than one purchaser, each must sign,[61] although in the case of trustees the signature of a single trustee is sufficient.[62] A company signs through its secretary or other person with authority,[63] and a partnership through all its partners or a representative partner nominated by a majority.[64] It is thought that an agent can sign if duly authorised by a power of attorney.[65] After submission, the return and payment are checked by the Revenue and, if everything is in order, an official certificate (SDLT 5) is issued. Without the certificate the deed cannot be registered in the Land Register, GRS, or Books of Council and Session.[66]

There has been considerable disquiet in the legal profession in relation both to the complexity of the forms, and to the delay which they involve. This is at least partly because stamp duty was form-free and allowed immediate payment, in some cases over the counter. The concern is particularly about the enforced delay in registration. Unlike in England and Wales, where a constructive trust comes into effect, a purchaser of land in Scotland is vulnerable to the insolvency of the seller during the period between payment of the price and registration of the disposition or other deed.[67] The longer the delay in registration, the greater the vulnerability. The Revenue has responded to these concerns by allowing personal presentation of the return at the Stamp Office in Edinburgh but limited, usually, to cases where no letter of obligation has been issued by the sellers' solicitors or the letter excludes searches in the Companies Register. Presentation must be made within two working days of the effective date of the transaction. A handwritten SDLT certificate is issued.[68] In other cases the classic letter of obligation covers a period of 21 days after settlement, which should give enough time for receipt of the certificate and registration.

Self-certificates

For transactions which are not notifiable, no land transaction return is 15–14 made and no certificate issued. But a certificate is still required if the deed is to be registered. This is a "self-certificate", a certificate by the

---

[60] Finance Act 2003, Sch.10, para.1(1)(c).

[61] Finance Act 2003, s.103(4).

[62] Finance Act 2003, Sch.16, para.6.

[63] Finance Act 2003, s.100(2).

[64] Finance Act 2003, Sch.15, paras 6 and 8.

[65] That assumption, at least, is made by the Inland Revenue. See *SDLT Bulletin 6* (available on *http://www.inlandrevenue.gov.uk/so/bulletin6.pdf*).

[66] Finance Act 2003, s.79.

[67] Now confirmed by the House of Lords in *Burnett's Tr v Grainger*, 2004 S.L.T. 513.

[68] For the Revenue's statement, see Reid and Gretton, *Conveyancing 2003*, pp.147–9.

purchaser, in the prescribed form, that no land transaction return is required in respect of the transaction.[69] The self-certificate must be signed by the purchaser, or all the purchasers if more than one.[70] The rules for trustees, partnerships and companies are the same as for land transaction returns.[71]

---

[69] Finance Act 2003, s.79(3)(b) and Sch.11, para.2. The prescribed form is contained in the Stamp Duty Land Tax (Administration) Regulations (SI 2003/2837), reg.8 and Sch.1.
[70] Finance Act 2003, s.103(4).
[71] And are discussed in para.15.13.

CHAPTER 16

POST-SETTLEMENT CLAIMS

Introduction

This chapter deals with claims which may arise after settlement of a   16–01
transaction has taken place. The subject has three aspects. The first is
whether, after settlement, the missives can to any extent still be founded
on as a basis for a claim. The second aspect, which relates only to defects
and limitations in the title, is whether a claim can be made under the
warrandice clause in the disposition. The third aspect is whether it may
be possible to have the disposition, or other deed, judicially rectified.
The third aspect is considered in the next chapter.

CLAIMS UNDER MISSIVES

Up to 1997

The law was changed fundamentally by the Contract (Scotland) Act   16–02
1997, but something must first be said about the pre-1997 law, as
essential background to the current law and practice.

At common law there was a rule that missives were superseded by the
disposition.[1] Thus Lord Watson in *Orr v Mitchell*: "Where a disposition
in implement of sale has been delivered to and accepted by a purchaser
it becomes the sole measure of the contracting parties' rights, and
supersedes all previous communings and contracts however formal."[2] Or,
as Lord Meadowbank put it: "When communings and correspondence
result in regular title deeds, you are to consider everything previous to
the actual title as burnt."[3] The scope of the doctrine was, however, as
unclear as its doctrinal basis. The general view was that it applied only to
those matters which were common to both the missives and the
disposition. Thus, if the boundaries differed, the disposition prevailed.[4]
But as to matters about which the disposition was silent, the missives
remained in force: matters of this sort were called "collateral". But the
1981 decision of the Second Division in *Winston v Patrick*,[5] threw

---

[1] For further discussion of the pre-1997 law, see pp.334–343 of the first edition of this
book, and also: Reid (1981) 26 J.L.S.S. 414; Scottish Law Commission, *Report on Three
Bad Rules in Contract Law* (Scot. Law Com. No.152, 1996).

[2] (1893) 20 R. (HL) 27. See also *Lee v Alexander* (1883) 10 R. (HL) 91.

[3] *Hughes and Hamilton v Gordon*, June 15, 1815, Fac. Coll.

[4] Even this was by no means certain: see *Anderson v Lambie*, 1954 S.C. (HL) 43.

[5] 1980 S.C. 246, 1981 S.L.T. 41.

everything into confusion. Few cases have ever caused such consterna-
tion amongst conveyancers. The case[6] decided that collateral obligations
did not, after all, survive the delivery of the disposition, or, at least, that
while some of them might, others did not. Conveyancers responded to
Winston by adding to missives a clause declaring that they would *not* be
superseded by the subsequent disposition, but would remain in force for
a certain period (usually two years). But there was a logical difficulty
here: the supersession doctrine, in killing the missives, would kill the
non-supersession clause contained therein. And the courts duly so held,
at any rate in some cases.[7] So conveyancers came back and began to add
the non-supersession clause to the disposition as well, though even this,
according to some decisions, was ineffective.

   Winston was obscure, and the whole subject grew yet more obscure as
other decisions rapidly accumulated in the law reports attempting to
explain it, generally unsuccessfully and sometimes contradicting each
other. It would have been easy, if unrewarding, to write an entire book
on this subject, which, in its mix of labyrinthine complexity, conceptual
incoherence and practical unworkability quickly became a disgrace to the
Scottish conveyancing system. It is a matter for regret that the Inner
House, or House of Lords, never had the opportunity to reconsider
Winston (or indeed the earlier authorities) and thus rationalise the law.
The job had to be done by legislation in the shape of the Contracts
(Scotland) Act 1997.

1997 onwards

16–03   Section 2 of the Contract (Scotland) Act 1997 provides that

> "where a deed is executed in implement . . . of a contract, an
> unimplemented, or otherwise unfulfilled, term of the contract shall
> not be taken to be superseded by virtue only of that execution or of
> the delivery and acceptance of the deed."

Thus, the supersession doctrine, which had caused such chaos, was killed
off in a single sentence.

   Of course, despite this radical simplification and rationalisation,
problems may still arise. Suppose, for instance, that the extent of the
property as identified in the missives is different from that identified in
the disposition. This often happens as a mistake, and it is the missives
which reflect the true agreement. In that case the disposition can be
rectified under section 8 of the Law Reform (Miscellaneous Provisions)
(Scotland) Act 1985.[8] But sometimes there is no mistake and the
disposition does indeed represent the final intentions of the parties. In
cases such as this the 1997 Act should not be construed as meaning that
the missives prevail over the disposition. In a practical sense the 1997
Act deals chiefly not with such cases, but with collateral obligations, such

---

[6] Which concerned a missive clause about local authority consents.

[7] It is typical of the confusion in this area that other decisions took exactly the opposite
view.

[8] See Ch.17.

as those concerning moveables, the physical condition of the property, and local authority consents.

After *Winston,* non-supersession clauses generally had a cut-off period, typically two years. If the purchasers wished to sue the sellers for breach of some missive clause, they had to do so within that time. The period was a compromise one. The sellers would, in most cases, like to be free of the contract as soon as they received the money, while the buyers usually wanted time to find out whether the sellers' obligations had been properly implemented.[9] Since the 1997 Act, non-supersession clauses have come to be replaced by supersession clauses. The point is this: missives will now presumptively remain in force notwithstanding settlement. That suits the buyers. But the sellers are likely to be unhappy at the idea that they will remain liable, potentially,[10] until negative prescription has run in their favour. Hence the old compromise is still what parties want: a two-year enforceability period. But, whereas in the old days that was to be achieved by contracting *against* supersession for the two-year period, now it is to be achieved by contracting *into* supersession *after* two years.[11] Such a clause might run:

> "The missives of sale may not be founded upon[12] after a period of two years from the date of entry hereunder[13] except in so far as they are founded on in any court proceedings which have commenced within that period."

In the old days such a clause would normally be part of the original offer, since it was more likely to be the buyer than the seller who wanted the clause. Nowadays the position is reversed: the clause is more likely to be for the benefit of the seller than the buyer, and so if the offer omits it, the qualified acceptance should normally contain it. It is clear from the 1997 Act that the clause need appear only in missives,[14] and there is nothing to be gained from repeating it in the disposition.

This two-year period seems in most cases to be satisfactory, but sometimes it turns out to be too short. This is particularly likely to happen if there is a missive clause dealing with a question which is likely to take some time to resolve. For instance, it may be that the sellers had

---

[9] Since most obligations in missives are the sellers', the continued enforceability of missives is chiefly for the benefit of the buyers. But in some cases they can be for the benefit of the sellers, though more often in commercial sales than domestic ones.

[10] Of course, in most cases there never will be any actual liability since the sellers will have fully performed all their obligations.

[11] The lawfulness of supersession clauses is recognised by s.2(2) of the Contract (Scotland) Act 1997.

[12] Or "shall cease to be enforceable." For the term "enforceable" in this context see *Smith v Lindsay & Kirk,* 1998 S.L.T. 1096, revised 2000 S.C. 200. See further Reid and Gretton, *Conveyancing 1999,* p.41.

[13] Does this mean contractual date of entry or actual date of entry? See para.3–25(7). If the clause fails to specify when the clock starts to tick, it may be invalid: *Lonergan v W. & P. Food Service Ltd,* 2002 S.L.T. 908.

[14] 1997 Act, s.2(2): the rule that missives survive "is without prejudice to any agreement which the parties to a contract may reach (whether or not an agreement incorporated into the contract) as to the supersession of the contract." Formerly repetition in the disposition was required because the rule was that missives did not survive.

agreed to pay for certain remedial construction work. It is notorious that building work often takes longer than expected. In such cases the buyers' solicitors should seek to negotiate a longer period, and, if this proves impossible, must ensure that the two-year period does not slide by without the appropriate action being taken. *Hamilton v Rodwell*[15] is an illustration of how things can go wrong. Here the seller was bound to pay for certain repairs, and part of the price was put on joint deposit receipt, which would be payable to the seller once he had done so. The seller never did pay for the repairs, and the purchasers had to. They accordingly claimed the sum in the D/R. But by this time the two-year period had elapsed and the missives were unenforceable. It was held that the purchasers had no right to the money. (But where this left the money is obscure, since one could equally argue that, since the missives had expired, the seller had no right to it either.)[16]

Finally, it should be noted that a supersession clause cannot be attacked on the ground that it is an attempt to contract out of the law of prescription.[17]

WARRANDICE CLAIMS UNDER THE DISPOSITION[18]

Introduction

16-04   Warrandice is a guarantee, expressed or implied, of good and unencumbered title. In dispositions there are three degrees of warrandice,[19] which are, in ascending order, simple, fact and deed, and absolute. The higher includes the lower, so that if a claim could be made under simple warrandice, it could also be made under fact and deed warrandice, and if a claim could be made under fact and deed warrandice, it could also be made under absolute warrandice.

Simple warrandice

16-05   Simple warrandice is a guarantee that the granter will do nothing subsequently to prejudice the title of the grantee. The content of this guarantee is minimal, for in most cases there is nothing that a granter could do to incur liability. If Ann dispones to Beth with simple warrandice, Ann can thereafter do nothing to affect the title, because Ann is no longer owner. Simple warrandice would however cover the following case. Ann grants a disposition to Beth on Monday, and fraudulently grants another disposition of the same property to Chris on

---

[15] *Hamilton v Rodwell*, 1998 S.C.L.R. 418; *Hamilton v Rodwell (No.2)*, 1999 G.W.D. 35–1706. See Reid and Gretton, *Conveyancing 1999*, p.4.

[16] For another illustration see *Albatown Ltd v Credential Group Ltd*, 2001 G.W.D. 27–1102, discussed in Reid and Gretton, *Conveyancing 2001*, p.63.

[17] Thus, it was held for non-supersession clauses, and the same logic seems to apply to supersession clauses. See *Ferguson v. McIntyre*, 1993 S.L.T. 1269.

[18] The fullest account is Reid, in D.J. Cusine (ed.), *Scots Conveyancing Miscellany: Essays in Honour of Professor J. M. Halliday* (1987). See also Reid, *Property*, paras 701–719.

[19] In addition there is warrandice *debitum subesse* which is implied in onerous assignations of debt. This is a guarantee that at the date of the assignation the debt is payable to the cedent.

Tuesday. Chris completes his title by registration on Wednesday. Assuming that Chris has acted in good faith, Beth has no remedy against Chris. But Beth can claim from Ann on the footing of warrandice, even simple warrandice.

Fact and deed warrandice

Fact and deed warrandice is a guarantee that the granter will do and has done nothing which could prejudice the title of the grantee. It thus covers what simple warrandice covers, but also covers past acts by the granter as well. Take the previous example and suppose that Beth had completed title first. Would Chris then have a claim against Ann? Not under simple warrandice, because the disposition by Ann to Beth was, at the time when Ann granted warrandice to Chris, not a future act but a *past* one. But if the warrandice by Ann to Chris was fact and deed warrandice, Chris would have a claim against Ann.   16–06

Absolute warrandice

Absolute warrandice guarantees the grantee against defects and limitations in the title whether caused by the granter or not. Thus, suppose that Ann dispones to Beth a farm, with absolute warrandice. It later turns out that title to one area of ground is bad, this area actually being part of the title of the neighbouring farm, though in terms of possession being part of the first farm. The reason for this is that the previous owner—Ann's predecessor—had sold several hectares to the neighbour, including the area in question, but that due to the wrong positioning of a fence the area remained in the possession of the first farm. Ann is liable to Beth in warrandice. She would not have been liable if she had granted to Beth only simple, or fact and deed, warrandice, because the defect did not arise from her own act.   16–07

Wording of warrandice clause

In practice, the warrandice is always expressed in the conveyance, usually as the final clause before the testing clause. The forms are: "I grant simple warrandice"; "I grant warrandice from my own facts and deeds"; "I grant warrandice". The last of these means absolute warrandice.[20]   16–08

Which type of warrandice?

If there is no warrandice clause, the law will imply one. In outline, the rule is that simple warrandice is implied in conveyances by way of gift, and absolute warrandice is implied in sales. But implied warrandice is overridden by express warrandice. Thus, if a disposition by way of sale grants simple warrandice only, the implication of absolute warrandice is excluded.   16–09

In sales by trustees or executors the practice is to grant fact and deed warrandice personally, and to bind the trust (or executry) estate in

---

[20] Titles to Land Consolidation (Scotland) Act 1868, s.8.

absolute warrandice. The practice in sales by heritable creditors is similar. The creditor grants fact and deed warrandice personally and binds the debtor (the former owner) in absolute warrandice.[21]

Missives do not usually make provision about warrandice. The grantee is in that case entitled to the type of warrandice which is implied or is normally granted in transactions of that type. If there is anything dubious about the title, or part of it,[22] a decision needs to be made at missives stage about what sort of warrandice should be granted, and this will simply mirror what the missives themselves provide about good and marketable title. Sometimes a property with a doubtful title is sold for full value: in such cases the warrandice should normally be absolute. But if the queries about the title mean that the parties have bargained for a significantly below-market price, then the warrandice should normally be fact and deed warrandice only, for in this latter case it is the buyer who is assuming the risk. Sometimes absolute warrandice is granted unthinkingly even if the missives provide that title is to be taken as it stands.

Remedies under warrandice

16–10   Warrandice is enforced by a claim for damages. If the defect in title is such that the disponee loses the property entirely, the quantum of damages is the market value of the property. If the defect is a lesser one, the quantum is the diminution in market value. Thus, suppose that Ann dispones a house to Beth, and it then emerges that the garden ground is burdened by a servitude of way in favour of a neighbouring property. In a warrandice claim, the court will hear evidence as to what the market value would have been if the servitude had not existed, and as to the actual market value subject to the servitude. The difference is then the. measure of Beth's loss and of Ann's liability to Beth.[23] Probably no claim can be entertained for solatium.[24]

What does warrandice cover?

16–11   Warrandice is generally said to be a guarantee that the title is (i) good and (ii) unencumbered, and this is true as far as it goes. But no liability under warrandice can arise in respect of the first of these guarantees unless and until there has been judicial eviction,[25] that is to say a decree declaring the existence of a better right in some third party.[26] However,

---

[21] It is arguable that a purchaser should ask for absolute warrandice from the selling creditor: see para.19–37.

[22] For it is perfectly competent to grant absolute warrandice for part of the property disponed and lesser warrandice for some other part.

[23] The leading case is *Welsh v Russell* (1894) 21 R. 769.

[24] *Palmer v Beck*, 1993 S.L.T. 485 *per* Lord Kirkwood at p.492.

[25] The word "eviction" is perhaps misleading, and it must accordingly be borne in mind that it has a special meaning in the context of the law of warrandice. The word has been used in this special sense for time immemorial.

[26] *Clark v Lindale Homes Ltd*, 1994 S.C. 210, one of the most important cases on the law of warrandice. See also *Palmer v Beck*, 1993 S.L.T. 485. If the action is settled without decree, there is still eviction provided that there was no good defence: *Watson v Swift's J.F.*, 1986 S.L.T. 217.

it seems that there are some differences in the way the doctrine works in the Land Register as opposed to the GRS. In the GRS a person may have a recorded title to property, but that title may be void in part or whole. But in the Land Register that cannot normally happen. Since title flows from the Register itself, if the Keeper accepts an application, the person registered will in general actually have the registered rights. Hence with the Land Register the law is probably that the test for "eviction" is whether or not the Register is actually rectified against the disponee.[27] If it is rectified, the disponee has pretty clearly been "evicted", but unless and until this occurs the disponee still has what was disponed (because title flows from the Register) even if the Register is inaccurate. However, the general principle just stated, if correct, leaves at least two further questions open. One is what happens if the Keeper refuses to register the disponee, either wholly or in part. There can be little doubt that that would amount to "eviction". The other is what happens if the Keeper accepts the application, but with exclusion of indemnity. In that case there is probably no "eviction" in the relevant sense for the reasons already given. However, in this case there will usually be a concurrent claim under the missives, for which see below.

So far what has been discussed has been the first aspect of warrandice, namely that the title shall be good. The guarantee as to unencumbered title is somewhat different. In this case, eviction is not required to trigger liability. A claim under warrandice can be made in respect of any encumbrance which was unknown to the purchaser at the time when warrandice was granted.[28] The second point requires emphasis. Thus, if land is subject to a servitude in favour of a neighbour, and the grantees were aware of this, they cannot subsequently turn round and sue the granters under warrandice. If they were unhappy with the position, they should have raised the point before settlement.[29] This is one of the reasons why a disposition narrates all the burdens which affect the land, so as to make absolutely clear what the grantees are acquiring. The second aspect of warrandice also works slightly differently as between the Land Register and the GRS. If a title sheet does not disclose an encumbrance, then the encumbrance does not exist, so that the possibility of a breach of the second aspect of warrandice is less likely for properties in the Land Register. However, encumbrances that are "overriding interests" are effective whether or not they appear in the Register, and in respect of such encumbrances there is little difference as between the two registers.

Leases are treated differently from other encumbrances, and appear not to give rise to a warrandice claim.[30] However, where it is intended to convey property with vacant possession, it is nowadays standard practice to state this fact expressly in the deed,[31] so that in such a case the existence of a lease would give rise to a claim.

---

[27] *Mutch v Mavisbank Properties Ltd*, 2002 S.L.T. (Sh. Ct) 91.

[28] The relevant date is delivery of the disposition.

[29] Thus Roman law: D.19,1,1,1. But in earlier Roman law it was otherwise: *Orata v Gratidianus*, (91 B.C.) Cicero, *De Officiis* 3, 67. For discussion see Rodger, in P. G. Stein and A. D. E. Lewis (eds), *Studies in Justinian's Institutes* (1983).

[30] *Lothian and Border Farmers Ltd v McCutchion*, 1952 S.L.T. 450. The correctness of this decision is, however, not wholly free from doubt.

[31] This is done in the entry clause: "with entry and vacant possession" (or "actual occupation"). The entry clause is discussed further in para.11–19.

Concurrent claim under missives

16–12   The requirement of eviction can be circumvented by making a claim
under the missives. Missives normally contain a guarantee of title, and in
so far as the missives survive settlement,[32] this guarantee will also
presumably survive. Hence, if the buyers discover, after settlement, that
their title is not good and marketable, the sellers will normally be liable
in terms of the missives. Eviction is not required.[33] For as long as they
remain in force, therefore, missives are likely to provide a more
attractive basis of claim. But as and when the missives have been
superseded, which is most cases will be after two years, any claim will
have to be based on the warrandice only.[34]

Transmission of warrandice

16–13   Suppose that Ann sells land to Beth, and Beth later sells to Chris. A
defect in title then emerges. Chris can sue Beth under the warrandice
which Beth granted to him. But he may not wish to do this. Perhaps
Beth is bankrupt, or has disappeared. Can Chris claim from Ann? The
answer is that he can, because the clause of assignation of writs which
will normally have been part of the disposition by Beth to Chris[35]
operates as an assignation to Chris of Beth's warrandice rights against
Ann.[36]

   This, however, is subject to certain qualifications. Ann can be liable to
Chris only to the extent that she would have been liable to Beth if Beth
had not sold to Chris: *assignatus utitur jure auctoris*. Thus, if Ann had
granted only simple warrandice to Beth, she would be unlikely to be
liable to Chris. Or if the defect was caused by Beth's act, or by diligence
by Beth's creditors, Ann cannot be liable to Chris.[37] Moreover, Ann's
liability may be barred by negative prescription.

---

[32] Discussed at the beginning of the chapter.

[33] Reid, *Property*, paras 707 and 710.

[34] For discussion of this question see Steven, 1998 S.L.T. (News) 283.

[35] This clause is now implied: Land Registration (Scotland) Act 1979, s.16. See
para.11–16.

[36] Stair, II, iii, 46. If, however, Chris sues Beth, then it appears that Beth can sue Ann.
See *Christie v Cameron* (1898) 25 R. 824; *Cobham v Minter*, 1986 S.L.T. 336.

[37] Warrandice (even if absolute) does not extend to future acts by a successor in title.

CHAPTER 17

JUDICIAL RECTIFICATION OF DOCUMENTS

Wrong words or no words

Drafting being an imperfect art, deeds sometimes contain mistakes. 17–01 For instance, words may have been missed out, or included without good reason, or the wrong words may have been used, or words which are unclear.[1] Often this is no more than a clerical error. Something went wrong in the typing, or the dictating, and the error is not picked up until it is too late. Less commonly there has been a failure to understand what the client actually wants. Where this happens it is usually because the solicitor has not received, or insisted upon, adequate instructions. For example, the client may have failed to mention the informal agreement reached with the seller (or buyer) over a glass of sherry, with the result that the missives fail to include (or exclude) that elusive lock-up garage in the centre of town.

In general the best way to sort out a mistake is to produce a new version of the document. Missives can be amended, or a fresh disposition executed and registered. But this is not always possible. Too much time may have passed, so that the original parties are dead, or untraceable. Or, more seriously, the mistake may have grown into a dispute, for it is likely to benefit one party at the expense of the other. Recipients of windfall benefits are not always willing to relinquish them, and may seek to argue that the deed was what they had intended all along.[2] Indeed the dispute may be genuine enough, for parties in negotiation can quite easily be unclear on what precisely was agreed.[3]

Errors which cannot be rectified by agreement can sometimes be rectified judicially. By section 8 of the Law Reform (Miscellaneous Provisions) (Scotland) Act 1985 ("the 1985 Act") a power is conferred on the court to rectify documents which fail to express accurately the parties' intentions.[4] There is concurrent jurisdiction in the Court of

---

[1] There is a growing tendency to use rectification as a means of resolving ambiguity or uncertainty of language—quite often by a party which loses the argument on interpretation. See *e.g. Howgate Shopping Centre Ltd v Catercraft Services Ltd,* 2004 S.L.T. 231.

[2] *e.g. Cruickshank Botanic Gardens Trs v Jamieson,* 2001 G.W.D. 19–735.

[3] *e.g. Rehman v Ahmad,* 1993 S.L.T. 741.

[4] This provision implemented the Scottish Law Commission's *Report on Rectification of Contractual and Other Documents* (Scot. Law Com. No.79, 1983). See also W. W. McBryde, *The Law of Contract in* Scotland (2nd ed., 2001), paras 8–102—8–107.

Session and sheriff court.[5] In practice it is for the applicant to suggest the changes which are required, although further changes may be put forward by the court.[6] In recent years applications for rectification have become more common as their value has come to be recognised.

Three types of case

17–02 The key provision is section 8(1), which is in the following terms:

"Subject to section 9 of this Act, where the court is satisfied, on an application made to it, that

(a) a document intended to express or to give effect to an agreement fails to express accurately the common intention of the parties to the agreement at the date when it was made; or

(b) a document intended to create, transfer, vary or renounce a right, not being a document falling within paragraph (a) above, fails to express accurately the intention of the grantor of the document at the date when it was executed,

it may order the document to be rectified in any manner that it may specify in order to give effect to that intention."

From this it will be seen that an application for rectification may be made in respect of:

(i) Documents intended to "express" an agreement, *e.g.* written contracts such as missives.

(ii) Documents intended to "give effect" to an agreement, *i.e.* to implement agreements, such as dispositions in implement of missives of sale.

(iii) Documents (not falling within (i) and (ii)) intended to create, transfer, vary or renounce a right.[7] Into this class fall documents which are not merely unilateral in form[8] but are unilateral in substance, such as dispositions by way of gift.

Type (i)

17–03 The three types are listed in ascending order of chance of success. Applications in respect of type (i) documents seem never to be granted.[9] The reasons are not hard to find. For an application to succeed it is

---

[5] Law Reform (Miscellaneous Provisions) (Scotland) Act 1985, s.8(9). For the procedure, see I. D. Macphail, *Sheriff Court Practice* (2nd ed., by C. G. B. Nicholson and A. L. Stewart), Vol.1 (1998), paras 24.07 and 24.08. See also Rules of the Court of Session 1994, Ch.73.

[6] *Renyana-Stahl Anstalt v MacGregor*, 2001 S.L.T. 1247 at para.46 *per* Lord Macfadyen.

[7] s.8(1).

[8] Most conveyancing deeds are unilateral in form.

[9] *Shaw v William Grant (Minerals) Ltd*, 1989 S.L.T. 121; *Angus v Bryden*, 1992 S.L.T. 884; *Rehman v Ahmad*, 1993 S.L.T. 741; *Belhaven Brewery Co. v Swift*, 1996 S.L.T. (Sh. Ct) 127; *Bovis Construction (Scotland) Ltd v Glantyre Engineering Ltd*, 1997 G.W.D. 32–1609; *Baird v Drumpellier & Mount Vernon Estates Ltd (No.2)*, 2002 G.W.D. 12–427.

necessary to show that the document fails to express the agreement of the parties. But usually there was no clear agreement prior to the document itself. Type (i) documents are usually contracts (such as missives of sale) which are the product of close negotiation. It would be rare for the parties to reach a clear informal agreement first which is later reduced to writing. Much more commonly, the parties are negotiating up to the last moment, so that underlying agreement is achieved at the same moment as the signature of the document itself.[10] In those circumstances it is difficult to show that the written text is wrong. That, after all, is the text which the parties signed up to. Anything before that was no more than a negotiating position, abandoned by the time of the final text. The whole justification for the use of writing is that informal negotiations are discarded. Doubtless an obvious error could be rectified. For example, if missives mis-transcribe "31 High Street" as "13 High Street", the mistake is easily demonstrated. But mistakes which suit neither party could be corrected consensually and do not require an application to the court. This suggests that s. 8 is available mainly in cases where it is not needed. If a mistake, or alleged mistake, suits one party but not the other (for example, an offer to purchase for £171,000 instead of £117,000, as intended), rectification is unlikely to succeed.[11]

Type (ii)

Type (ii) documents give effect to an earlier agreement, written or oral. Most deeds used in day-to-day conveyancing fall into this category. Thus a disposition gives effect to missives of sale, or a standard security to the loan agreement with the bank or building society. It has been held in the sheriff court that the parties to the agreement must be same as those to the deed.[12] Common intention is viewed objectively,[13] and is not the less compelling for being based on ignorance of a material fact.[14] 17-04

If the prior agreement was in writing, it will usually be obvious whether an error has been made. For example, if missives are concluded for the sale of property X, and the disposition conveys property Y as well, it is reasonable to conclude that property Y was added in error and that the deed should be rectified.[15] Conversely, if the disposition is consistent with the missives, rectification is unlikely to succeed. There is no better evidence of the parties' intentions than the written document in which they were expressed.[16] In theory it would be possible to argue that the written contract was itself inaccurate and should be rectified, but this turns a type (ii) case into a type (i) case, with predictable results.[17] A

---

[10] *Rehman v Ahmad*, 1993 S.L.T. 741 at 751I-L and 753B *per* Lord Penrose.

[11] *Bovis Construction (Scotland) Ltd v Glantyre Engineering Ltd*, 1997 G.W.D. 32–1609. If, however, the mistake was known to the other party at the time of the offer, the doctrine of unfair advantage may provide a remedy. See *Angus v Bryden*, 1992 S.L.T. 884.

[12] *Delikes Ltd v Scottish & Newcastle plc*, 2000 S.L.T. (Sh. Ct) 67. For criticism, see Reid and Gretton, *Conveyancing 2000*, pp.119–20.

[13] *Rehman v Ahmad*, 1993 S.L.T. 741 at 752A *per* Lord Penrose.

[14] *Co-operative Wholesale Society Ltd v Ravenseft Properties Ltd*, 2003 S.C.L.R. 509.

[15] *Oliver v Gaughan*, 1990 G.W.D. 22–1247. See also *Aberdeen Rubber Ltd v Knowles & Sons (Fruiterers) Ltd*, 1995 S.C. (HL) 8.

[16] *Howgate Shopping Centre Ltd v Catercraft Services Ltd*, 2004 S.L.T. 231. Sometimes, though, the document itself is unclear, as in *McClymont v McCubbin*, 1995 S.L.T. 1248.

[17] *Angus v Bryden*, 1992 S.L.T. 884; *Baird v Drumpellier & Mount Vernon Estates Ltd (No.2)*, 2002 G.W.D. 12–427.

different approach is to argue for a change of mind since the date of the contract.[18] This is made more difficult by section 8, which focuses on intention as at the date of the contract.[19] To accommodate changes of mind it would be necessary to argue that the deed was intended to give effect, not to the written contract in its original form, but to the contract as varied by some later and informal agreement. Later intention would then become relevant. Again, success is likely to be denied.[20]

If the earlier agreement is not in writing, there may be difficulties in proving its terms, and rectification will be correspondingly harder to achieve. As with type (i) cases, it will not always be possible to separate out the agreement from the written deed which followed.[21]

Type (iii)

17–05   While in cases of the first two types it is necessary to show that the written document departs from the common intention of the parties at the time of the underlying agreement, in type (iii) cases there is no underlying agreement and hence no common intention. A type (iii) deed is unilateral, and made without reference to a previous agreement. Examples might include an unheralded gift of land, made by disposition, or an *inter vivos* deed of trust.[22] Under s. 8(1)(b) the concern is with the intention of the granter alone, and an application succeeds if it can be shown that the deed does not give effect to the granter's intention as at the date when it was executed. In theory it ought to be easier to show the intention of one person than of two. If the granter is also the person applying for rectification, there may be no one who can contradict his or her assertion that the deed was blundered. But a court might not always be convinced. The Scottish Law Commission took a cautious view[23]:

> "In the case of unilateral writings proof of the granter's intention will be inherently more difficult, for he is less likely to have communicated with any other party. It may therefore be difficult to establish what his true intention was and to what extent this has been misrepresented in writing. Moreover, a court would not be satisfied that a document was defectively expressed purely on the basis of an assertion that the writing was not what the granter had intended."

Certainly a donor would not be able to withdraw a gift under the guise of rectification.

---

[18] *Renyana-Stahl Anstalt v MacGregor*, 2001 S.L.T. 1247.

[19] Scot. Law Com. No.79, para.3.5. The relevant part of s.8(1) provides that the court must be satisfied that "a document intended to . . . give effect to an agreement fails to express accurately the common intention of the parties to the agreement at the date when it was made". "It" here refers to the agreement and not to the document: documents are not "made".

[20] *George Thompson Services Ltd v Moore*, 1993 S.L.T. 634.

[21] *Huewind Ltd v Clydesdale Bank plc*, 1996 S.L.T. 369; *Royal Bank of Scotland v Shanks*, 1998 S.L.T. 355.

[22] *Hudson v St. John*, 1977 S.C. 255.

[23] Scot. Law Com. No.79, para.3.8.

The boundary between types (ii) and (iii) is not easily drawn. Since a type (iii) case is likely to be the easier to establish, there is a temptation to try to bring documents under this heading. Initially the courts took a broad view of type (iii). In one of the early leading cases, Lord President Hope gave the distinction as being between unilateral and bilateral documents. All unilateral documents came within type (iii).[24] But the view now taken—surely correctly—is that a type (iii) deed is one which does not implement a previous agreement.[25] The grantee must have had no prior entitlement to the grant. This means that most unilateral deeds are classified as type (ii) documents, and that type (iii) cases will be rare.

Which documents?

Section 8 applies to all documents other than those of a testamentary 17–06 nature.[26] It is no objection that the document has been recorded in the GRS, or formed the basis of registration of a title in the Land Register.[27] There seem no reason why documents executed before the provision came into force should not qualify.[28] Perhaps surprisingly, there is no requirement that the document effects, or records, a juridical act.[29] The person seeking rectification need not have been a party to the document,[30] so that for example an owner of land could apply for rectification in respect of an earlier deed in the titles.

Mistakes in one document can lead to mistakes in another, and for that reason the court is empowered to order the rectification of any other document which is defectively expressed by reason of the defect in the original document.[31] A typical example would be an error in the description in a disposition which was then carried forward into a standard security.[32]

Which mistakes?

In principle, section 8 applies to all mistakes, both of commission and 17–07 omission. The mistakes may touch fundamentals. For example, section 8 has been used to change the description of the property being conveyed or over which rights are being created.[33] Words can be added, deleted,

---

[24] *Bank of Scotland v Graham's Tr,* 1992 S.C. 79 at 86, 1993 S.L.T. 252 at 253L *per* Lord President Hope: "The document with which we are concerned is a unilateral deed, not an agreement, so the relevant provision for present purposes is para.(b)."(The report in Session Cases mistakenly refers to "para.(a)".)

[25] *Royal Bank of Scotland v Shanks,* 1998 S.L.T. 355.

[26] s.8(6).

[27] s.8(5).

[28] The provision came into force on December 30, 1985: see s.60(2)(d). The deed rectified in *Bank of Scotland v Graham's Tr,* 1992 S.C. 79 was executed and recorded prior to that date, although the point was not raised.

[29] At least in type (ii) cases. This seems to mean that if Alan contracts with Barbara to write a sonnet but actually writes a limerick, Barbara can ask the court to rectify the verse.

[30] *Delikes Ltd v Scottish & Newcastle plc,* 2000 S.L.T. (Sh. Ct) 67 at 70 *per* Sheriff Principal C. G. B. Nicholson Q.C.

[31] s.8(3).

[32] Scot. Law Com. No.79, para.5.1.

[33] *Oliver v Gaughan,* 1990 G.W.D. 22–1247; *Beneficial Bank plc v Wardle,* 1996 G.W.D. 30–1825.

and substituted. Furthermore, section 8 is not confined to errors in expression but extends also to errors in expectation—to cases where the words themselves were correct but the result thereby achieved was wrong and contrary to the parties' intentions. In the leading case a bank's letter of consent was rectified on the basis that, while the words were those which the parties intended to use, their legal effect was not what was intended.[34] If pressed too far, this runs the risk of being a charter for incompetent conveyancing, rescuing even the wildest errors and misapprehensions on the part of the draftsman.

In fact there are important limitations. Only the actual terms of the deed may be rectified. Section 8 cannot be used to cure defects of execution, such as the absence of a signature, or a signature by the wrong person;[35] nor can it be used to change the parties to a deed.[36] Further, the court is not bound to grant rectification. Section 8(1) says "may" and not "shall".[37] In the exercise of this discretion regard will be had to various factors[38] including the extent of the changes proposed. It has been said that:[39]

> "Rectification of a deed is one thing, but wholesale alteration of contractual terms is another which may go beyond the power conferred by the statute."

Similarly, the court has warned that:[40]

> "The more extensive the amendments proposed by a party, the more questionable may become the exercise of even a wide discretionary power in particular circumstances . . . There is a qualification inherent in most if not all general discretionary powers that they require to be exercised within reasonable limits."

The way in which this qualification will be applied remains to be seen. But it may be assumed that the extent of alterations will be measured by legal effect rather than by number of words.[41]

---

[34] *Bank of Ireland v Bass Brewers Ltd*, 2000 G.W.D. 20–786, 2000 G.W.D. 28–1077, discussed in Reid and Gretton, *Conveyancing 2000*, pp.118–9. The court having allowed a proof, rectification was later awarded as of consent. For a case where the court was less disposed to help, see *Co-operative Wholesale Society Ltd v Ravenseft Properties Ltd*, 2003 S.C.L.R. 509.

[35] *Bank of Scotland v Graham's Tr*, 1992 S.C. 79 at 88 *per* Lord President Hope. In that case the problem of the granters having signed once rather than (as was demanded by the structure of the deed) twice was solved by rectifying the standard security so that only one signature was required. But if there had been no signature at all, the deed could not have been rescued.

[36] *Bank of Scotland v Brunswick Developments (1987) Ltd (No.2)*, 1999 S.C. (HL) 53.

[37] *Bank of Scotland v Brunswick Developments (1987) Ltd (No.2)*, 1997 S.C. 226 at 231D *per* Lord President Rodger.

[38] In the case of a deed of conditions, for example, the good and harmonious governance of the community to which it relates: see *Sheltered Housing Management Ltd v Cairns*, 2003 S.L.T. 578 at paras 17ff. *per* Lord Nimmo Smith.

[39] *Huewind Ltd v Clydesdale Bank plc*, 1996 S.L.T. 369 at 375D *per* Lord Justice-Clerk Ross.

[40] *Norwich Union Life Insurance Society v Tanap Investments V. K Ltd*, 1999 S.L.T. 204 at 211F–G *per* Lord Penrose.

[41] *Norwich Union Life Insurance Society v Tanap Investments V. K Ltd*, 1999 S.L.T. 204 at 211L–212A *per* Lord Penrose.

A striking feature is the way in which s. 8 has been used for mistakes which are mere conveyancing blunders. In one case the box marked "THE PROPRIETOR" in a standard security had been left blank, so that the security ostensibly had no granter, though in fact the owner had executed the deed. The omission was repaired by rectification.[42] In another, also involving a standard security, the property was insufficiently described. Again the missing details were able to be added.[43] This is rectification as the conveyancer's friend. For mistakes in conveyancing, s. 8 provides a final line of defence.

Standard of proof

The court must, as usual, be satisfied on a balance of probabilities,[44]   17–08 and may have regard to all evidence, whether written or oral.[45] Missives of sale can be consulted even after expiry due to a supersession clause.[46] In practice there may be a reluctance to overturn a written document on the basis of prior communings which were expressed orally, to say nothing of the difficulty of proving such communings.

Protection of third parties

Documents may affect more than the immediate parties, particularly   17–09 in the case of deeds which create real rights. A person in this position could defend the application on the merits if it is brought to his or her attention.[47] More importantly, s. 9 of the 1985 Act excludes rectification altogether if it would adversely affect, to a material extent, a person who relied on the document in its unrectified form (or on an entry on the Land Register made on the basis of such a document). Reliance involves acting or refraining to act, and must have been reasonable and without knowledge, actual or constructive, of the mistake. It is not reasonable to rely on a deed if the mistake is obvious.[48]

Thus suppose Anne, by mistake, conveys too much land to Brian. Brian registers his title in the Land Register. Two years later Brian grants a standard security to the Caledonian Bank. The Bank relies on the entry on the Land Register. Anne then seeks rectification, both of the disposition and of the standard security.[49] Rectification should succeed as to the disposition but not as to the standard security.[50] By

---

[42] *Bank of Scotland v Graham's Tr*, 1992 S.C. 79.

[43] *Beneficial Bank plc v Wardle*, 1996 G.W.D. 30–1825. As these cases suggest, it is easier to add words which are not there than to substitute words which were included in error. For erroneous words may confer a windfall benefit which leads to rectification being opposed. Perhaps the only completely safe conveyancing deed is a blank sheet of paper subscribed by the granter?

[44] *Rehman v Ahmad*, 1993 S.L.T. 741. And see Scot. Law Com. No.79, paras 4.3–4.6.

[45] s.8(2).

[46] *Renyana-Stahl Anstalt v MacGregor*, 2001 S.L.T. 1247.

[47] *Norwich Union Life Insurance Society v Tanap Investments VK Ltd (No.2)*, 2000 S.C. 515.

[48] *Co-operative Wholesale Society Ltd v Ravenseft Properties Ltd*, 2001 G.W.D. 24–904, 2002 S.C.L.R. 644.

[49] Rectification of the Land Register would also be required, for which see below.

[50] So that this plot of land will revert to Anne, but burdened by the security. It might be argued that the security too should be rectified, since if that led to rectification of the Register under the 1979 Act, the Bank would be protected by indemnity. But in that case the keeper would be prejudiced.

contrast, an unsecured creditor does not usually lend in reliance on the register and would not be protected against rectification.[51] Not all examples are so straightforward, however. In practice, indeed, a case under s. 9 is not easily made out. Thus before a third party can be said to have relied on a document, he or she must be shown to have been familiar with the very term which is now the subject of rectification.[52] And even if such close familiarity can be demonstrated—which is unlikely to be easy—there is the further hurdle of showing that the act (or refraining from acting) was properly attributable to the term now to be rectified and not to some other cause.[53]

A practical difficulty is that the court may not always know about third parties. Where real rights are concerned a search of the register should be undertaken. In Land Register cases the court can require the Keeper to list those persons who have been given details of the relevant title sheet.[54] But some people will fall through the net, if only because not all real rights are registered. Here the 1985 Act makes special provision. A third party who was unaware of the application for rectification but later finds out can apply to the Court of Session within two years. But no application may be made later than five years after the original order. The court has power either to reduce the rectifying order or to require the original applicant to pay compensation.[55]

Effect of the order

17-10   A rectification order, in a conveyancing matter, will generally change the real rights in a property. When does that change take effect? In other words, when does the order have real effect? It would be natural to suppose that this took place with effect from the date of registration in the property register. But in fact the provisions of the 1985 Act are complex and in some respects puzzling. The following is an attempt to explain them.

Entering the Land Register

17-11   If the property is in the Land Register, the order does not have immediate real effect. Real effect requires registration. Rectifying a deed achieves nothing of itself, for title flows from the Register and not from the deed. Thus, in order to be effective, rectification of the deed must be followed by rectification of the Register itself.[56] One kind of rectification is thus followed by another. Contrary to the usual rule, the Land

---

[51] The same applies to a trustee in sequestration or liquidator, as the representative of the ordinary unsecured creditors. See *Bank of Scotland v Graham's Tr*, 1992 S.C. 79.

[52] *Shetland Housing Management Ltd v Cairns*, 2003 S.L.T. 578.

[53] *Jones v Wood*, Dumfries Sheriff Court, October 27, 2003, unreported; discussed in Reid and Gretton, *Conveyancing 2003*, pp.104–06.

[54] s.9(6). How much use this will be is unclear. Often the only parties who will have requested details will be law firms, credit reference agencies, and search firms, all of whom will normally be acting for others.

[55] s.9(7), (8).

[56] As with reductions, it may be taken that the effect of rectification of a deed requires to enter the Register by rectification and not by registration. See *Short's Tr v Keeper of the Registers of Scotland*, 1996 S.C. (HL) 14.

Register may be rectified even where this is to the prejudice of a proprietor in possession.[57] No indemnity is payable.[58] But *bona fide* proprietors will often have been able to prevent the initial rectification of the deed, on principles already discussed.[59]

Entering the GRS

For property in the GRS, the order has real effect immediately, even 17–12 without recording. But there is an incentive to record,[60] in that an unrecorded order cannot be pled against a third party who, in good faith and for value, acquires right to the land after rectification but before its recording.[61] This has the odd result that the rectified deed is deemed to have one text in a question with that third party but a different text in a question with everyone else, including those who inspected the Register prior to rectification.[62]

Retroactivity

The order has real effect when made (GRS) or when registered (Land 17–13 Register), but the 1985 Act provides that the date when the real effect comes about is not the date when it begins to operate. The order is retroactive in effect, so that after the order takes real effect the document is deemed always to have been written in its rectified form.[63] But the court has power to modify this rule to take account of the position of third parties acting in reliance on the unrectified document.[64]

Retroactivity may make sense for personal rights, but it hardly does so for real rights. A deed recorded in the GRS is deemed always to have been recorded in its rectified version[65]; and an entry on the Land Register rectified in response to the rectification of the underlying deed is deemed always to have been so rectified.[66] The results are scarcely satisfactory. Suppose that in 2000 Alice conveys Whitemains and Blackmains to Bruce. Bruce registers his title in the Land Register. In 2004 both the disposition and the Register are rectified to exclude Whitemains, and Alice is entered on the Register as owner. Who owned Whitemains in 2002? The answer depends on the date of the question.

---

[57] 1979 Act, s.9(3)(b). This includes a proprietor who acquires in good faith after the rectification of the deed but before the rectification of the Register. There is thus no equivalent in the Land Register of s.46(2) of the 1924 Act. (Notwithstanding s.29(2) of the 1979 Act, the *Short's Tr* litigation took for granted that s.46 did not apply to the Land Register.)

[58] 1979 Act, s.12(3)(p).

[59] 1985 Act, s.9(1)—(3).

[60] What is recorded is the extract decree.

[61] 1924 Act, s.46(1). By contrast with s.9(1) to (3) of the 1985 Act, there is no requirement of prejudicial reliance.

[62] This latter point arises from the fact that—unlike reduction (on which s.46(2) is modelled)—rectification operates retrospectively. So it is better to buy immediately after rectification than immediately before. But a person who buys immediately before may sometimes be able to have the rectification set aside under s.9(7) of the 1985 Act.

[63] s.8(4).

[64] s.9(4), (5).

[65] s.8(5).

[66] 1979 Act, s.9(3A).

In 2002 the answer to the question is "Bruce". In 2004, following rectification, it is "Alice". So it is correct to say that Bruce, not Alice, owned the property in 2002, and it is equally correct to say that Alice, not Bruce, owned the property in 2002: a historical fact changes according to when it is asserted.

If the rectification were to be reduced, to accommodate the interests of third parties, the answer in 2006 might once again be "Bruce".[67] But the question has not changed, only the answer. The Land Register, it appears, has not been telling the truth. In property law it is awkward to rewrite history in this way. For example, obligations are quite often imposed on the "owner" of property, whether by statute,[68] or common law,[69] or by real burdens. Can Bruce, forced to perform such an obligation in 2002, demand compensation from Alice in 2004, and if so under what principle?

The position is worse if Bruce has granted subordinate real rights, particularly if they were unregistered and so not known to the court at the time of the application for rectification. For example, in 2001 Bruce might have granted a 15-year lease of Whitemains to Cara, and a servitude to David. In 2004, following rectification, both would become void, retrospectively, as having been granted *a non domino*. In theory Cara or David would have until 2009 to have the initial rectification reduced, and their rights restored.[70] But since Alice is a proprietor in possession, and in good faith, it is not clear that such a reduction could be given effect to on the Register.[71]

Reduction

17-14   Depending on the circumstances, reduction can sometimes be used as an alternative to rectification. For example, if in error a disposition conveys too much land, the disposition could be adjusted by means of a partial reduction.[72] Reduction is not, in general, retroactive in effect. A difficulty with reduction is that there is no special provision allowing rectification of the Land Register against a proprietor in possession, and some reductions will fall at this hurdle.[73]

---

[67] Under 1985 Act, s.9(7). This assumes, possibly incorrectly, that the reduction is itself retrospective in effect. Further, for reasons explained below, it is not clear that such a reduction could ever get on the Register.

[68] *e.g.* Building (Scotland) Act 2003, ss.28 to 30.

[69] *e.g.* the common interest obligation of maintenance in respect of boundary walls.

[70] s.9(7), (8). However, as mentioned earlier it is not clear that a reduction would operate retrospectively. If not, the lease and servitude would still have been granted *a non domino* and their validity would now depend on the law of accretion.

[71] Section 9(3)(b) of the 1979 Act applies only to a rectification "consequential on the making of an order under" s.8. It is far from clear that a reduction of a s.8 order under s.9 is "consequential" in the sense of the provision.

[72] *Aberdeen Rubber Ltd v Knowles & Sons (Fruiterers) Ltd*, 1995 S.C. (HL) 8.

[73] *Short's Tr v Keeper of the Registers of Scotland*, 1996 S.C. (HL) 14. But s.9(3)(a)(iii) of the 1979 Act (fraud or carelessness) may sometimes apply.

CHAPTER 18

HOME LOANS

Introduction

Loans secured over residential properties are commonly known, in 18–01 non-legal language, by the English term "mortgage". This common usage has now been adopted by the Scottish Parliament in the shape of the Mortgage Rights (Scotland) Act 2001 (asp 11), though the word is used only in the title, and not in the body of the Act. "Mortgage" is the term the clients are likely to understand, though they are usually fuzzy about its precise meaning. Clients typically use the word to mean the whole package, not just the security. Thus, they include the loan, the life policy and so on. The average client will also say that "the First National Bank of Pitlochry gave me a mortgage". The opposite is true. The lender grants the loan. The debtor grants the security. That clients often think of a mortgage as an asset is curious. It is not an asset but a liability. The misconception is one that financial institutions do little to dispel.

The Scottish equivalent for the English term "mortgage" is heritable security.[1] There is now only one type of heritable security, the standard security. The term "home loan" is also quite common and we will sometimes use it here, though it is imprecise. For instance a standard security can be over any heritable property, and not just residential property.

The importance of heritably secured loans can hardly be overstated. There are at any given time more than a million home loans in Scotland,[2] and the total amount on loan is more than £40 billion.[3] This chapter is concerned with the home loan market and the home loan packages available. Almost of this chapter would be equally applicable on the other side of the border. The next chapter gives some account of the law and practice of heritable security, where of course Scotland and England diverge.

---

[1] Actually this is an oversimplification since in English law the term "mortgage" can apply to security over assets other than land.

[2] Emma McCallum and Ewen McCaig, *Mortgage Arrears and Repossessions* (2003), p.49. The survey date was 2000 and the number estimated was 1,036,786. The figure will have risen significantly since then. The figure is by loans not properties: thus a property with two secured loans is counted twice in the figures. The figure is for home loans: commercial and agricultural loans are excluded. To put the figure into perspective, there are very roughly two million title units in Scotland.

[3] Emma McCallum and Ewen McCaig, *Mortgage Arrears and Repossessions* (2003), p.48, estimates the figure for 2000 at £38,271,000,000. The figure will have risen significantly since then. The figure is for home loans in Scotland. It does not include commercial and agricultural lending.

The lenders

18–02   Once upon a time, house purchase loans were often obtained privately, sometimes by the solicitor putting two clients in touch with each
other, one with money to lend, and the other with a house to buy,
though, of course, institutional lending was also common. Nowadays,
private lending is rare. Until the 1980s the main providers of home loans
were the building societies. Now other financial institutions have a large
share of the market. There have been two main reasons for the change.
The first is that historically the commercial banks almost never made
home loans, mainly because such banks disliked long-term loans. In the
1980s that attitude changed. The second reason is the Building Societies
Act 1986 enabled building societies to "demutualise" *i.e.* to convert into
commercial banks, and many did so. Major building societies have thus
become major banks and in doing so have maintained their activities in
the home loans market. Whereas 25 years ago building societies had
most of the market, those that survive today have less than 25 per cent.
In a survey of the Scottish market carried out in 2000, the top ten
mortgage lenders had between them two thirds of the market, and eight
of these lenders were commercial banks.[4] There are about 150 mortgage
lenders active in the UK market.

Building societies

18–03   Unlike the commercial banks, building societies are non-profit cooper-
atives. They are juristic persons (corporations) whose members are
(subject to some qualifications) their depositors and borrowers. Thus,
clients who have a home loan with a building society are members, and
so, for instance, can vote at general meetings, etc. It follows that a
building society has no interest in exploiting its borrowers. Building
societies claim that, because of their structure, they can offer loans on
better terms than the commercial banks, and independent surveys
confirm that this is true, though the difference is not a big one. Building
societies were once restricted to lending only for house purchase and
only on first-ranked security. These rules have been relaxed to some
extent but home loan finance remains their core business.

Mortgage brokers

18–04   Mortgage brokers, also called mortgage intermediaries, arrange loans,
especially for those whose creditworthiness may be uncertain. Brokers
are normally paid a commission for new business by the lenders, and, if
they arrange a life assurance policy, by the life assurance company.

The Council of Mortgage Lenders

18–05   The Council of Mortgage Lenders is a voluntary organisation whose
membership includes almost all UK mortgage lenders. One of its
functions is to publish the *CML Lenders' Handbook for Scotland*. This

---

[4] Emma McCallum and Ewen McCaig, *Mortgage Arrears and Repossessions* (2003), p.s47.
They were, in order, (i) Halifax (ii) RBS (iii) Abbey National (iv) Bank of Scotland (v)
Clydesdale (vi) Northern Rock (vii) Lloyds TSB (viii) Alliance & Leicester (ix) Dun-
fermline Building Society and (x) Yorkshire Building Society.

used to be a print publication but is currently available only on the CML website.[5] All conveyancers need to be familiar with it. Part I sets out standard terms that all the CML lenders have agreed on. Part II sets out terms of individual lenders.

Regulation of the market

Hitherto the home loan system has been largely unregulated, though 18–06 the Consumer Credit Act 1974 has played a certain role. To some extent there was voluntary self-regulation, especially through the Mortgage Code Compliance Board (an organisation separate from the CML), which, as its names indicates, published a (voluntary) Mortgage Code. But as from October 31, 2004 the sector is under statutory regulation by the Financial Services Authority (FSA)[6] acting under powers conferred by the Financial Services and Markets Act 2000. In the new system there are four "regulated activities" which cannot lawfully be carried on except with authorisation by the FSA: these are lending, administering, advising on, and arranging "regulated mortgage contracts".[7] This means that law firms so acting will need SFA authorisation.[8]

One secured loan or more?

The normal practice is to obtain all the finance for house purchase 18–07 from a single lender. This is worth mentioning because in some other countries it is common to obtain a cocktail of loans from different lenders, each lender taking security and the whole package making up the total amount needed. However, owners may, after having bought, take out another secured loan with a different lender: such loans are usually called second mortgages.

When a house is sold, the modern practice is for the sellers to redeem the existing secured loan (from the proceeds of sale) and for the buyers to arrange their own loan. It is in theory possible for the buyers to take over the existing secured loan (a fact that will be reflected in the price paid) and to obtain a top-up loan as required. This was common in the nineteenth century, but today is almost unknown. In some countries, in contrast, it is the norm.

Types of home loan—general

A heritable security secures a loan. The loan is the principal: the 18–08 security is the accessory. A home loan is a loan that happens to be secured, and the numerous different packages available vary chiefly in the loan terms, not in the security terms. However, sometimes a lender may ask for additional security, such as a security over a life assurance policy, or a guarantee from a third party.

---

[5] *http://www.cml.org.uk/*.
[6] *http://www.fsa.gov.uk/*.
[7] Financial Services and Markets Act 2000 (Regulated Activities) (Amendment No.2) Order 2003 (SI 2003/1475).
[8] See further Cullen (2004) 49 J.L.S.S. April/44.

Term loans and on-demand loans

18-09   A loan may be an on-demand one or it may be for a term. In the latter case the borrower has the use of the money for the defined period and cannot be asked to repay it until then, though normally interest payments will be due. Sometimes the loan is repayable in a single payment at the maturity date, while in other cases it may be payable by instalments. In a term loan the debtor will normally have no right to pay off the loan early, though this is subject to agreement to the contrary. If the borrower is in material breach of a term loan the lender normally has the option to accelerate the loan, ie to convert it into an on-demand loan. Home loans are intended for long-term borrowing (up to 25 years and occasionally longer) and so are normally term loans.

Early repayment

18-10   At common law a term loan cannot normally be repaid early, unless either (a) the contract so provides, or (b) the creditor is happy to accept early repayment. The fact that a loan is secured by standard security does not alter that rule.[9] However, in practice one or other of these usually applies. Quite often the loan contract will provide that although the borrower is entitled to repay early, in that event an "early repayment charge"—also called a "redemption penalty"—is due. These charges may be substantial and clients should be aware of them before agreeing to the loan. They tend to be used most commonly where a special loan deal is being offered that is particularly beneficial to the borrower in the first year or two. Such deals would be unworkable if the borrower could simply remortgage with a new lender as soon as the initial period came to an end. Early repayment charges thus make possible deals that would otherwise be impossible.

Payment dates

18-11   Traditionally payments to lenders were made twice a year, at Whitsunday and Martinmas. Nowadays payments are almost invariably monthly.

Market interest rates

18-12   In the UK there is no legal control of interest rates. Lenders and borrowers are free to negotiate whatever they like. In practice market forces operate so that a lender who demands too much will find itself without customers. Naturally rates in practice vary according to the risk to the lender. A secured loan will generally be at a lower interest rate than an unsecured loan. A loan to a person of undoubted creditworthiness will be at a lower interest rate than to someone who has been sequestrated three times in the past twelve years. In lending at lower rates in such cases institutions are not being charitable. There is competition between lenders and market forces reign.

---

[9] Redemption of Standard Securities (Scotland) Act 1971, s.1.

There exists a widespread idea that the Bank of England sets rates. That is not true in law but is to a substantial degree true in practice. The Bank of England has a rate (once called the Bank Rate, later the Minimum Lending Rate and today the Repo Rate). Nobody is legally bound to have any regard to this rate but its influence in the market is immense. Hence changes in the Repo Rate will in practice rapidly cause changes in home loan rates.

Timing of rate changes

A change of rate sometimes comes into effect the month after it is 18–13 announced. In other cases there is an annual adjustment. Thus, the rate is adjusted every April or whatever. The benefit to borrowers is that their payments are fixed for 12 months at a time. Although the rate *payable* is adjusted annually, the rate *chargeable* is normally adjusted whenever the general rate changes. For example, suppose that in October a lender cuts its rate from 8 per cent to 7 per cent. The borrowers continue to pay at the old rate until April. During the interval they are thus overpaying, and this is taken into account at the annual adjustment.

Fixed interest rate

Once upon a time the interest on home loans was fixed at the outset 18–14 and could not change. This made sense when market interest rates were fairly stable. But nowadays market rates are less stable. Thus, if the rate is a fixed one, it may soon be above or below the market rate. If market rates fall, borrowers will be likely to pay off the loan and take out a new one at a lower rate, whereas if market rates rise, borrowers will stay with the loan. The risk is thus a one-way bet in favour of the borrowers, unless an early repayment charge can be made. In current practice it is quite common to borrow at a fixed rate for a period of some years, with the position being protected by an early repayment charge, but rates fixed for long periods (*e.g.* more than 10 years) are rare.

Variable interest rate

If the rate is a variable one, how is it determined? The reasonable 18–15 approach would be to refer to some independently determined rate. This is common in commercial loans, where the rate is often tied to LIBOR.[10] In home loans the traditional way of setting a variable rate was for the loan contract to refer the rate to the Commissioners on the Rate of Interest on Landed Securities in Scotland. This venerable body, organized under the auspices of the W.S. Society, meets twice a year and sets a rate for the next six months, at the current market rate. Their rate is published in the legal press. However, nowadays few loans are tied to this rate. The great majority of home loans have a clause allowing the lender to fix the rate. The lender can do this at any time and simply

---

[10] London Inter-Bank Offered Rate. This is the constantly changing rate at which banks lend to and borrow from each other on the London Money Market. A commercial loan might thus be set at, for instance, LIBOR + 2.

writes to borrowers to notify changes. This is an astonishing arrangement: in what other kind of debt can creditors increase the interest rate at any time without the consent of the borrowers? The risk to the borrowers is obvious: what happens if the lenders fix the rate at 1,000,000 per cent?[11] In practice, of course, this does not happen, partly because to do so would ruin the commercial reputation of the lenders, and partly because lenders which acted in such a way would be at risk of losing their authorisation to conduct banking or credit business. So the lenders set the rate to keep more or less in line with market rates. Each lender will usually have its "standard variable rate" (SVR), and because of market forces different SVRs are similar. But individual loans may or may not be set at the SVR.

The Miles Report

18-16   In 2004 the Treasury published the Miles Report on the mortgage system.[12] The Report found that "a great many households—particularly amongst first-time buyers—attach overwhelming weight to the initial monthly repayment on mortgages. They focus much less on where the burden of debt repayments might be some way ahead, even though mortgage debt is long-lived. And where debt is at variable rates there is great uncertainty about how affordability will evolve. Many borrowers have a poor understanding of the risks involved with different mortgages."[13] Moreover, "many short-term fixed and discounted variable-rate mortgage deals are cross-subsidised by other variable-rate mortgages paying much higher interest rates. Cross-subsidisation from established borrowers, for example those paying standard variable rates that could be as much as 200 basis points above the lowest rates, is intrinsically undesirable and unfair."[14] The Report recommends that the FSA should compel lenders (and advisers) to provide better information to borrowers, to make the products more easily understandable, to end cross-subsidisation and to make it easier to take out long-term fixed-rate loans—"long-term" in this context meaning fixed for ten years or more. It also recommends legislative changes to make interest stabilisation easier.

Some types of deal as to interest rate

18-17   Often the interest is simply the lender's SVR. But there are numerous variants available. One has already been mentioned—the rate that is fixed for the lifetime of the loan—but this is rare in current practice. Another is the rate that is fixed for an agreed period, such as, say, three years, after which it reverts to the SVR. Sometimes there is a variable rate but with a maximum (a "cap"). Sometimes there is both a maximum and a minimum—a cap and collar. Quite common is the discount loan in

---

[11] Whether the borrowers might have a defence in private law is arguable.
[12] David Miles, *The UK Mortgage Market: Taking a Longer-Term View: Final Report and Recommendations* (H.M. Treasury, 2004).
[13] p.6.
[14] p.7.

which the rate is a certain number of points below the SVR for an agreed period. During this period the rate varies as the SVR varies, but always with the discount.

There is the low-start or deferred-interest system under which the rate payable is for the first so many months (*e.g.* 24 or 36) both (1) a fixed rate and (2) a rate which is below the market rate. The low fixed-rate means the rate payable not the rate chargeable. The balance (chargeable but not payable) is added on to the capital. So after the grace period, not only do the borrowers start to pay full rate, but also their total indebtedness will have increased. So after the grace period, they will be paying, to the end of the loan, more than they would have done if they had opted for a more conventional loan.

Some lenders may offer a lower rate on a large loan. Higher rates are likely to be charged if the borrower has a poor credit record, or if the amount borrowed is a high proportion (*e.g.* 90 per cent) of the value of the property, for in such cases the risk is, or is perceived to be, higher.

When comparing interest rates it is important to look at the APR the annual percentage rate as calculated in terms of the Consumer Credit Act 1974. The APR is a standardised way of calculating an interest rate, designed to make comparison easy.

Flexible mortgages, offset mortgages, and current account mortgages

There are other types of deal which do not directly concern the 18–18 interest rate. In the flexible mortgage the borrowers have a degree of flexibility as to how much they pay in any given month. In an offset mortgage the rate is charged on the net balance, taking into account any credit balance on another account, such as a current account. A current account mortgage (CAM) is similar: here the home loan is in essence an overdraft on the current account. This too can benefit the borrower. Most people prefer, however, to keep their home loans separate from their other bank accounts.

The term

The "term" means the length of time the loan is to run. This is 18–19 negotiable,[15] but the usual periods are multiples of five years, the commonest term being 25 years. Usually a lender will be reluctant to agree to a term which would run beyond the borrower's retirement age. In most cases the loan is repaid much sooner than the term, because the property is sold. The average lifespan of a home loan is only about seven years.

Loan agreements—whether backed by security or not—almost always have an acceleration clause whereby the lender is entitled to demand repayment in full, ahead of term, if there is an "event of default". An event of default is a breach justifying acceleration. Usually failure to pay an instalment of capital or of interest is not an immediate event of default, but rather becomes one if the default continues for a defined period, such as one month or two months.

---

[15] And can sometimes be renegotiated later, *e.g.* if the borrower gets into financial difficulties. A lengthened term can mean reduced monthly payments.

Paradoxically there is sometimes also a clause tucked away saying that in any case the whole loan is repayable on demand irrespective of any default. We say "paradoxically" because an on-demand loan does not need an acceleration clause: indeed the two things contradict each other. Loans are either repayable on demand, or they are not. They cannot be both.

Types of term loan: introduction

18–20   Loans may be divided into on-demand loans and term loans. The latter have many subtypes. In the roll-up loan nothing is due until the term date, so that interest is rolled-up. Because of the way compound interest works, the capital—the total amount due—snowballs, so such loan contracts are unusual. (They are occasionally used in equity-release mortgages.) In an interest-only loan, interest is regularly paid during the life of the loan, so that (unlike a roll-up loan) the total sum due does not increase, but neither does it decrease. The whole capital falls due in one lump sum at the term date. Another type of loan contract, called the capital-and-interest method, or the amortisation method, requires the interest to be paid regularly and the capital to be paid off in instalments, so that in fact there is not a single term date but rather a series of term dates. Thus if the loan is for 20 years, and if the contract requires repayment of part of the capital each month, then there are $20 \times 12 = 240$ term dates. During the course of the 20 years the capital decreases.

If the capital instalments are all of equal amounts, the effect would be that, over the years, less and less interest would be due, so that total annual payments to the lender would fall off over time. By the same token, in such a loan contract the payments by the debtor are front-loaded. That is often acceptable in commercial loan contracts, but in domestic cases is generally unsuitable, since the borrower's earning power is unlikely to be at its peak in the early years. Hence long ago a system was devised whereby the monthly payments are kept constant during the whole lifetime of the loan. This is such a standard method that when people speak of the "capital-and-interest" method this is what they generally mean. To it we now turn.

The capital-and-interest method

18–21   The borrower pays (every month, or whatever) a sum which has within it two elements, namely (a) the interest due and (b) part of the capital. The amount of the latter is calculated so that the whole capital will have been repaid by the end of the term. The expression "repayment" method is often used for this type of loan contract, but since all loan contracts require repayment it is misleading and we will not use it here.

The monthly payment stays constant throughout the term, apart from any changes which may result from alterations to the interest rate, but the proportion of that constant payment that represents capital is constantly changing in an upwards direction, and, conversely, the interest element is constantly dwindling. In the early years almost all of the monthly payment is interest. As the years go by, more and more of the capital is paid off, and so the total annual interest bill gradually falls. As it falls, more and more of the monthly payment can be ascribed to capital. Near the end of the life of the loan, almost all the monthly payment is of capital. The monthly payment is mathematically calculated to ensure that the loan will be fully paid off at exactly the term. The calculations are quite complex in theory but of course in practice there are preprinted tables and software programmes. Each year the lender sends the borrower a statement showing how much capital has been repaid.

This method has, historically, been the most popular way of structuring home loan contracts. It is not difficult to understand, and the borrower has the assurance that it will, if kept up, ensure the repayment of the whole loan by the end of the term. There is also the comfort of seeing, in the annual statement, the amount of the loan falling year by year.

The interest-only method

The other method is to pay nothing but interest during the term, thus keeping the capital constant. The capital is then paid off in a lump sum at the end of the term. These are occasionally called "bullet" loans or "balloon" loans but currently the normal term is an "interest-only loan". (This expression is perhaps slightly misleading, because it suggests that only interest is paid. That is true until maturity, but at maturity the capital must be repaid.) To ensure that there will be money to repay the whole loan at term, the borrower will enter into some kind of savings scheme (in this context known as the repayment vehicle) which, all being well, will generate enough money. Some lenders positively require the borrower to do this, as a term of the loan contract. Other borrowers merely recommend to the borrower that this be done. 18–22

Both this method and the capital-and-interest method are commonly used in home loans. Traditionally, lenders were reluctant to offer interest-only mortgages since it meant tying up the capital for the whole term,[16] or at least potentially so.[17] During the 1970s and 1980s interest-only loans gradually became dominant. In recent years, however, there has been a strong trend back to old-fashioned capital-and-interest home loans.

There are various kinds of repayment vehicle. Some of them may have tax advantages. This was true of the endowment vehicle, which was the original and best-known type of repayment vehicle, and the removal of its special tax status was one reason for its decline. It does not need to be said that tax rules constantly change. But because of its historical role, and because life assurance is in any case important for home loans, we begin with life assurance, then look at endowment mortgages, and thereafter look briefly at some other repayment vehicles.

---

[16] Indeed, it used to be the case that lenders would offer this package only at a higher rate of interest than for a repayment mortgage.

[17] In fact most mortgages will be paid off ahead of time.

Types of life assurance

18–23   There are many different sorts of life assurance available. But the basics are as follows.

(1) *Term assurance.* If the life assured[18] dies within the next 15 years (or whatever period is agreed) the life office will pay the sum assured. But if s/he dies even one day later, nothing is payable. This is cheaper, in terms of premiums, than the following two types, for the simple reason that in most cases the life office never has to pay out a single penny. An even cheaper variant is the reducing term assurance, in which the sum assured declines as the years pass, to zero at the end of the term.[19]

(2) *Whole of life assurance.* A whole of life policy matures on death, whenever that is. This is more expensive in terms of premiums because no one is immortal, and so the life office has to pay out one day.

(3) *Endowment assurance.* An endowment policy matures on the death of the life assured, but if the assured is still alive at a stated date (the 65th birthday for instance) the policy matures anyway. This is, in premium terms, the most expensive form of assurance. The life office is bound to pay some day, and at all events not later than the stated date. Endowment policies have now become unpopular and some companies have stopped offering them. But historically they have been of huge importance and there are many millions still in existence.

In the first two types (term assurance and whole-of-life assurance) the sum payable on death is generally a predetermined sum stated in the policy itself. But in the third (endowment assurance) this is not usually the case.[20] There are two main types of endowment policy where the sum payable is not fixed but flexible. In the traditional "with-profits" endowment, the policy states a fixed sum which is the minimum which will be paid. But over the years "bonuses" are added to the policy, the amount of which will depend on the investment success of the life office. When the policy matures, the sum payable will normally be well in excess of the guaranteed minimum. These endowment policies have long been a popular way of combining life assurance with savings. A popular variant is the "low-cost with-profits" endowment. Here the minimum sum payable at the maturity date is less than the minimum sum payable at death. However, the policy holder hopes that the bonuses to be added over the years will more than make up the difference. These are only the basic types. In practice, there is a myriad of different endowment options. One variant which is worth mentioning is the low-start, low-cost, with-profits endowment, where the monthly payments to the life office are in the early years lower than they would otherwise be, and higher in the later years.

Although endowment policies are in the form of life assurance policies, they are functionally a mixture of life assurance and savings. As savings, they are likely to perform better, in the longer term, than

---

[18] The "life assured" is to be distinguished from the "policy holder". In practice they are often the same person, but they need not be.

[19] Such policies are widely used as "mortgage protection policies". See later.

[20] If it is, the endowment policy is a "without profits" policy. These are rare.

deposits, while avoiding the potential for extreme volatility that affects direct equity investment. However, they are opaque products. Policy holders are likely to know little about how the funds are invested or how the successive bonuses are determined.

The level of premium depends on various factors, including the age and health and sex of the life assured. Alex, aged 40, a heavy drinker, smoker and drug abuser, who works as a mercenary in central Africa, will not get such favourable terms as Tom, a healthy 21-year-old who avoids all drugs and hazardous activities, such as sexual intercourse, except under medical supervision. Mother nature (not father nature) decrees that most men live shorter lives than most women, so that women pay lower premiums than men, as the risk to the life office is lower.

The life assured is the person on whose death the policy will become payable. The policy holder is the person to whom, or to whose representatives, the money will be payable on maturity. This is usually in the first instance the same person as the life assured, but need not be. Thus, a woman might take out a policy on her husband's life: he would be the life assured but she would be the policy holder.[21] Joint policies are possible, and sometimes are used by couples. There are two main types: those payable on the first death and payable to the survivor, and those payable on the first death and payable to the estate of the first to die. Joint policies payable on the second death are possible but rare. It is (to coin a phrase) strange but true that life offices themselves get muddled about these different types of joint policy. Indeed it is sometimes difficult to determine from the policy documents themselves which kind of joint policy it is. So if clients take out a joint policy this point should be clarified.

A life policy is normally assignable, which is to say that the holder can transfer it to someone else, by reason of sale or otherwise. The "insurable interest" restrictions apply only for the creation of a policy. Once created, a policy can be assigned to someone who has no insurable interest. The assignee then becomes the policy holder, and if the policy matures will be the person paid by the life office. As will be seen, such assignations are common. It must not be forgotten that every assignation requires intimation to the life office.

Life policies normally acquire a capital value as time goes on. For instance, if there is an endowment policy with a maturity value of £50,000, which will mature next year when the life assured is 65, the *present* value of the policy is therefore of a similar figure. Thus the life office would be prepared to pay a large sum to be freed of their liability to pay the money next year. This—the sum a life office is prepared to

---

[21] A familiar example from commerce is "key person insurance" whereby a business takes out insurance on the life of a key employee, typically a director. It should be noted, however, that the law restricts the right to take out life assurance over the life of another, for reasons of public policy. The person taking out the policy must have an "insurable interest". One spouse has an insurable interest in the life of the other, and a business has an insurable interest in the life of an employee.

pay to be freed of its obligations—is called the surrender value. In practice, however, the surrender values which are offered by the life offices are not generous, and a better price can usually be obtained by selling the policy.

Life assurance and home loans

18-24   Life assurance interacts with residential conveyancing in two ways. The first is that the lender is likely to recommend, and may insist, that the borrower takes out what is called a mortgage protection policy. This is term life assurance where the term is the life of the mortgage and the maturity value is the loan. The policy is often of the reducing type, so that at any stage the amount covered by the policy will be the current amount of capital due, which, if the capital-and-interest method is used, is a steadily declining figure.[22] The idea is that if the borrower dies during the life of the loan, there will be a fund out of which the loan can be paid off. The one case where the lender will not recommend, or insist on, a mortgage protection policy is where the home loan is of the endowment type, since that has inbuilt life assurance. To that we now turn.

Endowment mortgages

18-25   In an endowment mortgage the borrower takes out an endowment policy with a life office and a loan with the lender. The maturity period of the policy is the same as the term of the loan. Thus, if the borrower dies during the term, the policy matures and pays off the loan. If the borrower survives to term, the policy matures at exactly the right moment to pay off the loan. Unless it is a non-profit endowment (which is rare) there will usually be bonuses as well, so that after the loan has been paid off there will, with luck, be a surplus. During the life of the loan the borrower pays the lender interest only. The borrower thus has two monthly payments to make, one to the lender, of interest, and the other to the life office, of premiums.

At one time the life policy was invariably assigned to the lender, but nowadays most lenders do not require it, though there is usually a contractual right to demand an assignation. If the policy is assigned it works as additional security. If there is default the lender could surrender the policy to the life office or auction it, though this seldom happens as in practice the lender simply sells the house. If the borrower dies, the whole maturity value of an assigned policy is paid by the life office to the lender because the latter is the holder, even if the amount involved is greater than the debt. The lender then deducts the amount of the loan and pays the balance to the executor or whoever is entitled to

---

[22] However, level term assurance is also often used. This would mean that if, for example, the borrower died 15 years into a 25-year mortgage, there would be a surplus left after repaying the loan.

the reversion to the policy.[23] Usually, of course, the borrower does survive to the age of 65 or whenever. If so, well and good. The life office pays the maturity value to the lender, which then pays any free balance to the borrower.

If the life policy is a low-cost, with-profits endowment, the minimum sum guaranteed to be payable on death is not less than the capital of the debt. But, unlike a conventional endowment, the sum payable at maturity at the end of the term is not so guaranteed. The borrower simply hopes that the accumulated bonuses will be enough to pay off the loan at that stage, and, even better, will deliver a surplus.

Most existing home loans are either endowment or capital-and-interest, although few new home loans are of the endowment type. How do they compare with each other in practice? With the endowment method the monthly payment to the lender is smaller than it would be with the capital-and-interest method, but this does not mean that the endowment method is cheaper, because there are the assurance premiums to take into account too. But as against this the person with a capital-and-interest loan must also pay premiums on a mortgage protection policy, though because this is term assurance only the premiums will be fairly low.

Endowment mortgages can be less flexible than capital-and-interest mortgages in a number of respects. Early repayment of an endowment mortgage may be harder because capital has not declined. To release the capital value of the endowment policy, sale or surrender is required, which can be complicated and which may not realise a fair value.[24] Changing the term of the loan is harder with the endowment method because it normally involves renegotiating the life policy. Again, whereas it is usually easy to convert from capital-and-interest to endowment, the converse is more difficult, both for practical reasons and because if an endowment policy is surrendered, a loss usually results. So once into the endowment system, the borrower tends to be locked in. Again, the investment element in an endowment mortgage is inflexible in that the borrower is tied to a single company for the period of the loan.

The rise and fall of the endowment mortgage

Endowment mortgages reached their peak in the 1980s. In the past 18–26 few years they have declined dramatically in popularity. Whilst the number of new endowment mortgages being set up is small, the number of existing ones is large. The following table shows the rise and fall.[25]

---

[23] Questions of great difficulty—and of great practical importance—can arise as to who is deemed to have paid off the loan. The first to die? The survivor? Both, equally? See Gretton (1987) 32 J.L.S.S. 303 and (1988) 33 J.L.S.S. 141, but the subject awaits a full study. See also the important case of *Christie's Exr v Armstrong*, 1996 S.L.T. 948.

[24] Early repayment in order to sell the existing house and to buy another, of the same or greater value, presents no difficulty in an endowment mortgage, for the policy can be used to finance the new mortgage. However, problems may arise if the owner wishes to sell but not to buy another house, or wishes to buy another house but of a lower value.

[25] From the House of Commons Treasury Select Committee Report, *Restoring Confidence in Long-term Savings: Endowment Mortgages* (March 11, 2004), p.8. Ultimate data source: Association of British Insurers.

Percentage Share of UK Mortgage Market

Year	Capital-and-interest	Endowment	Other
1969	88	9	3
1970	88	7	5
1971	86	8	6
1972	80	12	8
1973	72	17	11
1974	73	16	11
1975	74	16	10
1976	72	18	10
1977	71	21	8
1978	67	25	8
1979	64	27	10
1980	69	23	9
1981	74	20	6
1982	73	20	7
1983	41	54	5
1984	38	61	1
1985	42	57	1
1986	28	70	2
1987	18	80	2
1988	14	83	3
1989	18	79	3
1990	20	76	4
1991	18	77	5
1992	21	68	12
1993	26	59	15
1994	30	56	14
1995	35	46	16
1996	38	32	24
1997	41	34	26
1998	43	34	25
1999	47	28	25
2000	60	17	23
2001	72	9	19
2002	82	5	13

Alleged flexibility

Endowment mortgages were often promoted on the footing that it was 18–27 a sort of transferable mortgage, which could be continued when the owner needed to move house. This quotation from someone described as a "borrower" illustrates this: "I will probably move in a couple of years, and then who knows? I don't want to have to take out a new mortgage every time I move up the ladder. With an endowment, you can top it up to cover the extra borrowing and it will still be repaid 25 years after you bought your very first house. This system seems more sensible in this day and age."[26] There is very little in this. On moving house a client must "take out a new mortgage" regardless of what type of mortgage his old house was on. It is just as easy to "move up the ladder" in the repayment system as in the endowment system. Those hoping to gain commission by selling endowment policies—and these commissions were lucrative—might nevertheless say the sort of things just quoted. Or again take the following from *What Mortgage* magazine:[27] "With a repayment mortgage you have to start again, paying it off from scratch, if you move to another property. An interest-only loan has a separate payment vehicle which still stands even if you buy a more expensive property." This, and the previous quotation, is indicative of the sort of sales pitch which sells, or used to sell, endowment mortgages. It ignores the fact that with the endowment mortgage no part of the debt will have been repaid, and it omits to mention that if a more expensive property is being bought the existing repayment vehicle will normally have to be topped up.

The great endowment mortgage crisis

Once upon a time endowment mortgages were the best. Their 18–28 favourable tax treatment, and the fact that inflation tended to push stock market prices up in nominal terms while the capital of the mortgage remained fixed, meant (in the typical case) that not only would the loan be paid off but there would also be a surplus.

But eventually the tax privileges were withdrawn, while inflation, which had been so marked a feature of most of the second half of the 20th century, fell to a low level. As a result the inflationary upward movement of share prices slowed markedly. In 2001-2003 the UK stock market moved down sharply. Many endowment policies, particularly those of the popular low-cost type, began to look unlikely to realise enough, at maturity, to pay off the home loan. It became apparent that the growth projections issued by the insurance industry were often unrealistic, so that the premium levels had often been set at too low a level. It emerged that many people had been told that an endowment policy would be certain to pay off the home loan. That was "mis-selling". In legal terms it was misrepresentation.

The FSA required insurers to send out "re-projection letters". These came in three varieties. The nice ones were the Green Letters. These

---

[26] *Which Mortgage*, September 1992, p.21.
[27] December 1998, p.18.

said that "your endowment policy is on track to repay the target amount at the end of the term". (But even a Green Letter might be a disappointment to the consumer who had been led to expect a surplus.) Amber Letters said that "there is a significant risk that your endowment policy may not pay out the target amount at the end of the term". The Red Letters said that "there is a high risk that your endowment policy may not pay out the target amount at the end of the term." About three-quarters of all re-projection letters have been Red. These letters also contained advice about what to do if there was a projected shortfall, and also how to complain and seek compensation if the consumer felt that he or she had been mis-sold the policy.[28] The FSA imposed a compensation scheme on the industry but which is without prejudice to a consumer's common law rights.

On March 11, 2004 the House of Commons Treasury Select Committee published a report, *Restoring Confidence in Long-term Savings: Endowment Mortgages.*[29] The title is indicative of the damage done. The Report said that "the insurance industry has a poor track record for asset allocation."[30] It said that:

> "around 80% of endowment policies are now unlikely meet their target of repaying the original mortgage, with an average shortfall across policies of £5,500. The shortfall on policies is likely to grow over time, but the current figures nevertheless suggest a collective shortfall across the endowment mortgage market that is already approaching £40 billion. The industry initially failed to give policy-holders adequate information about the shortfalls emerging across the endowment mortgages market . . ."[31]

It also reported that:

> "The industry was also slow to respond to intense regulatory pressure to improve the marketing of low-cost endowment mortgages. The regulator initially warned in late 1999 that the standard of endowment mortgage marketing was inadequate. Continued problems surfaced in summer 2000 and the FSA had to take further action in the autumn of 2000. So far, five firms have been fined £5.2 million and over £670 million has been paid out in compensation to endowment policyholders. The available evidence suggests that between 50% and 60% of all policyholders believe their policies were mis-sold . . ."[32]

Where complaints have been made "many companies have not handled complaints fairly and the FSA has intervened repeatedly on this issue.

---

[28] Complaining is fairly straightforward: details can be found on the FSA website at *http://www.fsa.gov.uk/*. The endowment crisis has spawned numerous firms that offer to make claims on behalf of consumers.

[29] Available on the House of Commons website *http://www.parliament.uk/*.

[30] p.4.

[31] p.3.

[32] p.3

Even so, for some companies the Financial Ombudsman Service . . . is finding in favour of the consumer in over 50% of cases. This suggests that much of the industry is still locked into an unacceptable culture that focuses upon short term sales rather than long term customer care."[33]

However, some of the outrage over endowment mortgages is, perhaps, excessive. For many years endowment mortgages were an excellent idea. They almost always paid off the home loan and generally produced a handsome surplus as well. Even after the disappearance of the favourable tax treatment there was a case to be made for them. It is possible that many people who took out endowment mortgages without being warned of the risks would have made the same decision anyway.

Other repayment vehicles for interest-only loans

A variant on the endowment mortgage is the unit-linked endowment. 18–29 The life office invests in a unitised fund and the maturity value is the value of the units at maturity.[34] These have a higher risk/reward ratio than conventional endowments. If the investments do well, the customer does better than in a conventional endowment, and vice versa. protection. The ISA[35] mortgage is also a riskier repayment vehicle which does, however, have tax advantages. In a pension[36] mortgage the repayment vehicle is a personal pension scheme which matures at retirement age (which will be the same date as the term of the loan). Part of the pension will be commuted into a lump sum which pays off the loan. The rest of the pension remains to give a regular income. There is no assignation to the lender, since pension funds are non-assignable. The borrower will also have to take out a mortgage protection life policy as in the case of a repayment mortgage. The attraction of the pension mortgage is that pension schemes receive favourable tax treatment. Disadvantages are that the system may compel retirement at the agreed time, and that there is no surrender value. Pension mortgages are available only to the self-employed.

Foreign currency mortgages

A foreign currency mortgage is one denominated in a foreign currency 18–30 such as Euros or Japanese yen or Swiss francs. In other words, though the house is in Scotland the loan is in dollars, or whatever, and must be repaid in dollars. There is no law compelling people to transact in sterling. Foreign currency loans are attractive when sterling interest rates are significantly higher than interest rates in the foreign currency in question. Because of the possibility that sterling might depreciate against the other currency, thereby increasing the debt in sterling terms, foreign currency loans are risky and only for the financially sophisticated.

---

[33] p.4.

[34] As with low-cost, with-profit endowment, there is a life assurance element whereby if the borrower dies, the life office guarantees as a minimum to pay off the loan.

[35] Individual Savings Accounts. The predecessor of the ISA was the PEP (Personal Equity Plan) and thus there exist some PEP mortgages though no new ones can be created.

[36] Or PPP—Personal Pension Plan.

Indexed mortgages

18–31   An indexed mortgage is one where the capital of the loan is index-linked, so that the total debt increases with inflation. The benefit to the borrower is that because his capital is secure in real terms the lender can afford to charge a lower rate of interest. To this extent the idea is similar to that of a foreign currency mortgage. They are, however, rare. The Building Societies Act 1986 authorises building societies to lend on this basis.

Equity share mortgages

18–32   An equity share mortgage is where the borrowers and lenders are owners in common of the house. The borrowers have a mortgage only in respect of their share. Thus, this is cheaper for them. The contract provides for the transfer of the other share to them in slices, until they own it all. The price payable for each slice is fixed by an index or by arbitration. The idea is to help poorer people who could not afford to take a secured loan over the whole property. Such arrangements are not common. Deals of this sort can sometimes be set up with a housing association. The buyers pay the association rent for the slice not (yet) owned by them. A variant of this idea is where the sellers sell only a 50 per cent (or whatever) share, with the other 50 per cent to be bought by the buyers after (say) five years, or sooner at their option, at a value to be fixed by an independent valuer. The buyers need initially to get a loan only to cover the 50 per cent.

Non-purchase home loans

18–33   This chapter deals with loans for house purchase. But a person may already own a house and wish to use it as security for a loan for some other purpose. We will not discuss such loans here, apart from certain particular aspects.

Buy-to-let loans

18–34   Until recently loans to enable a person to buy a house to let it out were almost unknown. Banks were not interested in long-term lending. Building societies would lend only to owner-occupiers. Moreover, in addition to the absence of a supply of funds, there was no demand, since the Rent Acts meant that rent levels were kept at a below-market rate. Investing in rented property was only for those with a death wish. But all that has changed. "Buying to let" is now popular and banks are willing to lend.

Remortgages

18–35   A remortgage is where a new home loan is taken out and the proceeds used to pay off the old one. This is done where for one reason or another the borrowers prefer the terms of the new loan. The preference for change will have to be fairly strong because of the costs involved. These are: (i) re-survey fee (ii) an administrative charge by new lender and (iii) legal expenses. However in recent years competition among lenders has led to special offers for new business, and as a result consumers have been increasingly changing from one loan to another.

Further advances

A further advance is where the borrower borrows more money from 18–36 the same lender. This is common for home improvements. Lenders are usually willing to make a further advance for this purpose, so long as there is sufficient equity.[37] Likewise a further advance is usually easily obtainable to pay for a large but unexpected repair, since the lender has an interest in ensuring the good condition of the property. Because the original standard security will almost invariably have been for all sums due and to become due, it automatically covers the new advance.[38] Lenders will usually wish to know the purpose for which the further advance is sought, and will often impose restrictions, especially in the case of building societies.

Second mortgages

A second mortgage is where there is a further secured loan which, for 18–37 whatever reason, is not from the existing lender. There are some institutions which specialise in these. As a postponed heritable security, it ranks second. A notice of second charge should be sent to the first lender under section 13 of the 1970 Act.

Equity release mortgages—lifetime mortgages

People who have reached the age of, say, 70 will normally have paid 18–38 off the home loan and retired. But the pension may not be very good. Why live in semi-poverty while they are sitting on a valuable asset, which, when they die, will merely enrich their heirs? Why not release some of the equity and spend it while still alive? This is the reasoning behind what are called equity release mortgages, home income mortgages, or lifetime mortgages. The way it works is that the elderly person borrows and secures the debt on the house. Interest only is payable,[39] the capital being repayable at death. The proceeds of the loan are typically used to buy an annuity. Part of the income from the annuity is used to pay the interest on the loan. The rest is free extra income. When the person dies, the capital is repaid. The net effect is that the value of the estate at death is less than it would otherwise have been. The money has, instead, been spent by the owner while still alive. Insurance companies offer annuities, and some have prepackaged equity release schemes. Because the cost of an annuity depends on life expectancy at commencement, these schemes only make sense for older people. The amount of

---

[37] Equity in this context means market value of the property minus secured debt.

[38] Subject to s.13 of the Conveyancing and Feudal Reform (Scotland) Act 1970.

[39] Unless it is a roll-up mortgage, in which interest is not paid but is accumulated with capital. These roll-up mortgages can be arranged on a drawdown basis, whereby the elderly person does not borrow the full amount at once but only as and when needed.

the loan is typically about 25 per cent of the value of the property. Thus most of the value is still available to the heirs.

There are many variants on the market. One variant—sometimes called a home reversion—is actually not in the form of a loan at all. In this, there is a sale and lease-back. The company thus becomes legal owner, and the elderly person becomes tenant, at a nominal rent of say £5 per annum, the lease lasting to death. Sometimes the owner sells only a share of the property, *e.g.* 50 per cent. The price paid by the reversionary company will not be the current market price, but a discounted figure, discounted to reflect the fact that the company does not recover its investment until the death of the planholder.

Such schemes can be a good way of rescuing an elderly person from unnecessary poverty. But they can have drawbacks too. In the first place, if the person dies soon after the scheme is set up, the annuity company makes a large profit, the heirs suffer a large loss, and the elderly person only gets little benefit. This, of course, is a risk inherent in any annuity deal. Naturally it can work the other way round too, as with any annuity: if the person lives to 110, the annuity company suffers a large loss, and the elderly person can die happy in the knowledge of having done what was probably the best business deal of his or her life. Secondly, the estate is less than it would otherwise be. Whether this matters or not depends on the circumstances. If the elderly person has no spouse or children, this may be no problem. But if the person wants to leave a good estate to his or her heirs, this scheme may be inappropriate. Finally, the interest rate on the loan may be variable whereas the annuity is normally fixed. This is fine if interest rates fall, but can be a disaster if they rise. There have been many people who entered into an equity release deal and later came to regret it. The modern, and wise, trend is therefore for the interest to be a fixed rate.

Equity release schemes have frequently come in for strong criticism. While they can be valuable, they need very careful consideration. The money released may diminish welfare benefits.[40] There may be tax consequences. And of course the estate will in due course be smaller than it would otherwise have been.

How much can be borrowed?

18–39   Here only ordinary house purchase loans are dealt with. Two factors determine how much can be borrowed. The first is the status of the borrower, and the second is the value of the house. But exactly how these factors will be applied varies from lender to lender, and also varies from one year to another. So what follows is only a general picture. The lender will take details about the borrower, especially about her/his income. In general, a lender will advance up to about 3.5 times the income, calculated before deductions for tax, national insurance and so forth. Often there are joint borrowers (*e.g.* husband and wife) both with incomes. In that case the practice is to lend about 3.5 times the larger income plus the smaller income. Thus if the larger income is £50,000 and the smaller is £30,000, the maximum loan would be (3.5 × £50,000) +

---

[40] Many elderly people fail to claim all the benefits to which they are entitled.

(£30,000) = £205,000. Another approach is to lend up to 2.75 times the combined income. That would be 2.75 × (£50,000 + £30,000) = £220,000. Extra income, such as overtime, may be included or excluded or included at a reduced weighting, according to the policy of the lender.

The other factor determining the amount borrowable is the value of the property. Once again, practice varies, with some lenders prepared to offer up to 90 per cent of value, others 95 per cent others 100 per cent, while yet other figures may be encountered. Indeed, lenders are free to lend more than 100 per cent of value, and this occasionally happens. The percentage[41] is calculated, not on the purchase price, but on the valuation obtained by the lender from its surveyor. Often the valuation figure is lower than the final purchase price, since a lender's surveyor may take a cautious approach. This point is important since it is often not appreciated by clients. Thus, if a 90 per cent loan is available, and the property is valued at £100,000, but bought for £110,000, the purchaser will then have £20,000 still to find.

There are thus two maximum figures, one based on status and the other on value. Which applies? The answer is, whichever is the lower. Thus, suppose that the couple in our earlier example wish to buy a house which the surveyor values at £250,000. And suppose that the lender is prepared to lend only up to 80 per cent of valuation, *i.e.* £200,000. The status-based maximum was £205,000. So the lender will lend up to £200,000. If the house is in fact bought for £250,000, the clients will have to find £50,000 out of their own pockets, plus the expenses involved in house purchase.

Some lenders have an absolute maximum which they are prepared to lend, but this is seldom a problem. Most have no limit, and for those that do the limit is usually high, such as £500,000.

Borrowers often tend to assume that if the lender is prepared to lend a given figure, then they can afford to meet the repayments on that loan. It is easy for the solicitor to make the same assumption. But the rules used by lenders for determining maximum loans based on status are mechanical and may be inappropriate to the individual borrower, who may in fact not be able to afford the loan which the lender is prepared to give. The solicitor should point this out to the clients. A particular danger is that a large loan is taken out and then interest rates rise.[42] An affordable loan may cease to be affordable. Since a sharp rise in interest rates may trigger a fall in property prices, the buyers are stuck with a loan they cannot afford on a house which is worth less than they paid for it. In this connection, the standard income multiplier tends to rise as interest rates fall, the current standard figure of 3.5 being historically high. Those borrowing at that multiplier are taking a risk. Over the years there has been an increasing tendency to borrow more. The proportion of first-time buyers in the UK who borrowed more than three times their annual income was about 5 per cent in 1985. Now it is about 45 per cent[43]

---

[41] Known as the LTV figure, *i.e* loan to value.

[42] "When choosing between mortgages, many borrowers attach great weight to the level of initial monthly repayments and too little to the likely overall cost of borrowing over the life of the loan. Many borrowers' understanding of interest rate risk is poor." Miles Report (above), p.1.

[43] See p.17 of the Miles Report (above).

Sometimes, if the lender will not offer enough, it may be possible to obtain a top-up loan from a second lender, secured on the property on a postponed basis. Banks or insurance companies may be willing to offer this. Of course, the interest rate for a top-up loan will be higher, and may impose on the borrower monthly outgoings greater than can be afforded. But most lenders make it a requirement that the balance of the funds come from the borrowers' own resources, so that any arrangement of the kind described would need the lenders' consent.[44]

Evidence of income: self-certified loans

18–40   Lenders generally seek confirmation of income, either by being authorised to contact the salaries department of the borrower's employer, or by asking to see wages slips.

Non-status loans, also called self-certified loans, are where the lender relies on the borrower's own statement of his/her financial circumstances. They are typically used for self-employed borrowers where sufficient audited accounts are not available. Normally in a non-status loan the maximum borrowable is only around 70 per cent of the property value. In addition to this ordinary use of non-status loans, some lenders offer non-status loans (usually remortgages) to people who are or have been in financial difficulties, often at high rates of interest.[45] Such people are tempted because their financial problems undermine their credit status, thus making conventional borrowing harder.

High LTV advances

18–41   "LTV" is jargon meaning "loan to value". If lenders give a loan at a high percentage of valuation, they may insist that a guarantee be obtained from an insurance company. This is called a mortgage indemnity guarantee (MIG). Currently, most lenders will insist on a MIG where the loan exceeds a certain percentage—typically 90 per cent—of valuation. The reason for this is that high percentage loans involve a greater risk to the lenders, for if there is default there is a greater danger that the forced sale of the property will not recoup the whole loan.[46] For a MIG a one-off premium is payable by the borrowers, called a mortgage indemnity premium. The cost of this depends on the circumstances, and varies considerably from lender to lender, but can be expensive.[47] This

---

[44] The *CML Lenders' Handbook for Scotland*, para.5.8 says: "You must ask the borrower how the balance of the purchase price is being provided. If you become aware that the borrower is not providing the balance of the purchase price from his own funds and/or is proposing to give a second charge over the property, you must report this to us if the borrower agrees . . . failing which you must return our instructions and explain that you are unable to continue to act for us as there is a conflict of interest." ("Second charge" is CML-speak for a second-ranking security.)

[45] The advertisement may say "CCJs welcome". A CCJ (county court judgment) is roughly the equivalent in England of a sheriff court decree, the point being that such lenders are prepared to lend to people with a dubious credit record.

[46] About 80 per cent of mortgage enforcement cases involve mortgages where the original LTV was 90 per cent or over. See Emma McCallum and Ewen McCaig, *Mortgage Arrears and Repossessions* (2003), p 52.

[47] Thus for a 95 per cent loan on a house worth £100,000 the MIG might cost as much as £1,790. (Data from the Consumers Association website: *http://www.which.net/*.)

premium is payable by the borrower. It comes as a shock to many borrowers, and clients must be warned in advance. In addition, if there is default and the insurers have to pay, the insurer is subrogated and so can sue the borrower. Thus, a MIG is purely for the benefit of the lenders, and not for the borrowers. Many borrowers do not seem to realise this. It should have been explained to them. It may be added that a MIG is often required in low-start loans too. As an alternative to a MIG, in cases of high LTV the lenders may make a special charge at the outset, often amounting to several hundred pounds.

The avaricious borrower

Some borrowers will try to obtain a larger loan by questionable means. It is common, in self-certified loans, for borrowers to overstate their income. A loan intended for commercial purposes (eg buy-to-let) may be presented as a loan for ordinary home purchase where the lender will not lend for commercial purposes or will lend only subject to conditions. A buyer may attempt to get the lender to think that the property is worth more than it is so as too boost the amount of the loan.[48] The wise solicitor will have nothing to do with such ploys.

18–42

---

[48] Such questionable methods seem to be used openly. For instance in the January 2004 issue (p.47) of *Mortgage Advisor* it is suggested that the borrower use what is called the "inflated purchase price" method, in which the price reported to the lender and the price actually paid are different.

CHAPTER 19

HERITABLE SECURITY

Introduction

19–01   Historically there have been various forms of heritable security. Three of them, the bond and disposition in security, the bond of cash credit and disposition in security, and the *ex facie* absolute disposition, were abolished by the Conveyancing and Feudal Reform (Scotland) Act 1970,[1] though the abolition was prospective, so that such securities granted before the Act continued to exist until discharge. A fourth form, the pecuniary real burden, lingered on, seldom used, until abolished by the Title Conditions (Scotland) Act 2003.[2] The 1970 Act created a new form, the standard security. This was a development of the old forms, with a new name. Much of the old law applies equally to standard securities. Since a standard security is a species of the genus, which is heritable security, a standard security can be, and often is, called a heritable security, and a standard security holder is often called a heritable creditor.

The standard security is a true or "proper" security, meaning that it is a subordinate real right. The real right of ownership remains with the debtor.

The role of the solicitor: advising the lending clients

19–02   The lending clients will in most cases be professional moneylenders such as banks who presumably know their own business, and who generally dictate the terms of the documents used, so that the role of the solicitor is mainly the technical one of ensuring that a valid security is constituted. But the letter of instruction must be checked to see what the lenders expect. In most cases the lenders will be members of the CML[3] and if so the terms of the *CML Lenders' Handbook for Scotland* must be complied with. It must always be borne in mind that if there is eventual default, and the lenders find themselves unable to recover in full, they will, as a matter of course, see whether there is any possibility of making a claim from the solicitors who acted for them.[4]

---

[1] Conveyancing and Feudal Reform (Scotland) Act 1970, s.9(4).
[2] Title Conditions (Scotland) Act 2003, s.117.
[3] For the CML see para.18–05.
[4] See para.1–21.

The role of the solicitor: advising the borrowing clients

The solicitors must check the documentation on behalf of the clients, 19-03 and bring to their attention anything which is significant, especially anything which they might one day blame the solicitors for not telling them. For instance, if the loan contract provides for an early redemption penalty[5] it is important that the clients be told this. It is also a good idea to draw to the clients' attention other matters, such as that letting the property is not allowed without the consent of the lenders.[6] If the loan is an interest-only one, the clients need to know that there may be a risk that the savings vehicle might not repay the loan at maturity. Evidence that such advice has been given should, of course, be preserved.

Spouses and similar cases

The issues here have been discussed in Chapter 1, but it is appropriate 19-04 to touch on them again here. If one person grants a deed, such as a standard security, for the benefit of another person there is a danger that the decision to do so was not a free and informed one. For this reason in such cases it is important that the parties be separately advised. The classic example is where husband and wife are co-owners of a property and wish to grant a standard security to secure the husband's business borrowings. It is important that the same solicitors do not act for both parties, and it is important that the solicitors acting for the wife take care to explain the meaning and effect of what she is signing, and to verify, as far as it is possible to do so, that her consent is genuine. The advice should be given in writing as well as in person.

To some extent this is common sense, but the issues became more important after *Smith v Bank of Scotland*[7] which held that if a wife could show that she had been induced to sign by her husband's misrepresentation or undue influence, she could rescind, unless the lender could show that it had taken active steps to ensure that her consent was free and informed. That decision has led to numerous later ones, refining the doctrine. The doctrine has proved unpopular in the Scottish judiciary, for in case after case *Smith* has been distinguished, until it has been distinguished almost to death.[8]

Where there are joint borrowers great care must be taken if one signs as agent of the other, because of the obvious danger of fraud. Indeed, CML lenders will not accept such a deed.[9] Moreover even where the standard security bears to be signed by both parties, experience shows that there is a danger that one signature may be forged: the cautious law agent will look carefully at both signatures. Of course, such forgeries can, and do, occur in other deeds, such as dispositions, but they are

---

[5] A surcharge payable if the borrower wishes to pay off the loan before the end of the term.

[6] 1970 Act, Sch.3, Standard Condition 6.

[7] 1997 S.C. (HL) 111. See para.1–11.

[8] Most of the cases and literature are cited in Eden (2003) 7 *Edinburgh Law Review* 107. The most important case since that article is *Royal Bank of Scotland plc v Wilson*, 2003 S.C. 544. See further Reid and Gretton, *Conveyancing 2003*, p.73.

[9] The *CML Lenders' Handbook for Scotland*, para.5.11.

particularly common in the case of standard securities. It is difficult to sell a house, with a forged signature, without one's partner finding out about it, but it is rather easier to raise a secured loan with a forged signature with at least a substantial chance of not being found out.

Pro forma **deeds**

19-05   Most lenders use preprinted forms of standard security, in which the task of the solicitor is simply to fill in the blanks.[10] These *pro forma* deeds generally make reference to what used to be called the schedule of variations but nowadays is usually called the mortgage conditions, a deed which the lender will have registered in the Books of Council and Session. Each lender has its own form. This deed lays down the standard conditions of loan for that lender, and to the extent that it is operates as a variation of the standard conditions in the 1970 Act. The borrower is thus presented with a contract of adhesion—take it or leave it. There is virtually no possibility of negotiation of terms.[11]

Procedure

19-06   The lenders will write to the solicitors formally instructing them to act. This letter contains various bits and pieces. One is the letter of instruction itself. Next there is a report on title, also called a certificate of title, with blanks to be filled in. After examining the title, the solicitors complete the report and return it to the lenders.[12] Next, there is a standard security with blanks. The standard security is preprinted in the lenders' preferred form. Thus, solicitors seldom have to draft complete standard securities themselves. The standard security is usually in duplicate. One is used as a draft and the other as the final version. Next, if this is to be an endowment mortgage there will be a preprinted assignation of the life policy, with blanks, once again in duplicate. Then there will be a copy of the lenders' Schedule of Variations. This means variations to the standard conditions. This should be examined and passed on to the borrowers. Next, there is, in the case of a building society, a copy of the Rules of the Society. This is important because the borrowers will normally become members, with voting rights, etc., and so it should be passed on to the borrowers. Lastly, there will be a Schedule of Writs. This is a bit of paper, mainly blank, on which will eventually be entered a list of all the title deeds, and which will be sent to the lenders with the deeds after completion of the transaction. A copy should be retained, so that the file will show what deeds are held by the lenders. Sometimes, depending on the circumstances, other documentation may also be needed. For instance, the lenders might require a guarantee from a third party.

Once the standard security and, if applicable, the assignation have been drafted and then engrossed, the engrossments are sent to the

---

[10] Examples can be found in Halliday, *op. cit.*

[11] That is to say, in ordinary home loans. This book does not deal with commercial conveyancing.

[12] The report must be handled with care because it may contain all sorts of unreasonable warranties.

borrowers for execution. This should be done several days before settlement. Neither the standard security nor the assignation need to be executed by the lenders, perhaps surprisingly. A few days before settlement the completed report on title (also called the certificate of title) is sent to the lenders.[13] This states that the title is good (if it is good), and draws attention to any points which the solicitors think the lenders should know. Payment of the loan is requested at the same time. The lenders remit the money to the solicitors, not to the borrowers. This used to be done by cheque but today is usually done by bank transfer. Now settlement can take place. If, after requisitioning the funds, a major problem crops up, such as a significant delay in settlement, the solicitors must notify the lenders. If there is a delay in settlement for more than a few days the lenders will want the money back again for the period until settlement does take place.

After settlement the standard security must be sent off without delay for registration. The fee charged by Register House for a standard security is smaller (currently £22) if the security accompanies a disposition. If the borrower is a company the standard security must also be registered in the Companies Register.[14] If there is an assignation of a life policy, the formal intimation must be sent to the life office. This too must be done immediately after settlement. When all the deeds are to hand they should be sent to the lenders for safekeeping.

Personal search and company search

In a typical conveyancing transaction the personal search covers both 19–07 the purchasers and the sellers. Usually, if a problem arises it is because there is something in the search affecting the sellers, but the purchasers' solicitors need to check the search against their own clients as well as against the sellers. The reason is that they have to make sure that the lenders are going to get a good security. It occasionally emerges that a purchaser is an undischarged bankrupt, surprising though this may seem, and has failed to disclose this fact to his solicitor.[15] So when acting for buyers it is important to check the Personal Register in relation to the buyers/ borrowers as well as the sellers. For the same reason, if the borrowers are a company, a company search will be needed.

Should a fresh personal search be made for a further advance? There is some uncertainty as to whether a supervening inhibition could affect a further advance,[16] but at all events if there is an inhibition the agent for the lender will wish to know that fact. And, obviously, if the borrower has been sequestrated, or granted a trust deed, the further advance will be refused. (The personal search will disclose sequestration and protected trust deeds as well as inhibition.) Similar remarks apply to the company search when there is a further advance. However, in practice lenders usually make further advances without the involvement of solicitors, and so searches are seldom made.

---

[13] See generally the *CML Lenders' Handbook for Scotland*, para.10.

[14] See para.25–05.

[15] There are several reported cases where a standard security has been granted by an undischarged bankrupt, most recently *Halifax plc v Gorman's Tr*, 2000 S.L.T. 1409. See further Ch.26.

[16] See G. L. Gretton, *Law of Inhibition and Adjudication* (2nd ed., 1996), Ch.9.

The six sources of rights and duties

19–08   In a loan secured by standard security it can be surprisingly difficult to determine what the rights and duties of the parties are. Those rights and duties in the typical case will have no fewer than six sources, and sometimes more. (i) The first is the loan contract. In a home loan this is usually contained in an offer of loan made by the bank and accepted by the borrower. (ii) The second is the standard security. (iii) The third is part II of the Conveyancing and Feudal Reform (Scotland) Act 1970. (iv) The fourth is Schedule 3 of that Act. Though this is part of the Act, it was designed to function as a standard-form contract. (v) The fifth is the schedule of variations, or mortgage conditions, which most lenders use. (vi) The sixth is the Mortgage Rights (Scotland) Act 2001. Indeed, there are yet other sources, such as the Consumer Credit Act 1974. Thus even quite simple questions about the rights and duties of the parties can be difficult to answer, especially since these six sources can easily fail to dovetail with each other.

The loan and the security

19–09   A standard security secures a loan. Unlike most of other rights, a security has no independent existence: it exists only in relation to another right, the secured obligation. In traditional language, it is an accessory right.[17] The obligation can exist without the security but the security cannot exist without an actual or at least potential obligation.

Although there must be an obligation which is secured, the obligation does not have to be the debt of the granter of the security. It is possible for the owner of property, Jack, to grant a standard security over it for the debt of Jill. In that case, Jack has no personal liability. Suppose that Jill's debt is £200,000 and Jack's property is worth £180,000. If Jill defaults and the creditor forces the sale of the house, Jack will lose his house, but he will not be liable for the shortfall of £20,000. This sort of arrangement is sometimes called third party security. Thus whilst in a typical standard security the proprietor and the debtor are the same person, this does not have to be the case. Third party security should not be confused with a similar state of affairs, where a third party grants a cautionary obligation (guarantee) and then grants a standard security to secure that obligation. For instance, in the example suppose that Jack had guaranteed Jill's debt and had granted a security for that guarantee. In that case Jack would be personally liable (contingently on Jill's default) for up to £200,000. In this latter case the security granted by Jack secures his *own* obligation (the cautionary obligation)[18] whereas in the first example the security secured an obligation of Jill's.

A standard security can secure a specific debt of a definite amount, such as a loan of £100,000. Or it can secure a specific bank account, where the overdraft may rise and fall and rise again, so that what is secured is a fluctuating amount. Or it can secure "all sums due or to become due" by the debtor to the creditor. This third possibility is the

---

[17] See *e.g. Trotter v Trotter*, 2001 S.L.T. (Sh. Ct) 42.
[18] Of course, the cautionary obligation itself secures Jill's obligation.

commonest in practice. It is convenient because it means that if any further advance will automatically be covered by the security. Without this system, lenders would be more reluctant to make a further advance, or would have to insist on a new standard security, which would be slow and expensive.

Whether a standard security is for all sums or not is determined by the wording of the bond element. Often a form A security (see below) will state the loan as a fixed sum, but later have a clause stating that the security is to be good not only for the loan but for all sums. Alternatively, a form A security may not state the amount of the loan at all, but merely have words obliging the grantor to pay to the grantee all sums, for which obligation the security is granted. The wording of the standard security ought to make it clear what obligations are secured, and usually it is clear. But not always.[19] Although the "all sums" clause is convenient it can cause problems. Suppose that Jane has a home loan with a bank and also has a current account with the same bank. The current account is in overdraft. The standard security will secure both the home loan account and the current account, and indeed any other sums she may owe. If she wishes to sell, the bank could refuse to discharge the security except against repayment of everything that is owed. Jane may not realise this. When she discusses the sale with her solicitors, they should check not only the home loan account but also ask if other debts exist.

Forms A and B

The 1970 Act[20] says that the security deed[21] can include the secured 19–10 obligation, or it can merely identify that obligation, which itself is to be found outwith the security deed. A standard security containing the secured obligation is a form A security, while a standard security which refers to but does not contain the secured obligation is called a form B security. Both forms are given in Schedule 2 to the Act, and either can be used. In the case of home loans form A is the norm, while in commercial cases form B is the norm. The meaning and effect of form A are defined in s. 10 of the 1970 Act. Form A is not perfectly drafted. But strict compliance with this and the other styles is not necessary.[22]

Interest rate

Form A requires the interest rate to be stated. As true fixed-interest 19–11 loans are rare, this creates a problem. The old practice was to state the rate in force at the time the security was entered into, with a further

---

[19] For problems see *Hambros Bank v Lloyds Bank*, 1999 S.L.T. 49; *Hambros Bank v Lloyds Bank (No.2)*, 1999 S.L.T. 649; *Norwich Union Life Insurance Society v Tanap Investments V.K. Ltd*, 1998 S.L.T. 623, 1999 S.L.T. 204, 2000 S.C. 515; *Royal Bank of Scotland v Shanks*, 1998 S.L.T. 355; *Hewit v Williamson*, 1998 S.C.L.R. 601; *Société General S.A. v Lloyds TSB Bank*, 1999 G.W.D. 37–1822.

[20] Sections 9 and 10 and Sch.2.

[21] The term "standard security" is used to mean both the deed and the subordinate real right created by the ensuing registration.

[22] Halliday, *op. cit.*, para.52–31.

provision to the effect that it was variable. Nowadays the usual practice is not to state the initial rate, but merely that the rate is variable. It is generally accepted that this is sufficient compliance with form A. Details about interest will then be given in the Schedule of Variations, which is referred to in the security itself.[23]

Description

19-12   The property subject to the security must be sufficiently identified by a conveyancing description. The rules are the same as for dispositions.[24] If a standard security is being granted over property which is being split off at the same time, there is a problem in that the description of the property has not yet been registered. In that case the split-off plan should be done in duplicate, one for the disposition and one for the standard security.[25]

The standard conditions

19-13   Schedule 3 of the 1970 Act sets forth the "standard conditions" which, except in so far as varied, apply to every standard security. The idea is to provide a ready-made contract.[26] These conditions can be varied, and usually are. Most institutional lenders have a Schedule of Variations which is long and tedious but important. These variations can be embodied in the standard security itself. But the normal practice is to register them in the Books of Council and Session. Each standard security simply refers to the registered schedule, and this reference is part of the pre-printed style. Although the standard conditions were intended as a ready-made contract, the 1970 Act fails to keep consistently to this idea. Thus some parts of the standard conditions are in fact mandatory requirements that the parties cannot vary.[27] Indeed, the relationship between the body of the act and the standard conditions is often a difficult one.

It has been mentioned above that the terms of a secured loan are often obscure because of the multiple sources of the rights and obligations of the parties. An example is the basic question of whether the loan is an on-demand loan or whether it is a term loan, repayable over, say, 20 years. Often the borrower has agreed a term loan, and a term loan is what is expressly set forth in the offer of loan which the borrower has accepted. Yet whilst the offer was made in a style standard for that lender, the same lender may using a Schedule of Variations that says that all loans are on-demand loans.[28] If a form A standard security is

---

[23] For a valuable account of common clauses dealing with interest, see D.J. Cusine and Robert Rennie, *Standard Securities* (2nd ed., 2002), para.3.32.

[24] As to which see Ch.12. For no good reason the rules used to be different where the property was in the GRS, but they were made the same by the Abolition of Feudal Tenure etc. (Scotland) Act 2000, Sch.12, para.30(23)(a).

[25] ROTPB, paras 6.70 and 8.47.

[26] *cf.* the standard-form articles of association in company law.

[27] See s.11.

[28] Indeed sometimes it will say in different places that it is an on-demand loan and that it is a term loan.

used, that creates a presumption that the loan is an on-demand one.[29] The result is confusion. However, in most cases neither the lender nor the borrower will actually look at the Schedule of Variations unless the latter gets into financial difficulties.

Another clause common in Schedules of Variations says that the borrower may neither transfer ownership nor grant any second security, unless with the lender's consent. This clause is arguably pointless. A standard security, being a real right, would be unaffected by any such transaction anyway. If the borrower breaks this condition, and if the loan is a term loan, the lender could in theory accelerate the loan. But if the borrower is keeping up the monthly payments it is difficult to see why the lender would wish to do that, while if the borrower is not keeping up then the lender could accelerate anyway.

Transfers subject to security

In the absence of the sort of clause just mentioned, a borrower is free **19–14** to transfer ownership without the lender's consent. This is uncommon in practice since the main reason for transfer is sale and a buyer will normally insist on an unencumbered title. Such arrangements, when they happen, are generally family transactions. An example would be where the husband owns the house (or a half share of the house), and there is a separation agreement under which he is to transfer the house (or his share of it) to his wife.

If property is transferred subject to a security, neither personal liability nor real liability is affected. Personal liability for the loan remains with the borrower. Real liability stays with the property. Thus, in the event of default the house could be sold even though it is in new ownership, but the new owner is not personally liable for the loan.[30]

If is desired to transfer ownership to another person, keeping the loan and security in place, and for the outgoing owner to be freed of liability and for the incoming owner to take on liability, there are two possibilities. The first is for the disponer and disponee to agree that the latter will pay the loan, and that if for any reason the disponer is made to pay it, the disponee will indemnify the disponer. This is good as far as it goes, but since the lender has not agreed to the arrangement the disponer is still liable, and so still at risk. If, for instance, the disponee later became bankrupt, the disponer would end up paying the debt. A more satisfactory method, therefore, is to obtain the lender's agreement. This can be done by discharging the old loan and security and putting in place a new secured loan. Another method that achieves the same substantive result is to have a bond of corroboration and discharge.[31] This is a tripartite deed, signed by the old owner, the new owner, and the lender. "Corroboration" means that the new owner is accepting personal liability under the loan contract. "Discharge" means that the lender is

---

[29] 1970 Act, s.10.

[30] Subject to the Conveyancing (Scotland) Act 1874, s.47 and the Conveyancing (Scotland) Act 1924, s.15.

[31] Such a deed is now classifiable as a "deed of variation" within the meaning of s.16 of the 1970 Act.

discharging the old owner of any personal liability. In addition, of course, there must be the disposition. The old owner cannot be quit of personal liability merely by disponing the property, nor by the fact of another person assuming liability. Discharge requires the consent of the lender.

An example of a slightly different arrangement is where Eve owns a house, subject to a standard security, and marries Adam, and the couple agree on common ownership. A simple disposition of a half share will achieve this, though if the standard security has a prohibition on transfer then the consent of the lender will be required. But even then the result would be that while ownership was shared, the woman alone would be the debtor. Hence it is usual in such a case to have a deed of variation of the standard security whereby the husband assumes joint and several liability for the loan.

Joint borrowers

19–15   Often there are two borrowers, such as husband and wife. What normally happens in such a case is that they are jointly and severally liable for the loan, and that each one-half *pro indiviso* share is burdened with the whole loan. Sometimes they make future joint borrowings from the same lender. Assuming that the standard security contains, as it usually does, an "all sums due and to become due" clause, then the future loans will be on the same footing as the original one.

Problems can arise where future loans are made to only one of the parties. For example, Jack and Jill are co-owners and grant a standard security for a joint loan. Some years later Jack borrows money from the same lender. The loan is made to him alone. Will this loan be covered by the standard security? If so, does it affect only Jack's *pro indiviso* share or does it affect Jill's too? Is she personally liable for it? The answers depend on the facts of each case. Some banks use styles that expressly provide that any debt, incurred at any time, owed to the bank by either party burdens the whole property, and that each party is personally liable for it, even though the debt may be incurred without her consent or even knowledge.[32] Whether the use of such clauses in consumer transactions is ethical is open to debate. Possibly they might be challenged under the Unfair Terms in Consumer Contracts Regulations 1999.[33] A majority of institutional lenders use styles that are less clear and that may cover only joint debts. For instance they provide that the deed covers debts due by "the borrower", a term that is defined as meaning Jack and Jill. Although such deeds almost always have a clause declaring liability to be joint and several, it is arguable that that clause does not extend the class of debts that is covered, but merely states the nature of the liability for such debts as are covered, and that only debts that are due by both are covered.[34] It is unsatisfactory that such a cloud of uncertainty and potential unfairness should exist, quite unnecessarily, as to everyday deeds. In practice there is seldom much chance of persuading the lender

---

[32] For an example see *Royal Bank of Scotland plc v Wilson*, 2003 S.C. 544.
[33] SI 1999/2083.
[34] See Reid and Gretton, *Conveyancing 2003*, p.79.

to change the wording, but the clients should be told of the possible implications.

This sort of problem used to be rare. Until the 1980s building societies provided most of the lending for house purchase and improvement, and did not normally lend for other purposes. The chance that Jack might later borrow from the building society without Jill's knowledge was thus slight. But in the 1980s building societies started to offer the sort of facilities formerly offered only by banks while banks started to offer home loans.

Problems can arise on the death of one party, especially where the loan is paid off by the maturing proceeds of an assigned life policy. Thus in *Christie v Armstrong*[35] Ms Armstrong and Mr Christie bought a house in common with a survivorship destination. They had a joint loan secured on the house, and also by an assigned policy over Mr Christie's life. Soon after the house had been bought, Mr Christie died, intestate, and the proceeds were, naturally, paid by the life office to the lender. The loan was thus extinguished, and Ms Armstrong was now sole owner, by virtue of the destination. Mr Christie's daughter was confirmed as her father's executor. Ms Christie argued that the whole loan had been repaid out of her father's estate (the policy) and that therefore Ms Armstrong should pay back to the estate one half. She sued Ms Armstrong. The argument was sustained in principle, but it was also held that proof was necessary to ascertain the intentions of the deceased[36] since it might have been his intention that there should be no right of relief in the circumstances which emerged.

Although the specific facts of *Christie* will not arise often, the points at issue are potentially relevant in a variety of cases. One unusual feature of *Christie* was that the life policy was only over one party's life. More common is the joint policy. Suppose that the whole policy matures on the first death and (being an assigned policy) immediately pays off the loan. Who has paid it off? Presumably that depends on to whom, or to whose estate, the proceeds would have been payable, had the policy not been assigned. Some joint policies are payable to the estate of the first to die, while others are payable to the survivor. Which way the policy is written thus can make a large difference.

Finally, it often happens that one of the borrowers pays the whole of each monthly payment to the lender, or at least more than half of it. Later they become estranged. The overpayer argues that he has a right of relief against the underpayer. This is the same issue as in *Christie* though arising in a different way. The underpaying party will claim that there was an unwritten understanding that relief would not be claimed. The overpayer is likely to deny this. The wise course is to have a pre-purchase agreement on such matters, but this seldom happens.

Matrimonial Homes (Family Protection) (Scotland) Act 1981

Standard securities normally require documentation under the 1981   19–16 Act, because the lender needs to be protected against latent occupancy rights. The documentation will be a renunciation or a consent, or an affidavit, as appropriate.

---

[35] 1996 S.C. 295.
[36] How those intentions were to be ascertained is not so easy to see.

Variations

19-17 By "variations" is here meant not the variations of the standard conditions, which are stated in the original security itself, but subsequent variations, made after the security has already been registered. The subject is covered in section 16 of the 1970 Act. This states that variation is not appropriate where discharge, or restriction, or assignation would be appropriate. Where the term to be varied is contained in the original standard security as registered, the variation must itself be registered, but if the term to be varied is itself not registered, the variation need not be registered. For example, in a form B security, a variation of a term in the (unregistered) loan contract would not have to be registered. It is unclear what the sanction is for failing to register a variation. An unregistered variation would still be binding contractually as between the parties. Presumably, therefore, the sanction would be that third parties would not be affected. But it is not easy to think of an illustrative example, especially as section 16(4) provides that even a registered variation does not affect real rights acquired by third parties prior to the variation.[37]

Such matters as further advances and changes in interest rate can be handled by a deed of variation, but in practice are not so handled. As to the first, virtually all standard securities are for "all sums due or to become due", and as for the second, there is normally a provision for a floating interest rate, whereby changes are made informally. Hence, deeds of variation are rare. Sometimes a deed of variation is used when a couple split up, and one of them takes on the whole property and also the loan. It is also sometimes used when a single owner marries and the spouse, as well as taking a half-share of the title, also becomes jointly liable for the loan.

Standard securities over long leases

19-18 Long leases can be registered in the Land Register or the GRS.[38] Standard securities can be granted over such leases.[39] Few residential properties are held on leases of substantial duration, and indeed since 1974 it has been effectively impossible to create long leases of residential property.[40] But a small number of older properties are held on leasehold title. Until the 2000 Act there was no limit on long leases of commercial property, but a maximum of 175 years has now been imposed.[41] As with the 1974 Act this provision is not retrospective.

The lenders' solicitors must check the terms of the lease, on such matters as ish, onerous conditions,[42] irritancy, need for landlords' consent to transactions, and rent. (The latter is usually nominal for

---

[37] If this is in fact the true meaning of that subsection.
[38] Registration of Leases (Scotland) Act 1857, s.1; Land Registration (Scotland) Act 1979, s.2(1)(a)(i).
[39] 1970 Act, s.9(2), (8)(b).
[40] 1974 Act, Pt.11.
[41] 2000 Act, s.67.
[42] Though bearing in mind that leasehold casualties were abolished by the Leasehold Casualties (Scotland) Act 2001.

residential long leases.) If the security is being granted simultaneously with the grant of the lease, the validity of the title of the landlords must be verified. But if the lease already exists, and the leasehold title sheet contains no exclusion of indemnity, that is normally sufficient, though the real burdens should be noted and considered. If the lease is in the GRS rather than the Land Register, prescription will usually have resolved any defect that there may have been in the landlords' title at the time when the lease was granted, either by curing that defect, or by fortifying the lease itself. But if the lease was granted only recently the validity of the landlord's title must be verified.

Tenants

Sometimes owners want to let to tenants. In that case the lender must approve.[43] In practice, however, this is often ignored. A tenancy given without the heritable creditor's consent is voidable.[44]   19-19

Assignation of standard securities

Assignations of standard securities are dealt with in section 14 of the 1970 Act. An assignation is where the lenders transfer the loan and the security for it to a third person, for whatever reason. The assignation must be recorded. Once that is done, the assignees are substituted for the original creditors in all the rights, both personal and real. The rule *assignatus utitur jure auctoris* applies, as it generally does in assignations of any type, so that any defence which the debtors could have pled against the cedents (assignors) can equally be pled against the assignees. Thus, suppose that the price paid by the assignees is based on the assumption that a certain amount is still due under the security, and that assumption turns out to be false, and that the true sum is lower. In that case the debtors cannot be liable for more than the true amount, even though the assignees were in good faith.[45] Assignation is simple enough in the case of a fixed-sum standard security, but such securities are rare. If the standard security is for all sums, difficult problems can arise.[46]   19-20

It is quite common for lenders to sell a mortgage portfolio, such as £25,000,000 worth of mortgages. The sellers (the original creditors) are paid an agreed price, and the buyers take over the rights under the mortgages. Quite often the individual standard securities are not assigned, so as to save expense. In that case, the sellers remain the heritable creditors, and the sale does not affect the borrowers. Indeed, they may not even know that a sale has taken place. Thus, for instance,

---

[43] 1970 Act, Sch.3, Standard Condition 6.

[44] *Trade Development Bank v Warriner and Mason (Scotland) Ltd*, 1980 S.C. 74. However, the law in this area is complex. Special, and unresolved, problems arise if the tenancy falls under the Rent (Scotland) Act 1984 or the Housing (Scotland) Act 1987. See *Tamouri v Clydesdale Bank plc*, 1996 S.C.L.R. 732; *Cameron v Abbey National*, 1999 Hous. L.R. 19.

[45] In which case, the assignee will normally have a claim against the cedent in warrandice.

[46] See *e.g. Watson v Bogue*, 1998 S.L.T. (Sh. Ct) 125, 1998 S.C.L.R. 512; *Sanderson's Trs v Ambion Scotland Ltd*, 1994 S.L.T. 645; D. J. Cusine and Robert Rennie, *Standard Securities* (2nd ed., 2002), Ch.6; Gretton, 1994 S.L.T. (News) 207.

they keep up payments to the same party, who then passes on such payments to the buyers. In other words, the sale is simply a contractual arrangement between the two financial institutions. This is called sale by sub-participation.

There can be no question of an assignation of a standard security by the *debtor*. The debtor can transfer ownership of the property, but since the debtor is owner that transfer is by disposition not assignation.[47] As for liability under the loan, that cannot be transferred, except with the creditor's consent.

Restrictions

19–21   A restriction[48] is a discharge by the creditor, but limited to part of the property. An example would be where Jack sells a slice of garden to his neighbour, Jane. Jane would insist on a deed of restriction from Jack's heritable creditor. A creditor is not normally obliged to grant such a deed, and so Jack will have to be persuasive. However, sometimes a creditor agrees in advance to grant restrictions. For example, a company buys a site and plans to build 40 houses, which will be sold one by one. The company has to borrow to carry out the development, and the loan is secured over the site. As each house is finished it is sold, but each buyer will insist on an unencumbered title. So the bank will grant a restriction for that house. This will have been envisaged in the original contract between the builder and the bank. The contract will provide, for example, that in return for the deed the bank must be paid 75 per cent of the sale price, thereby ensuring that as the extent of the security is reduced the outstanding loan is also reduced.

Restriction can be effected by a separate deed of restriction, duly registered. It is more common, however, for the lender to execute the disposition as a consenter to the effect of restricting the security.[49] A form 2 will be needed in either case.

Discharges: in general

19–22   Discharges are regulated by section 17 of the 1970 Act. On complete repayment the lender must grant a discharge to the borrower, which is then registered. The expense of this falls on the borrower. The statutory style[50] is far from perfect. It requires that the discharge state that it is "in consideration of £ . . . being the whole amount secured by the standard security aftermentioned". But it can be difficult to know what sum to fill in. For example, a company grants a standard security for its current account, which is sometimes in credit and sometimes overdrawn. Ten years later the company decides to change its bank, at a time when the

---

[47] Only incorporeals are transferred by assignation. The debtor's reversionary right under an *ex facie* absolute disposition was incorporeal and so was transferable by assignation.

[48] Regulated by s.15 of the 1970 Act.

[49] The 1970 Act makes no provision for effecting a restriction in this way, but there can be no question of its validity, under the common law of heritable security. The Act is not a code, but has to be supplemented frequently by the common law.

[50] Sch.4, form F.

account happens to be in credit. A discharge is required. What sum can be filled in? There never was a principal sum. There was, instead, just an account with many thousands of credit and debit entries. Another case where the statutory style is inappropriate is where the lender agrees to discharge the security without full repayment of the loan.[51] It is hard to see, in any case, why a clause of this sort is required. At common law it is not necessary to state the reason or cause of granting. In practice, deeds often depart considerably from the statutory style, and indeed there can be little doubt that a discharge which wholly omitted the consideration clause would be valid. But it is wise to adhere to the official style as nearly as is reasonably possible.

Usually, the security being discharged is an all-sums security. Here, a peculiarity of the official style must be noted, namely that the all-sums aspect not only must be mentioned, but in fact affects the wording of the discharge at two separate points. In the following the words which are italicised must be inserted for the discharge of an all-sums security: "in consideration of . . .[52] *being the whole amount secured by the standard security aftermentioned* paid by . . . hereby discharge a standard security *for all sums due or to become due*".

The discharge is normally a separate deed. But it can alternatively be endorsed on the original standard security, and some standard securities have a preprinted form of discharge at the end. Another possibility is that the discharge can be incorporated as part of a disposition. Thus, if A wants to dispone to B, and the plan is to discharge a standard security which X has, X could execute the disposition as well as A, as consenter, to the effect of discharging the security.[53] In whichever way the discharge is done, a form 2 will be needed.

Section 18 makes provision for the case where the lender fails to grant a discharge. This, again, is inadequately drafted, for various reasons, including the fact that it assumes that repayment of the loan is being offered at the same time. This is the same mistake as before: by the time the discharge is wanted there may be no outstanding loan.

A standard security, like any security, is an accessory right, meaning that it can have no existence separate from the debt which it secures.[54] Hence, once the debt is gone, the security secures nothing, and so is implicitly discharged.[55] Therefore, the discharge is simply evidential. The (ex-)debtor wishes it to be granted as evidence that the property is now unencumbered. However, this is true in an unqualified way only of fixed-sum standard securities. By contrast, suppose that a standard security is granted for an overdraft. Over the years the account is sometimes in debit and sometimes in credit. It must not be supposed that the moment the debit balance disappears, the security is discharged. Therefore, in the

---

[51] This would be unusual, but it can happen, for instance where there is a commercial loan secured over several properties.

[52] In a domestic standard security there is inserted here the loan figure stated in the original security deed.

[53] As with restriction, the 1970 Act does not expressly authorise this, but once again there can be no doubt of its competency under the common law.

[54] See *e.g. Trotter v Trotter*, 2001 S.L.T. (Sh. Ct) 42. And see *Albatown Ltd v Credential Group Ltd*, 2001 G.W.D. 27–1102, and Reid and Gretton, *Conveyancing 2001*, p.91.

[55] *Cameron v Williamson* (1895) 22 R. 393.

case of all-sums standard securities, the discharge is more than merely evidential.

Discharges: separate debts

19-23   It would be natural to suppose that if the clients pay the lenders the amount outstanding on the home loan, plus any early redemption penalty, the lenders will discharge the security. In most cases that would be right. But sometimes one finds that the clients owe money to the same lenders under another contract. For instance, they might have a home loan and also an overdraft. The standard security will in practice be so devised as to secure the overdraft as well as the mortgage debt.[56] Hence, if the creditor is offered the amount due under the mortgage, it can still refuse to discharge the security so long as the overdraft remains in existence. Usually where this happens the amounts due under the other contract are not large, and either they can be paid off, or the lender can be persuaded to discharge the security anyway. Indeed, usually lenders in this situation are happy to co-operate, though they will often insist that the new home loan (on the new house) is with them as well. The reason for this is that the new standard security will then cover the existing overdraft or whatever in addition to the new home loan. But occasionally problems crop up, most often where the clients are in business and so may have borrowed from the lender to finance the business. A creditor is normally entitled to refuse to discharge a security not only if there is an additional debt, such as an overdraft, but also if the client is liable to the lender on a guarantee. For instance, Smith is director and chief shareholder of Smith Ltd. Smith Ltd has an overdraft with the bank, for which Smith has—as is usual in such cases—given the bank a guarantee. The bank would (subject to certain qualifications) be entitled to refuse to grant a discharge of the security for Smith's home loan so long as the overdraft was in place.

Ideally, one should therefore (i) ask the clients whether they have any other debts to the lender, apart from the home loan, or any guarantees, and (ii when asking the lender for a redemption statement ask them to confirm that there are no liabilities other than the home loan.

Death

19-24   If the debtor dies, in most cases the loan will be paid off. There is usually a source of funds for this, since in most cases a debtor will have taken out life assurance which will at least cover the amount of the loan. In the unlikely event that this does not happen, whoever takes over the property (the spouse, or a legatee, etc.) must undertake, as a condition of taking the property, to pay off the loan. For the purposes of succession, the debt is deemed a burden on the heritable estate, and thus does not, for example, diminish *jus relictae.* However, if the debt is secured not only by the standard security but also by an assignation in

---

[56] Because the standard security will cover all sums due by that debtor to that creditor.

security of a life policy, the debt is, for succession purposes, notionally ascribed both to the land and to the policy.[57]

The death of the creditor is much less usual, because the creditor is seldom a natural person. If he or she is, then the security and the loan which it secures simply forms part of the estate to be administered by the executor and transferred to a beneficiary, or sold. The debt (which, from the creditor's viewpoint, is an asset) is deemed heritable in the succession to the creditor's estate.[58]

Consumer Credit Act

A loan which is under the limit (£25,000 currently) may be a "regulated agreement" under the Consumer Credit Act 1974.[59] The impact of this on conveyancing is that if a standard security is granted to secure a regulated agreement, the standard security itself falls under the statutory regime, with various implications, including the format of the documentation and the rights of the parties, including rights and procedures on default.[60] However, in practice not many standard securities are affected, for the following reasons. First, most standard securities are for sums over £25,000. Secondly, if the lender is an exempt institution such as a local authority, the statutory provisions do not apply. Next, the provisions do not apply if the borrower is a registered company. Finally, they do not apply if the lender is a purely private lender. Thus, if Jack borrows £20,000 from his aunt, the statutory provisions do not apply, unless she is a professional moneylender.

19-25

Ranking

Only certain aspects of the complex subject of ranking[61] can be dealt with here. Ranking is partly dealt with by the 1970 Act itself and partly by the common law.

The most important fact about a standard security is that it is a real right, and, like most other real rights, will obey the rule *prior tempore potior jure*.[62] So the first to be registered ranks first. Thus, if Adam holds a first-registered standard security for a loan of £50,000, and Barbara has a second-registered security for a loan of £25,000, and there is default and the house is sold for £60,000, after deduction of expenses, Adam takes £50,000 and Barbara takes the balance of £10,000. If, however, the two securities had been registered at the same time they would have

19-26

---

[57] *Graham v Graham* (1898) 5 S.L.T. 319; Gretton (1987) 32 J.L.S.S. 303 and (1988) 33 J.L.S.S. 141. The area is one of great difficulty, and the two articles cited are far from the whole truth.

[58] Subject to s.117 of the Titles to Land Consolidation (Scotland) Act 1868.

[59] The 1974 Act was being reviewed when the present edition was being prepared and reform is possible.

[60] For instance, on default the lender must first serve a "default notice" prior to calling up, etc. This default notice under the Consumer Credit Act 1974 must not be confused with the notice of default under the 1970 Act itself. There are cases where a default notice must be followed by a notice of default.

[61] See Halliday, paras 57-27—57-42; D. J. Cusine and Robert Rennie, *Standard Securities* (2nd ed., 2002), Ch.7.

[62] Earlier by time, stronger by right.

ranked *pari passu*, with the result that Adam would have received £40,000 and Barbara £20,000. Creditors are free to enter into a ranking agreement, the meaning of which is self-explanatory. Such agreements, though common in commercial cases, are rare in domestic ones.

Account must also be taken of section 13 of the 1970 Act. If Adam's security is for all sums, a potential problem exists. For after the second security is granted, Adam might lend further sums, which would have the effect of eating up the equity[63] on which Barbara had relied. So common law developed a rule[64] whereby if Adam knew that a second security had been granted, any further advance by him could not prejudice the second security. The substance of this common law rule is given statutory force by section 13. Only voluntary further advances by Adam are so affected. Thus, interest accumulating is unaffected. And if the further advance had already been contracted for, it is unaffected.[65] The knowledge of Adam of the existence of the second security is a matter of actual knowledge. No formal notification procedure is laid down. But the practice is for Barbara, or her solicitor, to send what is sometimes called a notice of second charge to Adam. If her solicitor fails to do this that may constitute negligence. Section 13 is not very clearly drafted and there has been controversy as to its exact meaning. The main issue is this: if the first creditor, after receiving notice, does make a further advance, is that advance secured but postponed or is it unsecured? It is difficult to see any clear answer.[66]

Preparing postponed securities

19–27   Schedule 2, note 5 to the 1970 Act says that "where the security subjects are burdened by any other standard security . . . which ranks prior to the standard security which is being granted" the new standard security should refer to the fact twice, the second time being in the warrandice clause. The purpose of this provision is unclear. If the property is already burdened then the earlier security ranks first anyway.

It sometimes happens that an owner is granting two securities at the same time, to Sue and to Tom, and that the mutual intention of the three parties is that Sue's security should have priority. That can be achieved by good timing: ensuring that Sue's security is registered first, even if only by one day. But it easy for things to go wrong: if Sue delays to register, one can hardly expect Tom to wait for her. Hence the situation sometimes arises in which Tom's security is registered first, but is worded in conformity with Schedule 2, note 5 to the 1970 Act. In that case the law is probably that Tom's security ranks first until Sue's is

---

[63] Meaning, in this context, market value minus secured debt.

[64] *Union Bank v National Bank* (1886) 14 R. (HL) 1.

[65] This would be rare in domestic cases. But commercial loans are often "drawn down" in "tranches".

[66] See Gretton (1980) 25 J.L.S.S 275; Halliday (1981) 26 J.L.S.S. 26; Gretton (1981) 26 J.L.S.S. 280.

registered, and then Sue's ranks first and Tom's second.[67] But the law is by no means free from difficulty.[68]

Property insurance

The Standard Condition 5 requires the debtor to insure the property. 19–28 Most lenders will offer the borrower a choice of, say, six insurance companies. The level required is normally reinstatement value rather than market value. The cover should be increased to keep in line with inflation. Most policies have an automatic annual increase linked to inflation. Some lenders pay the premiums themselves and charge the borrower, while others leave it to the borrower to make the payments. Sometimes the policy is in the joint names of the lender and the owner, sometimes in the name of the lender, sometimes in the name of the borrower, and sometimes in the name of the borrower with the name of the lender endorsed on the policy. All these raise difficult theoretical questions as to the respective interests in the policy of the two parties, and also as to insurable interest. The lender is not concerned with contents insurance.

Acceleration

If the loan secured is an on-demand loan, the creditors can insist on 19–29 repayment at any time, though section 19 of the 1970 Act provides that the first step towards enforcing their rights under the security itself is to serve a calling-up notice. If the loan is a term loan, the contract, if properly drafted, will have an acceleration clause. This is a clause, standard in all term loan contracts, secured or unsecured, whereby if the debtors default in a defined way (such as being in arrears for more than 21 days on any instalment) the creditors may, at their option, convert the loan into an on-demand loan and call for repayment of the whole debt at once. For obvious reasons, no acceleration clause is needed in an on-demand loan.

Sometimes term loans have no acceleration clause. This might cause problems. Take this example. Anne lends Tom £50,000, and the loan contract says that it is repayable in two equal instalments, the first after two years and the second after four. The contract is silent as to acceleration. A standard security is granted for the loan. After the two years no payment is made. Anne enforces by sale. How much can she take from the sale? £50,000? Or just £25,000? The argument for the latter is that at the time of the sale only £25,000 was due and resting owing. Section 27 of the 1970 Act, which deals with what is to happen to the sale proceeds, simply says that the lender is paid "the whole amount due under the standard security", which in this context is ambiguous. The matter seems never to have been tested in court, and it seems that

---

[67] The qualification of the warrandice clause in itself probably does not have this effect. See *Leslie v McIndoe's Trs* (1824) 3 S. 48. The court in *Trade Development Bank v Crittall Windows*, 1983 S.L.T. 510 disapproved *Leslie*, but, contrary to what is said in the headnote, did not overrule it.

[68] For discussion see D. J. Cusine and Robert Rennie *Standard Securities* (2nd ed., 2002), para.7.04. See also ROTPB, para.6.74.

there has been no discussion in the literature either. In practice, it is generally assumed that where a term loan is secured by standard security, a right of acceleration is implied, so that in our example Anne could take the whole £50,000. And there is also an argument that common law implies a right of acceleration in every loan contract for any breach which amounts to a material or repudiatory breach.

Arrears

19-30 Arrears can arise for all sorts of reasons. The main ones are loss of employment and marital breakdown.[69] In practice, solicitors are not often called on to advise a borrower who is in arrears, since such people do not usually turn to their lawyer. But sometimes they do. Often a debt counsellor can give the best advice. Home loan arrears do not exist in isolation from the rest of the clients' affairs. The solution may be a change of lifestyle. But in what follows we will look specifically at ways of cutting the mortgage payments.

The clients should contact the lenders. Most lenders are reluctant to take enforcement action at an early stage. Such action involves administrative costs and is never good publicity. Some lenders have ethical standards and wish to give borrowers a chance to get back on their feet. So, although creditors may not say in so many words, they are usually prepared to put up with some arrears on a temporary basis. The theory is that they will be more understanding if the borrowers get in touch with them to explain their problems. Debtors who are in financial trouble are naturally reluctant to contact their creditors, but it is often wise to do so. This may delay enforcement action, and in some cases a deal can be struck.

If the financial problems are likely to be temporary, some sort of renegotiation of the loan may be advisable. The lenders may agree to a payment holiday or a period of reduced payments. But it must be borne in mind that during this time interest will continue to accumulate. Another idea is for payments to be put on an interest-only basis for several months. But this is possible only for capital-and-interest loans, as in others the monthly payments to the creditors are already interest-only. However, sometimes it is possible to arrange for an endowment policy to be put on ice for a period. But even for capital-and-interest loans this idea is often not of much use, since in the early years, when the problems are most likely to arise, most of the monthly payment is interest anyway. A common tactic for cases where the problems are likely to be temporary is to switch to a new loan, either with the same lender or a different one. A difficulty here is that a history of arrears may already have damaged the borrower's credit-rating. Yet another possibility is extending the term of the loan, which will result in reduced monthly payments. If the problems are not short term, the best advice may be to cut the mortgage payments by selling the house and buying a cheaper one, with a smaller loan. This advice is too seldom given. But here too there may be a problem, which is that the sale price may be insufficient to pay off the secured debt—in other words, the problem of negative equity.

---

[69] See Emma McCallum and Ewen McCaig, *Mortgage Arrears and Repossessions* (2003).

In some cases the social security system will help, though there is always a substantial period in which no assistance is available, and the system is much less generous than it used to be.[70] The clients should contact the local social security office.

One other possibility is a mortgage-to-rent scheme. Here a housing association buys the property and lets it back to the sellers. The clients thus avoid having to flit. Moreover there may be substantial benefits in terms of social security payments, because whereas public assistance for paying a mortgage is difficult to get, rent will often be paid through housing benefit.

If the worst comes to the worst and the borrowers are put out on the street by the lenders, they will normally qualify to be rehoused by the local authority under the homelessness legislation.[71] If this looks like happening, the debtors should get in touch with the local housing department without delay, though the housing department should already have been alerted by the lenders.[72]

Negative equity

What is called the "equity" in a property is the market value minus 19–31 the secured debt. Thus if the property is worth £250,000 and there is an loan of £100,000 secured by standard security, the equity is £150,000. If the secured debt is greater than the market value, the property is said to have negative equity. This can happen where a loan at a high percentage of the value is followed by a market slump. Or it can happen intentionally: there is no rule of law saying that a secured loan has to be less than the value of the collateral. Negative equity is a problem for both lenders and borrowers. It is a problem for the lenders because, if the borrowers default, sale of the property will not pay off the debt. It is a problem for the borrowers because it will be difficult to sell the house and buy a new one, because the sale will not generate enough money to pay off the existing loan. However, some lenders are prepared to allow negative equity to be transferred. For instance, Alice buys a house for £200,000 with a £175,000 loan. Property values then fall. By agreement with the lender Alice sells it two years later for £150,000 and buys another house for £125,000. Assuming that she pays the expenses, she can repay £25,000 of the loan and now has a property worth £125,000 with a secured loan of £150,000. The lenders are at risk, but were at risk anyway.

Borrowers sometimes ask if they can walk away from a home loan, that is to say, hand the keys to the lender and give up the property and thereby be freed of the debt.[73] The answer is that such an action does not free the borrower of the debt. A borrower is personally liable for any

---

[70] The rules are to be found in the massive Income Support (General) Regulations 1987 (SI 1987/1967), as amended. See generally N. J. Wikeley and A. I. Ogus, *Law of Social Security* (5th ed., 2002).

[71] Currently contained in the Housing (Scotland) Act 1987 as amended by various statutes including the Homelessness etc. (Scotland) Act 2003.

[72] Homelessness etc. (Scotland) Act 2003 (asp 10) s.11. See para.19–38.

[73] This question is asked only where there is negative equity. No rational person would wish to walk away from a property which had positive equity.

shortfall suffered by the lender after a sale. In practice, however, lenders will sometimes not seek to recover the shortfall.[74] But even then the borrower is likely to be listed with the credit reference agencies as a bad risk.

In practice most sales fails to recoup what is due, so far from there being a balance payable to the ex-borrowers, there is a shortfall.[75] The reasons are complex. One reason is that defaults are commonest with high LTV loans. In the second place, most defaults are in the early years of the loan, by which time market values may not have risen much, if at all. A third reason is that the accumulated unpaid interest has to be added to the debt, and the interest is compound interest. A fourth is that the enforcement process is expensive, and the expenses are paid first out of the proceeds. A fifth is that the borrowers, in financial difficulties, may not have maintained the property adequately, with loss of value as a result. A sixth is that the property will be marketed without furnishings, something which tends to make a property less attractive to buyers.

Enforcement: introduction

19–32   First terminology. The term "repossession" is sometimes used, but it is inaccurate. The creditor never had possession and so regaining possession is not possible. Leaving repossession on one side, even possession is not in itself an objective of the enforcement process, except incidentally, to assist the sale of the property.

In most cases the question of the enforcement of a standard security does not arise.[76] Most lenders in general are careful to lend only to those whom they believe to be creditworthy. But enforcement, though unpleasant, is sometimes necessary. Without the possibility of enforcement the system would not work, and most people agree that the system is a good one, because it enables people to buy their homes when they otherwise would be unable to do so.

In most countries the sale process is supervised by the court. In practice this tends to be slow, and to result in a sale price substantially less then the market price—in some countries less than half. The main reason for this is that to obtain full value properties should be sold in the ordinary way. In Scotland the property is indeed sold in the ordinary way. Thus, if one looks at the property pages of the local newspaper, some of the properties will be creditor sales, but there is no way to tell which. The effect is that a fair market price, or something near it, is normally obtained. This fact benefits the creditor or the debtor or both,

---

[74] A practical problem is that they often do not have a current address for the borrower.

[75] Emma McCallum and Ewen McCaig, *Mortgage Arrears and Repossessions* (2003), p.54.

[76] There are considerable difficulties in determining the number of standard securities that are enforced by sale in any given year. Emma McCallum and Ewen McCaig, *op. cit.*, p.19 gives figures of 2,560, 2,847 and 3,102 for the years 1997, 1998 and 1999 respectively. The debate on September 20, 2000 on the Homelessness (Scotland) Bill in the Social Inclusion Housing and Voluntary Sector Committee of the Scottish Parliament suggests a rather lower figure. (See col.1372 of the proceedings.) The number of cases in which the enforcement process *begins* is, naturally enough, considerably higher than the number of *final sales*. The trend in recent years has been an upward one. Whether that is wholly explained by the steady increase in home ownership, or whether other factors might be involved as well, is unclear.

according to circumstances. It benefits the creditor, by making full recovery of the loan more likely. It benefits the debtor, for the higher the price the more the debt is reduced, and, once the debt is paid off, the more the debtor will be paid. For instance, suppose that the loan is £150,000. A sale at £130,000 gives the debtor nothing, leaves him or her with a continuing debt of £20,000, and is a problem for the lender, in trying to recover the balance. An increased price of £140,000 would benefit both parties. A price of £160,000 would pay off the loan and give the debtor £10,000 cash.[77] If there are other creditors, they are benefited as well. The selling creditor has no financial interest to obtain more than £150,000. Hence the law imposes an obligation to obtain to best price reasonably attainable.[78] But the fact that the property will be marketed in the ordinary way tends to mean that it will sell for full value anyway.

The law about the enforcement of standard securities is a subject of great and unnecessary complexity: it is a veritable maze.[79] Part of the law is in the 1970 Act, part is common law, part is in the Mortgage Rights (Scotland) Act 2001 and one or two bits are in the Heritable Securities (Scotland) Act 1894.[80]

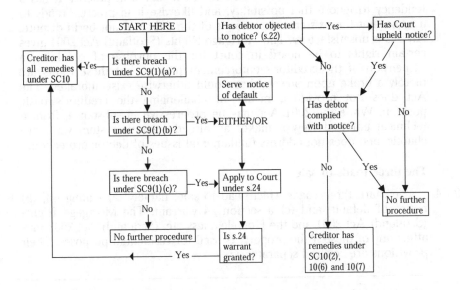

---

[77] In this example the expenses of enforcement, which can be substantial, are ignored.

[78] 1970 Act, s.25. See para.19–39.

[79] We give a flow chart, but no warrandice is granted. The chart may not be an accurate interpretation of the Act. Even if it is, it omits important points, especially the procedures introduced by the Mortgage Rights (Scotland) Act 2001, and it ignores certain obscurities. One of the sources of difficulty is the way that the provisions are divided between the body of the Act and Sch.3. The provisions refer to each other in a confusing way. They overlap partially, and sometimes are even mutually inconsistent.

[80] The 1894 Act is not of much importance today because most of it was superseded by the 1970 Act. Other provisions are found in the Consumer Credit Act 1974, if the mortgage is regulated by that Act, which, however, is not generally the case.

Remedies

19-33   The creditor has a whole battery of remedies, including personal
action, summary diligence, poinding of the ground, adjudication, removing the debtor and letting the property, and so forth. But to a large
extent these remedies are of theoretical interest only since in practice the
creditor will almost always opt to sell.[81] So that is what we will deal with
here.

There is no requirement that creditors obtain decree for payment.
That is a curious fact. In the second and third roads to sale (see below)
the debtors have a chance to state their position in court, though even
then the procedure is not that of an action of payment, so that the court
will be in the odd position of having to determine whether a debt is due
outwith the context of such an action. In the first road the debtors have
no opportunity to appear in court, unless the creditors seek declarator,[82]
and so if they dispute liability they must take the initiative themselves,
for instance by raising an action of declarator and interdict, and perhaps
suspension and reduction, against the creditors.[83] Actually the problem is
systemic in the Act. Although it recognises the possibility that some
standard securities will not be payable on demand, in practice it has a
tendency to ignore that possibility, and likewise it in practice tends to
assume that the existence or amount of the debt will not be in dispute.
All this is unsatisfactory. The Mortgage Rights (Scotland) Act 2001 gives
certain rights to be heard in court for the purpose of obtaining a
suspension of the creditor's enforcement powers, but these rights are
merely a brake upon powers that would otherwise exist unbraked. The
Act does not provide a means of challenging the creditor's basic
position. While the 2001 Act may be progressive in substance, from a
technical point of view it makes an already chaotic system yet more
chaotic, and does not address fundamental issues of debtor protection.

The three roads to sale

19-34   There are three roads which lead to sale, namely (a) calling up, (b)
notice of default, and (c) a section 24 warrant. The Mortgage Rights
(Scotland) Act 2001 and the Homelessness etc. (Scotland) Act 2003 may
affect any of these if the property is used for residential purposes. Their
provisions are covered separately.[84]

---

[81] With or without taking possession in the formal sense of that term. As to the rights
and liabilities of a heritable creditor in possession, see Scottish Law Commission, *Report
on Real Burdens* (Scot. Law Com. No.181, 2000), paras 13.7 and 13.8. A heritable creditor
in possession is liable for outstanding obligations due under real burdens but subject to a
right of relief against the debtor: see Title Conditions (Scotland) Act 2003, ss.10 and
123(2)(b).

[82] And in practice where such declarators are raised they focus on the powers of the
creditor and not on the core issue of what money is due. For an example where the
defender did resist on the ground that no debt was due see *J. Sykes & Sons (Fish
Merchants) Ltd v Grieve*, 2002 S.L.T. 15

[83] The subject is too large and complex to enter into here. See *Wilson v Target Holdings*,
1995 G.W.D. 31-1599 and *Gardiner v Jacques Vert plc*, 2002 S.L.T. 928. The debtor does
have an extremely limited statutory right to query the sum due: 1970 Act, s.19(9); but even
this has been restrictively construed: *Bank of Scotland v Flett*, 1995 S.C.L.R. 591.

[84] para.19-38.

The first road: calling up

The calling-up process is covered by section 19 of the 1970 Act. The 19–35
creditors serve a calling-up notice which requires repayment of the
whole debt within two months.[85] If the two-month period expires without
payment, the power of sale emerges automatically. The Act does not say
what circumstances justify the service of this notice. There is no problem
if the loan is an on-demand one, or if, though a term loan, there is an
acceleration clause which has been activated. In practice, one or other of
these will virtually always be the case.

This procedure is extra-judicial. But in practice it is common for
creditors to follow it up by an action of declarator that the right to sell
has emerged. It is obviously prudent to do so, and moreover if the
debtors refuse to give up possession a court action is needed anyway.

The second road: notice of default

Notices of default are governed by sections 20 and 21 of the 1970 Act. 19–36
The notice states what the default is, and calls upon the debtors to cease
to be in default within one month, failing which the enforcement powers
emerge. The Act uses the word "default" in different ways at different
places and it is sometimes unclear what is meant.[86] But a failure to make
a payment to the lenders will count as a "default" under Standard
Condition 9(1)(b), and thus entitle the creditors to issue a notice of
default. A key difference between this procedure and a calling-up notice
is that the latter requires repayment of the whole debt, whereas a notice
of default requires only that arrears be brought up to date. The debtors
can, if they wish, challenge the notice in court.[87] If the debtors do not
dispute the notice, the creditors are likely in practice to raise an action
of declarator for the same reasons as apply in the calling-up procedure,
above.

The calling-up procedure and the notice of default procedure are
often alternatives.[88] In practice there is a certain tendency amongst
institutions to use the former for residential standard securities and the
latter for commercial ones.

The notice of default should not be confused with the default notice
which is needed in cases under the Consumer Credit Act 1974. If the
standard security is regulated by that Act, a default notice will be needed
in addition to the calling-up notice or notice of default.

The calling-up notice and the notice of default are in one sense
parallel procedures, but in another sense they are not. A notice of

---

[85] It is important to observe the formalities in order to secure evidence that the notice
has been served. For discussion of detail see C. Waelde (ed.), *Professor McDonald's
Conveyancing Opinions* (1998), p.169.

[86] For an interesting discussion see D. J. Cusine and Robert Rennie, *op. cit.* (2nd ed.,
2002), para.8.14. And see *Bank of Scotland v Millward*, 1998 S.C.L.R. 577 holding that the
calling-up procedure and the notice of default procedure are not mutually exclusive. Note
that Standard Condition 10 gives a variety of powers upon default, but in fact this is
contradicted by the body of the Act which does not allow all these powers upon all
defaults.

[87] 1970 Act, s.22.

[88] *Bank of Scotland v Millward*, 1998 S.C.L.R. 577.

default presupposes some sort of breach of contract on the part of the debtors, or at least it presupposes that the creditors think that there has been such a breach. By contrast, a calling-up notice does not presuppose such a breach. In an on-demand loan the creditors may serve a calling up notice whenever they choose, breach or no breach. However, a calling-up notice may arise out of a breach. The classic example would be where there is a term loan with a clause of acceleration for breach. There is breach, the creditors accelerate, and then call up.

The third road: the s.24 warrant

19–37   Lastly, there is the section 24 warrant. This is an application by the creditors to the court stating that the debtors are in default and asking for permission to sell. When is this route used? Probably the only case where it has to be used is where the creditors wish to sell, not because of any failure to pay, but because the debtors have become insolvent.[89] This is not very common. But section 24 is also available, as an option, for cases under Standard Condition 9(1)(b), namely any breach of the security. Whether section 24 is available for breach under Standard Condition 9(1)(a) (failure to comply with a calling-up notice) is unclear. If the creditors can prove that the statutory requirements are met, the court has no discretion to refuse a section 24 warrant, subject always to the 2001 Act.[90] Where the debtors are a company in liquidation, the issue of a section 24 warrant for sale prevails over the rule[91] that any disposition of the property of a company in liquidation is void.[92]

Section 24 is not a declaratory procedure. Heritable creditors often raise actions to declare the existence of their rights, but such actions presuppose that such rights have already emerged, for instance by reason of the expiry, without payment, of a calling-up notice. By contrast, a section 24 application asks the court to *confer* powers.[93] A sensible practical course for creditors is to frame a writ which is both (a) a declarator and (b) an application for warrant. Such an action will be simultaneously a common law action and a statutory one. It should seek ejection of the debtors[94] and should also seek both declarator of the power of sale and warrant to exercise that power.[95]

---

[89] Standard Condition 9(1)(c).

[90] *Halifax Building Society v Gupta*, 1993 S.C.L.R. 583.

[91] Now contained in the Insolvency Act 1986, s.127.

[92] *UDT Noters*, 1977 S.L.T. (Notes) 56; *UDT v Site Preparations Ltd*, 1978 S.L.T. (Sh. Ct.) 14 and 21.

[93] See *Bank of Scotland v Fernand*, 1997 S.L.T. (Sh. Ct) 78, in which a declaratory action failed because the creditor should, instead, have been seeking a warrant. In practice declarators and s.24 actions are, understandably, merged with each other: this case distinguishes them. The style in the first edition of Halliday (para.39–61), which was widely adopted in practice, was essentially declaratory, but the *Fernand* decision suggests that this is incompetent. The style in the new edition (para.54–63) is an improvement in this respect because the third crave is "to grant warrant".

[94] Assuming the debtors to be in natural possession.

[95] The style in the first edition of Halliday (see above) did not seek this expressly, but only mentioned the powers of a heritable creditor in lawful possession. The trouble was that the power of sale is treated in the Act as distinct from the powers of a creditor in possession. The style in the new edition of Halliday (above) wisely adds express reference to the power of sale.

Residential property

The Mortgage Rights (Scotland) Act 2001[96] applies to "any standard 19–38
security over an interest in land used to any extent for residential
purposes".[97] The Act identifies certain benefited persons. The main
beneficiary is the debtor, but there are numerous others. For instance,
not only cohabitants but even former cohabitants are in some cases
beneficiaries under the Act. The Act confers on the beneficiaries the
right to apply to the court. If they do nothing the Act does not help
them. They must apply to the court before the calling up notice, or the
notice of default, has expired. If the creditor is seeking a section 24
warrant the beneficiary must make the application before the warrant is
granted. If an application is timeously made, the court can "suspend the
exercise" of the creditor's powers of enforcement rights "to such extent,
for such period, and subject to such conditions as the court thinks fit".[98]
The four factors that the court must consider are:

"(a)　the nature of and reasons for the default
　(b)　the applicant's ability to fulfil within a reasonable period the
　　　　obligations under the standard security
　(c)　any action taken by the creditor to assist the debtor to fulfil
　　　　those obligations, and
　(d)　the ability of the applicant and any other person residing at
　　　　the security subjects to secure reasonable alternative
　　　　accommodation."[99]

If the court makes a suspension order, the order must be registered in
the Register of Inhibitions and Adjudications[1] so that any person with an
interest—including the Keeper—will know that no power of sale exists.[2]
To ensure that the beneficiaries are alerted to their rights, the Act
requires that creditors who wish to enforce must serve certain notices
addressed to the occupier. No separate notice is required for the debtor,
since the calling up notice or the notice of default will, as amended by
the 2001 Act, contain the necessary information. Amendments made to
the 1970 Act by the Homelessness etc. (Scotland) Act 2003 further

---

[96] See further Mark Higgins, *Repossessions: The Mortgage Rights (Scotland) Act 2001*
(2002); D. J. Cusine and Robert Rennie, *Standard Securities* (2nd ed., 2002); Reid and
Gretton, *Conveyancing 2001*, pp.75–85.
[97] Mortgage Rights (Scotland) Act 2001, s.1(1).
[98] s.2(1).
[99] s.2(2).
[1] s.3. Since suspension orders are property-specific, one might have expected that
registration would have been in the Land Register or GRS.
[2] The style of notice is been prescribed by the Mortgage Rights (Scotland) Act 2001
(Prescribed Notice) Order 2001, SSI 2001/419. Nothing is said as to whether the notice is
to be registered against the debtor's name or the creditor's. The Keeper is sensibly
registering it against both.

require that, in the case of property used to any extent for residential purposes, a notice be served on the local authority.[3]

The sale

19-39   The power of sale emerges when: (i) a calling-up notice has not been complied with at the end of the two months; or (ii) when a notice of default has neither been complied with nor challenged in court within the one-month period; or (iii) when a notice of default has been challenged but the challenge has been unsuccessful; or (iv) where a sale warrant has been granted under a section 24 application. In all cases the power emerges only if there is not in force a suspension order under the 2001 Act.

To sell, the creditors will wish to get the debtors out of the property. (This is not required by law. But in practice buyers will not proceed if the debtor is still in possession.) Often the debtors flit of their own accord. But if they do not, court procedure will be required. This issue has caused difficulties because of the obscurities of the Act.[4] Matters have, however, been somewhat clarified by an Act of Sederunt,[5] and the position now seems to be as follows. If the creditors have issued a calling-up notice or notice of default which has not been complied with, they should seek ejection of the debtors under section 5 of the Heritable Securities (Scotland) Act 1894. If they make a section 24 application without seeking ejection, the application is a summary one. But if they wish to combine a section 24 application with a warrant to eject, they can do so, but the action must proceed as an ordinary action. If the property is not occupied by the debtor but by a tenant, and the tenancy predates the security, then it is a prior real right, and the creditor can sell the property only subject to the tenancy. If the tenancy postdates the security then presumptively it is subject to the security.

Once the power of sale has emerged and possession has been obtained, the property can be sold. Sometimes this is done by an in-house solicitor for the lenders, and sometimes by an outside firm. The marketing happens in the same way as for any other property. Roups are rare except as a last resort to shift property that has not sold in the more conventional way. If there is more than one security, it is possible for the postponed creditors to sell. If both creditors wish to sell, the law makes no provision as to which is to do it. The custom, however, in such cases is that the first-ranked creditors will do the sale unless otherwise agreed.[6] it was held that where first-ranked standard security holders had taken possession, they could interdict a second-ranked heritable creditor from selling.

---

[3] 1970 Act, ss.19B, 21(2A), and 24(3)(c), (4A) (inserted by the Homelessness etc. (Scotland) Act 2003, s.11 and Sch.). At the time of writing these provisions were not in force, and no regulations had yet been made, under s.11(3) of the Act prescribing the form of notice.

[4] See, *e.g.*, Jamieson, 1989 S.L.T. (News) 201.

[5] SI 1990/661.

[6] *cf. Skipton Building Society v Wain*, 1986 S.L.T. 96, though how much that case decides is arguable.

Section 25 of the 1970 Act imposes a duty to advertise and a duty to get the best price reasonably obtainable. These come to much the same thing. If the creditors advertise properly then they should get the fair market price, while conversely a fair market price is unlikely to be achieved without proper advertising. The 1924 Act[7] contained detailed provisions as to advertisement in relation to bonds and dispositions in security, but these were not repeated in the 1970 Act. In practice, however, the 1924 rules are often followed, to avoid any dispute about the sufficiency of the advertising.[8] But NSEAs are sometimes feeble about advertising. Sometimes they do not even put in a newspaper advertisement at all but merely list the property in their free handout. In land registration cases the Keeper appears to take the view that this is sufficient, but many would disagree.[9] Difficulty may arise when the purchasers' solicitors ask for evidence of proper advertisement. The normal practice is to get from the newspaper publisher a certificate of advertisement, whereby the publishers confirm that such and such an advertisement appeared in the paper on such and such days.

If the lenders failed to obtain the best price they are liable in damages.[10] The quantum is the difference between the actual price and the price that should have been obtained: the fact, if it is a fact, that the sale was not properly conducted is not in itself a basis for damages.[11] In practice the burden of proof in damages actions of this sort is a fairly high one.[12] A creditor who delegates to professionals may in some circumstances be liable for the negligence of the latter.[13] It has been held that the debtor cannot interdict sale.[14]

Missives are concluded in the usual way. Usually no moveables will be included, since the creditors normally have no right to sell them.[15] However, some lenders include in their standard conditions a right to sell any moveables in the premises. In that case they will be selling not as security holders but as agents. There are some technical problems in this connection, and where such a sale of moveables happens the selling creditors will not warrant title to the moveables. Selling creditors will

---

[7] s.28.

[8] *cf.* Halliday, para.54–43. See also D. J. Cusine (ed.), *The Conveyancing Opinions of Professor J. M. Halliday* (1992), p.314.

[9] For further discussion see McDonald (1994) 7 Prop. L.B. 5.

[10] *Royal Bank of Scotland v Johnston*, 1987 G.W.D. 1–5.

[11] *Newport Farm Ltd v Damesh Holdings Ltd* [2003] All E.R. (D.) 114, a New Zealand case, is instructive.

[12] *Dick v Clydesdale Bank*, 1991 S.C. 365. For a recent example where a claim for damages failed see *Davidson v. Clydesdale Bank*, 2002 S.L.T. 1088. Generally on the duty to obtain the best price see D. J. Cusine and Robert Rennie, *Standard Securities* (2nd ed., 2002), para.8.40.

[13] *Bisset v Standard Property Investment plc*, 1999 G.W.D. 26–1253. See Reid and Gretton, *Conveyancing 1999*, pp.52–4.

[14] *Associated Relays v Turnbeam*, 1988 S.C.L.R. 220; *Gordaviran Ltd v Clydesdale Bank*, 1994 S.C.L.R. 248. But the proposition that interdict is under no circumstances competent seems to us a doubtful one.

[15] Unless the creditor has resorted to the diligence of poinding of the ground, which is occasionally done, though more often in commercial than in domestic cases. Debtors sometimes use the moveables as a ground for attacking the creditor: see *e.g. Gemmell v Bank of Scotland*, 1998 S.C.L.R. 144. See also *Harris v Abbey National*, 1996 Hous. L.R. 100.

indeed be more reluctant than ordinary sellers to warrant certain other things, such as that the central heating is in good working order.

The disposition is granted by the creditors.[16] The debtors' signatures are not required, which is just as well, for in most cases they would not be made forthcoming. The practice is for the selling creditors to grant fact and deed warrandice personally and to bind the debtors in absolute warrandice. It is, however, arguable that this practice is unreasonable. If it turns out that there is a problem about the title, the debtors will normally not be worth suing.[17] It is arguable that the selling creditors should grant absolute warrandice. But purchasers who want this would have to stipulate for it in the missives.

The normal Land Register reports should be obtained against the property and the sellers and also against the debtors though it is unlikely that any entry in the personal register could affect the sale. Thus, an inhibition against the debtors after the security was created but before the sale is irrelevant.[18]

Documentation under the 1981 Act is not required in relation to the selling creditor (in respect of whom the house could never be a matrimonial home), but is still required in respect of the debtor. This should have been obtained at the time the security was granted in the first place.

The risk of future challenge

19–40   Might the buyers find their title open to challenge by the former owner on the ground of some irregularity in the sale? There are few definite answers here. There is a statutory provision in section 41 (as amended) of the 1924 Act[19] which says that a buyer will be protected by good faith. However, the actual wording of the section is obscure and leaves open many issues. Both form 1 and form 2 ask the applicant to state "whether the statutory procedures necessary for the proper exercise of such power [power of sale under the standard security] been complied with." If the applicant ticks the "yes" box, and does so negligently or fraudulently, then the possibility arises of rectification of the register, though such rectification would have to be preceded by reduction of the disposition in the applicant's favour. The Keeper normally relies on what the applicant says in this connection, without further checks.[20]

The safe course to take when acting for a purchaser is the cautious one. In particular, it is wise to insist on certificates of advertisement and on the calling-up notice or whatever other steps were used to lead to the sale, including any decrees. Moreover, these need to be kept because it is possible that the Keeper may wish to check them too. In many cases the creditors will have obtained a decree under section 24. In that case there is usually no question as to their power to sell, though there may still be

---

[16] For a style see Halliday, *op. cit.*, para.54–47.
[17] If they were fully solvent, there would have been no need for a forced sale in the first place.
[18] *Newcastle Building Society v White*, 1987 S.L.T. (Sh. Ct.) 81; G. L. Gretton, *Law of Inhibition and Adjudication* (2nd ed., 1996), Ch.9.
[19] As applied by s.32 of the 1970 Act.
[20] ROTPB, para.6.73.

questions as to the exercise of that power. The purchasers should, of course, see the decree and take a copy of it.

A theoretical point

A standard security is a *jus in re aliena*, that is to say a real right, but 19–41 not a real right of ownership. The debtors have the real right of ownership. Though this is generally well understood, a common mistake is to suppose that the creditors become owner as soon as they take possession. This is not correct. The debtors remain the owners until the moment when ownership passes to the buyers, which, of course, is at the moment when the disposition in their favour is registered. The creditors never become owners, unless there is a decree of foreclosure[21] which is extremely rare.

When is the right of redemption cut off?

Up to what point do the debtors still have the right to pay off the debt 19–42 and so save the property? The issue is seldom of importance, for if the debtors could pay they would have done so at an earlier stage. But the point is worth a few words. Section 23(3) of the 1970 Act says that under the notice of default procedure the debtors have the right to redeem right up to the moment when missives of sale are concluded. This is sensible, but no parallel provision exists for the other two roads to sale. A guess would be that the same rule would apply, since it is the only reasonable rule. However, it may be that in such a case the debtors would have to serve a notice of redemption.[22]

What happens to the proceeds of sale?

The distribution of the proceeds of sale is governed by section 27 of 19–43 the 1970 Act. The creditors hold the proceeds in trust, first for payment of the expenses of sale, secondly for payment of any prior secured debt, thirdly for payment of his own secured debt and any other secured debt having an equal ranking, fourthly for payment of any postponed secured debt, and fifthly, for payment to the debtor.[23] Payment at any of these levels can be made only to the extent that there are funds remaining from the previous levels. In *Halifax Building Society v Smith*,[24] Sheriff Principal Caplan said: "Professor Halliday in his commentary on the Act . . . suggests that the tabulation in s. 27 represents one of the better characteristics of modern draftsmanship. If this is so the terms thereof seem nevertheless to have sown a considerable amount of doubt and confusion." In complex cases the creditors will not want to take the risk of distributing the fund themselves, but will instead raise a multiple-poinding, so that the court can decide who gets what. In some cases, especially if there is an arrestment, they will generally have little choice but to take the multiplepoinding route.

---

[21] 1970 Act, s.28.
[22] See *Forbes v Armstrong,* 1993 S.C.L.R. 204.
[23] This text is a rough paraphrase of the statutory wording.
[24] 1985 S.L.T. (Sh. Ct.) 25.

Diligence[25]

19-44   Sometimes another creditor of the debtor has inhibited before the sale. This will not normally affect the secured creditor's power of sale.[26] Whether it will give the inhibitor any right to share in the proceeds of the sale has been a matter of controversy and conflicting decisions. If, however, a creditor has adjudged, and has registered the decree, then that creditor falls to be treated as a secured creditor with a ranking determined by the date of registration.

Sometimes another creditor will seek to arrest in the hands of the selling creditor. This is because upon sale, if a surplus emerges, the debtor-creditor relationship is reversed, and the (ex-) debtor becomes a creditor and the (ex-)creditor a debtor. Thus, suppose Adam has a loan from a bank, with £40,000 outstanding, and there is default, and the bank sells. After deduction of expenses the bank holds a surplus of £50,000. Adam is no longer the bank's debtor for £40,000 but its creditor for £10,000, and this is an asset which is arrestable by his other creditors. The arrestment must be in the hands of the selling creditor, not the selling creditor's solicitors.[27] The arrestment must be laid on, at latest, before distribution has taken place. There is some uncertainty as to how early the arrestment can take place, but it has been held[28] that it is competent as soon as the selling creditor has taken possession, *i.e.* well before missives of sale will have been concluded, let alone the price received.

Disburdenment

19-45   Section 26 of the 1970 Act provides that on the sale by the creditor the property is disburdened automatically of the security and of any postponed or *pari passu* security. Prior securities are not automatically discharged, but this is really a merely theoretical point. For one thing, if there is more than one security the sale is normally by the first-ranked creditor anyway. Moreover, if the sale were by a postponed creditor, the proceeds would have to be paid in the first instance to the first creditor in terms of section 27, so that security would be discharged by payment. The rule is "pay up, discharge down", and the "paying up" will normally result in "discharging up" too.

---

[25] See G. Maher and D. J. Cusine, *Law and Practice of Diligence* (1990); G. L. Gretton, *Law of Inhibition and Adjudication* (2nd ed., 1996), and *Stair Memorial Encyclopaedia*, Vol.8.

[26] *Newcastle Building Society v White*, 1987 S.L.T. (Sh. Ct.) 81; G. L. Gretton, *op. cit.* (2nd ed., 1996), Ch.9.

[27] *Lord Advocate v Bank of India*, 1991 S.C.L.R. 320.

[28] *Abbey National Building Society v Barclays Bank plc*, 1990 S.C.L.R. 639. It is open to argument whether this decision is correct. *Royal Bank of Scotland v Law*, 1996 S.L.T. 83 proceeded on somewhat different facts but the two decisions are not easy to reconcile.

CHAPTER 20

ASSIGNATIONS

Introduction

Assignation is the transfer of incorporeal property. For instance, 20–01 debts, intellectual property rights and insurance policies are transferred by assignation. As with other transfers, it is important to distinguish between the obligation to convey, or to transfer, and the conveyance or transfer itself. Thus an agreement to assign is precisely that, and no more.[1] It is like missives. Likewise a delivered but unintimated deed of assignation is like a delivered but unregistered disposition. As with other transfers, a right may be assigned for all sorts of reasons, including sale and donation.

Some types of assignation are subject to special rules. Thus, there are special rules on the assignation of standard securities.[2] There are also special rules on the assignation of intellectual property rights,[3] of leases,[4] of company shares[5] and of company bonds (*i.e.* debentures and loan stock).[6] (The word "assignation" is not normally used for the transfer of shares and bonds, but that is merely a linguistic oddity: such transfers are, definitionally, assignations.) This chapter does not deal with these special types of assignation, but with the general law of assignation, and also the special rules applying to the assignation of life policies. Mandates will also be mentioned.

Rights assignable, not obligations

Only rights are assignable, not obligations. This is common sense. If 20–02 obligations could be assigned, then a person could borrow money and at once assign the obligation to repay, choosing, say, a tramp as an assignee. For a new obligant to be substituted in an obligation—a process known as *delegation*—the creditor's consent is therefore required.[7] By contrast, rights can be assigned without the consent of the

---

[1] See *e.g. Bank of Scotland Cashflow Ltd v Heritage International Transport Ltd*, 2003 S.L.T. (Sh. Ct) 107.

[2] See para.19–20.

[3] See Reid, *Property,* paras 811, 1006, 1197, 1227, 1248.

[4] See Halliday, *op. cit.,* Ch.46.

[5] Stock Transfer Act 1963, and, for "dematerialised" shares the Uncertificated Securities Regulations 2001 (SI 2001 No.3755).

[6] These are subject to the same legislation as company shares.

[7] There are one or two minor exceptions to the principle. One is that the contract may itself permit delegation. Another is to be found in the law of leases: an assignation of a lease not only works as an assignation of the cedent's rights but also as a delegation of the cedent's obligations.

debtor.[8] An assignation of contractual rights will thus not normally mean that the assignee undertakes the cedent's contractual obligations.[9]

General law of assignation[10]

20–03 Assignation involves two steps, namely (i) the delivery of the deed of assignation and (ii) the intimation, *i.e.* the notification to the third party concerned.[11] The relationship between them is very similar to the relationship between (i) the delivery of a disposition and (ii) registration. In both cases the grantee's right remains personal until title has been completed.

A statutory style of assignation is given in the Transmission of Moveable Property (Scotland) Act 1862.[12] This is optional, but in practice the statutory style tends to be followed, more or less. In fact, the common law is very lenient as to style: almost anything goes.[13] Indeed, the Requirements of Writing Act does not require assignations of incorporeal moveable property to be in writing.[14]

The question of how intimation is made is a complex one. At common law it had to be done in a *formal* manner, and it was not sufficient that the third party simply *knew* of the assignation. Case law has sometimes wobbled on this point, but it is thought that the law remains unchanged.[15] There is an optional statutory method, and in practice this is generally used: this is given in the 1862 Act (above). This provides for intimation by recorded delivery post. A copy of the assignation must be attached.[16] Nowadays, this can be a photocopy.[17] The intimation need not be probative and in practice normally is not. The intimation is made by the assignee (or by the assignee's solicitors).[18] The 1862 Act does not

---

[8] Again, there are some exceptions. In particular, the original contract between debtor and cedent may expressly or implicitly exclude assignation: see *e.g. James Scott Ltd v Apollo Engineering Ltd*, 2000 S.L.T. 1262.

[9] See *e.g. Alex Lawrie Factors Ltd v Mitchell Engineering Ltd*, 2002 S.L.T (Sh. Ct) 93.

[10] This chapter cannot give a full account of this complex area of law. See Halliday, Ch.8; William W. McBryde, *The Law of Contract in Scotland* (2nd ed. 2001), Ch.12; Reid, *Property*, paras 652–662; Nienaber and Gretton, in R. Zimmermann, D. Visser and K. Reid (eds), *Mixed Legal Systems in Comparative Perspective: Property and Obligations in Scotland and South Africa* (2004), pp.787–818. For the history of assignation, see Luig, in K. Reid and R. Zimmermann (eds), *A History of Private Law in Scotland* (2000), vol.1, pp.399–419.

[11] In the assignation of real rights, intimation is replaced by registration or possession: see Reid, *Property*, para.657.

[12] See Halliday, paras 8–07—8–11 for examples based on this statute.

[13] See, *e.g.*, *Laurie v Ogilvy*, Feb. 6, 1810, Fac. Coll.; *Carter v McIntosh* (1862) 24 D. 925; *Brownlee v Robb*, 1907 S.C. 1302.

[14] Requirements of Writing (Scotland) Act 1995, s.11(3)(a). This seems to take leniency too far.

[15] To what extent informal intimation is valid is "one of the long slow burning questions in the law": William W. McBryde, *op. cit.*, para.12–112.

[16] Like the common law of intimation, this presupposes that there has been a written assignation. An unwritten assignation thus seems to be incapable of intimation. This adds to the puzzle of why the 1995 Act does not require assignations to be in writing.

[17] The 1862 Act says that the copy must be "certified as correct" but it does not say how or by whom. In practice, intimations are usually by the assignee's solicitors, who do the certification.

[18] According to *Libertas-Kommerz GmbH v Johnston*, 1978 S.L.T. 222 it can be by the cedent.

give a style of intimation. In practice, the style is much the same as for intimations of assignations of life policies, for which see below. Because of the importance of intimation, evidence of it is desirable. The usual course is to ask the debtor to acknowledge receipt of the intimation.

The right assigned passes at the time of intimation.[19] Thus, suppose that Mary gives Peter a personal bond for £10,000, and Peter assigns this to Anne on Monday. Anne intimates to Mary on Wednesday. But on the previous day, Tuesday, Henry, a creditor of Peter, arrests in the hands of Mary. At the date of the arrestment the bond still belongs to Peter, and so the arrestment attaches it, and thus prevails over the right of Anne. This is a principle of vital importance.

Another important principle is *assignatus utitur jure auctoris,* meaning that the debtor (Mary) can plead against the assignee (Anne) any defences which she could have pled against the cedent (Peter). Thus, if Peter obtained the bond from Mary by fraud, Mary could plead the fraud as a defence to Anne, even though the latter took the bond from Peter for value and in good faith.

In many cases it is preferable to embody a debt obligation not in a personal bond but in a negotiable instrument, such as a promissory note or a bill of exchange. The main reasons are that intimation of transfer is not necessary, and that the *assignatus utitur* rule does not apply. Thus, in the first example, if Mary had given Peter not a personal bond but a promissory note, Anne's right would prevail over Henry's. And in the second example, if this had been a promissory note, Anne would be unaffected by Peter's fraud, assuming that she was in good faith.[20]

General law of assignation in security

Incorporeal property can, as well as being assigned outright, be assigned in security (*cessio in securitatem debiti*). The idea is that the assignee holds the property as a security for a debt owed by the cedent. If the debt is repaid, the assignee will assign the property back to the cedent: this is called retrocession. If the debt is not repaid, the assignee realises the property.   20-04

Thus, suppose in the example that Peter assigns the bond to Anne as a security for a debt owed by him to her. If he defaults, Anne can enforce the bond against Mary. Or Anne could sell the bond. An assignation in security makes the assignee the legal holder of the incorporeal property. The cedent is divested.[21] Thus, suppose that the bond provides for repayment by installments. Mary would pay these installments to Anne, not to Peter, for as long as Anne continued to be the legal holder of the bond. Of course the assignee in such a case is under a duty to account to the cedent for moneys received, for the assignee cannot recover more than is owed by the cedent. Thus, if a bond for £10,000 were assigned in security of a debt for £7,000, and the assignee is paid the £10,000 by the

---

[19] Stair, III, i, 6.

[20] Because she would be a holder in due course: Bills of Exchange Act 1882, ss.29 and 38(2).

[21] Contrast, *e.g.*, a standard security, where, despite the security, the debtor remains legally the owner of the property. Although Peter is divested of his right *against Mary*, he has a right *against Anne* in respect of the bond.

debtor in the bond, the assignee must return the excess of £3,000 to the cedent.

An assignation in security, whether of a life policy or not, can be either in the form of an outright assignation (*i.e.* an *ex facie* absolute assignation coupled with a separate document setting forth that it is truly only an assignation in security),[22] or an assignation expressly in security.[23] The latter seems more common in practice, at least for life policies.

Assignations in security are nowadays not very common except for life policies, for which see below. The form of an assignation in security is similar to that of an outright assignation.

Assignations of life policies

20–05   Like other rights, life policies can be assigned either absolutely or in security. Such assignations used to be common, but now are rare, partly because endowment home loans have become uncommon and partly because even where there is one the lender will often not insist on an assignation. However, if there is an existing endowment home loan with an assigned life policy, and the loan is being repaid, the policy must be assigned back, ie retrocessed.

There is a simple statutory style of assignation in the Policies of Assurance Act 1867,[24] which is optional, but in practice is followed. The Act does not, however, give a style of intimation.[25] The usual practice is to send the intimation in duplicate, asking the life office to return one copy with an acknowledgment of receipt on it. The Act requires the life office to issue written acknowledgment of receipt of intimation, on payment of a fee of 25 pence.[26]

Retrocession

20–06   Life policies are frequently assigned in security in connection with endowment mortgages.[27] When the loan is paid off the policy is retrocessed ie re-assigned. It must not be overlooked that the retrocession must be intimated in the same way as the original assignation. In most cases, the home loan is paid off not on maturity, but on a sale, and in that case the sellers may be using the same policy as a security for their next secured loan. So the retrocession may have to be followed immediately by a new assignation. This is done even where the same lender is involved in both the old and the new home loan. Thus, suppose that Rachel has an endowment home loan with Bank X. Her life policy is with LifeCo, and this policy has been assigned to Bank X as a security for the loan. She sells her house and buys another. This too is to be financed with an endowment home loan with Bank X. When she sells the

---

[22] See Halliday, para.8–78 for an example.

[23] See Halliday, paras 8–76 and 8–77 for examples.

[24] For an example based on this style see Halliday, para.8–31.

[25] Which it refers to as "notice of assignment". For styles see Halliday, para.8–35. See also D. J. Cusine and R. Rennie, *Standard Securities* (2nd ed., 2002), paras 2.09 and 3.36.

[26] This figure has not been increased since 1867, and nowadays, being trivial, is not charged.

[27] See paras 18–23 *et seq.*

first house she will pay off the existing loan. The standard security will be discharged by Bank X, and Bank X will also retrocess the life policy to Rachel, with intimation to LifeCo. In respect of the new house there may immediately follow a new assignation by Rachel to Bank X, with a new intimation to LifeCo (plus a new standard security by Rachel to Bank X over the new house). All this must be done in the right order. In principle, there is no reason why it should be done this way. If the lender remains the same it seems safe to leave the policy in its original assigned state, provided that the original assignation is so framed as to cover all debts, present and future, due by Rachel to Bank X. But the practice is to retrocess and then assign once again.

Implications of divestiture

Where incorporeal property is assigned in security, the assignee 20-07 becomes the legal holder of the property. This can be a significant point in a number of contexts. Two will be mentioned here. In the first place, suppose that Rachel dies while the home loan is still outstanding. In that case the policy matures. LifeCo owe the whole maturity value, bonuses and all, to Bank X. This is so even if, as will normally be the case, the total maturity value is greater than the home loan debt due to Bank X. Thus, suppose that the maturity value of the policy is £80,000 and the home loan debt due by Rachel to Bank X is £55,000, LifeCo will pay the whole £80,000 to Bank X, for the simple reason that Bank X is the legal holder of the policy. Bank X will pay itself what it is owed out of the proceeds. The surplus value (£25,000) is then owed by it to Rachel's executors.[28] Thus, although the surplus value belongs to Rachel's estate, it is not owed to the estate by LifeCo. LifeCo owes nothing to Rachel's estate, because although Rachel was the "life assured", she was not, at the time of her death, the holder of the policy. The surplus value is owed to Rachel's estate by Bank X. And of course it will pay it over to Rachel's executor[29] without fuss.

The second point concerns postponed securities. Rachel (whom we will now suppose to have recovered from her life-threatening illness) is not now the policy holder. She only has a reversionary right. But her reversionary right itself has a value, namely, the surplus value over and above the home loan debt. She might wish to assign this reversionary right to Steve, and she may wish to do this either outright or in security. Her reversionary right is itself incorporeal property, and can be assigned. To whom should intimation be made? Not to LifeCo. The reasons is that Rachel is not, strictly speaking, assigning the policy. She is not, at present, the holder of the policy, so she cannot assign it. She is assigning her reversionary right, which is a personal right not against LifeCo but against Bank X. Therefore intimation should be made to Bank X.[30] Assignations of reversionary rights are not common but they are occasionally encountered. The effect is to vest the reversion in Steve. For

---

[28] Assuming that the reversionary right to the policy was still vested in Rachel at her death.

[29] Once the executor has been confirmed.

[30] *Ayton v Romanes* (1895) 3 S.L.T. 203.

example, suppose that Rachel assigns to Bank X, and later assigns the reversion to Steve in security of a debt due by her to Steve. Rachel then succumbs to the grim reaper. The policy has a final maturity value of £80,000. The home loan debt is £55,000. The debt due by Rachel to Steve is £20,000. What happens is as follows. LifeCo pays £80,000 to the Bank X. LifeCo is now out of the picture. Bank X takes £55,000. The surplus of £25,000 it pays over to the holder of the reversion, Steve. Bank X is now out of the picture. Steve takes £20,000. Steve then pays over the value of the sub-reversionary right, namely £5,000, to Rachel's executor. Everyone is now happy, including, we hope, Rachel.

Personal bond

20-08   An assignation in security is a security for a debt, and so there should be a document (such as a personal bond) setting forth the terms of the loan contract. This can be done *in gremio* of the assignation itself,[31] but usually the loan contract will be in another document, such as a personal bond or a 1970 Act form A standard security. In that case the assignation should simply refer to that other document.

Enforcement clause

20-09   If Rachel lives and keeps up her repayments,[32] the question of enforcement does not arise. Nor does it arise if Rachel dies, for in that case the maturity value is paid direct to the creditor. The question of enforcement arises if Rachel, while alive, defaults on her repayments to Bank X. In that case Bank X will, in all probability, not seek to enforce its security over the policy, but will enforce the standard security over the house, by sale. This will normally pay off the debt, and the policy can then be retrocessed. But Bank X wish to have the possibility of enforcement against the policy, for otherwise they would not have insisted on the assignation in the first place. This would be important if, for instance, the market value of the house proved to be smaller than the debt due, which occasionally happens. A security over a life policy can be enforced in two ways, namely surrender and sale. In a surrender, the policy holder (Bank X) renounces the policy, and in exchange the life office (LifeCo) makes a payment, called the surrender value. In a sale, the policy is auctioned. Someone will buy it as an investment, taking the benefit when, eventually, Rachel dies.

The right to enforce by surrender or sale is implied in an assignation, but in most cases these rights are also conferred expressly.[33] Obviously, enforcement cannot happen unless the borrowers default on the loan, but normally one would wish to ensure that the right to sell or surrender the policy did not emerge instantly upon default. Otherwise borrowers

---

[31] See, *e.g.*, Halliday, paras 8–76 and 8–77.

[32] *i.e.* the repayments on the debt secured by the assignation in security. This will typically secure all sums due. Failure to keep up the premiums to the life office is typically made an event of default.

[33] It will often be found that these provisions are written into the Schedule of Variations (Mortgage Conditions) referred to in the standard security. The assignation of the policy then simply has a short clause referring to the Schedule of Variations.

might be one day late in making the monthly mortgage payment and find that the next day, without telling them, the lenders had sold the policy. A warning period, such as seven days, is thus sometimes written in. In practice, however, assignations are often silent on the matter, but the risk is small, because lenders are seldom in a hurry to sell or surrender a life policy.

Mandates

The term "mandate" has a number of meanings. In conveyancing 20–10 practice it usually means an instruction by a client (Alan) to his solicitor (Genius & Co.) to pay, out of moneys belonging to Alan which come into Genius & Co.'s hands, to a creditor of Alan. For example, suppose that Alan is buying a house and there is a delay in obtaining his home loan, which is to come from Bank X, which specialises in mortgage lending. Alan arranges bridging finance with his ordinary bank (Bank Y). As a condition of this, Bank Y has Alan sign a "mandate", which is a letter signed by Alan and addressed to Genius & Co., requiring the latter to pay to Bank Y the proceeds of the loan as and when this money is received by Genius & Co.[34] This gives Bank Y a certain degree of assurance that it will be repaid. Or the bank may obtain a mandate for the payment of the proceeds of the sale of the old house. The mandate will be expressed to be irrevocable without the consent of Bank Y. Sometimes the bank will ask the law firm to confirm that it will honour the mandate, but in general this request should be resisted, since it comes close to being a cautionary obligation on behalf of the client.

An obvious question is whether such mandates amount to an assignation of the future proceeds of the building society loan or of the sale. The question can arise in a number of circumstances. One example would be where another creditor of Alan serves an arrestment on Genius & Co., thereby attaching funds held for Alan. The answer to this question is far from clear.[35] To avoid the difficulty, some banks use a document which is in the form of an assignation,[36] rather than a mandate. If a mandate has been used, and a problem arises as to its effect (*e.g.* where there has been an arrestment), the solicitor should refuse to release any money except on the basis of an agreed settlement between all interested parties. If such agreement cannot be arrived at, a multiplepoinding may be unavoidable.

---

[34] Bank X will make over the loan moneys not directly to Alan but to Alan's solicitors.
[35] The subject is complex. See, for instance, *National Commercial Bank v Millar's Tr*, 1964 S.L.T. (Notes) 57 and *Hernandez-Cimorra v Hernandez-Cimorra*, 1992 S.C.L.R. 611. For discussion see Gretton (1994) 39 J.L.S.S. 175.
[36] In particular, using the words "do hereby assign".

CHAPTER 21

GENERAL CONVEYANCES

INTRODUCTION

Unregistered holders and completion of title

21-01   Delivery of a conveyance does not make the grantee owner. For that
the further step of registration is required.[1] During the period between
delivery and registration the grantee has rights but also vulnerabilities.[2]
He or she is able to grant certain deeds which, normally, only an owner
is able to grant. Usually, too, possession can be taken, under the entry
clause in the conveyance. But because ownership remains with the
granter, the grantee is vulnerable to the granter's insolvency, or to a
competing grant which is registered first.[3] Traditionally a person holding
land on a delivered but unregistered conveyance was known as an
"uninfeft proprietor", but the term, never satisfactory,[4] was rendered
obsolete by the abolition of the feudal system. The replacement proposed by the Title Conditions (Scotland) Act 2003 is *unregistered holder*,[5]
although it remains to be seen whether it becomes established in day-to-
day practice.[6]

Registration is sometimes described as *completion of title*. An unregistered holder therefore is one who holds on a title which is incomplete.

Normally the period between delivery and registration is only a matter
of days. Concerned to limit their vulnerability, grantees will generally
register as quickly as possible. But in one type of case the grantee may
be slow to register or, more commonly still, will not register at all. That
case is where the conveyance is a "general conveyance".

General conveyances and special conveyances

21-02   A *special conveyance* is one that conveys a particular property that is
identified in the deed. A standard example is the ordinary disposition. A
general conveyance differs in that it contains no description (or an

---

[1] *Sharp v Thomson*, 1995 S.C. 455, reversed on a different point, 1997 S.C. (HL) 66.
[2] Reid, *Property*, para.644.
[3] para.11-27.
[4] For "proprietor" suggested the ownership which would be conferred only by
registration.
[5] Title Conditions (Scotland) Act 2003, s.128(1), Sch.14, para.7(3)(a), substituting
"unregistered holder" for "uninfeft proprietor" in s.3(6) of the Land Registration
(Scotland) Act 1979.
[6] For the difficulty of terminology in this area, see para.11-07.

insufficient description) of the property. It may seem surprising that a conveyance of land should lack a description, but it does happen in certain types of case. A non-exhaustive list of conveyances which are, or depending on the circumstances may be, general in character is:

(i) Testament (will).
(ii) Trust deed for behoof of creditors. This is a general conveyance by the debtor of his or her assets to a trustee.[7]
(iii) Act and warrant in a sequestration. This is an interlocutor which conveys the debtor's assets to the trustee in sequestration.[8]
(iv) Deed of assumption and conveyance in favour of new trustees.[9]
(v) Decree appointing a trustee or a judicial factor.[10]
(vi) Legislation transferring land to a public body. For instance, when local government reorganisation took place in 1996, land was transferred by statute from the old councils to the new.[11] The latter do not become owner merely by virtue of the statutory vesting: that vesting has the effect of a disposition, but, like a disposition, no real right is acquired without registration.

Reasons for not registering

Often, the grantees of general conveyances do not complete title but choose to remain as unregistered holders. For this there are a number of possible reasons. In the first place, the risk from non-registration may be small. In a general conveyance the property often derives from a person who is inactive, dead or is a now-defunct public body. There may be little prospect of supervening insolvency, or of a second grant of the same property.[12]   21-03

In the second place, registration may in the circumstances be troublesome and expensive. Since the property is not identified in the deed, it must be identified of new for the purposes of registration. In some cases that is a difficult and unwelcome task. Registration may also be expensive, particularly if the conveyance encompasses a number of different properties. And finally, for GRS properties, there is the further barrier that a general conveyance is not eligible for recording as it stands. Instead a new deed must be prepared, known as a notice of title, which describes the particular property or properties and gives details of

---

[7] See para.26–04.
[8] See para.26–02.
[9] See para.22–16.
[10] Conveyancing Amendment (Scotland) Act 1938, s.1.
[11] Local Government (Scotland) Act 1994, s.15; Local Authorities (Property Transfer) (Scotland) Order 1995 (SI 1995/2499).
[12] But not always. *Burnett's Tr v Grainger*, 2004 S.L.T. 513, illustrates the potential value of completion of title by a trustee in sequestration. In that case the bankrupt had, some time previously, sold a house and granted a disposition. By completing title on the act and warrant the trustee was preferred to the disponee who had failed to register. See para.26–02.

the general conveyance. The conveyance itself is not sent to the Register. We return to the subject of notices of title later in the chapter.[13]

Finally, and as already mentioned, the grantee can perform certain juridical acts without completing title, so that the benefit of registration may seem out of proportion to the trouble and the cost. In particular, the grantee is able to sell the property and to grant a valid disposition. That is the subject of the next section.

JURIDICAL ACTS

Which acts?

21-04   Even without registration, the grantee of a conveyance can perform certain juridical acts in relation to the property. This is a matter of statutory concession. As the grantee is not owner, any grant is, naturally, *a non domino*. Nonetheless, it is convenient that a person in the position of an unregistered holder should be able to grant a number of standard deeds. In doing so, the person is transferring or burdening, not ownership itself, but rather the (personal) right to become owner. Statute does the rest.

Only a limited range of acts is permitted for the unregistered holder of land. Thus the holder can:

- convey the land, by disposition;[14]
- grant a standard security;[15]
- create real burdens;[16]
- if the right held is a lease, assign the lease or renounce it;[17] and
- if the right held is a standard security, assign, restrict, vary or discharge the security.[18]

But other acts leading to the creation of real rights are not allowed. Thus an unregistered holder cannot, for example, grant a lease, or a deed of servitude (although a servitude could be granted or reserved within a disposition).[19]

Deduction of title

21-05   The statutory concession just described is restricted to an unregistered holder, *i.e.* to the grantee of a delivered but unregistered conveyance (or equivalent). And the holder must be able to *deduce title*, that is to say, to

---

[13] para.21–11.
[14] Conveyancing (Scotland) Act 1924, s.3.
[15] Conveyancing and Feudal Reform (Scotland) Act 1970, s.12.
[16] Title Conditions (Scotland) Act 2003, ss.4(2)(b), 123(1).
[17] 1924 Act, s.24.
[18] 1924 Act, s.3, applied by the 1970 Act, s.32; 1970 Act, Sch.4, note 1.
[19] D. J. Cusine and R. R. M. Paisley, *Servitudes and Rights of Way* (1998), para.4–08.

demonstrate the conveyance (or, it may be, the series of conveyances) by which he or she is linked with the owner. The owner is the person who holds the last completed (*i.e.* registered) title;[20] and the conveyance or conveyances which provide the link to that person are known as *midcouples* or *links in title*. Thus suppose that Lorna is sequestrated, and an act and warrant is issued in favour of her trustee in sequestration, Michael. Michael sells to Norman without first completing title. On these facts the owner is Lorna, the unregistered holder is Michael, and the midcouple is the act and warrant. It will be seen that the validity of the proposed disposition rests on the validity of the act and warrant; and from the point of view of its grantee (Norman), a midcouple gives a power to grant which the granter would not otherwise have had.

Midcouples

Most conveyances do not function as midcouples. A disposition, for 21–06 example, is usually granted and registered without further ado, and so avoids the suspended animation of non-registration, and the patient wait for the day when its grantee might grant a further deed in which its role is merely to deduce title. A conveyance which is registered at once is thus effective in its own right, rather than being merely a cause of effectiveness in other, and later, deeds.

In practice most midcouples are general conveyances which the grantee has chosen not to register.[21] But any conveyance is *capable* of being a midcouple,[22] and even special conveyances are sometimes used in this way. In particular, confirmations of executors[23] and docket transfers[24] are not recorded directly in the GRS and so, for GRS titles, are invariably found in the role of midcouples. The same is true of English probate or letters of administration insofar as affecting land in Scotland.[25]

There is one exception. Although a testament or will is a general conveyance, its capacity to function as a midcouple is restricted. We return to this subject in the next chapter.[26]

If not all conveyances are in practice midcouples, there can be no midcouple which is not a conveyance. In particular, the right of a purchaser under missives of sale, or of a beneficiary under a trust, is not capable of being used as a midcouple. So an acquirer who has concluded missives but not taken delivery of the disposition is not an unregistered holder in the sense meant here, and cannot dispone the property deducing title through the missives.

---

[20] Since one of the main occasions giving rise to unregistered proprietors is an executry, the owner is in practice quite often dead.

[21] para.21–02.

[22] 1924 Act, s.5.

[23] See paras 22–05 and 22–06.

[24] See para.22–07.

[25] Administration of Estates Act 1971, s.3. See generally James Currie, *Confirmation of Executors* (8th ed., by Eilidh Scobbie, 1995), Ch.14.

[26] para.22–04.

Title on the Land Register

21-07   The rules about (a) whether a person is in a position to deduce title, and (b) if so, what sorts of deeds such a person can grant are the same regardless of whether the property is in the Land Register or is still in the GRS. However there does exist one important difference between the two registers. If the property is still in the GRS, a deed by an unregistered holder must contain a clause called a clause of deduction of title (discussed below). Such a clause is unnecessary if the property is in the Land Register.[27] It is sufficient to present the Keeper with the midcouple or midcouples which validate the deed.[28] But that is only a change in way deeds are drafted, and not a change in the substantive law, which still requires an unregistered granter to be able to deduce title.

First registrations

21-08   In a first registration, if the applicant does not have a disposition direct from the existing owner, not only must the disposition be backed up by the necessary midcouples, as where the property is already in the Land Register, but the disposition must contain a clause of deduction of title. Such a clause simply lists the midcouples, using a style laid down in the Conveyancing (Scotland) Act 1924. This begins by detailing the last recorded title, and then explains how the present person has acquired right to the property. Thus suppose that Michelle buys property in 1994 and is sequestrated in 2004. Her title is in the GRS. The trustee in sequestration, Nigella, wishes sell without first completing title. She grants a disposition to the buyer, Oliver. The disposition must contain a clause along these lines:[29]

> "Which subjects were last vested in the said[30] Michelle Morag MacLeod whose title thereto is recorded in the said Division of the

---

[27] 1979 Act, s.15(3). This says that it is not necessary to deduce title, but that there must be sufficient midcouples. The point is merely terminological: what s.15(3) means is that no clause of deduction is needed.

[28] Terminology and concepts are surprisingly difficult, however. Take a standard example. Andrew, the registered owner of land, dies. Brenda, his executor, obtains confirmation. As unregistered proprietor she grants a disposition to Colin. Colin applies for registration. He presents two conveyances to the Keeper: the confirmation and the disposition. Taken together, these provide the links between Colin and the last owner (Andrew), but only the confirmation is a midcouple in the strict sense. This is because the disposition would be invalid, as granted *a non domino*, but for (i) a statutory rule to the contrary (1924 Act, s.3) (ii) which is brought into operation by the confirmation. Thus the confirmation plays a secondary, supportive role in establishing the validity of the disposition. It is thus a midcouple and not a principal deed. This is seen more clearly if the deed granted by Brenda is a standard security and not a disposition. Colin's application for registration is in respect of the security and not the confirmation, so that even after registration *Brenda* (the grantee of the confirmation) lacks a completed title. Another way of approaching the matter is to say that a midcouple is a conveyance which links to the owner, not the applicant for registration (Colin) but the granter of the deed in his favour (Brenda).

[29] 1924 Act, s.3, Sch.A, form 1. But see ROTPB, para.5.75. The Keeper's practice is wrong.

[30] The person with the last recorded title must be designed, but she may have been designed earlier in the deed, in which case a simple reference is sufficient.

General Register of Sasines on the fourth day of September in the
year nineteen hundred and ninety-four[31] and from whom I
acquired right by the said[32] act and warrant in my favour."

It will be observed that the statutory style of deduction has three parts:
(i) identification of person with the existing GRS title; (ii) date of that
title; and (iii) the midcouple or midcouples. More is said about clauses
of deduction of title at the end of this chapter.

Title continuing in the GRS

In most cases, either the property is already in the Land Register or
the present transaction will switch the property into that Register. But in
a few types of case the property is still in the GRS and will remain there
for the time being. An example would be where Roberta owns a house,
her title being in the GRS, and dies. Her executor is Sally. Roberta's will
leaves the house to Timothy. Sally dispones to Timothy. This disposition
will be recorded in the GRS. It will need a clause of deduction of title,
deducing title through the confirmation in Sally's favour. The system is
precisely the same as in first registrations except that the midcouple (in
the example given, the confirmation) is not sent to the Register.

21-09

Preservation of midcouples

If the midcouple is a deed,[33] such as deed of assumption and
conveyance, or a docket transfer, the traditional practice was to register
it in the Books of Council and Session. That happens less often
nowadays, since once the title has been registered in the Land Register
the underlying deeds lose much of their significance, and in any case a
copy is retained by the Keeper.[34] In GRS transactions the midcouple is
not presented for recording, and registration in the Books of Council
and Session is a convenient means of ensuring that it does not become
lost.

21-10

General conveyance: completion of title

Often the grantee of a general conveyance does not trouble to
complete title but is content to remain as unregistered holder on an
indefinite basis. But sometimes this is not so. The method of completing
title then depends on whether the property is in the Land Register or the
GRS.

21-11

If the title is already on the Land Register, the position is straightforward, for in principle there is no difference between a general conveyance and a special conveyance. The conveyance is presented to the

---

[31] Or simply "which subjects were last vested in the said Michele Morag MacLeod as
aforesaid" if the information has already been given in an earlier part of the same deed.

[32] The midcouple must be specified fully, but here this has been done earlier in the same
deed.

[33] As opposed to a decree, which is already preserved in the register of the court in
question.

[34] Almost always, that means that it can be inspected, and a copy obtained: see
para.8–21.

Keeper in the usual way along with the appropriate application form and, if it is in order, registration will then follow. The same is true for GRS titles if the conveyance was granted for valuable consideration and so triggers first registration in the Land Register. If, in either case, the deed was the last of a sequence of unregistered conveyances, the earlier deeds act as midcouples for the applicant's own deed and so must accompany the application.[35]

The position is different for titles remaining on the GRS. As already mentioned,[36] a general conveyance[37] cannot be presented for recording in its own right but must instead be used as the midcouple[38] for a further deed known as a *notice of title*.[39] A notice of title is executed, not by the grantee of the general conveyance, but by a solicitor. It narrates that the last recorded title and the midcouple were presented to the solicitor, and that accordingly the grantee "has right as proprietor" to the property in question, which is then fully described. The notice also contains a clause of deduction of title, much as in a disposition. A statutory form of deed is provided and must be followed as closely as possible.[40]

CLAUSES OF DEDUCTION OF TITLE

Introduction

21-12   In this final section we consider some aspects of clauses of deduction of title in greater detail. It seems worth repeating that such clauses are not needed for Land Register titles. Accordingly the discussion which follows is relevant only to GRS transactions and to first registrations.

Some cases where the clause is not required

21-13   A clause of deduction of title is unnecessary where the granter already has a completed title. For instance, suppose that Penelope and Quintus buy a house with a survivorship clause in the title, and the title is in the GRS. Quintus then dies. Under the law of survivorship destinations, Penelope is deemed to have a completed title in the whole property the

---

[35] 1979 Act, s.3(6). This is because the midcouples establish the validity of the applicant's conveyance. This is the situation previously discussed in para.21–07.

[36] para.21–03.

[37] In theory a notice of title could also be used for a special conveyance, but in most cases this would be a pointless complication as direct recording has been allowed since 1858. See para.8–23. One case where a notice of title remains necessary is where the grantee of a special conveyance dies before the deed can be recorded, for death removes the possibility of recording: see Titles to Land Consolidation (Scotland) Act 1868, s.142.

[38] Thus, by contrast to the position on the Land Register, the general conveyance is merely a midcouple, *i.e.*, a source of validity of a subsequent deed (the notice of title). For property on the Land Register there is no notice of title.

[39] Notices of title were introduced by the 1924 Act, s.4 as an alternative to notarial instruments. Thereafter notarial instruments were rapidly supplanted in practice but were not formally abolished until 2004, by the Abolition of Feudal Tenure etc. (Scotland) Act 2000, s.76(2), Sch.13. For a discussion, see Scottish Law Commission, *Report on Abolition of the Feudal System* (Scot. Law Com. No.168, 1999), paras 7.27–7.33.

[40] 1924 Act, s.4, Sch.B. The normal form is form 1 of Sch.B.

moment that he dies.[41] Hence when she comes to dispone, it is not necessary for the disposition to contain a clause of deduction of title. The disposition should simply mention the survivorship clause and the fact of Quintus's death.

Next, a trustee in sequestration did not have to deduce title under the old law.[42] But the rule appears to be different for post-1985 sequestrations.[43] Liquidators, administrators and receivers do not need to deduce title since dispositions by them are considered as being dispositions by the company itself.

Thirdly, where a standard security holder sells, no deduction is required. It might be argued that this rule is anomalous. But the idea is that the standard security operates as an authorisation to the creditor to convey on behalf of the owner (in the event of default), so the position is comparable to a sale by an agent, where of course no deduction is needed.

Errors in deductions

It is not uncommon to find an error in a clause of deduction of title in 21–14 a deed recorded in the GRS. In general, such an error will be fatal, in the sense that the deed will fail to give a valid title. However, the problem can usually be solved without much difficulty.[44] Suppose that Ulrica owns a property that is still in the GRS. She dies. Her confirmed executor is Vernon. Vernon does not complete title but dispones to Walter, to whom Ulrica bequeathed the property. The disposition is recorded in the GRS. It fails to include a clause of deduction of title; or perhaps it contains one but it is bungled. Despite the recorded deed Walter is not the owner. His title is void. However, the disposition is still valid as a midcouple, because it is a conveyance. Walter could thus complete title by recording a notice of title with a clause deducing title though (a) the confirmation and (b) the disposition. This could be done even at one remove. Thus suppose that Walter were to die without having recorded the notice of title. His executor, Xerxes, is confirmed and dispones to Yvonne, to whom Walter bequeathed the property. This disposition could include a clause of deduction of title deducing through (a) Vernon's confirmation to Ulrica's estate (b) the disposition by Vernon to Walter, and (c) Xerxes's confirmation to Walter's estate. There is no limit to the number of midcouples that may be used.

The problem of errors does not arise once a property has been transferred to the Land Register, because although the right midcouples must exist there is no requirement that they be listed in the deed.

---

[41] para.23–05.

[42] Bankruptcy (Scotland) Act 1913.

[43] Bankruptcy (Scotland) Act 1985. The reason is that s.100 of the Bankruptcy (Scotland) Act 1913 provided that a disposition by the trustee in sequestration took effect as if it had been granted by the bankrupt with the consent of the trustee. The notional granter was thus infeft, and so deduction was not required. The 1985 Act seems to contain no equivalent provision.

[44] It rather seems that this point was overlooked in *Haberstich v McCormick*, 1975 S.L.T. 181, though the facts of that fact are not quite clear.

The word "vest"

21–15   The term "vest" is an ambiguous one. In the 1924 Act it is used to signify a completed title. Thus, when a deduction of title clause says that the subjects were "last vested in" someone it means that the last completed title was in that person. It should, however, be noted that the word is sometimes also used in a broader sense. Thus, in the law of succession, "vesting" is used to mean the acquisition of an indefeasible beneficial right.[45] Again, sequestration "vests" the estate of the bankrupt in the trustee, but this of itself gives the trustee a real right only for certain types of property, not including heritage.[46]

Some examples

21–16   We give here, at the risk of repetition, some typical examples of clauses of deduction of title. Clauses such as these are needed only where the property is still in the GRS, but the underlying principles are equally applicable where the property is in the Land Register.

(a) Anne owns property. She dies. Boris is confirmed as executor. Clare is the beneficiary. Boris can, without completing title in his own name, dispone to Clare, deducing title through the confirmation:

> "Which subjects were last vested in the said Anne . . . whose title thereto is recorded in . . . on . . . and from whom I acquired right as executor foresaid by said confirmation in my favour."[47]

(b) The same, but instead of disponing to Clare, Boris grants to Clare a docket transfer.[48] The result of this is that Clare is unregistered holder.[49] Clare could thereafter complete title by recording a notice of title, deducing title through the confirmation in favour of Boris and the docket in favour of herself. Or she could, without completing title herself, dispone to someone else, deducing title in the same way.

(c) As (b). But Clare does not complete title. Clare dies. David is confirmed as Clare's executor.[50] David could record a notice of title, or dispone, deducing through (i) Boris's confirmation to Anne (ii) the docket to Clare, and (iii) David's confirmation to Clare's estate.

> "Which subjects were last vested in Anne [*design*] whose title thereto was recorded in . . . on . . . and from whom I acquired right as executor foresaid by (one) confirmation in favour of Boris as executor of the said Anne issued by the Commissariot of . . . at . . . on . . . (two) docket endorsed on a certificate of the last-

---

[45] For discussion of this tricky subject, see Gretton (1986) 31 J.L.S.S. 148; Maher (1986) 31 J.L.S.S. 396; Gordon (1987) 32 J.L.S.S. 218; Patrick (1988) 33 J.L.S.S. 98; and Styles (1989) 34 J.L.S.S. 338.

[46] Bankruptcy (Scotland) Act 1985, s.31. See para.26–02.

[47] In such a case the narrative clause will already have designed Anne and specified the confirmation.

[48] Succession (Scotland) Act 1964, s.15(2). See para.22–07.

[49] Because the docket will not be recorded.

[50] This may seem a complex case, but is quite common in practice.

mentioned confirmation by the said Boris in favour of the said Clare dated . . . and (three) said confirmation in my favour as executor of the said Clare dated as aforesaid"

(d) Alfred, Brenda and Chris are trustees with a completed title. Alfred resigns and Brenda dies. Chris executes a deed of assumption and conveyance appointing Donna and Elaine as new trustees.[51] This deed could be recorded in the GRS,[52] but let us suppose that it is not recorded. The three trustees (Chris, Donna and Elaine) can complete title by notice of title deducing through the deed of assumption and conveyance. The clause would run on the following lines:

"Which subjects were last vested in the said Alfred . . . and Brenda . . . and Chris . . . as trustees foresaid whose title thereto was recorded in . . . on . . . and from whom, following the resignation of the said Alfred . . . by minute of resignation dated . . . and registered in the Books of Council and Session on . . . and also following the death of the said Brenda . . . on . . ., the said Chris . . . and Donna . . . and Elaine . . . acquired right as trustees foresaid by deed of assumption and conveyance by the said Chris . . . as trustee foresaid in favour of the said Chris . . . and Donna . . . and Elaine . . . as trustees foresaid dated . . . and registered in the Books of Council and Session on . . ."

As this example shows, the practice is that in a deed of assumption and conveyance, the granter is one of the grantees.

(e) Alan and Beth are own a property is common, with no survivorship clause. Alan dies and Beth confirms as Alan's executor. Beth is also the legatee of Alan's half share. Beth as executor dockets that half share to herself as an individual. Beth then sells the whole property. The deduction, which is needed only in respect of *Alan's* half share, would run:

"Which subjects were last vested to the extent of a one half *pro indiviso* share in the late Alan [*design*][53] whose title thereto is recorded in . . . on . . . and from whom I acquired right by (primo) confirmation in my favour as executor of the said Alan . . . issued by the Commissariot of . . . at . . . on . . .[54] and (secundo) docket endorsed on a certificate of said confirmation by me as executor foresaid in favour of myself as an individual dated . . ."

(f) Suppose in the last example that Beth is sequestrated after she had granted the docket to herself, and that Cornelius, her trustee in sequestration, dispones to Darius. Here the two halves of the property will need separate deductions:

---

[51] See para.22–16.

[52] If it has a proper conveyancing description of the heritable property in the trust.

[53] No designation is needed if Alan has been designed earlier in the deed, in which case the wording is "in the said Alan".

[54] Or "said confirmation" if, as is likely, it has already been specified earlier in the deed.

"Which subjects were last vested to the extent of a one half *pro indiviso* share in the late Alan . . . [*design*] whose title thereto is recorded in . . . on . . . and from whom I as trustee in sequestration foresaid acquired right by (one) confirmation in favour of the said Beth . . . as executor of the said Alan . . . issued by the Commissariot of . . . at . . . on . . . (two) docket endorsed on a certificate of said confirmation by the said Beth . . . as executor in favour of herself as an individual dated . . . and (three) the said act and warrant in favour of myself as trustee in sequestration foresaid, and which subjects were last vested to the extent of the other one half *pro indiviso* share in the said Beth . . . whose title thereto is recorded in . . . on . . . and from whom I as trustee in sequestration foresaid acquired right by said act and warrant."

CHAPTER 22

TRUSTS AND EXECUTRIES

Introduction

When someone dies, the body, the soul and the property pass on. The 22–01
body is buried or cremated. The fate of the soul is not a matter for the
law. As for the deceased's estate, two questions arise. The main one is:
who gets what? This is the province of the law of succession, and of
inheritance tax. But there is also the question of how who gets what, or
in other words how the successors are to obtain title. Every death thus
involves a conveyancing problem of getting rights out of the dead and
into the living.

The law before 1964

Before the 1964 Act there were two separate systems, according to 22–02
whether moveable or heritable property was involved. For moveables,
the process was (subject to minor qualifications) that the executor
obtained confirmation from the sheriff, acting as commissary. Confirmation is a type of decree. This procedure was used in both testate and
intestate cases. This is still the law. But the executor had, as such, no
right to administer the heritage. The administration of the heritage itself
could happen in two ways. In the first place, if the deceased was
intestate, the heritage passed to the heir.[1] The law, in ascertaining the
heir, preferred males to females and, subject to certain exceptions, the
elder to the younger: the system thus displayed two mortal sins of
modern theology, namely sexism and ageism. If there were children, the
heir was the eldest son. If there were only daughters, the daughters were
co-heirs, under the name heir-portioners. In the absence of issue, the
heir[2] would be a collateral heir, such as a brother, for always males were
preferred to females. The procedure was that the heir petitioned the
sheriff for a decree of service.[3] This decree then operated as a
conveyance in his favour. Alternatively, he could complete title by the
clare constat procedure, which involved application to the superior. Both
of these procedures were abolished by the 1964 Act, though they
remained competent in respect of pre-Act deaths.

---

[1] The heir's right could, however, be subject to a liferent in favour of the relict, under
the doctrine of terce (in favour of a widow) and courtesy (in favour of a widower).

[2] The full title was heir-at-law or heir-of-line, the two terms being synonymous.

[3] There were two types of service, special and general. Special service was appropriate
for property in which the deceased had a completed title, and general service for other
property. For service before the 19th century reforms, see Erskine, III,viii, 59.

In the second place, if the deceased was testate, the heritable property would pass to whomever was entitled to it under the testament. There are, in theory, two types of testament, or will, namely the will or testament strictly so called, and the trust disposition and settlement. In the former, the legacies are made direct to the legatees, while in the latter everything is conveyed to trustees (who in practice would be the same as the executors for the moveables), with the legatees having the status simply of beneficiaries under a trust.[4] After the nineteenth century reforms, if there was a will (in the narrow sense) then either the legatee or the executor could deduce title through the will. (If the executor did so, he would, of course, then convey to the legatee.) But if there was a trust disposition and settlement only the trustee could complete title.[5]

The pre-1964 law, which has just been stated in only the briefest fashion, is important not only by way of background to the modern law, but also because knowledge of it can still be relevant in current practice. The pre-1964 law still applies to pre-1964 deaths. Consequently, if the last recorded title to land is in the name of someone who died before the 1964 Act, it is necessary to employ the pre-1964 law to make up title. It might be thought that this never happens nowadays, but in fact such cases still occasionally crop up. Thus, Mr Campbell buys a small farm in 1958, and his title is recorded. He dies intestate in 1962, and his son, Mr Campbell the second, takes over the farm, but no legal steps are taken to make up title. The son dies intestate in 1991 and his son, Mr Campbell the third, takes over, again with no legal steps being taken. Mr Campbell the third now wants to sell, but the GRS shows his grandfather as the person with the most recent completed title.[6] It will be necessary to establish whether the beneficial right to the farm did indeed pass in 1962 to Mr Campbell the second (which is a question for pre-1964 law) and then whether it further passed in 1991 to Mr Campbell the third (which is a question for post-1964 law). Assuming that the present Mr Campbell is the person beneficially entitled, there remains the technical problem of enabling him to grant a valid title to a purchaser. This in turn means finding midcouples to link the present Mr Campbell with the 1958 recorded title.[7]

The law since 1964

22–03   The 1964 Act made radical changes, both as to who gets what and as to the mechanics of transfer. On the latter point, it extended the confirmation procedure to cover heritage as well as moveables. That

---

[4] In a trust disposition and settlement typical wording would be: "I . . . assign dispone and convey to my said trustees my whole means and estate heritable and moveable real and personal wherever situated which shall belong to me at the time of my death . . . but these presents are granted in trust only for the following purposes . . . (Tertio) to convey and make over to . . . my house at 17 Carey Gilson Street Kirkcudbright." A will in the narrow sense simply says: "I bequeath to . . . my house at 17 Carey Gilson Street Kirkcudbright . . . and I appoint . . . as my executor."

[5] See, generally, ss.19 and 20 of the Titles to Land Consolidation (Scotland) Act 1868 and s.46 of the Conveyancing (Scotland) Act 1874. For full discussion see John Burns, *Conveyancing Practice* (4th ed., 1957, by Farquhar MacRitchie) and John Burns, *op. cit.* (4th ed., 1932). The 19th century reforms thus extended the role of the executor to heritage in testate cases.

[6] In feudal language, the person last infeft.

[7] For discussion of this particular type of case, see Allan (1978) 23 J.L.S.S. 438.

made the service procedure redundant and accordingly it was abolished, though it remains competent in relation to the estate of anyone who died intestate before 1964.[8] Hence, in intestate cases, title to land is now obtained through confirmation. For testate cases the situation is rather more complex, there is a choice. Title can be taken in such cases either through confirmation or through the will.

Title through the testament

Although a clause of deduction of title is never necessary in a 22-04 disposition of registered property,[9] the underlying law is the same for registered conveyancing as it is in GRS conveyancing. All that has altered is that the *clause* may be omitted. It remains the law that a granter without a completed title must be *able* to deduce title.[10] In the following, therefore, references to deduction include references to dispositions of registered property, with the one qualification that in such dispositions the clause itself will not appear.

After the 1964 Act was passed, there was some uncertainty as to whether title could come only through the confirmation, or whether it could come through the testament (if there was one) as an alternative. To resolve the doubts, the Law Society of Scotland submitted a memorial to the Professors of Conveyancing, and the views which they expressed have been universally accepted.[11] They held that an executor can indeed take title through a will,[12] but they were divided as to the position of a legatee. Because the law on the latter point is uncertain, deduction through a will *by a legatee* is almost never attempted in practice, and a title which depended on such a deduction would not be regarded as a good and marketable title.[13] There is no case law on the subject.

One drawback which can arise in GRS conveyancing where an executor deduces title through the will is that the protections afforded by section 17 of the 1964 Act[14] do not apply. However, the general view is that this drawback is not so serious as to justify an objection to a title which involves deduction through the will. In most cases there is no point in deducing through the will since confirmation will have been obtained in any case. Its utility is therefore restricted to the situation where there is no other estate of the deceased which would require confirmation.

---

[8] Titles to Land Consolidation (Scotland) Act, 1868, s.26A, inserted by the Abolition of Feudal Tenure etc. (Scotland) Act, s.68.

[9] Land Registration (Scotland) Act 1979, s.15(3).

[10] para.21-07.

[11] See (1965) 10 J.L.S.S. 153 and (1966) 11 J.L.S.S. 84.

[12] And so *a fortiori* title can be deduced by a trustee through a trust disposition and settlement. The Professors added that "we strongly recommend that the confirmation should be used in preference to the will as a link in title".

[13] However, it seems that the Keeper is in some cases prepared to accept deeds by legatees where there is no confirmation: ROTPB, para.5.33.

[14] See para.22-14.

Confirmation

22-05   The general law and practice of confirmation falls outwith the scope of this book.[15] But because of the importance of confirmation as a conveyancing document something needs to be said about it here. Four general points should be noted.

In the first place, confirmation is a conveyance, from the deceased to the executor. It is a judicial conveyance, and may be compared in this respect with the act and warrant in a sequestration. However, unlike an act and warrant, it is a special conveyance, in that it lists the various items of the estate of the deceased. Logically, therefore, if the property is still in the GRS it should be possible for the confirmation to be recorded directly in the GRS so as to make the executor owner (in trust).[16] This, however, is never done in practice, and since in conveyancing settled practice tends to mature into settled law, it may be that a confirmation could not be so recorded. At all events, the attempt is never made. The issue does not arise for property in the Land Register, as in that case the confirmation itself is sufficient to authorise registration.[17]

Second, an executor is a species of trustee under the 1921 Act and the Trusts (Scotland) Act 1961,[18] and also, to certain extent, at common law. This is important, because it means that the general body of trust law[19] applies to executors. For example, where an executor dies without having completed the administration of the estate, the rules of lapsed trusts can be applied. Or again, a purchaser from an executor has the protection afforded to any purchaser from a trustee under section 2 of the Trusts (Scotland) Act 1961. Again, the persons beneficially entitled to succeed, whether as legatees, or by legal rights, or prior rights, or as heirs *ab intestato,* are in the position of beneficiaries of a trust, the executor being the trustee. It is common for wills to declare that the executor is to be a trustee, but this would seem to be superfluous, at least under modern law.

The third point about confirmation is that it is not necessary to put in a full conveyancing description of the heritage, but merely "such a description as will be sufficient to identify the property or interest therein".[20] However, it is quite common to see a full conveyancing description used, and indeed when in doubt it should be used. Occasionally, dreadful descriptions are found in confirmations, from which it is impossible to know what land is in question. If the property concerned is simply a house, a postal address will usually be satisfactory. But in other types of property something fuller may be necessary. If the property is in the Land Register, a full conveyancing description is particularly easy, for all that is needed is the title number.

---

[15] See James Currie, *The Confirmation of Executors in Scotland* (8th ed., 1995 by Eilidh M. Scobie).

[16] As was observed by Professor A. J. McDonald at (1965) 10 J.L.S.S. 71 at 72.

[17] 1979 Act, s.3(6). See para.21–11.

[18] s.2. Originally this was true only of executors nominate, but s.20 of the 1964 Act extended the 1921 Act to executors dative.

[19] Or most of it, at any rate.

[20] Act of Sederunt (SI 1966/593).

Fourth, once confirmation has been issued the sheriff clerk, acting as commissary clerk, will issue, if asked, not only the confirmation itself but also one or more "certificates of confirmation".[21] A certificate is a briefer document which refers to a single item of estate, and states that that item has been included in the confirmation. The point is that the executor will want to keep the confirmation itself, while the person taking the land—either a beneficiary or a purchaser—will also want it as a midcouple. The problem is solved by the certificate of confirmation, which is delivered to the grantee.

The confirmation as a link in title: registration

A confirmation does not of itself transfer title to the executor. It is a 22–06 conveyance of land and, like any conveyance of land, it can give no real right of itself: completion of title by registration—in the Land Register or the GRS as appropriate—is necessary for a real right to be obtained.

If the property is in the Land Register the executor simply applies on a form 2, enclosing the confirmation or a certificate of confirmation. If the property is in the GRS, completing title will not trigger a first registration. The executor must expede and record a notice of title deducing title through the confirmation.[22]

Although the executor can complete title in this way, it is uncommon to do so without special reason, such as that the administration of the estate is likely to be prolonged. More usually the executor conveys to the buyer or beneficiary without having first completed title.

Disposition to a beneficiary without prior completion of title

There are two ways in which an executor can convey property to a 22–07 beneficiary without first having completed title. The simplest is just to grant a disposition, the confirmation being the midcouple. If the property is in the GRS a clause of deduction of title is required. The alternative is the docket procedure given by section 15 of the Succession (Scotland) Act 1964.[23] What happens is that the executor endorses on the certificate of confirmation (or on the confirmation itself, though that is rare in practice) a docket nominating the beneficiary as the person entitled to the property in question. The docketed certificate is then normally registered in the Books of Council and Session, though that is not a requirement of law.

The docket of itself does not give the beneficiary a real right, because a real right requires registration in the Land Register or GRS. The docket can be used as a basis for registration in the Land Register but probably cannot be directly recorded in the GRS.[24] So if the property is still in the GRS the beneficiary, now holding the docket, has to take further steps to complete title. This is done by preparing and recording,

---

[21] These are regulated by Act of Sederunt (SI 1971/1164).

[22] para.21–11.

[23] The style is given in Sch.1 to the Act. Because of the wording of the style, it is uncertain whether it could be used where property is to be conveyed in implement of a deed of family arrangement. In such cases a simple disposition should be used.

[24] The point is an open one, but such direct recording is never attempted in practice.

in the GRS, a notice of title, with a clause of deduction of title listing as midcouples (a) the confirmation and (b) the docket.[25]

Alternatively, the beneficiary could hold the property indefinitely on the basis of the docket, without ever completing title. Eventually the beneficiary could then sell and dispone to a third party. If the property is in the Land Register, no clause of deduction is needed. Otherwise the disposition should deduce through (a) the confirmation and (b) the docket. It is quite common in practice for a beneficiary not to complete title but to hold on the basis of the docket. But this is hardly satisfactory, and in our view title should always be completed immediately.

A docket can be in favour of the executor as an individual, and this is quite common, for the executor is often a beneficiary and sometimes the sole beneficiary. In that case, the wording on the docket is simply that the executor does hereby nominate herself/himself, and so forth.

The docket procedure is puzzling. It is deed that conveys property. But the law already provides such a deed, namely the disposition. A disposition is no harder to draft than a docket. Indeed, of the two the docket is the more problematic, for if the nomination is not worded correctly the docket is probably invalid,[26] whereas the validity of a disposition does not depend on its narrative clause. Moreover, if the property is in the GRS the use of the docket means that two deeds (the docket and the notice of title) are needed instead of just one (disposition) for the beneficiary to complete title. Why the 1964 Act introduced the docket is a mystery.[27] The frequent use of the procedure in practice is probably explained by specialisation and departmentalisation in law firms. Those who do wills, trusts and executries do not do dispositions (which are the business of conveyancers), but they do do dockets.

Disposition to a buyer without prior completion of title

22-08   There are various reasons why the executor may sell the property, instead of transferring it to a beneficiary. Where this happens the docket procedure is not available, and an ordinary disposition must be used.

Leases

22-09   The present work does not generally deal with leases. However, if a lease is involved one complication deserves mention. The executors may have to assign the lease to the appropriate beneficiary within one year, failing which the lease is vulnerable to termination by the landlord.[28]

---

[25] See para.21-16(b).
[26] Authority on this issue is absent.
[27] Did the draftsperson think that a docket would confer a real right?
[28] Succession (Scotland) Act 1964, s.16. See further Angus McAllister, *Scottish Law of Leases* (3rd ed., 2002), Ch.8; M. C. Meston, *The Succession (Scotland) Act 1964* (5th ed., 2002); Reid and Gretton, *Conveyancing 2000*, pp.63–6. The reported cases are *Lord Rotherwick's Trs v Hope*, 1975 S.L.T. 187; *Gifford v Buchanan*, 1983 S.L.T. 613; and *Sproat v South West Services (Galloway) Ltd*, 2000 G.W.D. 37–1416. For the liability of a solicitor for overlooking s.16, see *Paul v Ogilvie*, 2001 S.L.T. 171.

Where the deceased did not have a completed title

Complexities sometimes arise where the deceased did not have a 22–10 completed title. Take the following case. Alan owns a house and dies intestate. Beth, his widow, is entitled to the house under prior rights. She is also the executrix dative. She confirms to her late husband's estate, and executes a docket transfer in her own favour, but does not complete title. Some years later she dies. Her will leaves the house to her niece Christine, whom she also nominates as her executrix. Christine confirms to her aunt's estate. The last person with a completed title was Alan. Christine can validly dispone (to herself as beneficiary, or to a purchaser). She is linked to the last recorded or registered title by an unbroken chain of valid midcouples, namely: (a) Beth's confirmation to Alan's estate; (b) the docket transfer in favour of Beth; (c) Christine's confirmation to Beth's estate. If the property is in the GRS these midcouples will have to be listed in the clause of deduction of title.[29] If the property is in the Land Register such a clause is not necessary, but the existence of the unbroken chain of valid midcouples is just as necessary as for a GRS title.

Lapsed trusts

Now consider a variation on the above case. Suppose that although 22–11 Beth confirmed to her late husband's estate, and although she was beneficially entitled to the house by virtue of prior rights, she did not grant a docket to herself, or otherwise transfer the property to herself as an individual. Here there is a problem. Beth had the beneficial right. Christine can confirm to that beneficial right, *i.e.* to Beth's beneficial right in the estate of Alan. But the title is still stuck in Alan's executry, for there has been no transfer out of his executry. In other words, there is a "lapsed trust".

A trust is said to lapse where (1) there is still trust property undistributed but (2) there are no acting trustees, usually because all the trustees are dead. That is what has happened here. There are various ways of unscrambling a lapsed trust.[30] Those mentioned below are applicable to all types of trust, including executries, except for the third, which is applicable only to executries.

In the first place, where the beneficial right is absolutely vested and no further trust administration is required with respect to that property, the beneficiary can apply to the court for an order authorising him to complete title.[31] This procedure is, however, almost never adopted in practice.

In the second place, anyone with an interest can petition the court for the appointment of a new trustee.[32] The petition will itself suggest to the

---

[29] para.21–16(c).
[30] The following is a list of the main ones. There are some others, such as the appointment of a judicial factor.
[31] Trusts (Scotland) Act 1921 Act, s.24. The decree is then a midcouple.
[32] 1921 Act, s.22. Curiously, this section does not in fact mention the death of the sole trustee (or all trustees) as a ground of petition. But the section has always been construed as covering such cases, and indeed is seldom used for any other purpose. See W.A. Wilson and A.G.M. Duncan, *Trusts, Trustees and Executors* (2nd ed., 1995), Ch.21.

court a suitable person to act. The decree then operates as a midcouple in favour of the person appointed. Such petitions are quite common.

In the third place, where the executor has died, a new executor can be appointed to the estate. In the example, this would mean someone else becoming executor to Alan. That person could then dispone to the ultimate beneficiary of Beth's estate, the disposition incorporating the consent of Beth's executor.[33] A new executor appointed in this way is called an executor *ad non executa, i.e.* an executor appointed to an estate which had not been "executed" by the original executor.[34]

The fourth method, frequently used in practice, is the procedure set out in section 6 of the Executors (Scotland) Act 1900. Under this procedure, the executor (Christine) of the executor (Beth) can confirm to the unexecuted estate. This will involve confirming to the house twice in the same inventory. In the main body of the inventory, Christine would confirm to Beth's beneficial right to Alan's estate. Then, in an appendix to the inventory, Christine would enter the house itself. Confirmation issued in such terms operates as a midcouple in favour of Christine. She can then dispone (to herself, if she inherits from her aunt) the deduction of title running through (i) Beth's confirmation to Alan's estate and (ii) her own confirmation to her aunt's estate. One qualification to be noted is that this procedure is competent only where no further acts of administration are required in the trust or executry which has lapsed. In other words, it is available only where the only thing needed is to convey the property to the person beneficially entitled. This, however, is usually the case.

Lapsed trusts are a nuisance. So where it is anticipated that a trust will continue for some time, it is wise to have more than one trustee. In ongoing trusts there may, of course, be additional reasons for having more than one trustee, for difficult decisions may need to be taken, and two or three heads will be wiser than one.

In the example, it would not have been sufficient for Christine merely to confirm to her aunt's beneficial right to Alan's estate. Of course, such confirmation is necessary, for what may be called the internal purposes of Beth's executry, or in other words such aspects as beneficial succession to Beth, and tax liabilities for her estate. But such confirmation would be ineffectual for conveyancing purposes. The reason is that the entry in Christine's confirmation to Beth's estate concerns only Beth's beneficial right to the house, and title cannot be deduced through a mere beneficial right.[35] Hence the necessity of confirming to the title itself in an appendix under section 6 of the Executors (Scotland) Act 1900, or adopting some other means of rescuing title from the lapsed trust.

---

[33] In such a case, of course, it would be for Beth's executor to determine the person to whom the property should be conveyed. Alan's new executor would then simply follow that request. Alternatively Beth's executor could request Alan's new executor to convey to her, in her capacity as Beth's executor. The position would be the same if a new trustee to Alan's estate had been appointed under s.22 of the 1921 Act.

[34] The process is a common law one, subject to the Executors (Scotland) Act 1900, s.7.

[35] But only through a conveyance: see para.21–06. Once more the point is made that in the case of registered property no clause of deduction is needed (1979 Act, s.15) but nevertheless precisely the same midcouples are required as in the case of GRS property.

Destinations

Destinations are the subject of Chapter 23, but a few words are 22-12
appropriate here. If there is a survivorship destination in the title there is
no need for confirmation in respect of that property, on the first death,
because the survivor is deemed automatically the owner of the whole. Of
course, on the second death there will have to be confirmation to the
property. More strictly, there will have to be confirmation on the last
death, for one can have a survivorship destination among three or more
people, such as three sisters. Where, after the first death, the survivor
dispones, no deduction of title is necessary because deduction of title is
required only where the title of the granter is not complete. The fact of
the earlier death is stated in the narrative clause.

A quite separate issue under the same heading of destinations is
whether, in an *inter vivos* disposition in favour of trustees, it is necessary
to add a survivorship destination. Though it is quite common to do so, it
is unnecessary and indeed in principle inappropriate. Trust ownership is
joint ownership.[36] Each trustee does not have a "share" of the property.
There is thus no question of such a non-existent "share" *passing,* on the
death of one trustee, to the other trustees. When one trustee dies, he
simply drops out of the picture. His death does not *enlarge* the rights of
the others. The title is a single one, under joint administration.

Purchasing from an executor or trustee

In a purchase from an executor or trustee, it is not necessary to verify 22-13
that there is a power of sale, because in such cases section 2 of the Trusts
(Scotland) Act 1961 protects the purchaser. Good faith is not required.
In other words, if an executor or trustee sells in breach of trust, the
beneficiaries must pursue their remedy against the delinquent trustee,
not against the purchaser. Such cases are, however, rare, partly because
breach of trust is rare and partly because in most cases trustees have an
implied power of sale.[37]

However, in such cases it may be necessary for the purchaser to
examine the will or other deed of trust for a quite separate reason. A
spouse of the beneficiary of the property may have had occupancy
rights.[38] Hence a consent or an affidavit may be required. Examination
of the will or other trust deed may then be required to determine who
should grant the consent or affidavit.

Lastly, a purchaser from a confirmed executor is protected, if in good
faith, against the unlikely event of the subsequent reduction of the
confirmation.[39]

---

[36] As to which see para.22-15.

[37] Trusts (Scotland) Act 1921, s.4. In the unlikely event that they do not have it, they can
usually acquire it from the court: 1921 Act, s.5.

[38] See Ch.10.

[39] Succession (Scotland) Act 1964, s.17. Reductions of confirmations are in any event
extremely rare.

Purchasing from a beneficiary

22–14   Suppose that an executor or trustee has conveyed to a beneficiary, and the beneficiary comes to sell within the period of positive prescription, and the property is still in the GRS.[40] Is it necessary for the purchaser to check that the executor or trustee conveyed to the right person? In other words, does the purchaser need to check the terms of the will or other deed of trust? In the case of a beneficiary who has taken title from a confirmed executor, section 17 of the Succession (Scotland) Act 1964 provides that a purchaser from that beneficiary is protected,[41] provided that he is in good faith. No one is sure what good faith amounts to in this context. Some conveyancers think that the will must be checked in order to be in good faith, while others think not. The issue is unresolved.

Section 17 applies only where the beneficiary took title from a confirmed executor. In other cases where a purchase is from a beneficiary, the purchaser has no statutory protection. Thus, suppose that there is an *inter vivos* trust, and the trustees convey part of the estate, a house, to Alan. Alan then concludes missives to sell to Brenda. If the trustees should not have conveyed to Alan, Alan's title will be voidable. However, if Brenda is in good faith, she will be protected at common law.[42] Hence the position is in fact effectively the same as under section 17 of the 1964 Act.[43]

Joint property

22–15   Where there is more than one trustee, or executor, they hold as joint owners, not owners in common.[44] Indeed, trust ownership appears to be the only case where joint ownership is possible for heritable property. Joint owners, unlike owners in common, do not have identifiable shares. If there are two owners in common, each has a half share, if three, a third, and so on *i.e.* they have aliquot shares.[45] But nothing like that is the case for trustees. If there are two trustees and they assume a third, it would be quite wrong to suppose that the "share" of the first two fell from a half to a third. It is because the title is joint that, when one trustee dies, there is no "share" to pass to his estate. Instead, the surviving trustees carry on as before, owners of the whole. The position is the same if one trustee resigns.

---

[40] The issue here discussed is less likely to be relevant if the property is in the Land Register.

[41] *i.e.* protected against the possibility that the beneficiary's title was reducible because the executor should have conveyed to someone else, or because the confirmation itself was reducible.

[42] At common law, voidability does not transmit against a disponee who gives value and is in good faith.

[43] Indeed, s.17 is to that extent merely declaratory of the common law.

[44] The term *pro indiviso* ownership applies to both cases. For the differences between common and joint property, see Reid, *Property*, paras 17 *et seq.*

[45] Unless some other, unequal, division has been expressly provided for.

Assumption

Trustees, including executors nominate (but not executors dative),[46] 22–16 can normally assume new trustees.[47] This is rare in executries, but common in long-running trusts. It is done by a deed of assumption and conveyance.[48] This can take the form of a special conveyance, but is more usually done as a general conveyance, *i.e.* as a conveyance of the whole trust estate without specification of any particular property. If some of the existing trustees are to continue, the practice is to convey to themselves and to the new trustee or trustees, so that the granters will also be among the grantees. The new trustee or trustees adds a docket at the foot accepting office. The deed is, as a matter of good practice, registered in the Books of Council and Session. It is wise to complete title in the name of the new body of trustees,[49] but this is not always done. Naturally, the deed of assumption is a midcouple, and title can be deduced through it.

Resignation

A trustee can normally resign, unless he or she is the sole trustee.[50] A 22–17 sole trustee who wants to resign must assume a new trustee first. A minute of resignation[51] by a trustee should, as a matter of good practice, be registered in the Books of Council and Session. The resignation must be intimated to the other trustees. The effect of resignation is to divest the resigning trustee.[52] That this can be achieved without conveying is due to the fact that the co-ownership of trustees is not ownership in common but joint ownership.

Execution of deeds by trustees

The practice is to ensure that conveyancing deeds are signed by all the 22–18 trustees, including any whose title is completed by registration. But it is unclear whether this is legally necessary or whether majority execution is sufficient: some solicitors will accept the latter. Section 7 of the 1921 Act may perhaps mean that a majority is sufficient, but its terms are obscure.[53]

---

[46] Succession (Scotland) Act 1964, s.20, proviso. Though incompetent, the attempt is occasionally made.

[47] Trusts (Scotland) Act 1921, s.3.

[48] See s.21 of and Sch.B to the 1921 Act for the statutory style.

[49] If the property is still in the GRS this will require a notice of title.

[50] 1921 Act, s.3. There are various exceptions stated in the section. Note also that an executor dative cannot resign: 1964 Act, s.20.

[51] 1921 Act, s.19 and Sch.A.

[52] 1921 Act, s.20.

[53] The proper construction of s.7 is uncertain. It is limited to dispositions to non-beneficiaries who are acting in good faith. It is unclear what presuppositions were being made as to the existing state of the law. In *Harland Engineering Co. v Stark's Trs*, 1913 2 S.L.T. 448, 1914 2 S.L.T. 292 it was held in the Outer House that a majority suffices. The case was reclaimed on a question of expenses, and in the Inner House some doubt was expressed as to whether the substantive decision had been correct. The law was thus obscure, and s.7 made it more so.

Warrandice by trustees

22–19   In a disposition to a beneficiary the practice is for the trustees or executors to grant fact and deed warrandice only.[54] If the disposition is to a purchaser the practice is to grant fact and deed warrandice and to bind the trust estate in absolute warrandice.

Charitable and religious trusts

22–20   Special conveyancing rules apply to many religious and educational trusts.[55] The general rule here is that of automatic completion of title. In other words, as, over the years, the trustees change, so each new set of trustees is deemed to have a completed title, the title of the original trustees continuing, by a fiction, in favour of their successors. Hence, as and when the present trustees require to grant a deed, they do not deduce title, for deduction of title is not required by a registered granter. These rules thus come close to giving corporate status to the body of trustees. Similar rules apply where there is an *ex officio* trustee.[56]

In practice, the terms of the original trust will often impose restrictions on the trustees, limiting their power to sell the land. The zealous landowner who, in 1877, gave the land and money for the building of a chapel for the Congregation of the Auchnashuggle Free Reformed United Presbyterian New Covenant Church of Scotland wanted to make sure that the building would never be used for any other purpose. The present congregation (the last left in Scotland) has decided to merge with the Church of Scotland, and wants to sell the chapel. Can this be done? The question, which is one of some difficulty, is a problem for the sellers and not for the purchaser, who will be protected by section 2 of the Trusts (Scotland) Act 1961.

Liferents[57]

22–21   Viewed from the perspective of property law, there are two quite different types of liferent. In the true or "proper" liferent, both liferenter and fiar have real rights. The fiar has the real right of ownership,

---

[54] For warrandice generally, see paras 16–04 *et seq.*

[55] Titles to Land Consolidation (Scotland) Act 1868, s.26. For discussion see Halliday, para.39–18, and D. J. Cusine (ed.), *Conveyancing Opinions of Professor J. M. Halliday* (1985), no.153. The precise meaning of s.26 is by no means clear.

[56] Conveyancing (Scotland) Act 1874, s.45. This uses the term "*ex officio*" in the section heading. In the body of the section the reference is to "the holder of any place or office or proprietor of any estate." The expression "place or office" is suggestive of public law rather than private law. An example would be a charitable trusteeship vested in the Church of Scotland minister, for the time being, of a particular parish. However, in practice a broader interpretation of the expression is generally accepted: see *e.g. Mailler's Trs v Allan,* 1904 12 S.L.T. 595, *Vestry of St Silas Church v Trs of St Silas Church,* 1945 S.C. 110 and *Balgowan Trustees, Petitioners,* 1999 S.L.T. 817. See also ROTPB para.5.35. But no authoritative definition seems to exist. The idea of a trusteeship vested in the proprietor for the time being of an estate is also problematic. What happens if the estate is divided, or is co-owned? Conveyancers should be cautious in their use of s.45.

[57] See generally, W. J. Dobie, *Manual of the Law of Liferent and Fee in Scotland* (1941); S. C. Styles, "Liferent and Fee", in *The Laws of Scotland: Stair Memorial Encyclopaedia,* Vol.13 (1992).

burdened by the subordinate real right of liferent. The fiar can sell, but naturally the buyer will obtain the same right, which is to say ownership encumbered by the liferent. There are no trustees. But proper liferents are uncommon. In practice, they seldom exist except as a result of a home-made will.[58] More common is the trust liferent, also called the improper liferent or beneficiary liferent. Here there is just one real right, namely the real right of ownership of the trustees. The rights of the liferenter and the fiar are beneficial rights under the trust. When the beneficial liferenter dies, the trustees dispone to the beneficial fiar. Before this happens, the beneficial fiar can, if he or she wishes, sell the beneficial right. But as with the sale of any beneficial right under a trust, the sale is given effect to not by disposition but by assignation, for what is being conveyed is an incorporeal right, a personal right against the trustees.

It sometimes happens that the liferenter no longer wishes to live in the liferented property. He or she may wish to move to a smaller house, or a house in a different place, or move in with relatives, or to a nursing home. A well-drafted will or other deed of trust will have anticipated this possibility by allowing the trustees to sell, and providing that the proceeds of sale (whether invested, or used to buy another house) will be subject to the same division of rights between the beneficial liferenter and the beneficial fiar. If the deed is silent the same thing can still happen provided that both parties agree. But it may be that the beneficial fiar is awkward. Or it may be that the beneficial fee is unvested. Or it may be that the beneficial liferenter has become incapax. In such cases there can be doubts as to whether the trustees have an implied power of sale. If necessary, the consent of the court may be sought.[59] In most cases, however, a power of sale will exist.[60] At all events, the problem is the concern only of the trustees, not of the purchaser.[61]

Some further examples

Jack died in 1985, owner of a house. He left a trust disposition and 22–22 settlement directing his trustees to hold for his widow Mary in liferent and his daughter Kate in fee. The trustees confirmed and completed title. Mary lived in the house until her death in 1990. Thereafter Kate lived in the house. But the trustees never got round to granting a disposition to Kate. Kate died in 2004. She left a trust disposition and settlement giving the house to her son Paul. Paul, however, does not wish to keep the house. He concludes missives to sell the house to Tom. How should the disposition to Tom be drafted?

In the first place, Paul, the seller, cannot dispone. He is not owner, nor is he linked to the recorded or registered title by any midcouples. Nor can Kate's trustees dispone. It is indeed true that where there is a trust

---

[58] In such a case, to give effect to the proper liferent in conveyancing terms, the executor would grant a disposition "to A in liferent and to B in fee" and title sheet in the Land Register will reflect this.

[59] *e.g.* under s.5 of the 1921 Act or s.1 of the Trusts (Scotland) Act 1961.

[60] *Mauchline, Petr*, 1992 S.L.T. 421.

[61] Who is protected by the Trusts (Scotland) Act 1961, s.2.

the title is usually vested in the trustees, with the beneficiary having a personal right. But here the right vested in Kate's trustees is itself a personal right only. There are thus, so to speak, two levels of personal right. Kate's trustees cannot dispone because they are not the owners and, like Paul, are not linked to the recorded or registered title by any midcouples. The current completed title is that of Jack's trustees, and only they can grant the disposition. They hold for Kate, and since her death, for her trustees. They must therefore dispone to the person selected by Kate's trustees. The latter in turn must obtain a conveyance either to Paul himself or to Paul's nominee, *i.e.* Tom. In other words, Paul tells Kate's trustees to convey to Tom, and Kate's trustees then tell Jack's trustees to convey to Tom. The disposition is thus granted by Jack's trustees, and bears the consent of Kate's trustees and of Paul. The real seller, Paul, is thus in conveyancing terms merely a consenter. If the title is in the GRS no clause of deduction of title is called for since the granters hold a completed title.[62] The narrative clause will refer to Jack's trust disposition and settlement and its terms, to Mary's death, to Kate's death, to Kate's trust disposition and settlement and its terms, to the confirmation in favour of Kate's trustees, and to the sale by Paul to Tom.

Would it have made any difference if Jack's trustees had never completed title? The answer is, very little. The last completed title would in that case be Jack's. Neither Paul nor Kate's trustees would be in a position to deduce title, because they would have no midcouples linking them to that last title. Kate's trustees have confirmed to her beneficial right to Jack's estate, and title cannot be deduced through a mere beneficial right. The disposition would be granted by Jack's trustees in the same terms as above. The only difference is that, in a GRS case, there would be a clause deducing title through the confirmation in favour of Jack's trustees.

Take another example. Hamish and Morag acquired a house in common in 1961. There is no survivorship clause. Morag died in 1963. Her will (which was a will in the narrow sense) left her half share to Hamish, who was also appointed executor. Hamish confirmed, but not to the house.[63] Hamish did not complete title. Hamish continued to live in the house until his death in 1989. His will left the house to his son Fergus. Fergus confirmed to his father's estate and granted a docket transfer to himself, but did not complete title before his death in 1998. Fergus died intestate and the house passed by prior rights to his widow, Elspeth. Elspeth confirmed as Fergus's executor. Elspeth wishes to sell the house. How is title to be granted to the buyer?

Morag's estate is governed by pre-1964 law. Hence Hamish could have recorded a notice of title to her half share, either to himself as executor or directly to himself as an individual, in both cases using Morag's will as the midcouple. He did not do this. But his right to use the midcouple as an individual passed to his executor, Fergus.[64] Fergus could thus have

---

[62] If the title is in the Land Register such clauses are not needed anyway.

[63] Before the 1964 Act confirmation to heritage was, subject to minor qualifications, incompetent.

[64] The a right to use a midcouple as an individual passes on death, but the right to use a midcouple as a trustee in general does not pass on death, but lapses.

completed title as his father's executor, the midcouples being (i) Morag's will and (ii) his own confirmation to his father's estate. Or he could have disponed direct to himself as an individual, deducing in the same manner. However, in point of fact he did not complete title, but simply granted to himself a docket transfer. But this itself is a good midcouple. Once Fergus's executor has confirmed, she can dispone, deducing title through (i) Morag's will (ii) Fergus's confirmation to Hamish's estate (iii) the docket transfer by Fergus to himself, and (iv) Elspeth's confirmation to Fergus's estate. In other words, these facts do not create a lapsed trust. If, however, Fergus had not executed a docket transfer to himself, there would be a lapsed trust.

It will be observed that the above concerns Morag's half share only. Hamish's original half can also be disponed by Elspeth, however, deducing title through (a) Fergus's confirmation to Hamish's estate (b) the docket transfer by Fergus to himself and (c) Elspeth's confirmation to Fergus's estate.

In the example, Elspeth is selling as executrix. This, of course, is perfectly competent, even though the ultimate beneficial right is vested in her as an individual. The example could be varied so that after confirming to Fergus's estate she granted a docket transfer in her own favour as an individual. In that case the disposition to the purchaser would be from her as an individual, not as executrix. If the property is in the GRS, both halves of the deduction clause would have an additional midcouple, namely the docket in her favour.

CHAPTER 23

DESTINATIONS

Introduction

23–01   There are two sorts of destinations. The first is the destination-over, which is found in testaments and deeds of trust of various sorts. For instance, a will might provide that the testator's house is to go to Tara, whom failing to Yvonne. Thus, if Tara dies before the testator, Yvonne takes the house.[1] The second sort of destination is the special destination, which is found in conveyances of heritable property.[2] The only common form in modern practice is the survivorship special destination. Thus, Ann and Brian Bell[3] take title to a house in the form "to the said Brian Bell and the said Ann Minto or Bell[4] equally between them and to the survivor of them". This means that each takes a one half *pro indiviso* share, but each half share is subject to a destination in favour of the other. If Ann dies first, her share passes to Brian, and vice versa.[5] Thus the destination is really a shorthand for "half to Ann whom failing to Brian and the other half to Brian whom failing to Ann."

The reason why both devices share the name "destination" is that in both cases a deed which gives right to property makes provision for what is to happen to that property in the event of the death of the grantee.

There are two types of destination-over, the conditional institution and the substitution.[6]

---

[1] If a legatee predeceases, the legacy lapses, *i.e.* becomes void. A destination-over thus has the effect of preventing such lapse. There are also certain other principles of succession law which can prevent lapse, notably the *conditio si institutus sine liberis decesserit.*

[2] Special destinations in moveable property can, in theory, exist in certain types of case, but are almost unknown in practice. A destination-over can be of moveables just as much as of heritage.

[3] Usually one is dealing with spouses but survivorship destinations are, of course, competent in all types of case. For instance, from time to time one sees siblings buying property with a survivorship clause, and also unmarried couples.

[4] We give the husband's name first purely as a reflection of common practice.

[5] Because nature decrees that men have shorter average lifespans than women, survivorship clauses operate more frequently in favour of women than of men.

[6] The *substitutio vulgaris* of Roman law corresponds to our conditional institution rather than to our substitution. Our substitution is a form of the fideicommissary substitution (*substitutio fideicommissaria*) of the civil law. Another form of the fideicommissary substitution is the tailzie (entail). Tailzies, long unimportant in practice, were abolished by the Abolition of Feudal Tenure etc. (Scotland) Act 2000, s.50.

Conditional institutions

In conditional institution, the first grantee of the property is the 23–02 institute and the person who is to take the property in the event of the institute's death is the conditional institute. The conditional institute can take the property only if the institute has died before the date of vesting. Thus, suppose that a will leaves a house to Tara whom failing to Yvonne and that this is by way of conditional institution. Tara dies before the testator. Yvonne then takes the property as legatee. However, suppose that Tara dies one day after the testator. In that case the legacy was vested in Tara. On Tara's death the property does not pass to Yvonne but forms part of Tara's estate.[7] In that case, Yvonne's contingent right is said to "fly off".

Suppose, however, that Tara did not die. She would then receive a disposition from the testator's executor. The disposition would simply be in favour of her, Tara, not in favour of "Tara whom failing Yvonne", even though that was the wording of the will. For Yvonne's right has flown off by the fact of Tara's survival of the date of the vesting.[8]

Substitutions

In a substitution, Tara is again called the institute but Yvonne is called 23–03 the substitute. Substitution includes the effects of conditional institution, but additional effects as well. Thus, suppose that there is a will leaving a house to Tara whom failing Yvonne and Tara predeceases the testator. Then the house goes to Yvonne, just as in conditional institution. Or again, if Tara survived but Yvonne predeceased, the effect is the same as in conditional institution, namely that the property passes to Tara.

The difference between the two types of destination-over emerges where *both* Tara *and* Yvonne survive the date of vesting. Suppose (to take the earlier example) that Tara dies the day after the testator. Since we are now dealing with a substitution and not a conditional institution, the legacy, although it had vested in Tara, passes to Yvonne on Tara's death. The testator's executor must convey to Yvonne, not to Tara's executor. Suppose, however, that Tara does not so die. In that case she will receive a disposition from the testator's executor. The form of the disposition should be to "Tara whom failing Yvonne". In other words, where a destination-over in a will or deed of trust is a substitution, the conveyance which gives effect to it should copy out the terms of the destination, thereby converting the destination-over into a special destination.[9] But this will be true only where both Tara and Yvonne survive

---

[7] Strictly what forms part of Tara's estate is a personal right against the testator's executor to insist upon a transfer of the property. Since Tara will not have had time to take a conveyance, the testator's executor will convey to Tara's executor, who will in turn convey to whoever is entitled to the property in Tara's succession. (That person might be Yvonne, of course, but probably is not.) Or, more simply, the conveyance could be direct by the testator's executor to the latter person, the conveyance incorporating the consent of Tara's executor.

[8] In most wills the date of vesting is the date of the testator's death. But sometimes it is postponed, and the same applies to many *inter vivos* trusts.

[9] A special destination is itself a substitution. Hence there are two sorts of substitution: a substitution in a will and a substitution in a conveyance.

the date of vesting. If either predeceases, the conveyance will incorporate no special destination.

Again, suppose a will leaves a house to "Peter and Robert and the survivor". If this is a substitution, the executor must convey to "Peter and Robert and the survivor of them".[10] If, however, the destination-over in the will is a conditional institution, the executor simply conveys to Peter and Robert.[11]

Where a special destination has to be used in a conveyance to a beneficiary, it is preferable that this be done in a disposition rather than a docket.[12] But there can be little doubt that a special destination in a docket transfer would be valid.

Identifying which is which

23–04   In a testament or deed of trust the property may be given simply to "A whom failing B" or to "A and B and the survivor". How is it possible to tell whether this is a conditional institution or a substitution? In the first place, the deed may make it clear which is intended, and a well-drafted deed will always do this. If conditional institution is intended (and this is the most common case) this is typically done by saying: "To Tara whom failing by her predecease to Yvonne". This makes it clear that Yvonne is to take if and only if Tara predeceases. If the will or deed of trust does not make the intention clear, the common law supplies certain rules as to presumed intention.[13] These are as follows. (1) If the property in question is moveable, conditional institution is to be presumed. (2) If the property in question is heritable, substitution is to be presumed. (3) If the property is a mix of moveables and heritage, conditional institution is to be presumed.[14]

Special survivorship destinations to purchasers

23–05   Special destinations inserted in a conveyance to beneficiaries under wills or trusts are not common in practice. The vast majority of special destinations are contained in conveyances to purchasers, in which case they are inserted at the request of such purchasers. Such destinations can be of various types.[15] Much the commonest is the ordinary survivorship destination. Here, two (or more) persons buy a house in common, the title being granted, at their request, to them both and the survivor of them. The usual case is spouses, but sometimes cohabitants do this, and it can also be found in other cases, such as siblings who live together. It is possible to have more than two parties involved. For instance, three sisters might buy a house with the disposition to "A and B and C equally

---

[10] Unless both Peter and Robert otherwise request.

[11] Unless Peter and Robert positively request a survivorship destination to be inserted.

[12] Docket transfer under s.15(2) of the Succession (Scotland) Act 1964. See para.22–07.

[13] The case law is of enormous bulk, but the following three rules are a fairly accurate summary.

[14] For example a legacy of a house and its contents. And a legacy of residue will often be mixed.

[15] A full account is to be found in John Craigie, *Scottish Law of Conveyancing: Heritable Rights* (commonly called *Heritable Rights*) (3rd ed., 1899).

between them and to the survivors and survivor of them". That would give each a one third *pro indiviso* share in common ownership. If B then died, half of her share[16] would pass to A and the other half of her share to C, thus leaving A and C with a half of the whole. If C then died her half share of the whole would pass to A, who would thus then be the sole owner.

In most cases when two or more people buy a property a survivorship destination is inserted.[17] However, that should never be done without the express instructions of the clients. The reason is that the substantive effect of a survivorship destination is that of a legacy of the share of the property. Thus, if Kate and Luke buy a house with a survivorship destination, the substantive effect is that Luke is making a legacy to Kate of his half share, and vice versa. This requires instructions from the clients. Indeed, the need for instructions is especially strong because, as will be explained below, in most cases the effect of the destination cannot be defeated by a later testament: whereas a legacy is revocable, a quasi-legacy by means of a survivorship destination is usually irrevocable. Suppose that Kate and Luke become estranged. She makes a will leaving her half share to her sister. Soon afterwards, she dies. The legacy is likely to be ineffective, so that the half share will pass to Luke under the destination. The point must be explained to the clients, and their informed wishes ascertained. It should be borne in mind, and explained to the clients, that if each party wishes his or her share to pass, on death, to the survivor, this can also be secured by each party making a will to that effect. This presents little practical difficulty since it is common for people to make wills, or new wills, when buying a house.

An argument often heard in favour of the use of survivorship destinations is that on the first death the share passes to the survivor automatically, without need for confirmation or conveyance.[18] This can indeed be useful. However, in most deaths involving a person who owns heritage, confirmation will be needed anyway, in which case the fact of automatic completion of title confers little benefit. It should also be said that special destinations frequently bring up difficult issues of law and have often resulted in litigation,[19] which cannot be welcomed by clients. Judges and legal writers have doubted the wisdom of using special destinations, and the view of the authors of this work is that clients should not be advised to use them in ordinary cases, and that, if they are used, this should be done only after careful discussion with the clients and clear instructions from them.[20] There can be circumstances when special destinations are useful.

Terminology

The distinction between conditional institution and substitution has 23–06 been explained above. In a special destination, the second party can only be a substitute, not a conditional institute, for the institute cannot die

---

[16] *i.e.* a sixth of the whole.
[17] For a survey, see Nichols (1990) 35 J.L.S.S. 189.
[18] See para.23–07.
[19] See, for instance, Lord Cooper's remarks in *Hay's Tr v Hay's Trs*, 1951 S.C. 329.
[20] Confirmed in writing.

before vesting. Thus, if property is disponed to Ann and Brian and the survivor, Ann is institute for a one-half share, and Brian is the substitute for that share, and, for the other half share, Brian is the institute and Ann is the substitute. Another term for a substitute in a special destination is "heir of provision". This means a person who inherits not by the general law of succession but by a special provision[21] in the title to some property. One other terminological point worth noting is the "clause of return". A clause of return is a special destination where the substitute (or heir of provision) is the granter of the conveyance which creates the destination. Thus, if Fred dispones to Gina whom failing to Fred himself, that is a clause of return. Or suppose a wife, owning a house, dispones it to herself and her husband equally and to the survivor. Then the destination attached to her resulting half share would be an ordinary special destination, but the destination attaching to her husband's half share would be a clause of return.

Where husband and wife (or siblings or others) take title, their title is said to be *pro indiviso* whether or not there is a survivorship destination and whether or not any survivorship destination that has been used is or is not capable of evacuation.[22] Further, the use of a survivorship destination, even one not capable of evacuation, does not convert the ownership from ownership in common to joint ownership.[23] The only case of joint ownership of heritage is ownership by trustees.[24]

Completion of title

23–07   When the institute in a special destination dies, the property passes to the substitute, unless the destination has been evacuated. But how does the substitute complete title? The answer depends on whether the special destination is a survivorship one, or some other type.

If, as is nowadays almost always the case, the destination is a survivorship destination, the substitute is deemed to have a completed title automatically by simple fact of the death of the institute.[25] Thus, suppose that two people buy a house, and take title "to and in favour of the said Ian Dewar Macdonald and Shona Beatrice Brodie or Macdonald equally between them and to the survivor of them". Ian then dies, the property still being owned by the two of them. Shona obtained a completed title in the whole property when Ian's heart ceases to beat. No conveyance to her of his half share is needed: his death itself operates as a registered conveyance. This seems to be the only case in our law when ownership of heritable property can pass from one person to another without an actual recorded or registered conveyance. It is, thus, a somewhat anomalous doctrine. It was introduced by the case of *Bisset v Walker*.[26] There are good grounds for thinking that that decision was incorrect. But, of course, false legal doctrines, once they become

---

[21] *Provisio hominis*, or, in the ablative, *provisione hominis*.

[22] For evacuation, see paras 23–08 *et seq.*

[23] *Munro v Munro*, 1972 S.L.T. (Sh. Ct.) 6 held the contrary, but is incorrect. The law is settled.

[24] See, further, Reid, *Property*, para.34.

[25] Unless the destination has been evacuated, for which see paras 23–08 *et seq.*

[26] Nov.26, 1799, F.C.

settled and accepted, become true doctrines, and the doctrine of automatic completion of title is now, and has long been, settled and accepted as good law.[27]

In the rare cases of other types of special destination, the rule is different. Thus, suppose that property is disponed to "Tara whom failing to Yvonne". Tara completes title and later dies. Yvonne takes the property, of course, but she does not automatically acquire a completed title. A conveyance to her by Tara's executor is required, and Tara's executor has no choice but to grant it.[28]

Evacuation of special destinations *mortis causa*

A special destination may be "evacuated" either *inter vivos* or *mortis* 23–08 *causa*. *Inter vivos* evacuation is discussed below. *Mortis causa* evacuation is effected by bequeathing the property to some person other than the substitute (heir of provision).

This subject has two aspects. First, there is the question of power to evacuate. If there is no power, a purported evacuation will be null, and the legatee will not take the property, which, notwithstanding the legacy, will pass to the substitute. Secondly, *if* power to evacuate does exist, there is the question of how it is competently exercised.

Power to evacuate *mortis causa*

In the first place, the conveyance creating the special destination may 23–09 have a provision expressly stating whether or not it can be evacuated *mortis causa*, though such clauses are uncommon in modern practice. If there is such a clause and it forbids evacuation, the traditional practice was to ensure that the deed was executed by the grantee/s as well as by the granter. But this is probably not strictly necessary, for by acceptance of the disposition a grantee is deemed to accept its terms. An evacuation clause is simple to draft. After the destination follow some such words as the following: "But expressly declaring that the said grantees and each of them shall have full right and power" (or "no right and power") "to evacuate the foregoing destination".

If the deed has no express clause, the law has certain presumptions. The power to evacuate is presumed to be excluded in cases of marriage contracts, clauses of return and in cases where there is an implied contract not to evacuate. In other cases power to evacuate is presumed.[29] It is the third of these which is much the most important in practice.

---

[27] We have replaced the old name of "automatic infeftment" with the correct modern one of "automatic completion of title" but the old term may in practice survive.

[28] Succession (Scotland) Act 1964 Act, s.18(2). Note the words in that section: "if such conveyance is necessary". In most cases no such conveyance is necessary because in most cases there will be automatic completion of title. Before the 1964 Act, Yvonne would have completed title by a special process called service as heir of provision.

[29] However, it is uncertain whether a special destination can be evacuated if it was inserted in a conveyance to a beneficiary. See *Massy v Scott's Trs* (1872) 11 M. 173; *Robertson v Hay-Boyd*, 1928 S.C. (HL) 8 *per* Lord Dunedin; Lord McLaren, *Wills and Succession as administered in Scotland* (3rd ed., 1894), pp.629–630; R. Candlish Henderson, *The Principles of Vesting in the Law of Succession* (2nd ed., 1938), p.328.

The leading case, which virtually invented the doctrine of the implied contract not to evacuate, is *Perrett's Trs v Perrett*.[30] This case, and later cases which elaborated the doctrine,[31] holds that where there is a survivorship destination, and both parties have contributed to the price,[32] there is a presumed contract that neither can evacuate. If, however, only one party paid the price, there is a presumed contract that that party can evacuate but that the other party cannot. In determining whether both parties have contributed to the price, it has been held that the narrative clause of the deed is conclusive.[33] This is a practical point to be watched. Some conveyancers tend, in cases of a purchase by husband and wife, to declare in the narrative clause that both have paid the price, and they do this as words of style without checking the true facts. If in truth it was, say, the wife who paid the whole price, the narrative clause will destroy the power of evacuation she would otherwise have had.

To leave the question of power to evacuate to implication is unsatisfactory. The clients must have some definite intention about the matter. The deed should expressly declare the destination to be evacuable or non-evacuable. (Or to be evacuable by one party and non-evacuable by the other.) Unfortunately such declarations are not very common.

Exercise of power to evacuate *mortis causa*

23-10   If there is no power to evacuate, a legacy will be null. But if there is power, the legacy will still be null unless it complies with a statutory form.[34] This is an important point to note when drafting a will.

Evacuation by death of substitute

23-11   A special destination becomes null where the substitute (heir of provision) dies before the institute. Thus, suppose that property is disponed to Tara whom failing to Yvonne, and Yvonne then dies. The destination is evacuated by Yvonne's death, and if Tara were to die the next day the property would simply be part of her estate, so that Yvonne's representatives would have no rights. Or again, suppose that husband and wife own their house in common with a survivorship destination. The husband dies. His share passes to his widow. She then dies. The destination attached to her original half share of the house became void when her husband died. So the whole house becomes part of her estate. Her husband's representatives have no rights.

---

[30] 1909 S.C. 522. The case is unimpressive and arguably wrong. But it became settled law and so cannot now be questioned: see *Shand's Trs v Shand's Trs*, 1966 S.C. 178.

[31] *Renouf's Trs v Haining*, 1919 S.C. 497; *Taylor's Exrs v Brunton*, 1939 S.C. 444; *Brown's Tr v Brown*, 1943 S.C. 488; *Hay's Tr v Hay's Trs*, 1951 S.C. 329. For a review, see Morton, 1984 S.L.T. (News) 133.

[32] Equal contribution is not necessary.

[33] *Gordon-Rodgers v Thomson's Exrs*, 1988 S.C. 145. But it is not conclusive if both parties so agree: *Hay's Tr v Hay's Trs*, 1951 S.C. 329. There exists a logical difficulty: how can the effect of a destination at death depend on what is or is not subsequently conceded?

[34] Succession (Scotland) Act 1964, s.30. For case law see *Stirling's Trs*, 1977 S.L.T. 229; *Marshall v Marshall's Exr*, 1987 S.L.T. 49; *Gordon-Rodgers v Thomson's Exrs*, 1988 S.C. 145.

Waiving the bar to evacuation

The substitute may agree to authorise the institute to evacuate 23–12 (assuming that power to evacuate did not already exist). This can be done by a probative deed, which does not have to be registered, though registration in the Books of Council and Session would be good practice. Even better would be a new conveyance which would have a clause expressly authorising evacuation. Thus, if Jack and Jill are co-owners with a survivorship destination which is not capable of evacuation, they could dispone to themselves with a clause authorising evacuation. The practical benefit of this method is that the waiver of the bar to evacuation could not be overlooked at a later stage. However, waivers of the bar to evacuation are almost unknown in practice. What does occur from time to time in practice is the voluntary discharge of a destination. The difference is this: the first leaves the destination intact, but allows it to be evacuated *mortis causa*,[35] whereas the second actually destroys the destination. Moreover, waiving the bar is relevant only if the destination is otherwise non-evacuable, whereas discharge is relevant both for evacuable and for non-evacuable destinations.

Voluntary discharge of destination

The substitute may waive the destination in his favour altogether. This 23–13 is done by a new conveyance of the property, omitting the existing destination. Thus, suppose that Jack and Jill have a house with a survivorship destination in the title. They wish to discharge it. The practice in such a case is for them to dispone the property to themselves, with no survivorship clause in the deed. The result is that they become simple co-owners, without any destination.

Could a survivorship destination be discharged by probative unre-gistered deed? Such a deed would certainly discharge the destination in one sense.[36] But it might be that on the first death automatic completion of title would still operate, the position then being that the substitute would be under an obligation to convey to the executor. If this is the law,[37] this would obviously be an inconvenient outcome. Hence the practical importance of ensuring that a discharge of a destination is embodied in a registered conveyance.[38]

Evacuation *inter vivos* by conveyance

Evacuation *inter vivos* means some act, other than a will, which defeats 23–14 a special destination. Voluntary discharge (see above) is thus a sort of *inter vivos* evacuation. But a special destination can also be evacuated by a conveyance. Thus, suppose that property is disponed to Tara whom

---

[35] Which may or may not happen.

[36] *Redfern's Exrs v Redfern*, 1996 S.L.T. 900.

[37] Which it seems to be. See *Redfern's Exrs v Redfern*, 1996 S.L.T. 900, though there may be scope for debate as to the meaning of the decision.

[38] The potential problem would not exist in the case of destinations not of the survivorship type, for the doctrine of automatic completion of title does not extend to such destinations.

failing Yvonne. If Tara subsequently dispones the property to Zenon, then Yvonne's contingent right is defeated. For a special destination can operate only where the institute still owns the property at the date of her death. Thus, a person who owns property, or a share of property, which is subject to a destination, can always defeat that destination by alienating the property (or share therein) *inter vivos,* and this is true even if there is no power of *mortis causa* evacuation.

There is some older authority[39] suggesting that evacuation can be effected only by onerous *inter vivos* alienation (typically sale), and not by gratuitous *inter vivos* alienation (donation or gift). But the clear trend of the modern authorities is that it does not matter whether the alienation is onerous or not.[40] Thus, if Jack and Jill hold their house subject to a survivorship destination, and if Jack gratuitously dispones his half share to his brother, and then dies, a modern court would almost certainly hold that Jill had no rights in that half share.

A trap

23–15   There exists a well-known trap into which the unwary solicitor may fall.[41] It happens typically as follows. Adam and Eve own a house in common with a survivorship destination. Adam goes off on the razzle-dazzle leaving Eve to cope with the house and the children. She sees her lawyer, he sees his lawyer, and it is agreed that he will make over his half share of the house to her. The court department of the wife's law firm send down a note to the conveyancing department asking them to draw up a conveyance. A conveyance of the half share is accordingly prepared and Adam signs it. It is registered. Eve is now owner of the whole house. A year or two later she dies. Her original half share is still subject to an unevacuated destination in favour of that scum-of-the-earth, Adam. So it passes to him. This is almost certainly not what had been intended when the settlement between the parties was reached.[42] From a practical point of view, the problem arises because the deal has been put together in the respective court departments of the firms, who have passed the conveyancing to the conveyancing department for implementation, without proper discussions.

If the problem comes to light while Eve is still alive and still owns the property,[43] what can be done? Adam could be approached to assist in putting matters right, by a deed renouncing the destination.[44] Or she

---

[39] See, *e.g., Grahame v Ewen's Trs* (1824) 2 S. 612 (NE 522); *Gillon's Trs v Gillon* (1890) 17 R. 435; *Macdonald v Hall* (1893) 20 R. (HL) 88.

[40] *Steele v Caldwell,* 1979 S.L.T. 228; *Smith v Macintosh,* 1989 S.L.T. 148.

[41] First drawn to attention by an article by "GL" at 1977 S.L.T. (News) 197 and later by D.A. Johnstone at 1985 S.L.T. (News) 18. That the trap genuinely does exist has been confirmed by *Gardner's Exrs v Raeburn,* 1996 S.L.T. 745.

[42] One might seek to argue that Adam has conveyed to Eve all rights he has, and therefore he cannot retain his claim under the destination. The difficulty is that by the terms of the disposition he conveys only such rights as he has *in the half share being transferred.* The destination in his favour relates to the *other* half share.

[43] She can, of course, sell the property and if she does so Adam's contingent rights will fly off.

[44] para.23–13.

could dispone the property to a nominee, which would wash out the undesired destination.[45]

The whole problem can and should be avoided. The correct practice is for the disposition to be a disposition of the whole property, not merely Adam's half share. The disposition is granted by both Adam and Eve, with Eve as the sole disponee. This, on being registered, will wash the destination out of the title.

Conveyance by the survivor

Suppose that title is taken by Jack and Jill with a survivorship 23-16 destination, and Jack dies, so that Jill automatically acquires a completed title to his share. She thus now has a completed title to the whole. She then sells. If the property is still in the GRS, Halliday[46] says that the disposition by Jill should contain a clause of deduction title in respect of the half share formerly owned by her husband, the midcouple being the fact of Jack's death. Although a conveyance in such terms would be valid, in fact no clause of deduction of title is required. The reason is that a clause of deduction is needed (if the property is in the GRS) only where the granter does not have a completed title.

However, where Halliday's style is not used, it is wise, though not strictly necessary, to make reference in the disposition to Jack's death, in order to show how it is that Jill has a completed title to the whole. This can be done in the narrative clause. That clause will narrate that title was taken by such-and-such a disposition to Jack and Jill and the survivor, and that Jack died on such-and-such a date without having evacuated the said destination, etc.

Verifying evacuation or non-evacuation

If Jill sells, how can the buyers, and the Keeper, be sure that Jack's 23-17 share did indeed pass to her? That depends on establishing a negative fact, namely non-evacuation, and that can be awkward to do. They can verify that Jack did not alienate his share *inter vivos.* They can verify the existence of the survivorship destination, and they can verify the death of Jack by asking for the death certificate.[47] But how can they be sure that Jack did not evacuate the destination by will? In most cases the destination will not have been capable of evacuation *mortis causa,* and this fact can normally be ascertained from the deed which created it. Even there, however, there is the possibility that Jill had by unregistered deed authorised Jack to evacuate, and that he did so. This risk is, however, small. The risk would be greater where the destination was capable of evacuation *ab initio,* though this is less common in practice. It has been suggested by Burns[48] that when buying from someone in Jill's position "a purchaser has no duty of inquiry", which presumably means

---

[45] This may cause practical problems (but not insuperable ones) if there is a heritable security.

[46] Halliday, para.37-60.

[47] This should always be done.

[48] John Burns, *Conveyancing Practice* (4th ed., 1957), p.259.

that in a case of latent evacuation a purchaser would be protected by good faith. Whether this is correct, however, must be speculative. The Keeper's practice is to seek either (a) written confirmation from the applicant's solicitor or (b) an affidavit from the seller that the destination was not evacuated.[49]

Verifying evacuation is easier than verifying non-evacuation. But nevertheless there may be difficult questions as to whether the power to evacuate existed, and the Keeper's policy in such cases is to "take a cautious approach".[50]

Destinations and leases

23-18　　A destination in a lease[51] is subject to different rules from a destination in a disposition or feu disposition, the reason being that the landlord, as well as the substitute, is presumed to have an interest, by virtue of the doctrine of *delectus personae*. But destinations in assignations of leases are probably subject to the ordinary rules, though the point is uncertain.[52]

Destinations and liability

23-19　　Suppose that when Jack dies, he is insolvent, and that his estate is then sequestrated. Does Jill keep Jack's share free from the claims of the creditors? Or can Jack's trustee in sequestration demand either that she return the share or pay its value? This question has caused considerable controversy. The better view is that Jill is liable for its value.[53]

---

[49] ROTPB, para.6.17. If the applicant is a buyer, it is not clear how the applicant's solicitor would be in a position to give the Keeper the necessary assurance. Indeed, the applicant's solicitor will be seeking the necessary assurance from the seller.

[50] ROTPB, para.6.17.

[51] The destination clause in a lease is sometimes also called the alienation clause.

[52] See Gretton, 1982 S.L.T. (News) 213 for full discussion.

[53] *Fleming's Tr v Fleming*, 2000 S.C. 206. For discussion see Reid and Gretton, *Conveyancing 1999*, pp.64–6.

CHAPTER 24

PARTNERSHIPS

Introduction

This chapter deals with ordinary partnerships[1] and limited part- 24-01
nerships,[2] but not with limited liability partnerships.[3]

The firm itself normally has no title

A partnership has its own separate juristic personality, distinct from its 24-02
partners.[4] But this personality is more restricted than that of other
juristic persons. Until recently, a partnership, unlike a corporation, could
not itself own land directly. Title had to be held by trustees for the firm.
Whilst this restriction has been removed,[5] practice has not changed. It is
more or less unknown in practice for title to be taken in the name of the
firm itself. This chapter deals, therefore, with the normal case.

In theory it does not matter who the trustees are. They need not be
partners. The practice, however, is to appoint as the trustees some or all
of the partners. If the number of partners is large, it may be unwise to
make all of them trustees, if only because this can cause inconvenience
at a later stage, when a large number of people will have to execute a
disposition or whatever. Being a trustee confers no real advantage on a
partner. The economic interest in the firm rests on the fact of being a
partner and not on the fact of being trustee.[6]

The three levels of right

Where a partnership holds land, there are three levels of right. In the 24-03
first place, at the top level there is the title of the partners, or some of
them, as trustees for the firm. Heritable property held by a firm is thus
simply part of the general law of trusts, and this is the master key for

---

[1] Under the Partnership Act 1890.

[2] Under the Limited Partnership Act 1907.

[3] For which see the next chapter.

[4] The Partnership Act 1890 (ss.1 and 4(2)) announces that it will use the term
"partnership" to mean the relationship between the partners and the word "firm" to mean
that separate juristic person that arises out of that relationship. However, the rest of the
Act often ignores this terminological distinction.

[5] Abolition of Feudal Tenure etc. (Scotland) Act 2000, s.70.

[6] However, in some firms, the heritable property is not partnership property at all, but is
owned by one or two partners in their own interest, and merely made available to the firm.

understanding the law. A trust must, of course, have a beneficiary, which in this case is the firm itself, as a separate juristic *persona.* The firm thus comes in at the second level. The partners themselves are not the beneficiaries of this trust. The partners come in at the third level. They hold rights, not in the firm's property itself, but in the firm, of which they are the owners. Their interests are rather like the interests of the members of a company. Shareholders hold shares in the company, not in the company's property.[7]

In general, a trust requires a deed of trust, which in the normal case will be the disposition to the partners as trustees, which will declare that the property is vested in the disponees in trust. The trust is a "bare trust", which is to say that the trust purposes are simply to hold for the benefit of a single beneficiary (the firm) and to dispose of the property at the direction of that beneficiary.

A trust presupposes a beneficiary. The question of whether the beneficiary of this trust is (a) the firm or (b) the partners of the firm is sometimes not properly focused.[8] Dispositions to firms sometimes state that the disponees are to hold in trust for the firm, and sometimes that they are to hold in trust both for the firm and for the partners present and future thereof. It seems open to question whether this latter style is correct. The general view, both traditional and modern, is that the beneficiary of the trust is the firm. To make both the firm and the partners the beneficiaries is to depart from this simple conception and may produce odd results. Thus, suppose that Mr Ant and Ms Bee take title in trust for the firm of Messrs. Ant & Bee and for the partners present and future thereof. Such a clause appears to say that there are, at least at this stage, three beneficiaries, namely Messrs. Ant & Bee, Mr Ant and Ms Bee. Does this mean that the beneficial right is divided into thirds? That seems to be the meaning, but it cannot be the real intention. The point might seem merely theoretical, but it could become a live one in some cases of insolvency. In addition, is it really intended that, for example, a so-called salaried partner should have a beneficial right which is ostensibly equal to that of the senior partner? On the contrary, it is the partnership deed, and variations to it made from time to time, which does and should determine the rights and interests of the several partners.[9] Thus, the better practice is simply for the disposition to declare that the disponees hold in trust for the firm.

Of course, there is a sense in which the firm's property is held for the benefit of the partners. But it is equally true to say that company property is held, in an indirect manner, for the benefit of the share-holders. But a company does not hold its property in trust for the shareholders. and they are not beneficiaries in the legal sense of that term. Likewise partners, though in a functional or economic sense they may be the "owners" of the land of the firm, are not legally in the position of beneficiaries. The beneficiary is the firm. The role of the partners is to own the beneficiary.

---

[7] See Gretton, 1987 J.R. 163.

[8] For instance J. Bennett Miller, *Law of Partnership in Scotland* (2nd ed., 1994), p.401 seems to say both that the trust is for the firm and that it is for the partners. It is difficult to see how both could be true.

[9] See Halliday, para.11–09.

Heritable property brought in by one partner

It sometimes happens that an incoming partner brings in heritable 24–04 property. This may happen either where a new partner joins an existing firm, or, more commonly, where a sole trader takes in partners and contributes the heritable property. A familiar example is where a farmer, owning his own land, takes his sons into partnership with him. In such a case the original disposition of the land to the partner who has the completed title obviously cannot itself be the deed of trust. Ideally, in such cases the partnership deed should identify the land as property of the firm, and in that event the partnership deed will be the deed of trust. Sometimes the partnership deed is silent on the point, and disputes can then arise as to whether the land is property of the firm or not (that is, a dispute as to whether the partner with a completed title holds for himself/herself or holds as trustee for the firm). An alternative approach would be for the incoming partner to dispone to himself/herself and the other partners, with the disposition declaring the trust, but in the typical case this will hardly be worthwhile.

Deeds granted by a firm

A disposition or other deed by a firm should not be granted simply by 24–05 the firm itself, because the firm itself is not the legal owner.[10] The deed must be granted by the trustees. Whether all trustees with a completed title must sign, or a majority is sufficient, is a difficult and unresolved question.[11] The prudent approach is to have all sign.

Need the firm itself be a party?

The trustees with a completed title may not account for all of the 24–06 current partners. If not, is it necessary that the other partners be party to the deed? It is good practice for this to be done[12] but it is not strictly necessary.[13] The partners hold as trustees for the firm, and section 2 of the Trusts (Scotland) Act 1961 enacts (in effect) that where trustees sell trust property, the purchaser's title shall not be challengeable on the ground that the sale was in breach of trust. Thus, even if the sale was without the firm's consent, a purchaser will have a good title. This rule also applies to the grant of standard securities, though not to gratuitous deeds. Despite the modern rule, the pre-1961 practice of taking all current partners into the deed has continued, and this is sensible, if only to put the matter beyond dispute as between the partners themselves. Occasionally in dispositions the firm itself, as well as all the partners, is a consenter, though this is hardly necessary. In standard securities, however, the lender will usually require the personal bond element to be entered into by the firm itself as well as by all the partners,[14] and it is

---

[10] In theory it might be but this is never the case in practice.

[11] See para.22–18.

[12] See Halliday, para.37–53.

[13] See Halliday, para.2–157. Banks often insist that it is done where they are the grantees of a standard security by a firm.

[14] If the firm is personally bound, then the partners will be as well. But lenders nevertheless like all the partners to sign.

often found that the lender will expect the firm itself to be a co-granter of the security element of the deed, though as has been said this is not actually necessary.[15]

Outgoing partners

24-07   Suppose that the firm of X buys property, the title being taken in the name of Adam, Brenda, Charles, David and Erica, the partners at the time, as trustees for the firm of X. Later Adam, Brenda and Charles retire. If the firm then sells the property, can the disposition be granted by David and Erica on their own, or do the retired partners have to be brought in? The answer is the latter. Adam, Brenda and Charles are no longer partners, but they are still trustees, and hold the property as such. There is no rule of law to the effect that the trustees for a firm and its partners must be the same. It is possible to be a partner without being a trustee and conversely it is possible to be a trustee without being a partner. So the fact that these persons have retired as partners has no effect on their continuing status as trustees with a completed title. They should therefore sign the deed, or resign as trustees.[16]

Resignation of trustees

24-08   It may be inconvenient to get hold of a retired partner. So the simplest way of avoiding the problem is to have an outgoing partner execute a minute of resignation. By this is not meant resignation as a partner, though that will be required as well, but resignation as a trustee. This can be signed at the time s/he resigns as a partner. The deed should be done in conformity with section 19 of the Trusts (Scotland) Act 1921. The Act prescribes a style in Schedule A, but this often requires a certain amount of modification in partnership cases. The deed of trust referred to in the style is usually the original disposition to the firm. The resignation extinguishes the title of the resigning trustee.[17] The reason for this is that trust property is joint property not common property. A sole trustee cannot resign.

Assumption of trustees

24-09   Such resignations may excessively thin out the number of trustees with a completed title, and accordingly it may be wise from time to time to have additional partners assumed as trustees.[18] It may be convenient to modify the statutory style of deed of assumption so as to convert it into a conveyance of the specified property, from the existing trustees to themselves (unless they are at the same time resigning) and the new trustees.[19] If the property is still in the GRS, there is an advantage in

---

[15] If (see below) the standard security has to be signed by a former partner, the deed should be so drafted as to make it clear that that person incurs no personal liability.
[16] *cf.* C. Waelde (ed.), *Professor McDonald's Conveyancing Opinions* (1998), p.16.
[17] Trusts (Scotland) Act 1921, s.20.
[18] 1921 Act, s.21 and Sch.B.
[19] This is authorised by the statutory style.

that the grantees may then complete title by recording the deed direct, without need for a separate notice of title.[20]

Dissolution

If the partnership is dissolved, this has no direct effect on the title, 24–10 which continues to be held by the trustees. The beneficial right in the trust may pass to one partner or to a group of partners, but that is a separate issue. Thus, a disposition will generally be necessary, the identity of the grantee being determined by the circumstances of the dissolution. In a typical case there will be a minute of dissolution which will regulate the matter. However, if the minute of dissolution directs that the property is to pass to a successor firm, the title could be left as it is. For, in that case, the minute of dissolution operates as an assignation of the beneficial right to the new firm, and all that is needed is for that to be intimated to the trustees.

Does an outgoing partner need to dispone?

Even if an outgoing partner has a completed title, it would be 24–11 mistaken to grant a disposition of any particular share in the heritage to the remaining or incoming partners. Title is held as joint property not as common, and there is no share which can be separately dealt with.[21] Although the departing partner may be handing over his or her share in the firm, that has nothing to do with the state of title. Hence, the only thing an outgoing partner, who is a joint owner, should do is to resign as trustee at the same time as resigning as partner.

In most cases, the only conveyance which is or may be rendered necessary by changes in the membership of the firm is a deed of assumption and conveyance of new trustees. Halliday[22] has an interesting paragraph on this subject. He takes the view that where the title was originally taken to "A, B and C the partners of the firm of A, B & Co. and the survivor of them as trustees for the said firm of A, B & Co. and the partners thereof present and future", a deed of assumption and conveyance is appropriate. But where the original title does not refer to future partners, he takes the view that any change in the constitution of the firm may amount to a change in the trust purposes, with the result that the existing trustees should grant a disposition to trustees for the firm as newly constituted. The same would be true where the firm is dissolved and replaced by a new firm carrying on the same business. With respect, we doubt this view of matters. If the firm is dissolved and reconstituted, then the trustees hold for whoever it is that succeeds to the firm's beneficial right, for which see above. If, however, what has happened is merely a change in the membership of an existing firm, then the title can be left as it stands, for the identity of the beneficiary is unchanged. In either case it seems to make little difference in what form the original disposition was drafted.

---

[20] A general conveyance (*i.e.* one in which the property is not sufficiently described) requires a notice of title: see para.21–11.

[21] para.22–15.

[22] Halliday, para.11–78.

Incoming partners

24-12   Just as an outgoing partner with a completed title does not cease to hold that title merely by ceasing to be a partner, so likewise an incoming partner does not become a trustee merely by becoming a partner. To become a trustee it is necessary to be assumed as such. Thus, suppose that title is taken in the names of Alan, Beth and Carla, and at the time of sale the current partners are Carla, Deirdre and Edmund, and that there has been no resignation (as trustees) by Alan or Beth and no assumption (as trustees) of Deirdre or Edmund. The disposition falls to be granted by Alan, Beth and Carla. Deirdre and Edmund should adhibit their consent, though even this is strictly speaking not required for the validity of the deed.[23]

Incapacity, death, or sequestration of partners

24-13   Incapacity will normally entail ceasing to be a partner, but it does not terminate ownership. Moreover, if a guardian has been appointed, the guardian has no power to deal with trust estate. Since an incapax trustee cannot execute a deed of resignation as trustee, it may be necessary to have the trustee removed.[24]

Death or sequestration of one partner can bring about the dissolution of the firm[25] but in practice partnership deeds commonly provide that the firm shall continue notwithstanding these events. The death of a partner extinguishes any title to heritable property. This is because trustee property is owned jointly and not in common.[26] So any partner who has died can be left out of account entirely, though a copy of the death certificate should be put up with the titles, and the death should be narrated in the next deed. For the case where the death is of the sole, or sole surviving, partner with a completed title, see below.

The sequestration of a person who happens to be a trustee under some trust has no effect on the trust property. This is true both at common law and by statute.[27] In addition, such sequestration generally has no effect on the bankrupt's status as trustee. There is no rule of law that a bankrupt cannot be a trustee[28] The bankrupt thus continues as trustee, though not usually as partner, and so will have to be one of the granters of any future deed affecting title. The trustee in sequestration has no right or title to the firm's property itself. The trustee's right is solely a right to the bankrupt partner's share in the partnership. The same is true, *mutatis mutandis*, of the case where a partner grants a trust deed for behoof of creditors.

---

[23] para.24–06.

[24] Under s.23 of the Trusts (Scotland) Act 1921.

[25] Partnership Act 1890, s.33. As part of their major review of the 1890 Act the Scottish Law Commission and the Law Commission have recommended continuity as a default rule. See *Report on Partnership Law* (Scot. Law Com. No.192, 2003), Part VIII.

[26] para.22–15.

[27] Bankruptcy (Scotland) Act 1985, s.33.

[28] Though a bankrupt cannot be a trustee of a charitable trust: Law Reform (Miscellaneous Provisions) (Scotland) Act 1990, s.8.

Lapsed trust

If the sole trustee, or sole surviving trustee, dies, the result is a lapsed 24–14 trust. This can be sorted out in the ordinary way, such as by a petition for new trustees under section 22 of the Trusts (Scotland) Act 1921 Act or (in most, though not all, cases) by procedure under s. 6 of the Executors (Scotland) Act 1900.[29] Since a firm can itself now own heritable property,[30] s. 24 of the 1921 Act could also be used, but in practice the vesting of title in the firm is usually regarded as undesirable.

Contracting out

It has been said above that an outgoing partner does not cease to be a 24–15 trustee, unless he resigns as such, and likewise that an incoming partner does not become a trustee, unless he is assumed as such. Could these rules be contracted out of? In other words, could it be provided that every resigning partner (or partner becoming insane) should automatically cease to be a trustee, and that every incoming partner automatically be deemed to be assumed as trustee? These are difficult questions. It is possible to have trustees *ex officio*, so that it might be thought that it could be provided that every partner for the time being would be a trustee *ex officio*. Indeed, if this could be done it would not even be necessary for future partners to complete title or deduce title, because of the provisions of section 45 of the 1874 Act. But given the uncertainty about what is meant by "*ex officio*", such an idea cannot be recommended.

Might there be a consensual provision that an outgoing partner would automatically cease to be a trustee? In principle this might seem unobjectionable, but again it cannot be recommended in practice. There seems to be no authority for such a device. Moreover, section 19 of the Trusts (Scotland) Act 1921 presupposes that any resignation by a trustee will be a resignation *de praesenti* whereas the suggested idea would involve a resignation *de futuro*. Although resignation *de futuro* is arguably competent, the prudent conveyancer should seek to avoid attempting it.

Bankruptcy of firm

A partnership may be sequestrated as such, either with or without the 24–16 sequestration of its individual partners.[31] The firm's trustee in sequestration probably cannot grant a disposition of its heritable property. The problem here is that the title is held not by the firm itself but by trustees for the firm. Thus, while the trustee in sequestration has power of sale, the disposition must be granted by the trustees for the firm. This seems unsatisfactory in a practical sense, especially if the trustees are themselves bankrupt, as is likely to be the case. It might be argued, on the other side, that section 31 of the Bankruptcy (Scotland) Act 1985 vests

---

[29] See, further, Halliday, para.37–32.
[30] Abolition of Feudal Tenure etc. (Scotland) Act 2000, s.70.
[31] Bankruptcy (Scotland) Act 1985, s.6.

the property in the trustee. But what is vested? Vesting is *tantum et tale* and what the firm had was not title but only a beneficial right.[32] Again, it might be argued that the sequestration of the firm dissolves it and so each partner is deemed to have a share. But this is probably not an accurate way of stating the position.[33] In addition, even if true it would take us no further because title would still be stuck inside a trust. All that would have changed would have been the identity of the beneficiary.

Where a firm is sequestrated, it often happens that the partners are also sequestrated, or grant trust deeds, and it commonly happens that the insolvency practitioner who is trustee of the firm is also trustee for the partners. Will this fact be of assistance? Probably not. For (see above) a bankruptcy trustee has no right to deal with property which is vested in the bankrupt only in trust. The result may seem absurd: we have an insolvency practitioner who is trustee for the bankrupt firm and also for all the bankrupt partners, yet he cannot, on his own, grant a disposition of the firm's property, if this line of reasoning is correct.

What sometimes happens in practice is that the firm's trustee in sequestration does grant the disposition,[34] without getting the trustee-partners to sign. If the argument outlined above is correct, this procedure is improper. The practical advice is that the disposition should be signed not only by the firm's trustee in sequestration but also by those trustees with a completed title, even if themselves bankrupt. This may be unsatisfactory from the practical point of view, but in the absence of any clear provision on the point in the legislation, and in the apparent absence of authority, it seems the wise approach. The trustees with a completed title would be under an obligation to co-operate.[35]

---

[32] If Ms Smith is a beneficiary under her aunt's trust, and is sequestrated, no one would suggest that the title held by the aunt's trustees could pass to Ms Smith's trustee in sequestration.

[33] There is authority that a sequestrated firm still exists as a juristic *persona*, the effect of sequestration being to dissolve the contract (the partnership) rather than the personality (the firm): see *Stewart & Macdonald v Brown* (1898) 25 R. 1042.

[34] In a GRS case, deducing title through the act and warrant.

[35] For further discussion of the problem of the bankruptcy of a firm, see William W. McBryde, *Bankruptcy* (2nd ed., 1995), paras 9.62–9.65.

CHAPTER 25

COMPANIES AND LIMITED LIABILITY PARTNERSHIPS

Introduction

This chapter deals with companies and, briefly, with limited liability 25-01 partnerships. The last of these is included in this chapter because, despite its name, it is more like a company than a partnership.

Intra vires and *ultra vires*

The Companies Act 1989 abolished the *ultra vires* doctrine as far as 25-02 outsiders are concerned.[1] The result is that those dealing with a company need not concern themselves with the question of whether the company is acting within its powers. Good or bad faith is irrelevant. However, the post-1989 rule only affects the external operation of the *ultra vires* doctrine. The doctrine still applies internally, and the board of directors must not breach the company's constitution.

Whilst the external aspect of the doctrine has been abolished, there remain some qualifications. Three in particular are worth noting. The first is that the abolition applies only to companies incorporated under the Companies Acts. Most other juristic persons are still subject to the common law rules about *ultra vires*.[2] The second is that charitable companies were excepted from the abolition, so that the external aspect of the *ultra vires* rule still applies to them.[3] The third is that section 320 of the Companies Act 1985 provides that in certain cases a disposition by a company to one of its directors, or *vice versa*, is voidable unless approved by the company in general meeting.[4]

Powers of directors and the exercise of those powers

The directors act for the company. But they do not have that power 25-03 individually. An individual director can do nothing. Company law sees the directors as a collective entity, namely the board. The board is the

---

[1] Companies Act 1985, s.35(1), substituted by the Companies Act 1989, s.108: "The validity of an act done by a company shall not be called into question on the ground of lack of capacity by reason of anything in the company's memorandum".

[2] For a striking example, see *Piggins & Rix Ltd v Montrose Port Authority*, 1995 S.L.T. 418.

[3] Companies Act 1989, s.112.

[4] See *e.g. Micro Leisure Ltd v County Properties & Developments Ltd.*, 1999 S.C. 501.

"organ" by which the company acts.[5] An individual director can act for the company only in so far as power has been duly conferred—which, of course, is very common in practice.[6]

There exists some tension between the rules of company law, which have just been outlined, and the rules about execution of deeds contained in the Requirements of Writing (Scotland) Act 1995.[7] Schedule 2, para.3(1) of the 1995 Act says that "where the granter of a document is a company, the document is signed by the company if it is signed on its behalf by a director, or by the secretary . . . or by a person authorised to sign. . ." Suppose that an offer is made to a company to buy some land. The board of directors meets and discusses the offer. By a five to one majority, the vote is not to accept. The dissident director signs a letter of acceptance on behalf of the company. Is there a contract of sale?[8] Company law says no, but the 1995 Act seems to say yes. In practice the counterparty (the buyer in the example) will sometimes (especially in higher-value transactions) insist on seeing a certified copy of a board resolution. The law may perhaps be that decisions must be made by the board (or by a person duly authorised by the board), but that the implementation of the decision can be by a single signature. That would lead to the conclusion that in the example there is no contract. However it is far from certain that this is indeed the law.[9]

It can happen that while an act would be valid if properly authorised by the company, the directors of the company, when entering into it, were exceeding their powers as laid down in the company's memorandum and articles. Here again, however, the Companies Act 1989 will, in general, protect a third party,[10] and though the protection requires good faith,[11] such a party is not in bad faith merely because he knows that the directors have exceeded their powers,[12] which seems to amount to saying that good faith is not necessary.

Designing the company

25–04   Juristic persons, like natural persons, must be designed in conveyancing deeds. Companies have traditionally been designed by giving the

---

[5] The other "organ" is the general meeting, considered as an entity rather than as an event.

[6] Thus a "managing" director has general powers. An individual director can also bind the company if s/he has ostensible authority: see *e.g. Freeman & Lockyer v Buckhurst Park Properties*, [1964] 1 All E.R. 630.

[7] A similar issue can in principle arise in partnership law: see the Law Commission and Scottish Law Commission, *Report on Partnership Law* (Scot. Law Com. No.192, 2003), paras 9.88, 9.93 and 9.97.

[8] The tension between company law and the 1995 Act becomes even greater if the acceptance was signed by the company secretary. In the eyes of company law the role of company secretaries is limited to administrative matters.

[9] The discussion in the text has focussed on validity rather than probativity. Conveyancing deeds by companies will in practice be probative. The resulting presumptions are useful from a practical standpoint, but do not solve the underlying problem. (For the rules on probativity see ss.3(1), 3(1A) and 3(1C) of the 1995 Act all as substituted by Sch.2, para.3(5) of that Act.) For probability see para.14–18.

[10] Companies Act 1985, ss.35A and 35B, substituted by the Companies Act 1989, s.108.

[11] Companies Act 1985, s.35A(1), as substituted.

[12] Companies Act 1985, s.35A(2)(b), as substituted.

name and registered office. Whilst this is legally sufficient, during the 1990s this came to be regarded as less than best practice, which is to include the registration number as well. The main reason for this is that companies can change their names fairly easily,[13] and can even assume names previously held by other companies. It is indeed possible for companies to swap names, so that ABC Ltd assumes the name of XYZ Ltd while XYZ Ltd assumes the name of ABC Ltd.[14] Thus the fact that property was bought by ABC Ltd and is now being offered for sale by ABC Ltd does not prove that the seller is the owner.[15] By contrast, a company registration number is a birthmark. Names may come and go, but the number stays the same.

The traditional view is that a more exacting standard is applied to company names than to the names of natural persons, so that even very minor errors are fatal.[16] In an opinion which has become well-known, Professor Halliday stated that the mere omission of an apostrophe in the name of the disponing company was fatal,[17] and that certainly represents the traditional approach of conveyancers.[18] However, a minor error is probably not fatal if coupled with the correct company number, since the number is actually the superior form of designation.

Registration of charges[19]

When a company grants a standard security it must be registered not only in the Land Register, or GRS, but also in the Companies Register. The latter must happen with 21 days of its registration in the Land   25–05

---

[13] And can also change the registered office.

[14] *cf. F. J. Neale (Glasgow) Ltd v Vickery*, 1973 S.L.T. (Sh. Ct.) 88. Many people find it hard to believe that the law allows this sort of thing.

[15] The problem is made worse by the fact that the two companies are likely to be associated and thus very likely have the same registered office.

[16] It is easy to go wrong: the client company may itself not use the exactly correct form in its stationery.

[17] D. J. Cusine (ed.), *The Conveyancing Opinions of Professor J. M. Halliday* (1992), p.265. And see C. Waelde (ed.), *Professor McDonald's Conveyancing Opinions* (1998), p.14.

[18] Whether this ultra-strict approach would be followed by the courts is a large subject which cannot be entered into here. The issue is one which crops up quite often. The following cases deal with mis-designation of companies in various different contexts (and it should be realised that the context is important, so that their relevance for conveyancing may be restricted): *Goldsmith (Sicklesmere) Ltd v Baxter* [1969] 3 All E.R. 733; *Re Vidiofusion Ltd* [1975] 1 All E.R. 76; *Richards and Wallington (Earthmoving) Ltd v Whatlings*, 1982 S.L.T. 66; *Lin Pac Containers (Scotland) Ltd v Kelly*, 1983 S.L.T. 422; *Unisys v Eastern Counties* [1991] 1 Lloyds Rep. 539; *Allied Irish Banks plc v GPT Sales and Services Ltd*, 1995 S.L.T. 163; *Bank Tejarat v Hong Kong & Shanghai Banking Corporation* [1995] 1 Lloyds Rep. 239; *Prudential Assurance v Smiths Foods*, 1995 S.L.T. 369; *Modern Housing Ltd v Love*, 1998 S.L.T. 1188.

[19] For details see Gretton (2002) 6 *Edinburgh Law Review* 146. The Scottish Law Commission has provisionally proposed abolition of the requirement that standard securities be registered in the Companies Register: see *Discussion Paper on Registration of Rights in Security by Companies* (Scot Law Com. D.P. No.121, 2002), paras 3.15–3.12.

Register or GRS.[20] Failure to register will cause the security to be null,[21] though the debt secured remains a valid debt. Registration out of time is possible but only with the authority of the court.[22] This authority is not always granted, and, when it is granted, is generally subject to conditions. If a solicitor realises that he has failed to make timeous registration he should, in the typical case, petition the court immediately. Failure to register is a common error, and amounts to negligence.

When the Keeper registers a standard security in the Land Register, he can offer a guarantee to its validity only if it is registered in the Companies Register within 21 days of its registration in the Land Register. Hence the certificate issued by the Registrar of Companies[23] confirming due registration should be exhibited to the Keeper. Without it the Keeper will have to exclude indemnity for the security in respect of the possibility of its non-registration in the Companies Register. Of course, the certificate cannot be produced at the time of registration in the Land Register, because registration in the Companies Register happens after registration in the Land Register. But the gap will be only a matter of days, so that the certificate from the Registrar of Companies can be sent to the Keeper well before he issues the land certificate and charge certificate.

Buying from a company: the search

25–06   When taking a deed from a company it is necessary to make sure that the company is duly incorporated and is not in insolvency. The main dangers are: (i) striking off[24] (ii) liquidation (iii) receivership, and (iv) administration. All these can be checked, and must be checked, by a search in the company file at the Companies Office. The Keeper does not provide searches in the Companies Register. Such a search can be obtained through independent searchers or by direct inspection. Direct inspection is nowadays usually done digitally, though the "Companies House Direct" service. A search in the Companies Register is also needed if the property is in the GRS and a company has held title during the prescriptive progress. The correct name of the company, and also its registered number, should be put on the memorandum of search. Company searches are available in both interim and final form, so that the interim report can be seen on the eve of settlement and the final report a few weeks later.

---

[20] The present rules are to be found in ss.410 *et seq.* of the Companies Act 1985. The Companies Act 1989 replaces these with new provisions inserted in s.395 *et seq.* of the 1985 Act, the present sections bearing those numbers being repealed. However, it now seems improbable that these provisions will ever be brought into force.

[21] Companies Act 1985, s.410. Actually the section says, not that the security is void, but only that it is void as against certain parties, namely a future liquidator, a future administrator, and any creditor. The exact meaning of this is obscure: for practical purposes it can be equated with nullity.

[22] Companies Act 1985, s.420. There is an extensive body of case law on this and its English equivalent, s.404.

[23] Companies Act 1985 s.418.

[24] Companies Act 1985, s.652.

Scottish companies are registered at the Companies Office in Edinburgh.[25] English and Welsh companies are registered at the Companies Office at Cardiff/Caerdydd. In law these are separate. But for most administrative purposes they function as a single entity, and indeed Edinburgh is now called a mere "regional office" of the Cardiff/Caerdydd "headquarters", a description unsound in law but true in substance.[26] Each company has its own file, now held in digital form.[27] It is up to the Registrar how to keep the data,[28] except that the legislation provides for a so-called "Register of Charges" in which is placed information about security rights granted by companies. This term suggests that there is a single register, used by all companies. That is not so. A separate register is kept for each company, and it is merely a part of the file (now a digital file) for that company. Solicitors often request the searchers to search merely in the "Register of Charges", which is insufficient because such a search will not disclose important information, such as liquidation. However, in practice searchers will normally report back if there has been a liquidation, even though not expressly so asked.

Length of search

The usual practice is to ask for a search against the selling company 25-07 beginning from the date of the company's incorporation, or October 27, 1961, whichever is the later,[29] and ending 22 days after the registration of the disposition. This period is calculated to ensure that anything which has happened before the recording of the disposition will have had time to enter the company file. Of course, if the company being searched against is not the current seller, but, say, a previous owner, it is necessary only to search up to 22 days after the date when the disposition granted by that company was registered.

What is being searched for?

Standard securities will be disclosed by the Companies Search, but 25-08 they will in any case be known from the form 10 or 12 report. Floating charges will also be disclosed, but they, in principle, should not matter to a buyer since they do not prevent the company from selling, and such sale will automatically discharge the floating charge in relation to the subjects sold. This is one of the key differences between a standard security and a floating charge: a standard security is a real right and thus attaches to the property, even if ownership changes, but a floating charge is not a real right, unless and until it crystallises, when it becomes one. A person who acquires property subject to an uncrystallised floating charge thus acquires unencumbered property.

However, there are two dangers. The first is that the floating charge will often contain a clause forbidding the company from selling its

---

[25] 37 Castle Terrace, Edinburgh, EH1 2EB.
[26] There is a single website: *http://www.companieshouse.gov.uk/*.
[27] Originally they were kept in paper form, later in microfiche, and since 2002 digitally.
[28] Companies Act 1985, s.707A.
[29] October 27, 1961 is the date when charges became registrable.

heritable property without the consent of the charge holder. No one knows whether such a clause could prejudice the title of a buyer,[30] but equally no one would wish to take the risk of it. The second danger is that the charge might have attached (crystallised) by liquidation or receivership.[31]

The memorandum for search should thus seek information about registered charges, liquidation, receivership, and also about administration. It should further inquire whether the company has been struck off.[32] Lastly, it is common to ask the searchers to report the names of the registered directors and secretary. This is to enable the purchaser to be sure that the disposition is signed by persons authorised to sign it.[33] However, this step is not usually taken where the company is a large and respectable one.

Certificate of non-crystallisation

25–09   A floating charge is automatically discharged on a sale of property, provided that it has not attached (crystallised).[34] This is because a floating charge can affect only that which belongs to the debtor company. The effect of attachment is to convert the floating charge into a "fixed" charge, which is a real right, with the result that the company can no longer alienate property free of the charge. So what the buyer should ask for[35] is a certificate from the chargeholder certifying that the charge has not attached, and also that it will not be made to attach for a stated period, such as 21 days from the date of the certificate.[36] This is called a certificate of non-crystallisation. Since it is common in a floating charge to have a clause forbidding sale of heritage without the consent of the charge holder, it is advisable for the certificate to contain such a consent as well. Banks are often prepared to go further and grant a certificate which actually releases the property being sold from the ambit of the floating charge. This is slightly preferable, because, unlike a classic certificate of non-crystallisation, it is not fettered by a time-limit, so that if there is a delay in settling the transaction, there is no need to go back to the bank for a fresh certificate.

The problems in this area (from the standpoint of a purchaser from a company) have been considerably lessened by the decision of the House

---

[30] *Trade Development Bank v Warriner & Mason (Scotland) Ltd*, 1980 S.C. 74 could be used as a basis for an argument that a purchaser would be affected, but the argument is by no means conclusive. The subject is a large one. Apart from anything else it could be argued that a prohibition on alienation is repugnant to the essence of a floating charge.

[31] Companies Act 1985, s.463; Insolvency Act 1986, s.53.

[32] Under s.652 of the Companies Act 1985. Such striking-offs are extremely common. Of course, a dissolved company has no power to sell or dispone.

[33] Companies must register the names of the current directors and secretary: Companies Act 1985, s.288. There is an argument that a purchaser in good faith would be protected if the signatories of the disposition were not properly appointed, but the issue is complex and a search on the point is a sensible precaution.

[34] The two terms mean the same. The first is Scottish, and the second English, but the English term is widely used.

[35] And stipulate for in the missives.

[36] For an example, see J. H. Sinclair, *Handbook of Conveyancing Practice in Scotland* (4th ed., 2002), para.35.

of Lords in the celebrated case of *Sharp v Thomson* [37] in which it was held that as soon as a selling company delivers a disposition to a purchaser the property is deemed to be released from the ambit of the floating charge.

Letter of obligation and certificate of solvency

The solicitors for a company will normally grant a standard letter of 25-10 obligation, but this will not normally cover the company search. The final company search might contain an entry which did not show up on the interim report, such as liquidation. The practice is, therefore, to require some or all of the directors to grant what is sometimes called a certificate of solvency, guaranteeing that the company is not insolvent and will not become so prior to the registration of the grantee's title.[38] Both this and the certificate of non-crystallisation should be stipulated for in the missives.

Some of the same considerations apply where a previous owner within the prescriptive period was a company, though in that case the certificates of non-crystallisation and of solvency are not normally required because the situation can be fully checked from the company search, which should be with the title deeds. If it is not, then another search will be necessary. This also must be stipulated for in the missives.

Search against buying company

A law firm acting for a purchaser which is a company is wise to 25-11 instruct a company search against its client. For example, a law firm does not want to find itself buying on behalf of a company that has been struck off under section 652 of the Companies Act 1985. In many cases the purchasing company is granting a standard security over the property being acquired, and in that case the lender will in any case insist on a company search.

Lending to a company on standard security

Although a floating charge will not, subject to some qualifications, 25-12 concern a purchaser from a company, it will usually concern someone taking a standard security. This is because floating charges usually have a clause[39] whereby future standard securities are postponed to the floating charge. It is, therefore, particularly important for the lender to ascertain whether any prior floating charge has been granted, and if so, on what terms. Since a floating charge can be registered up to 21 days after its creation there exists a potential blind period.[40]

---

[37] 1997 S.C. (HL) 66. See further para.11–27.

[38] For an example, see J. H. Sinclair, *Handbook of Conveyancing Practice in Scotland* (4th ed., 2002), para.7.35.

[39] Under the Companies Act 1985, s.464(1).

[40] See *AIB Finance v Bank of Scotland*, 1995 S.L.T. 2 for the dramatic implications. The 21-day rule is, of course, absurd and has long been recognised as such. The Scottish Law Commission has proposed that a floating charge should be created only on registration: see *Discussion Paper on Registration of Rights in Security by Companies* (Scot. Law Com. D.P. No.121, 2002), paras 2.3–2.11.

Foreign companies

25-13   The company may not be Scottish. It may be incorporated elsewhere,
such as England, France, Liechtenstein, the Isle of Man, or the Cayman
Islands. How can one be sure that it is not dissolved or being dissolved
or otherwise unable to give good title? And how can one know whether
the persons signing the disposition are authorised to do so on behalf of
the company? If the company is from outwith the UK, it is advisable for
the other party to insist on seeing an "opinion letter" letter from a law
firm in the country concerned,[41] certifying that the company is duly
incorporated, and so forth. Since styles for such letters are difficult to
find, we offer the following, which is for a secured loan, but which may
be adapted according to circumstances:[42]

> "So far as we are aware, having made due enquiry:
>   (i) The borrower is a corporation with full juristic personality,
> and is duly incorporated, duly organised, validly existing and in
> good standing under the laws of Ruritania. Its corporate existence
> is not limited in time.
>   (ii) The execution, delivery and performance by the borrower of
> the [loan agreement] [personal bond] [other] and standard security
> are within the borrower's corporate powers, have been duly
> authorised by all necessary corporate action and they do not
> contravene
>
>   (a) the constitution of the borrower (whether in the form of
> memorandum and articles of association, charter, bye-laws corpor-
> ate statutes or otherwise) or
>   (b) any legislative provision (whether statute, regulation,
> enactment or otherwise) or rule of law in force under the laws of
> Ruritania.
>
>   (iii) No authorisation or approval (including exchange control
> approval) or other action by, and no notice to, or filing or
> registration with, any governmental, administrative or other public
> agency, authority or court is required under the laws of Ruritania,
> except for [specify] which have been duly obtained or made and are
> in full force and effect.
>   (iv) Any decree obtained in the Scottish courts by the lender
> against the borrower in relation to said [loan agreement] [personal
> bond] [other] and standard security would be accorded full faith
> and credit under the laws of Ruritania.
>   (v) The persons signing the [loan agreement] [personal bond]
> [other] and standard security namely . . . are duly authorised to do
> so on behalf of the borrower under the laws of Ruritania.
>   (vi) No insolvency proceedings have been opened against the
> borrower in the courts of Ruritania, or in any public agency or

---

[41] Or from the foreign company's Scottish solicitors, if they are prepared to grant such a
letter.

[42] There is no such thing as a perfect style, and no doubt this style would be susceptible
of improvement.

authority with power to open insolvency proceedings, and no other orders have been issued by any Ruritanian court or public agency or authority which could prejudice the effectiveness of the [loan agreement] [personal bond] [other] and standard security."

Obtaining such a letter will increase costs, but that is because a foreign company has decided to involve itself in Scottish heritable property. The costs will be borne by the company itself. Whether such a letter is necessary for a company incorporated in another part of the UK, *i.e.* in England and Wales or in Northern Ireland, is arguable. In practice it is seldom done.

Limited liability partnerships[43]

Limited liability partnerships ("LLPs") have full juristic personality, 25–14 and are more akin to companies than to ordinary partnerships, or to limited partnerships.[44] Like companies, they come into being by registration.[45] They have a registered office, and a registered number, and what has already been said about companies is equally applicable: LLPs should be designed by name, number and registered office. If they acquire heritable property, they do so in their own name, like companies. The *ultra vires* doctrine does not apply.[46] Unlike companies, but like ordinary partnerships, each member acts for the firm. Thus in LLPs there is nothing that precisely corresponds to the board of directors of a company. Even if the partner exceeds his or her authority, the firm is bound, unless the counterparty was in bad faith.[47] LLPs can grant security rights, including standard securities and floating charges,[48] in the same way as companies, and the rules about registration of charges[49] apply to LLPs as they do to companies.

---

[43] See Bennett (2001) 54 Prop. L.B. 1.

[44] "The law relating to partnerships does not apply to a limited liability partnership": Limited Liability Partnerships Act 2000, s.1(5).

[45] The LLPs Register is kept by the Registrar of Companies.

[46] "A limited liability partnership has unlimited capacity": Limited Liability Partnerships Act 2000, s.1(3).

[47] Limited Liability Partnerships Act 2000, s.6.

[48] Limited Liability Partnerships (Scotland) Regulations 2001 (SSI 2001/128).

[49] Companies Act 1985, Part XII.

CHAPTER 26

INSOLVENCY

Introduction

26–01   This chapter deals mainly with purchases from an insolvent estate. Purchases from a heritable creditor are dealt with elsewhere.[1] The whole subject is a complex one and we will give only an outline.[2] Five forms of insolvency are considered in this chapter, namely (i) sequestration (ii) trust deeds for behoof of creditors (iii) liquidation (iv) receivership and (v) administration.

Sequestration

26–02   A petition for sequestration can be either by the debtor or by a creditor. When this happens the court at once causes a notice to be registered in the personal register.[3] Under section 14 of the Bankruptcy (Scotland) Act 1985 this has the effect of an inhibition. Unless the petition is by the debtor, the entry will be called a warrant to cite, which means only that the petition has been presented, not that sequestration will happen, or, to use the technical term, "be awarded".[4] Once sequestration has been awarded an interim trustee in sequestration is immediately appointed. The latter's powers are, however, limited. In due course the permanent[5] trustee in sequestration will be appointed— typically the same person as the interim trustee. The court will issue an interlocutor called the act and warrant, which is a judicial conveyance to the trustee of the assets of the bankrupt. It is a general conveyance, which is to say that no property is identified.[6] The effect is to vest all the property in the trustee, but this is like a disposition which has been delivered but not registered: the trustee is not owner but merely an unregistered holder.[7] Nonetheless the trustee can sell without first having

---

[1] Ch.20.

[2] For insolvency law generally, see William W. McBryde, *Bankruptcy* (2nd ed., 1995); Donna McKenzie Skene, *Insolvency Law in Scotland* (1999); J. B. St Clair and J. E. Drummond Young, *Law of Corporate Insolvency in Scotland* (2nd ed., 1992); J. H. Greene and I. M. Fletcher, *Law and Practice of Receivership in Scotland* (2nd ed., 1992); though these works do not have extensive coverage of conveyancing questions.

[3] Bankruptcy (Scotland) Act 1985, s.14.

[4] The interlocutor granting the petition is delightfully called the award of sequestration. Congratulations, Jimmy, you're bust.

[5] An odd term, since the trustee is not permanent. The term is used as a contrast with the interim trustee.

[6] para.21–02.

[7] para.21–01.

completed title, and until recently this was what usually happened in practice. But before selling the trustee is able to complete title, as such, in his or her own name, and this course of action is nowadays increasingly the norm.[8] If the property is still in the GRS, this means recording a notice of title, deducing title through the act and warrant as the midcouple.[9] If the property is in the Land Register the trustee applies with the act and warrant on a form 2.

Everything acquired by the bankrupt after sequestration also passes to the trustee. But eventually—normally after three years—the bankrupt is discharged,[10] which means that anything acquired thereafter may be kept, even though the debts have not been paid in full. The discharge of the bankrupt does not, however, mean that any assets which the trustee has not realised return to the ex-bankrupt. Unless they have been "abandoned" by the trustee, which is unusual, any unrealised assets remain subject to the sequestration. Thus the trustee can sell them even after the bankrupt's discharge. However, if (a) there is unrealised heritable property, and if (b) the trustee has not completed title, and if (c) the trustee has not renewed the section 14 notice,[11] the bankrupt will be able to deal with such property again.[12] This state of affairs might seem unlikely to crop up in practice, but it sometimes does.

Another state of affairs which seems incredible but does sometimes happen is that while still undischarged the bankrupt acquires heritable property and grants a security over it. Although the law is unsettled, it seems likely that the security is invalid[13] It is true that the general creditors would then, through the trustee, make a windfall gain, but that is always the potential result when a person lends to an undischarged bankrupt. It should be recalled that in a case of this sort a discharge does not free the bankrupt of the debt to the bank, for the loan is a post-sequestration debt: discharge frees a bankrupt only from pre-sequestration debts.

In many cases, especially "small asset" cases, the trustee is the Accountant in Bankruptcy. As well as acting as trustee, he also administers the Register of Insolvencies and generally oversees the bankruptcy system.[14] The Register of Insolvencies contains more information about sequestrations and trust deeds than the Personal Register.

Buying from a trustee in sequestration

The key document in a sequestration is the act and warrant, vesting 26–03 the estate in the trustee. Accordingly, the buyer must see this, and the Keeper too will require to see it.[15] It constitutes the midcouple for

---

[8] The benefits are illustrated strikingly by *Burnett's Tr v Grainger*, 2004 S.L.T. 513.

[9] para.21–11.

[10] Bankruptcy (Scotland) Act 1985, s.54. In England and Wales the period has recently been reduced to one year and legislation to the same effect seems likely to Scotland.

[11] The renewal must be registered timeously: *Roy's Tr, Noter*, 2000 S.L.T. (Sh. Ct) 77; *Tewnion's Tr, Noter*, 2000 S.L.T. (Sh. Ct) 37. For discussion see Reid and Gretton, *Conveyancing 2000*, pp.101–03. Whilst there is a deadline for the registration of a s.14 renewal, there is no deadline for the alternative, which is to complete title.

[12] Conveyancing (Scotland) Act 1924, s.44.

[13] See *Alliance & Leicester Building Society v Murray's Tr*, 1994 S.C.L.R. 19, *Royal Bank of Scotland plc v Lamb's Tr*, 1998 S.C.L.R. 923; *Halifax plc v Gorman's Tr*, 2000 S.L.T. 1409. For discussion see Reid and Gretton, *Conveyancing 2000*, pp.98–101.

[14] *http://www.aib.gov.uk/*.

[15] ROTPB, para.5.40.

conveyancing purposes and, if the property is still in the GRS, the disposition will have a clause deducing title through it, unless the trustee has already completed title.[16] It is good practice, though perhaps not strictly necessary, for the buyer to require evidence that the seller is a qualified insolvency practitioner.[17] It is likewise prudent to stipulate that there has been due registration in the Personal Register.[18] Any outstanding heritable security must be discharged. This can be done either by an ordinary discharge or by the consent of the heritable creditor embodied in the disposition by the trustee.[19] However, inhibitions against the bankrupt need not be discharged.[20] If the property is residential, there is the problem of section 40 of the Bankruptcy (Scotland) Act 1985. This provides that where the property is a family home (as defined) then the trustee, before selling, must obtain certain consents.[21] The section does not make it clear what happens if the trustee sells without obtaining such consents: the cautious purchaser must assume the worst.[22] There are practical problems here: what happens if the trustee has not obtained consents on the view that they are not needed? How can the purchaser be satisfied? How can the trustee show that the house was not a "family home"? There seems to be no neat solution. In practice a written assurance from the trustee should be acceptable, and is acceptable to the Keeper.[23]

Trust deeds for behoof of creditors

26–04   A trust deed for behoof of creditors is similar to sequestration but is extrajudicial. The deed which the debtor voluntarily signs is a general conveyance to the trustee.[24] As in sequestration, the trustee can complete title or sell without having done so. The trust deed may enter the Personal Register but does not have to.[25] A trust deed is said to be "protected" if certain procedures have successfully been gone through: its protected status means that the creditors cannot challenge it. A protected trust deed will appear in the Register of Insolvencies.[26]

Buying from a trustee under a trust deed

26–05   The key document in a trust for behoof of creditors is the trust deed itself. This should have been registered in the Books of Council and Session and an extract must be produced. Registration in the Register of

---

[16] para.21–08.

[17] Insolvency Act 1986, s.388.

[18] Under s.14 of the Bankruptcy (Scotland) Act 1985. Registration under this section has the effect of an inhibition against the bankrupt. The obligation to register is placed on the clerks of court, who, however, occasionally fail in this duty. One danger is that another party might, in the absence of this registration, take a deed in good faith from the bankrupt.

[19] In such a case either the trustee or the heritable creditor can sell. There is a procedure for determining which it is to be, but the purchaser is protected from any failure to go through that procedure properly: Bankruptcy (Scotland) Act 1985, s.39(7). If the heritable creditor sells, the disposition does not have to be consented to by the trustee.

[20] Bankruptcy (Scotland) Act 1985, s.31(2); ROTPB, para.6.25.

[21] See generally William W. McBryde, *Bankruptcy* (2nd ed., 1995), paras 9–66 *et seq.*

[22] See William W. McBryde, *op. cit.,* para.9–79.

[23] ROTPB, para.5.42.

[24] paras 21–01–21.03.

[25] Bankruptcy (Scotland) Act 1985, Sch.5, para.2.

[26] Bankruptcy (Scotland) Act 1985, s.1A(1)(b)(ii).

Insolvencies is not required unless the trust deed is a "protected" one. Title will be deduced through the trust deed, unless the trustee has already completed title in his own name. The remarks made in connection with sequestration (about section 40 of the Bankruptcy (Scotland) Act 1985) are probably equally applicable in this type of case. But, in addition, the "anti-dealings" provisions of the Matrimonial Homes Act,[27] though they do not restrict the powers of sale of a trustee in sequestration, are capable of adversely affecting the powers of sale of a trustee under a trust deed. So the seller must satisfy the purchaser that there are no adverse matrimonial occupancy rights. Lastly, a purchaser should normally stipulate that the trust deed be a protected one.[28] Provided that it is so protected, it is not necessary that any inhibitions against the bankrupt be discharged. However, any outstanding heritable security must be discharged. Evidence should be obtained that the seller is a qualified insolvency practitioner.

Liquidation

Liquidation (also called winding up) is governed by the Insolvency Act 1986. It is made subject to much of the law relating to sequestrations, which it therefore resembles in many but by no means all respects. Unlike sequestration, liquidation is available for solvent as well as insolvent companies. Again, whereas sequestration is always judicial, liquidation can be either judicial ("compulsory liquidation" or "winding up by the court") or extrajudicial ("voluntary liquidation"). The two divisions do not coincide: both solvent and insolvent companies can go into either kind of liquidation. Another difference is that whereas in sequestration there is a conveyance to the trustee (even if the trustee may often choose not to complete title upon that conveyance) in liquidation there is no such conveyance.[29] What happens is that the liquidator replaces the board of directors and in that way assumes control over the company's assets. A company in liquidation still exists as a juristic person: dissolution happens at the end of liquidation.

26-06

In a winding up by the court, an interim liquidator is appointed, like the interim trustee in sequestration. In addition, there may be a provisional liquidator, who can be appointed to manage a company while a liquidation petition is being considered by the court. Thus, the existence of a provisional liquidator means that the company is not in liquidation, but that it soon may be. Liquidation appears in the Companies Register and in the Register of Insolvencies, but not in the Personal Register. Fuller details as to registration are given in the table at the end of this chapter.

---

[27] Matrimonial Homes (Family Protection) (Scotland) Act 1981, s.6(1). See Ch.10.

[28] See the Bankruptcy (Scotland) Act 1985, Sch.5, as amended by the Bankruptcy (Scotland) Act 1993.

[29] Apart from s.145 of the Insolvency Act 1986, which is almost never applied in practice. In addition, there is s.25 of the Titles to Land Consolidation (Scotland) Act 1868 (as substituted by the Abolition of Feudal Tenure etc. (Scotland) Act 2000, s.76(1), Sch.12, para.8(9)) which enables a liquidator to complete title. We cannot discuss this interesting provision here.

Buying from a liquidator

26–07   If the liquidation is a compulsory one, the key document is the interlocutor ordering liquidation—the winding up order. If the liquidation is a voluntary one, the key document is the special resolution of the company. In either case the buyer must examine it. The interlocutor or resolution should have been registered in the Companies Register. A winding up order should also have been registered in the Register of Insolvencies. The liquidator's appointment should have been registered in the Companies Register and in the Register of Insolvencies. Evidence should be obtained as to the liquidator's status as an insolvency practitioner, as for sequestrations. Outstanding heritable securities must be discharged, for, as with sequestrations, a liquidator has no power to sell property free from security rights. The question of whether outstanding inhibitions need to be discharged is unclear. Our view is that if the liquidation is a compulsory one the liquidator has power to dispone free of inhibitions, but that for voluntary liquidations it is prudent to insist on their discharge. However, the Keeper has taken a somewhat different approach, considering that the liquidator cannot sell free from an inhibition, except one created within 60 days prior to the liquidation.[30] So long as that is his approach the law agent for a buyer will be similarly cautious. If there is a floating charge, the chargeholder must consent to the sale, and if a receiver has been appointed under the charge, the receiver must consent.[31]

There is normally no vesting of the company's property in a liquidator. Approximately speaking, the liquidator simply replaces the board of directors.[32] Hence, the disposition is from the company itself, though the practice is to make the liquidator a co-disponer with the company itself. The liquidator signs, with a witness. It is not necessary to affix the company's seal, though this is commonly done. There can, however, be vesting in a liquidator, either under section 25 of the Titles to Land Consolidation (Scotland) Act 1868[33] or under section 145 of the Insolvency Act 1986. In those cases the company is divested and the liquidator invested. But they are rare in practice.

Receivership

26–08   Receivership is a means of enforcing a floating charge. If there is no floating charge there can be no receivership. It is normally extrajudicial: the chargeholder executes an "instrument of appointment" which makes the charge attach (crystallise) and which appoints a receiver to run the company. Judicial receivership is competent but rare. The receiver displaces the board of directors for almost all purposes. When the charge

---

[30] ROTPB para.6.26.

[31] In that case, consent by the charge holder is not necessary. In cases where consent is required, it should be incorporated in the disposition.

[32] A company in liquidation still exists as a juristic person. It continues to exist as such until dissolution. It is dissolution, not liquidation, which marks the end of the juristic personality. A company in receivership or administration also still exists as a person.

[33] As substituted by the Abolition of Feudal Tenure etc. (Scotland) Act 2000, s.76(1), Sch.12, para.8(9).

attaches it becomes a real right of security, in favour of the chargeholder. But the chargeholder cannot deal with the property attached: that can be done only by the receiver. Thus, there is a curious asymmetry[34]: the chargeholder has the real right of security but no power to do anything about it (apart from the appointment of the receiver) while the receiver has the power to enforce but no real right is vested in him. A company may be simultaneously in liquidation and receivership: in that case the receiver normally has precedence over the liquidator.[35] Receivership does not appear in the Personal Register or Register of Insolvencies, but only in the Companies Register.

One problem thrown up by *Sharp v Thomson*[36] is that in some cases the receiver's power of sale cannot be relied upon, because although the property still belongs to the company it is subject to a delivered, though unregistered, disposition to a purchaser and so escapes the receivership. In practice the problem seems not to be a major one and the Keeper will normally register a purchase from a receiver without exclusion of indemnity.[37]

By virtue of the Enterprise Act 2002, floating charges created after September 15, 2003 cannot be enforced by receivership, except for six narrowly-defined categories.[38] Instead floating charges must be enforced by means of liquidation or administration.

Buying from a receiver

In a receivership, there are two key documents, which must be seen 26–09 and copies of which should be kept. The first is the floating charge itself. This must be checked carefully, to see that it was properly executed, and to see that it covers the property now being sold.[39] It must also be verified that the charge was duly registered within the 21-day period.[40] The second key document is the instrument of appointment. This is the deed by which the charge holder appoints the receiver.[41] The buyers should verify that it was validly executed, that the appointee accepted the appointment,[42] and that the receivership was duly registered.[43] They should also verify that the receiver is a qualified insolvency practitioner.

It sometimes happens that there is more than one receiver. In that case the purchaser should insist that both of them execute the disposition. However, if the company is simultaneously in receivership and in liquidation, it seems that there is no need to ask the liquidator also to

---

[34] Much in the law of floating charges and receivership causes difficulty to the rational mind.

[35] *Manley, Ptr*, 1985 S.L.T. 42.

[36] 1997 S.C. (HL) 66. See further para.11–27.

[37] ROTPB, para.5.37.

[38] Insolvency Act 1986, ss.72A—72H as substituted by the Enterprise Act 2002.

[39] A floating charge describes the property it affects not specifically but generically. The standard phrase is "the whole property and undertaking" of the company, and this will cover all heritage, present and future. But occasionally a floating charge is restricted, *e.g.* to the moveables. Such a charge would obviously be no basis for selling the heritage.

[40] Companies Act 1985, s.410.

[41] In theory, a receiver can be appointed by the court, but this never happens in practice.

[42] Insolvency Act 1986, s.53(6).

[43] Insolvency Act 1986, s.53(1).

consent.[44] A receiver executes the disposition in the same manner as a liquidator, and the practice is for the deed to run in the name of both the company and its receiver.

A floating charge granted within two years prior to liquidation can be subject to challenge by the liquidator on the ground that it was granted to secure a pre-existing debt.[45] But there would appear to be no danger to a purchaser where there has been no liquidation at the time of the sale. The potential danger arises only where (1) there is a concurrent liquidation; (2) the sale is by the receiver and not the liquidator; (3) the liquidator does not consent; and (4) the charge was created within the period of challenge. Even in such cases the charge will usually be at least partly valid because of section 245(2).[46] There seems to be no generally accepted good practice, but it is suggested that where (1), (2) and (4) apply the receiver should be required to satisfy the purchaser, either by obtaining the liquidator's consent, or by giving an indemnity, or by providing a title insurance policy, or by producing evidence that section 245 is inapplicable.

Whether outstanding heritable securities need to be discharged is a complex question, but in general the purchaser should insist on this, or on a court order enabling the receiver to sell free of them.[47]

There is a parallel problem for inhibitions against the company. An inhibition which precedes the creation of the charge must be discharged, or the receiver must obtain judicial authority to sell free of it.[48] An inhibition created at a later stage seems not to affect a receiver's power of sale. However, the Keeper's current practice is to exclude indemnity where the selling receiver has not obtained either a discharge of the inhibition or the authority of the court to sell free of it.[49]

Administration

26–10   Like liquidation and receivership, administration is a process for companies only. There is no vesting in the administrator, who takes control of the assets by taking control of the company itself. Administrations are at present not common, but the effect of the Enterprise Act 2002 is likely to be that they will become so, because in respect of post-2003 floating charges they will take over the function of receivership. An administration is commenced by an "appointment" which may be by (a) the court (b) the company (c) the directors of the company or (d) a floating charge holder.

---

[44] Subject to what is said below.

[45] Insolvency Act 1986, s.245. In some types of case the challenge period is only one year.

[46] Whereby a floating charge is protected from challenge to the extent that it secures new money advanced after its creation. The rule in *Devaynes v Noble* (1816) 1 Merivale 529 (called, with English logic, *Clayton's Case*), adopted into Scots law by *Royal Bank v Christie* (1841) 2 Rob. 118, operates in favour of the charge holder in such cases.

[47] Insolvency Act 1986, s.61.

[48] Insolvency Act 1986, s.61.

[49] ROTPB, para.6.23. See further *Armour & Mycroft, Ptrs*, 1983 S.L.T. 45; G. L. Gretton, *Law of Inhibition and Adjudication* (2nd ed., 1996); C. Waelde (ed.), *Professor McDonald's Conveyancing Opinions* (1998), p.176.

Buying from an administrator

The key document is the appointment: this must be checked by the 26-11 buyer, as should the administrator's status as an insolvency practitioner. The appointment should have been registered in both the Companies Register[50] and in the Personal Register.[51] Fuller details as to registration are given in the table at the end of this chapter.

The disposition typically runs in the name of both the company and its administrator, and is executed in the same way as by a liquidator. Ordinarily there is no power to sell free of security rights (*e.g.* a standard security), except with the consent of the creditor concerned, which would involve a discharge, either as a separate deed or in gremio of the disposition. However, the court can authorise a sale without consent,[52] and consent is never required in respect of floating charges.[53] Although the point is uncertain, an administrator probably cannot sell free of an inhibition, unless at the direction of the court.[54]

Warrandice, warranties and take-it-or-leave-it

Buyers from an insolvency practitioner will find that the sort of 26-12 undertakings and warranties that they could hope for in an ordinary purchase are difficult or impossible to obtain. The attitude of the seller is, understandably, rather a take-it-or-leave-it one. For instance, the usual practice is for absolute warrandice to be granted on behalf of the insolvent person or company and fact and deed warrandice on behalf of the insolvency practitioner. The former is in practice of little value because the person is not worth suing. The latter is equally unlikely to be of value because if there is a title problem it will almost never be covered by fact and deed warrandice. Thus buyers from an insolvency practitioner, unlike ordinary purchasers, are effectively receiving no warrandice worth speaking about.

This is but one aspect of a general theme in insolvency conveyancing: the buyers must accept matters as they are, satisfy themselves, and absorb any risk there may be. As well as the warrandice issue, the seller will be reluctant to warrant the planning position or the building control position or that there is a good title to any moveables included in the sale, and so on. The qualified acceptance is thus likely to knock out many provisions which, in an ordinary case, the seller would be prepared to leave in, or merely to modify. On the whole the buyers must reconcile themselves to the situation, for the seller will usually not budge. But all this means that the buyers' solicitor needs to proceed with extra care, for there is unlikely to be any comeback against the seller if problems emerge.

---

[50] Insolvency Act 1986, Sch.B1, para.46(4). (Schedule B1, inserted by the Enterprise Act 2002, replaces the previous Part II of the Act.)

[51] Insolvency (Scotland) Rules 1986 (SI 1986/1915), r.2.19, as amended by the Insolvency (Scotland) Amendment Rules 2003 (SI 2003/2111).

[52] Insolvency Act 1986, Sch.B1, para.71.

[53] Insolvency Act 1986, Sch.B1, para.70.

[54] ROTPB, para.6.27. The changes in the law of administration do not seem to have affected matters in this respect.

A related point is that the right of the trustee, or liquidator, or receiver, or administrator, to sell the property will, subject to minor qualifications, be no better than that originally held by the insolvent person or company. So if Donald Debtor buys land, but his title is bad, his trustee in sequestration will, generally speaking, have no better right to sell the land than Donald had. Thus, in addition to the specialities applicable to the insolvency itself, the buyers' agent must make the usual examination of title.

Has the seller gone through the right hoops?

26–13   Some of the matters touched on in this chapter are requirements imposed by legislation on the seller, of an administrative nature, and sanctioned typically by fines (e.g., registration of a liquidation in the Companies Register.) Non-compliance with requirements of this sort will thus tend to affect the seller rather than the buyers. However, buyers often require evidence that these hoops have been duly gone through. Though arguably unnecessary, such requirements cause no difficulty since a competent seller will have ensured compliance. The positive argument for buyers making these requirements is that there might possibly be situations in which buyers might have to defend their title on the basis of good faith.

Designation

26–14   The narrative clause of the disposition should narrate the insolvency and design the insolvency practitioner by reference to it, as well as in the ordinary manner. For instance, a disposition by a trustee in sequestration would typically run: "I . . . permanent trustee in sequestration on the sequestrated estate of . . . conform to act and warrant . . . and as such trustee unregistered holder[55] of . . .".

Buying from a non-Scottish insolvency practitioner

26–15   This chapter is confined to purchasers from a Scottish insolvency practitioner, *i.e.* where the insolvency process is a Scottish one. From time to time a non-Scottish individual or company will have heritable property in Scotland and become formally insolvent under the laws of some other country. That other country is most commonly England, but other jurisdictions can be involved. The subject of "cross-border insolvency" is a complex one that cannot be entered into here, except to say that normally the foreign insolvency practitioner's power of sale will be recognised.[56]

Registration and insolvency: a summary

26–16   The principle that rights and events that affect third parties should be in the public domain—the publicity principle—applies not only to real rights but to other aspects of law too, including insolvencies. The

---

[55] For this, post-feudal, terminology, see para.11–07.

[56] For the common law, see *Ayara v Coghill*, 1921 1 S.L.T. 321. The main legislative provisions are the Insolvency Act 1986, ss.72 and s.426; the Insolvency Act 2000, s.14; and the EU Regulation on Insolvency Proceedings, 1346/2000.

following is a summary of the main current rules. They are not entirely satisfactory.[57]

What?	Where?	When?	Why?
Sequestration			
First deliverance	Personal Register; Register of Insolvencies	Forthwith	Bankruptcy (Scotland) Act 1985, s.14
Appointment of permanent trustee	Register of Insolvencies	Forthwith	Bankruptcy (Scotland) Act 1985, s.25
Trust deed			
Protected trust deed	(a) Personal Register; (b) Register of Insolvencies	(a) At any time; (b) Immediately on expiry of notice period	(a) Bankruptcy (Scotland) Act 1985, Sch.5, para.2; (b) 1985 Act, Sch.5, para. 5(1)(e)
Liquidation			
Resolution for voluntary winding up	Companies Register	Within 15 days	Insolvency Act 1986, s.84(3)
Winding up petition	No registration[58]		
Winding up order	Companies Register; Register of Insolvencies	Forthwith	Insolvency Act 1986, s.130(1), read with Scotland Act 1998, Sch.8, para.23(2), (3)
Appointment of provisional liquidator	Companies Register; Register of Insolvencies	Forthwith	Insolvency (Scotland) Rules 1986,[59] r.4.2(1)(a), (aa)

[57] For the question of the importance of publicity in connection with insolvency, and the problems of the existing law, see the Scottish Law Commission, *Discussion Paper on Sharp v Thomson* (Scot. Law Com. D.P. No.114, 2001), especially Part 4.

[58] Though there must be a notice in the Edinburgh Gazette, and, unless the court decides otherwise, in a newspaper: see Rules of the Court of Session 1994 (SI 1994/1443), r.74.22.(1)(c); Sheriff Court Company Insolvency Rules 1986 (SI 1986/2297), r.19(6)

[59] SI 1986/1915. As with all legislation, the Rules must be consulted in their amended form.

Appointment of interim liquidator	Register of Insolvencies	Within 7 days	Insolvency (Scotland) Rules 1986, r.4.18(4)(a).
Appointment of liquidator	Companies Register; Register of Insolvencies	Within 7 days	Insolvency Act 1985, s.109(1); Insolvency (Scotland) Rules 1986, rr.4.18 and 4.19
Receivership			
Receivership	Companies Register	Within 7 days	Insolvency Act 1986, ss.51(1) and s.54(3)
Administration			
Petition for administration	Personal Register	Forthwith	Insolvency (Scotland) Rules 1986, r.2.3
Appointment of administrator	(a) Companies Register; (b) Personal Register	(a) Within 7 days; (b) forthwith	(a) Insolvency Act 1986 Sch.B1, para.46(4); (b) Insolvency (Scotland) Rules 1986, r.2.19(2)(e)

CHAPTER 27

TENEMENTS, NEW HOUSES, AND THE RIGHT TO BUY

TENEMENTS

General

To the ordinary person a "tenement" conjures up images of sombre 27–01
stone buildings from Victorian times or earlier. But to the lawyer a
"tenement" is simply any flatted building, whether new or old, purpose-
built or converted, residential or commercial. At the time of writing all
such tenements were governed, as for several hundred years before, by a
body of common law known as the law of the tenement.[1] But the law of
the tenement was due to be replaced by a new Tenements (Scotland)
Act 2004, implementing for the most part recommendations by the
Scottish Law Commission.[2] The bill was introduced to the Scottish
Parliament at the beginning of 2004 and at the time of preparing this
edition was expected to be passed, and to come into force on the day
appointed for the abolition of the feudal system (November 28, 2004).[3]
For the purposes of this chapter the bill is taken as being the law, and is
in this chapter referred to as the 2004 Bill.[4]

Default rules and title rules

Like the common law of the tenement before it, the new statutory law 27–02
is no more than a default code. If the titles are silent, the statutory the
rules will govern the tenement (including tenements built before the
code was enacted). But if the titles provide, the titles prevail.[5] In practice
titles are rarely silent, except in the case of the very oldest tenements,
and yet are rarely comprehensive, except, sometimes, in the case of the
very newest. The result is that most tenements are governed both by the
titles and, insofar as the titles are silent, by the statutory code. In

---

[1] See, for that law, Reid, *Property*, paras 227–51.

[2] Scottish Law Commission, *Report on the Law of the Tenement* (Scot. Law Com. No.162,
1998; available on *http://www.scotlawcom.gov.uk*). The *Report* is an indispensable guide to
the legislation.

[3] Stage 2 of the bill was completed on June 15, 2004.

[4] Of course the possibility that the bill will not be passed, or will be passed in a different
form, cannot be excluded.

[5] 2004 Bill, ss.1(1) and 4. All section numbers given in this chapter are to the Bill at the
end of Stage 2.

considering the rules governing a building, conveyancers must have regard to both.

Traditionally, title provision was made in the split-off deed for each flat. The split-offs would usually be granted by the original developer as soon as the construction was complete, although sometimes the flats were let out at first and only sold gradually over a period of years. Thus, one sometimes comes across a tenement built in, say, 1890 with the break-offs being granted from, say, the 1930s onwards. In more modern developments there is usually a deed of conditions,[6] to which each break-off refers. This is obviously more convenient. It is also generally true that the more modern the development the more complex the conditions are. A split-off of a flat in 1890 may just have a few words about the roof and the back green. A modern deed may have pages of provisions.

Two main topics are covered by the statutory code, and also by the titles. One is the allocation of ownership within the building. The other is management and maintenance.

Allocation of ownership: the statutory code

27–03   On allocation of ownership, the new statutory code virtually re-enacts the previous law, while taking the opportunity to resolve doubts and fill in gaps. The rules are individualistic rather than communal, with a tenement being viewed as a group of self-contained houses built, by some odd chance, one on top of the other. Thus the proprietor of a flat owns, not only the airspace which the flat occupies in the building, but also the walls, ceilings and floors.[7] Nothing is shared. An outside wall is owned in its entire thickness. Each section of outer wall belongs to the corresponding flat, so that if one looks at the outside of a tenement with the eyes of a legal eagle there is a series of horizontal title stripes. A wall which forms a boundary with another flat is owned to the mid-line,[8] after which it is part of the adjoining flat.[9] The roof, and roof space, are part of the highest flat in the building, and the solum (*i.e.* the ground on which the tenement is built) and foundations are part of the lowest flat.[10] That leaves only (a) the common entrance, stair and corridors, and (b) the garden and other ground to be accounted for. The former—referred to in the legislation as the "close"—is the common property in equal shares of the owners of all flats accessed by it, *i.e.* excluding only those main-door flats with no door to the common passage.[11] The latter is owned, in sections, by the owners of those "bottom flats most nearly adjacent".[12] Ancillary parts such as chimney stacks, rhones, down pipes,

---

[6] See para.13–11. Deeds of conditions for flats are commoner in the Glasgow area than elsewhere. For an example, see Halliday, para.34–38.

[7] 2004 Bill, s.2(1).

[8] Or the *medium filum*, in the Latin form beloved by conveyancers. The term is geometrically inexact since it is in truth not a line (*filum*) but a plane (*planum*). But nobody ever says *medium planum*. Conveyancers seldom perceive the beauties of mathematics, and sometimes even say "mid-point".

[9] The same is true for the boundary between the floor and the ceiling of the flat underneath.

[10] 2004 Bill, s.2(3), (4).

[11] 2004 Bill, s.3(1), (2). The close includes both the roof above and the solum beneath: s.2(5).

[12] 2004 Bill, s.3(3). But paths are common property under s.3(4).

entryphone systems and the like are allocated according to a functional test. A part which serves one flat only is a pertinent of that flat (only), while a part which serves two or more flats is owned in common by the owners of the flats in question.[13]

Allocation of ownership: title provisions

Titles usually vary the default rules by increasing the parts which are to be owned in common. The titles typically make the roof, solum, foundations, external walls and back green common property. This is not an unmitigated blessing. Common property requires agreement among owners who have been thrown together largely by chance and who may be little inclined to co-operate. And it can lead to unexpected and unwanted consequences. If, for example, external walls are common property and not, as the default rules would have it, the sole property of the owner of the flats in question, the result is that in every flat two walls (at least) are the property of everyone in the building. That includes the inside surface as well as the outside. This means that anything added to the wall—from wallpaper to an Adam fireplace—becomes, by accession, the property of everyone in the building, and that not even the wallpaper could be changed, in strict law, without their agreement.[14] As a general guide to drafting it may be said that common property is an appropriate response where the purpose to allow everyone the *use* of something—as, for example, in the case of the back green. But it is not an appropriate response where the purpose is simply *common maintenance*. That is better achieved by maintenance burdens and without altering the rules of ownership; and in fact common maintenance is usually the result of the statutory code without the need for express provision.[15]

Solum

As has been seen, the default rule is for the solum to be owned solely by the owners of the lowest flat or flats in the building.[16] Some solicitors when acting for purchasers will object to a title of an upper flat which does not have a share in the solum. But in fact the solum has little significance.[17] If a tenement were to be burnt down or demolished, ownership of the solum would not determine the disposal of the site. In terms of the new legislation, no owner is able to re-build without the agreement of everyone else or except where required to do so by the titles; and any owner—even the owner of an upper flat with no right to the solum—can insist on the sale of the site and the division of the proceeds.[18] As a practical matter, the prospects of re-building are increased by the statutory requirement that the tenement be insured against fire and other risks.[19]

27-04

27-05

---

[13] 2004 Bill, s.3(4), (5). Common ownership is in equal shares except for chimney stacks where shares are allocated on the basis of number of flues.

[14] See in particular *Rafique v Amin*, 1997 S.L.T. 1385.

[15] See para.27-07.

[16] 2004 Bill, s.2(4).

[17] See D.J. Cusine (ed.), T*he Conveyancing Opinions of Professor J.M. Halliday* (1992), p.154.

[18] 2004 Bill, s.18. By s.16 demolition does not by itself affect ownership.

[19] 2004 Bill, s.15.

Roof void and space above the roof

27–06   Sometimes a top owner wishes to build an upper floor in the roof void. Under the statutory code the roof void belongs to the owner of the top flat,[20] but title deeds often vary this. If they merely say that the "roof" is owned in common, without also specifying the roof void, the latter is probably not included, and so remains subject to the default rule.[21] Sometimes a top proprietor has built a room in a commonly owned roof space without obtaining dispositions from the other parties. This obviously can cause major problems and when buying a top flat for a client it is wise to check whether there has been a roof void extension and if so whether the title to the extension is good.[22] The description in the Land Register is usually too meagre to provide much assistance one way or the other.

A top owner cannot lawfully build an extra storey. The airspace above the roof belongs to the owner of the solum[23] — in practice either the owner of the lowest flat (the default rule) or all the owners in the tenement (the normal variation effected by the titles). But in a case where the roof is pitched, a top owner who owns the roof also owns, and can build into, the airspace above the slope of the roof as far as the roof's highest point.[24] In this situation dormer windows are therefore unobjectionable.

Management and maintenance: the statutory code

27–07   Virtually no provision for management and maintenance was made by the common law.[25] The new statutory code is radically different. A detailed Tenement Management Scheme is set out in the schedule to the statute and applies except where alternative provision is made in the titles.[26] Decisions under the Scheme may be made by a simple majority, with or without a meeting, although if no meeting is held all owners must be consulted, except where it is impracticable to do so.[27] Most decisions will be about maintenance, but owners are also empowered to appoint a manager or factor and to arrange a policy of common insurance.[28] Once a decision on maintenance has been taken, the estimated cost can be collected in advance, thus reassuring both the owners and the contractors that the bills will be paid.[29] "Maintenance" includes cleaning and gardening, and also improvement which is

---

[20] 2004 Bill, s.2(3).

[21] For a different view see C. Waelde (ed.), *Professor McDonald's Conveyancing Opinions* (1998), p.50.

[22] For a cautionary tale see (1991) 36 J.L.S.S. 77.

[23] 2004 Bill, s.2(6). In theory this could be altered by the titles but in practice it is never done.

[24] 2004 Bill, s.2(7).

[25] Except that by the doctrine of common interest, any owner could insist on the repair of any part (such as the roof) which was necessary for support or shelter, with the owner meeting the cost. Common interest disappears under the new law but a unilateral right to insist on repairs touching on support and shelter survives: see the 2004 Bill, ss.7 and 8.

[26] 2004 Bill, s.4.

[27] Tenement Management Scheme, r.2.

[28] Tenement Management Scheme, r.3.1.

[29] Tenement Management Scheme, r.3.2–3.4.

reasonably incidental to maintenance.[30] Only "scheme property" can be maintained under these powers, but the definition is wide, extending to (i) all common property (ii) all property which is to be commonly maintained in terms of the titles, and (iii) the following key parts of the building (if not already included under (i) and (ii)): the solum, foundations, external walls, roof, and any load-bearing wall, beam or column.[31]

Liability for maintenance of scheme property is shared among the owners. If the property is owned in common, liability depends on size of *pro indiviso* share (and a person who did not own would have no liability).[32] Otherwise the rule is that the owner of each flat pays the same except where the flats are of unequal size, defined as occurring where the floor area of the largest flat is more than one and a half times that of the smallest, in which case liability is calculated by floor area.[33] Liability, it will be noticed, is largely separated from ownership, and a non-owner will often be bound to contribute to the cost of maintenance.

One major change concerns the roof. Under the common law of the tenement the roof was the sole property of the top owner or owners, and had to be maintained by that owner or owners unless the titles provided otherwise—which they did usually but not always. Under the new law the roof is scheme property and falls to be maintained by everybody. This means that in acting in the purchase of a top flat it is no longer necessary to examine the titles of the other flats. If the title to the top flat contains a maintenance burden, that will in practice[34] fix the liability; and if there is no burden, liability will be determined by the Tenement Management Scheme.

Management and maintenance: title provisions

Usually there is express provision in the titles for repair of the roof 27–08 and various other parts.[35] Assuming that this accounts for the full cost,[36] and is properly constituted as a real burden,[37] it prevails over the default rules set out in the Tenement Management Scheme. But the Scheme rules will apply in respect of any scheme property not provided for in the titles.

Sometimes titles specify the share of liability in fractional terms (*e.g.* one-eighth) or percentage terms (*e.g.* 12.5 per cent). That is the simplest

---

[30] Tenement Management Scheme, r.1.5.

[31] Tenement Management Scheme, r.1.2.

[32] Tenement Management Scheme, r.4.2(a).

[33] Tenement Management Scheme, r.4.2(b).

[34] Strictly, only if the whole cost of roof maintenance is duly apportioned among the flats. If the figures fail to add up, the maintenance burden is considered to have failed and the position is regulated by the Tenement Management Scheme: see the 2004 Bill, s.4(6).

[35] In practice there is no sharp division between repair and improvement, and this fact can give rise to disputes. See *e.g. McLay v Bennett*, 1998 G.W.D. 16–810; *Quantum Claims Compensation Specialists v Findlay*, 2002 G.W.D. 22–733. As already mentioned, "maintenance" is defined for the purposes of the Tenement Management Scheme (by r.1.5).

[36] 2004 Bill, s.4(6).

[37] See further Ch.13. Under the former law it was sometimes doubted whether an obligation to contribute to maintenance (as opposed to a direct obligation to maintain) was valid as a real burden on the ground that no actual figure was given. But these doubts have been removed, retrospectively, by the Title Conditions (Scotland) Act 2003, s.5(1).

and most convenient. But often it will be found that liability is divided either according to the ratio of the feuduty or according to the ratio of the rateable value.[38] Feuduty has disappeared and residential property is no longer subject to rates, but burdens based on the old values are still valid.[39] When calculating liability on the basis of the feuduty it should be borne in mind that in the old money the pound sterling was divided into 20 shillings, and each shilling was divided into twelve pence (and each penny was two halfpence, and each halfpenny two farthings). For example £2/12s/6d = £2.625.

Titles may also make provision for decision-making. Sometimes this is no more than a declaration that a majority can agree on repairs, but in modern developments of any size there is often provision for residents' associations, committees, factors, annual meetings, and the like. It is only where no provision is made at all that the default rule in the Tenement Management Scheme (for decision by majority) applies.[40]

Some drafting points

27–09   In preparing a deed of conditions for a new block of flats the default law of the statutory code must be kept in mind. So far as ownership is concerned, an increase in the common property allowed by the statutory code is worth considering but, for reasons mentioned earlier,[41] should be modest in extent.

Issues of management and maintenance of such parts as the roof etc. are potentially more troublesome in practice than issues of ownership of such parts. Broadly, there are four options. (i) One is to say nothing in the deed, with the result that the Tenement Management Scheme applies in full. (ii) A second is to make partial provision so that the Scheme applies in some respects (*e.g.* allocation of liability) but not in others (*e.g.* decision-making). (iii) A third choice is to make full, but different, provision, so that there is no scope for the Scheme to apply. (iv) A final choice is to disapply the Tenement Management Scheme in favour of the Development Management Scheme,[42] as expressly permitted by the legislation.[43] Where this is done the Tenement Management Scheme is wholly superseded. The first option may be suitable for small developments, and the last for large developments. But in most cases the choice will be between the second and third options. Where the second option (partial provision) is selected, it is highly desirable to begin with the Tenement Management Scheme and to produce a new, integrated scheme which combines the statutory scheme with the preferred alterations of the drafter. In that way the rules governing the tenement will be contained in the one place. What is particularly to be avoided is a few clauses in a deed of conditions which cover some, but not all of, the

---

[38] This is competent even although the relevant figures are not found in the deed (or, therefore, in the register): see the 2003 Act, s.5(2), and para.13–10 above.

[39] The old rateable values are still accessible: Abolition of Domestic Rates Etc. (Scotland) Act 1987, s.5.

[40] 2004 Bill, s.4(4).

[41] para.27–04.

[42] See para.27–11.

[43] 2004 Bill, s.4(2).

ground, making it necessary to move from deed of conditions to Tenement Management Scheme and back in order to work out the applicable rules.[44] Where a new scheme altogether is to be produced (the third option), there remains much to be said for following the attractively simple style and organisation of the two statutory schemes.

Statutory notices

Statutory repairs notices were discussed in an earlier chapter.[45] In 27–10 tenements they can be a convenient solution for the failure of the owners to reach agreement; and at any rate they are used much more for tenements than for property of any other type.

It is common practice for the local authority to serve a notice on all the flats, even though not all are liable under the statutory code, or by virtue of the titles, and even though the problem in question (*e.g.* wood rot in certain joists) does not affect all the flats. This blanket-bombing is lawful, and if the council does the work it will normally bill all the owners.[46] If that happens, readjustment in terms of the titles (or the general law) is usually possible,[47] but that readjustment is simply as between the parties, and does not affect the council.

The development management scheme

A second model scheme—the Development Management Scheme— 27–11 was introduced by the Title Conditions (Scotland) Act 2003.[48] This is optional and, for the most part, freely variable, and can be used both for tenemental and non-tenemental property. It is brought into operation by execution and registration of a deed of application by the developer or other owner.[49] The central idea is that the development should be governed by a manager acting on behalf of a residents' association which is a body corporate (but not a company). Detailed provision is made in respect of powers, meetings, annual budgets, service charges, and so on; and it is possible, and probably necessary, to add use restrictions, which would then be rules of the Scheme rather than real burdens. In fact the Scheme itself is missing from the 2003 Act, as are a number of supporting provisions, and is to be included in an order made by the UK Government under section 104 of the Scotland Act 1998.[50] At the time of writing no order had been made although one was expected.[51] Once

---

[44] This will still usually be necessary for tenements conveyed before the entering into force of the 2004 Bill.

[45] paras 4–28–4–31.

[46] Though whether this is authorised by the legislation is arguable: see Reid (1990) 35 J.L.S.S. 368 at pp.371–372. The issue is touched on, but not settled, in *Dana v City of Edinburgh District Council*, 1994 G.W.D. 15–913.

[47] But if the work was in respect of scheme property, all owners are liable under the Development Management Scheme, r.4.1(d).

[48] Title Conditions (Scotland) Act 2003, Part 6.

[49] 2003 Act, s.71.

[50] The residents' association was assumed to be a business association and hence a reserved matter under the Scotland Act 1998, Sch.5, Part II, head C1.

[51] It is likely to follow closely the draft scheme set out in Sch.3 of the draft bill included in the Scottish Law Commission's *Report on Real Burdens* (Scot. Law Com. No.181, 2000; available on *http://www.scotlawcom.gov.uk*). Part 8 of that *Report* is a valuable guide to the scheme.

the provisions are enacted and in force, the Development Management Scheme will provide an attractive alternative to proceeding, in the traditional way, by deed of conditions and real burdens; but its relative complexity makes it suitable mainly for large developments.

NEW HOUSES[52]

Missives

27–12   For second-hand houses, the terms of missives are a matter for negotiation. But in the case of new houses the builders usually have a standard style, the terms of which are presented as being non-negotiable. Generally, it is in the form of an offer addressed to the builders to be signed personally by the prospective buyers. The builders promptly add their acceptance. Often the buyers receive no legal advice, and simply arrive at a law office clutching the concluded contract in their hands. By this stage they may already have paid a deposit of perhaps 1 per cent, and maybe also a "reservation fee" of perhaps £500.[53] Even if the buyers see their solicitors before signing anything, the builders may refuse to consider alterations of the terms. Usually they are one-sided documents. They may amount to this: that the buyers will pay the price whenever the sellers ask for it, whether or not the house has actually been built, whether or not it has any defects, and whether or not the support works (roads, sewers, etc.) have been constructed. Often there is no proper description of the property being bought. The missives may absolve the sellers of the need to show good and marketable title or clear searches or planning permission or building warrants or completion certificates or road bonds. The missives may also reserve to the sellers the right unilaterally to alter the design of the house or the shape of the plot.[54] The Housing Improvement Task Force, set up by the Scottish Executive, has concluded that such missives "leave the consumer in an unacceptably weak position, particularly if buyers are persuaded to sign the contract on the developer's premises, without having an opportunity to take legal advice first."[55]

If legal advice is indeed sought, the solicitors can hardly but advise that the terms should be altered. The builders will resist, but if threatened with the loss of the sale will in practice often agree to be less unreasonable. At all events, if unfair missives are entered into, the buyers' solicitors must inform their clients of the possible dangers, and do this in writing.

One possible remedy is the Unfair Terms in Consumer Contracts Regulations 1999.[56] These apply to contracts where one party is in

---

[52] See Allan (1980) 25 J.L.S.S. 17; Brymer (2002) 60 Prop. Law Bull. 1.

[53] Whilst deposits in commercial conveyancing are common, in residential conveyancing they are not. New houses are the exception.

[54] Not all builders' missives have such provisions.

[55] Housing Improvement Task Force, *Stewardship and Responsibility: A Policy Framework for Private Housing in Scotland* (2003), para.204. The Task Force recommended (paras 207–08) that the Scottish Executive review the subject, seeking a compromise between the interested parties but with the prospect of legislation if no agreement could be reached.

[56] SI 1999/2083.

business and the other is a consumer. The exceptions to the Regulations do not mention sales of heritable property, but the term "goods or services" suggests that only sales of corporeal moveables are covered.[57] The same terminology is used in the English-language version of the Directive[58] which is transposed by the Regulations. However, the other official languages of the E.U. use terms applicable to sale of property of any description, including heritable property.[59] It is an open secret that the English version is a poor one. The modern practice of the courts is to construe legislation which transposes E.U. law in the light of the E.U. law itself, which in this case seems intended to apply to builders' missives.

Disposition

Builders almost always use *pro forma* dispositions, and sometimes a 27-13 copy of this is part of the missives. It will contain real burdens either directly or by reference to a deed of conditions, and of course the clients must decide whether these burdens are acceptable. It is important to check the terms of the disposition carefully. There is a temptation to assume that the builders' solicitors have done a reasonable job. Surprisingly often this is not so. For instance, there may be errors in the description of the property, or the common parts, or amenity areas, and so on. Sometimes the purchasers' solicitors point out some defect only to be met with the reply that the *pro forma* has already been examined by ten other firms without objection. They should not be intimidated by such a reply. If the defect is a real one, so much the worse for the other ten firms, and their clients.

A perennial problem with new houses is that the company prepares plans for the development, but the houses and their boundary fences and walls when built may not correspond exactly with the plans. The company will typically offer a disposition with a plan based on the design plan. This may look beautiful and precise,[60] but it may not correspond to what is on the ground. These problems potentially exist in both GRS and Land Register cases. In the latter the Keeper's practice is to delay issuing land certificates to purchasers until the development is complete, so as to minimise the danger of the sort of problems just described. This, however, is not wholly satisfactory for the earlier purchasers. Another implication is that a P16 Report cannot usually be obtained for the purchase of one of the earlier properties.[61]

---

[57] "Goods" typically means corporeal moveables, as in the Sale of Goods Act 1979.

[58] 93/13/EEC.

[59] Thus the French text speaks of "*biens*", a term whose meaning is certainly not restricted to corporeal moveables. It means property in a broad sense, including immoveable property. Other official versions of the text (*e.g.* "Güter" in the German) use similar broad terms. See further Thomson (1995) 40 J.L.S.S. 490.

[60] Or it may not. Some plans offered by builders are extraordinarily sloppy. They may contain no measurements and no means of anchoring the plot to existing physical features.

[61] The Keeper runs a scheme called the Estate Plan Approval System. Where building companies participate in this the problems are much reduced.

Public law consents[62]

27–14   New houses require various consents in public law. The main ones are planning permission, and building warrant with completion certificate. These should be stipulated for in the missives and exhibited at or before settlement. The missives ought also to stipulate for a road bond where road construction is necessary.

Building faults and the NHBC

27–15   The builder's obligations are governed by the terms of the contract, read against the background of the common law, under which a builder is obliged to do work competently.[63] If faults emerge then the builder must (depending on the terms of the contract) pay damages. But what if the builder becomes bankrupt? (Bankruptcies in the building trade seem to be particularly common.) In most cases the builder will be a member of the National House Builders Council (NHBC).[64] This organisation inspects houses in the course of construction and offers to purchasers a 10-year insurance policy, called Buildmark Insurance. The buyer does not pay a separate premium for this. The cost is borne by the builder and is thus in effect included in the overall price. The cover is more extensive for faults notified in the first two years than in the next eight: during the latter period only major faults are covered.[65] The NHBC also covers the risk that the builder might become insolvent before the house has been completed. The missives for a new house should normally stipulate for an NHBC guarantee. The insurance is for the benefit of the owner for the time being. Thus if a builder builds a house and sells to Jack, and five years later Jack sells to Jill, the Buildmark Insurance does not have to be assigned. But the policy should be handed over to Jill on settlement. Standard-form offers generally provide that if the house was built within the past ten years it must be covered by Buildmark Insurance.

NHBC is the largest, but not the only, example of a "building standards indemnity scheme", and it may be that the builder participates in some other acceptable scheme. If not, there should be certification from an independent expert.[66] A standard-form certificate can be found in the *CML Handbook*.[67]

PUBLIC SECTOR HOUSING: THE RIGHT-TO-BUY LEGISLATION

Introduction

27–16   One of the slogans of Thatcherism was "a property-owning democracy". Soon after coming to power in 1979, the Conservatives introduced legislation to allow the tenants of council houses, and tenants

---

[62] See Ch.4.

[63] *Owen v Fotheringham*, 1997 S.L.T. (Sh. Ct) 28.

[64] *http://www.nhbc.co.uk/*.

[65] But establishing liability can be fraught with difficulty: see *Cormack v National House Building Council*, 1998 S.L.T. 1051, and *Hughes v Barratt Urban Construction (Scotland) Ltd*, 2002 G.W.D. 12–353, 2003 G.W.D. 13–452. See also Deutsch (2001) 41 Civil Practice Bull. 2.

[66] But the real value of such certificates may be limited.

[67] For the CML see para.18–05.

renting from certain other types of landlord, compulsorily to purchase their houses or flats at below-market prices. The Scottish legislation was at first contained in the Tenants Rights Etc. (Scotland) Act 1980 and is now in the Housing (Scotland) Act 1987, as amended, especially by the Housing (Scotland) Act 2001. These provisions are commonly called the "right-to-buy" legislation. Over the years the legislation has generated a large body of case law and the following is only an overview.[68]

The detailed rules have changed over the years, but a broad distinction can be made between tenancies entered into before September 30, 2002 and those entered into after that date, when the Housing (Scotland) Act 2001 came into force. We will call these older and newer tenancies.

The rules for older tenancies

Those eligible to buy are tenants of at least two years' standing, 27–17 holding a "Scottish secure tenancy"[69] from a local authority, or certain other public-sector landlords. Certain exceptions exist.[70] The amount of the discount—*i.e.* the amount by which the price is less than a fair market price—depends partly on whether the property is a flat or a house and partly on how long the applicant has been a tenant. For a flat the discount ranges from a minimum of 44 per cent to a maximum of 70 per cent. 2 per cent is added for each year after the initial qualifying period of two years. For a house the discount ranges from 32 per cent to a maximum of 60 per cent, with 1 per cent being gained for each year. Thus a tenant of flat of three years' standing would get a discount of 46 per cent, and a tenant of a house of nine years' standing would get a discount of 39 per cent.

The rules for newer tenancies

For tenancies starting on or after September 30, 2002 the rules are less 27–18 favourable to tenants. The initial qualifying period is five years rather than two. The discount is the same regardless of whether the property is a flat or a house, but is lower than before. The minimum is 20 per cent and the maximum is 35 per cent, but the discount cannot exceed £15,000. The discount rises by 1 per cent for each year after the qualifying period. Thus a tenant of six years' standing would get a discount of 21 per cent and a tenant of 19 years' standing would get a discount of 34 per cent, in each case, however, capped at a maximum discount of £15,000. The Scottish Ministers have power to designate certain areas as "pressured areas". In such areas the right to buy is suspended, but only for newer tenancies.

---

[68] A valuable introduction is the Scottish Executive's booklet *Your Right to Buy your Home* (2002).

[69] The standard form of public sector tenancy, regulated by the Housing (Scotland) Act 1987.

[70] For instance, some types of tied property, property specially adapted for the infirm, and so on. These exceptions have generated a great deal of litigation.

Procedure

27-19   The first step is to complete and submit the official "application to purchase" form.[71] The landlord will then arrange for the property to be valued, at its own expense. The landlord should then, within two months of receiving the application to purchase, make a formal offer to sell, at the valuation figure less the applicable discount. The tenant then has two months after that to decide whether or not to accept. A tenant who considers that the landlord is not following the legislative requirements can take the matter to the Lands Tribunal.

The buyers' solicitors should carefully check the terms of the offer to sell. They should ensure that the discount has been calculated correctly. They should ideally inspect the property, because there may be problems about shared amenity areas, access routes and so on. Council properties were not originally constructed with individual ownership in mind.

Missives are concluded when the tenant sends to the landlord a "notice of acceptance" of the offer to sell. Thereafter matters cease to be regulated by the legislation,[72] and so ordinary law and conveyancing practice apply. For instance, if the tenant dies after missives but before settlement, the tenant's rights pass to his or her executor.[73]

Clawback: repayment of discount

27-20   If the new owner "sells or otherwise disposes" of the property within three years from the date of the notice of acceptance, the discount or part of it is repayable.[74] If this happens in the first year, the whole discount is repayable; if in the second year, the proportion falls to 66 per cent; if in the third year it falls to 33 per cent. After the expiry of the three year period no discount is repayable. This contingent obligation to repay all or part of the discount is secured to the former landlord by a standard security, known as the discount standard security. The precise meaning of the provisions dealing with repayment of discount[75] has been the subject of some controversy.[76] The discount standard security ranks after a standard security securing a loan for the purchase price.[77]

Funding from a family member

27-21   It is quite common for a tenant—and especially an elderly tenant, who usually qualifies for maximum discount—to exercise the right to buy at the suggestion of, and with finance provided by, a grown-up child, or other relative, or a friend (we will use the term "funder"). The arrangement is then commonly that when the tenant/purchaser dies, the

---

[71] Currently as prescribed in The Right to Purchase (Application Form) (Scotland) Order 2002 (SSI 2002/332). This contains useful explanatory material.

[72] Apart from possible repayment of the discount.

[73] *Cooper's Exrs v City of Edinburgh District Council*, 1991 S.C. (HL) 5.

[74] Housing (Scotland) Act 1987, s.72.

[75] Housing (Scotland) Act 1987, ss.72 and 73.

[76] *Jack's Exrs v Falkirk District Council*, 1992 S.L.T. 5; *Clydebank District Council v Keeper of the Registers*, 1994 S.L.T. (Lands Tr.) 2; *McDonald's Tr v Aberdeen City Council*, 2000 S.C. 185.

[77] Housing (Scotland) Act 1987, s.72(5).

property will pass to the funder. This can be done simply by a will, but the risk to the funder is that a will is revocable. Sometimes some form of contract is entered into, or a trust created in favour of the funder. The danger of such schemes is that if they are entered into within the three-year period they may amount to a "disposal", thereby triggering liability to repay the discount. "A disposal under section 72", it has been said, "need not involve a formal conveyance. It is sufficient that the former tenant puts it out of his power to deal with the house as owner."[78] Moreover, if liability is triggered, the full 100 per cent discount would be repayable because the "disposal" would typically be at the time of the purchase, and thus within the first 12 months after the exercise of the right to buy.[79]

It is difficult to be certain as to whether such schemes trigger liability, because the legislation does not define "disposal". However, in practice repayment may not be demanded simply because the ex-landlord is unaware of the arrangement. It is difficult to give reliable advice as to how to arrange matters so as to avoid entirely the danger of triggering liability for discount. One safe method is simply to secure the finance by standard security, but that will not affect the question of who will take the property on death. Moreover, if the value of the house rises, the amount secured will no longer reflect the value of the house. Another possibility is to confer on the relative an option to buy (on the death of the tenant/purchaser) at a fixed sum (representing the original finance), which option can then be secured by standard security. Such an option would probably not be a "disposal" in itself, though it would become one at the date of its exercise, which, however, with any luck would be outwith the three-year period.

We cannot here give detailed analysis of this complex subject, but will conclude with two words of warning. The first is that such arrangements can be complex to draft and set up, not only because of the need to steer round the "disposal" rules, but also because of the need to regulate matters properly between the parties, for instance in relation to insurance, upkeep, the possibility that the tenant/purchaser might wish to move house, and so on. The second warning is that in all such arrangements different solicitors must act for each party.

---

[78] *McDonald's Tr v Aberdeen City Council*, 2000 S.C. 185 at 192H *per* Lord Gill.

[79] Actually if the agreement is entered into *before* the right-to-buy missives have been concluded, then there is an argument (perhaps an absurd one), based on the wording of s.72, that it is not a qualifying disposal.

INDEX